T5-AXM-933

The Gregg Press
Science Fiction Series

David G. Hartwell and L. W. Currey, *Editors*

Science-Fiction Studies, Second Series
edited by R. D. Mullen and Darko Suvin

Science-Fiction Studies

Second Series

Selected Articles on
Science Fiction 1976–1977

Edited with Notes by
R. D. MULLEN *and* DARKO SUVIN
and with an Introduction by
MARC ANGENOT

GREGG PRESS

A DIVISION OF G. K. HALL & CO., BOSTON, 1978

This original anthology photographically reproduces selected articles as they were first published in Volumes 3 and 4 (issues 8–13, March 1976–November 1977) of *Science-Fiction Studies*. Paginations for the original journal appearances of articles are given at the beginning of each article. The trim size of the journal is 6 by 9 inches.

Printed on permanent/durable acid-free paper and bound in the United States of America.

Published in 1978 by Gregg Press, A Division of
G. K. Hall & Co.,
70 Lincoln Street, Boston, Massachusetts 02111.

First Printing, June 1978

Library of Congress Cataloging in Publication Data

Main entry under title:

Science-fiction studies II.

(The Gregg Press science fiction series)
"First published in volumes 3 and 4 . . . of Science-fiction studies."
1. Science fiction—History and criticism—Addresses, essays, lectures. I. Mullen, Richard D., 1915– II. Suvin, Darko, 1930–
PN3448.S45 809.3′876 78-5586
ISBN 0-8398-2444-0

Contents

The Sociology of Science Fiction

Introduction

WHEN *Science-Fiction Studies* was created in 1973, its founders had the ambition to open up science fiction criticism to a number of new points of view, to broaden its horizons, to break up with the comfortable purring of anecdotal and thematic commentary inherited from the Golden Age (or Tin Age) of fandom. The critical opening that *Science-Fiction Studies* was determined to effect can be summarized in three ways:

1. An opening on the *history,* including ancient forms of cognitive estrangement. From the Hellenistic period to 19th century, the imaginary voyage, the Land of Cockayne, the fictional utopia, the alternative satire, and other narratives of rational conjecture are, in our view, both formally contiguous and historically ancestral to present forms of SF, and therefore contribute to illuminate them.

We were determined not to approach such early SF in the state of mind of a lover of ruins. For us, the century-old history of utopian thought is still vivid; its underground tradition still influences today's literary production, and in particular most of the highest achievements in SF. Moreover, we considered extremely provincial and narrowminded those bogus, shoddy and forgetful "Histories" of SF whose "Antiquity" is represented by Jules Verne and H. G. Wells, "Renaissance" by Hugo Gernsback from *Modern Electrics* to *Amazing Stories,* and "Classicism" by the so-called Golden Age of the 1940s.

SF criticism at the time was a strange though well-known

phenomenon: a marginal group, rather critical towards established hierarchies and values, unconsciously ends up reproducing in its own field the ideological hoax of literary establishment—artificial creation of a standard history, setting up of a canonic corpus and an official pantheon, passwords, disbarments and excommunications. It finally came to pass that SF had nothing to envy the mainstream. It was better then to try and locate SF in the complex network of actual history with its dynamics of conflicting forms, themes, and world views.

2. An opening on *other cultures* and literary traditions, in order to question the hidden chauvinism of Anglo-Saxon SF criticism. We have tried to diffuse critical information about contemporary Slavic, Germanic and Romance SF—till the time when we will be able to deal with Japanese or Hindi texts! This attempt to reach a truly cosmopolitan (or indeed internationalist) perspective has fortunately coincided with the book market's discovery of foreign SF writers: most importantly Italo Calvino, Stanislaw Lem and the Strugatski brothers, as well as Klein, Merle, Franke, Abé, etc. At the same time, foreign "classics" were translated, such as Defontenay, Rosny the Elder, Lasswitz, Witkiewicz—and it was even discovered with amazement that others, such as Jùles Verne, were available in English only in clumsy, unfaithful, and bowdlerized "translations."

3. An opening on the various methodologies of *contemporary literary theory*—genre morphology, narrative semiotics, Freudian and Marxist criticism. Such an ambition might also have seemed ambiguous. Were we simply trying to give SF, coming out of its ghetto, an institutional, "academic" recognition? To offer it a small jump seat in the Concert Hall of Canonic Literature? The fan critics sometimes suspected the editors of *Science-Fiction Studies* to be a kind of frogmen of the academic establishment sent to spy out the shores of SF before their annexation is attempted. On the contrary: in this second half of the 20th century, the official institution of literature is sinking, and we are not eager to refloat it. It was simply a matter of "taking SF seriously"—as has been said many times in the pages of the journal. What was meant by this "seriousness"?

Anecdotal (not to say gossipy) and thematic (not to say paraphrastic) SF criticism was for a long time all there was, and it was, in our opinion, incapable of a true *critique*. Hence this paradox: everybody went on saying that SF is the "only alive literature today," "the literature of the future," but such archaic, outdated, and irrelevant concepts were used to describe it that they completely discredited it in "mainstream" criticism.

It is a general rule in sciences that the object under scrutiny codetermines the methodological tools to be used for scrutinizing it. If SF today is a form of literature fit to reflect the growing complexity of historical becoming, then it requires a "totalizing" or encompassing critical approach and excludes as inadequate and mystifying every compartmentalizing—be it the impoverishing hyperformalism, the ahistorical reductionism of the so-called archetypal approach, the narrow provincialism of anecdotal commentary, the bogus subjectivism of impressionistic criticism, or the shabby terrorism of some mechanical "ideological explanations."

Every scholarly journal worthy of that name is obliged to display an intelligent tolerance towards opinions and methods, yet at the same time to define criteria with precision and rigor. This is the everyday problem of editorial work: we simply hope, taking one with the other, that *Science-Fiction Studies* has had—and might continue to have—reasonable success in balancing these principles.

I will not try to measure how far *Science-Fiction Studies* has been able to comply with the program sketched above in its first five years. I would say right away that, in spite of the work that has been done, it seems to us that almost everything remains to be done: in SF what is most striking is the size of problems that have never been dealt with in a critical way; the number of writers—both American and foreign—whose work deserve an extensive analysis; and the variety of economic, sociological, philosophical, and aesthetic aspects that remain to be circumscribed and studied thoroughly. Such remarks call for a reasonable modesty in assessing what has so far been achieved; they also urge us to persevere in opening the journal to an ever wider compass of opinions and methods, provided they see SF as a potentially cognitive genre, within a complex but manmade history.

The central problem in paraliterary criticism arises from the confrontation of aesthetic and/or political value judgments with the present situation of the book market and the film industry. In the U.S., both are exclusively profit-oriented, with their alienating and worn-down narrative recipes which make for the overwhelming success of ideological fakes of the *Foundation* Trilogy, *Star Trek* or *Star Wars* type. (Obviously the situation is somewhat different in the U.S.S.R. and some other Warsaw Pact countries, but it is after all not fundamentally different. Only the kind of alienation has changed from profit pressures to direct bureaucratic pressures. This still leaves the SF critic with the same dilemmas as those I am now getting at, concentrating on the situation in capitalism where most of *Science-Fiction Studies* contributors work and write.)

The SF critic should, no doubt, first of all describe the empirical state of affairs, gathering as much information as he can on the production and consumption of these cultural commodities, describing in the most rigorous way the narrative features and their functions; but there comes a moment when he cannot proceed without an overall value judgment (which in my opinion is a political one). The traditional method of "I like/I dislike" seems after all to be a bit subjective.

However, the critic's position is likely to be rather uncomfortable. Every hyper-bestseller and every billion-dollar movie that invades the market brings a contradiction that can be described as the *Star Wars* syndrome: endless discussions among "specialists" who enjoyed the movie while sharing very good critical reasons to hate it. In the social sciences and humanities, there is no place for an external and truly objective observer. "The partial identity of subject and object" (Lucien Goldmann) makes it impossible to eliminate personal equations. It also implies that social contradictions are reflected in the observer's mind. The critic may be able to describe accurately a literary text; he will not be able to explain its rhetorical, ideological and social determinations without having recourse to a network of methods sufficiently complex and rigorous to at least partly dissolve the blind spot of personal choices and prejudices. To illuminate in such a way a given stylistic or ideological pattern does not amount to approving or disapproving, rejecting or praising; but on the other hand, any all-encompassing point of view contains, explicitly or not, immanent value judgments.

The above axioms and preoccupations have not changed since *Science-Fiction Studies* was created. No doubt we came up against various ideological, ethical and aesthetical resistances. We feel nonetheless that the studies in SF are developing a hopeful dynamic and that the journal has played—and can still play—a positive role at this juncture.

The essays gathered in this second series of selected articles from *Science-Fiction Studies,* 1976–1977 (a first volume, including articles from 1973–1975, was published by Gregg Press in 1976) reflect rather clearly the various orientations I have described—even though they are only a selection of the journal content (most bibliographies, certain polemical discussions, and the whole section of book reviews and notes were eliminated). The reader will find in the present anthology several original studies on writers of the first rank, such as Cordwainer Smith, Samuel R. Delany, and Ursula K. Le Guin. Another SF writer—a French one, Gérard Klein—analyses with insight the aesthetic and political significance of Le Guin's work. Other foreign novelists, such as Stanislaw Lem, have their work examined by various contributors. David N. Samuelson's essay on Walter M. Miller, Jr. is a good example of analysis of an interesting writer, appreciated by the general readership, but somewhat neglected by the critics.

The historical orientation of *Science-Fiction Studies* is illustrated by a series of essays on "SF Before Wells" that mostly correspond to a special issue (#10) of the journal. Jack London's centenary was commemorated in #9 with Nadia Khouri's penetrating study and Darko Suvin's and David Douglas' "Jack London and His Science Fiction: A Select Bibliography" (not reprinted in this collection).

Issue #13 was devoted to "The Sociology of SF": no doubt, this issue is far from covering every aspect of SF considered from a sociological point of view, including the "external" sociology of book industry, market and readership, and the "internal" criticism of ideology and world views. Gérard Klein's

"Discontent in American Science Fiction" has the merit of offering an overarching sociocritical hypothesis that is worth being discussed.

In order to illustrate what I said above on the need for dealing with SF seriously and not complacently, I would like to point out Charles Elkins' essay on Isaac Asimov: it was time to say that "the King is naked"—that is what Elkins does soundly and rigorously.

This collection of selected articles from *Science-Fiction Studies* will be the last one coedited by Dale Mullen. Professor Mullen has, alas, resigned as editor and publisher of *Science-Fiction Studies,* effective at the end of 1978, though he will continue his connection with the journal in some formal capacity. *Science-Fiction Studies* will go on in Montreal under the joint editorship of Darko Suvin, Charles Elkins, Robert Philmus and Marc Angenot.

It is up to the reader to judge our efforts and results—and to let us know his/her comments, objections and suggestions. We hope that so far *Science-Fiction Studies* has done significant and useful work and—as is customary for SF writers and critics—we look expectantly towards the Future!

Marc Angenot
McGill University

Notes on Contributors

Peter S. Alterman's dissertation at the University of Denver is "A Study of Four Science Fiction Themes and Their Function in Two Contemporary Novels." **Marc Angenot,** McGill University, has published extensively in French on science fiction and paraliterature. **Albert I. Berger,** whose master's thesis on SF was published in the *Journal of Popular Culture,* 5(1972):867–943, has for his *SFS* articles drawn on the materials for the dissertation he is writing in history at Northern Illinois University. **Alex Eisenstein** has published articles on SF in various magazines and has written SF stories in collaboration with his wife, Phyllis. **Charles Elkins** teaches at Florida International University. **William B. Fischer,** Emory

University, is doing a dissertation at Yale in German literature. **S. C. Fredericks,** Indiana University, who has published on both Greek literature and science fiction, here brings his two interests together. **Dieter Hasselblatt's** publications in German include *Grüne Männchen vom Mars,* 1974. **Jerzy Jarzębski** is a Polish editor and critic. **Wolfgang Jeschke** is a freelance writer and editor in West Germany. **Michael Kandel V** is a direct descendant of that Michael Kandel who back in the 1970s translated a number of Stanislaw Lem's books into English. **David Ketterer,** Concordia University, whose *New Worlds for Old,* 1974, stirred up considerable controversy in SF circles, is now working on a book on *Frankenstein*. **Nadia Khouri** teaches at Dawson College in Montreal. **Gérard Klein,** an economist, is well-known in France as an SF author and editor; among his novels in English is *The Overlords of War,* translated by John Brunner. **Bernt Kling,** audio-visual editor of the German-language *Science Fiction Times,* is co-author of *Romantik und Gewalt* (Romanticism and Violence).

Ursula K. Le Guin's most recent book is a collection of short stories set in a mythical European kingdom, *Orsinian Tales* (1976). **Stanislaw Lem** was the only nonscientist invited to participate in the Soviet-American CETI symposium of September 1971; the paper he presented there appears in the Russian publication *Problema CETI* (Moscow, 1975). **George Locke,** the well-known book-seller specializing in rare SF, has done important work in SF bibliography, including *Voyages in Space* (1975). **Christie V. McDonald** teaches at the Université de Montréal. **Walter E. Meyers,** North Carolina State University, has published articles on linguistics and folklore. **Charles Nicol,** Indiana State University, who reviews modern fiction for such magazines as *Harper's* and *National Review,* is currently engaged in editing a collection of articles on Nabokov. **Patrick Parrinder,** University of Reading, edited the Critical Heritage volume on H. G. Wells; his 1970 monograph, *H. G. Wells,* in the Writers and Critics series, has recently been published in this country by Putnam's. **Robert Plank,** Case Western Reserve University, has published numerous essays and one book on the psychological significance of science-fiction concepts. **David N. Samuelson,** California State University, Long Beach, has published articles on Heinlein, Brunner, Delany, Clarke, and other SF writers, in *SFS, Extrapolation,* and other places. **Scott Sanders,** Indiana University, is the author of a book on D. H. Lawrence as well as of numerous critical and scholarly articles. **Rudolf Stefen** has since 1969 been the chairman of the West German Federal Bureau for Examining Youth-Endangering Writings, and since 1973 the editor-in-chief of the journal *Medien-&-Sexual-Pädagogik.* **Michael Stern,** Harvey Mudd College, is writing his dissertation at Yale on Weberian and Durkheimian models of social structure in 19th-century English fiction. **Roy Arthur Swanson,** University of Wisconsin-Milwaukee, has edited journals in, written articles on, and published translations from Greek and Latin literature. **David Winston** is on the faculty of a theological institute associated with UC Berkeley. **Gary K. Wolfe,** Roosevelt University, has an essay in Thomas D. Clareson's *Many Futures, Many Worlds* (1977) and is at work on a book-length critical study of science fiction.

Science Fiction Before Wells

S.C. Fredericks

Lucian's *True History* as SF

(from SFS *3: 49–60, March 1976)*

After crossing the river, we found something wonderful in the grapevines. The part which came out of the ground, the trunk itself, was stout and well-grown, but the upper part was in each case a woman, entirely perfect from the waist up. Out of their finger-tips grew the branches, and they were full of grapes. When we came up, they welcomed and greeted us. They even kissed us on the lips and everyone that was kissed at once became reeling drunk. They did not suffer us, however, to gather any of the fruit, but cried out in pain when it was plucked. Some of them actually wanted us to embrace them, and two of my comrades complied, but could not get away again. They were held fast by the genitals, which had grown in and struck root. Already branches had grown from their fingers, tendrils entwined them, and they were on the point of bearing fruit like the others any minute.

"The king of the inhabitants of the Sun, Phaethon," said Endymion king of the Moon, "has been at war with us for a long time now. Once upon a time I gathered together the poorest people in my kingdom and undertook to plant a colony on the Morning Star which was empty and uninhabited. Phaethon out of jealousy thwarted the colonization, meeting us halfway at the head of his dragoons. At that time we were beaten, for we were not a match for them in strength, and we retreated. Now, however, I desire to make war again and plant the colony."

Habitues of SF would respond to these two passages from Lucian's *True History*[1] as if they revealed the kinds of cliches that have made the genre notorious. The first, wittily describing men seduced, then incorporated, by an alien life-form, would fally naturally enough under the rubric "First Encounter." The second might be equally familiar as a paragraph from a 'thirties'

"Space Opera" with its commonplace theme of interplanetary imperialism and warfare. Indeed, one critic has written: "I will merely remark that the sprightliness and sophistication of *True History* make it read like a joke at the expense of nearly all early-modern science fiction, that written between, say, 1910 and 1940."[2]

This observation compares Lucian and modern SF without neglecting *True History*'s all-encompassing dimension of irony and satire. It thus has the advantage over one type of SF criticism which has consistently tried to analyze the work solely in terms of what Sam Moskowitz and Damon Knight have called "the sense of wonder." Representatives of this kind of analysis—the list would include J.O. Bailey, R.L. Green, and, most recently, P. Versins in his *Encyclopedie* article on Lucian—respond to the sheer newness and imaginativeness of Lucian's speculative ideas: a flight to the moon, a well and a mirror in that other world where doings on earth may be heard or watched respectively, ice sailing, heavier-than-air flight by the lunar Volplaners, tree-top voyaging in Book 2.[3] Indeed it is fair to say that almost everything in the work is touched with a sense of wonder in a strictly *fictional* manner because Lucian's ironic narrator constantly registers his amazement and incredulity at each new experience during his *voyage extraordinaire*. This interest in the strange and bizarre, and the thrill of experiencing it, is built into the very fictional structure of the work.

Yet it is also true that these speculations are never proposed as scientific or any other kind of realizable possibilities; they remain, as the author tells the reader explicitly in the Preface, only intellectual amusements, valuable for lubricating the mind while relaxing it from the weary concerns of everyday existence. As such, they remain in the realm of literary fantasy and do indeed resemble the "almost anything is conceivable" speculations which appeared in the "wonder tales" of American magazine SF of the thirties and forties—provided that one ignores Lucian's self-effacing irony.

Consequently, this "amazing ideas" approach can take us only so far. It pinpoints one major reason for Lucian's new-found popularity in the Renaissance when creative thinkers like More and Erasmus were inspired to translate many of his works and imitate them in their own writings. The Renaissance world and Lucian's narrator alike shared a thirst for new knowledge and new experiential horizons.[4] It also suggests why Lucian seems, almost uniquely among the ancients, so "modern" in outlook, inasmuch as the modern world since the voyages of Columbus and the Copernican revolution has grown accustomed to having its imaginative limits transcended time and time again with each new scientific discovery. But this kind of criticism cannot show if there is a deeper, more strictly intellectual purpose at work in *True History*, nor if there is a science fictional significance to its form and general import as distinct from this or that particular item of content. Elements of spontaneous daydream and fairy-tale, in displaced form, are certainly present, but there is also a more rigorous cognitive side to the work which precludes our allying Lucian solely with the dreaming pole of SF represented by modern writers like Burroughs, Kuttner, and Farmer.

A more fruitful intellectual approach to *True History* might be borrowed from the "history of ideas" criticism originated by A.O. Lovejoy and G. Boas, and adapted to fictional moon voyages by Marjorie Nicolson. In this kind of criticism it is assumed that literature registers important changes in a given society's imagination due to new scientific or philosophical ideas; literature thus acts as a barometer of major alterations in the symbolic potential of any age.

Certainly there are sciences exploited for imaginative effect in the work. Geography appears in the opening of the travelogue although it is almost at once transformed into a totally imaginative kind that mocks contemporary romancers who fabricated outrageously fictive accounts of voyages and travels for their readers.[5] Astronomy makes an appearance in the famous account of the narrator's trip to the moon in Book 1, and although Lucian's knowledge is totally conventional and derivative at least he does describe the heavenly bodies as other worlds on a par with our own (§1:10).[6] Anthropology and natural history (and weird combinations of both) are prevalent throughout the work, but in neither of these sciences did the Greeks make their most outstanding empirical contributions. Throughout its long history in Greek culture the anthropological mode of thought remained, like history, a speculative rather than empirical science, and too often it seems to involve conceptualizations of folk beliefs and myths—conventional themes of the Golden Age and the Noble Savage are displaced onto foreign peoples who are then compared with the home culture for critical/satirical purposes.[7] With the notable exceptions of Aristotle and Theophrastus, natural history seldom escaped the Greek anthropocentric outlook, and Lucian is superior to his contemporaries in his sensitivity to animal life like insects, spiders, mollusks, and fishes.[8]

Even in such limited cases as these, *True History* reveals how significantly both the human and physical sciences had affected the Greek imagination by altering the forms of its thinking as well as its content. The Greek worldview had developed profoundly since Homer, and the geographical, astronomical, biological, and anthropological journey of Lucian's narrator is of a completely different intellectual order than the non-conceptual, still largely mythicized landscape traversed by Odysseus.[9]

However, this line of reasoning will not take us very far because it restricts the scope of Lucian's imagination too severely. Besides the sciences already mentioned, Lucian touches on theology, philosophy, literary scholarship, utopian thought, and historiography. All of these are essential to the cognitive appeal of the work, and for that reason a much more comprehensive view of the Greek accomplishment in the world of ideas is necessary if we are to judge the total science-fictional impact of *True History* properly.

Here we must take into account the entire tradition of Greek intellectual enquiry from Thales to Galen. The Greeks' accumulation of positive knowledge in these centuries was a considerable improvement over that of their Near Eastern predecessors.[10] More significant, the Greeks discovered many methods for acquiring new knowledge, made them explicit, and so formulated their principles that they could be taught to others. Thus to their credit go many intellectual disciplines which can be termed "sciences" in the sense of organized forms of investigation which can lead to new results within their own domains: philosophy, theology, history, literary scholarship, linguistics, grammar, and political science, as well as a number of practical and theoretical sciences in the strict modern sense.[11] For this reason alone they may justly be regarded as the prototypical theorists in Western tradition: "With the Greeks a new and most important element did enter science. This is the element of speculative philosophy, which constitutes the specific quality, the real originality, of Greek science."[12] This is what is suggested by the title of Bruno Snell's classic, *The Discovery of the Mind*:[13] the human intellect had encountered the world of ideas, entities which could be identified, analyzed, and classified by the workings of reason. It is this most abstract dimension of Greek thought—this recognition of a non-material order of reality, distinct from ordinary, commonsense experience but open to rational enquiry—to which Lucian responds in *True History*.

The essential function of Lucian's fiction is epistemological—to focus on this rationalizing and conceptualizing tendency in Greek thought. His is the greatest satire in antiquity about what can happen when theoretical speculation, unhampered by personal observation, experience, and common sense, runs rampant.[14] We should not be so quick to term his attitude "unscientific" or "anti-intellectual" as to recognize in it a sound corrective to the perpetual vulnerability of Greek intellectuals, scientists included, in this area, for much of their otherwise brilliant work was vitiated by a habit of arbitrarily erecting all-encompassing theories on the basis of *a priori* convictions. In Ronald Paulson's evaluation, "Man, things as they are, and things as they are not make up the elements of Lucian's world; and in this triangle the emphasis clearly falls on the overstructured life and mind materialized in the elaborate structure of things as they are not."[15] Thus even if it is self-purportedly not "true," the *True History* is certainly "cognitive" in its overall intention. Lucian's satire, even at its most facile, is intellectual rather than moral or social.[16] It is satire of, and about, ideas.

This will go far to explain the presence in *True History* of so many literary parodies as motivated by something other than the impulse of our writer to show off his knowledge in the manner of a rhetorician of the Second Sophistic. Most often Lucian does not directly satirize the intellectual disciplines we have been talking about; rather he indirectly imitates, with distortions for humorous effect, the literary modes of expression employed by such disciplines.[17] Here, too, we must allow for a cognitive/epistemological purpose, for the recent work of G.D. Kiremidjian on the "Aesthetics of Parody"[18] abandons the conventional but uncritical assumption that parodies are only humorous attacks against earlier writers' works. This author identifies parody as an essentially epistemological form which clarifies, and makes us more fully aware of, the manner in which we acquire knowledge. Thus, whether we speak of Lucian "imitating" or "satirizing," the object of his criticism is not content, but form; not a thing, but an idea and the expression of an idea. This is also why the older source criticism—the endless cataloguing of items that Lucian read or used—is bound to be sterile, for it can get no further than to say Lucian is derivative; it has no means of describing the intellectual dynamics of *True History*.

However, we may be doing a disservice to the author even in so attempting to defend his reputation. For in concentrating on either the fanciful or the satiric/parodic we may ignore the fact that Lucian also often achieves an authentic sense of reality. One of the older interpreters notes how "through the whole narrative he holds us captive by his air of verisimilitude."[19] This is what Scholes and Kellogg mean by their technical term, "the mimetic": "The mimetic...owes its allegiance, not to truth of fact but to truth of sensation and environment, depending on observation of the present rather than investigation of the past."[20] An excellent instance of "truth of sensation and environment" occurs immediately after the Preface in which it is boldly stated that the story is going to be entirely a lie. Then the author performs a perfect about-face and introduces a "realistic" (in the strict literary sense) rationale for his fictive narrator's travels:

> One day, setting out from the Pillars of Hercules and heading for the western ocean with a fair wind, I went avoyaging. The motive and purpose of my journey lay in my intellectual activity and desire for adventure, and in my wish to find out what the end of the ocean was, and who the people were that lived on the other side. On this account I put aboard a good store of provisions, stowed water enough, enlisted in the venture fifty of my acquaintances who were like-minded with myself, got together also a great quantity of arms, shipped the best sailing-master to be had at a big inducement, and put my boat—she was a pinnace—in trim for a long and difficult voyage. (§1:5-6)

The passage, in fact, deceptively combines two levels of realism: the first part establishes the credentials, perspective, and motivation of the narrator, and makes him seem a reliable witness; the second is involved with the realia of the ship, its crew, and the first days of the voyage (subsequently to lead into a storm). There is nothing to suggest fantasy here. This is all matter-of-fact and empirically reasonable.

The ability to write fiction in this mimetic mode remained limited in ancient fiction according to Scholes and Kellogg, who reinforce the general conclusions of Erich Auerbach's classic, *Mimesis*. In this particular quality Lucian has to be recognized as a master for his time, though he is by no means as sophisticated as modern SF authors, for the modern novel has had a tremendous positive influence on the competence of writers to deliver mimetic touches.[21]

However, there is a second type of mimesis in *True History*, based not on our own normal/empirical experience, but on an alternative experience which is merely parallel to our own. An example of what I mean occurs after the story has already become quite fantastic. The ship suddenly takes flight and the narrative shifts to an extraterrestrial perspective:

> For seven days and seven nights we sailed the air, and on the eighth day we saw a great country in it, resembling an island, bright and round and shining with a great light. Running in there and anchoring, we went ashore, and on investigating found that the land was inhabited and cultivated. By day nothing was in sight from the place, but as night came on we began to see many other islands hard by, some larger, some smaller, and they were like fire in color. We also saw another country below, with cities in it and rivers and seas and forests and mountains. This we inferred to be our own world. (§1:10).

Here Lucian cleverly understates his narrator's first encounter with the moon and other heavenly bodies. The catalogue of extraterrestrial wonders will come later in the story; now he concentrates on our sense of familiarity, with "islands" and a land which is "inhabited and cultivated." The last sentence of the passage further shows that our world, from the narrator's stance on the moon, appears as just another land "below," but it is otherwise indistinguishable from the extraterrestrial lands.

Thus there are two types of mimesis: one imitating the "zero world" of normal, verifiable experience,[22] the other creating an analogy to normal experience in another, estranged world. Whereas the first type is an imitation of life, the second is a life-like reification of an impossibility. For this very reason, Lucian seems to be at the opposite cognitive pole from the ancient pseudo-scientific romancers. Lucian protests from the outset that everything in his narrative is false, then provides us with a sense of the real throughout the fictive journey in our own as well as other worlds. He does so not in order to deceive us into believing his own fictions, but to make us return from his various fictional worlds with the realization that it is easy for the artificial and unreal to appear natural and real.

This, then, seems to be a critical place for providing a new, more satisfying rationale for Lucian as a prototypical SF writer. Because of its powerful mimetic dimension his narrative must not be reduced solely to being satire nor to being a sequence of literary parodies. Like a modern SF writer, Lucian takes the sciences and other cognitive disciplines available to him and pictures alternate worlds which can dislocate the intellects of his readers in such a way as to make them aware of how many of their normal convictions about things were predicated upon cliché thinking and stereotyped response—in areas as diverse as religious belief, aesthetic judgement, and philosophical theory.[23] The "places" visited by the protagonist-narrator are, therefore, intellectual loci, and much more of Lucian's geography is figurative then literal. We really travel with the narrator through a sequence of conceptions and speculations which comment satirically and critically on men's habits of mind in the real world.

Consequently, *True History* may properly be regarded as SF because Lucian often achieves that sense of "cognitive estrangement" which Darko Suvin has defined as the generic distinction of SF, that is, the depiction of an alternate world, radically unlike our own, but relatable to it in terms of significant knowledge.[24]

The most significant and detailed of Lucian's analogical universes[25] is that of the heavens, and it is unfortunate that so much critical energy has been expended on the fanciful interplanetary flight and not enough on Lucian's portrayal of the workings of an alternate universe. The flight proper is only the rhetorical vehicle, of little fictional importance to the work itself, while the real tenor is the moon world.

The passage in which this world appears may be analyzed conveniently into two sections. The first (§1:11-21) deals with the war between the moon and the sun, both sprawling, mongrel empires analogous to the Hellenistic monarchies which antedated Rome. Not only does Lucian describe the armies on both sides, their offensive and defensive weapons, their mounts, their tactics and strategies, but he enters this world thoroughly and rigorously enough to give a quasi-medical description of a wound (§1:16) and the terms of the treaty which concludes the war (§1:20).

The second part of the passage (§1:22-25) turns to the alternate anthropology and biology of the lunar world. We find an account of the natives' clothing (how manufactured and how worn, §1:25), their diet (§1:23), their physiology and internal organs (§1:24), and their distinctive alimentary, urinary, excretory, and reproductive systems (§1:22-23); Lucian's subtlety extends so far that he can go beyond the idea that the lunar folk are all males to say that they do not even have the word for "women," just the merest hint of an analogical language (§1:22) which corresponds to its own distinct culture.

The lunar world is also important for introducing the motif of giganticism. Mosquitoes, ants, spiders, birds, vegetables, and cloudcentaurs are all of monstrous proportions, and their huge dimensions are, in turn, reinforced by the outrageously large numbers and varieties of alien beasts and quasi-human forms which are reported. This is, of course, a specimen of the grotesque in literature, a disruption of normal perspective for the imaginative/cognitive effect of making us rethink the function of things and their relationship with one another—e.g., ants used as battle mounts, vegetables for boats, and nuts and seeds for weapons and armor.[26] Giganticism as Lucian employs it thus leads to a distancing effect, so that we can come to view our own behavior with greater detachment and irony when we see it projected onto radically different beings like the Moonites. Warfare, another motif which recurs, suggests the same kind of distancing effect.[27]

Thus, the lunar world represents a parallel "other world" with all the complexities of earth itself. This is a fully articulated analogical universe whose differences from our own operate at more than one level, illustrating Darko Suvin's view that "SF takes off from a fictional ('literary') hypothesis and develops it with extrapolating and totalizing ('scientific') vigor."[28] But it also exemplifies one parameter of Lucian's style, for he never again portrays another world with such thoroughness of detail; his subsequent alternate worlds are deliberately conceived more sketchily.

Other universes may be evaluated more briefly. The second total world, the inside of the whale (§1:30-2:2), contrasts not only with the real world, but also with the extraterrestrial one just preceding it. Here the narrator encounters two Greeks, father and son, living apart from other men. This is a wonderful anticipation of the Robinson Crusoe genre because these two men have been able to construct a complete civilized (i.e., Greek) existence by imposing their own social norms and technological knowledge (e.g., viticulture) on nature, and they have functioned as fully civilized men though isolated for 27 years. This passage is, therefore, science-fictional because it shows how man alters his environment, how he molds his world to shape his needs and his values.[29] It is a microcosmic model of normal culture which offers a sort of minimum definition of civilization, including its inherent propensity for war (as soon as the castaways join forces with the narrator and his allies, they make war on the various fish-and-mollusk races in the whale and totally exterminate them). It also confronts the pastoral ideal satirically and critically, for the narrator soon experiences overwhelming boredom in this allegedly idyllic existence, terms it a "prison" (§1:39), and applies his ingenuity to escape. His negative feelings about this forced sojourn in a "closed" universe are, therefore, harmonious with his original desire for an "open" universe with its possibilities for exploration and new knowledge.

Many of the analogical universes represent alternate *cultures* rather than entire worlds. Among these, the most important is Elysium, the Isle of the Blessed (§2:5-27). It is an example of utopian fiction, but its entire value is satirical inasmuch as only the dead can inhabit this perfect society; the living, as the narrator soon discovers, are disqualified from citizenship. Besides radically shifting the perspective from living to dead men, Lucian includes all manner of cognitive disciplines within his critical scope and lets us see their limits by contrasting them with the rules and lessons of everyday real life.[30] His favorite technique in these cases is to take a famous dead personage about whom there has raged some theoretical controversy, then let him respond to his critics. In conversation with the narrator, Homer, for example, refutes all the theories of the Alexandrian critics about his real name, his birthplace, and details surrounding poetic composition (§2:20); Pythagoras and Empedocles are handled more briefly in the same manner. In this way, in this lengthy and witty section of the travelogue, Lucian manages to comment on many fields of organized knowledge: philosophy of many schools (§2:17-18), poets and poetry, legal science and the law courts, historians, theologians, and myth theorists (especially Euhemerists).

Lucian's fictional utopia is more like its modern counterpart than its Platonic inspiration because he acknowledges that the perfect society is only a speculative/imaginative possibility. Its value lies in its being a model by means of which human ambitions and yearnings for a more perfect existence can be judged in light of the norms of everyday, imperfect society.

Soon after being exiled from Elysium, the travelers reach Tartarus (§2:29-32), the Underworld of Greek mythology, here described as a dystopia—the first of its kind in SF—to contrast with utopian Elysium. The pumpkin-pirates, nut-sailors, and dolphin-riders (§2:27-39) very briefly suggest still other alternate human cultures.

Still another group of alternate worlds is consciously nonhuman in conception. First, there are two "metaphorical universes," thoroughly dominated by one recurrent image: Dionysus' wineland (§1:7) and Galatea's milk-and-cheese land (§2:3). Here Lucian's description of landscapes comprised totally of wine or milk products respectively—although in origin based on well known myths—suggests an alternate ecology (all of it potable or edible). All the other nonhuman worlds are concerned to portray alien races distinct from, but analogous to, men. The simpler examples include the vine-nymphs (§1:8-9); the bullheads, a race of minotaurs (§2:44); the asslegs, a cannibalistic race of shape-changing women (§2:46); and the race of feuding giants on floating islands (§1:40-42). Although all of these "monsters" were obviously inspired by myths and legends, in Lucian they belong to a different intellectual order altogether, for there is not even the slightest trace of supernatural or mythic atmosphere about them; rather, they are scrutinized in terms of fictive natural history and anthropology.

The men of Corkland and their country (§2:4) involve a combination of the alternate ecology and alternate human culture types. The creatures of Lamptown (§1:29) are even more remarkable since Lucian has here created the image of a non-animate race going about the business of civilization. It is the merest hint at the robot theme, for these creatures are the products of human technology, tools (the narrator even has a discussion with his own lamp about things at home!), which are envisioned as alternate life-forms. The most intriguing instance in this entire category, however, is the Isle of Dreams (§2:32-35), which is populated by a nonmaterial race whose universe works by dream logic, so that Lucian can suggest a set of alternate physical laws (really, in fact, mythicoreligious laws) for this particular universe, and by so doing he anticipates the modern "weird tale."

Finally, two lands are totally and explicitly literary illusions: Aristophanes' Cloudcuckooland from his comedy, *Birds* (§1:29), and Circe's isle from Homer's *Odyssey* (§2:35-36). Both of these offer contrasts with the other imaginary lands in such a way as to keep the reader conscious of fictional illusions; he is not allowed to forget the artificiality and contrivance of all the alternate worlds. The atmosphere of verisimilitude is thereby disrupted, and Lucian signals his reader that he cannot benefit from this narrative by thinking of it as "real" in any sense—any values will have to be solely literary or imaginative ones. These two worlds thus reinforce the ironic Preface, linking Lucian to "metafictional" literature in which a literary narrative includes a second-order commentary on the nature, value, or truth of literature itself.

Still, there remains the "other world" across the Western ocean which was the original object of the narrator's journey but is never reached.[31] In Elysium (§2:27) Rhadamanthus prophesied that the journey would ultimately take him there, but of course in the famous non-ending of *True History* the narrator puts the reader off with his last lie by saying that the adventures in the "other world" will be reserved for another volume. Lucian is letting us know, of course, that he can go on generating these fanciful worlds without limit, and the world of the imagination—unlike the real world of late antiquity[32]—remains indeterminately open.

Hence, if we look at Lucian one way, he is an intellectual pluralist. Like the philosophers, he is impressed—and is the last good mind in Graeco-Roman antiquity to be so impressed—by the accomplishment of the Greek intellectual tradition. Like the scientists, he possesses an inquisitive mind which shows traces of the old Ionian pre-Socratic curiosity about the tremendous variety in nature and human society alike. With imaginative writers, he is an authentic fantasist, influenced immensely by Aristophanes and Athenian Old Comedy with its bold flights of fancy intermingled with a serious interest in intellectual issues. Lucian's fable even questions the unity of truth (is it one or many?) and the problematical relationships among diverse approaches to truth.

But if we look at him from another angle, he is a thorough sceptic who recognizes that there is an element of make-believe in every manifestation of mind. He is particularly aware of the prevalence of myths and the perpetual recrudescence of old myths in new disguised forms (e.g., philosophical utopia instead of mythical Elysium), and—a closely related phenomenon—he is aware of the degeneration of thought into pseudo-science which gives a scientific format to imaginary themes of every origin. He also recognizes the paradox that results from the concept of "truth" among his philosophical predecessors: "true" had a tendency to become identified with "real," yet once a product of reason was hypostasized and regarded as possessing a metaphysical reality, it was also doomed to appear unreal when judged in light of common sense and the workings of everyday, normal life.

The preceding analysis proposes, in conclusion, that a science-fictional interpretation of *True History* can take us a step beyond the more limited kind of satirical criticism which views the work as a humorous critique of those speculations which have become divorced from the facts of the real world. The many estranged worlds of *True History* reveal a dynamic and disequilibrious relationship between the mind and its imaginative products on the one hand and the real world on the other. If the disparities between the ideal and real realms are obvious, Lucian yet implicitly represents the most ancient example of what we have come to know as SF intellectual non-conformism. There are no absolutes for Lucian, only a continuing process of the mind creating new conceptions which in turn make the mind more fully conscious of its own workings. His is a mind both open and self-reflective.

NOTES

1. The two passages are condensed from the standard English translation by A.M. Harmon in Volume 1 of the Loeb Classical Library edition of Lucian (Cambridge, Mass., 1913), *True History* §1:8 and §1:12 respectively (the references are to the standard book:

paragraph divisions). Harmon unfortunately bowdlerizes Lucian's best obscene puns and fantastic sexual ideas. Paul Turner's recent translation, *True History and Lucius or The Ass* (Midland Books, Indiana University Press, 1974) is lively and attractive but not literal enough for my purposes here, and its format is not congenial to scholarly reference.

I have checked all references and translations against the Greek text in Volume 1 of the Oxford Classical Text edition of Lucian by M.D. Macleod (1972).

I wish to thank R.D. Mullen for originally suggesting the topic of this paper.

2. Kingsley Amis, *New Maps of Hell* (New York, 1960), p. 28.

3. The best account of Lucian's fantastic ideas may be found in J. Bompaire, *Lucien Écrivain* (Paris, 1958), pp. 657-77. Although the author is overly fond of source criticism (a fault he shares with the general run of Lucianic scholarship in classical philology), this work remains the most important single book on Lucian.

4. In his second sentence (§1:5), the fictional narrator identifies as the motive and purpose of his journey his "intellectual activity and desire for adventure," and his "wish to find out what the end of the ocean was, and who the people were that lived on the other side."

5. The ancient testimonia state that *True History* was intended as a parody of Antonius Diogenes' lost work, *Of the Wonderful Things Beyond Thule* (whose protagonist also reached the moon). For geography as a Greek science, see J.O. Thomson, *History of Ancient Geography* (Cambridge, 1948). Morris Cohen and I.E. Drabkin, *A Source Book in Greek Science* (New York, 1948), pp. 143-81, emphasize the empirical results of Greek geographical science.

6. At that, however, the heavenly bodies are conceived as *islands* in the sky, and this is just one detail which suggests that Lucian is deliberately returning to pre-Socratic natural philosophers like Anaximander and Anaxagoras—perhaps a satirical anachronism.

7. See A.O. Lovejoy and George Boas, *A Documentary History of Primitivism and Related Ideas in Antiquity* (Baltimore, 1935), and H.C. Baldry, *The Unity of Mankind in Greek Thought* (Cambridge, 1965).

8. In a very important article, Jerry Standard, "Lucianic Natural History," in *Classical Studies Presented to Ben Edwin Perry* (Urbana, Ill., 1969; Illinois Studies in Language and Literature, vol. 58), pp. 15-26, demonstrates convincingly that Lucian was a competent observer of nature and was acutely sensitive to details of anatomy and animal behavior—so that even his most wildly fictitious and imaginary plants and animals are enlivened by quasi-realistic touches. Witness, e.g., the narrator's dissection and inspection of one of the fishes native to the river of wine on Dionysus' island (§1:7). Cf. J.D. Rolleston, "Lucian and Medicine," *Janus* 20(1915):83-108.

9. See Bompaire (Note 3), p. 659, note 2, for a lengthy catalogue of parallels for *True History* in the *Odyssey*.

10. Documentation at length in Cohen and Drabkin (Note 5), and in Benjamin Farrington, *Greek Science: Its Meaning For Us* (Penguin Books, 2nd edn revised for the 2nd time, 1969). Both of these outstanding books were explicitly conceived as revisionist in order to correct a view of Greek science which had become a cliché—that it did not produce empirical results, did not use proper observational or experimental techniques, and led only to impractical theories which were both unverified and unverifiable.

11. Farrington (Note 10), rightly includes these ancient disciplines within the scope of his book. For theology specifically, see Werner Jaeger, *The Theology of the Early Greek Philosophers* (Oxford, 1947); for history, J.B. Bury, *The Ancient Greek Historians* (New York, 1909); for literary scholarship, R. Pfeiffer, *History of Classical Scholarship from the Beginnings to the End of the Hellenistic Age* (Oxford, 1968).

12. Benjamin Farrington, *Science in Antiquity* (Oxford, 2nd edn, 1969), p. 17. This book emphasizes the theoretical and speculative side of Greek science and especially its associations with Greek philosophical speculations, whereas the other book, cited above in note 10, emphasizes technology and practical results. S. Sambursky, *The Physical World of Late Antiquity* (London, 1962), p. x, speaks of "the extraordinary flair of the Greek mind for rational speculation in the right direction."

13. English trans., T.G. Rosenmeyer (Harper Torchbooks, 1960), esp. pp. 227-45, "The Origin of Scientific Thought."

14. His major competition appeared some 600 years earlier: Aristophanes' *The Clouds*, which described the first "think tank," Socrates' *phrontisterion*, a precursor of Swift's Laputa and Bacon's Solomon's House.

15. *The Fictions of Satire* (Baltimore, 1967), p. 42.

16. I concur with Darko Suvin, "On the Poetics of the Science Fiction Genre," *College English* 34(1972-73):377, when he identifies Lucian as a cognitive writer whose satirical/critical perspective combines "a belief in the potentialities of reason with methodical doubt in the most significant cases."

17. For a thorough but mechanical account of Lucian's parodies, see Bompaire (Note 3), pp. 599-655. Lucian states in the Preface (§1:2) that everything in his story is a "more or less comical parody of one or another of the poets, historians, and philosophers of old, who have written much that smacks of miracles and fables." However, as I argue later, the author's self-announced intention notwithstanding, the work as a fictional unity is more than just a sequence of parodies.

18. *Journal of Aesthetics and Art Criticism* 28(1969):231-42.

19. F.G. Allinson, *Lucian: Satirist and Artist* (Boston, 1926; *Our Debt to Greece and Rome*, vol. 8), p. 118. For further examples of realism in Lucian, see Bompaire (Note 3), pp. 471-536.

20. *The Nature of Narrative* (Oxford, 1966), p. 13.

21. Lucian's own brand of realism is based, rather, on the clarity and simplicity of his style and the near perfection of his Attic diction. He had also mastered the technical lessons of the Platonic dialogue which is the most perfect representative of the mimetic in ancient Greek literature. Yet it is also an authentic part of his enduring appeal that Lucian reads as well in translation as in the original Greek.

22. I borrow the term, "zero world," from Suvin (Note 16), derived in turn from Stanislaw Lem. Cf. Scholes and Kellogg (Note 20), p. 113, who view *True History* as a long narrative satire which is "continually threatened both by the aesthetic impulse to tell an interesting story and by the representational and illustrative tendencies to focus attention on either the real or the ideal world."

23. Paulson (Note 15), p. 41, remarks: "...(Lucian's) purpose is the very general one of discomfiting the reader, shaking up his cherished values, disrupting his orthodoxy."

24. Suvin (Note 16), esp. pp. 372-5 and note 4. Cf. his more recent article, "Science Fiction and the Genological Jungle," *Genre* 6(1973):251-73. The expression has also been taken up by Robert Scholes, *Structural Fabulation* (Notre Dame and London, 1975), pp. 29 and 46-7.

25. For the "analogical model" and analogical universes in SF, see Suvin, "Poetics" (Note 16), pp. 379-80, and "Genological Jungle" (Note 24), pp. 264-5.

26. Examples of giganticism besides moon flora and fauna: the giants on floating islands (§1:40-42); the gigantic craft of the pumpkin-pirates and nut-sailors (§2:37-38); the great kingfisher and its egg (§2:40-41), a precursor of the Roc in the Arabian Nights.

27. The examples besides the war between Phaethon and Endymion: the war with the fish races inside the whale (§1:35-38); the feuding giants on islands (§1:40-42); pumpkin-pirates, nut-sailors, and dolphin-riders (§2:37-39).

28. "Poetics" (Note 16), p. 374.

29. I acknowledge a debt to Fredric Jameson, "Generic Discontinuities in SF," SFS 1(1973):58.

30. See John Ferguson, *Utopias of the Classical World* (Ithaca, 1975), pp. 174-6, for Lucian's Elysium in the history of ancient utopian literature. The author suggests that Lucian's parody of utopia has a critical purpose: "Political theory which ignores the hard facts of material existence is in the last resort sterile" (p. 176).

31. The notion of another continent or island outside the boundaries of the known world of course goes back ultimately to Plato's description of Atlantis in the dialogues *Timaeus* and *Critias*. Ferguson (Note 30), *passim*, demonstrates that later Greek thought took the theme up mostly for utopian speculations, transferring descriptions of better human societies to imaginary landscapes. The theme remains speculative until late pagan/early Christian times when it finally degenerates into the pseudo-scientific conviction that such places really existed.

32. Considering the period in which he wrote, Lucian should be given all due credit for the freshness and vigor of his intellect. On the one hand, ancient science in the second century was, at best, in its senescence, although the period is famous for two scientific monuments—the medical corpus of Galen and the geocentric astronomy of Ptolemy—both of which unfortunately came to impede the progress of modern science because of their tremendous prestige. On the other hand, Lucian's age was clearly falling back into a reliance on the religious consciousness, in pagan and Christian thought

alike, as well as in the numerous quasi-religious philosophies of the times. See E.R. Dodds, *Pagan and Christian in an Age of Anxiety* (Cambridge, 1965), for a discussion of the increasing irrationalism in the era.

The truly remarkable fact is that Lucian so often surmounts the limits of his times in *True History* and other works: cognitive limits of Greek speculative thought and of ancient education with its excessive rhetorical emphases, as well as the limits inherent in the audience of the Second Sophistic. Despite Edward Gibbon's famous assessment of the period of the Antonine emperors as an era of unprecedented peace and prosperity for Roman citizenry as a whole, it was undeniably a dull lackluster era in terms of literature and ideas. Anachronism and archaism were the dominant modes of sensibility in literature, and higher culture in general was being stifled by the worship of tradition. For the intellectual sterility of the age, see B.A. van Groningen, "General Literary Tendencies in the Second Century A.D.," *Mnemosyne* 18(1965):41-56. Paulson (Note 15), p. 41, remarks: "Lucian is...the epitome of the satirist who writes at what he takes to be a time of extreme stodginess and reaction, when values have become standarized and rigid."

David Winston

Iambulus' *Islands of the Sun* and Hellenistic Literary Utopias

(from **SFS** *3: 219–227, November 1976)*

The original of Iambulus' narrative (written sometime between 165 and 50BC)[1] has perished, and were it not for the excerpts made by Diodorus Siculus in his *Bibliotheke* (§§2:55-60) we should have to rely on two meagre references in Lucian and Tzetzes. In introducing his parody of imaginary-voyage literature, *True Histories*, Lucian singles out Ctesias and Iambulus as representative. The latter, says Lucian, wrote much that was incredible about the lands in the great sea, but though obviously fabulous, it was not an unpleasing story. Ionnes Tzetzes (*Chiliades* §§727-30) noted that Iambulus wrote of round animals found in the islands of the Ethiopians, of double-tongued men who could converse with two different people simultaneously, and numerous other things. From Diodorus' excerpt, we may, in spite of its disorder, reconstruct the form and content of the work in some detail.

1. Iambulus' Narrative. Entitled *Islands of the Sun* or possibly *The Adventures of Iambulus in the Southern Ocean*, it probably contained chapters in a sequence similar to the following: 1) Birth and Education of Iambulus; 2) Incidents Leading to his Discovery of the Islands of the Sun; 3) Geographical and Astronomical Description of the Islands; 4) Constitution and Customs of the Islanders; 5) Religion of the Islanders; 6) Language and Learning of the Islanders; 7) The Animals of the Islands; 8) Sojourn of Iambulus at Palibothra and his Return to Greece or Asia Minor. These headings will be followed in my account of Iambulus' story, which in Diodorus is narrated in the third person.

Chapters 1-2. There was a certain Iambulus who had an early passion for learning, but who upon the death of his merchant father, plunged into commercial enterprise. On the way through Arabia to the spice-bearing country (i.e. the Somali coast), he was seized by brigands and ultimately carried off to the Ethiopian coast where he was compelled to participate in a ritual for the purification of that land: A boat containing a six-month food supply was rigged for him and a companion, and they were ordered to put to sea and to steer south until they arrived at a blessed isle inhabited by virtuous folk. If they reached the island safely, they would not only secure personal bliss but also confer peace and prosperity upon the Ethiopians for six hundred years. But if they should grow afraid and turn back, they would incur the sharpest penalties and bring disaster on the whole nation. After sailing over a vast and tempestuous sea for four months, they put in at the island foretold them, where some of the natives met them and drew their boat to shore. The islanders, crowding around, were amazed at the strangers, but behaved decently toward them, and shared with them whatever they had.

Chapter 3. The island was circular in form, with a circumference of about five thousand stades (1000 kilometers). It was part of an archipelago consisting of seven islands, all of about equal size, equidistant from each other, and following the same laws and customs. Although at the equator, the natives enjoyed a most temperate climate; moreover, the fruits there ripened the year through, even as the poet writes: "Pear upon pear grows old, and apple on apple, yea, and clustered grapes on grapes, and fig upon fig" (*Odyssey* §§7:120-21). Day and night are of equal length, and at noon nothing casts a shadow, since the sun is directly overhead. Of the constellations known to us, the Bears and many others are entirely invisible.

The natives spend their time in the meadows, the land supplying many things for sustenance. For by reason of the island's productivity and the mild climate, foods are produced of themselves in greater quantities than necessary. A certain reed growing there in great plenty, a span broad, bears abundant fruit resembling white vetch; it waxes and wanes with the moon. After gathering this reed, the natives steep it in warm water, until it becomes the size of a pigeon's egg: then, having crushed it and kneaded it skilfully with their hands, they mould it into loaves which when baked are of excellent sweetness. The island also has abundant streams, the warm ones good for bathing and overcoming fatigue, while the cold ones are deliciously sweet and healthful. Even the sea about the island, which has violent currents and ebbs, is sweet to the taste. Fruit trees grow there abundantly and spontaneously, including the olive tree and vine. The natives catch many varieties of fish and birds. The immense snakes are harmless to man, and have deliciously sweet flesh. Clothing is made from certain reeds having a bright velvety down in the center, which they gather and mix with pounded oyster shells, thus making wonderful purple garments.

Chapter 4. The inhabitants of this island are very different from those who live in our part of the inhabited world, both in the peculiar nature of their bodies and in their way of life. They are over six feet tall, and their bones flex to a certain extent and straighten out again like the sinewy parts. Their bodies are very soft to the touch, yet far more vigorous than ours; if they lay hold of any object with their hands, no one can force it from their grip. They have hair on the head, eyebrows, eyelids, and chin, but on the other parts of the body not even the slightest down is visible. They are remarkably handsome and well-proportioned in their body contours. The openings of their ears [or nostrils?] are much wider than ours and have valve-like coverings. Their tongues are two-pronged up to a point, and they cut up the inner portion even further so that it is doubled up to the root. Their phonetic potential is accordingly very diversified, for they can reproduce not only every articulate language used by man, but even the multi-toned warbling of birds, and in general every phoneme. But the most incredible feat of all is their ability to carry on conversation simultaneously with two people, responding to the questions of one with one fork of the tongue, while conversing familiarly about current events with the other fork.[2]

They live in clan groupings, not more than four hundred to a group. Each grouping is ruled by its oldest member, who is something like a king, and obeyed by all. On completion of his one hundred and fiftieth year the ruler puts an end to his life in accordance with the law, and the next oldest succeeds to the rule. They alternately serve one another, some of them fishing, others working at the crafts, others occupying themselves in other useful matters, and still others—except for the very aged—performing public duties in cyclic rotation. They do not marry, but possess their women in common, and raising the children as communal wards they love them equally. While still infants, they are frequently exchanged by their nurses, so that not even the mothers will recognize their own. Since there is thus no rivalry among them, they live free from partisan strife, placing the highest value upon inner harmony. Each grouping maintains a peculiar large bird, whereby a test is made to determine the psychic state of the infant children. They mount the babies upon the birds, and those who endure the aerial flight they rear, but those who get airsick and panicky they cast out as of an undeserving temperament and unlikely to live long.

Although everything is abundantly and spontaneously supplied to them, the islanders nevertheless do not indulge their pleasures without restraint, but practise simplicity and eat only to sufficiency. They prepare meats and all roasted or boiled foods, but they do not know other dishes, such as the numerous condiments and sauces concocted by cooks. Their whole way of life follows a prescribed order: not that they eat in a public area or the same foods, but specified days have been constituted for eating sometimes fish, sometimes fowl, at other times the flesh of land animals, and at others olives with the simplest side dishes.

They are extremely long-lived and mostly free from disease. Anyone maimed or with any bodily defect is compelled by an irrevocable law to do away with himself. When they reach the age of one hundred and fifty, it is their custom to voluntarily remove themselves by using a strange plant: whoever lies upon it falls imperceptibly and gently asleep and dies. They bury their dead at low tide, covering them with sand; when the tide comes in a mound is formed.

Chapter 5. As gods they revere the all-encompassing heavens, the Sun, and in general, all the celestial bodies. At their feasts and festivals, hymns and songs of praise to the gods are recited and sung, but especially to the Sun, after whom they name both the islands and themselves.

Chapter 6. Every branch of learning is diligently pursued by them, but their chief concern is with astrology. They employ an alphabet representing twenty-eight different phonetic values but comprising only seven characters, each of which can assume four different forms. They do not write their lines horizontally as we do, but vertically downward.

Chapter 7. They have a very odd sort of small animal: it is round and very similar to a tortoise, and its skin is crossed by two yellow diagonal lines, at each end of which it has an eye and a mouth. Though seeing with four eyes and using four mouths, it collects all its food through one gullet into one intestine. All its inner organs are similarly single; but all around its underbelly there are many feet enabling it to walk in any direction it pleases.[3] The blood of this animal has a wondrous property: it immediately glues together any living member that has been severed; even if a hand or a similar organ is severed, by means of this blood it can be glued on again while the cut is fresh. The same is true of any other part of the body excepting the vital regions.

Chapter 8. After a seven-year stay, Iambulus and his friend were shipwrecked in shoals off India, and while his companion perished, Iambulus was taken up from the coast by native villagers to the king at Palibothra, a distance of many days from the sea. Since the king was fond of the Greeks and a supporter of learning, he regarded Iambulus with great favor. Finally, after receiving safe conduct, Iambulus travelled first to Persia and later safely home to Greece [or a Greek-speaking country]. Iambulus considered his adventures worth recording, and added a good deal of information about India unknown to his contemporaries.

2. Extraordinary Voyages and Utopian Themes in Greek Literature. The Hellenistic age witnessed an extraordinary flowering of geographical and travel literature, very striking in its profuseness and variety. This kind of literature was not, to be sure, a new interest with the Greeks. To appreciate the fascination such writings had always had for the Greek mind, one need only recall the epic adventures of Odysseus, the *Arimaspeia* of Aristeas of Proconnesus, the almost painful elaboration on Io's peregrinations in Aeschylus' *Prometheus*, and the texts of the Ionian pioneers of historical-geographical writing culminating in Herodotus' medley. With the conquests of Alexander, however, this literature attained new dimensions. Eyewitness accounts of Greek generals, admirals, roving ambassadors and special envoys followed each other in rapid succession. A bare enumeration of their names would suffice to indicate the magnitude of a vast literature which has almost totally disappeared.[4] This Hellenistic overflow may well be compared to a similar phenomenon which occurred in 16th-17th century Europe.

By a very natural development, there sprang up from the main branch of travel literature two considerable offshoots, the *travel fantasy*—a frankly fictive account of exotic travel adventures with no attempt to lend an air of reality to the narrative—and the *voyage extraordinaire*. Though the travel fantasy has perished, the name of Antiphanes of Berge and his famed tall tale survive to testify to the many travel yarns which flourished in this age.[5] Our chief concern, however, is with the "extraordinary voyage," since it was this form that Iambulus chose for his utopian narratives. The choice was a logical one, for unlike the travel fantasy, the mark of authenticity carefully contrived by its author commends the extraordinary voyage to a wider audience and lends its imaginary contents the prestige of the real and concrete: the utopian community it described is not a wild dream which can be shrugged off, but a cold, hard fact. Before proceeding to examine Iambulus' methods of authentication, let us observe the similar methods employed by the extraordinary voyages before him.

The earliest known utopian composition written in the form of an extraordinary voyage is the *Peri Hyperboreon* of Hecataeus of Abdera, a contemporary of Alexander the Great. Painting an elaborately idealized picture of the mythical Hyperboreans, Hecataeus added much geographical and astronomical data, which were sufficiently striking in their simulated authenticity to cause geographers to make detailed attempts at identification with specific sites. Combining the various fragments, we get the following geographical-astronomical picture: in the northern Amalchian sea, there lies opposite the land of the Celts an island not smaller than Sicily, called Helixoia. It is inhabited by the Hyperboreans, i.e. people who live beyond the point whence the north wind (Boreas) blows. The island is very fertile and productive, and owing to its extremely temperate climate it yields two crops a year. It is said that the Moon appears from this island to be only a very short distance from the Earth, so that its Earth-like prominences are visible, and that Apollo visits the island every nineteen years, the period in which the stars complete their heavenly movements returning to their former positions. The Hyperboreans speak a language peculiar to themselves, and are very friendly to the Greeks, especially the Athenians and Delians, who inherited this good will from the most ancient times. In fact, certain Greeks are said to have visited the Hyperboreans, leaving behind them costly votive offerings with Greek inscriptions.

So turn now[6] to the *Hiera Anagraphe* of Euhemerus of Messana (ca. 300 BC), an extraordinary voyage with a special philosophical-religious theory as its purpose. It seems to have been an elaborately detailed work in at least three books, and exhibits every mark of a careful effort at authentication. Euhemerus speaks of his many voyages in his official capacity on behalf of King Cassander of Macedonia (301-297 BC) and specifically of a long southerly ocean-voyage he once made from the eastern coast of Arabia Eudaemon (i.e. from that NE part of Arabia lying opposite the modern Baluchistan), which took him to the Panchaean isles. A detailed description of three of these islands follows, including the names of the notable cities Hyracia, Dalis, Oceanis, and especially Panara, whose citizens are called "Suppliants of Zeus Triphylius" (Zeus of the three tribes). Whenever he can, Euhemerus gives exact dimensions and distances on and between the three islands; from Panchaea's eastern promontory one can catch a glimpse of India through the misty distance. Another realistic touch is the elaborate description of the nature of frankincense and its preparation on the island of Hiera, to which may also be added that there is nothing very strange or incredible in Euhemerus' account of the political setup of the Panchaeans. Finally, perhaps following the lead of Hecataeus, Euhemerus provides scientific documentation for his religious theory that the gods were nothing more than great rulers from the remote past deified for their admirable deeds on behalf of men, by referring all his information in this area—aside from supposed conversations with the priests—to various inscriptions, and especially to a gold stele in the sanctuary of Zeus Triphylius on which are inscribed in summary fashion, in the writing employed by the Panchaeans (apparently Egyptian hieroglyphics), the deeds of Uranus, Cronus and Zeus. Combining geographical and botanical detail with sober political narrative, Euhemerus produced a most persuasive *voyage extraordinaire*, which easily deceived Diodorus into taking it as straight history.

Iambulus' extraordinary voyage can now be seen in its proper setting. Uniting all the techniques of his predecessors, he uses astronomical, geographical, botanical, zoological and anthropological data of all sorts to authenticate his narrative. It should be noted that one of the most accurate and influential of the genuine voyage narratives, the *Paraplous* of Nearchus, was especially rich in scientific information, above all astronomy, meteorology, and botany. Iambulus' marked use of such data, therefore, is clearly understandable. The scientific charlatan employs an abundant scientific terminology to convince the audience that he is rigorously scientific;[7] similarly, Iambulus affects the best scientific-voyage terminology of the age in an effort to win the confidence of his audience. His unusual success can today be measured only by the long list of geographers who have taken him in full earnest and have bravely defended him against his defamers.[8]

In general, Greek literary genres are sharply defined, and each has a set of themes (*topoi*) peculiar to itself. Conforming to this usage, Iambulus' work exhibits themes frequently found in the Greek utopia. The Sun-islands are circular in form, the favorite geometrical pattern for a utopian country. So, for example, Plato's Atlantis is composed of a series of concentric circles of land and sea, and Hecataeus' temple of Apollo on the island of the Hyperboreans is spheroid. Similarly, the utopian climate is always pleasant, there is always an abundance of sweet and healthful spring water, and a super-abundant food supply. Further, utopians are usually tall and well-built. Iambulus' Sun-men are also long-lived and free from disease, but most utopians outstrip them in this matter: the Uttarakuru of Sanskrit sources live one thousand (or 10,000) years, and so too the Hyperboreans; according to Herodotus the Ethiopians live to 120 years or more, and Onesicritus in *Pos Alexandros ekhthe* (in Strabo, *Geography* §15:1:34) attributes 130 years to the people of Musicanus; the Meropes of Theopompus live twice as long as ordinary mortals, and never know disease. Utopians, however, not only live pleasantly, but also die pleasantly. On the island paradise of Syria (*Odyssey* §§15:403-14), Apollo of the silver bow and Artemis slay the happy natives with their gentle shafts; in Hesiod's Golden Age men die as overcome with sleep (*Works and Days* §116); the inhabitants of Theopompus' Eusebes die laughing. Similarly, Iambulus' Sun-men have a magical plant which induces the sleep of death.

Finally, most utopians expel their visitors as evil-doers. After a stay of seven years, Iambulus and his comrade are cast out as incorrigibly prone to evil ways. Homer's Phaeacians similarly send strangers back where they came from (*Odyssey* §§7:32-33). Examples from later, 18th century utopias are Swift's Gulliver and Foigny's Sadeur, ultimately ejected as unfit for a perfect, rational society.

Iambulus' Sun symbolism is especially understandable when we realize its specific connection with justice and righteousness. The prophet Malachi (§3:20) spoke of "the Sun of Justice," a figure of speech then current in the Near East, from the ancient Babylonian literature to the Orphic hymns.[9]

Summing up, Iambulus' main source beside travel narratives on India was the Greek utopian tradition of extraordinary voyages which preceded him (as well as various philosophical works). Shaped by his imaginative genius, however, these varied elements blended into a distinct utopian art-form, which found a permanent place in European literature.

3. Cockayne Utopianism. The earliest detailed analysis of Iambulus was that of Rohde, who remarks that Iambulus' basic theme was that the perfect condition of man lies in the simplest and most primitive state of nature. This was in accord with the doctrines of the elder Stoics, who described the rawest state of nature as the ideal arrangement of human society.[10] Farrington is equally convinced that Iambulus' Sun-isle is a Stoic utopia and adds that "it exhibits in the most unmistakable way the intimate connection between Stoic and Chaldean conceptions of the universe and society." The seven islands correspond with the Sun, Moon and five planets (already noted by Pöhlmann). The reed which waxes and wanes with the Moon illustrates the sympathy imagined to exist in Chaldean astrology between heaven and earth. It is because the inhabitants are Sun-men that their society is based on egalitarian communism, and the island's location on the equator is a symbol of the equality which prevails there.[11]

The most penetrating appraisal of Iambulus' utopia, though somewhat distorted by an overpowering zeal for socialist theory, is that of Pöhlmann, who notes that Iambulus' narrative is the first political romance known to us, and represents the high-water mark of the Greek poetic utopia. Its author is in fact a socio-economic Jules Verne. Diodorus has unfortunately emphasized the fantastic element, giving little of the social and economic. It is abundantly clear, however that the whole Sun-state is one large communist association (or unification of such associations: "systemata"), whose aim is nothing less than a fully communist regulation of the entire economic and social life—possibly under the influence of Aristonicus' uprising. The collectivism of the Sun-state is strongly authoritarian, with a ruling "hegemon" in each group whose power is life-long, and who is not elected. But what might have been an irksome collectivism is softened considerably by the richness of the earth's productivity, which diminishes the necessity of human labour and leaves a maximum amount of leisure for intellectual pursuits. The fantastic element, Pöhlmann further argues, was necessary if Iambulus wanted to satisfy his audience, who expected it in this genre of literature. Moreover, just as much of his novelistic framework was drawn from the current literature, so do his ideas correspond to current streams of thought, reminiscent of Platonic, Cynic, and Stoic ideas, which were then, so to speak, in the air.[12]

The first to deny that Iambulus' utopia is stoic was Richter, who agrees with Rohde that the Sun-men are a people in their pristine power and beauty, living in blissful peace, in the simplest sort of organization, based on primal natural rights, but argues that there was nothing specifically Stoic or Cynic in that.[13] Tarn points out that Iambulus' work is a patchwork of ideas typical for the Hellenistic age (true or quasi-scientific details, speculation on the ideal state, travel story, romance, desire for the simple life). Like H.G. Wells, Iambulus was a vivid story-teller, and his utopia is reminiscent of Wells' *Men Like Gods.*[14] Similarly, Africa writes: "Like Montaigne's cannibals, Iambulus' happy Indians are a romanticized composite of travellers' tales, held up as an existent ideal to mortify corrupt Europeans, and The Isles of the Sun are closer to Melville's *Typee* than to More's *Utopia.*"[15]

This multiplicity of opinion, at first sight baffling, is essentially the result of a lack of precision in defining the various kinds of utopianism and of an adequate terminology in this area. I propose to designate the utopianism which is unwilling to confine its program to a transformation of social and political patterns, but beguilingly seeks to overhaul the very structure of the natural world, as *Cockayne utopianism*—borrowing a word from a widespread folk motif, the Land of Cockayne, with which it shares its peculiar flight into fantasy. In Cockayne, Nature is refashioned to the author's liking, and her beneficence charms our anxieties away. While Cockayne utopianism is an unrestrained expression of man's hidden desires, utopianism proper is an expression of the reflective mind and in accord with philosophical ideals.[16] The utopist's mood is one of rebellion against the given. His utopian dream is an explosion of the poetic spirit, and beneath the glowing colors lies concealed his quarrel with the Lord: "If only God had plied his craft better!..." I shall now endeavor to show that Iambulus' *Island of the Sun* is an unmistakable example of Cockayne utopianism.

The distinguishing mark of Cockayne utopianism is not its vision of a new social order, but of a *new natural order* which necessarily entails the former.[17] It says, in effect, that what we need is a new Heaven and a new Earth—and a new race of men. This is exactly what Iambulus has conjured up before our eyes. His island enjoys perfect climatic conditions, and its automatic productivity yields an overabundance of everything. All foods (including snake-meat) and all liquids (including the seawater) are deliciously sweet and healthful. The islanders themselves are physically no ordinary mortals. They are all well over six feet, built like football players, with an inimitable hand-grip, and a wonderfully pliable bone structure. Severed limbs they glue right back on by means of a potent blood-extract, while their natural resistance makes them practically immune to disease. Ear valves keep out unnecessary noise and a two-forked tongue both speeds up their work and adds an unusual variety and zest to their conversation. Everything, in fact, exemplifies beauty, symmetry, and vigour. The islands form perfect circles (symbols of perfection), are seven in number (a number loaded with every conceivable form of symbolism), are all of about equal size, are equidistant from each other, and follow the same laws and customs. The people, perfectly alike physically and mentally, are divided into groupings, each numbering about four hundred members, who enjoy a life-span of 150 years (though they apparently could live much longer if they had so wished) whereupon they freely and pleasantly take their exit of life. This passion for symmetry, sometimes called the geometrical spirit, is an unfailing charactertisic of our genre.[18] Though pleasingly held within bounds in Iambulus, it is sometimes carried to enormous extremes.

To sum up, a super-race lives on a super-island, where all is beauty and symmetry. No philosopher, grappling with the complexities of reality and seeking the way to a new and better life in spite of them, would deny that Iambulus' solution is much simpler and more effective. He would insist, however, that the Cockayne element removes Iambulus' vision from the realm of serious philosophical speculation. This is not to deny, of course, that Iambulus may genuinely reflect many philosophical ideas. But for him they form part of an *imaginative* matrix from which he draws the various elements of his utopian construction. Thus his narrative seems shaped by opposed designs. At one end Iambulus seeks to approach the real as best he knows, at the other he seeks to escape it as completely as he can. That is why his techniques of authentication wrought such havoc among later geographic commentators. But his tendency to evade reality in the solution of social problems has been equally mischievous. Some see in his utopia the ideal of primitive simplicity, while others find in it an authoritarian collectivism. Both are wrong. There is nothing primitive about multilingual people, expert in every branch of learning, clad in beautiful purple, and enjoying a varied diet of all sorts of roasts and an abundance of oil and wine. On the other hand, there is nothing authoritarian about collectives which operate without the aid of a judiciary or central government, where every office or duty (however menial) is constantly rotated, and where labour is at a minimum. A most difficult paradox of real life has thus been resolved with the aid of Cockayne, which has graciously bestowed on the Sun-children the boon of natural virtue and absolute equality. These incorruptible utopians walk amid abundance, yet practice moderation and simplicity. Their well-oiled organization, thoroughly communist and all-regulating, operates, nevertheless, through separate and uncoordinated units, without coercion or central control. Everybody loves everybody. All hail to Iambulus!

NOTES

1. The grounds for this dating may be found in my dissertation, "Iambulus: A Literary Study in Greek Utopianism," Columbia University, 1956.

2. Cf John Ferguson, *Utopias of the Classical World* (US 1975), p 209, n 14: "The late Sir Richard Paget, owing to a peculiarity of the voice-box, could sound two notes simultaneously. His daughter inherited this capacity, and they used to sing quartets."

3. A delightful sketch of this weird creature, with severed hands and legs strewn all about it, is in Leo Africanus, *Description de l'Afrique*, ed. Jean Temporal (Lyon 1556), vol 2, *La Navigation de Iambol, marchant* Grec, p 116.

4. See Franz Susemihl, *Geschichte der Grieschischen Literatur in der Alexandrinerzeit* (Leipzig 1891), 1:649-701, who lists over forty authors.

5. Antiphanes spoke of a city so cold that human speech freezes there as it is uttered, and only on its melting in the summer can one hear what has been said. For the subsequent elaborations of this story in European and American literature, see Eugene S. McCartney, "Antiphanes' Cold-Weather Story and its Elaboration," *Classical Philology* 48(1953):169-72. Lucian's parody of the fantastic-voyage literature, his *True Histories*, indicates its extensive proportions and popularity.

6. I have omitted from this discussion Amometus' book on the Attacorae, which was classified by Pliny with Hecataeus' work on the Hyperboreans (*Natural History* §6:55) and was probably also written in the form of a voyage extraordinaire. Unfortunately, all we know about it is that the Attocorae were said to have dwelt on the bay of the same name, sheltered by sunbathed hills from every harmful wind, and enjoying the same kind of climate as the Hyperboreans. Magasthenes seems to have referred to them when he mentioned "Indian Hyperboreans" (Strabo, *Geography* §15:1:57). Fragments of Amometus (lived during the reign of Ptolemy I or II) are in C. Müller, *Fragmenta Historicorum Graecorum* §2:396. For the Sanskrit sources describing the Uttarakuru, see C. Lassen, "Berträge zur Kunde des Indischen Alterthums aus dem Mahabharata," *Zeitschrift für die Kunde des Morgenlandes* 2(1839):62-70. These sources describe an Indian Cockayne: Uttara Kuru is the land of unbroken delights, not too cold or warm, free from disease, sadness, and worry. The earth is dust-free and aromatic, while the rivers flow along golden beds, rolling pearls and precious stones instead of pebbles. The trees always bear both fruits and all sorts of materials and multi-colored clothing, and every morning from their branches hang the most beautiful women, who, through a curse of Indra, must die again every evening. Cf Lucian, *True Histories* §§1-8. See also Erwin Rohde, *Der Griechische Roman and Seine Vorläufer*, 3d edn (Leipzig 1914), pp 233-34, and Bimala C. Law, *Geographical Essays* (UK 1937), 1:29.

7. See, for example, the fascinating account of pseudo-science by Martin Gardner, *In the Name of Science* (US 1952). Two classics of pseudo-science are the 750-page *Glazial-Kosmogonie* by Hans Horbiger, "filled with photographs and elaborate diagrams, heavy with the thoroughness of German scholarship, and from beginning to end totally without value," and *The New Geology* by George M. Price, "disproving" evolution (Gardner, pp 37, 128). The analogy is, of course, inexact, since the pseudo-scientist usually believes he is truly scientific.

8. Gian Battista Ramusio, "Navigatione di Iambolo mercantate antichissimo," in his *Delle Navigationi et Viaggi* (Venezia 1550), 1:188-90; also John Harris, *Navigantium atque itinerantium Bibliotheca* (London 1764), 1:383-85; E. Jacquet, "De la relation et de l'alphabet indien d'Iamboule," *Nouveau Jornal Asiatique* 19, 2d ser., tome 8 (1831), pp 20-30; E. Stechow, "Kannte das Altertum die Insel Madagascar?" *Petermann's Geographische Mitteilungen* (1944), pp 84-85; Christian Lassen, *Indische Alterthumskunde* (Leipzig 1858), 3:253-71.

9. See Franz Joseph Dölger, *Die Sonne der Gerechtigkeit und der Schwarze*, Liturgiegeschichtliche Forschungen, Heft 2 (Münster 1918), pp 83-100; also the same author in *Antike und Christentum* 5(1936):138-40, and W.W. Tarn, "Alexander Helios and the Golden Age," *Journal of Roman Studies* 22(1932):140+147-48.

10. Rohde (Note 6), pp 243-60.

11. Benjamin Farrington, *Head and Hand in Ancient Greece* (UK 1947), pp 55-87.

12. Robert von Pöhlmann, *Geschichte der Sozialen Frage und des Sozialismus in der Antiken Welt*, 3d edn (Munich 1925), 2:305-24. Upon the death of Attalus III (133 BC) and his deeding of the Pergamene kingdom to Rome, Aristonicus, illegitimate member of the royal

family, claimed the throne for himself. Compelled to retire to the hinterland and recruit new forces, Aristonicus appealed to the dispossessed poor and slave populations, offering the latter liberty and the former, it seems, a sparkling social program. These new recruits were specifically designated Heliopolitae (Strabo, *Geography* §14:1:38 C646), a fact which in the opinion of Pöhlmann (2:404-06) and W.W. Tarn (*Alexander the Great* [UK 1948], 2:411-14) suggests a definite relationship between Aristonicus' social program and the Hellenistic utopian literature, especially Iambulus.

On the other hand, M. Rostovtzeff (*Social and Economic History of the Hellenistic World* [UK 1941], 2:808), soberly comments that "the evidence is slight and inconclusive," and that "the name Heliopolitae may equally well be connected with the oriental belief in the Great Sun, the Supreme God of oriental solar henotheism, the God Justice and the protector of those who have suffered wrong." So too writes J.W. Swain ("Antiochus Epiphanes and Egypt," *Classical Philology* 39[1941]:78): "It seems more likely that the name was taken from some Anatolian cult with which the rebels would be more familiar than they were with Greek philosophy." Rostovtzeff's explanation is also preferred by D.R. Dudley ("Blossiuis of Cumae," *J. of Roman Studies* 31[1941]:98), V. Vavřinek (*La Revolte d'Aristonicos*, Rozpravy Československe Akademie Ved 67 [Prague 1957], p 43), F. Bömer, *Untersuchungen über die Religion der Sklaven in Griechenland und Rom* [1961], 3:165ff), T.W. Africa ("Aristonicus, Blossius and the City of the Sun," *Int. Rev. Soc. History* 6[1961]110-24), J. Vogt (*Sklaverie und Humanität*, Historia Einzelschr. 8 [Weisbaden 1965], p 43), and C. Mossé ("Les Utopies égalitaires a l'époque hellénistique," *Revue Historique* 93[1969]:297-308).

But Pöhlmann's suggestion is accepted by Joseph Bidez (*La Cité du Monde et la Cité du Soleil chez les Stoiciens* [Paris 1932]), Hugh Last (*Cambridge Ancient History*, 9:104), G. Cardinale ("La Morte di Attalo III e la Rivolta di Aristonico," *Saggi di Storia Antica e di Archeologia* [Rome 1910], pp 300-301), Benjamin Farrington (Note 11), Esther V. Hansen (*The Attalids of Pergamon* [US 1947]), and most recently John Ferguson (*Utopias of the Classical World* [US 1975], pp 124-29). Finally, it is regarded as perhaps valid by Julius Beloch ("Sozialismus und Kommunismus in Alterthum," *Zeitschr. f. Sozialwissenschaft* 4[1901]:360) and Franz Altheim (*Alexander und Asien* [Tübingen 1953]).

13. Waldemar Richter, *Iambulus* (Beilage zum Osterprogramm des Gymnasiums Schaffhausen, 1888).

14. Tarn (Note 12, 1st par.); cf Elizabeth Visser, *Iamboulos en de eilanden van de Zon* (Groningen 1947).

15. Africa (Note 12, 2d par.).

16. These classifications have not been invented but simply introduced from other utopian literatures. The term "voyage extraordinaire" was introduced—according to Geoffrey Atkinson, *The Extraordinary Voyage in French Literature Before 1700* (US 1920), page x—by Gustave Lanson in his *Manuel Bibliographique de la Littérature Française Moderne* (Paris 1914). For a detailed discussion of the problems involved in the classification of the imaginary voyage and cautions about extensions of the classification "voyage extraordinaire" for general use, see P.B. Gove, *The Imaginary Voyage in Prose Fiction* (US 1941), especially pp 93-122.

17. See Paul Hazard, *The European Mind* (US 1953), pp 26-27. For its use in Indian and Japanese tradition, see *Aware of Utopia*, ed. David W. Plath (US 1971), pp 28-29.

18. It is almost certain that many other utopias imitating the style and technique of Iambulus were composed in the Greco-Roman age. The fact that Lucian singles out Iambulus for special mention in the opening pages of *True Histories* is a clear testimony to his popularity with Greco-Roman readers, and it is inconceivable that he was not imitated by other writers. Further, though Hellenistic utopian literature has for the most part disappeared, Iambulus seems to have had a distinct influence on the 17th-century utopias by Tommaso Campanella (*Civitas Solis* or *Città del Sole*, 1623) and Gabriel Foigny (*Terre australe connue* or *Les Aventures de Jacques Sadeur*, 1676). Though Campanella lacks entirely the Cockayne concept, many elements of his City of the Sun are strikingly similar to those of Iambulus' Islands of the Sun, as are many elements of Foigny's Cockayne utopia and *voyage extraordinaire*. Iambulus was easily accessible to Campanella in the Italian translation of Ramusio (Note 8) and to Foigny in the French translation of Leo Africanus (Note 3). Although the loss of his work has made Iambulus a shadowy figure in the history of Greek literature, I hope this article has succeeded in restoring some of the flavor of his work and in indicating its importance in the utopian tradition.

Roy Arthur Swanson

The True, the False, and the Truly False: Lucian's Philosophical Science Fiction

(from SFS *3: 228–239, November 1976)*

Lucian of Samosata, the Greco-Syrian satirist of the second century A.D., appears today as an exemplar of the science-fiction artist. There is little, if any, need to argue that his mythopoeic Milesian Tales and his literary fantastic voyages and utopistic hyperbole comport with the genre of science fiction;[1] but much remains to be observed of the substance of his contribution to this genre, particularly with regard to his estimates of fiction as potentially, and often actually, superior to scientific cognition (the "philosophy" of the ancient world) in the elucidation of truth and as a check upon the excesses of introverse cognition. The following essay proposes a view of Lucian's "true fictions" as truth-serving fiction, of his manner of exposing false values and misdirections in "philosophy," and of his warranting identification as a writer of philosophical science fiction. Clarification of the phrase "true fictions" will include etymological comment on the word "true" in its Greek form and some attention to the proper translation of the title provided for his literary fantastic voyaging, a title variously rendered as "A True Story," "(The) True History," and "True Histories." The term "philosophical science fiction" is to be understood, not as referent to science fiction written by a philosopher, or in a philosophical vein, but as indicative of science fiction written by, in this case, a satirist about philosophy; an illustrative parallel would be Aristophanes's *Clouds* as philosophical comedy.

1. Truth-serving Fiction. It is Lucian's concept of truth-serving which the careful reader of the *True Tales* would do well to attend, and her or his attendance ought to be marked by an awareness of Lucian's skill in the technique of inversion, by means of which he exposes a good many reversals of sensible value. An explanation of "True Tales" as a translator's title preferable to those already mentioned will be offered below. Lucian prefaces his *True Tales* with a statement that he is submitting reading which provides, not only relaxing entertainment after the rigors of serious study, but also food for thought. He then notes that he presents falsehoods and that he deals with poets, historians, and philosophers who have done the same. The chiastic sequence in his note can be expressed in the form of a ratio: the pleasant (charíen) is to thought (phronésein) as falsehoods (pseúsmata) are to poetry/history/philosophy. He concludes his preface with a claim that his own lying is superior to that of philosophers because it is not presented as though it were truth: to admit that one is lying is to be truthful. The comic paradox is that falsehood can be a form of truth (telling the truth that one is lying) just as Socratic ignorance can be a form of knowledge (knowing that one does not know).

Lucian's tales are "true" in the sense that they are truly, or really, tales. They are true to their fiction. Poets, historians, and philosophers who pass tales off as factual truth are false to their own modes of expression. Lucian is less than profound in differentiating between obvious fiction which stimulates thought and fiction which elicits credibility by means of verisimilitude; but he does proffer the perennially necessary reminder that thinking and believing are different and distinct kinds of mental activity and that it is best not to confuse them. He tells us that his tales are utterly false to fact, and he makes them so blatantly false to fact that we are constantly secure from the tentacles of belief. Then, as we relax with the entertainment he provides, we are entirely free to think. We are not compelled to think, as readers of philosophy feel themselves to be; but we are free to do so if we choose. If we do so, there is much to provoke and enlarge our thought, as presumably there is not in the work of writers who offer entertainment exclusively for its own sake or in that of writers who place a stage of credibility under their entertainment or embellish their entertainment with realistic props and scenery, all by way of promoting, for its own sake, a willing suspension of disbelief. Lucian confronts us with a suspension of belief, to the end that we may obtain a pension of thought.

The adjective *alēthḗs* means "true" in the sense of "genuine" as well as in the sense of "factual"; a genuine tale is not a factual narrative; and Lucian implicitly reminds us that there is no truth in a true tale, that is, in a tale that is truly a tale. The Greek adjective, moreover, is implicit with the sense of "awareness." It is derived from a combination of the words *a* (not) and *lanthánein* (to escape notice). Our English word "true" is etymologically inseparable from the area of "belief" and is at best merely a practicable translation of *alēthḗs*. Real thought begins in awareness, and it may end in, or be cut short by, belief. Belief is, positively speaking, an acknowledgment of an inescapable fact or datum; negatively speaking, it is an acceptance of a fiction as a fact. When we read Lucian's *True Tales* we are done with belief as soon as we acknowledge his fiction as inescapably fiction. We may then go on either to enjoy the fiction as fiction or to do this and to think about it as well.

We may, for example, simply regale ourselves with a picture of the Morning Star (Eosphorus) as a neutral colony between the ridiculous Sun people and the equally ridiculous Moon people; or we may go on to ponder the significance of the Morning Star as transversal to the day (Sun) and the night (Moon). Our thinking would then bring us to the scientific periphery of astronomy or to the literary periphery of allegory, or to both; if to both, then we would be in the world of science and fiction, to which the genre of science fiction is transversal.

Given the virtual synonymity of "science" and "philosophy" with respect to the ancient West, Lucian's science fiction could rightly be called "philosophy fiction," except for the fact that, in modern context, the term is much more applicable to a work like Voltaire's *Candide*. For this reason, among others, the most descriptive generic phrase relative to *True Tales* is "philosophical science fiction." As we shall see, Lucian presents philosophers as practitioners of cognition who serve their cognitive methods much more than they serve truth. From this and from his presentation of philosophy as the servant more of its own ends than of truth we can conclude that Lucian looks upon philosophy as predispositional to belief, which all too frequently breeds unawareness. Conversely, he looks upon fiction as serving truth by means of its constant sustenance of awareness. Were Lucian writing science fiction today, he would doubtless bring us to science, as we know it, through a fiction which would not let us remain complacent with the acknowledgment of data.

From a Lucianic perspective the staying power of a science-fiction work like H.G. Wells's *The First Men in the Moon* consists in its invalid science, the incredible Cavorite, for example, or the assumption of vegetation and life on and in the moon. The validity of one-sixth G brings the Bedford-Cavor moonshot too close to credibility; but this bit of scientific accuracy proves only momentarily to distract us. We are brought to science and allegory as Lucian would bring us to them when we meet the concept of intelligent life transformed into pure function and when we see science (Tsi-puff) and philosophy (Phi-oo) in the ultimate self-service to which Lucian saw science-philosophy tending to reduce itself. Serendipitously, perhaps, Wells's novel is more effective today than when he wrote it because we of the Apollo and Viking Program years are much less likely than Wells's contemporaries to be offset by credence and, accordingly, much more free to think.

In histories of philosophy and literature Lucian is never accorded the status of a great thinker. Plato's distinctions between thought (diánoia) and belief (pístis)[2] have never been, nor are ever likely to be, in danger of challenge or supersession by the works of the satirist, whose importance in intellectual history merits due recognition nevertheless. Lucian's talent is in stimulating thought and in ridiculing the process by which thought is translated into or terminated by belief. His remedy for thought which, turned back upon itself, becomes belief is to invert belief and start anew. In *True Tales* he turns belief upside-down: "One must not believe [pisteúein] in any of the events about which I write," he says in his preface after insisting, "I shall state only one truth, and that is that I am lying [toûto alētheúso hóti pseúdomai]." Our belief, then, can be directed only to falsehood in his series of tales which are true, as tales, only because they are false.

In *True Tales* and in some of his dialogues Lucian exposes philosophy, ostensibly a mode of inquiry into truth, as being patently effective, once it has come to a terminus in belief, only to the degree that it serves falsehood. His subsumption of philosophy to fiction is to be equated with the science-fiction writer's subsumption of science to fiction: science, ostensibly a mode of inquiry into truth, is literarily effective to the degree that it serves fiction. Lucian thrice asserts his veracity as he narrates his "true tales": "I hesitate to say, lest you call me a liar" (§1:25); "he will see that I am telling the truth" (§1:26); and "I knew that I had never been a liar" (§1:31). His assertions are false, and yet they are true to his prefatory admission of falsehood. The connotative dimensions of the title of his literary fantastic voyage are appreciable in proportion as we infer his comic sophistry, namely, the false is the true.

The textual tradition unfortunately attaches two titles to the piece. The earlier codices (tenth/eleventh centuries) have *alētheîs historíai* (true histories); later codices (thirteenth to fifteenth centuries) have *alēthê diēgḗmata* (true tales). "True tales" carries the connotation of "true fiction" that accords with Lucian's oxymoronic distinction between true falsehood and false (or pseudo-) truth. "True histories" means literally "true narrations of what one has learned by inquiry" and accords with Lucian's theme of intellectual exploration. Lucian's most recent editor, M.D. MacLeod (Oxford, 1972) elects *alēthê diēgḗmata*, the choice dictated by the remarks in this essay as well. In English the word "history" lacks virtually any connotation of "falsehood"; "story" retains the denotation of "true" as well as of "fictitious," but regularly means, in the context of literature, "a fictional composition"; "tale" retains fewer vestiges than "story" of the denotation "true" and is regularly "a deliberate lie" or "a falsehood." If we translate the title of Lucian's work as "True Histories" or as "True Stories," we may savor the etymological cognition of "story" with *historía* and the fact that both share the root *weid-*, which means "wisdom."[3] The translation "True Tales" is preferred in this essay because it does not preclude interpretations contrary to those presented herein; but the choice most in keeping with the interpretations presented here would be "True Fictions," a title than which one more suited to Lucian's veritable genre of philosophical science fiction would, in the writer's opinion, be exceedingly difficult to discover.

Immediately after concluding his preface with a caution that his readers must disbelieve him, Lucian begins the narration of his tales with an explanation that one of the reasons for his setting out on the journey which he is to recount was the officiousness of his intellect (hē tês dianoías periergía), that is, his intellectual curiosity. The other reason, apart from his desire to see what was at the end of the [Atlantic] Ocean, was his eagerness for new experiences (pragmátōn kainôn epithumía). The statement of these reasons confirms the theme of intellectual exploration.

The fantastic voyage takes up somewhat more than thirty-two months. Specifically, Lucian accounts for one hundred and fifty-one days, twenty-seven months, and "some days." There are approximately thirty-five different adventures associated with at least twenty-one different locales. The umbilicus of the narration is the reported sojourn of twenty months and twenty days inside the whale. Part I concludes with the twenty months, plus eight days, in the whale; and part II begins with the twelve days during which the escape from the whale is finally made. Except for the initial visit to Wineland, eighty days beyond the Pillars of Heracles (Straits of Gibraltar), and the concluding imprisonment in the whale, the voyaging in part I is all celestial: Moon, Sun, Morning Star, Lychnopolis (Lamptown), and Nephelococcygia (Cloudcuckooland).

Nephelococcygia is the air-borne ornithic realm to which impressionable and hopeful humans and gods seek admission in Aristophanes's comedy *Birds*, the first play of his utopian triad; the second and third plays in this triad are *Thesmophoriazusai* and *Ecclesiazusai*.[4] Lucian and his shipmates cannot visit this bird-built utopia which they sight on the ninety-ninth day of their voyage, because of a crosswind; but Lucian expresses satisfaction that Nephelococcygia actually exists and that doubts of its existence were unfounded: Aristophanes, he says, was "a wise and truthful man" (§1:29). Some twenty months later, in the narrative, Plato is discovered to be absent from the Elysian Field on the Island of the Blessed because of his residence elsewhere, namely, in the Republic which he had created. Lucian expresses no satisfaction over the existence of Plato's utopia, and he says nothing whatsoever to the effect that Plato was a wise and truthful man.

If, in accordance with his prefatory caution, nothing is to be believed in Lucian's narrative, then we may want to assume that his actual views of Aristophanes and Plato are the reverse of those he presents or suggests. A careful reader will not leap to this assumption; he or she will recognize that it is the series of fantastic events which are incredible and not the narrator's reactions to those series of events, or to those thoughts to which the events give rise in him, or to the character of individual or collective participants in the events. Lucian's editorial or evaluative views, relevant to the fantastic and its thought-provoking accouterments, constitute a device by means of which he invites our evaluation of both the subject and objects of fantasy.

Our evaluation of philosophy as an enterprise of fantasy is invited by the event of the Heroes' Banquet on the Elysian Field of the Island of the Blessed. At this banquet the heroes of fiction and the poets are in the company of the philosophers. We see Homer, Hesiod, Eunomus, Arion, Anacreon, Stesichorus, Aesop, Hyacinthus, Narcissus, Hylas, Rhadamanthus, Theseus, all of the demigods, Palamedes, Nestor, Odysseus, Achilles, and all of the Trojan Warriors except Ajax, along with Cyrus the Elder, Cyrus the Younger, Anacharsis, Zamolxis, Numa, Lycurgus, Phocion, Tellus, and all of the sages except Periander. The disparate assemblage reduces the philosophers to a contingent in an epic catalogue: Socrates, Aristippus, Epicurus, Diogenes, Empedocles, and Pythagoras. Lucian specifically calls our attention to Ajax's absence from the company of Trojan Warriors and Periander's absence from the company of sages. The overt exclusion of Ajax is a humorous deference to the notion that a warrior who commits suicide, as Ajax did, is *déclassé*. The overt exclusion of Periander honors the tradition that his place among the Seven Sages belonged properly to Myson of Chenae. Plato's absence from the company of philosophers is explicitly accounted for, as has been noted. If, however, unworthiness is implicit in the absence of Ajax and Periander from their respective groups, the fact of Plato's absence, despite the reason stated for it, must implicate Plato in an unworthiness which is concurrently established by the intimation of his inferiority to Aristophanes. In the comic epic catalogue the creators and creatures of fiction enjoy equal status with the philosophers except for the fact that the former quite outnumber the latter. This particular scene is a graphic tableau of philosophy-and-fiction. We cannot believe in the actual existence of the heroes of fiction, nor can we attach believability to the poets whose craft is fiction. More importantly, we cannot attach believability to the philosophers who form part of this assemblage, which is disparate in its mixture of historical with fictional personages and yet homogeneous in its common stratum of falsehood. Evaluating the significance of Lucian's juxtaposition of fiction-creators, fiction-creatures, and philosophers is much the same thing that we do in pondering the significance of Samuel R. Delany's mélange of mythmakers, myth-creatures, and mathematicians in *The Einstein Intersection*.

Lucian's mélange brings philosophy within the sphere of fiction and evokes an evaluation of philosophy that is comically charted in a number of his dialogues. The substance of his philosophical satire—that is, his satire of philosophy—is to be discerned in at least four dialogues which are more complementary than ancillary to the context of *True Tales*.

2. False Values in Philosophy. Lucian's caricatures of philosophers in *Lives for Sale*[5] are consonant with Aristophanes's caricature of Socrates in *Clouds*. Both writers satirically deride the exploitation of philosophers' thoughts and methods; both writers use the philosophers themselves as representatives, not of the respective philosophers' methods, but of what the philosophers' efforts had spawned. Lucian identifies the real targets of his satire in *The Resurrected, or, The Fisherman*;[6] they are, not Socrates, Aristotle, and the others, but the self-proclaimed Socratics, Aristotelians, Pythagoreans, and the like. These are the pseudo-intellectuals who, "to judge from their conduct, have read and contemplated" the philosophers "only to practice the reverse" of what the philosophers recommend (*Fisherman* 34).

The philosophers who are put on the market in *Lives for Sale* are, accordingly, representative of the "philosophies" which bear their names. The prices they bring indicate a scale of relative value or worth. Socrates is sold to the fifth customer for two talents (approximately a pre-inflationary twenty thousand dollars). Aristotle is sold to the eighth customer for twenty minas (about three thousand dollars, taking the mina to be roughly equivalent to one hundred and fifty dollars). Chrysippus and Pythagoras are purchased by the seventh and first customers for, respectively, twelve minas and ten minas. Then there is a huge drop in prices, proportional to the drop from Socrates's sale figure to Aristotle's. The sixth customer buys Epicurus for two minas and the ninth buys Pyrrho for one mina. In a third proportional price drop, the second customer gets Diogenes for two obols (about fifty cents). Aristippus, offered to the third customer, and Democritus and Heraclitus, both offered to the fourth, cannot even be sold.

The prices may represent a correspondence to Lucian's evaluation of the propounded philosophies, but Lucian regularly shows an affinity with Cynicism (Diogenes's school) and, given his penchant for the inverse, it is safer to view his prices here as inversely proportional to philosophical value. This need not mean that the unsold philosophers, or philosophies, would be more to Lucian's liking than Diogenes, or Cynicism; instead, they would be the most valuable, on this scale, by reason of their having virtually no pseudo-proponents in Lucian's time.

The Cynic Menippus of Gadara had a positive influence upon Lucian, who, like him, checked philosophy with satiric humor. The allegorical figure, Dialogue, who in *Twice Accused*[7] is doubtless Lucian's spokesman, acknowledges a debt to the old "dog" (a reference to the fact that kynikós, or "cynic," means "of *or* like a dog"), that is, to Menippus, whose bite is hidden in laughter. Menippus is Lucian's spokesman in *Menippus, or, Prophecies of the Dead*:[8] the Cynic berates pseudo-philosophers in almost the same words used by Lucian himself in *Fisherman*. Menippus also figures in other of the underworld dialogues as an exemplar of good sense.

The suggestion here is that, in *Lives for Sale*, Socrates is the most insidious of the marketed philosophers, bringing a price that corresponds to his detrimental influence, and that the unsold philosophers are the least insidious in that they have practically ceased to manifest any influence. False values are, at an inverse rate, falsely valued. Aristotle, Chrysippus, and Pythagoras are then much more costly to humankind than Epicurus, Pyrrho, and Diogenes, which last three remain mere nuisances.

In the order in which the philosophers are offered up to the buyers—(1) Pythagoras, (2) Diogenes, (3) Aristippus, (4) Democritus and Heraclitus, (5) Socrates, (6) Epicurus, (7) Chrysippus, (8) Aristotle, and (9) Pyrrho—the central, or focal, position is occupied by Socrates. He is showcased in a sale of commodities which are priced on a rising scale of negative values.

When, in *Fisherman*, the resurrected philosophers condemn Lucian for having denounced them in *Lives for Sale* and other dialogues, Diogenes, serving as an illustration of Lucian's irony, complains that he was the most grossly insulted in being pictured as having a market value of only two obols. Philosophy herself presides over the trial to which the philosophers bring Lucian, and Truth serves as one of the jurors. Lucian is acquitted after appeasing the philosophers by insisting that he was ridiculing, not the philosophers themselves, but the false schools and the deceptive practitioners of their philosophies. The greater irony, however, consists in Lucian's implication that what the pseudo-philosophers perpetrate in the names of the philosophers is similarly perpetrated by the philosophers themselves in the name of philosophy. The philosophers are taken in by Lucian, whose defense includes no explanation of his scale of prices; and it is Diogenes who, with his two-obol selling price still unexplained, retracts his accusation and expedites the exoneration of Lucian. It is Diogenes, again, who joins Lucian in fishing for the philosophical charlatans: a Cynic is hooked and thrown back as worthless; subsequently a Platonist, an Aristotelian, and a Stoic are hooked and thrown back as small fish.

The fishing episode exposes the schools of Diogenes, Socrates, Aristotle, and Chrysippus as equally worthless in the presence of Philosophy and Truth. It is also to be noted that Philosophy and Truth are personified as two separate entities. Their being other than one and the same permits the further inference that Philosophy does in the name of Truth what the philosophers do in the name of Philosophy.

Diogenes is less costly to humankind than the other marketed philosophers, but, with regard to truth, he is as worthless as they are. The genuine practice of Cynicism, however, serves truth much better than Diogenes serves philosophy and much better than Diogenes's adherents, with one exception, serve Diogenes. The exception is Menippus, who is not put up for sale in Lucian's dialogue and whose writings have informed Lucian's own practice of Cynical humor. Menippus neither appears nor is mentioned in *Lives for Sale* and *Fisherman*: Lucian is Menippus's spokesman in these dialogues, just as Menippus is Lucian's in others.

Lucian seeks to restore a scale of values by establishing the superiority of truth to philosophy, of philosophy to philosophers, and of philosophers to their adherents. In only the one case he reverses the direction of superiority: Menippus, the adherent, is superior to Diogenes, the philosopher.

In *Fisherman* Lucian satirizes the reversal of his scale of values. Philosophy, at best a servant of Truth, is personified not only as a peer of Truth but also as *prima inter pares*. She is the judge, and Truth is merely a juror. The reverse should prevail: Truth should be the judge, and Philosophy a juror. The philosophers, moreover, should serve, not Philosophy, as Diogenes does, but Truth, as we may infer that Menippus does. Finally, the philosophers' adherents compound this deranged allegiance and falsify the values of inquiry by serving, neither the philosophers they represent nor Philosophy, but only themselves. Lucian's Menippean Cynicism is to be interpreted as a direct service to Truth.

3. The Truly False in Philosophical Science Fiction. In the four dialogues cited, the satire on the false values and misdirections of philosophy is very broad. In *True Tales* the target of the satire is the same, but the satire becomes a subtle constituent of the very broad fantasy in the tales of voyaging. This shift, in concert with the structure of *True Tales*, exhibits a skillful rendition of philosophy as an inverse constituent of fiction.

Part II of *True Tales* comprises travels and adventures on the sea and on various islands and concludes with a shipwreck on a new land, or new continent (hetera gê). The narrative presents a dramatic inversion in its placement of the celestial voyage in part I and the terrestrial-marine adventures in part II. One would ordinarily expect the island adventures to stand as prelude to the awesome extra-terrestrial episodes. Lucian takes us directly and almost immediately to the moon and sun, and then brings us back to earth for the bulk of the narrative. As philosophical science fiction, this is an equivalent of philosophy's abandonment of tangible human moorings for flights into the abstract. By counter-exaggeration satire can bring philosophy, or the philosophically inclined, back to concretion. Lucian assigns this role to satire as Menippus and Aristophanes before him had done and, with regard to modern science, as Samuel Butler, Eugene Zamyatin, Vladimir Nabokov, and Thomas Pynchon long after him would do. In his work, fiction redeems philosophy, as, in the work of many serious science-fiction writers, fiction redeems science.

Effective science fiction does not transform science into fantasy, even though it may give the appearance of doing so; it brings us back to the limitations of science by means of fantasy or fiction, just as Lucian brings us back to the limitations of philosophy through satiric fiction and the fantastic voyage.

The voyage in *True Tales* is defined as one of exploration. The exploration is identified as both intellectual and entertaining, the entertainment being the satisfaction of the desire for new experiences; this amounts to a restatement of the Roman satirist Horace's *utile et dulce*. Lucian claims the intellectual stimulation and the entertainment for himself: he, the narrator, had undertaken his literary voyaging in these his own interests; but, at the same time, he is like that writer who, in Horace's words, has blended the useful with the pleasant by equally delighting and instructing his reader ("qui miscuit utile dulci/lectorem delectando pariterque monendo," *Ars poetica* §§343-4). If the ratio, science:*utile*::fiction:*dulce*, is valid, then the science-fiction writer is recognizably *qui miscet utile dulci*—the effective science-fiction writer, that is, like Lucian. In his satiric science fiction Lucian evinces the ratio in his own literary art while simultaneously offering to his reader the prescriptive ratio: science (or philosophy) should be to *utile* as fiction is to *dulce*. That the prescription has not been filled by philosophers is precisely what he satirizes; and his satire is itself an example of the proper blend of utility and entertainment.

The voyage of exploration does not end where Lucian's narrative ends. He neatly inverts Vergilian epic by ending his narrative *in mediis rebus*. The *Aeneid* opens with a shipwreck on a strange coast; and *True Tales* concludes with a shipwreck on a strange coast.[9] Lucian's conclusion is anything but haphazard. It may strike us as abrupt, leaving us as it does with our unsatisfied curiosity about the new land and with our wondering how the narrator returned to tell the tale which he falsely promises to finish. Actually, Lucian has entertained us and has given something to think about to those of us who are disposed to think. The entertainment is over, but the intellectual exploration goes on into the figuratively new land that has been discovered. The new land defines the total series of adventures, and the reader can find Lucian's way back to the Pillars of Heracles by recapitulating the adventures in reverse.

A look at this conclusion, as an illustration of Lucian's structural nicety, will incidentally provide an opportunity to observe the degrees to which translators can either guide or mislead us. Harmon translates the final period as follows:

Thus far I have told you what happened to me until I reached the other world, first at sea, then during my voyage among the islands and in the air, then in the whale, and after we left it, among the heroes and the dreams, and finally among the Bullheads and the Asslegs. What happened in the other world I shall tell you in the succeeding books.

Like Harmon, Casson breaks Lucian's fluid period into two sentences; but he improves upon Harmon in clarity and by rendering *hetêra gê* as "new continent" instead of the almost extra-terrestrial sounding "other world":

You now know our story up to the moment we reached this new continent: our adventures on the sea, during our trip around the islands, in the air, and, after that, inside the whale; then, after escaping from there, our further adventures among the Heroes, the dreams, and, finally, the Bullheads and Asslegs. What happened to us on the new continent I will tell in the subsequent volumes.

Turner destroys the passage by rendering the whole of it in this decapitated version:

Thus we finally landed on the continent at the other side of the world; and what happened to us there, I will tell you in another book.

Turner, who has also deprived Latinless readers of their immediate opportunity individually to interpret Thomas More's "Abraxa" by his translating it as "Sansculottia,"[10] has here chosen for no defensible reason to delete the very important summary sequence in the concluding period.

The summary lists the objects of exploration in an intriguingly challenging order: (1) the new land, (2) the sea, (3) the islands, (4) the air, (5) the whale, (6) the heroes, (7) the dreams, (8) the Bullheads and Asslegs, (9) the new land. "The air" is referent to the celestial voyaging and should, chronologically, precede "the sea" in this catalogue, unless we constrain "the sea" to denote the area covered during the initial embarkation. Nonetheless, "the islands" should definitely follow "the whale" in a sequential list of the adventures. The chronological sequence would properly read (in a translation that is literal save for the rearrangement of the emphasized words and phrases):

These, then, up to [my reaching] *the new land*, are the things that happened to me *in the air*, and afterward *in the whale*, and, when we had escaped, *on the sea*, and in sailing to *the islands*, and among *the heroes* and *the dreams*, and finally among *the Bullheads and the Asslegs*, and I shall set down in subsequent books the things [that happened] on *the new land*.

What may appear to be a lack of care in Lucian's closing period is in all probability the reverse of carelessness. The oddly arranged sequence affronts temporal order to no real purpose; but it affronts balance to significant purpose. If, in his unchanged text, we take "the new land" as *a* and "the sea/the islands" as *b*, then "the air" would be *c*, "the whale" *d*; "the heroes/the dreams/the Bullheads and Asslegs" (as part of the sea-and-island voyaging) would reiterate *b*; and, with the repeated "new land," the balance-sequence is identifiable as *a b c d b a*. The chiastic balance is upset by either *c* or *d*. Taking the focal episode of *d* ("the whale) as representing the pivot of the story, and taking *c* ("the air") as representative of an abortive flight, we may establish the intellectual, cognitive, or logical extraneity—and by the same token the crucial satirical importance—of *c*. The celestial voyaging, indicative of the flights of philosophy (science, or cognition in general), is clearly—with its grotesque wars, etc.—out of place in intellectual exploration. The philosophers come in for their specific ridicule at the Heroes' Banquet on the Elysian Field; we have noted this ridicule to consist chiefly in their being classed with poets as producers of falsehoods. Philosophy itself is, in Lucian's equation of it with celestial flight, ridiculed as falsehood itself. Philosophy is thereby that which lends imbalance and eccentricity to intellectual exploration; and Lucian stimulates us intellectually by moving us to think about philosophy in this way. He brings philosophy down to earth, where, in his opinion, it belongs, and recommends it to the service of truth against its apparently inevitable service to itself. The exploration of the new land is thereby the equivalent of the proper intellectual frontier; and that is where Lucian leaves us at the end of his narrative.

The interstitial subtlety of Lucian's narrative eludes most of his commentators, who neglect attention to his structural precision, his imagistic and thematic sequences, and the thought that he spent on thinking as an activity susceptible of being inhibited by belief.[11] He does not condemn philosophy unreservedly any more than Pynchon condemns science out of hand. It is appropriate to say that to Lucian there is a point at which philosophy tends to become worthless, a point whose co-ordinates are (1) philosopher-adherents serving themselves, (2) philosophers serving philosophy instead of truth, and (3) philosophy serving itself instead of truth.

Too many measurements of the depth of Lucian's thought have been prompted by his persistent and quantitative ridicule of major philosophers instead of being drawn from his qualitative ridicule of excessively abstract philosophy and pseudo-philosophy and from his studious admiration of Menippus as a sensible philosopher.[12] It does not follow from the very real possibility of Lucian's being wrong, much less from his genius for entertainment, that his thought is no more than superficial. Aristophanes, Plautus, Terence, Horace, Persius, and Juvenal are not great thinkers, but scholars and commentators show no inclination regularly to calibrate the profundity of these comedians' and satirists' thought. Aristophanes puts philosophy (the new science) up in the air by showing Socrates hoisted in a basket to get nearer to the clouds he studies. Aristophanes, however, like the others just mentioned, writes in verse and, except for *Clouds* in his case, directs no consistent ridicule at philosophy and its schools. Lucian is acclaimed as a prose artist, and yet the manner in which his art provides an experience of errant philosophy's ineptness is seldom critically examined; appreciation is reserved for the stylish humor openly evident in the superficies of his work. There is substance beneath that polished surface in which hasty commentators see only their own reflection, just as there is a real concern for philosophy implicit in Lucian's satire of it.

The episode of the Island of Dreams (§§2:32-5) is, for example, on the surface merely an elaborate personification of sleep and dreams. Beneath the surface, however, it is a complex allegory of the nature and effects of sleeping and dreaming and a subtle excursus on the true and the false. Lucian and his crew overtake the elusive Island of Dreams and sail into it through the Harbor of Sleep. In Classical myth, death and resurrection are transmuted into a journey to the Underworld; Lucian transmutes sleep and waking into a form of this journey, and the clue to his doing so is his inclusion of the Underworld's gates of ivory and horn. He cites Homer as mentioning only these two gates—the ivory gate for the egress of false dreams and the gate of horn for the egress of true dreams—when, by his extension of the myth, there are in fact four. Vergil is not cited, although again there is an inversion of Vergilian epic as the sailors *enter* through the ivory gate, from which Aeneas makes his *exit*. Lucian's additional two gates are those of iron and clay, egress for fears and for dreams of murder and violence. True dreams are not necessarily dreams that come true any more than true tales are necessarily true to fact; true dreams are real or actual dreams and are experienced only in sleep. A true dream, then, is as false to the facts of waking life as a true tale is false to actual fact. A false dream is a calculated or contrived dream, either a daydream deliberately indulged in while one is awake or a nurture of one's fears and hopes. Lucian's *hoí te phoberoi kai phonikoi kai apēneîs* (fear-filled, murderous, and violent dreams) is characteristically truncated by Turner and rendered simply as "nightmares." Casson has "nightmares and dreams of murder and violence." Harmon is superior to both of his successors in translation with "fearful, murderous, revolting dreams." Unfortunately, Harmon goes on to translate *Taraxíōna* (Taraxíōn = Anxiety) as "Nightmare." Nightmares are real, or true, dreams; and fears and anxieties are false dreams. Lucian's gates of iron and clay open out from the Plain of Sloth (tô tês blakeías pedíon), the area of false sleep. They open on the idle dreams that are fostered by their germinal, sloth; these are the idle dreams that spread passivity, intensify introversion, and never lead to action. Lucian's gates of horn and ivory face the coastal inlet and the sea. The ivory gate opens for the waking dreams of exploration, for the active imagination, and for dreams that foster quests in service to truth; it is neighbor to the horn gate of true dreams borne in sleep.

Lucian has differentiated the false dreams wrought by sloth from the false dreams that sustain action. The horn gate is the gate of true and earned repose, or pleasant dreams; it is the gate of entertaining fiction. The ivory gate is the gate of true exploration, the gate of utile fiction and sensible philosophy. The iron and clay gates are the gates of self-indulgent, dogmatic, and excessively abstract philosophy.

The two temples in Dream City are those of Night and Alektryon (the Rooster). The Rooster Temple is near the port; and behind it, to the right and left, are, respectively, the Temple of Night and the Palace of Sleep. The rooster, herald of dawn and wakefulness, is properly enshrined near the locale of embarkation and the ivory gate, that is, near the sources of wakeful action and of the false dreams concomitant with wakeful action.

The two great shrines in Dream City honor, respectively, Deceit (Apátē) and Truth (Alḗtheia). That they are twin shrines should go without saying. Their juxtaposition recalls the parity of philosophers and poets on the Island of the Blessed and further informs Lucian's theme of fiction's being as good a servant, if not a better servant, of truth than philosophy is: on the one hand, Deceit (fiction) is the complement of Truth; on the other hand, philosophy's pilgrimage is to Deceit and Fiction's is to Truth. That the two shrines complement each other, like the gates of ivory and horn and like the ivory-gated resolution of philosophy and fiction (or, science and fiction), says more about Lucian's understanding and appreciation of philosophy than his translators and many of his readers are prepared to admit.

Lucian and his crew remain for thirty days and thirty nights,[13] in sloth and sleep, on the Island of Dreams, which lies, significantly, between the Islands of the Damned and the island Ogygia. Then, aroused by a thunderclap, they leave the island and on a reverse odyssey make their way *to* Ogygia, just as Odysseus, aroused from his enervating sloth and slumber, had made his escape *from* Ogygia, and from the passive existence with which Calypso had tempted him, to new adventures.

Lucian's philosophical science fiction imbues us with the sense that philosophy and fiction are complementary explorations into truth and that philosophy tends abortively to claim success in an exploration which fiction is content both to sustain and constantly to renew. He states in his preface that poets incur his reproach less than philosophers because those who profess philosophy do much the same thing as poets do, the implication being, as we have noted, that poets are faithful to their calling and philosophers are not. Casson takes this to be a "crack at Plato's Myth of Er told in Book 10 of *The Republic*." Harmon likewise adjudged it a "slap at Plato's Republic (x.614 A *seq.*), as the scholiast says." Actually, Lucian would be more likely to applaud Plato's overt recourse to fiction in a philosophical work than to find fault with Plato's commixture. Lucian could not but have approved Plato's persistent use of poetic devices in the *Republic* along with his many citations from poets.[14] By falling back on myth in the last book of the *Republic*, Plato tacitly admits the shortcomings of the philosophical exploration of truth and openly illustrates his ideas by means of a fable. Lucian's prefatory statement is on the surface an expression of tolerance for the writers of fiction.[15] Its deeper signification, adumbrated by the fact that Lucian is himself a writer of fiction, lies in its corollary: both fabulists and philosophers falsify, but philosophers are the more deserving of reproach because they generally affect not to do so.

"Philosophy's task is not to resolve a contradiction through mathematical or logico-mathematical invention but to make clear the mathematical situation that bothers us, the situation that exists *prior to* the resolution of the contradiction":[16] Lucian would consider this statement by Ludwig Wittgenstein to be one worthy of Menippus. He would find the statement congenial to his task of taking to task the philosophers and quasi-philosophers who have presumed to exceed their task. He would see in it his own fictionist's preference of clarification by means of falsity to obfuscation created by a presumption to resolve. The opening proposition of Wittgenstein's *Tractatus Logico-Philosophicus* is "Die Welt ist alles, was der Fall ist" ("The world is all that is the case"): Lucian's early termination of his two weeks of celestial voyaging in *True Tales* is his way of saying the same.

NOTES

1., For example, Brian W. Aldiss includes Lucian in *Billion Year Spree: The True History of Science Fiction* (US 1973 xiv+339; UK 1973), and the SF anthology *Past, Present, and Future Perfect*, ed. Gregory Fitz Gerald and Jack C. Wolf (Fawcett pb 1973) includes a selection from "A True Story." The title of Aldiss's history may be something of a comic overture to Lucian and is, if so, a far more commendable note than his exceptionable statement, "We no longer expect anything but entertainment from Lucian..." (p 59). There are three convenient translations of Lucian: A.M. Harmon et al., *Lucian with an English Translation* (8 vols., UK-US 1913-1967); Lionel Casson, *Selected Satires of Lucian* (US 1962 pb & hb); Paul Turner, *Lucian: True History and Lucius or The Ass* (US 1958, pb 1974; UK 1958) and *Lucian: Satirical Sketches* (Penguin pb 1961).

2. See *Republic* §10.

3. In any case, the singular—"True History" (Turner), "True Story" (Harmon, Casson), or "True Tale"—is misleading. Lucian's effort is a collection of tales or episodes, not a sequentially plotted story; the arrangement of the episodes is more important than any patent connection of events from episode to episode.

4. Patric Dickinson's translation, *Aristophanes: Plays* (2 vols., UK-US 1970), is lucid and informative. His second volume includes the entire utopian triad.

5. In Harmon Vol. 2 and Casson as "Philosophies for Sale" and in Turner Penguin as "Philosophies Going Cheap" [! Some of them are far from "cheap."].

6. In Harmon Vol. 3 as "The Dead Come to Life, or The Fisherman," in Casson as "The Fisherman," and in Turner Penguin as "Fishing for Phonies."

7. In Harmon Vol. 3 as "The Double Indictment, or Trial by Jury."

8. In Harmon Vol. 4 as "Menippus, or The Descent into Hades" and in Turner Penguin as "Menippus Goes to Hell."

9. We need not beg Lucian's familiarity with Horace or Vergil. Even if he had never heard of the Roman satirist or the Roman epic poet, an entirely unlikely supposition, given his travels in Italy and his patronage by the emperor Commodus, his artistic concerns would still have paralleled theirs in these matters. Those who object to the suggestion that Lucian inverts Vergilian epic may yet recognize an inversion of the Odyssean narrative which opens with the shipwrecked Odysseus on Ogygia, the details of which shipwreck are supplied in *Odyssey* §12.

10. *Thomas More: Utopia* (Penguin pb 1965), p 69. Turner explains his "rash conjecture" in his glossary, s.v., and notes the possibility of a connection of "Abraxa" with "Abraxas." The wiser course would be the retention of "Abraxa" in the main text. This would visibly sustain the possibility of a connection with "abrektos" (a + brachth-), the meaning of which Greek term ("unwetted") would describe the peninsular Abraxa before it became, in a kind of geographical baptism, the island Utopia.

11. Many Lucianologists, particularly Lucian's translators, have automated their attitudes to Lucian's thought and to his appraisal of philosophy. Casson says that "[t]o Lucian all philosophy is worthless," as though Cynicism were alien to philosophy and as though Lucian had not accepted Plato's distinction between thought and belief. Harmon, disregarding the fact that Lucian had willfully abandoned his profession of rhetoric in favor of devoting his later life to his writings, cavalierly pontificates that Lucian "was not a philosopher nor even a moralist, but a rhetorician, that his mission in life was not to reform society nor to chastise it, but simply to amuse it." Turner insists that Lucian's "main appeal must be as a writer, not a thinker." Casson, again, says, "Lucian as a thinker is consistent and honest (most of the time) but no great intellect." He also claims that Lucian's treatment of philosophy "shows how superficial his thought can be."

12. For a valid and unprejudiced estimate of the depth of Lucian's thought see S.C. Fredericks, "Lucian's *True History* as SF," SFS 3(1976):49-60.

13. Both Turner and Casson, but not Harmon, miss the imagistic sequence (horn-ivory, Night-Alektryon, sleep-sloth, night-day) by translating Lucian's *heméras...triákonta kai ísas nýkas* (thirty *days* and as many *nights*) as "a month."

14. For details of Plato's poeticisms see F. Blass, *Die Rhythmen der attischen Kunstprosa* (Leipzig, 1901): "On Attic Prose Rhythm," *Hermathena* 14.82, 1906; C.L. Brownson, *Plato's Studies and Criticisms of the Poets* (US 1920).

15. Lucian's statement, literally translated, reads: "Encountering all of these [i.e., Ctesias of Cnidus, Iambulus, Homer, and other writers of the fabulous (mythṓdē)], then, I have not zealously reproached the fellows for falsifying, noting indeed this kindred habit even among those professing philosophy." Turner's rendition: "I do not feel particularly shocked by this kind of thing, on moral grounds, for I have found that a similar disregard for truth is quite common even among professional philosophers"; Casson's: "Now, I've read all the practitioners of this art and I've never been very hard on them for not telling the truth—not when I see how common this failing is even among those who profess to be writing philosophy." Turner's "on moral grounds" and Casson's "failing" are extracontextual. Harmon's translation of the passage remains the most reliable: "Well, on reading all these authors, I did not find much fault with them for their lying, as I saw that this was already a common practice even among men who profess philosophy."

16. Ludwig Wittgenstein, *Philosophische Untersuchungen* I.125: Es ist nicht Sache der Philosophie, den Widerspruch durch eine mathematische, logisch-mathematische, Entdeckung zu lösen. Sonden den Zustand der Mathematik, der uns beunruhigt, den Zustand *vor* der Lösung des Widerspruchs, übersehbar zu machen.

Darko Suvin

The Alternate Islands: A Chapter in the History of SF, with a Select Bibliography on the SF of Antiquity, the Middle Ages, and the Renaissance

(from **SFS** *3: 239–248, November 1976)*

In the first part of Thomas More's *Utopia* (1516), a long discussion of England's social ills culminates in Hythloday's famous description of the destruction of the medieval peasantry:

> Your sheep...which are usually so tame and so cheaply fed, begin now, according to report, to be so greedy and wild that they devour human beings themselves and devastate and depopulate fields, houses, and towns.... there are noblemen, gentlemen, and even some abbots, though otherwise holy men, who.... leave no ground to be tilled; they enclose every bit of land for pasture; they pull down houses and destroy towns, leaving only the church to pen the sheep in.[1]

This passage, embedded in the acute analysis of what the nascent capitalism meant to the people (it is quoted by Marx in *Capital*), is a masterpiece of humanist sarcasm. The noblemen that turn into earthquakes razing entire districts, the holy men that are brutally indifferent to their spiritual flock and leave churches standing only as profitable sheep-pens, the land which is no longer communal tilling ground for a stable yeomanry but a private enclosure for rich landlords that throw tenants out on the roads to beg and rob, finally the erstwhile meek sheep that have now turned into man-devouring beasts—all this, couched in the careful verisimilitude of a traveller's report from exotic countries, amounts to a picture of *a world upside-down* being born in the shambles of the natural one. Rejecting all half-way and reformist solutions to such radical evils, the second part of *Utopia* will therefore present a radically different model of sociopolitical life—a country that governs itself as a classless extended family.

1. The Sociopolitics of Happiness: *Utopia* and its SF Context. The country Utopia—whose punning name means a good place which is (as of now) nowhere—is an England re-created in a more perfect shape. It is an island of the same size and subdivisions as England, but round instead of triangular; it has the same natural resources, pegged to an economy based on agriculture, but it is a just and happy country because it has abolished private property in land and other means of production. Instead of the monarchic pyramid where power flows from above downward, it is, at least in principle, a democratic centralism that acknowledges no political elite, with a power pyramid established from below upward. Where Europe slavishly worships obscene war and gold, Utopia despises both; while it sometimes has to fight wars, it uses gold for chamber-pots and slaves' fetters. It lives a distributive, egalitarian, pre-industrial communism; much like tribal societies, or medieval villages and guilds, it is federalist and patriarchal. Its organization is of a piece with its way of life, the best example being the network of equidistant halls where the daily meals are an occasion for pleasurable communion in both physical and spiritual nourishment. Hythloday's review of such "laws and customs" in Utopia is a model of clarity and forcefulness, which answers the objections of his dialogue partners (including a "More" manipulated for self-protective irony) simply by the gesture of pointing. It finds this "best state of society" based on the pursuit of a finally ethical pleasure attainable only in a social order with a truly common economy and culture. Happiness for each reached by economic justice for all is the final goal of a possible social organization—a startingly subversive idea.

Utopia is thus the reaffirmation of a world consonant to human nature. This "new island" at the antipodes puts the upside-down monstrosity of European class society back on its feet: the estrangement is a de-alienation. Yet a static human nature working itself out in a family model—both concepts taken from medieval Christianity—makes for a certain clogging rigidity of relationships in Utopia, in contradiction to its fundamental ideal of a higher Epicureanism. The Utopians possess slaves (criminals and war prisoners), an official religion (albeit mostly deistic and tolerant of all creeds except—an unforgivable lapse!—atheists), and barbarous provisions against adultery. Also, the representative democracy is tempered by a permanent rule of the Elders, the family fathers, and the learned. Together with a proper subsistence-economy concern for husbanding resources, this subordinates freedom to an egalitarian balance, enforced where necessary by stringent measures (e.g. the travel restrictions). For all its dry wit, there is an air of schematic blueprint, of groundplan without adornments, about More's picture of Utopia, But finally, it is an open-ended narrative (the Utopians accept Greek learning and show interest in Christ's collectivism), the first picture of an egalitarian communism with a relatively well-defined tolerance.

More's *Utopia* subsumes all the SF forms of its epoch (in which it thus fulfills the same function as Wells does for recent SF history). It fuses the permanent though unclear folk longings for a life of abundance and peace with high-minded intellectual constructs of perfect—i.e. communist—human relations known from Antiquity on: it translates the Land of Cockayne and the Earthly Paradise into the language of the philosophical dialogue on the ideal state and of the Renaissance discovery-literature as reinterpreted by More's unique blend of medieval collectivism and Christian humanism. Let us take a brief look at these forms and More's synthesis.[2]

Cockayne is a universal folk legend of a land of peace, plenty, and sloth, well known already in Antiquity, and refurbished—probably by vagrant student-poets—in the Middle Ages. In that Nowhere, rivers flow with cream or wine, roasted fowls fly into your mouth, and sausages run around crying "Eat me, eat me!" It is already an inverted world which relates to human needs, and like utopia proposes a strictly materialistic solution. It can therefore be transformed into utopia by relying on human intervention instead of on a magical parallel world, and all utopias, beginning with More, will retain its abhorrence of human degradation by war, toil, and hunger. Next in the family of wondrous lands are the Blessed Islands at the limits of the Ocean. Found already in tribal tales, Chinese and Mesopatamian legends, and Homer, such an Elysium was originally a place of magical fertility and contentment to which the blessed heroes were admitted in the flesh. In the Middle Ages, such locations in far-off seas, including the Celtic legendary island, came to be considered as the EARTHLY PARADISE, which was situated in this world and whose inhabitants (before religious rewritings) were not disembodied but simply more perfect, endowed with happiness, youth, and immortality.

Echoes of such folk legends are heard in Dante's account of Ulysses' final heroic voyage toward the Earthly Paradise, during which he is sunk by a jealous God intent on preserving his monopoly over the right of passage. In fact, Dante's *Comedy* incorporates in its astrophysical and metaphysical universe almost all SF elements transmitted to More through the Middle Ages, when—after Augustine of Hippo's *Civitas Dei*—"the utopia is transplanted to the sky, and called the Kingdom of Heaven" (Mumford):[3] the *Comedy* subsumes discussions of several ideal political states, traditions of the damned and blessed places, the search for the perfect kingdom, and Dante's own superb vision of the perfectly just City of God.

More was well aware of such subgenres as the Earthly Paradise, but he rejected their place outside history, in a magically arrested time (often entailing the hero's instant aging upon return). Bidding also "a curt farewell" to the mythical conservatism of a Golden Age of happy forefathers, he resolutely located Utopia in an alternative human attainable present, momentous just because non-existent among Europeans. As in Plato's *Republic*, which looms large in the backgroud, human destiny consists of men and their institutions; but diametrically opposed to Plato, the just place can result from a heroic deed such as King Utopus's cutting off the "new island" from the tainted continent. Men's norms and institutions are not the province of religion and magic but of sociopolitics, and time is measured in terms of creative work. That is why Utopia differs radically from Plato's curious combination of caste society and ruling-caste communism. Plato's dialogue develops an argument for a timelessly ideal (today quite anti-utopian) blueprint, set up in order to escape popular, monarchic, or imperfectly oligarchic government. More's dialogue dramatically unfolds an actually present state of classless self-government. More lacks all sympathy for both Plato's erotic communism and his caste system. As for the notion that a just state depends on a community of goods, More was much closer to the early Christian fathers and peasant insurgents (such as John Ball) who extolled communism than he was to Plato. Besides, this notion was so widespread in Hellenic literature before and after Plato that Aristophanes could mock in the *Ecclesiazusae* (i.e. Assembly-women) a female try at instituting egalitarian communism without money or toil, and in *The Birds* a Cloudcuckooland where "everything is everybody's" and things illegal in Athens or on Olympus are deemed beautiful and virtuous. All such references—characteristically surviving only in fragments of rebuttals—speak of a set-up where

> ...all shall be equal, and equally share
> All wealth and enjoyments, nor longer endure
> That one should be rich, and another be poor.
> (*Ecclesiazusae* §§590-91, tr. Rogers)

Such an *omnia sint communia* is from that time on the constant principle separating consistent utopian literature from the established society.

When Hythloday is introduced to "More," he is compared to Plato, but also secondarily to Ulysses, the hero of wondrous voyages to the island of Circe, of the Phaeacians, etc. The genre of IMAGINARY VOYAGE, as old as fiction, was the natural vehicle of the Earthly Paradise and utopian tales, though it often led simply to entertaining worlds whose topsy-turviness remained more playful than didactic. But it could also lead to just peoples in happy lands at the limits of the world, from the Hyperboreans to Ethiopians, from Plato's Atlanteans to Euhemerous's Panchaeans (and in the Middle Ages from Mandeville's Sumatrans to the subject of Prester John). The nearest in spirit to More is a fragment of Iambulus (circa 100 BC) about the equatorial Islands of the Sun where the usual magically fertile nature enables men to live without private property and state apparatus, in a loose association of communities. In their joyous work, such as picking fruit, each in turn serves his neighbor. They practice erotic communism, eugenics, and euthanasia (at the age of 150); the sciences, especially astronomy, are well developed but the liberal arts are more valued as leading to spiritual perfection. Written at the time of the great Mediterranean slave and proletarian revolts, Iambulus presents a plebeian Hellenic negation of the warring empires, the privatization of man, and the division of labor. His gay islanders live in the fields, under the open southern sun; and his account of their radical collectivism (found by a voyager-narrator later expelled for his harmful habits) is the best that has even fragmentarily survived from the host of similar voyagers' tales.

Such tales were renewed by the great geographical discoveries: Hythloday is also introduced as a participant in the voyages of that Vespucci who had lent his name to America and set Europe abuzz by describing the "perfect liberty" of Red Indian tribal communism and Epicureanism. Thomas More transformed all such strange new horizons, with their potent dissolving effects, into a systematic verbal construction of *a particularized community where sociopolitical institutions, norms, and personal relations are organized according to a more perfect principle than in the author's community* (as literary utopias could be defined). This estranged place is presented as an *alternative history*; whoever its author, however he twists utopian cognition, it always flows out of the hope of repressed and exploited social classes, and expresses their longings for a different but this-worldly other world. Sudden whirlpools in history which both further and permit its appearance in literature—the times of Iambulus, More, Fourier, Morris, or indeed our own—have therefore the makings of great ages of SF. For utopias are social-science fiction, the sociopolitical variant of the radically different peoples and locations of SF—*the sociopolitical subgenre of SF*. All later SF, necessarily written against the background of the readers' societies, will be situated between utopian and anti-utopian horizons—not the least when it attempts to deny its utopian heredity.

More's greatness resides thus not only in ethics or prose style. Beyond that, *Utopia* supplied both the name and the logically inescapable model for later literary utopias. Their hallmark is a rounded and isolated location (valley, island, planet) articulated in a panoramic sweep showing their inner organization as a formal, ordered system. This system is utopia's supreme value: there are authoritarian and libertarian but no unorganized utopias. The coming about of the new order must be explained as the installation of a new social contract; in the Renaissance the contract-maker is usually a founding hero, but later it will increasingly be a democratic revolution openly as in Morris's socialist revolution or transposed into cosmic analogs as tenuous as Wells's gas from a comet. Lastly, utopias are presented by a dramatic strategy which counts on the surprise effects of its presentations upon the reader. Though formally closed, significant utopian writings are in permanent dialogue with the readers, i.e. open-ended—as in More.

2. The Dissociation of Play and Truth: Rabelais to Bacon. More conveyed "full sooth in game." François Rabelais's imaginative voyage through a sequence of wonderful places boisterously perfected such a fusion of urgent truth and witty play to deal with the full compass of earthly preoccupations and possibilities. But already in the last books of his pentalogy on the giants Gargantua and Pantagruel (1532-64) the joke got grimmer and thinner. By the time of Campanella and Bacon, the formal exercise of utopia had dissociated intellectual gravity from plebeian play; in the process, "truth" itself grew increasingly ideological.

Gargantua's and Pantagruel's sallying out of Utopia to Paris and the ends of the world, and their insistence on the drink and food of the body as well as of the spirit, are symbolic for Rabelais's integration of sensual with philosophic materialism, of folk chronicles about the deeds of enormous and valiant giants with an uproarious intellectual critique of the sum total of contemporary life. This critique is inescapable because it reaches from rational argument and farce to the colossal deployment of synonyms and neologisms, idioms taken literally and fields encompassed encyclopedically. Language itself is no longer god-given but a medium of human labor, enjoyment, and folly; it is formally presented as such in the SF parable of the congealed words in Book IV. The sequence of events, too, bodies forth a gay and dynamic process of imbibing knowledge from the various provinces of reality passed in critical review—from war and education in the first two books, through marriage and sex in the third, to the wondrous and horrible island's religion, law, and finance in fourth and fifth. The basic attitude of this work is "a gaiety of spirit" equated with the wine of the grape as well as the wine of learning and freedom, of friendliness and life itself. Such a draught is a blasphemous transubstantiation in which matter becomes its own conscious and cognitive enjoyment, substituting for service of the divine (*divin*) that of the vine (*du vin*). The folk enjoyment in gigantism is not separated from goodness and wisdom. Rather, matter is treated as not only the sole reality but also the supreme good, of which there can never be too much. Rabelais's whole work is one huge navigation toward liberated matter and unalienated man. This cognitive "imaginary voyage" is the exploration of a dangerous freedom: "You must be the interpreters of your own enterprise" is the final conclusion.

Thus "pantagruelism" is the liberation of a human quintessence from the impure actuality, an unbridled creation of a new human nature scorning contemporary unnatural Europe—as when Pantagruel makes out of the bad, aggressive king Anarch a good though henpecked hawker of green sauce. It oscillates between sheer fantasy and simple inversion. The latter is seen in the anti-abbey or "free university" of Thélème, set against the old educational and monastic institutions; formally, this is the most clearly utopian passage in Rabelais, though it is not his boldest creation but an elite assembly of young people noble enough to follow the inner-directed commandment of "DO WHAT YOU WILL." More important, "pantagruelizing" entails assimilating the whole reality of that age and regurgitating it transmuted by his laughing philosophy, just as Gargantua comprehended whole countries in his throat and regurgitated the narrator who visited them. To that end, Rabelais employs with a serene greediness all available SF traditions and all forms of delighted estrangement—Greek satire and medieval legends, Plato and Villon, More and Lucian. Almost incidentally, he produced some episodes of SF which will stand as its constant yardstick.

Rabelais adapted the episode in Gargantua's throat and the whole marvelous voyage in the second half of his opus from the classical tradition subsumed in Lucian of Samosate. In *True Histories* (ca. AD 160), Lucian laughingly settled the score with the whole tradition of vegetative myths, from the mythological tales themselves, through Homer's voyages, to the popular Hellenistic adventure-romances. His journey to various wondrous islands, his flight to the Moon, Morning Star, and Sun, his life inside a huge whale, in Cloudcuckooland, on the Island of the Blessed, etc., is a string of model parodies each translating a whole literary form into a critical—i.e. cognitive—context. The island of vine-women is a parody of Circe's and other islands of erotic bliss, and the war of the Selenites against the Heliotes introduces aliens and combats more grotesque than in any romance or myth; but both are also models of later SF meetings and warfare with aliens. Lucian uses the mythical scheme of journeys based on the vegetative cycle of death and rebirth, darkness and day, closing and opening, for ironic subversion. Its spectrum ranges from ironic events, situations, and characters, through parodic allusions and wordplay, to direct sarcasm. For example, his tongue-in-cheek extrapolation of colonial warfare into interplanetary space is rendered utterly ridiculous by a farcically pedantic and scabrous description of the semi-human Selenites. Lucian's whole arsenal of demystification amounts to a value-system in which vitality is equated with freedom. Being confined to the country within the whale with its oppressive fish-people is Lucian's equivalent of an infernal descent, after his flight through imperialist heavens. The humanistic irony embodied in esthetic delight of "Lucian the Blasphemer" became the paradigm for the whole prehistory of SF, from More and Rabelais to Cyrano and Swift.

In More and Rabelais, this tradition led to the "alchemical" procedure of creating a new homeland by a transmutation of the baser elements in the old country (England or the Touraine), so that Rabelais's fictive narrator called himself "Abstractor of the Quintessence." However, in actuality the marvelous countries became colonies, More died beheaded, Rabelais barely escaped the stake: knowledge and sense were again viciously sundered by religious wars and monarchist absolutism. In the profound crisis of the age, the first wave of the revolutionary middle class had separated itself from the people, and been destroyed or absorbed by church and state. At the beginning of the 17th century this was clearly spelled out by the burning at the stake of Giordano Bruno, the philosopher who had proclaimed an infinite universe with an infinite number of autonomous worlds. The new power cast a spell even over utopists. In southern, Catholic Europe Campanella reinstated astrology, that fantastic pseudo-science of absolutism, as the guiding principle of his *City of the Sun* (pbd 1623); in northern, Protestant Europe Bacon perspicaciously hit upon a natural science behaving as an esoteric religion as the wave of the future in *New Atlantis* (pbd 1627). Tommaso Campanella, though formally prolonging Iambulus's and More's line, describes a perfect theocracy somewhere behind India, in the seas of the old caste empires and on an island so large it is almost a continent. The traditional utopian abolition of private ownership, the stimulating ideas on dignifying labor and education, are of little avail in a community run by a monastic bureaucracy whose impersonal, militaristic order regulates all relations, from times for sexual intercourse to the placing of buttons, in strict and grotesque detail fixed by astrology. For the explosive horizontal explorations of the Renaissance, Campanella substituted a doctrinaire vertical which descends from the Sun of Power to men. More's urbane talk between friendly humanists became here a one-track exposition from one top oligarch to another.

Francis Bacon's "great instauration," based on the rising force of capitalist manufacture and its technological horizons, was in the following three centuries to prove more virulent than Campanella's monastic nostalgia. For Bacon the social system is an open question no more; rather, the key for transforming the world is a power of nature exercized by, and largely for, a politically quite conservative, quasi-Christian priestly hierarchy. The organized application of technology in New Atlantis is not a breakthrough to new domains of human creativity or even (except for some agricultural and biological techniques) of natural sciences; the only use mentioned for "stronger and more violent" engines is in artillery, for the old destructive purposes. Conversely science becomes a patriarchal, genteel, and highly ceremonial religion, and it could be characterized—much like its later offshoot, Saint-Simonism—as "Catholicism minus Christianity." Scientists are a self-sufficient aristocracy of experts manipulating or "vexing" nature and other men; as opposed to Plato, More, and Rabelais, their "science does not so much exude from wisdom as wisdom exudes from science" (White)[4] and gold is not a sign of baseness but of permanent abundance in possessions and power. The very name of Bacon's country aims to improve Plato both by correcting his account of Old Atlantis and by presenting a New Atlantis whose old perfection has withstood not only political but even geological contingencies (the narration ends with an indication that its science can prevent earthquakes, floods, comets, and similar).

The major positive claim of New Atlantis is that it delivers the goods—abundance of things and years, and social stability—by employing the lay miracles of science. At that historical epoch, even such a filling in of extant technical possibilities, without a radical change in human relationships, constituted a huge and euphoric programme, and the goal of the "research foundation" of Salomon's House is formulated as "the knowledge of causes, and secret motions of things; and the enlarging of the bounds of human empire, to the effecting of all things possible," but though this science is guarded by experts who can, interestingly enough, refuse to divulge dangerous discoveries, it is by its own definition ethically indifferent: nuclear bombs and gas ovens in concentration camps are some of the "things possible to effect." *New Atlantis* is starry-eyed over inquiring into the "secret motions and causes" of fruits, winds, sounds, and clocks, yet it does not think of inquiring into motions and results with respect to the mother of the family condemned to seclusion, or to the population sundered from Salomon's House. It is thus a foretaste of that combination of technology and autocracy which in fact became the basis of European empires at home and abroad. At this point, the utopian tradition fell under the sway of an upper-class ideology which staves off human problems by technocratic extrapolation, by quantitative expansion promising abundance within a fundamentally unchanged system of social domination. Bacon's "science" thus turns out to be as mythical as Campanella's astrology, though more efficient. As a verbal vision, *New Atlantis*—with its heavy insistence on a power hierarchy and resplendent signs of public status, observation which becomes interesting only when enumerating grandiose projects, and a general adman's abuse of adjectives suggesting opulence—is in fact much inferior to the fanatic splendor of *The City of the Sun*. It is symptomatic for the quality of imagination in the ensuing age that his work (one of Bacon's poorest) should have become the master of its thought. The "outrageous piece of 'miraculous evangelism'" (Chambers) which founded New Atlantis, its stuffy ceremonials and barbarous human relations completes the picture of this "curious alliance of God, Mammon and Science" (Dupont).[5]

Thus the developing utopian tradition dragged into the open the latent contradictions in More's crypto-religious construction of Utopia. After the Rabelaisian flowering, Campanella and Bacon mark a reaction against Renaissance libertarian humanism, whose logical next step was the end of utopia as an independent form. The official repression would have worked toward this in any case; but it would not have succeeded so swiftly and well had not the utopian camp been betrayed from within. Having lost a fertile connection with the popular longings, utopia—for all the tries of the 18th-century "state novel" (*Staatsroman*)—disappears from the vanguard of European culture until Fourier and Chernyshevsky. Ironically, Bacon fought medieval scholasticism but inaugurated a new dogmatism of technocracy, and Campanella rotted for decades in papal prisons but announced a return to the closed, mythic world-model of Plato. History is cruel to "final solutions."

NOTES

1. Thomas More, *The Complete Works of St. Thomas More*, Volume 4, ed. Edward Surtz, S.J., and J.H. Hexter (US 1965), pp 65-67.
2. The following paragraph is argued at greater length in my essay "Defining the Literary Genre of Utopia," *Studies in the Literary Imagination* 6(Fall 1973):121-45.
3. Lewis Mumford, *The Story of Utopias* (1922; US 1962 iv+315), p 59.
4. H.B. White, *Peace Among the Willows: The Political Philosophy of Francis Bacon* (The Hague 1968), p 106.
5. R.W. Chambers, *Thomas More* (1935; UK 1938 416p, p 362); V. Dupont, *L'Utopie et le roman utopique dans la littérature anglaise* (Toulouse and Paris 1941), p 146.

WORKS ON THE SF OF ANTIQUITY, THE MIDDLE AGES, AND THE RENAISSANCE: A SELECT BIBLIOGRAPHY

General histories of society, culture, literature, or science have not been included, nor works of methodological importance only. As a rule, the first English-language edition is cited, and the short form of the title is used. The city of publication is given only for books not published in the United States or the United Kingdom.

1. General works (including those on history and theory of utopian thought).

Bakhtin, Mikhail. *Rabelais and His World*. US 1968.
Beer, Max. *The General History of Socialism and Social Thought*. I-II. UK 1957.
Berneri, Marie Louise. *Journey Through Utopia*. UK 1950.
Biesterfeld, Wolfgang. *Die literarische Utopie*. Stuttgart 1974.
Bloch, Ernst. *Das Prinzip Hoffnung* I-II. Frankfurt 1959.
Cawley, Robert Ralston. *Unpathed Waters*. US 1940.
Ceserani, Gian Paolo. *I falsi Adami*. Milan 1969.
Cioranescu, Alexandre. *L'avenir du passé*. Paris 1972.
Comparative Literature Studies, Vol. 10, No. 4 (Dec 1973)—special issue on "Utopian Social Thought in Literature and the Social Sciences."

Desroche, Henri. *Les Dieux rêvés*. Paris 1972.
Dupont, V. *L'Utopie et le roman utopique dans la littérature anglaise*. Paris 1941.
Duveau, Georges. *Sociologie de l'utopia*. Paris 1961.
Elliott, Robert G. *The Shape of Utopia*. US 1970.
Eurich, Nell. *Science in Utopia*. US 1967.
Gibson, R.W., and J. Max Patrick. *St. Thomas More: A Preliminary Bibliography*. US 1961.
Gove, Philip Babcock. *The Imaginary Voyage in Prose Fiction*. US 1941.
Marin, Louis, *Utopiques*. Paris 1973.
Morton, A.L. *The English Utopia*. UK 1952.
Mucchielli, Roger. *Le Mythe de la cité idéale*. Paris 1960.
Mumford, Lewis. *The Story of Utopias*. US 1922.
Negley, Glenn, and J. Max Patrick. *The Quest for Utopia*. US 1952.
Revue des sciences humaines 155 (1974)—special issue on "l'Utopie."
Ruyer, Raymond. *L'utopie et les utopies*. Paris 1950.
Schwonke, Martin. *Vom Staatsroman zur Science Fiction*. Stuttgart 1957.
Seeber, Hans Ulrich. *Wandlungen der Form in der literarischen Utopie*. Göttingen 1970.
Studies in the Literary Imagination, Vol. 6, No. 2 (Fall 1973)—special issue on "Aspects of Utopian Fiction."
Suvin, Darko. *La Science-fiction entre l'utopie et l'anti-utopie*. Montreal 1976.
Villgradter, Rudolf, and Friedrich Krey, eds. *Der utopische Roman*. Darmstadt 1973.
Wandlungen des Partadiesischen und Utopischen. Berlin 1966.

2. Antiquity and the Middle Ages. See also section 1 above, especially Beer, Biesterfield, Bloch, Ceserani, Cioranescu, Eurich, Gove, Morton, Mumford, Villgradter-Krey, and *Wandlungen*, and section 3 below, especially Beger, Förster, Liljegren, Patch, Seibt, and Süssmuth.

Ackermann, Elfriede Marie. *"Das Schlaraffenland" in German Literature and Folksong*. US 1954.
Altheim, Franz. *Der unbesiegte Gott*. Hamburg 1957.
Babcock, W.H. *Legendary Islands in the Atlantic*. US 1922.
Baldry, H.C. *Ancient Utopias*. UK 1956.
Bar, Francis. *Les Routes de l'autre monde*. Paris 1946.
Barker, Ernest. *The Political Thought of Plato and Aristotle*. UK 1959.
Bidez, Joseph. *La Cité du Monde et la Cité du Soleil chez le Stoïciens*. Paris 1932.
Boas, George. *Essays on Primitivism and Related Ideas in the Middle Ages*. US 1948.
Bompaire, J. *Lucian écrivain*. Paris 1958.
Bonner, Campbell. "Dionysiac Magic and the Greek Land of Cockaigne." *Trans. & Proc. Amer. Philological Assn.* 41 (1910).
Cocchiara, Giuseppe. *Il paese di Cuccagna*. Turin 1956.
Coli, Edoardo. *Il Paradiso Terrestre dantesco*. Florence 1896.
Cornford, Francis M. *Plato's Cosmology*. UK 1937.
Curtius, Ernst Robert. *European Literature and the Latin Middle Ages*. US 1953.
Ferguson, John. *Utopias of the Classical World*. US 1975.
Finley, M.I. "Utopianism Ancient and Modern." In *The Critical Spirit*, ed. Kurt H. Wolff and Barrington Moore, Jr. US 1967.
Fredericks, S.C. "Lucian's *True History* as SF." SFS 3 (1976).
Giannini, A. "Mito e Utopia nella letteratura Greca prima di Platone." *Rendiconti del Ist. Lombardo, Classe di Lettere* 101 (1967).
Graf, Arturo. *Miti, Leggende e Superstizioni del Medio Evo*. Bologna 1965.
Gronau, Karl. *Der Staat der Zukunft von Platon dis Dante*. Braunschweig 1933.
Guggenberger, Alois. *Die Utopie vom Paradies*. Stuttgart 1957.
Kampers, F. *Mittelalterliche Sagen vom Paradiese*. Köln 1897.
Lovejoy, Arthur O., and George Boas. *Primitivism and Related Ideas in Antiquity*. US 1935.
Manuel, Frank E., and Fritzie P. Manuel. "Sketch for a Natural History of Paradise." *Daedalus* 101 (1972).
Merkelbach, Reinhold. *Roman und Mysterium in der Antike*. Munich & Berlin 1962.
Patch, Howard Rollin. *The Other World*. US 1950.
Pöhlmann, Robert von. *Geschichte der sozialen Frage und des Sozialismus in der Antike* I-II. Munich 1912.
Rohde, Erwin. *Der griechische Roman und seine Vorläufer*. Leipzig 1876.

Salin, Edgar. *Civitas Dei*. Tübingen 1926.
———. *Platon und die griechische Utopie*. Munich & Leipzig 1921.
Schuhl, Pierre-Maxime. *Etudes sur la fabulation platonicienne*. Paris 1947.
Swanson, Roy Arthur. "The True, the False, and the Truly False: Lucian's Philosophical SF." SFS 3 (1976).
Vallauri, G. *Euhemero di Messene*. Torino 1956.
Visser, Elizabeth. *Iamboulos en de eilanden van de Zon*. Groningen 1947.
Westropp, Thomas Johnson. "Brasil and the Legendary Islands of the North Atlantic." *Proc. R. Irish Acad.* 30 (1912).
Winston, David. "Iambulus' Islands of the Sun and Hellenistic Literary Utopias." SFS 3 (1976).

3. More's *Utopia*. See also section 1 above, especially Beer, Berneri, Bloch, Cawley, Cioranescu, Dupont, Duveau, Elliott, Gibson-Patrick, Gove, Martin, Morton, Suvin, Villgradter-Krey, and *Wandlungen*; section 2, especially Kampers, Patch, and Westropp; and section 4 below, especially Bierman and Massô.

Adams, Robert P. "The Philosophic Unity of More's *Utopia*." *Studies in Philology* 38 (1941).
———. "The Social Responsibilities of Science in Utopia, New Atlantis, and After" *J. of the History of Ideas* 10 (1949).
Ames, Russell. *Citizen Thomas More and His Utopia*. US 1949.
Beger, Lina. "Thomas Morus und Plato." *Zc. für die gesamte Staatswiss.* 35 (1879).
R.W. Chambers. *Thomas More*. UK 1935.
Dermenghem, E. *Thomas Morus et les Utopistes de la Renaissance*. Paris 1927.
Donner, H.W. *Introduction to Utopia*. UK 1945.
Dudok, G. *Sir Thomas More and His Utopia*.
Förster, Richard. "Lucian in der Renaissance." *Archiv für Literaturgesch.* 14 (1937).
Gallagher, Ligeia, ed. *More's Utopia and Its Critics*. US 1964.
Heiserman, A.R. "Satire in the *Utopia*." PMLA 78 (1963).
Herbrüggen, Hubertus Schulte. *Utopie und Anti-Utopie*. Bochum-Langendreer 1960.
Hexter, J.H. *More's Utopia*. US 1952.
Liljegren, S.B. *Studies on the Origin and Early Tradition of English Utopian Fiction*. Uppsala 1961.
Marc'hadour, Germain. *L'Univers de Thomas More*. Paris 1969.
Miles, Leland, "The Literary Artistry of Thomas More." *Studies in English Literature* 6 (1966).
Morris, William. "Introduction." In Thomas More, *Utopia*, UK 1893. (Reprinted in this issue of SFS.)
Nelson, William, ed. *Twentieth Century Interpretations of Utopia*. US 1968.
Sanderlin, George. "The Meaning of Thomas More's *Utopia*." *College English* 12 (1950).
Schoeck, R.J. "'A Nursery of Correct and Useful Institutions': On More's *Utopia* as Dialogue." *Moreana* 22 (1969).
Seibt, Ferdinand. "Utopie in Mittelalter." *Historische Zc.* 208 (1969).
Sullivan, Frank, and Maijie Padberg Sullivan. *Moreana* [annotated bibliography] I-IV. US 1964-68. Index US 1971.
Surtz, Edward L., S.J. The Praise of Pleasure. US 1957.
———. The Praise of Wisdom. US 1957.
——— and J.H. Hexter. "Introduction." In *The Complete Works of St. Thomas More* IV, US 1965.
Süssmuth, Hans. *Studien zur Utopia des Thomas Morus*. Münster 1967.
Sylvester, R.S. "'Hythlodaeo Credimus.'" *Soundings* 51 (1968).
Traugott, John. "A Voyage to Nowhere with Thomas More and Jonathan Swift." In *Swift*, ed. Ernest Tuveson. US 1964.
L'Utopie à la Renaissance. Bruxelles and Paris 1963.

4. Other Renaissance Works. See also section 1 above, especially Bakhtin, Beer, Berneri, Bloch, Cawley, Cioranescu, Desroche, Dupont, Duveau, Gove, Mumford, Schwonke, Suvin, Villgradter-Krey, and *Wandlungen*; and section 3, especially Adams 1949, Dermenghem, Süssmuth, and *L'Utopie*.

Badaloni, Nicola. *Tommaso Campanella*. Milan 1965.
Beaujour, Michel. *Le Jeu de Rabelais*. Paris 1969.

Bierman, Judah. "Science and Society in the *New Atlantis* and Other Renaissance Utopias." PMLA 78 (1973).
Blodgett, Eleanor Dickinson. "Bacon's *New Atlantis* and Campanella's *Civitas Solis*." PMLA 46 (1931).
Bock, Gisela. *Thomas Campanella*. Tübingen 1974.
Diéguez, Manuel de. *Rabelais par lui-même*. Paris 1960.
Doren, Alfred. "Campanella als Chiliast und Utopist." In *Kultur- und Universalgeschichte. Walter Goetz su 60. Geburtstag*, Leipzig & Berlin 1927.
Farrington, Benjamin. *The New Atlantis of Francis Bacon*. UK 1965.
François Rabelais: IVe Centenaire de sa Mort. Geneve & Lille 1953.
Greene, Thomas M. *Rabelais*. US 1970.
Kaiser, Walter. *Praisers of Folly*. US 1963.
Lefebvre, Henri. *Rabelais*. Paris 1955.
Lefranc, Abel. *Les Navigations de Pantagruel*. Paris 1905.
Marin, Louis. "Les Corps utopiques rabelaisiens." *Littérature* (Feb 1976).
Massô, Gildo. *Education in Utopia*. US 1927.
Nicolson, Marjorie. *Science and Imagination*. US 1956.
Paris, Jean. *Rabelais au futur*. Paris 1970.
Sainéan, Lazare. *La Langue de Rabelais*. Paris 1922.
Saulnier, V.L. *Le Dessein de Rabelais*. PLaris 1957.
Scholtz, Harald. *Evangelischer Utopismus bei J.V. Andreae*. Stuttgart 1957.
Spitzer, Leo. "Le pretendu realisme de Rabelais." *Modern Philology* 37 (1939).
White, H.B. *Peace Among the Willows: The Political Philosophy of Francis Bacon*. The Hague 1968.
Wiener, Harvey S. "'Science or Providence': Toward Knowledge in Bacon's *New Atlantis*." *Enlightenment Essays* 3 (1972).

Christie V. McDonald

The Reading and Writing of Utopia in Denis Diderot's *Supplément au voyage de Bougainville*

(from SFS *3: 248–254, November 1976)*

Roland Barthes has suggested that utopia is familiar to every writer because his task—or his pleasure—is to bestow meaning through the exercise of his writing, and he cannot do this without the alternation of values, a dialectical movement akin to that of a yes/no opposition.[1] Such is the polarity between nature and culture in Diderot's *Supplément au voyage de Bougainville* in which the description of Tahiti (a "natural" society) becomes a springboard for critique of (the then) present-day European culture. Indeed, the binary opposition between the two poles effectively seems to produce a moral statement about culture and thus generates a meaning within the text, and yet something seems to go awry when the apparent simplicity of the thematic statement is not borne out at other levels of the text. In the heterogeneous and plural meanings produced within this single work we find an acute questioning of the relationship between utopia, the problem of origins, and the text as writing.

The banal opposition between nature and culture in the 18th century bespeaks of a continuing preoccupation with origins—whether those of the self, of language, or society—which constitutes not only the initial but the crucial phases of the utopian process. Within this opposition, present-day society (be it ours or Diderot's) partakes of the artifice of culture and thus estranges man from his true inner self, whereas "nature" emblematically signals the return to both the individual and the collective transparency of man's being. The meaningful difference between the two is similar to the contradiction engendered in traditional utopias between the reader's observable society and its opposite, the newly discovered or ideal society. It is the negative relationship—that of contradiction and antithesis—rather than the concept of perfection which interests us here. Utopia, it would seem, arises from a series of oppositions—here/elsewhere, real/imaginary, etc.—which constitutes the fundamental contradiction.

The *Supplément au voyage de Bougainville* consists of five parts (each in dialogue form) in the editions standard since 1935, but of four parts in earlier editions.[2] In Part 1 two interlocutors ("A" and "B") discuss Bougainville's 1771 non-fictional narrative of his voyage round the world[3] and prepare to read through together a "supplement" to it. Part 2 begins the reading with the speech of an elder Tahitian who, in addressing Bougainville, deplores both the intrusion of the European colonizers and the ill effects of their corrupting ways. In Parts 3-4 Orou, a Tahitian, engages his European guest, the Almoner, in a conversation which ranges from religious beliefs to differing sexual mores. Part 5 (Part 4 of the earlier editions) presents the final dialogue between "A" and "B" in which they comment and elaborate upon the preceding conversations.

Diderot clearly sets up the binary opposition between nature and culture in the distinction between Tahiti and Europe. Yet there is no single continuous narration to guide the reader; rather, the oppositions are created through a series of dialogues in which the voices align themselves according to one side or the other. In addition, each protagonist takes a dual role: he speaks both as an individual in his own voice and as a representative of the collectivity to which he belongs. It can be said that at one level dialogue requires interlocutors and, minimally, an addresser and an addressee ("destinateur" and "destinataire"). Emile Benveniste has shown that the first-person pronoun "I" can never be isolated from the implicit second-person "thou" ("je"/"tu"). He has shown further that one presupposes the other in opposition to the third-person (or, as he says, non-person) pronoun "he"/"she"/"it."[4] For Benveniste it is this reciprocity between "I" and "thou" which makes possible all social bonds. That is, language is the sole means by which one may reach another, and "society in its turn only holds together through the common use of signs of communication."[5] Ideally, then, there should be a rigorous continuity between the premises which underlie the individual speech act and those which subtend the larger political structure. But it is precisely here that the coherence of Diderot's text breaks down; it is in the curious asymmetry between the presuppositions concerning individual speech and the more explicit ideological statement that the *Supplement* indicates preoccupations other than the strictly moral ones. Thus the debate relating to colonization and sexual freedom is but the surface of an exploration, by far more troubling, of the relationship between interlocutors and the social context (present or future) in which language as communication remains possible.

The two subtitles of the work, which in English would be *Dialogue Between A and B* and *On the Disadvantage of Linking Moral Ideas to Certain Physical Actions*, indicate priorities within the text. The work is above all a fictional supplement to Bougainville's narrative. Yet whereas Bougainville's autobiographical account is rendered by a single narrator, Diderot's recap splinters into two voices, "A" and "B," who in turn introduce others. Finally, the actual dispute is a moral one.

The presentation of the opposition between nature and culture cannot be dissociated from the complex network of voices through which it becomes manifest and whose function is neither identical nor complementary. The fragmentation of the dialogues, alternating between the "A" and "B" conversation and the inner or interspersed dialogues (between the Old Man and his implicit addressee, Bougainville, on the one hand, and Orou and the Almoner, on the other), puts into question any cohesive thematic meaning of the work. A more detailed—though extremely brief—discussion is necessary to demonstrate this.

The first part of the text, entitled "judgment of Bougainville's Voyage," opens with a most anodyne conversation between "A" and "B" about the weather. "A" says: "This superbly starred arch under which we met yesterday, and which seemed to guarantee a beautiful day, has not kept its word" (455/§1).[6] This remark initiates a discussion which is at once the beginning of the text that we are reading and also the continuation of another text, the tale of Madame de la Carlière—a short story written by Diderot during the same year.[7] Since the beginning is indeed less a beginning than a continuation, the protagonists tacitly evoke reflexion upon their dialogue as the re-writing, or re-inscription, of another's discourse—even if, in this case, the other text is Diderot's own. In themselves the interlocutors appear divested of psychological characteristics, for the reader knows and learns nothing about them; their anonymity is total. What is striking is that, in addition to their roles as continuators of a displaced dialogue, they are also readers both of Bougainville's voyage and the *Supplement* as well, and as such they remain indispensable to one another. The necessity for their mutual presence becomes explicit when "B" refuses to give a copy of the Supplement to "A," insisting that they read together. In this manner the dialogue between them serves to introduce and conclude the episode of the *Supplement* that we are reading. From time to time the voice of an anonymous narrator intrudes, but far from the surreptitious intervention of a unifying authorial voice, these fragmentary interruptions only further weaken the coherence of the dialogues.

Such dispersion would seem to disallow the notion of subjectivity within the so-called "characters" because of a constant movement from subject to subject and the ensuing dislocation within the axis of the speaking voice. The quest for origins focuses less on the concept of an internal world which is to be discovered and highly prized, than upon the social relationships which insure social cohesion and communication. Any such statement concerning the individual subject (as self) must have immediate consequences for the corresponding ideological position. Here the status of the referent is of particular importance because access to it comes only through the interlocutors. Let us concentrate for a moment on the representation of Tahiti as the Old Man portrays it in his speech. Addressing his compatriots he invites them to rejoice in the departure of the Europeans, and he then delivers an attack upon the corruption so inveterate in the society of the colonizers that it could not but contaminate the Tahitians' happiness. The entire speech, or harangue as it is called, is constructed upon antitheses destined to evoke Tahiti in strict contrast to European society: happiness/unhappiness, freedom/slavery, health/illness, life/death. However, the rhetoric of antithesis only partially masks a twisting of the nature/culture polarity since the so-called opposition consists more precisely of a moral gradation between two differing societies: one is healthy and hence closer to nature, while the other is corrupt and therefore further removed from nature. Finally, the Old Man speaks neither about nature nor even about Tahitian society. Rather, his discourse projects an ideological critique of the excesses and abuses of society as an institution which, far from rejecting civilization, tends to confirm the value of the social structure; the norm is actually reinforced by the focus on transgression.

Yet, although the referent, and the reference points, seem well delineated in the *Supplement*, they constantly overlap and interfere with one another: first, there is the voyage which Bougainville recounts in his own work; the *Supplement* then takes up the narration of this same voyage through the dialogue; lastly, Tahiti is described by the Old Man in opposition to Bougainville's society. By maintaining a constant distance from any realistic representation of Tahiti, and by playing upon the multiple sources of the work (ranging from Bougainville's text to Rousseau's *Second Discourse*), the text calls attention to its own fictive status and becomes thereby self-referential. The seemingly innocuous deviation from the nature/culture opposition signals a radical questioning of any referent exterior to the text. Just as the Old Man is not a true primitive, his harangue is not written in his own language, for indeed his discourse betrays "ideas and turns of speech which are European" (459/§2). Not only has there allegedly been translation from Tahitian to Spanish and then to French, but the text clearly does not seek to rehabilitate traces of a more 'natural' language. The Old Man may speak in the name of his society, but he does so in a classical and artificial discourse meaningful only within that society which he would so bitterly oppose.

In contrast to the Old Man, who purports to be the spokesman for all Tahiti, Orou and the Almoner—interlocutors of part three—speak both in their own right and their own names, and yet the function of their dialogue is every bit as socially motivated as that of the Old Man. Each speaker takes a position which diametrically opposes that of his interlocutor on moral questions (marriage, adultery, incest), but the dialogue never pretends to be grounded in a subjectivity—and hence also an intersubjective relationship—which goes beyond language. One interlocutor views himself in his difference to the other only in order to assure social communication. In this manner the opposition between Tahiti and Europe, as it is recapitulated within the dialogue between Orou and the Almoner, serves less as a genetic quest for man's inner reality than as a privileged moment in which language reflects the mechanisms of its own functioning. The question of phylogenesis, as that of ontogenesis, is for example quickly disposed of when "A" asks how Bougainville would explain the origin of certain particularities of nature, and "B" responds that Bougainville "explains nothing; he is merely a witness" (459/§1). At the same time, however, though he declares impossible the knowledge of man's primitive history, "B" does recognize the compelling attraction of all questions of origin. At the mere sight of certain places—in this case the island called Lanciers—"there is no one who would not wonder who had placed man here; what kind of communication men might once have had with the rest of their species; what became of them when they multiplied within the confines of a small space" (460/§1).

A certain symmetry does arise in the confrontation between Tahiti and Europe as it is evoked within the respective dialogues of the Old Man and Orou, for the discussion in both cases emphasizes the crucial problem of property. For example, in the Old Man's speech images of illness, corruption and contamination by colonialism dominate as he demonstrates how the purity of Tahitian culture has been infected by the irruption of property—of the "mine and yours" syndrome. Orou, on the other hand, in his dialogue with the Almoner, puts into question the institutions of European culture and, in particular, marriage as a symptom of the decay of civilization. Then "B" explains that marriage too is a question of property: "It is man's tyranny that has converted the possession of women into property" (509/§4).

Not only is there symmetry between the two inner dialogues but also an inverse relationship connecting the individual voice (Bougainville and Orou have proper names) to the collective voice (the Old Man and the Almoner, each as representative of his society):

NATURE	CULTURE
The Old Man	[Bougainville]
Orou	The Almoner

Each word, each sentence uttered by an interlocutor takes on meaning only in relation to the person whom he addresses and who is at the same time his opposite. This reciprocal exchange leads directly to another one, the spatial opposition between Tahiti and Europe. Thus the dialogue recapitulates the process of utopian antithesis by integrating the axis of the referent to the process of uttering (what

Benveniste calls 'énonciation') by the individual speaker, and everything would seem to function smoothly: as the subject speaks he implicitly reflects upon the opposition between Tahiti and Europe which in turn opens up the larger question of communication as the foundation of all society.

The lack of an intersubjective model as the external structure which would define language internally is not without paradox here. It is not clear in the *Supplement*, for example, under what conditions social discourse becomes possible. It would seem, moreover, that the symmetrical and ordered oppositions within the interspersed dialogues (all those excluding "A" and "B") assure the continuation of a social language which never totally puts itself into question. The moral contradiction between Tahiti and Europe leaves culture pretty much intact—corrected, reprimanded perhaps, but never totally censured. The constant maintenance of a distance between Tahiti and Europe, as between the self and other in dialogue, belies a desire for unity which is analogous to the ideal of a *mapa mundi* ('mappemonde' or global map) of knowledge. Diderot evokes this image in the article entitled "The Encyclopedia" from the *Encyclopedia* itself. The image of the map to convey not only the possibility for progress through knowledge but also the very project of the text (entitled the *Encyclopedia*) indicates the importance of assemblage and unification as a means of mastery. "B" never loses sight of this implicit desire, for he says: "The act of ordering is always the act of making oneself the master of others" (512/§4). Finally, the inner dialogues, which fit neatly into the division between Tahiti and Europe, can be read as the fictive history of a division internal to man. "B" declares: "There existed a natural man: an artificial man was introduced into this man; and there occurred within the cave a continual war which lasts throughout life" (512/§4). Such a fall from unity implies, of course, the possibility of redemption.

The dialogue between "A" and "B" is different from the inner dialogues; it disperses meaning with a seeming alacrity while the others seek unity, a moral statement, from the firm opposition between Tahiti and Europe. A brief sketch of the ideological implications corresponding to the two levels of dialogue will suggest at least a partial explanation for the asymmetry between them.

The dialogues between the Old Man and Orou remain firmly anchored within the polarity nature/culture (however mitigated the opposition may have become in its moral ramifications) which generates a whole series of antitheses closely allied to those mentioned earlier: absence/presence, before/after, etc. This notion of dialogue implies, as its extension or prolongation, a concept of utopia that depends upon an internal necessity of distance.[8] Diderot's presentation of Tahitian customs figures as a moral critique of European culture with no pretense to any revolutionary change, for the vision of a culture open to progress and evolution depends upon the traditional model of the city—an image evoked explicitly by Diderot in the article "Encyclopedia." Dialogue must presuppose language as communication within such a logocentric system in order to make possible the ideal of reciprocity between moral geography and discourse. Both of these apparently converge at the focal point: the book which we are reading. However, it becomes increasingly clear that, within the spatial sphere of the text and through the explicit reflexion of "A" and "B" upon the act of reading, a kind of dispersion takes place which irremediably disrupts the ideal of unity.

There is no exact counterpart to the schematic opposition which comes out of the dialogues between the Old Man and Orou within the dialogue between "A" and "B" since theirs does not split according to the same ideological distinctions. Though "A" and "B" may at certain moments show a penchant for one or the other position, neither takes a strong line, and when it comes to opting in favor either of civilization or the free reign of the instincts (in any case an illusion since Tahiti also has its taboos), "B" tallies things up and retreats to a position of moral prudence, not to say indecision:[9] "Let us imitate the good almoner, a monk in France, a primitive in Tahiti" (515/§4). As for the relationship between the two interlocutors, questions are asked, answers given, but in the last analysis one is hard put to distinguish between the two. In addition to the lack of psychological depth in these "characters," their dialogue cannot lead to any reconciliation of the voices since they seem to merge and separate indifferently. Indeed, their voices, like their sentences, seem strangely seated both inside the text which we are reading and outside of the text which they themselves are reading (a book of the very same title). Thus paradoxically situated within and without the text, they become agents of a constantly displaced meaning whereby the reality of any referent is repeatedly short-circuited and subverted. "B" states equivocally: "This is not a fable; and you would have no doubt about Bougainville's sincerity if you knew the supplement to his voyage" (464/§1). We may decode this as follows: that we will learn to read properly not through this most decipherable text of Bougainville's but rather through the one which is inscribed in it, the *Supplement*. For the act of reading cannot be dissociated from the act of writing here.

This interference or interruption—within the dialogue between "A" and "B"—in the emission of a distinct ideological meaning corresponds implicitly to the definition which Louis Marin proposes for the term 'utopique' and which, for us, is the second level of utopia. Marin situates the definition for this term, on the one hand, at a neutral point that falls into neither one or the other of the poles of the utopian contradiction (or antithesis) and, on the other hand, in the "plural"—that is, what he considers to be the dispersed field of utopian discourse.[10] The slippage of utopia into its adjectival form ('utopique') signals a model quite radically different from the well-ordered and transparent city which emerges from the harmonious oscillation of opposites; it would seem, on the contrary, to reject the binary system and call for a new revolutionary practice. For such a slippage suggests a movement within which transcendent truth and meaning are no longer the absolute guarantors for either language of the individual subject, in search of his own origins, or for society as the reflection of an Other reality beyond this world. This second sense of utopia is then the unhinging or deconstruction of the first.

What is most fascinating about the *Supplement*, and this holds true for other texts by Diderot as well, is that it not only conveys the two separate levels but holds them in a state of tension, a state of impossible co-existence, and it does so with unrelenting persistence. The lack of distinction between "A" and "B" indicates quite strongly that the critical and conceptual apparatus of the speaking subject does not function at the same level as within the other dialogues: theirs is a false critique, a false synthesis, and it is asymmetrical to the polarity between Tahiti and Europe. However, the more evident this becomes, the more evident it is too that the reader cannot reduce the assymmetry to a simple antithetical confrontation: the positions are simply not "totalizable." Thus if in a sense the text called the *Supplement to Bougainville's Voyage* speaks of utopia, in another sense utopia is a manifestation of the text, and textuality, which, it would seem, plays itself to the limit by oddly refusing to recognize (and thus to resolve) the consequences of its own functioning. Or is the meaning perhaps elsewhere? In any event, the trap is set, for to ask if one has seen what Diderot wanted us to see is to seek out a single voice in an irreducible plurality of voices, a unity in dispersion.

NOTES

1. Barthes refers to the concept of utopia not only in this traditional sense—generated by paradigmatic oppositions—but also in the new sense which he ascribes to it: that sense immanent in the Text as writing. See *Barthes par lui-même* (Paris 1975), and also *S/Z* (Paris 1973), for the important concepts of "readability" and "writability" ("le lisible" and "le scriptible").

2. The text was completed in its first form in 1771, and though intended for Grimm's *Correspondance littéraire* it was not published at that time; the state of this first version is not known. The work was published finally in 1796 in its revised form by Vauxelles, and this

was the established text from Naigeen (1798) to Assézat (1875). Later work by Viktor Johanssen on a Leningrad manuscript revealed important additions (presumably made in 1778-79), the most notable being the digression about Miss Polly Baker; this latter manuscript was the one edited by Gilbert Chinard (see Note 7).

3. Louis-Antoine de Bougainville, *Voyage auteur du monde* (Paris 1771).

4. See "De la subjectivité dans le langage," *(Problemes de linguistique générale* I (Paris 1966), 258-67.

5. Ibid. II (Paris 1974), 91.

6. 455/§1=page 455 of Denis Diderot, *Supplément au voyage de Bougainville* (Paris: Garnier, 1961) or Part 1 in presumably any four-part edition. All quotations from the *Supplement* in this essay are from the cited edition in my own translation. **Editorial Note.** There are several translations as *Supplement to Bougainville's Voyage*: the one I have used in editing this essay is in *Diderot, Interpreter of Nature: Selected Writings*, ed. Jonathan Kemp, tr. Jean Stewart and Jonathan Kemp (UK 1937), pp 146-91. —RDM.

7. Denis Diderot, *Supplément au voyage de Bougainville*, ed. Gilbert Chinard (Paris 1935), pp 46-48. Chinard cites other similarities between the two texts and concludes that they seem to be variations on the same theme.

8. For Saint Augustin, in the *City of God*, two cities were formed from the love of the sons of Adam: the city of men who love God and the city of men whose love has turned away from God. The two cities are eternal, but in the middle there exists a neutral space where man passes the duration of his life, though he belongs, by predestination, to one or the other of the two eternal cities even during his stay on earth. The city of God comprises truth, good, order, and peace while the city of the damned incorporates error, evil, disorder, confusion. In short, one is the repudiation of the other.

9. I would like to express my gratitude to Norbert Spehner for his remarks on this subject.

10. *Utopiques: jeux d'espace* (Paris 1973), p 9.

William B. Fischer

German Theories of Science Fiction: Jean Paul, Kurd Lasswitz, and After

(from **SFS** *3: 254–265, November 1976)*

Science fiction is a recent form of literature and an even newer topic of literary criticism. While many excellent interpretations have already been written, there is still no lack of unexamined material or unanswered questions. One of the most fundamental problems of SF criticism concerns the theory and definition of SF—its aesthetics or poetics. At least four major issues are involved: 1) the manner in which the content, methods, and outlook of science interact with the artistic temperament to produce the attitudes and themes of SF; 2) the nature of SF as a literary form; 3) the reciprocal interplay of author, text, and reader in the creation and reception of texts and in the evolution of a concept of genre; 4) the consideration of SF and SF criticism from literary traditions other than modern Anglo-American SF in the formulation of theories about the general nature of SF.

One major body of SF and SF criticism which has been unduly neglected is the one produced by German writers. In this essay I will discuss early German theories of SF, with particular attention to two writers, Jean Paul Friedrich Richter (1763-1825) and Kurd Lasswitz (1848-1910), whose work spans a period of over a century. Both participated, as theoreticians and writers of fiction, in the development of German SF. Their ideas and those of other German SF critics deserve a place in the history of SF and can also contribute much to the application of the concepts and methods of literary criticism to the study of SF.

The prehistory of German SF can be traced at least as far back as the Renaissance and Kepler's *Somnium* (c. 1610, pbd 1634). None of the few German utopias and imaginary voyages written during the next two centuries, however, are as well known or as important to the history of SF as those written in England, France, and Italy.[1] It was only after the middle of the eighteenth century that science even began to become a significant part of German literature. The impact of the Scientific Revolution on world-view and poetic imagery can be detected in some lyric poetry, for example the hymns of Friedrich Gottlieb Klopstock (1724-1803).[2] Many critics have noted the importance of science for Goethe, who was an able student of many sciences, and for the German Romantics, some of whom had formal scientific training.[3] The effect of modern cosmology and Newtonian physics on poetic consciousness is also apparent in several poems by Friedrich Hölderlin (1770-1843), such as "Keppler" (sic) and "Die scheinheiligen Dichter," both written shortly before 1800. None of these writers, however, can reasonably be considered authors of German SF, nor did they address themselves at any length to the philosophical and aesthetic questions raised by the interaction of science and literature. Even less did they—or for that matter most other German writers of the time—concern themselves in their fiction to any notable degree with technology, the social impact of the Industrial Revolution, or serious utopian thought. Here, as in industrialization and the development of a national state, Germany lagged behind Great Britain, France, and the United States. Perhaps the German literary community was too busy dealing with the issue of German nationalism or investigating the artistic implications of *Faust* or *Wilhelm Meister* to devote much thought to science, industrialization, or speculation about what society might be like after Germany finally became a nation. The contrast between German literature and British and American literature of this period, which was so important for the later development of Anglo-American SF, is readily apparent.

1. At the end of the eighteenth century there did appear one major statement about science and literature by a German writer. It is to be found, curiously enough, among the several whimsical prefaces and stories which accompany the novel *Leben des Quintus Fixlein* (1796) by Jean Paul Friedrich Richter (1763-1825), who is better known by his pseudonym Jean Paul. Jean Paul's relation to German Classicism and Romanticism has been warmly debated, and he is usually placed outside the main current of German literature. His literary excellence and originality, however, are widely acknowledged, and his reputation as an aesthetician is established by his *Vorschule der Ästhetik* (1804).

Jean Paul's discussion of cosmology, fantasy, and literature is couched as the "Dedication to My Foster-sister Philippine" which precedes the delicate, even fey story "Der Mond: eine phantasierende Geschichte."[4] Jean Paul, or rather the narrator of the story, begins the "Dedication" by describing the discrepancy between the cosmology of modern science and the older fantastic cosmology whose sentimentality and anthropomorphism, he says, still govern the thoughts of frivolous girls:

> In none of my books, my dear foster-sister, have I yet expressed my ridicule about how you girls make so much of the Moon. It is the plaything of your hearts and the nest-egg around which you set the other stars when you hatch fantasies from them.... But one could quarrel about something else, too, namely that you would rather love and look at the dear old Moon and the Man who lives there than get to know them—as is your custom with men who live here below the Moon.... Dearest, there is even the question of whether you yourself still know that the Moon is but a few square miles smaller than Asia. How often I had to drum it into your head before you could retain the fact that on the Moon not only does the day last half a month, but also—something even more worth hearing—the night.... I have it on good authority that

> you don't even remember what kind of a Moon the Moon has overhead—our Earth is the Moon's Moon, you silly thing, and to whoever is up there it looks no bigger than a wedding-cake. [*Werke*, 4:50-51]

Such familiarity with modern science in a German writer of the late 18th century is noteworthy but not unique. What is remarkable about Jean Paul is that he makes science an important ingredient of his philosophical outlook and his literature as well. The story-teller's flippant remarks about his foster-sister and the mysteries of modern astronomy give way to an earnest assertion that the study of the cosmos revealed by modern science "gives man an exalted heart, and an eye which reaches beyond the Earth, and wings which lift one into the Incommensurable, and a God who is not finite, but rather infinite" (*Werke*, 4:51). The serious tone is appropriate, for it soon becomes apparent that Jean Paul intends something more than a comment on the lag between modern science and popular consciousness. His observations about the differences between the modern and the old-fashioned cosmologies are the foundation for a statement about the effects of modern science on the world-view, themes, and images of poetry. In a passage which can count as an early attempt to resolve the problem of the "Two Cultures," Jean Paul declares that literature and modern science are not incompatible:

> One may have fantasies about everything under the Moon, and about the Moon itself too, as long as one does not take the fantasies for truths—or the shadow-play for a picture-collection—or the picture-collection for a natural-history collection. The astronomer inventories and assesses the sky and misses by only a few pounds; the poet furnishes and enriches the heavens.... The former lays measuring-lines about the Moon, while the latter lays garlands about it—and also about the Earth. [*Werke*, 4:51]

I would suggest that in this brief passage Jean Paul is offering a program for a new kind of literature much like SF, and that in his conception of the new type of "fantasy" he also touches on issues which have continued to occupy the attention of SF critics and theorists.[5] The elliptical syntax and eccentric terminology make it difficult at first to discern the exact meanings of the distinctions between "fantasies" ("Phantasien"), "truths" ("Wahrheiten"), "shadow-play" ("Schattenspiel"), "picture-collection" ("Bilderkabinett"), and "natural-history collection" ("Naturalienkabinett"). But the general purport is evident and the choice of such puzzling imagery in fact contributes to the argument. Jean Paul seems to be examining the differences between imagination (including the creation of fiction) on the one hand, and philosophical truths, historical and biographical facts, and the knowledge furnished by modern science on the other. The key word is "Phantasie," which refers not only to the daydreams of adolescents, but also to the faculty of imagination and its expression in the form of literature. According to Jean Paul the new fantasies and fictions do not claim to be statements of absolute fact ("Wahrheiten") and should not be considered as such; they have other functions and employ other categories of truth and validity than do philosophy, history, and science. Many modern theorists also suggest that a work of SF, despite its emphasis on concrete, realistic description and its use of the past tense and indicative mood, is not a prediction or prophecy but rather a "thought-model" or hypothesis in which author and reader explore future or alternate worlds. The reader, because he enjoys reading fiction and is interested in scientific speculation, temporarily and conditionally accepts the imaginary world as a real place. He then judges the fiction not according to its factual truth as a prediction of the future, but rather its validity and internal consistency as a plausible representation of an imaginary world, including its inhabitants and their culture.

In the next phrase Jean Paul formulates another distinction: the "shadow-play" of fiction is not to be mistaken for a "picture-collection." At the very least he is restating the notion that the new fantasies are not to be viewed as assertions which claim to express absolute truth. It is conceivable that he is also drawing our attention to the idea that the characters in the new kind of fantasy would perhaps have a different nature and function than those in other, more "realistic" fiction. Modern proponents of SF have argued similarly that the use of type characters or the avoidance of abnormal personalities in SF may have a legitimate function as part of the author's effort to make the imaginary world familiar and plausible.

The multiple meanings of "Bilder" make possible still another shift of argument. In a certain sense a work of literature, even though it does not claim to reproduce historical and biographical truth, can indeed be seen as a "Bilderkabinett," a collection of "representations," "images," or "figures." But the "images" of fantasy, even fantasy based on modern science, are not to be viewed as though they were parts of a "natural-history collection." Here, I think, Jean Paul is pointing out the distinction in content and function between science, including the non-fictional scientific text, and what we would call SF. The poet is given a certain license with reality, including scientific facts. He may create imaginary science, and he may use the cosmos of modern science as a background for speculations not immediately justified by present science. But he must also conform to the demands of fiction, which deals with living beings, not just with inanimate objects. To emphasize this difference Jean Paul contrasts the outlook and functions of the scientist and the poet. The astronomer, for example, measures the cosmos, while the practitioner of the new form of literary fantasy, like the writer of SF, speculates imaginatively about science and about life in the cosmos.

Even if the "Dedication" were nothing more than a comment about the impact of science on modern consciousness, it would be an important document for the attempt to trace the interplay of science and literature in the emergence of the type of sensibility which was a prerequisite for the creation of SF. But Jean Paul's remarks on science, imagination, and art, despite their brevity, irony, and eccentric style, make the "Dedication" even more significant for the history of SF. Although there was as yet no real SF to which he might have referred in his speculations about the new "fantasies," his own abilities as a writer and aesthetician, as well as his familiarity with the science of his time enabled him to analyze the impact of science on modern consciousness and to form conjectures about the possible literary expression of such interaction. At the end of the "Dedication," and often during the short stories "Die Mondfinsternis" (The Eclipse of the Moon) and "Der Mond," Jean Paul does indeed return to the old cosmology which had served poetry so well. But in the "Dedication" he anticipated, briefly but provocatively, a number of issues important to SF criticism.

By no means does the work of Jean Paul begin an essentially continuous tradition of German SF and SF criticism. At most one can distinguish a very minor and often historically discontinuous genre composed of science-oriented fantasies and whimsical pieces which resemble those of Lewis Carroll, Edwin A. Abbott, and C.H. Hinton.[6] Nor did any of the few German utopias of the late eighteenth or early nineteenth century, some of which describe imaginary science and technology, achieve any appreciable currency. The essential stylistic, thematic, and conceptual roots of German SF, like those of Anglo-American SF, are to be found instead in a later period, in technological fiction, the "future-war" story, the modern utopia, the tradition of middle-brow realistic fiction, and the direct confrontation of the author with science and technology in an industrialized society.

2. The real father of German SF was Kurd Lasswitz (1848-1910), who wrote a number of short stories, novellas, and novels, including his masterpiece, the two-volume novel *Auf zwei Planeten* (On Two Planets; 1897).[7] Lasswitz' personality, professional activity, literary works, and even his ideas about aesthetics show a juxtaposition and sometimes a happy synthesis of the sciences and the traditional humanities. Although he was a trained scientist, his education, like that of most

German intellectuals of the time, heavily emphasized the humanistic culture of Goethe's Weimar and of German Idealism. Indeed, it was as a teacher of philosophy as well as mathematics and physics that he spent thirty years at the Gymnasium Ernestinum in Gotha while writing his scientific works, histories of science and philosophy, essays on aesthetics, and SF. Lasswitz was deeply aware of his dual position as a descendant of German Classicism and an inhabitant of a modern world pervaded by science and technology. His confidence in his ability to bridge the gap between Goethe's Weimar and Bismarck's Germany was no doubt strengthened by his knowledge and near-adulation of Goethe and Kant, who had dealt so successfully with science as part of their humanistic lives.

Several times during his literary career Lasswitz examined the nature of the new kind of literature which he was helping to create. He first expressed his ideas in 1878 in the Preface to his two early novellas, the *Bilder aus der Zukunft* (Images from the Future; cited below as BZ). In the May 1887 issue of the general-interest liberal journal *Nord und Süd* he discussed "the poetical and the scientific views of nature" ("Die poetische und die wissenschaftliche Betrachtung der Natur," cited as PWBN). An essay on futurology in philosophy and fiction, "Über Zukunftsträume" (On Dreams About the Future; ZT), forms one chapter of the philosophical work *Wirklichkeiten* (1899). The two essays "Der tote and der lebendige Mars" (The Dead and the Living Mars; TLM) and "Unser Recht auf Bewohner anderer Welten" (Our Claims on Inhabitants of Other Worlds; URBAW) are Lasswitz' final word on SF. The latter appeared in the *Frankfurter Zeitung* on 16 November 1910, one day before his death; both are included in the posthumous volume *Empfundenes und Erkanntes* (1919), from which they are cited here. It would be impossible in these few pages to explore the full range and complexity of Lasswitz' thought or even to quote more than a few essential passages. I intend instead to summarize the major steps in his argument and to suggest its relevance to the major issues of modern SF criticism.

Lasswitz' essays on the aesthetics of SF reflect both his cultural heritage and his training in science. In its point of departure, conceptual organization, and terminology his course of reasoning resembles that of the treatises on aesthetics written by Kant, Goethe, Schiller, and, for that matter, Hegel and Schelling, who discuss art from psychological and cultural perspectives before turning to issues of artistic practice. Thus Lasswitz' theory of SF begins with the attempt to show that fiction about science reflects and satisfies basic human needs and is therefore a legitimate form of art. He states that it is human nature to speculate about the future of mankind and of human culture, because man has an intellect and a sense of curiosity, and also because "striving for improvement is the essence of human life" (ZT p 423). To these traditional philosophical notions Lasswitz adds the concepts and methods of modern science. He argues that man's confrontation with nature, especially the cosmos, is the initial impetus and recurring form of conceptualization for the attempt to comprehend human existence (PWBN pp 270-71). Thus science, as the German term "Naturwissenschaft" suggests, is not the mere collection of facts; rather it is intimately related to man's deepest philosophical, emotional, and cultural drives. In fact, as science progresses from superstition to a mature and systematic form of knowledge, it contributes more and more to man's effort to understand himself and his world and to transcend his intellectual and physical limitations. Astronomy, the study of the Universe, is therefore the particular "paragon of the sciences" (PWBN p 271), while technology is the modern expression of man's desire to gain practical mastery over his environment ("die technische Beherrschung der Natur," ZT pp 432, 435).

Lasswitz' knowledge of philosophy enables him to explore the implications of science and technology with particular acuity. Conversely, his scientific training adds new energy and relevance to his philosophical thought. As a Neo-Kantian he thinks of space and time as subjective modes of perception. As a modern scientist he also views space and time as objective, quantifiable concepts. Both space and time are used to measure and describe the physical world, and both can be treated—graphically as well as conceptually—as dimensions. Lasswitz also combines modern science with older concepts of historical and cultural development. To the ancient ideas of eschatological historical progression, cultural development, and the improvement of human nature, he adds the notion of extra-terrestrial life and the theory of evolution. One result is a belief—not without reservations—in the possibility of a "relative improvement of conditions through a gradual process of evolution" (ZT p 425). Another is a concept of the equivalence of travel through space and progression in time. Both ideas are of great importance to SF. The opening paragraphs of URBAW best express Lasswitz' thought:

> Ever since science has incontrovertibly made the Earth into a planet and the stars into suns like our own, we cannot lift our gaze to the starry firmament without thinking, along with Giordano Bruno, that even on those inaccessible worlds there may exist living, feeling, thinking creatures. It must seem absolutely nonsensical indeed, that in the infinity of the cosmos our Earth should have remained the only supporter of intelligent beings [Vernunftwesen]. The rational order of the universe [Weltvernunft] demands that there should necessarily even be infinite gradations of intelligent beings inhabiting such worlds.
>
> To this idea might be added the profound and inextinguishable longing for better and more fortunate conditions than those which the Earth offers us. Indeed we do dream of a higher civilization [Kultur], but we would also like to come to know it as something more than the hope for a distant future. We tell ourselves that what the future can sometime bring about on Earth must even now, in view of the infiniteness of time and space, have already become a reality somewhere. [URBAW p 163]

Even in his earliest writings, however, Lasswitz was aware that the concepts of philosophy and the content and method of modern science could be combined to produce visions of new worlds and cultures. Although in URBAW Lasswitz' interest was directed to non-terrestrial cultures, in the *Bilder aus der Zukunft* he described superior terrestrial cultures located in the future. In *Auf zwei Planeten* Lasswitz incorporated the equivalence of travel through space and progression through time. There he described the confrontation of contemporary terrestrial civilization with a superior alien culture, a conflict whose result is the gradual improvement of humanity.

We may question the validity and relevance of Lasswitz' cultural optimism, his rationalistic psychology, and his use of the concepts and terminology of Idealist philosophy. Nevertheless, these ideas and attitudes, in combination with his extensive knowledge of modern science, enabled him to reach conclusions about science, society, and the function of literature which are much the same as those which form the foundations of modern SF. Lasswitz believed that science and technology had become major determinants of history, society, and individual consciousness. He also shared the conviction that the impact of science on the modern world and its future could be explored in an artistically legitimate form. He even anticipated and explained the preference in SF for future or other worlds as settings, and for astronomy and physics as sources of themes and imaginary scientific content.

In his essays Lasswitz examined with considerable insight the kind of imagination encountered in SF. As an aesthetician and writer he understood the creation of art to be a matter of conception as well as execution. In SF, particularly, both of these processes are often viewed as consciously methodical acts. The writer must construct a detailed and consistent imaginary world which is distinctly different from our own and yet does not directly contradict modern science. He must then use his literary skills to gain our emotional and logical acceptance of that world. It is therefore not surprising to find in SF a concept of imagination which claims to be rational and systematic rather than absolutely unrestrained. There is also a corresponding preference for stylistic techniques which aim to encourage an impression of reality, rather than to create a sense of alienation or to remind the reader of the artificiality of the text.

Lasswitz' ideas about imagination and literary technique in SF are very similar to those of many later critics and writers of SF. In ZT and URBAW he bravely attempts to distinguish SF, which he calls "das wissenschaftliche Märchen" (ZT p. 441), from other fiction, especially fantasy fiction or "das Märchen" ("tale"); the issue is still a subject of considerable debate. Lasswitz suggests that science, viewed as a strict discipline, has neither the capability nor the mission to exceed the bounds of its knowledge in order to speculate freely about the future or other worlds (BZ p. iii, ZT p. 439, URBAW p. 164). If we wish to explore such ideas "we must turn to [the faculty of] imagination [Phantasie]," but such fantasy "need not be unbridled," as it is in fantasy fiction (ZT p. 439). The "bridle," as Lasswtiz repeatedly states, is provided not only by common sense, but even more by the concepts, methods, and standards of science. Like the scientist, the writer of SF, even though he has greater freedom of imagination, thinks in terms of hypotheses, quantifiable factors, and formulas:

Who can answer these questions [about the future]? Science cannot venture to do so, as long as it has not yet found the famous Universal Formula of Laplace, which answers all questions about the past and future and enables us to perceive the mechanism of the Universe in the same manner that this mechanism presents itself to the human intellect in the motion of atoms. And yet there is a magical agency by which we can anticipate this formula and with one fell swoop lift ourselves beyond the reality which slowly works itself out in space and time in accord with [the laws of] mass and energy. This magical agency which enables us to lift the veil of the future is imagination [die Idee]. Fiction [Dichtung] has the privilege of looking into the future. But if that which fiction narrates is really to inspire in us a sense of trust, then fiction must take counsel with reality and conform closely to experience. Many inferences about the future can be drawn from the historical course of civilization [Verlauf der Culturgeschichte] and the present state of science; and analogy offers itself to fantasy as an ally. [BZ pp iii-iv]

The scientific knowledge of a particular time is part of the common interest of humanity.... The picture of the nature of things which we form in this field is an essential element of the total content of the culture and can therefore also become a subject for literary treatment. But fiction gives form to this its raw material by transforming it into a part of the personal experience of fictional characters.

Now in this process fiction is much freer in its use of hypotheses than is science, whose business is to provide the objective knowledge. As long as he does not contradict the scientific knowledge of his time, the writer of fiction may expand the hypothesis in order to further those aims which he considers essential to his function. In science the hypothesis must receive its justification through the ongoing process of experience, while in fiction the hypothesis is justified simply by its psychological utility, i.e. by the effect which it creates by making objects and events vivid and plausible and by transforming them into elements of the reader's active emotional response. [URBAW p 167-68]

Lasswitz' choice of terminology makes it almost superfluous to emphasize once again the similarity of his ideas to those of later writers and critics of SF. The insight with which he outlined the process of "extrapolation" and the use of "analogs," key concepts in SF, is remarkable. His notion of the SF text as the formulation of a "hypothesis" also points the way toward modern theories of SF, which view the imaginary world as neither a pure fantasy nor an absolute prophecy, but rather as a "thought-model" similar to the theoretical models of reality proposed by the natural sciences.

In his earliest and latest essays Lasswitz also spells out the implications of this "scientific" concept of imagination in terms of literary aesthetics. As in the previous passages, he emphasizes plausibility, probability, and verisimilitude as principles of imagination and goals of literary style:

We have endeavored to relate nothing which cannot stand either as probable or at least as not completely impossible according to present knowledge.... Here the difficulty of artistic representation places a natural rein on fantasy; it is essential to find the proper mean between fantastic fabulation [Fabuliren] and didactic explanation. For that which is alien must be mediated to our understanding through that which is already familiar; this is not always simple to do and necessitates much and varied postulation [vielerlei Voraussetzung]. [BZ pp v-vi]

In the transformation [of speculations about science, the future, etc.] into literary form, the laws of nature and the soul may not be infringed without arousing the objection of the reader and interfering with the effect. For everything that occurs in a novel which is intended seriously as art must be capable of being related to our own experience, i.e. the contemporary view of natural laws and psychology; in short, it must be explainable and plausible. An effect which occurred simply by magic and could not be explained scientifically would be just as unusable poetically as a sudden, psychologically unmotivated transformation of a character.... Our sense of veracity tolerates no postulates which directly and absolutely contradict previous scientific and psychological experience. [URBAW pp 165-66]

As the two passages show, Lasswitz was aware that in SF the plausibility of the imaginary world is suggested and judged in several different ways. The sense of plausibility depends first of all on the creation of a general impression of correspondence between the imaginary world of the fiction and our own world of experience; or, as recent students of Realism express the idea, the fiction attempts to encourage a sense of "sharable experience" by suggesting the verifiability of its content.[8] But Lasswitz' notion of plausibility, like that of many if indeed not all writers of SF, also shows the direct influence of science. The scientific method, with its combination of hypothesis, projection, collection of data, and re-evaluation, is considered the model for sound imaginative speculation. The particular natural sciences, which furnish the categories and standards by which the real world is most validly observed and described, are the source of the individual criteria according to which the validity of the imaginary world is asserted and evaluated.

The next logical step in a theory about fiction in which the concept of imagination and standards of plausibility are based on science is the conclusion that science should be an important part of the content of the imaginary world and that such fiction might well look to science for help in creating particular stylistic techniques which would contribute to the impression of plausibility. In his theoretical essays Lasswitz mentions a number of themes and concepts of imaginary science which he considers appropriate and challenging subjects for the new kind of fiction. Among them are extraterrestrial life, space travel, solar energy, anti-gravity, synthetic food, and differences in psychological sensibility in non-terrestrial beings or in new environments (ZT p 442; URBAW and TLM, *passim*). Many of these ideas are important themes and motifs in later SF. Lasswitz also hints at some of the major structural patterns and stylistic tendencies of SF, for example the preference for exciting plots and heroic characters (ZT pp 435-37, 440-45).

Lasswitz' SF, however, offers a better indication of his notion of the stylistic techniques of SF. While his works are marred by a relative weakness in the representation of character and dialogue, even the early stories in BZ are quite successful as evocations of imaginary worlds in which science and technology are important elements. In the short stories written in the Eighties and Nineties Lasswitz refined his science-fictional techniques, expanded his thematic repertoire, and moved toward a maturer conception of the imaginary world as a "thought-model" interesting in its own right, rather than just as a satirical allegory of our own world. Lasswitz' conceptual powers and literary skills reached their highpoint in his modest best-seller, *Auf zwei Planeten*, which appeared in the same year as Wells's *War of the Worlds*. In this lengthy novel Lasswitz employs the archetypal SF idea of "first contact" to explore one of the fundamental themes of literature, the nature of humanity. Imaginary technology, speculation about alien biology, philosophy, character, and plot all play a role in the exposition of the theme. Many stylistic techniques which appear constantly in later SF are to be found in *Auf zwei Planeten*. Among them are technological neologisms, alien language, documental inserts, and pseudo-scientific and pseudo-historical discourses. Throughout the novel Lasswitz uses a measured, transparent, matter-of-fact narrative style calculated to win the reader's acceptance of the imaginary world.

Despite his foresight as an aesthetician and writer, Lasswitz was more conservative in his speculations about the subjects and functions of SF than has been borne out by later SF, although at the time his ideas would have seemed quite visionary. In his theoretical essays he also did little more than suggest the general stylistic characteristics of an SF that was still embryonic. Lasswitz was attempting to distinguish SF clearly from other literature, to establish its artistic legitimacy, and to argue the "scientific" nature of its form of imagination. He therefore concentrated on its more readily ascertainable features and emphasized its realistic and methodical nature. Later writers, better aware of both the possibilities and the supposed limits of their genre, would consciously seek to expand its boundaries and to achieve what had previously been considered unachievable.

3. A number of German writers and critics besides Jean Paul and Lasswitz have contributed to the discussion of science and literature, including SF. Except for the Nazi era, the modern tradition of SF theory and criticism in Germany is fairly continuous, although initially sparse. Until quite recently, however, almost all such discussion took place within larger contexts such as naturalism, realism, utopian thought, or mainstream literature. German SF did not diverge from the literary mainstream nearly as greatly as did Anglo-American SF. Similarly, SF criticism in Germany did not develop into a distinct discipline pursued by a cohesive community of writers and non-academic critics.

Technological consciousness, the theory of evolution, and the scientific outlook played a significant role in the social and aesthetic thought of the German naturalists. A major figure in such discussion was Wilhelm Bölsche (1861-1939), a writer, editor, and popularizer of science. Bölsche wrote a treatise about "the scientific foundations of poetry" (*Die naturwissenschaftlichen Grundlagen der Poesie*, 1887), as well as some speculative articles which explore themes familiar in later SF. Even more important as a landmark of SF theory and textual interpretation is his enthusiastic essay about *Auf zwei Planeten*, "Das Märchen des Mars."[9] The article does much to clarify the relation of Lasswitz' SF to that of Verne and Wells, to realism, and to the genres of fantasy and *Märchen*—questions which are by no means resolved yet. Another writer associated with the naturalists and realists was Hans Lindau, who published a biographical and critical essay on Lasswitz, as well as several book reviews.[10] He also added a longer (and better) biographical and interpretive introduction to Lasswitz' posthumous volume of essays, poetry, and stories, *Empfundenes und Erkanntes* (Things Felt and Known; 1919). The publication of *Auf zwei Planeten* in 1897 inspired a few other reviews in German journals associated with realism, naturalism, and liberalism. Perhaps the most perceptive of these are "Ein Robinson des Weltraums" (A Robinson Crusoe of Outer Space) by Fritz Engel (*Zeitgeist: Beiblatt zum Berliner Tageblatt*, 1897, No. 49; excerpted in *Das Magazin für Litteratur*, 18 December 1897) and "Weltphantasien" (Space Fantasies) by M. Kronenberg (*Die Nation*, 31 December 1898).[11]

At least three major essays exploring SF from quite different perspectives appeared during the years of the Weimar Republic: *Das naturwissenschaftliche Märchen* (The Scientific Tale; 1919) by Anton Lampa; " Weltraumschiffahrt, ein poetischer Traum und ein technisches Problem der Zeit" (Space Travel: a Poetic Dream and a Contemporary Technical Problem) by Karl Debus (*Hochland*, July 1927); and "Die phantastische Literatur. Eine literarästhetische Untersuchung" (The Literature of Fantasy: a Literary-Aesthetic Investigation) by Hans-Joachim Flechtner (*Zeitschrift für Ästhetik und allgemeine Kunstwissenschaft* 24 [1930]: 37-47). To these studies one might add Hans Dominik's observations on SF in his autobiography, *Vom Schraubstock zum Schreibtisch* (From the Workbench to the Writing-Desk; 1942). While Dominik's remarks scarcely constitute a systematic and profound analysis, they offer important indications of the internationality of his SF.

After 1933 the forced adaptation of literary criticism to Nazi party goals, the suppression of most German SF, and the termination of openly-conducted rocket research in Germany brought about an almost complete cessation of SF and SF criticism in Germany, although Dominik's SF novels continued to be published in mass editions because of their escape value and fascist ideology.[12] The post-war years have seen a modest rebirth of SF in Germany, as well as an impressive amount of SF criticism which Franz Rottensteiner reviewed recently in this journal (SFS 1[1975]:279-84).

For all its variety and occasional historical discontinuity, German SF criticism, both older and more recent, exhibits a number of persistent characteristics which are already apparent in Lasswitz and even in Jean Paul. In effect the German critics combine the strengths (and sometimes the weaknesses) of the two traditional schools of Anglo-American SF critics, the academic scholars and the "indigenous" community of writers, editors, fans, and critics. For the most part the German critics evidence a solid foundation in aesthetic theory and critical methods, an interest in philosophical and ideological discussion, a thorough knowledge of mainstream literature, and an impressive familiarity with both German and non-German SF. Each of these virtues, however, has its corresponding vice. One occasionally encounters a certain inflexibility of aesthetic concepts and terminology, a lack of attention to German SF, an insistence on associating or even confusing modern SF with other literary traditions whose importance to the development of SF may well be small, or a tendency to over-emphasize the political or philosophical implications of SF. These traits may well have to do with certain factors in the German intellectual tradition, as well as the lack of a clearly-defined native body of SF and readership community distinct from mainstream literature. Despite—or perhaps because of—such differences in background and critical orientation, German discussions of SF offer much valuable material to the student of SF. Jean Paul's provocative and remarkably prescient remarks on the new "fantasy" have a definite historical value and can also still contribute to our understanding of the fundamental relation between science and fiction. Even as early as the turn of the century, Lasswitz was able to explore the idea of SF with the special insights of a trained and experienced scientist, philosopher, and writer. The better recent studies, too, can compete with those written anywhere. In my own work with SF, including German SF, I have found such studies invaluable in the interpretation of primary texts and in the evolution of a descriptive definition suitable for SF in general and for German SF as a form of literature which, for all its differences from Anglo-American SF, exhibits many of the same philosophical attitudes, scientific themes, and stylistic techniques.

NOTES

All translations are my own. Where necessary I have sacrificed smoothness to achieve a closely literal rendition, since many of the texts are not readily available. For several reasons I have chosen to translate both "Phantasie" (in some instances) and the very difficult "Idee" as "imagination," even though the customary German word for "imagination" is "Einbildungskraft." I feel this translation is justified by the particular connotations of "Phantasie," as artistic imagination and the actual product of such imagination, and by the special meanings of "imagination" and "imaginary" in SF. The context in which Lasswitz uses "Idee" (BZ page iii) makes it clear that he means the process of imagination rather than "idea," "concept," "notion," etc. I have also translated "naturwissenschaft(lich)" and "wissenschaft(lich)" interchangeably as "science/scientific" (in the texts cited here there is no indication that the writers intend the latter to mean either "knowledge in general" or "scholarly learning"), and "Märchen" simply as "tale" rather than as the "folktale" or "fairy tale" into which it is often rendered when referring to Grimm's stories and similar texts.

1. Specialized bibliographies of early German utopias and imaginary voyages include Heinz Bingenheimer, *Transgalaxis: Katalog der deutschsprachigen utopisch-phantastischen Literatur aus fünf Jahrhunderten (1460-1960)* (Friedrichsdorf/Taunus 1959), and Carl von Klinckowstroem, "Liftfahrten in der Literatur," *Zeitschrift für Bücherfreunde* 3(1912): 250-64.

2. Cf Robert Ulshöfer, "Friedrich Gottlieb Klopstock: 'Die Frühlingsfeier,'" in *Die deutsche Lyrik*, ed. Benno von Wiese (Düsseldorf 1957), 1:168-84.

3. For example: Alex Gode-von Aesch, *Natural Science in German Romanticism* (US 1941); Rolf Denker, "Luftfahrt auf montgolfierische Art in Goethes Dichten und Denken," *Jahrbuch der Goethe-Gesellschaft* 26(1964):181-98; Fritz Usinger, *Tellurische und planetarische Dichtung* (Mainz 1964); Willy Hartner, "Goethe and the Natural Sciences," in *Goethe: A Collection of Critical Essays* (US 1968), pp 145-60.

4. All references are to Jean Paul, *Werke*, ed. Norbert Miller (München 1962).

5. In its thought and language the passage is reminiscent of the famous "golden world" passage near the beginning of Sidney's *Apology for Poetry* (1595); I would not consider a direct textual influence impossible. Despite the modern nature of his subject, Jean Paul, in his notion of aesthetics, clearly belongs to the classical tradition. In his view of art as *mimesis* he inclines toward Aristotle rather than Plato. Certainly the images of "garlands" and ornamentation in the passage quoted suggest the Platonic idea that art is removed from reality. But Jean Paul does not see art, including the new fantasies, as a misrepresentation or even a mere embellishment of reality; rather, art expresses a deeper, or at least another kind of truth. Jean Paul's discussion of the place of art between absolute philosophical truth and concretely observed fact reminds one very much of Aristotle's idea that the realm of art is located between the abstract ideals of philosophy and the individual, often imperfect actualities of biography and history.

6. Abbott, *Flatland* (1884); Hinton, *A New Era of Thought* (1888), *Scientific Romances* (first series, 1886, second series, 1902). The major German writers of such proto- or quasi-SF, besides Jean Paul, are Georg Christoph Lichtenberg (1742-1799), Gustav Theodor Fechner (1801-1887), and Paul Scheerbart (1863-1915).

7. The short stories, some of which appeared in *Nord und Süd*, are collected in the volumes *Seifenblasen* (1890) and *Nie und Nimmer* (1902). Willy Ley translated three of the stories as "When the Devil Took the Professor," "Alladin's Lamp," and "Psychotomy" in the January 1953, May 1953, and July 1955 issues of *The Magazine of Fantasy and Science Fiction*. There is an abridged version of *Auf zwei Planeten* in English: *Two Planets*, tr. Hans Rudnik, with Afterword by Mark R. Hillegas (US 1971).

8. I owe the term "sharable experience" and much of my understanding of realism to an unpublished essay, "Realism as Communication," by Prof. Peter Demetz. The association of Lasswitz, the writer of SF, with literary realism and naturalism, is not inappropriate, for he was in close contact with the German and foreign members of both schools, as is indicated by his long association with the journal *Nord und Süd* and with the publishing house of Emil Felber.

9. The various articles appeared over a number of years in the *Neue Deutsche Rundschau* and were reprinted in volumes of essays: "Das Märchen des Mars" in *Vom Bazillus zum Affenmenschen* (1909), "Luftstadt" in *Auf dem Menschenstern* (1900), and "Ob Naturforschung und Dichtung sich schaden?" (Whether Science and Poetry are Mutually Injurious) in *Weltblick* (1904).

10. "Kurd Lasswitz und seine modernen Märchen," *Nord und Süd*, September 1903, pp 315-33. See also Lindau's review of Lasswitz' *Nie und Nimmer* in the same issue, pp 413-14, and his eulogy of Lasswitz in *Kantstudien* 16, vii(1911):1-4.

11. Otherwise the scant secondary material on Lasswitz includes a eulogy by Otto Jauker in the *Deutsche Rundschau für Geographie* 33,vi(1911):279-80; a survey of Lasswitz' fiction and essays by Raimund Pissin in *Die Nation*, 3 Dec 1904, pp 153-54; an essay by Edwin M.J. Kretzmann, "German Technological Utopias of the Pre-War Period," *Annals of Science*, Oct 1938, pp 417-30; Mark Hillegas's essay on Wells, Lasswitz, and Orson Welles, "Martians

and Mythmakers: 1877-1938," in *Challenges in American Culture*, ed. Ray B. Browne et al. (US 1970), pp 150-77; two articles by Franz Rottensteiner, "Kurd Lasswitz, a German Pioneer of Science Fiction," in *SF: The Other Side of Realism*, ed. Thomas D. Clareson (US 1971), pp 289-306, and "Ordnungsliebend im Weltraum: Kurd Lasswitz," in *Polaris 1*, ed. Rottensteiner (1973); and Klaus Günther Just, "Ueber Kurd Lasswitz," in *Aspekte der Zukunft* (Bern 1972), pp 32-65, which subsumes two earlier essays on Lasswitz.

12.One might well speculate that Golden-Age Anglo-American SF profited from Germany's loss. In effect it was left to Anglo-American writers to explore the implications of modern physics and the German rocket research of the twenties and thirties. In doing so they had the assistance of German emigrés like Willy Ley, an admirer of Lasswitz, who under other circumstances might well have contributed as a writer and critic to a Golden Age of German SF.

George Locke

Wells in Three Volumes? A Sketch of British Publishing in the 19th Century

(from **SFS** *3: 282–286, November 1976)*

It is impossible within the scope of this brief article to explore every tributary of 19th-century British publishing which may have provided an occasional outlet for science fiction. I have concentrated instead on a few of the main streams in order to assess their relative importance to the development of the genre.

Mary Shelley's *Frankenstein* was first issued in 1818 in three volumes, at the tail-end of the "gothic novel" phase of English fiction. The gothic had flourished for some 20 years, and was circulated in the main to people who borrowed rather than bought their reading matter. Most of the novels were issued in more than one volume (the lender thus being able to extract several borrowing fees for a single story), and multi-volume fiction carried merrily on after tales of terror went out of fashion. Lending books became really big business in the 1840s with the growth of Mudie's circulating library and other chains. The hey-day of the multi-volume novel was probably in the 1870s and 1880s, when science fiction was finding a small but significant place in literature. The influence of the libraries was so strong that serious novelists (i.e. those who aspired to something more permanent than the parts-issue working-man's literature) were obliged to comply with the three-decker length of 700 to 1000 pages, which, although printed in large type, more often than not required considerable padding-out. It required a writer of considerable skill to write a first-class three-decker novel, and it is worth noting that many of the "classics" that had multi-volume first editions, like Le Fanu's *Uncle Silas*, were in fact reprints of magazine serials to which the kind of padding acceptable in three-deckers would have been the kiss of death.

The price of these books remained constant throughout their reign: ten shillings and sixpence per volume, typically 31/6 a title. They were thus beyond the reach of the average book-buyer, and most three-deckers found today are escapees from the libraries and consequently in poor condition. Print orders for the less popular authors were undoubtedly small, 500 copies or less, and many titles sought by collectors are today rare to the point of impossibility.

Science fiction as it developed is fundamentally fiction of idea, often of a single idea, and consequently the three-decker was not a good medium for the genre. Even when a small science-fiction boom occurred in the 1870s (stimulated by *Erewhon* and *The Coming Race*, both one-volume novels which the public could and did buy, and accompanied by at least a score of other works of modest length), the three-decker movement threw up only three or four examples, such as Edward Maitland's *By and By* (1873), a hard-core SF novel of the future; Mortimer Collins' *Transmigration* (1873), a fantasy of multiple incarnations of which the middle one is set on a utopian Mars; and Andrew Blair's anonymously published *Annals of the Twenty-Ninth Century* (1873), a hodge-podge of interplanetary travel and super-scientific inventions.

Mary Shelley's *The Last Man* (3v, 1826) and Jane Webb's *The Mummy* (3v, 1827) are usually described as gothics. But the tale of terror and the supernatural had by their time gone out of fashion and was soon to be demoted to the minute print of the cheap magazines and parts-issue "penny dreadfuls." Examination of the latter, incidentally, reveals an almost total preoccupation with the past and its horrors, both mundane and supernatural, so that the amount of science fiction to be found there, even in the form of isolated incidents, is infinitesimal. It was only when boys' periodicals, in the latter part of the century, shook themselves free of the penny-dreadful movement and took on a degree of respectability that science fiction (given an immense push forward by the translations of Jules Verne) began to appear in any quantity in the magazines.

But, to use the favorite words of the three-decker, I digress. Let me now list some of the multi-volume SF novels of the time. The anonymous *Eureka: A Prophecy of the Future* (3v, 1837) depicts an Africa divided into republics and Britain as a forgotten nation. Richard Eyre Landor's *The Fountain of Arethusa* (2v, 1849) has an account of a journey to a species of heaven, a physical world in the center of the earth illuminated by its own sun, followed by a series of philosophical discussions. Arthur Help's *Realmah* (2v, 1868) is a utopian curiosity. Percy Greg's *Across the Zodiac* (2v, 1880) is an acknowledged classic of interplanetary fiction. J.F. McGuire's *The Next Generation* (3v, 1871) and the anonymous *The Dawn of the Twentieth Century* (3v, 1882) are political what-would-happen-if Irish novels set in the near future. W. Minto's *The Crack of Doom* (3v, 1886) is a disappointingly light-weight comet-threat novel. I would guess that there are no more than another dozen multi-volume novels to be added to this list, with several of them marginal, like Fergus Hume's *The Island of Fantasy* and *The Harlequin Opal*, Arnold's *Phra the Phoenician*, and Mortimer Collins' *Miranda*. One, however, stands out as representing a kind of science fiction that could have benefitted from the three-decker long-novel concept, the anonymous *Annals of the Twenty-Ninth Century* (3v, 1874), which for all its lack of style, is a speculation of Stapledonian magnitude.

By the mid-1890s the British public has been weaned into the habit of buying hardcovers. Publishers in the latter part of the century had paid more and more attention to the hard-cover needs of their retail customers, and had reprinted many of the three-deckers in one volume at about 3/6. As more copies were sold to the public, print orders increased and prices came down. The libraries, now unable to make a profit from loaning 31/6 books, changed their policies and three-decker publishing came to an abrupt end. From the 1890s until the first world war, the majority of original hardcover novels had about 300 pages and retailed in one volume at six shillings, with reprints and reissues at 3/6 or even cheaper, while a respectable proportion of lighter-weight material first saw book publication in cloth at 3/6. No longer did a novelist desirous of seeing his work in hard covers have to write to a length unsuited to his theme.

The 25 years preceding the first world war saw many SF novels appear as single-volume hardcovers: future war and political speculations, interplanetary and lost-race stories, tales of the future, disaster stories (always popular with the British!), mad-scientist extravaganzas, etc. This aspect of Victorian SF publishing has perhaps been as well researched as any, for individual titles had a greater chance of survival than their multi-volume ancestors. The only comment I would like to make is that as research continues it becomes increasingly clear that a large proportion of these apparently original novels in truth saw previous publication in periodicals of one sort or another. I shall come to these in a moment.

One aspect of Victorian publishing, astonishingly analogous to the present vigorous original-paperback industry, has been largely neglected. Between 1880 and 1900 the railway bookstalls were stuffed to the brim with original paperback novels, known as "shilling shockers." The shilling shocker is often lumped by collectors of cheap Victorian literature with the "yellowback," a book published in paper-covered boards at, usually, two shillings. There is some logic to that; they were both products of the huge demand of the rapidly expanding railway-travelling public for inexpensive fiction. The yellowbacks, which began to develop mid-century and continued into the early 20th century, contributed little to the development of science fiction. A large proportion, particularly those published after 1870, were reprints of books previously published in cloth. Although titles like Hugh MacColl's *Mr Stranger's Sealed Packet*, Collins' *Transmigration*, and Arnold's *Phra the Phoenician* had yellowback editions, very few original yellowback SF works have so far been located.

The shilling shockers, on the other hand, were mainly original and usually short novels or short-story collections. Although shilling paperback originals existed earlier, contemporary writers suggest that the public's appetite for that sort of thing was whetted by the publication in 1883 of Hugh Conway's weird mystery thriller, *Called Back*. Sensationalism was the key to a successful shilling paperback, and among the most popular were an import from Australia, Fergus Hume's *The Mystery of a Hansom Cab* (1887) and Stevenson's *The Strange Case of Dr Jekyll and Mr Hyde* (1886). The latter is, of course, pure science fiction, and surely showed the way the genre would go.

The short-novel length favored by shilling-shocker publishers was ideal for exploitation by writers who had an idea for an SF story, and the following representative sample illustrates what I mean: "Grip," *How John Bull Lost London* (1882), scare story of an invasion through a channel tunnel; Stanley and Ritson Stewart, *The Professor's Last Experiment* (1888), in which a vivisectionist, motivated by Darwin's theories, gets to work on a winged, furry visitor from Mars; W. Grove, *A Mexican Mystery* (1889), of an engineer who creates a mechanical steam engine that comes to life; Grove, *The Wreck of a World* (1889), of a world in the future in which machines come to life, reproduce, and start slaughtering mankind; Fergus Hume, *The Year of Miracle* (1891), a plague-disaster story; Delaval North, *The Last Man in London* (1887), a dream story of the wanderings of the last man on earth, something of a predecessor to Shiel's *Purple Cloud*. Sensational plots, all.

Although often leaving much to be desired from the literary point of view, the shilling shocker seems to me to be one of the most important media in which SF developed in the 19th century. Research into this area of publishing has been minimal, because of the poor survival of those ephemeral little paperbacks. Even a bestseller like the detective story *The Mystery of a Hansom Cab* is exceedingly difficult to find in its original wrappers, and the fact that a good many had simultaneous editions in hardcover (usually at 1/6) does not appear to make them any easier to find.

I have already hazarded the guess that the total number of multi-volume SF works issued between 1818 and 1895 was about two dozen. I venture to suggest that when research into shilling paperbacks issued between 1880 and 1900 can claim a reasonable degree of comprehensiveness, the number of SF titles will be between 50 and 100.

(In parenthesis it may be noted that Wells' *The Time Machine* [1895] was issued in wraps at 1/6 and cloth at 2/6—in a format transitional between the shilling shocker and the more expensive hardback.)

Periodicals for adults had very little influence on the development of science fiction for most of the 19th century. Until the 1880s magazines were rather sharply divided between the cheap penny periodicals and the smarter shilling monthlies. The former, as indicated earlier, are poor sources for SF. The shilling monthlies, like *Blackwood's Magazine*, *Fraser's Magazine*, and *Dublin University Magazine*, and the later *Belgravia*, *London Society*, and *Cornhill* magazines, are more fruitful: an occasional story or satire definable as SF can be found in their pages, and once in a while an influential story appeared there, notably Chesney's "The Battle of Dorking" (*Blackwood's*, May 1871). But it was not until after two revolutions in magazine publication that the scene became favorable for the publication of SF as a deliberate, circulation policy rather than as an incidental oddity.

The first was the creation of *Tit-Bits* by George Newnes in the early 1880s. That penny weekly, publishing a miscellany of odds and ends culled from various sources, was an instant success, and when its format settled down after a year or two of experiment, it published a single short story and an installment of a serial in each issue. *Tit-Bits* published very little SF that I have been able to discover, and the rival Harmsworth publication *Answers*, almost equally successful, also published relatively little. A second imitator, however, *Pearson's Weekly*, was a leading promoter of the genre in the 1890s, and its publisher, C. Arthur Pearson, probably did more to advance the cause of SF than any other person at that time. Between 1893 and 1899, *Pearson's Weekly* published the George Griffith serials "The Angel of the Revolution," "The Syren of the Skies" (i.e. *Olga Romanoff*), "Briton or Boer?," and "Valdar the Oft-Born" (fantasy rather than SF); Rider Haggard's lost-race novel "The Heart of the World"; three future-war novels by Louis Tracy, "The Final War," "An American Emperor," and "The Lost Provinces"; and Wells' "The Invisible Man." Several of these became bestsellers in their book editions. The magazine also published a number of short stories in the genre.

Newnes was not satisfied with one publishing innovation. He took a hard look at the available monthly magazines. He saw a number of dull things that used no illustrations or only a small number of engravings, and he saw some others, like *Cassell's Family Magazine*, that used a sprinkling. Knowing that great technological progress was being made in the printing of pictures, he decided that the time was right for a glossy, profusely illustrated general-purpose magazine selling at 6d, and launched *The Strand* in 1891. It was immediately successful. It published a little SF during its first few years but probably owed much of its early success to the Sherlock Holmes stories it featured. Pearson established his inevitable imitation in 1896, *Pearson's Magazine*, and was soon using SF to boost the magazine's circulation in the same way that "The Angel of the Revolution" had put his *Weekly* on the map. Nearly the whole of 1897 was taken up with Wells' magnificent "The War of the Worlds." He followed that with Cutcliffe Hyne's Atlantis story "The Lost Continent" in 1899, and George Griffith's "Stories of Other Worlds" (i.e. *A Honeymoon in Space*) in 1900. By that time, of course, Pearson's rivals had caught on to the fact that SF was good for business, and *The Strand* managed to secure Wells' "The First Men in the Moon." Other magazines modeled on *The Strand* also featured SF regularly: *The Windsor Magazine, Harmsworth's Magazine* (later, *The London Magazine*), *Cassell's Magazine, The English Illustrated Magazine* (serializing E.D. Fawcett's "Hartman the Anarchist" and G.P. Lathrop's "In the Deeps of Time"), *The Royal Magazine* (with the serialization of Shiel's "The Purple Cloud"), and many others. Researchers have studied this aspect of Victorian SF intensively, but it does no harm to re-emphasize the importance of those periodicals to the evolution of the genre. They provided well-paying, even superbly paying markets to which good science fiction could be sold as readily as detective fiction (which came into its own by courtesy of the same developments in publishing) and it is unlikely that Wells would have made the monumental contributions to the genre that he did without them.

Consideration of 19th-century magazine science fiction does not stop with the *Tit-Bits* and *Strand* schools. Weekly and monthly all-fiction periodicals were to be found in abundance on the railway bookstalls. Most of them are so rare today that research into them has been as sketchy as that into shilling shockers, but SF is to be found in their pages when copies do show up. A Pearson (again!) publication called *Short Stories* was a particularly rich source in the 1890s, with serials such as Griffith's "Outlaws of the Air" and "Golden Star," Shiel's "The Empress of the Earth" (i.e. *The Yellow Danger*), and George C. Wallis's "The Last King of Atlantis." The last title, which never made it into book form, may well have inspired Pearson to commission Cutcliffe Hyne's Atlantean novel for the more prestigious *Pearson's Magazine* a couple of years later.

Also popular during the latter part of the 19th century were *The Illustrated London News* and other slick illustrated papers like *The Graphic, The Sketch*, and *Black and White*. Science Fiction had its fair share of those markets too: "Phra the Phoenician" occupied the serial slot in *The Illustrated London News* in the latter half of 1890; the multi-authored "The Great War of 1892" [i.e. *The Great War of 189-)* gave the newly created *Black and White* a huge initial boost in 1892; and Wells' "When the Sleeper Wakes" ran in *The Graphic* in the latter part of 1898.

To summarize, I believe that British science fiction found its feet in the shilling shockers and their editorial requirements for short novels, and was refined by the high standards demanded for the high fees paid by *Pearson's Magazine, The Strand*, and their competitors during the 20 years before the first world war. Suppose the three-decker had not been killed off in the 1890s. Suppose Newnes, Pearson, and Harmsworth had not revolutionized magazine publishing in Britain at the same time. Would Wells then have written all his scientific romances? I suspect not, and venture to suggest that his SF writing would have been confined to a few short stories, *The Time Machine*, and possibly one or two other novels (most probably *The Island of Dr Moreau* and *The Invisible Man*) before he moved on to *Kipps* and *The History of Mr Polly*.

I see Wells' science fiction as the product of the publishing trends of his time. Wells in three volumes? I shudder to think of the alternate universe where that might be so.

Morris, Wells, and London

Patrick Parrinder

News from Nowhere, *The Time Machine* and the Break-Up of Classical Realism

(from SFS *3: 265–274, November 1976)*

Critics of SF are understandably concerned with the integrity of the genre they study. Yet it is a commonplace that major works are often the fruit of an interaction of literary genres, brought about by particular historical pressures. Novels such as *Don Quixote*, *Madame Bovary* and *Ulysses* may be read as symptoms of cultural upheaval, parodying and rejecting whole classes of earlier fiction. My purpose is to suggest how this principle might be applied in the field of utopia and SF. While Morris's *News from Nowhere* and Wells's *The Time Machine* have many generic antecedents, their historical specificity will be revealed as that of conflicting and yet related responses to the break-up of classical realism at the end of the nineteenth century.[1]

Patrick Brantlinger describes *News from Nowhere* in a recent essay[2] as "a conscious anti-novel, hostile to virtually every aspect of the great tradition of Victorian fiction." In a muted sense, such a comment might seem self-evident; Morris's book is an acknowledged masterpiece of the "romance" genre which came to the fore as a conscious reaction against realistic fiction after about 1880. Yet *News from Nowhere* is radically unlike the work of Rider Haggard, R.L. Stevenson or their fellow-romancers in being a near-didactic expression of left-wing political beliefs. William Morris was a Communist, so that it is interesting to consider what might have been his reaction to Engels' letter to Margaret Harkness (1888), with its unfavorable contrast of the "point blank socialist novel" or "Tendenzroman" to the "realism" of Balzac:

> That Balzac thus was compelled to go against his own class sympathies and political prejudices, that he *saw* the necessity of the downfall of his favourite nobles, and described them as people deserving no better fate; and that he *saw* the real men of the future where, for the time being, they alone were to be found—that I consider one of the greatest triumphs of Realism, and one of the grandest features in old Balzac.[3]

It is not clear from the wording (the letter was written in English) whether Engels saw Balzac's far-sightedness as a logical or an accidental product of the Realist movement which in his day extended to Flaubert, Zola, Turgenev, Tolstoy and George Eliot. Engels' disparagement of Zola in this letter has led many Marxists to endorse Balzac's technical achievement as a realist at the expense of his successors. Yet the passage might also be read as a tribute to Balzac's social understanding and political integrity, without reference to any of the formal doctrines of realism. What is certain is that the "triumph" Balzac secured for the Realist school was in part a personal, moral triumph, based on his ability to discard his prejudices and see the true facts. Engels's statement seems to draw on two senses of the term "realism," both of which originated in the nineteenth century. Nor, I think, is this coincidence of literary and political valuations accidental. The fiction of Stendhal, Balzac and Flaubert in particular is characterized by the systematic unmasking of bourgeois and romantic attitudes. In their political dimension, these novelists inherit a tradition of analysis going back to Machiavelli, and which is most evident in Stendhal, who was not a professional writer but an ex-administrator and diplomat. Harry Levin defines the realism of these novelists as a critical, negational mode in which "the truth is approximated by means of a satirical technique, by unmasking cant or debunking certain misconceptions."[4] There are two processes suggested here: the writer's own rejection of cant and ideology, and his "satirical technique." Both are common to many SF novels, including *The Time Machine*, although in terms of representational idiom these are the opposite of "realistic" works. *News from Nowhere*, on the other hand, is the utopian masterpiece of a writer who in his life went against his class sympathies and joined the "real men of the future," as Balzac did by implication in his books. Morris has this in common with Engels (who distrusted him personally). Hostile critics have seen his socialist works as merely a transposition of the longings for beauty, chivalry and vanquished greatness which inform his early poetry. As literary criticism this seems to me shallow. Nor do Morris's political activities provide evidence of poetic escapism or refusal to face the facts. It was not by courtesy that he was eventually mourned as one of the stalwarts of the socialist movement.[5]

On the surface, *News from Nowhere* (1890) was a response to a utopia by a fellow-socialist—Edward Bellamy's *Looking Backward*, published two years earlier. Morris reviewed it in *The Commonweal*, the weekly paper of the Socialist League, on 22 June 1889. He was appalled by the servility of Bellamy's vision of the corporate state, and felt that the book was politically dangerous. He also noticed the subjectivity of the utopian form, its element of self-revelation. Whatever Bellamy's intentions, his book was the expression of a typically Philistine, middle-class outlook. *News from Nowhere* was intended to provide a dynamic alternative to Bellamy's model of socialist aspiration; a dream or vision which was ideologically superior as well as creative, organic and emotionally fulfilling where Bellamy's was industrialized, mechanistic and stereotyped. Morris was strikingly successful in these aims. The conviction and resonance of his "utopian romance" speak, however, of deeper causes than the stimulus provided by Bellamy.

News from Nowhere is constructed around two basic images or *topoi*: the miraculous translation of the narrator into a better future (contrasted with the long historical struggle to build that future, as described in the chapter "How the Change Came"), and the journey up the Thames, which becomes a richly nostalgic passage towards an uncomplicated happiness—a happiness which proves to be a mirage, and which author and reader can only aspire to in the measure in which they take up the burden of the present. Only the first of these *topoi* is paralleled in Bellamy. The second points in a quite different direction. *News from Nowhere* is a dream taking place within a frame of mundane political life—the meeting at which "there were six persons present, and consequently six sections of the party were represented, four of which had strong but divergent Anarchist opinions" (§1). The dream is only potentially a symbol of reality, since there is no pseudo-scientific "necessity" that things will evolve in this way. The frame occasions a gentle didacticism (in dreams begin responsibilities), but also a degree of self-consciousness about the narrative art. "Guest," the narrator, is both a third person ("our friend") and Morris himself; the change from third- to first-person narration is made at the end of the opening chapter. Morris's subtitle, furthermore, refers to the story as a "Utopian Romance." Many objections which have been made to the book reflect the reader's discomfiture when asked to seriously imagine a world in which enjoyment and leisure are not paid for in the coin of other people's oppression and suffering. It could be argued that Morris should not have attempted it—-any more than Milton in *Paradise Lost* should have attempted the task of justifying the ways of God to men. Morris, however, held a view of the relation of art to politics which emphatically endorsed the project of imagining Nowhere.

One of his guises is that of a self-proclaimed escapist: "Dreamer of dreams, born out of my due time,/Why should I strive to set the crooked straight?" *News from Nowhere* stands apart from these lines from *The Earthly Paradise* (1868-70), as well as from the majority of Morris's prose romances. Together with *A Dream of John Ball* (1888) it was addressed to a socialist audience and serialized in *The Commonweal. News from Nowhere* retains some of the coloration of *John Ball's* medieval setting, but, for a Victorian, radical medievalism could serve as an "estranging," subversive technique. Two of the major diagnoses of industrial civilization, Carlyle's *Past and Present* and Ruskin's essay "The Nature of Gothic," bear witness to the power of such medievalist imagination. Morris's own influential lectures on art derive from "The Nature of Gothic," and are strenuous attempts to "set the crooked straight" even at the cost of violent revolution and the destruction of the hierarchical and predominantly "literary" art of the bourgeoisie.[6] It is easy to find gaps between his theory of culture and his practice in literature and the decorative arts.[7] Nonetheless, his attack on middle-class art finds important expression in *News from Nowhere*, which is an attempt to reawaken those aspirations in the working class which have been deadened and stultified under capitalism. Genuine art for Morris does more than merely reflect an impoverished life back to the reader: "It is the province of art to set the true ideal of a full and reasonable life before [the worker], a life to which the perception and creation of beauty, the enjoyment of real pleasure that is, shall be felt to be as necessary to man as his daily bread."[8] *News from Nowhere*, however deficient in political science, is a moving and convincing picture of a community of individuals living full and reasonable lives. The "enjoyment of real pleasure" begins when the narrator wakes on a sunny summer morning, steps out of his Thames-side house and meets the boatman who, refusing payment, takes him for a leisurely trip on the river.

Morris's attack on the shoddiness of Victorian design and the separation of high art from popular art was pressed home in his lectures. In *News from Nowhere* he turns his attention to another product of the same ethos—the Victorian novel. Guest's girl-friend, Ellen, tells him that there is "something loathsome" about nineteenth-century novelists.

> Some of them, indeed, do here and there show some feeling for those whom the history-books call "poor," and of the misery of whose lives we have some inkling; but presently they give it up, and towards the end of the story we must be contented to see the hero and heroine living happily in an island of bliss on other people's troubles; and that after a long series of sham troubles (or mostly sham) of their own making, illustrated by dreary introspective nonsense about their feelings and aspirations, and all the rest of it; while the world must even then have gone on its way, and dug and sewed and baked and carpentered round about these useless—animals . [§22]

Morris introduced his poem *The Earthly Paradise* as the tale of an "isle of bliss" amid the "beating of the steely sea"; but the "hero and heroine" evoked by Ellen are also clearly from Dickens. (The "dreary introspective nonsense" might be George Eliot's.) Guest is seen by the Nowherians as an emissary from the land of

Dickens (§19). Both Morris and Bellamy shared the general belief that future generations would understand the Victorian period through Dickens's works. In *Looking Backward*, Dr Leete is the spokesman for a more bourgeois posterity:

> Judged by our standard, he [Dickens] overtops all the writers of his age, not because his literary genius was highest, but because his great heart beat for the poor, because he made the cause of the victims of society his own, and devoted his pen to exposing its cruelties and shams. No man of his time did so much as he to turn men's minds to the wrong and wretchedness of the old order of things, and open their eyes to the necessity of the great change that was coming, although he himself did not clearly foresee it. [§13]

Not only Morris would have found this "Philistine." But Morris's Ellen and Bellamy's Dr Leete are on opposite sides in the ideological debate about Dickens's value, which continues to this day. One of the earliest critics to register Dickens's ambiguity was Ruskin, who denounced *Bleak House* as an expression of the corruption of industrial society, while praising *Hard Times* for its harshly truthful picture of the same society.[10] Morris, too, was divided in his response. When asked to list the world's hundred best books, he came up with 54 names which included Dickens as the foremost contemporary novelist. The list was dominated by the "folk-bibles"—traditional epics, folktales and fairy tales—which he drew upon in his romances.[11] Dickens's humour and fantasy appealed to the hearty, extrovert side of Morris stressed by his non-socialist friends and biographers.[12] Yet he also reprinted the "Podsnap" chapter of *Our Mutual Friend* in *The Commonweal*,[13] and inveighed against Podsnappery and the "counting-house on the top of a cinder-heap" in his essay "How I Became a Socialist." It is the world of the counting-house on the cinder-heap—the world of *Our Mutual Friend*—whose negation Morris set out to present in *News from Nowhere.*

Not only do the words "our friend" identify Guest on the opening page, but one of the earliest characters Morris introduces is Henry Johnson, nicknamed Boffin or the "Golden Dustman" in honour of a Dickensian forebear. Mr Boffin in *Our Mutual Friend* is a legacy-holder earnestly acquiring some culture at the hands of the unscrupulous Silas Wegg; Morris's Golden Dustman really is both a cultured man and a dustman, and is leading a "full and reasonable life." He has a Dickensian eccentricity, quite frequent among the Nowherians and a token of the individuality their society fosters. This character, I would suggest, is strategically placed to insinuate the wider relation of Morris's "Utopian Romance" to nineteenth-century fiction.

The tone of *News from Nowhere* is set by Guest's initial outing on the Thames. Going to bed in mid-winter, he wakes to his boat-trip on an early morning in high summer. The water is clear, not muddy, and the bridge beneath which he rows is not of iron construction but a medieval creation resembling the Ponte Vecchio or the twelfth-century London Bridge. The boatman lacks the stigmata of the "working man" and looks amazed when Guest offers him money. This boat-trip is a negative counterpart to the opening chapter of *Our Mutual Friend*, in which Gaffer Hexam, a predatory Thames waterman, and his daughter Lizzie are disclosed rowing on the river at dusk on an autumn evening. Southwark and London Bridges, made of iron and stone respectively, tower above them. The water is slimy and oozy, the boat is caked with mud and the two people are looking for the floating corpses of suicides which provide a regular, indeed a nightly, source of livelihood. Dickens created no more horrifying image of city life. His scavengers inaugurate a tale of murderousness, conspiracy and bitter class-jealousy. Morris's utopian waterman, by contrast, guides his Guest through a classless world in which creativity and a calm Epicureanism flourish.

Two further Dickensian parallels centre upon the setting of the river. The Houses of Parliament in *News from Nowhere* have been turned into the Dung Market, a storage place for manure. Dickens scrupulously avoids the explicitly excremental, but in *Hard Times* he calls Parliament the "national cinder-heap," and a reference to the sinister dust-heaps of *Our Mutual Friend* may also be detected both here and in "How I Became a Socialist." It seems the Nowherians have put the home of windbags and scavengers to its proper purpose. In the second half of *News from Nowhere*, Guest journeys up-river with a party of friends; this again, perhaps recalls the furtive and murderous journey of Bradley Headstone along the same route. Headstone tracks down Eugene Wrayburn, his rival for the love of Lizzie Hexam. Guest's love for Ellen, by contrast, flourishes among friends who are free from sexual jealousy. Yet jealousy has not disappeared altogether, for at Mapledurham the travellers hear of a quarrel in which a jilted lover attacked his rival with an axe (§24). Shortly afterwards, we meet the Obstinate Refusers, whose abstention from the haymaking is likened to that of Dickensian characters refusing to celebrate Christmas. Even in the high summer of Nowhere, the dark shadow of Dickens is occasionally present, preparing for the black cloud at the end of the book under which Guest returns to the nineteenth century.

News from Nowhere has a series of deliberate echoes of Dickens's work, and especially of *Our Mutual Friend*. Such echoes sharpen the reader's sense of a miraculous translation into the future. In chapters 17 and 18 the miracle is "explained" by Hammond's narrative of the political genesis of Nowhere—a narrative which recalls the historiographical aims of novelists such as Scott, Disraeli and George Eliot. These elements of future history and Dickensian pastiche show Morris subsuming and rejecting the tradition of Victorian fiction and historiography. The same process guides his depiction of the kinds of individual and social relationships which constitute the ideal of a "full and reasonable life." Raymond Williams has defined the achievement of classical realism in terms of the balance it maintains between social and personal existence: "It offers a valuing of a whole way of life, a society that is larger than any of the individuals composing it, and at the same time valuing creations of human beings who, while belonging to and affected by and helping to define this way of life, are also, in their own terms, absolute ends in themselves. Neither element, neither the society nor the individual, is there as a priority."[14] SF and utopian fiction are notorious for their failure to maintain such a blance. But the achievement that Williams celebrates should be regarded, in my view, not as an artistic unity so much as a *coalition* of divergent interests. Coalitions are produced by the pressures of history; by the same pressures they fall apart. In mid-Victorian fiction, the individual life is repeatedly defined and valued in terms of its antithesis to the *crowd*, or *mass society*. The happiness of Dickens's Little Dorrit and Clennam is finally engulfed by the noise of the streets; characters like George Eliot's Lydgate and Gwendolen Harleth are proud individuals struggling to keep apart from the mass, while their creator sets out to record the "whisper in the roar of hurrying existence."[15] The looming threat of society in these novels is weighed against the possibility of spiritual growth. George Eliot portrays the mental struggles of characters who are, in the worldly sense, failures. She cannot portray them achieving social success commensurate with their gifts, so that even at her greatest her social range remains determinedly "provincial" and she can define her characters' limitations with the finality of an obituarist. She cannot show the source of change, only its effects and the way it is resisted. Dickens's despair at the irreducible face of society led him in his later works to fantasize it, portraying it as throttled by monstrous institutions and presided over by spirits and demons. His heroes and heroines are safe from the monstrous tentacles only in their "island of bliss." One reason why Dickens's domestic scenes are so overloaded with sentimental significance is that here his thwarted utopian instincts were forced to seek outlet. The house as a miniature paradise offsets the hell of a society.

It should not be surprising that a novelist such as Dickens possessed elements of a fantastic and utopian vision.[16] They are distorted and disjointed elements, whereas Morris in *News from Nowhere* takes similar elements and reunites them in a pure and uncomplex whole. Several of his individual characters display a Dickensian eccentricity, and they all have the instant capacity for mutual recognition and trust which Dickens's good characters show. Yet this mutual trust is all-embracing; it no longer defines who you are, since it extends to everybody, even the most casual acquaintances (Hammond, the social philosopher of Nowhere, explains that there are no longer any criminal classes, since crimes are not the work of fugitive outcasts but the "errors of friends" [§12]). Guest's sense of estrangement in Nowhere is most vivid in the early scenes where he is shown round London. Not only has the city become a garden suburb and the crowds thinned out, but the people he meets are instinctively friendly, responding immediately to a stranger's glance. They are the antithesis of Dickens's crowds of the "noisy and the eager and the arrogant and the forward and the vain," which "fretted, and chafed, and made their usual uproar."[17] The friendly crowd is such a paradox that Morris's imagination ultimately fails him slightly, so that he relapses into Wardour Street fustian:

> Therewith he drew rein and jumped down, and I followed. A very handsome woman, splendidly clad in figured silk, was slowly passing by, looking into the windows as she went. To her quoth Dick: "Maiden, would you kindly hold our horse while we go in for a little?" She nodded to us with a kind smile, and fell to patting the horse with her pretty hand.
>
> "What a beautiful creature!" said I to Dick as we entered.
>
> "What, old Greylocks?" said he, with a sly grin.
>
> "No, no," said I; "Goldylocks,—the lady." [§6]

Morris here is feeling his way toward the authentically childlike view of sexual relationships which emerges during the journey up-river. Guest begins to enjoy a gathering fulfillment, movingly portrayed but also clearly regressive. Annie at Hammersmith is a mother-figure, Ellen a mixture of sister and childhood sweetheart. Guest, though past his prime of life, feels a recovery of vigour which is, in the event, illusory; his fate is not to be rejuvenated in Nowhere but to return to the nineteenth century, strengthened only in his longing for change. Though he shares his companions' journey to the haymaking, his exclusion from the feast to celebrate their arrival is another inverted Dickensian symbol.[18] The return to the present is doubly upsetting to the "happy ending" convention (seen for example in Bellamy); for it is not a nightmare but a stoical affirmation of political responsibility. Guest's last moments in Nowhere show him rediscovering the forgotten experience of alienation and anonymity.

Dickens and George Eliot were moralists in their fiction and supporters of social and educational reform outside it. Morris worked to improve Victorian taste while coming to believe that there were no "moral" or "reformist" solutions to the social crisis. It was the perspective of the labour movement and the revolutionary "river of fire"[19] which enabled him to reassemble the distorted affirmation of a Dickens novel into a clear, utopian vision. His vision draws strength from its fidelity to socialist ideals and to Morris's own emotional needs. But Morris, for all his narrative self-consciousness, can only register and not transcend what is ultimately an aesthetic impasse. His book is *News from Nowhere, or An Epoch of Rest*; it shows not only the redemption of man's suffering past but his enjoyment of Arcadian quietism. In Nowhere pleasure may be had "without an afterthought of the injustice and miserable toil which made my leisure" (§20). Morris omits to describe how in economic terms leisure is produced, and how in political terms a society built by the mass labour movement has dispersed into peaceful anarchism. He stakes everything on the mood of "second childhood":

"Second childhood," said I in a low voice, and then blushed at my double rudeness, and hoped that he hadn't heard. But he had, and turned to me smiling, and said: "Yes, why not? And for my part, I hope it may last long; and that the world's next period of wise and unhappy manhood, if that should happen, will speedily lead us to a third childhood: if indeed this age be not our third. Meantime, my friend, you must know that we are too happy, both individually and collectively to trouble ourselves about what is to come hereafter." [§16]

It is true that the passage hints at further labours of social construction lying in store for man. Morris, however, prefers not to contemplate them. One is forced to conclude that in *News from Nowhere* the ideal of the perfection of labour is developed as an alternative to the dynamism of Western society. We are left with the irresolvable ambiguity of the Morrisian utopia, which peoples an exemplary socialist society with characters who are, in the strict sense in which Walter Pater had used the term, decadents.[20]

H.G. Wells first listened to Morris at socialist meetings at Hammersmith in the 1880s. Even for a penniless South Kensington science student, attending such meetings was an act of social defiance. But, as he later recalled, he soon forgot his "idea of a council of war, and...was being vastly entertained by a comedy of picturesque personalities."[21] He saw Morris as trapped in the role of poet and aesthete, yet in *A Modern Utopia* (1905) he readily acknowledged the attractiveness of a Morrisian earthly paradise:

Were we free to have our untrammelled desire, I suppose we should follow Morris to his Nowhere, we should change the nature of man and the nature of things together; we should make the whole race wise, tolerant, noble, perfect—wave our hands to a splendid anarchy, every man doing as it pleases him, and none pleased to do evil, in a world as good in its essential nature, as ripe and sunny, as the world before the Fall.[22]

Wells, in effect, accuses Morris of lacking intellectual "realism." His response to this appears to far less advantage in *A Modern Utopia*, however, than it does in his dystopian works beginning with *The Time Machine* (1895). *A Modern Utopia* is an over-ambitious piece of system-building, reflecting its author's eclectic search for a "new aristocracy" or administrative elite; *The Time Machine* is a mordantly critical examination of concepts of evolution and progress and the future state, with particular reference to *News from Nowhere*.

While Guest wakes up in Hammersmith, the Time Traveller climbs down from his machine in the year 802,701 A.D. at a spot about three miles away, in what was formerly Richmond. The gay, brightly-dressed people, the verdant park landscape and the bathing in the river are strongly reminiscent of Morris. The Eloi live in palace-like communal buildings, and are lacking in personal or sexual differentiation. On the evening of his arrival, the Time Traveller walks up to a hilltop and surveys the green landscape, murmuring "Communism" to himself (§6). The reference is to Morris rather than to Marx (whose work and ideas Wells never knew well). Wells has already begun his merciless examination of the "second childhood" which Morris blithely accepted in Nowhere.

From the moment of landing we are aware of tension in the Time Traveller's responses. He arrives in a thunderstorm near a sinister colossus, the White Sphinx, and soon he is in a frenzy of fear. The hospitality of the Eloi, who shower him with garlands and fruit, does not cure his anxiety. Unlike most previous travellers in utopia, he is possessed of a human pride, suspicion and highly-strung sensitivity which he cannot get rid of. He reacts with irritability when asked if he has come from the sun in a thunderstorm: "It let loose the judgment I had suspended upon their clothes, their frail light limbs and fragile features. A flow of disappointment rushed across my mind. For a moment I felt that I had built the Time Machine in vain" (§5). When they teach him their language, it is he who feels like a "schoolmaster amidst children," and soon he has the Eloi permanently labelled as a class of five-year-olds.

The apparent premise of *The Time Machine* is one of scientific anticipation, the imaginative working-out of the laws of evolution and thermodynamics, with a dash of Marxism added. Critics sometimes stress the primacy of the didactic surface in such writing.[23] But *The Time Machine* is not exhausted once we have paraphrased its explicit message. Like *News from Nowhere*, it is a notably self-conscious work. Wells's story-telling frame is more elaborate than Morris's, and Robert M. Philmus has drawn attention to the studied ambiguity Wells puts in the Time Traveller's mouth: "Take it as a lie—or a prophecy. Say I dreamed it in the workshop" (§16).[24] One of his hero's ways of authenticating his story is to expose the fabrications of utopian writers. A "real traveller," he protests, has no access to the "vast amount of detail about building, and social arrangements, and so forth" found in utopian versions (§8). He has "no convenient cicerone in the pattern of the Utopian books" (§8). He has to work everything out for himself by a process of conjecture and refutation—a crucial feature of *The Time Machine* which does much to convey the sense of intellectual realism and authenticity. The visit to the Palace of Green Porcelain parallels Guest's visit to the British Museum, but instead of a Hammond authoritatively placed to expound "How the Change Came," the Time Traveller must rely on habits of observation and reasoning which his creator acquired at the Normal School of Science.

In *The Time Machine* Wells uses a hallowed device of realistic fiction—the demonstration of superior authenticity over some other class of fictions—in a "romance" context. His aim is, in Levin's words, to "unmask cant" and debunk misconceptions. The truths he affirms are both of a scientific (or Huxleyan) and a more traditional sort. The world of Eloi and Morlocks is revealed first as devolutionary and then as one of predator and prey, of *homo homini lupus*. This must have a political, not merely a biological significance. No society, Wells is saying, can escape the brutish aspects of human nature defined by classical bourgeois rationalists such as Machiavelli and Hobbes. A society that claims to have abolished these aspects may turn out to be harbouring predatoriness in a peculiarly horrible form. This must become apparent once we can see the *whole* society. In Morris's Nowhere, part of the economic structure is suppressed; there is no way of knowing what it would have been like. In *The Time Machine* it is only necessary to put the Eloi and Morlocks in the picture together—whether they are linked by a class relationship, or a species relationship, or some evolutionary combination of the two—to destroy the mirage of utopian communism. The Dickensian society of scavengers cannot be so lightly dismissed.

In contrast to Morris's mellow Arcadianism, *The Time Machine* is an aggressive book, moving through fear and melodrama to the heights of poetic vision. The story began as a philosophical dialogue and emerged from successive revisions as a gripping adventure-tale which is also a mine of poetic symbolism. To read through the various versions is to trace Wells's personal discovery of the "scientific romance."[25] *The Time Machine* in its final form avoids certain limitations of both the Victorian realist novel and the political utopia. An offshoot of Wells's use of fantasy to explore man's temporal horizons is that he portrays human nature as at once more exalted and more degraded than the conventional realist estimate.

Imagining the future liberates Wells's hero from individual moral constraints; the story reveals a devolved, simian species which engages the Time Traveller in a ruthless, no-holds-barred struggle. The scenario of the future is a repository for symbolism of various kinds. The towers and shafts of the story are recognizably Freudian, while the names of the Eloi and Morlocks allude to Miltonic angels and devils. The Time Traveller himself is a variant of the nineteenth-century romantic hero. Like Frankenstein, he is a modern Prometheus. The identification is sealed in the Palace of Green Porcelain episode, where he steals a matchbox from the museum of earlier humanity, whose massive architectural remains might be those of Titans. But there is no longer a fit recipient for the gift of fire, and the Time Traveller's matches are only lit in self-defence. We see him travel to the end of the world, alone, clasped to his machine on the sea-shore. When he fails to return from his second journey we might imagine him as condemned to perpetual time-travelling, as Prometheus was condemned to perpetual torture.

There are few unqualified heroes in Victorian realistic fiction (this is a question of generic conventions, not of power of characterization). The zenith of the realist's art appears in characters such as Lydgate, Dorothea, Pip and Clennam, all of whom are shown as failures, and not often very dignified failures. They are people circumscribed and hemmed in by bourgeois existence. Intensity of consciousness alone distinguishes theirs from the average life of the ordinary member of their social class. As against this, Wells offers an epic adventurer who (like Morris's knights and saga-heroes) is close to the supermen of popular romance. His hero is guilty of sexual mawkishness and indulges in Byronic outbursts of temperament. But what distinguishes him from the run-of-the-mill fantasy hero is the epic and public nature of his mission. As Time Traveller he takes up the major cognitive challenge of the Darwinist age. He boasts of coming "out of this age of ours, this ripe prime of the human race, when Fear does not paralyse and mystery has lost its terrors" (§10). The retreat of superstition before the sceptical, scientific attitude dictated that the exploit of a modern Prometheus or Faust should be told in a scaled-down, "romance" form. Nonetheless, the Time Traveller shares the pride of the scientists, inventors and explorers of the nineteenth century, and not the weakness or archaism of its literary heroes.

There is a dark side to his pride. The scene where he surveys the burning Morlocks shows Wells failing to distance his hero sufficiently. The Time Traveller is not ashamed of his cruel detachment from the species he studies, nor does he regret having unleashed his superior "firepower." His only remorse is for Weena, the one creature he responded to as "human," and Wells hints that her death provides justification for the slaughter of the Morlocks. This rationalization is a clear example of imperialist psychology; but Wells was both critic and product of the imperialist ethos. Morris, who was so sharp about Bellamy, would surely have spotted his vulnerability here. It is not merely the emotions of scientific curiosity which are satisfied by the portrayal of a Hobbesian, dehumanized world.

News from Nowhere and *The Time Machine* are based on a fusion of propaganda and dream. Their complexity is due in part to the generic interactions which I have traced. Morris turns from the degraded world of Dickens to create its negative image in a Nowhere of mutual trust and mutual fulfilment. Wells writes a visionary satire on the utopian idea which reintroduces the romantic hero as explorer and prophet of a menacing future. Both writers were responding to the break-up of the coalition of interests in mid-Victorian fiction, and their use of fantasy conventions asserted the place of visions and expectations in the understanding of contemporary reality. Schematically, we may see Wells's SF novel as a product of the warring poles of realism and utopianism, as represented by Dickens and Morris. More generally, I would suggest that to study the aetiology of works such as *News from Nowhere* and *The Time Machine* is to ask oneself fundamental questions about the nature and functions of literary "realism."

NOTES

1. I use "realism" in a broadly Lukacsian sense, to denote the major representational idiom of 19th-century fiction. See e.g. Georg Lukacs, *Studies in European Realism* (US 1964). I also argue that "realism" in literature cannot ultimately be separated from the modern non-

literary senses of the term. No sooner is a convention of literary realism established than the inherently dynamic "realistic outlook" starts to turn against that convention.

2. Patrick Brantlinger, "*News from Nowhere*: Morris's Socialist Anti-Novel," *Victorian Studies* 19(1975):35ff. This article examines Morris's aesthetic in greater depth than was possible here, with conclusions that are close to my own.

3. Karl Marx and Frederick Engels, *On Literature and Art*, ed. Lee Baxandall and Stefan Morawski (US 1974), p 117.

4. Harry Levin, *The Gates of Horn* (US 1966), p 55.

5. The best political biography is E.P. Thompson, *William Morris: Romantic to Revolutionary* (UK 1955).

6. Morris's published lectures are reprinted in his *Collected Works*, ed. May Morris, vols. 22-23 (UK 1914), and some unpublished ones in *The Unpublished Lectures of William Morris*, ed. Eugene D. LeMire (US 1969). Three recent (but no more than introductory) selections are: *William Morris: Selected Writings and Designs*, ed. Asa Briggs (US-UK 1962); *Political Writings of William Morris*, ed. A.L. Morton (US—UK 1962); and *William Morris, Selected Writings*, ed. G.H. Cole (US 1961).

7. Morris took up the practice of handicrafts in 1860 and became, in effect, an extremely successful middle-class designer. His theories of the unity of design and execution were often in advance of his workshop practice. See e.g. Peter Floud, "The Inconsistencies of William Morris," *The Listener* 52(1954):615ff.

8. Morris, "How I Became a Socialist" (1894).

9. See note 6.

10. Ruskin commented on *Bleak House* in "Fiction—Fair and Foul," published in the *Nineteenth Century* (1880-1), and on *Hard Times* in *Unto This Last* (1860).

11. *Collected Works* 22:xiii ff.

12. J.W. Mackail records somewhat fatuously that "In the moods when he was not dreaming of himself as Tristram or Sigurd, he identified himself very closely with...Joe Gargery and Mr Boffin."—*The Life of William Morris* (UK 1901), 1:220-21. Cf. Paul Thompson, *The Work of William Morris* (UK 1967), p 149.

13. See E.P. Thompson (Note 5) pp 165-67. I have not managed to locate this in the files of *The Commonweal.*

14. Raymond Williams, *The Long Revolution* (UK 1961), p 268.

15. George Eliot, Introduction to *Felix Holt* (1866).

16. The fantastic and utopian elements in Dickens are associated with his genius for satire and melodrama: with his vision of the interlocking, institutional character of social evil, and his delight in sharp and magical polarizations between the strongholds of evil and those of beauty and innocence. The elements of traditional romance in Dickens's vision make him an exaggerated, but by no means unique case; a utopian element could, I think, be traced in every great novelist.

17. Dickens, *Little Dorrit*, §34.

18. Tom Middlebro' argues that both river and feast are "religious symbols"—"Brief Thoughts on *News from Nowhere*," *Journal of the William Morris Society* 2(1970):8. If so, this was true for Dickens as well, and I would see him as Morris's immediate source. The symbolism of the feast is present in all Dickens's works and has been discussed by Angus Wilson, "Charles Dickens: A Haunting," *Critical Quarterly* 2(1960):107-08.

19. Morris, "The Prospects of Architecture in Civilization" in *Hopes and Fears for Art* (1882).

20. Pater describes the poetry of the Pleiade as "an aftermath, a wonderful later growth, the products of which have to the full the subtle and delicate sweetness which belong to a refined and comely decadence." Preface to *The Renaissance* (1873). The compatibility of one aspect of Pater's and Morris's sensibility is suggested by the former's review of "Poems by William Morris," *Westminster Review* 34(1868):300ff.

21. *Saturday Review* 82(1896):413.

22. Wells, *A Modern Utopia* §1:1.

23. See e.g. Joanna Russ's remarks on *The Time Machine*, SFS 2(1975):114-15.

24. Robert M. Philmus, *Into the Unknown* (US 1970), p 73.

25. The most telling contrast is with the *National Observer* version (1894). For a reprint of this and an account of Wells's revisions of *The Time Machine* see his *Early Writings in Science and Science Fiction*, ed. Robert M. Philmus and David Y. Hughes (US 1975), pp 47ff.

Alex Eisenstein

The Time Machine and the End of Man

(from SFS *3: 161–165, July 1976)*

As many critics have observed, H.G. Wells was preoccupied very early with speculations on evolution, in particular the evolution of Man and the prospects of intelligent life, whatever its origins. *The Time Machine* (1895), *The War of the Worlds* (1898), and *The First Men in the Moon* (1901) are the best known examples of his interest in such matters, but certain of his shorter works also reflect this concern. Frequently, Wells would recapitulate and refine his major ideas, mining old essays for new story material or refashioning the elements of one tale in the context of another; various scholars have explored the interpenetration of these works in some detail.

In "The Man of the Year Million" (essay, 1893)[1] and *The War of the Worlds*, Wells outlined one model for the ultimate evolution of humankind. In both works, the culmination of higher intelligence is a globular entity, brought about by the influence of steadily advancing technology. In each case, it mainly consists of a great, bald head, supported on large hands or equivalent appendages, with thorax vestigial or entirely absent. The Martian is a direct analogue of the Man of the Year Million, as Wells himself indicated by citing his own essay in the body of the novel (§2:2).[2] The Selenite master-race of *First Men* is a kindred expression of this vision of enlarged intellect—especially the Grand Lunar, with its enormous cranium, diminutive face, and shriveled body. Of more special relevance to the Martians are the malignant cephalopods of "The Sea Raiders" (1896) and "The Extinction of Man" (essay, 1894), and as well the predatory specimen in "The Flowering of the Strange Orchid" (1894).

At least one scholar has referred to "The Man of the Year Million" as "another version" of *The Time Machine*, apparently because the domeheads take refuge underground from the increasing rigors of a cooling surface.[3] This connection is rather tenuous, at best; by such criteria, *First Men* also might be deemed a variant of *The Time Machine*. In fact, the Further Vision of the latter constitutes a curious inversion of the above essay, but scholars and critics have failed to perceive this relation. Their failure depends on a more primary error, which is this—the notion that Man is extinct at the climax of the novel.

That the progeny of Man is *not* absent from the final moments of the Further Vision should be evident from a passage that appeared (until recently) only in the serial version. This deleted episode is a philosophic bridge, a key to what happens at world's end. It introduces the successors of Eloi and Morlock: a hopping, kangaroo-like semblance of humanity and a monstrous, shambling centipede. According to Robert Philmus, "these two species must have descended in the course of time from the Eloi and the Morlocks; and again the 'grey animal, or grey man, whichever it was' is the victim of the carnivorous giant insects."[4]

Philmus accentuates the elements of degeneration and regression in Wells's Darwinian conjectures; thus he asserts that *The Time Machine* embodies a vision of the hominid line "irrevocably on the downward path of devolution."[5] The general validity of this viewpoint cannot be disputed; nevertheless, the extreme construction he places upon it leads him considerably astray. Though Wells used terms like "retrogression," "degradation," and "degeneration" in his essays, they were for him *relative* terms only. He would hardly have portrayed Man as reverting *literally* into so primitive a creature; such "devolution," I submit, is not in the Wellsian mode.

Philmus may have been encouraged in this faulty genealogy by the Traveller's observations of the Elysian world of the Eloi, which seems devoid of animal life, excepting a few sparrows and butterflies (§4b/288; §5a/292).[6] Of course, this stricture need not apply to the murky lower world, which could easily harbor all sorts of vermin. If butterflies prosper above, in a world of flowers, then centipedes should thrive below, in a realm of meaty table scraps and other waste. And at journey's end, "a thing like a huge white butterfly" makes a brief display, as a demonstration of what has survived the English sparrow (§11/328).

The Morlocks of Millenium #803, moreover, are not a race destined for perpetual dominance. This much is made clear by numerous facets of their existence—their lack of light, the disrepair of much of their machinery, their crude and inefficient method of harvesting Eloi. Although the Time Traveller refers to the Eloi as "cattle" and supposes that they may even be bred by the Morlocks (§7/311), the rest of the book does not show the latter practicing much in the way of husbandry. Indeed the absence of other land animals in the lush upper world may well be the result of earlier predations by the Morlocks. So the best assumption is that the relationship between the two races is unstable—that the Morlocks are depleting their latest dietary resource, which must eventually go the way of its predecessors.

The kangaroo-beast, therefore, can only be a tribe descended from the Morlocks, now scavenging the surface in the long twilight. The irony of the new situation is evident, and quite typical of the many ironic aspects of the novel: the hound is now the hare, the erstwhile predator has become the current prey.

The ancestry of this pathetic creature is confirmed by its morphology. Consider the appearance of the Morlock: "a queer little ape-like figure," "dull white," with "flaxen hair on its head and down its back" (§5b/299), and a "chinless" face, with "great, lidless, pinkish-grey eyes" (§6/306). Compare that with the Traveller's description of the later species: "It was...covered with a straight greyish hair that thickened about the head into a Skye terrier's mane.... It had, moreover, a rounded head, with a projecting forehead and forward-looking eyes, obscured by its lank hair" (325). The ape-like brow-ridge is a tell-tale vestige of the Morlocks, as well as the lank hair that now shields the creature's eyes. The shaggy visage identifies the kangaroo-man as a once-nocturnal animal only recently emerged from darkness. Another indicative trait is its rabbit-like feet, which are compatible with the "queer narrow footprints" of the Morlocks (§5a/292).

From a close inspection the Traveller surmises the nature of the beast: "A disagreeable apprehension flashed across my mind.... I knelt down and seized my capture, intending to examine its teeth and other anatomical points which might show human characteristics..." (326). He might also be looking for the signs of yesterday's carnivore.

This Morlock offspring is no longer extant in the climactic scene of the Further Vision, but it is not the Last Man observed by the Traveller. He arrives in the era of the giant land-crabs, then passes on to the time of the great eclipse, where nothing seems to stir—at first:

> I looked about me to see if any traces of animal life remained.... But I saw nothing moving, in earth or sky or sea. The green slime alone testified that life was not extinct.... I fancied I saw some black object flopping about...but it became motionless as I looked at it, and I judged that my eye had been deceived, and that the black object was merely a rock.

A neaby planet encroaches on the bloated sun; the eclipse progresses, becomes total, and then the shadow of heaven recedes:

> I shivered, and a deadly nausea seized me.... I felt giddy and incapable of facing the return journey. As I stood sick and confused I saw again the moving thing upon the shoal.... It was a round thing, the size of a football perhaps...and tentacles trailed down from it; it seemed black against the weltering blood-red water, and it was hopping fitfully about. Then I felt I was fainting. But a terrible dread of lying helpless in that remote and awful twilight sustained me while I clambered into the saddle. (§11/329-30)

The kangaroo-men hop about on elongated feet; the men of the year million hop about on great soft hands; the thing on the shoal hops about on a trailing mass of tentacles. This similarity in modes of locomotion is hardly a literary accident. In contrast, the Sea-Raiders never hop, but creep along at a steady pace when traversing solid ground.

In general form the Last Creature resembles a large cephalopod. Is it a primitive survivor from the ocean deeps, like *Haploteuthis* in "The Sea-Raiders," or is it a being like the Martians, the hypertrophic end-product of intelligent life? Most of the evidence points to the latter—a highly specialized and atrophied edition of genus *Homo*. Note particularly the size of the creature; it is about "the size of a football"—which is to say, about the size of a human head.

The Time Traveller contracts a "terrible dread of lying helpless" in the dying world soon after he becomes fully aware of the thing on the shoal. There seems to be a special revulsion attached to this monster, even though it can hardly pose a real threat to the Traveller. Before it commands his attention, he feels "incapable of facing the return journey"; afterward, the "dread of lying helpless" in its presence impels him to turn back forthwith. Consciously, the Traveller does not perceive the human ancestry of this apocalyptic organism, but apparently the unconscious realization of its true nature makes him flee the final wasteland. Not the oppressive conditions, nor the extinction of Man, nor even the approaching oblivion triggers his retreat; rather, he recoils from the knowledge, however submerged, of what Man has become.

And what has Man become? Certainly not the inflated intellect of a Martian, nor that of a Sea-Raider, despite the somatic affinities. In one important respect, the Last Man differs greatly from these other fantastic creations: it is a being without a face. Even *Haploteuthis* has a definite, mock-human visage—"a grotesque suggestion of a face." To be sure, the super-minds in the Wellsian canon—the million-year domeheads, the Martians, the Grand Lunar—all suffer from facial attrition, yet certain features, especially the eyes, always remain. Not so with the fitful creature on the beach; the swollen surface of its body seems utterly blank, devoid of perceptual apparatus, and its aimless, reflexive actions indicate that it is virtually mindless. In the end, then, Man has become little more than a giant polyp.

All these transmuted beings emphasize two primary functions of life: ingestion and cerebration. The intelligent Sea-Raiders, for example, come to earth in seach of a better feed. Both the Martians and the domeheads have actually surrendered their alimentary canals to cortical advances, and the Martians, like the man-eating squids, also come to Earth for new sustenance. The mindless tropism of the Strange Orchid impels it to siphon off human blood, whereas the Martians strive for the same end with a ruthless deliberation.

The ultimate survivor of *The Time Machine* is not a great brain; as with a polyp, therefore, all that is left is a great ravening stomach. (For this, too, its size is appropriate.) Here, in counterpoint to the Martian terror, is the Wellsian image of ultimate horror.

And so we confront a symbolic paradox: the same emblem represents both the zenith and the nadir of mentality; the opposition of head and stomach, of mind and body, is fused in this one corporeal form. In Wells's iconography, it stands for the ultimate degeneration, whether of body or mind. He disapproved less, we may suppose, of the absolute intellect, reserving his greatest dread for the other, the mindless all-devouring. Yet there can be little doubt that, despite sardonic ambiguities, as in "The Man of the Year Million" and *The First Men in the Moon*, he truly preferred neither; his best wish was that Man should master himself without ever losing the essence of humanity. To this end Wells devoted most of his long and active life, even unto *Mind at the End of Its Tether* (1945), where a faint hope still lingers that some ultra-human entity will arise to survive the impending decline of *Homo sapiens*. This was Wells's last desperate hope, and a very feeble one it was; nevertheless, near the end of his life, amid sickness and depression, that glimmer remained. As the nameless narrator of *The Time Machine* insists, when faced with the inevitable disintegration of Man: "If that is so, it remains for us to live as though it were not so" (Epilogue/335).

NOTES

1. First published in *The Pall Mall Gazette*, Nov 9, 1893, this essay, with title changed to "Of a Book Unwritten," appears in *Certain Personal Matters* (UK 1897), as does the other essay mentioned in this paragraph, "The Extinction of Man."

2. Another avatar appears in "The Plattner Story," against a setting remarkably suggestive of the Further Vision. Plattner, who is blown through a fourth *spatial* dimension, finds himself on a barren landscape of dark *red* shadows, backed by a *green* sky-glow. He watches the *rise* of a giant green sun, which reveals a deep cleft nearby. A multitude of bulbous creatures float upward, like so many bubbles, from this chasm. These are the "Watchers of the Living," literally the souls of the dead: "they were indeed limbless; and they had the appearance of human heads beneath which a tadpole-like body swung" (para. 26). Significantly, Wells had referred to his Men of the Year Million as "human tadpoles."

In many respects, this realm of the afterlife is a striking reversal of *The Time Machine*'s terminal wasteland, yet quite recognizably akin to it.

3. Gordon S. Haight, "H.G. Wells's 'The Man of the Year Million'," *Nineteenth-Century Fiction* 12(1958):323-26.

4. Robert M. Philmus, *Into the Unknown* (US 1970), pp 70-71.

5. *Ibid.*, p. 75.

6. §7/311 = Chapter 7 in the standard form of the text (i.e., as published in the Atlantic Edition, the *Complete Short Stories*, and almost all editions since 1924), or Page 311 of *Three Prophetic Novels of H.G. Wells* (Dover Publications, 1960). The chapterings of the standard

and Dover forms (with "a" and "b" added for convenience) collate as follows: 1a = 1; 1b = 2; 2 = 3; 3 = 4; 4a = 5; 4b = 6; 5a = 7; 5b = 8; 6 = 9; 7 = 10; 8 = 11; 9 = 12; 10 = 13; 11 = 14; 12a = 15; 12b = 16; Epilogue = Epilogue. The deleted passage, pages 325-27 of the Dover text, would appear between the first and second paragraphs of Chapter 11 in the standard text.

Nadia Khouri

Utopia and Epic: Ideological Confrontation in Jack London's *The Iron Heel*

(from SFS *3: 174–181, July 1976)*

A pedagogic Marxist program of revolutionary action set in an internecine Social-Darwinist world: such is the ideological substance of Jack London's *The Iron Heel.*

An emotionally charged humanist epic expressing the turn-of-the-century revolutionary socialist consciousness—the main plot—running parallel with annotated marginalia supposedly written seven hundred years later—the utopia—: such is its Janus-headed form of discourse.

1. It is customary to think of utopias as blueprints, detailed and ready-made. Here, *The Iron Heel* displays a peculiar genological complexity: it is a socialist utopia which could not afford to be a blueprint, yet could not help being a utopia, that is to say a desirable hypothetical better society in a hypothetical better time or place. Jack London suggested that better state in footnotes, divesting it of its frozen and exhaustive descriptiveness, and activated it by making it constantly comment on the epic from the point of view of a projected advantageous socialist future.

The formal organization of the novel underlines a somewhat strained discrepancy between the world of the epic and that of the utopia. The epic, with its Social-Darwinist struggle for existence and its Marxist revolutionary ideal, points in its every event to the utopian goal, all-pervasive in its very absence. The utopian footnotes, however, constantly abate the impact of the epic by impartially assessing the latter's emotional exaggerations in a hypothetical historical distancing. The aesthetic accommodation of such an ostensibly dynamic form of discourse as the epic with such a markedly static one as the classical utopia may in itself appear contradictory. However, by yoking ideological and generic tensions together and by conducting them towards a dialectical resolution, *The Iron Heel* significantly expresses the tensions of its own historical reality, and also ushers in—parallel to H.G. Wells's utopias—utopias that (both conceptually and narratively) do not in fact have to be static.

Socialist utopias as such stem from an ideological conflict with reality. By virtue of their happy otherness ("the best state of a commonwealth" and "a new island" in Thomas More's ancestral full title to *Utopia*), by their very stress on *difference from* rather than similarity to reality, they have been gestures of disapprobation. Claiming that the ills of society are products of historical material circumstances and that these can be altered, utopias offer an alternative view of being. Their constant generic trait is the symbolic resolution of the tensions engendered by a sociopolitically defective order. If socialist utopias are products of an alienated world, they are also its negations and plans for a new, de-alienated one. They are formal qualitative inversions: the prevailing values of the author's society are transformed into their opposites. In Henri de Saint-Simon's social organization, for example, the idleness and ineffectiveness of the ruling classes in early 19th century France turn to the producers' industry; in Charles Fourier's utopian communities, the Balzacian mercantilism of the country is resolved into passionate attraction and harmony; in Edward Bellamy's ideal Boston of *Looking Backward*, the extreme individualism of 19th century America is replaced by collective Christian Socialism in the service of the nation; in William Morris's humanized landscapes of *News from Nowhere*, the industrial barbarism and alienated drudgery of Victorian England are superseded by rest, creativity and life values. In London's *The Iron Heel*, the sharp and frictive class struggle of the early 20th century is both exasperated and provided with a horizon of a new age's brotherhood and stability.

The basic traits of qualitative inversion from chaotic opposition to a harmony in which individual and social come to terms, Jack London shares with his literary congeners. But where the utopias of Saint-Simon, Fourier and Bellamy (Morris seems a transitional case) are closed systems, his is emphatically open. Where they are detailed and exhaustive masterplans for a set of deterministic socio-economic interrelations, his is an unconsummated and non-causal assemblage of ideological data, still referable to the socialist utopian ideal, but intentionally inconclusive. The compelling priority here is not to design a commendable ready-made order, but *to be able to reach* such an auspicious *summum bonum*: that is why the overwhelming bulk of the text is the political epic-story and utopia is explicit only in the footnotes (though implied throughout). The previous socialist utopians had rationalist points of reference that made it possible for them to spell out the precise elements that would enter into their socio-economic models. Saint-Simon placed his faith in Newtonian cosmology and in the positivistic transformation of the new scientific materialism and industrial progress of his time. Fourier, the eccentric mathematician, calculated the socio-economic equations of his polymorphic utopian phalanxes. Bellamy shared the optimism of his middle-class compatriots in the power of technology and of a growing American nationalism to reform and unify society. Morris, the poet, politician and craftsman-artist, founder of a company working on the same principles as the medieval guilds, devised a eudemonist society in the image of his workshop. By the time Jack London wrote *The Iron Heel*, however, generations of utopian reformers had undergone a peculiar experience of violence, and the obstacles to the realization of an equitable order had taken an ominous turn. Socialist and all other movements against capitalist chaos had been ruthlessly crushed throughout the century. As historical horizons turned darker, the vision of an active struggle grew. The hope for the alternative society consequently placed the accent on the fight for the utopian goal rather than on the accomplishment of such a utopia. This struggle concretizes in *The Iron Heel* in the confrontation of such incompatible ideologies as Marxism, Spencerian Social-Darwinism and Nietzscheanism. In this regard *The Iron Heel* is merely an aesthetic sum of the conflicting social and ideological realities of the time. I shall try to show that London manages to merge and extend these ideologies into a finally socialist utopian combination, in which Marxism is the decisive dialectizing agent.

2. The Iron Heel is thus a dynamic utopia engaged in the process of overcoming historical obstacles. It is a utopia in the making and a future perfect assurance that it has been achieved pragmatically within the context of socialism. A "Foreword," supposedly written by the utopian Anthony Meredith, establishes the framework of the novel in utopian time—the year 419 of the Brotherhood of Man (B.O.M.) era, and in utopian space—the city of Ardis. The novel then proceeds in a looking backward fashion to recapture the events of a manuscript found in an ancient oak, a presumably authentic first-hand story revolving around Ernest Everhard, a socialist leader and militant of the early 20th century, and written 700 years earlier by his wife and collaborator Avis. Here London inflates his story with epic amplitude: as in the traditional epic, it is centered upon a heroic figure on whose actions the fate of society depends, and it is large in scale: as the *Odyssey* involved the whole Mediterranean or *Paradise Lost* the cosmic frame of Earth, Heaven and Hell, the socialist adventure in *The Iron Heel* spreads to the nation and gradually to the whole world in an international strike of workers. Everhard, like Achilles, Hector or Adam, is depicted as a figure of great importance. As the Trojan War in the *Iliad*, the adventures of Odysseus in his wanderings, the war in Heaven in *Paradise Lost*, the action of *The Iron Heel* is built on heroic deeds. Yet in this humanistic epic the destiny of man is man and his history is manmade. The supernatural figures of the traditional epic disappear. There is now only one epic hero: man; only one epic subject: the progress of humanity. Running parallel with this story of Everhard and his comrades, fighting for the socialist Cause in a wolfishly competitive world, are footnotes written by Meredith, intended as editorial clarification for the utopian readers of 419 B.O.M., explaining the obsolete values and terms of the internecine world of the manuscript.

The historical differences between the 20th century and the B.O.M. era are indicated by two contrasting levels of sensibility: the one self-conscious, idealized—the manuscript; the other rational, unromantic—the Foreword and the footnotes. The tone of the Foreword and the footnotes is factual, clinically informative, written in the calm and balanced spirit of the new age. It presents a gain in insight: "It cannot be said that the Everhard Manuscript is an important historical document. To the historian it bristles with errors—not errors of fact, but errors of interpretation. Looking back across the seven centuries that have lapsed since Avis Everhard completed her manuscript, events and the bearings of events, that were confused and veiled to her are clear to us. She lacked perspective. She was too close to the events she writes about."[1] Historical perspective means acuity in viewing events and an objective distance.

On the other hand, the tone of the manuscript is sharply subjective. The title of chapter I, "My Eagle," with its sudden symbolism, jolts the reader into an emotional dimension which is in stark contrast with the explicative literalness of the Foreword. "My Eagle" introduces an idealized hero concept which the footnotes deny. These achieve the objective of a distancing from empathy quite suitably: if the supposed utopian readers have not experienced, even remotely, the problematic struggles of the 20th century militants, since their utopia has been in existence for hundreds of years, how can they be expected to empathize? They can only frown or condemn. Moreover, London's technique of distancing or estrangement forces his contemporary reader out of a compassionate torpor which the tragic story of a unique hero might impose upon him: the reader's involvement in the story must be rational, objective and historical. And he must not forget that the tragedy of the hero has resolved itself in the victory of a whole world. To Avis Everhard's passionate "I think of what has been and is no more—my Eagle, beating with tireless wings the void, soaring toward what was ever his sun, the flaming ideal of human freedom. I cannot sit idly by and wait the great event that is his making, though he is not here to see. He devoted all the years of his manhood to it, and for it he gave his life. It is his handiwork. He made it," the footnotes comment, abating the emotional impact: "With all respect to Avis Everhard, it must be pointed out that Everhard was but one of many able leaders who planned the Second Revolt. And we, today, looking back across the centuries, can safely say that even had he lived, the Second Revolt would not have been less calamitous in its outcome than it was" (§1).

London here played with the aesthetic which Bertolt Brecht subsequently developed and called the *Verfremdungseffekt*, or the technique of estrangement whereby the onlooker is made to see objects and relations not merely by sympathizing with them, but especially by joining this sympathy to a critical detachment in view of their transformation.[2] Through this prefiguration of the Brechtian technique London managed to reject in the footnotes the idea of a unique hero and advance that of many heroes. *The Iron Heel* is a humanistic epic which praises the progress of reason, logic, brotherhood and justice, collectively felt and fought for. The evolution of the individual is intimately interwoven with the evolution of humanity, and the love story of Avis and Ernest with the destiny of the political struggle. However, if *The Iron Heel* is an epic, it is so only as long as the struggle lasts: it becomes an archaeological object when the struggle is over and won.

If in this humanistic epic there is to be a hero at all, then he has to be a public man and a polemic pedagogue (Ernest is at some point an orator on a soap-box addressing a crowd of working men). London organized his novel to emphasize the importance of theoretical preparation before revolutionary action. The manuscript is divided into two parts: the first half extending roughly from chapter 1 to chapter 10 and dealing with a theoretical education in historical materialism; the second one, going from chapter 10—suitably called "The Vortex"—to the end, dealing with revolutionary action. And the whole novel is indeed meant to be an instruction in both theory and practice.

Haranguing, attacking, exposing, ridiculing, debating, browbeating, demonstrating, persuading, predicting, the epic hero plays with rhetoric to enunciate the socialist philosophy. He has a mission of enlightenment directed against what is presented as the turbid erroneousness and viciousness of the world of capitalism. Proving arguments by discursive reason and logical disputation, he accuses the Church ministers:

> You are anarchists in the realm of thought. And you are mad cosmos-makers.... Do you know what I was reminded of as I sat at table and listened to you talk and talk? You reminded me for all the world of the scholastics of the Middle Ages who gravely and learnedly debated the absorbing question of how many angels could dance on the point of a needle. Why, my dear sirs, you are as remote from the intellectual life of the twentieth century as an Indian medicine-man making incantation in the primeval forest ten thousand years ago. [§1]

So much for idealist philosophies. Everhard then turns against the economy and sociology of capitalism. Evoking historical analogies to prove his point, he predicts the breakdown of the capitalist system in accordance with Marx's theory of surplus-value. He compares small businessmen to the machine-breakers of the 18th century: as these tried in vain to stop the Industrial Revolution that displaced them, so the small businessmen of the 20th century who try to break the great trusts will be forced to submit to their greater power. Persuasion is backed by historical evidence, by the "proof" device. And this leads deictically to the pedagogic statement: "That, gentlemen, is socialism, a greater combination than the trusts, a greater economic and social combination than any that has as yet appeared on the planet" (§8). Meanwhile demonstration, guidance, instruction gradually point the way to the power confrontation.

3. The virulent face to face between Ernest and the wealthy Philomath-club members is the climax of the first part of the novel. Socialist power challenges capitalist power and elicits the threatening response: "Our reply shall be couched in terms of lead. We are in power. Nobody will deny it. By virtue of that power we shall remain in power...We will grind you revolutionists down under our heel, and we shall walk upon your faces" (§5). Inescapably, violence is used to buttress those in power, and violence will be needed to overcome the obstacle. From chapter 10, "The Vortex," the narrative acquires a violent pace; it is swept into the whirlpool of the action. Terms like "Bloody strike," "smashed down," "riot clubs," "blood and revenge," "executed," "herded into bull-pens," "convulsed with industrial dissensions," "tales of violence and blood," "Riot, arson, and wanton destruction," "laborers were shot down like dogs," "Labor was bloody and sullen, but crushed," "maelstrom," "rack and ruin," carry the consciousness to arms. The mood unfolds in a succession of revolutionary terminology and situations: boycotts, sabotage, frame-ups, spying, guerrilla warfare, *agent-provocateurs.*

To grasp the full significance of this vocabulary one must visualize the colliding socio-economic interests of the time: the depression of 1873, the great railroad strike in Pittsburgh and the July riots of 1877, the great panic of 1893, the repeated instances of mass demonstrations of the unemployed in a time of internecine capitalism characterized by wild speculation which indeed ruled the world, and especially countries that were recently opened up—Australia, South Africa, Canada, South America, etc., wolfish economic ambitions, the establishment of trusts and combinations, the concentration of monopoly and large-scale production in a few hands—Vanderbilt, Moore, Pennsylvania, Morgan-Hill, Rockefeller, Harriman, Kuhn-Loeb, and the "big three" in the insurance field, Mutual, New York Life and Equitable. Power, struggle, revolution could become, either separately or interchangeably, the current catchwords in such a social climate.

The "Oligarchy" described in the novel as an "Iron Heel...descending upon and crushing mankind" (§Forward), is a development from that class of London's time which was supporting the status quo by misusing the catchwords of "struggle for existence" and "survival of the fittest" to uphold the idea that "the best competitors in a competitive situation would win, and that this process would lead to continuing improvement."[3] Herbert Spencer's Social-Darwinist theories, far more popular in the United States than in his own England, were welcomed by the ruling classes as helpful in persuading the working classes to accept the hardships of their life, and in preventing them from going in for reforms. On this matter one of the footnotes remarks:

> The oligarchs believed in their ethics, in spite of the fact that biology and evolution gave them the lie; and, because of their faith, for three centuries they were able to hold back the mighty tide of human progress—a spectacle, profound, tremendous, puzzling to the metaphysical moralist, and one that to the materialist is the cause of many doubts and reconsiderations. [§21]

Jack London himself, as quite a number of his contemporaries such as Theodore Dreiser, Clarence Darrow and Hamlin Garland, recognized the influence of Spencer on their formative years.[4] In the Foreword, even the utopian annotator does not conceal a certain admiration for Spencer: "Following upon capitalism, it was held even by such intellectual and antagonistic giants as Herbert Spencer, that Socialism would come." The systematization of knowledge in biology and sociology is repeatedly stressed in the novel. It is specifically in these two sciences that one is to find the assurance that the revolution will triumph:

Power will be the arbiter, as it always has been the arbiter. It is a struggle of classes. Just as your class dragged down the old feudal nobility, so shall it be dragged down by my class, the working class. If you will read your biology and your sociology as clearly as you do your history, you will see that this end I have described is inevitable. [§5]

The biology in *The Iron Heel* comes largely from Spencer, and the sociology from Marx. Spencer tried to synthesize the latest discoveries in biology (Darwin) and in physics—mainly investigations in thermodynamics of such people as Joule, Mayer, Helmholtz and Kelvin. This marked a departure from the old Newtonian view of a self-contained universe. In Spencer's system, the constant redistribution of matter and motion was divided between evolution and dissolution, evolution being the progressive integration of matter accompanied by the dissipation of motion, and dissolution being the disorganization of matter accompanied by the absorption of motion. The life process, being essentially evolutionary, meant an incessant change from incoherent homogeneity, exemplified by the lowly protozoa, to coherent heterogeneity.

If the United States was indeed during the last three decades of the 19th century in many respects *the* Social-Darwinist country, as well as one of Nietzschean individualism and power, it was also one with an already strong radical tradition: Abolitionism, Feminism, Unions, Cooperatives, Workers' Parties, Farmers' movements had their history in this country, and energetic attempts had moreover been made by disciples of Marx, such as Joseph Weydemeyer, Friedrich Sorge, Daniel de Leon, Eugene Debs and "Big Bill" Heywood to adapt Marxism to the conditions of American life.[5] Furthermore, there was a growing interest in and acquaintance with the socialism of such people as Henry George and certainly Bellamy. *The Iron Heel* synthesizes these elements and channels them towards a Marxist resolution: the final triumph of the socialist revolution.

3. Seen in this light, one can understand why the structure of the novel cannot be closed or specifically fixed or clear-cut. The two levels of *The Iron Heel*, manuscript and footnotes, are open-ended. The manuscript stops abruptly in the middle of a sentence, and the last footnote merely implies that there is no rounded resolution in the Aristotelian sense of the word:

This is the end of the Everhard Manuscript. It breaks off abruptly in the middle of a sentence. She must have received warning of the coming of the mercenaries, for she had time safely to hide the Manuscript before she fled or was captured. It is to be regretted that she did not live to complete her narrative, for then, undoubtedly, would have been cleared away the mystery that has shrouded for seven centuries the execution of Ernest Everhard. [§25]

Likewise, the structure of the two levels is linear. Manuscript and footnotes run parallel and never touch: they are separated by seven hundred years of social evolution.

The development from the society that the author is criticizing to the utopian organization is not specifically explained. There is a wide time-gap between epic and utopia. The dissolution of 20th century society and the evolution of the new order are not deterministic. We are faced, in geological terms, with different strata that were shaped by social revolutions analogous to physical earthquakes:

The Great Earthquake of 2368 A.D. broke off the side of one of these knolls and toppled it into the hole where the Everhards made their refuge. Since the finding of the Manuscript excavations have been made, and the house, the two cave rooms, and all the accumulated rubbish of long occupancy have been brought to light. [§18]

The extinctness of capitalist society is thus translated into seismic terms, and the interest in that era becomes archaeological. The desire for socialist change takes in London the shape of radical revolution: capitalism must become a lost civilization.

The Darwinist concept of evolution from the nebular mass that was the Earth, from lower species to higher and complex ones, turns in London to evolution from capitalist chaos to coherent socialist utopia. As in Spencer, the end-result of this evolutionary process is a state of biological equilibration which Spencer thought was inevitable because the evolutionary process cannot move infinitely towards increasing heterogeneity. In his *First Principles* he affirmed that dissolution followed evolution, disintegration followed integration; that in an organism this was represented by death and decay, but in society by the establishment of a balanced, harmonious, completely adapted state, in which "evolution can end only in the establishment of the greatest perfection and the most complete happiness."[6]

The Marxist use of the term "dissolution," however, signifies the dissolution of private property and the abolition of classes. The very economic evolution of private property bears in itelf the seeds of its own dissolution. And the antagonistic class this evolution has created, the proletariat, wins by abolishing both itself and private property. Only then can the principles of harmonious socialism be said to have been achieved. In *The Iron Heel*, the auspicious social balance of the Brotherhood of Man era is an inevitable outcome of both biological and socio-economic evolution. However, London's revolutionary historical consciousness and the Marxist ideological point of reference led him to repudiate the pseudo-Darwinian theory of passive and fatalistic adaptation to the conditions of life, and to draw instead on a dynamic program of action. In the face of those biological and historical forces, London sets the Marxo-Nietzschean titanic strength of Everhard, "a Superman, a blond beast such as Nietzsche has described" (§1). Mighty historical obstacles can only be overcome by superhuman power. Ernest (*ever hard*) struggling to dominate the cosmic antagonistic forces surrounding him and his class, and striving to affirm the convictions of the Cause, is not much different from Zarathustra straining to reach the top of the mountain. He uses his Will to Power, but it is the power of his own class.

Yet, as soon as the utopia is reached, the struggle for existence disappears. Terms expressing conflict and oppression such as "ramshackle house" (§3), "leg-bar" (§6), "lobby" (§9), "strike-breakers," "bull-pen" (§10), and "bluff" (§22) become unintelligible and have to be explained to the utopians. The Marxist perspective is projected to its logical conclusions. It becomes clear that the Spencerian view, having at its core the impossibility of controlling social evolution, was in fact anti-utopian and could not be used on its own. It was, nevertheless, the formal theory behind the social struggle for existence which London conveyed in every threateningly animal image of his novel. And it seemed that civilization was returning to the law of the jungle (a familiar Londonian theme), that "red of claw and fang" life (§3) in which the working class turned to cattle "herded in factory towns" (§2) or moved as "a raging, screaming, screeching, demoniacal horde" of "apes, tigers...hairy beasts of burden" (§23), a "roaring abysmal beast" (§21) finally "shot down like dogs" (§10) or lying "as the rabbits of California after a drive" (§24): "A slaughter-house was made of the nation by the capitalists" (§2). The struggle for Marxism in London is infused with that Spencerian bestiary. In the capitalist "organized wolf-pack of society" (§12), the Marxist Superman fights for a superhistory; the eagle "beating with tireless wings" (§2), the "roaring lion" (§2), strives to overcome the "wolf-struggle" (§3) with the brute power of his class-consciousness.

In the novel, Spencerian Social-Darwinism reflected Jack London's empirical background. Nietzscheanism gave the story its romantic motive force. Marxism provided its utopian horizon and sustained its unyielding ideological drive.

Yet, in the final analysis, the creation of a literary utopia depends not only on material preconditions—a conflictual genesis, for example—, but also on the fact that the alternative society is at the author's historical moment an accessible contingency. Social reactions shift with history, and utopias record them with figurative and rhetorical power. *The Iron Heel* was written at a strategic historical moment, when the confident persuasions of socialism had for the first time been validated in the Russian Revolution of 1905. Joan London went so far as to affirm that "without 1905, *The Iron Heel* would never have been written."[7] That might be a passionate exaggeration. Nevertheless, the events of that revolution most probably provided the novel with some important elements. The massacre of workers by Cossacks (the Mercenaries in the novel?), worker, student and peasant uprisings, the great general strike which paralyzed Russia in October, the national movements for liberation, and then the crushing of the December insurrection in Moscow, certainly have their echoes in the novel. And it might very well be that 1905 concretized in *The Iron Heel* the persistent utopian principle of hope beyond the pessimism of defeat.

NOTES

1. The text followed here is that of the Hill and Wang edition. See entry for *The Iron Heel* in the Suvin-Douglas bibliography in this issue of SFS.
2. See Ernst Bloch, "*Entfremdung, Verfremdung*: Alienation, Estrangement" in Erica Munk, ed., *Brecht* (NY: Bantam, 1972).
3. Richard Hofstadter. *Social Darwinism in American Thought* (NY: George Braziller, 1944), p 6.
4. Ibid., p 34.
5. See David Herreshoff, *American Disciples of Marx* (Detroit: Wayne State University Press, 1967) for an informative study on the propagation of Marxism in America.
6. Ibid., p 37.
7. Joan London, *Jack London and His Times* (Seattle: University of Washington Press, 1968), p 280.

Science Fiction Since Wells

David Ketterer

Science Fiction and Allied Literature

(from SFS *3: 64–75, March 1976)*

A paper was presented at the 1974 SFRA conference entitled, "The Rocket & the Pig, or Henry Adams Revisited, or Science Fiction Vindicated, in Thomas Pynchon's *Gravity's Rainbow*."[1] My knowledge of this paper derives from the conference program only; I was not present. However to judge from its title the argument must have that *Gravity's Rainbow* is a work of SF, indeed a superior example of the genre. Earlier the same year *Gravity's Rainbow* appeared amongst a list of books nominated for the newly-conceived Jupiter award—an award reflecting the evaluations of teachers of SF, an academic seal of approval, so to speak. Clearly a patent element of aggrandizement is at work here on the part of certain apologists for the genre. To be able to lasso a winner of the National Book Award and a Pulitzer Prize nominee for the SF corral is one way of combating the tendency of unfriendly critics to dismiss as juvenile the entire field. Unfortunately, having struggled through the 700-odd pages of *Gravity's Rainbow*, I can testify that it is not a work of SF in any real sense. Furthermore in my opinion it is not a particularly good book marred as it is by a kind of elephantiasis analogous to that displayed by the SF apologists of whom I am speaking. But that is by the way. The issue at hand is the sloppy critical approach which types works related to SF as, in fact, examples of SF. *Gravity's Rainbow*, like *The Education of Henry Adams*, is a work which may be seen as related to SF.

Pynchon's book is not an isolated example here. Mark Adlard, a British SF writer, comes close to calling Dante's *Divine Comedy* SF.[2] We are encouraged by Kingsley Amis to read *The Tempest* as SF.[3] Darko Suvin believes much of Blake's work to be SF.[4] Peter Nicholls, the editor of *Foundation*, is at work on a history of science fiction which begins with the epic of Gilgamesh and along the way makes references to *The Dunciad*, "The Rime of the Ancient Mariner" and *Hard Times*.[5] Surely, while all these works may contain science-fictional elements and to lesser and greater degrees have something in common with

SF, they are not themselves examples of SF. And, although what is and what isn't SF can be a matter of definition, there is absolutely nothing to be gained by expanding the definition of science fiction in order to include such cases. What is needed here is a new and larger category which would include both SF and the works which somehow insist upon being related to it. And in that context what is required is not so much an all-encompassing definition of SF as various defining distinctions between the different gradations of SF. Such a pluralistic approach is all the more necessary since we may be approaching a stage in the development of SF where an author's work may best be understood on its own terms rather than as an example of a particular genre.

1. I have proposed in *New Worlds for Old* that SF is best understood as an aspect of an encompassing tradition of what may be called apocalyptic literature.[6] Apocalyptic literature is conceived as one part of a tripartite circular sequence which also includes fantastic literature and mimetic literature. It is characterized by the creation of radically different other worlds which, by virtue of a reading convention, exist on a literal level in a credible relationship (credible whether on the basis of a religious faith or rationality) with the everyday world in the reader's head, thereby occasioning the destruction of that everyday world during the reading process. This admittedly somewhat inelegant formulation has the advantage that, while covering SF, it would also include works which appear to be related to SF. The distinction between apocalyptic literature and mimetic literature is reasonably clear cut—mimetic works attempt by way of certain conventions to reproduce the world of everyday experience. The distinction between apocalyptic literature and fantastic literature is apparently trickier to appreciate but it depends similarly upon an author's intention and ability to signal certain reading expectations. It is the intention of the apocalyptic writer to create a world which exists in a credible relationship with the putative real world; it is the intention of the fantastic writer to create a world which exists in an incredible relationship with the putative real world. The intentionality here does not altogether signal itself by way of subject matter. It is to be experienced or not experienced, as the case may be, through what Samuel R. Delany calls the level of subjunctivity, the glue between the words.[7] A writer can signal a desired level of subjunctivity both directly, by simply calling his work fantasy, SF, gothic romance or whatever, and indirectly by adopting a particular style. Herein lies the real distinction between SF and fantasy or, for that matter, the ultimate distinction between fantastic literature and mimetic literature.

The more rigorous kind of allegory where a relationship with the putative real world is to be sought on the subsurface level of translated meaning rather than on a surface level of scene and incident would belong, on that surface level, in my fantastic literature category. The categorization allegory, of course, involves the introduction of a parameter other than that which distinguishes the relationships between fictional worlds and the assumed real world. What is important is the relationship between semantic levels. Likewise with parody, where what is most relevant is the relationship between one literary world and another, a new parameter is required.

The term "speculative fiction" has been used somewhat confusedly, both as an alternative and more dignified interpretation of the initials SF and as a means of drawing attention to the wider possibilities of SF, seemingly in effect those possibilities that exist within the range of the apocalyptic imagination. On the one hand, the sense that SF exists within a larger and "nobler" literary structure is acknowledged, but on the other, SF itself is made to disappear. Why not then modify this usage and speak of science fiction—for such an animal does indeed exist and analysis can reveal its evolving forms—within the larger context of speculative literature? What is to be gained by apparently calling speculative literature apocalyptic literature? Well, for one thing the label speculative literature is often used to cover works of fantasy as well as SF and thus blurs what I consider to be a vital distinction. At the same time, if the variously faceted definition of apocalyptic literature which I have elaborated in *New Worlds for Old* is in any way convincing, I believe it allows for a much clearer mapping of the relationships between SF and its encompassing literary structure than does the term speculative literature. But in addition and of paramount importance, the apocalyptic concept acknowledges the sense of reality both physical and ultimately mystical which characterizes SF. To take my paradigm example in *New Worlds for Old*, it is surely much more convincing to speak of Edgar Allan Poe as an apocalyptic writer rather than a speculative writer. Perhaps, however, the term speculative fiction could be retained to describe those works on the bordering areas between SF and other aspects of the apocalyptic imagination or, indeed, of the fantastic and mimetic imaginations.

It should be apparent by now that this essay is very much a coda to *New Worlds for Old*. Partly in order to sharpen the focus of that book I largely limited my treatment of the classic, i.e. non science-fictional, apocalyptic imagination, to American literature. At the same time I hoped to point to the centrality of the apocalyptic imagination in American literature and thereby explain the peculiarly American nature of the SF genre. Of the major forces which have led to the development of SF—the new astronomy and the New World during the Renaissance, Darwinism and the Industrial Revolution during the nineteenth century—I believe that the New World concept was of primary importance. Clearly the era of geographical exploration in the seventeenth century provided a concrete analogue or "objective correlative" for the concurrent intellectual revolution. It is no accident that three early works of importance to the history of proto-SF, More's *Utopia*, Bacon's *New Atlantis* and Shakespeare's *The Tempest*, all display evidence of a New World awareness. Likewise, Verne and Wells pondered the significance of America.[8] And in terms of influence, Poe is to Verne what Hawthorne almost is to Wells.

However, my present concern is that larger subject implied but not treated at length in my book, the relationship between science fiction and those examples of the apocalyptic imagination which do not belong to the American literary tradition. What follows is a more or less chronological inventory, suggestive I hope and certainly not definitive, of literary forms, texts and writers of formal significance which I conceive as either existing exclusively within the confines of apocalyptic literature or alternatively capable of apocalyptic expression. Works of the apocalyptic imagination radically change and improve our understanding of a present reality, indirectly by presenting other worlds in space and time thus placing the present in a wider material context, or, more directly, by presenting other worlds out of space and time, thus placing the present in a transcendent visionary context. Such works effect the same transformation with most immediacy by devising new ontologies and radically reinterpreting aspects of the present—the nature of man, the nature of reality or the nature of an outside manipulator. When applied to individual works these distinctions coexist and overlap bewilderingly. But in the order given, they accord approximately with the chronological development of apocalyptic forms which I wish to survey here.

2. There are a number of genres or forms which developed early and depend for their interest largely upon the fact that outside of a localized area, the rest of the world was as unknown as the surface of the moon or Mars. Most histories of SF nod respectfully in the direction of the imaginary voyage and generally specify the *Odyssey*. The cosmic voyage is a perfectly natural development of the imaginary voyage. I see no essential formal difference between these two narrative structures. The affinity between the pastoral and SF has been noted by Darko Suvin and should receive some treatment in any scholarly approach to the history of SF.[9] There are various points of contact. The town/country duality like the male/female duality only needs to be taken literally in terms of contrasting worlds for all manner of science-fictional possibilities to become evident. Thus the proliferation of planet-cities and planets named Eden. At the same time, the centrality of the technology theme in SF invokes the pastoral by way of dialectical necessity. Furthermore, the strategy of the pastoral, as made familiar by William Empson, whereby the complex is transposed into the domain of the simple is one much imitated by writers of SF.[10] The pastoral, like utopian fantasy, is of course a form of satire and obviously that kind of satire which functions, as so much of it does, by creating an imaginary society which provides a distorted mirror image of man's own society, blends easily with SF giving rise to the dystopia theme.

To the extent that SF is future history, pre-history or alternative history, there are areas of overlap to be explored with myth (including the pastoral myth of an ancient Golden Age), legend and historical fiction—all forms concerned with other times. The more unknown, unauthenticated is the nature of the time past that is described, the more the work concerned may operate within the context of the apocalyptic imagination. But any successful realization of an historical society or situation will involve communicating a sense of scope, an awareness of trans-individual forces and a philosophical sense of the process of history similar to that required in sociological or large canvas SF. Fredric Jameson goes so far as to claim that "*SF is in its very nature a symbolic meditation on history itself*, comparable in its emergence as a new genre to the birth of the historical novel around the time of the French Revolution."[11] It is unquestionably true that the writer of historical fiction, like the writer of pastoral, utopian and dystopian fiction, and much of SF generally, is to a greater or lesser degree presenting a temporally removed society in order to comment on his own times. A historical subject will frequently present itself as offering suggestive parallels.

As for that apocalyptic tradition which deals in visionary worlds out of space and time, exhibit A (corresponding to the *Odyssey* as an example of other worlds in space and time) is Dante's *Divine Comedy*. Milton's *Paradise Lost* with its Heaven, Hell and Eden belongs in both of the other world camps. The visionary tradition culminates with the work of Blake, Shelley and the other Romantics. Since, as I believe, the overall thrust of SF, its outer edge, is visionary or mystical, one might legitimately expect the SF genre to be capable of comparable literary achievements. M.H. Abrams in *Natural Supernaturalism* describes what I understand to be the area of relationship between SF and Romantic poetry when he stresses the Romantic obsession with apocalypses of mind.[12] A good example of the more detailed kind of comparison which might be attempted is provided by Christopher Small's study of the connections between *Frankenstein* and *Prometheus Unbound*.[13] The relationship between the gothic novel generally and SF is well known and has recently been emphasized by Brian Aldiss in *Billion Year Spree*.[14]

Actually *Frankenstein* is perhaps the paradigm example of another important connection, that between SF and the natural sublime, if for the moment we can agree with Aldiss in typing *Frankenstein* as SF. Perhaps the best study of the sublime for present purposes is Marjorie Hope Nicolson's *Mountain Gloom and Mountain Glory* which chronicles the development of the natural sublime as distinct from the rhetorical sublime described by the pseudo-Longinus.[15] While Longinus did regard the power of forming great conceptions as essential to the achievement of the sublime it was not until the new astronomy and the new geology of the seventeenth century precipitated a new sense of the vastness of space and time that natural analogues were found for those sublime emotions previously associated directly with the deity. Mountains and oceans, once regarded as fallen disfigurements of the originally smooth surface of the mundane egg Earth were suddenly appreciated as evocative of the sublime emotions of terror and religious awe. But mountains and oceans were only terrestrial equivalents for that sublime horror and awe to be more accurately experienced by a consciousness of the immensities of interstellar space. Thomas Burnet in his extraordinary *The Sacred Theory of the Earth*, a work which occupies a pivotal position in the aesthetic history of the sublime, captures the essence of the natural sublime in the following passage:

> The greatest Objects of Nature are, methinks, the most pleasing to behold; and next to the Great Concave of the Heavens, and those boundless Regions where the Stars inhabit, there is nothing that I look upon with more Pleasure than the wide Sea and the Mountains of the Earth. There is something august and stately in the Air of these things, that inspires the Mind with great Thoughts and Passions; we do naturally, upon such Occasions, think of God and his Greatness: And whatsoever hath but the Shadow and Appearance of INFINITE, as all things do have that are too big for our comprehension, they fill and overbear the Mind with their Excess, and cast it into a pleasing kind of Stupor and Admiration.[16]

The relationship between all this and SF should be obvious although it has only recently been pointed out in print by Wayne Connelly in an article entitled "Science Fiction and the Mundane Egg."[17] What is to be regretted, of course, is that the rhetorical abilities of most SF writers are not equal to the occasions which SF offers for the experience of sublimity. The measure of excellence here is *Paradise Lost* which displays in an exemplary manner many instances of the sublime.

Certainly the various qualities involved in the sublime experience are readily obtainable in SF. Joseph Addison in his *Pleasures of the Imagination* (1712) emphasized the importance of the uncommon while Edmund Burke in *A Philosophical Enquiry into the Origin of our Ideas of the Sublime and Beautiful* (1757) stresses the value of obscurity because it excites fear of the unknown, specifically as related to the ideas of infinity and eternity. According to Burke, astonishment "is the effect of the sublime in its highest degree" but terror is the ruling principle of the sublime.[18] He claims that "the English *astonishment* and *amazement*, point out...clearly the kindred emotions which attend fear and wonder."[19] We have all, I am sure, heard of a magazine devoted to SF called *Amazing Stories*. A number of critics have concerned themselves with the importance of the power theme in SF. Burke argues that it is an awareness of the power implied by sublime phenomena which produces the emotion of terror. As I have suggested, perhaps the best example of this range of sublime qualities in SF, if it is SF, is Mary Shelley's *Frankenstein*. The monster is almost a projection of the qualities inspired by the book's Alpine setting, the same setting which so affected Burnet and many of the other testifiers to mountain glory.

The experience of a transcendent reality which in temporal terms can only be described as a kind of everlasting present does, of course, change our lived present reality in an immediate manner, very different from the way in which that reality is transformed by an awareness of other worlds in space and time. But radically new philosophical frameworks might be said to work on transforming a conventional reality even more directly. For the remainder of this paper I shall be concerned with kinds of literature which, because of their originality, effect analogously profound reinterpretations.

3. Peter Nicholls is fond of proclaiming that SF has less to do with physics than with metaphysics. My own approach supports this sense that SF is ultimately concerned with probing the nature of reality conceived on a universal scale. The term "metaphysical" might be applied to most of the writers that I would describe as apocalyptics—Dante and Goethe for example—but students of literature are more likely to think of the work of Donne and various other seventeenth-century poets. There appears to be as much doubt about the appropriateness of the label metaphysical poetry as the label SF, but that is not the only reason why it may be worthwhile looking for affinities between the two forms. Certainly metaphysical poets did make use of metaphysical ideas at a time when such ideas were undergoing a fundamental revolution. The metaphysical themes to be found in much SF, particularly the novels of Philip K. Dick and Stanislaw Lem, aim at being similarly disturbing and are often given similarly witty and playful expression. That balance of passion and thought which many critics have argued is the essential characteristic of metaphysical poetry is surely something to be aimed at in SF as is that "associated sensibility" which saw no disjunctions between art, science and religion. By means of logical rigour and a realistic precision of imagery, both metaphysical poetry and SF hope to give expression to the new and surprising. Of course, all literature which acknowledges in its world view the important role played by science and technology might be considered in some sense sympathetic to SF but, in order for such literature to be considered apocalyptic, developments in the sciences must be in some way correlated with the sense of a radically changed world. Such a correlation provides a basis for Donne's *Anniversaries* and allows one critic, Sona Raiziss, to speak of Donne's "apocalyptic mood."[20] If my argument for the importance of the apocalyptic tradition in American literature is acceptable, it is not surprising that the revival of interest in metaphysical poetry began in America. Nor is it surprising that one of Donne's satiric works—*Ignatius His Conclave*, which appeared shortly before the satiric "Anatomy of the World" in the *Anniversaries*—occupies a significant place in the history of SF.[21]

Work needs to be done on the literary hoax form and SF. In particular, it would be useful to untangle the conundrum of ontological issues involving the question of fiction and reality to which the topic gives rise. This article provides me with an opportunity for at least clarifying the problems. Sam Moskowitz has pointed to the importance of the newspaper hoax (e.g., Locke's "Moon Hoax" and Poe's "Balloon Hoax") in the development of American SF.[22] (The further connection between the "tall tale" and the hoax provides an additional argument for seeing a peculiarly American quality in SF; Mark Twain is the paradigm example of the tall tale to SF line of development.) In *New Worlds for Old* I disbar a number of Poe pieces from the category "straight" SF because they were originally conceived as hoaxes. The question which I evade in the book is whether or not a science-fictional hoax can be formally distinguished from a work of SF which is not conceived as a hoax or indeed a work of SF which has the unintentional effect of hoaxing its readers or listeners—I am thinking of the Orson Welles broadcast version of *The War of the Worlds*.

The literary hoax may take two forms—either the writer attempts to pass off a stylistic copy as an original or he attempts to pass off as factual a work of fiction. It only takes a moment's reflection to realize that the second category is likely to overlap with SF. Unlike the forger, who operates for financial gain, the hoaxer wants to prove something about human gullibility. For anything significant to be proven by the second kind of hoax, the "facts" described must be in some way startling or amazing like the "facts" of SF. The almanac form, which purports to forecast the future, proved an early model for the science-fictional hoax. Under the pseudonym Isaac Bickerstaff, Swift published a hoaxical almanac entitled *Predictions for the Year 1708*. The question then arises, should exploded hoaxes be categorized as SF first and hoaxes second or vice versa? Do the formal characteristics of the SF hoax—documentary presentation, a pervasive irony or sarcasm, a particular "Level of subjunctivity," to have recourse to Delany's concept again, its status as a "self-consuming artifact," to appropriate Stanley Fish's category[23]—suffice to distinguish it from SF proper? To take a specific instance, should George Adamski's accounts of his adventures with flying saucers and Venusians be read as literary hoaxes, as factual reports or as SF?[24] The hoax form strikes at the heart of the fact/fiction antithesis since, as employed by such writers as Poe and Twain, it carries the ultimate metaphysical implication that what we take to be reality is actually a hoax. It is by virtue of this characteristic that the literary hoax may be considered as an aspect of the apocalyptic imagination.

The Brechtian strategy of estrangement has received a good deal of critical attention and the importance of estrangement to science fiction has been explored by Darko Suvin.[25] In this context I only wish to emphasize that an estranged technique is yet another formal means of exchanging new worlds for old, in Brecht's case of replacing a false subjective view with a new objectivity and thereby effecting a radical transformation. This technique is as important an influence on the *nouveau roman* as on science fiction, and should be recalled when I come to speak of the relationship between the *nouveau roman* and SF.

It is rather surprising that the considerable affinity which exists between surrealism and SF has not attracted more attention. Certainly the surreal concept is frequently invoked in characterizations of particular works of SF. Brian Aldiss is partial to the surreal effect as is illustrated by the mix of fauna and technology in the generation starship gone to seed of *Non-Stop.* Michel Butor has pointed to descriptive passages in Verne's *20,000 Leagues Under the Sea* which are directly comparable to the later writings of the self-proclaimed surrealists.[26] Cordwainer Smith has produced a body of semi-surrealistic SF. But it is J.G. Ballard who more than any other writer has exploited that fertile area where surrealism and SF overlap.

Surrealism was a revolutionary movement dedicated to a new objectivity and the value of imagination (creative of bizarrely juxtaposed images) as a means of transforming our definition of reality, in order to allow for the existence of the marvellous. Important among the sources of surrealism is the gothic romance which fosters the suspicion that the world is dominated by forces not acknowledged by the rational mind. Unlike the Dada movement which preceded the development of surrealism and the work of Kafka and the absurdists which succeeded it, surrealism is founded upon an essential optimism. As I have argued in *New Worlds for Old*, the overall plot of science fiction is also optimistic.[27] Both surrealism and SF aim at a mystical yet somehow material state of unity. The surrealists employed the iconography of apocalypse to convey a sense of expanded reality rather than a sense of desperation. André Breton, a founder of surrealism, writes in *Le Seconde Manifeste du Surrealisme* (1929), "Everything tends to make us believe that there exists a certain point of the mind at which life and death, the real and the imagined, past and future, the communicable and incommunicable, high and low, cease to be conceived as contradictions."[28] The surrealist art of Salvador Dali which presents fantasy landscapes with a technique of photographic realism is comparable in approach and purpose to SF. If Dali's world is real, as its surface texture would suggest, then our definition of reality must be radically altered. In Dali's own words, "my whole ambition in the pictorial domain is to materialize the images of concrete irrationality with the most imperialistic fury of precision—in order that the world of imagination and of concrete irrationality may be as objectively evident as...the exterior world of phenomenal reality."[29] It should be noted that SF exploits both the discordant logically incoherent imagery of surrealism and the discordant but logically coherent imagery of metaphysical poetry.

If Anna Balakian's study *Surrealism: The Road to the Absolute* convinces, then surrealism is at least as successful as SF in bridging the gap between the worlds of science and art. She refers to the surrealist "spirit of cosmic adventure"[30] which is today the province of the scientist and the technician. The surrealist poet Guillaume Apollinaire, born in 1880, "predicted the space age along with its challenge to the human imagination."[31] The optimism, "force and vitality inherent in surrealism make of it the art-concept most in keeping with the productivity of the scientific age in which he flourished."[32] With the post-Einsteinian rejection of linear chronology and "the principle of causality, the scientist with his tools of reasoning confirms the surrealist's intuition that there can be a nondeterminist understanding of reality."[33] The old division between subjective and objective no longer applies. In describing the surrealist paintings of Tanguy, Anna Balakian speculates that "if man ever achieves his desire to be propelled on to other planets, what he will find...must resemble the objects and landscapes devised by Yves Tanguy."[34]

I have referred in *New Worlds for Old* to an affinity between the fictional universes of Kafka and Borges and the universe of SF.[35] Here I only want to underline the importance of Kafka. Kafka's "The Metamorphosis" is Tzvetan Todorov's concluding example in his structural analysis of the fantastic as a genre. Although Todorov's fantastic is not my fantastic but exists in the border area between my apocalyptic and mimetic categories, his remarks regarding Kafka do provide support for my contention that supernatural fiction and SF operate within a common form. After noting that the "event described in 'The Metamorphosis' [Gregor Samsa's transformation into an enormous insect] is quite as real as any other literary event," Todorov claims that "the best science fiction texts are organized analogously. The initial data are supernatural: robots, extraterrestrial beings, the whole interplanetary context. The narrative movement consists in obliging us to see how close these apparently marvellous elements are to us, to what degree they are present in our life."[36] We are given to understand that Kafka and SF relate two apparently incompatible genres bordering on Todorov's fantastic, the marvellous (which requires new laws of nature) and the uncanny (where the laws of reality remain unbroken). Todorov concludes that in Kafka and SF the *generalized fantastic* is the norm not the exception.

There is, finally, I believe, something to be gained by examining the strategy of the *nouveau roman*, a current manifestation of the anti-novel tradition, in relation to SF.[37] Based on the assumption that the naturalistic novel, deprived of its positivistic philosophical raison d'etre, can no longer be said to represent reality, indeed that the representation of reality is impossible, practitioners of the *nouveau roman* take pains to emphasize the unreality of their creations. The presentation, in extreme detail and with scientific precision, of the apparently external world as objects in consciousness, is a way of forcing the reader to see that the fictionality embodied in the material he is reading carries over into the world of consciousness which he inhabits. A truer reality is then at least implied by way of contrast as existing outside of the fiction and consciousness, a reality which is quite other than that experienced by the individual. It follows that the otherness of reality has some equivalence with the alien landscapes of SF, albeit most such landscapes are alien by convention and intentionality only. What I am suggesting is that SF writers might more successfully evoke the presence of the genuinely alien by exploiting the descriptive methodology of the "nouveau roman." After all, the matter of setting is of special importance in SF. The success of Stanislaw Lem's *Solaris* depends, I believe, largely upon his use of such a methodology in describing with intricate detail the varied structures thrown up by the "ocean" world. One might further hazard the suspicion that an awareness of the autonomy of literary language characteristic of the *nouveau roman* should assert itself whenever a writer works outside the purely mimetic tradition. Recently I had an opportunity to ask Brian Aldiss about his motivation in writing *Report on Probability A* where a style associated with the *nouveau roman* serves the ends of SF. He replied that this particular experiment resulted from his sense that the cool precise approach of such writers as Michel Butor and Alain Robbe-Grillet evoked a science-fictional quality, a way of looking at the world through alien eyes.

4. I would propose therefore, on the basis of both the foregoing survey and *New Worlds for Old*, that the most appropriate critical approach to SF is a comparative one. A chronological survey should include where appropriate, examples of and explanatory material concerning such matters as the pastoral, the imaginary voyage, utopian and dystopian satire (for example More's *Utopia* and Pope's *Dunciad*), historical fiction, metaphysical poetry, the literary sublime, romanticism and the Gothic Novel, Brechtian estrangement (*Galileo* would be the most appropriate example because the experience of estrangement applies to both form and content—Galileo's objectivity revealed a truer reality), surrealism, Kafka consciousness and the *nouveau roman*. Then there are those important texts which cannot be classified as SF, but which bear some important relations to the nature of SF—*Dr. Faustus*, *The Tempest* and *Gulliver's Travels*. Certainly the pervasive presence of the Faustian theme and the Prometheus myth in SF suggests that some attention be given to their existence in the very much broader tradition of world literature.

The main thread in such a chronological survey would of course be those works which are conceived as constituting the evolving tradition of SF including the evolving tradition of what might be called proto-SF (and here as I have indicated, where one draws the line is very much a matter of definition and personal choice). For example, once again, is *Frankenstein* best described as a gothic romance, proto-SF, or what? The purpose of the comparative approach is not so much to suggest that SF is worthy of attention because of the impressive literary materials which bear some relation to it but rather to suggest a potential fulfilment which SF may be capable of as a result of assimilating such materials.

It would be convenient at this point to instance some towering work of SF illustrating that this fulfilment is already in existence. Sadly this is not the case. Perhaps such an achievement would signal the death of SF as we know it. However since I began with reference to an acclaimed work which has been called SF but isn't, let me conclude by drawing attention to a work which won the 1973 W.H. Smith award for fiction in England and which is genuine SF but doesn't seem yet to have attracted that label. I am referring to Brian Moore's novella *Catholics*, originally published in 1972. Moore tells of the fashionably liberal state of the Catholic Church at the end of the twentieth century and the mission of a church agent to bring into line a group of renegade monks off the coast of Ireland who persist in performing the traditional mass in Latin and attracting thronging congregations. This sophisticated, convincing and well wrought futuristic account of the role of faith in a faithless age did not rate high if at all among the contenders for a Nebula or Hugo Award for 1972. The cause of SF will not be helped by widening the category to include established works of relational status, but neither will it be helped by a shrunken obsession with rockets and ray-guns which allows such a fine example of sociological SF as *Catholics* to pass by unrecognized.

NOTES

1. This paper was delivered by André Le Vot.

2. While noting that "The Divine Comedy was not serialized in the pulp magazines for technical and historical reasons which I imagine are clear to everybody," Adlard claims "I regard Dante as the supreme artist in those techniques I consider peculiar to the science fictional field." See "The Other Tradition of Science Fiction" in *Beyond*

This Horizon: An Anthology of Science Fact and Fiction (Sunderland, 1973), p.10.

3. See *New Maps of Hell* (New York, 1960), p.3.

4. Suvin writes of Blake, "His fantasies of cosmogonic history read like a gigantic inventory of later 'far out' SF, from Stapledon and E.E. Smith to Arthur Clarke and van Vogt." See "Radical Rhapsody and Romantic Recoil in the Age of Anticipation: A Chapter in the History of SF," *Science-Fiction Studies*, I (Fall, 1974), 260.

5. A chapter of this history appears, under the title "Science Fiction and the Mainstream: Part 2: The Great Tradition of Proto Science Fiction," in *Foundation*, 5 (January, 1974), 9-43.

6. See *New Worlds for Old: The Apocalyptic Imagination, Science Fiction, and American Literature* (New York and Bloomington, Ind., 1974).

7. See "About Five Thousand One Hundred and Seventy-Five Words," *Extrapolation*, 10 (May, 1969), 61-64.

8. Verne, in particular, was fascinated by America. Jean Chesneaux writes, "it is not by chance that in twenty-three of his novels, out of a total of sixty-four, the action takes place on American soil, either totally or in part, or that American characters play an important role." See Chapter IX, "The American Mirage and the American Peril," of *The Political and Social Ideas of Jules Verne* (London, 1972), p. 150. Wells wrote of *The Future in America* (1906) and *The New America* (1935). In his "Biographical Perspective" to *The Crystal Man: Stories by Edward Page Mitchell* (New York, 1973), Sam Moskowitz suggests that Wells may have derived ideas for his time *machine* and a scientific rationale for invisibility from the American, Mitchell, who got to those themes first in "The Clock that Went Backward" (1881) and "The Crystal Man" (1881). See pp. lxiii- lxv.

9. See Suvin, "On the Poetics of the Science Fiction Genre," *College English*, 34 (December, 1972), 376.

10. See *Some Versions of Pastoral* (London, 1935), *passim*.

11. See Jameson's contribution, "In Retrospect," to the forum, "Change, SF and Marxism: Open or Closed Universes?" *Science-Fiction Studies*, 1 (Fall, 1974), 275. Also relevant is Robert H. Canary, "Science Fiction as Fictive History," *Extrapolation*, 5 (December, 1974), 81-95.

12. See *Natural Supernaturalism: Tradition and Revolution in Romantic Literature* (New York, 1971), *passim*. See also Northrop Frye, *The Secular Scripture: A Study of the Structure of Romance* (Cambridge, Mass., 1975).

13. See *Ariel Like a Harpy: Shelley, Mary, and "Frankenstein"* (London, 1972), *passim*.

14. See especially Chapter I, "The Origins of the Species: Mary Shelley," in *Billion Year Spree: The True History of Science Fiction* (New York, 1973), pp. 7-39. According to Aldiss, "Science fiction was born from the Gothic, is hardly free of it now" (p. 18).

15. See *Mountain Gloom and Mountain Glory: The Development of the Aesthetics of The Infinite* (Ithaca, 1959).

17. "Science Fiction and the Mundane Egg," *Riverside Quarterly*, 5 (April, 1973), 260-67.

16. *The Sacred Theory of the Earth: Containing an Account of the Original of the Earth and of All the General Changes Which It Hath Already Undergone or Is to Undergo, till the Consummation of All Things* (London, 1684). The quotation is taken from the sixth edition of 1726, vol. I, pp. 188-89.

18. See *A Philosophical Enquiry into the Origins of our Ideas of the Sublime and Beautiful*, ed. J.T. Boulton (London, 1958), p. 57.

19. Ibid., p. 58.

20. See *The Metaphysical Passion: Seven Modern American Poets and the Seventeenth Century Tradition* (Westport, Connecticut, 1952), p. 9.

21. See Marjorie Hope Nicolson, "Kepler, the *Somnium*, and John Donne," *Journal of the History of Ideas*, 1 (June, 1940), 259-80; reprinted in *Science and Imagination* (Ithaca, 1956), pp. 58-79.

22. See the "Biographical Perspective" to *The Crystal Man*, pp. xi-xlvi.

23. See *Self-consuming Artifacts: The Experience of Seventeenth-Century Literature* (Berkeley, 1972).

24. See *Inside the Spaceships* (New York, 1955).

25. See "On the Poetics of the Science Fiction Genre," 374-375.

26. "Le point suprême et l'âge d'or" in *Répertoire: études et conferénces, 1948-1959* (Paris, 1960), pp. 130-62.

27. *New Worlds for Old, passim* but especially pp. 102, 124, 149.
28. Quoted in C.W.E. Bigsby, *Dada and Surrealism* (London, 1972), p. 38.
29. Ibid., p. 69.
30. *Surrealism: The Road to the Absolute* (London, 1972), p. 23.
31. Ibid., p. 45.
32. Ibid., p. 47.
33. Ibid., p. 246.
34. Ibid., p. 206.
35. *New Worlds for Old*, pp. 207, 210, 234-5.
36. *The Fantastic: A Structural Approach to a Literary Genre* (Cleveland and London, 1973), p. 172.
37. For some sense of the connections between SF and the *nouveau roman*, see Fredric Jameson, "Generic Discontinuities in SF: Brian Aldiss' *Starship*," *Science-Fiction Studies*, 1 (Fall, 1973), 64. For my overall sense of the *nouveau roman*, I am particularly indebted to Gabriel Josipovici, *The World and the Book: A Study of Modern Fiction* (London, 1971).

Gary K. Wolfe

Mythic Structures in Cordwainer Smith's "The Game of Rat and Dragon"

(from SFS *4: 144–150, July 1977)*

Discussions of the relationship between science fiction and myth usually begin to break down as soon as the question of basic definitions arises. There is little critical agreement as to the meaning of either term, and trying to establish some defensible relationship between two such slippery concepts begins very quickly to seem like an attempt to draw maps of clouds. But this should not be taken to mean, as it often is, that myth study has little to offer the study of science fiction or vice versa. In this paper, I will attempt to apply a specific methodology drawn from the study of myths conducted by Claude Levi-Strauss to a specific work that is generally received as science fiction, Cordwainer Smith's story "The Game of Rat and Dragon." The confluence of this particular method with this particular work arises partly out of the peculiarities of each, and should not be taken as an argument that all science fiction should be treated as myth, or that Levi-Strauss's methodology is the only proper approach to science fiction as myth.

But there is a compelling reason why the anthropological approach to myth may be of benefit to science fiction. We often encounter the claim that science fiction is a "modern mythology," but this is seldom accompanied by a discussion of what models are used for "mythology" or just what is meant by modern. Is science fiction modern only because it happens to be a contemporary popular genre, and is it myth only because it often deals with the heroic and the marvelous? As much could be said of fantasy or James Bond stories or Westerns. What of the relationship—explored by several critics—of science fiction to such universal systems of narrative interpretation as those of Northrop Frye or Joseph Campbell? Again we can accept the claim, but only with the awareness that it applies to most other kinds of narrative as well. It is not difficult to forge literary connections between science fiction and accepted bodies of myth, but such connections do little to elucidate the claim that science fiction can actually *function* as myth in our modern culture, in the same way that myths historically express the beliefs and aspirations of a people. In this broader context, myth is never mere escapism, nor is it the mere shell of surface narrative. And to look at science fiction in this context, we must look beyond the shape of narratives that simply *appear* to be mythic—such as heroic fantasies—into the real cultural content of such narratives, to the underlying beliefs and paradoxes. "In mythic imagination," Ernst Cassirer writes, "there is always implied an act of *belief*,"[1] and the discovery of the ways in which this belief has been codified and its paradoxes resolved through myth has been one of the major goals of such analysts as Levi-Strauss and Edmund Leach. In such analyses, focus is shifted from the narrowly literary aspects of the narrative to the functions of the myth within the culture that produced it. Certain recurrent actions associated with specific beliefs are discovered, and a link is forged not only to other myths, but to the social and intellectual life of the culture itself.

Whether or not such analysis can work with science fiction depends upon the extent to which we are ready to accept the notion that science fiction does indeed function as a way of ordering and expressing the myths of our culture, our common problems and beliefs. The question becomes even more problematical when we consider that science fiction is a literary genre with a rather specialized audience rather than a common body of folklore. However, there is mounting evidence that the mainstream of science fiction of the forties and fifties—perhaps because of its isolation from external literary influences, its vigorous internal cross-pollenation, and the force of that peculiar institution known as "fandom"—did indeed evolve into an almost tribal body of icons, themes, and beliefs. Both Donald Wollheim and James Gunn have commented on the "consensus future history" that science fiction developed during this period, and Wollheim goes so far as to cast out from the mainstream of science fiction any work that does not fit into his eight-stage "cosmogony."[2] Furthermore, it seems to be a habit among science-fiction writers to construct their own future histories—Blish, Heinlein, Stapledon, Simak, Dickson, are but a few examples besides Smith—and these future histories tend to be considerably more internally consistent than the "consensus," making it possible if not in fact preferable to look at a single work by one of these authors in the context of the author's own system.

Perhaps more than any other writer of future-history stories, Cordwainer Smith (Paul Linebarger) manages to impart to his tales the aspect of "strong time" of which Mircea Eliade speaks in describing the power of myth—"the prodigious, 'sacred' time when something *new*, *strong*, and *significant* was manifested."[3] Smith's stories, in the words of Franz Rottensteiner, constitute "an outlook, a world-view, colored and distorted as if transmitted by oral tradition."[4] Smith's narrators speak to an implied audience of an unimaginably distant future, to whom the fantastic inventions of the tales—the Up-and-Out, Scanners, habermen, pinlighters, go-captains, underpeople—are but as myths of an ancient and more powerful time.

The internal consistency of Smith's tales of the Instrumentality of Mankind has to some extent been established by J.J. Pierce in his introduction to the Ballantine collection *The Best of Cordwainer Smith*.[5] Because of this consistency, and because of the ways in which these stories partake of the icons and structures of the aforementioned "consensus" of mainstream science fiction, Smith's work seems an inviting area for the kind of structural mythic analysis which, if successful, can reveal some of the hidden beliefs and paradoxes that science fiction addresses. Specifically, there are three related themes in Smith that I think are central to much modern science fiction. First and most important is the antinomy of known and unknown and the means by which science fiction tends to validate the appropriation of the unknown and its assimilation into the known—the process of transforming Chaos into Cosmos, in Eliade's terms.[6] Second is the theme of beast or monster in science fiction, and the ways in which this image in its various manifestations relates to man's unconscious mind, his animal nature, and his terrestrial origins. The third theme is that of technology, and the apparent paradox in much science fiction that the more man tries to deny his autochthonous origins through technology, the more he is reminded of them.

All three themes are evident in the short and widely anthologized story "The Game of Rat and Dragon." While this story on one level is a highly imaginative treatment of conventional themes of romance and heroism, it is also a revealing treatment of science fiction as a codification, perhaps "mythification," of contemporary beliefs and concerns. There are four principal sets of actors in the tale: "pinlighters," or telepathic humans; "partners," or intelligent cats used to assist the pinlighters in their dangerous duties; "dragons" or "rats," primeval interstellar beings that destroy or drive mad humans in space; and the ordinary humans whom the pinlighters and their cats serve to protect from the dragons. Each set of actors plays a particular symbolic role in the antinomy of known-unknown. The known is represented by the ordinary humans and their planetary environments—the "'same old ticking world,'" says the pinlighter protagonist Underhill. "'Down here with the hot sun around us, it feels so good and quiet. You can feel everything spinning and turning. It's nice and sharp and compact. It's sort of like sitting around home.'" The unknown is clearly the realm of the dragons, which Smith describes in images of elemental chaos: "entities something like the dragons of ancient human lore, beasts more clever than beasts, demons more tangible than demons, hungry vortices of aliveness and hate compounded by unknown means out of the thin, tenuous matter between the stars." When telepaths try to read the minds of those damaged by dragons, they find only "vivid spouting columns of fiery terror bursting from the primordial id itself, the volcanic source of life."

Acting as a barrier between the known and the unknown are the two remaining sets of actors, the pinlighters and their cats. Although the pinlighters use advanced technology to fight dragons, their further dependence on cats from the bestial threat of the dragons suggests a more positive model of man's relationship to the animal world: his ability to work in concert with it. But this collaboration produces curious emotional attachments that are closer in many ways than the relationships pinlighters have with other humans. "'I've seen more pinlighters go crazy from monkeying around with Partners than I have ever seen caught by the Rats,'" Underhill is warned. Thus the pinlighters are regarded with a mixture of scorn and worship by other humans; when Underhill reads the mind of a nurse in a hospital where he is recuperating from a bout with the dragons, he sees himself visualized as a "radiant hero...very far away...better and more beautiful than people like her." Almost in the same instant, the nurse whirls on him and shouts, "'You pinlighters! You and your damn cats!'" The romantic hero becomes both an animal and a god.

Apart from the obvious heroic elements, how does such a story constitute a myth? In what is probably his best-known essay, "The Structural Study of Myth," Claude Levi-Strauss offers a clue. According to his analysis of the story of Oedipus, the diachronic elements of the various versions of the myth, when placed in a proper synchronic relationship, serve to resolve a fundamental paradox in the belief system of the culture that produced the myth. He organizes the "mythemes," or constituent narrative units of the tale, into four columns labeled according to what he regards as basic antinomies of the culture of Greece at that time: overrating of blood relations, underrating of blood relations, denial of the autochthonous origin of man, and persistence of the autochthonous origin of man. "It follows,"he writes, "that column four is to column three as column one is to column two," or "the overrating of blood relations is to the underrating of blood relations as the attempt to escape autochthony is to the impossibility to succeed in it."[7] Social reality (blood relations) serves to validate cosmological belief (autochthonous origins) by an identity of structure, even though nominally the two contradict each other in regard to the origin of man (bisexual reproduction vs. the belief that man is born of the earth).

Like the story of Oedipus, "The Game of Rat and Dragon" deals essentially with the acquisition of power through the defeat of a monster and the reassertion of man's autochthonous origins in spite of that power. The specific cultural problem that underlies Smith's story, and that in fact characterizes a great deal of science fiction, may be stated in two parts: first, as man tries through technology to incorporate the unknown into the known, he continually finds the unknown receding before him and remaining essentially intact but in a changing context; and second, the more man tries to overcome his autochthonous origins through the appropriation of space and power, the more he is confronted with the persistence of these origins in the form of monsters and his own vulnerability in the universe. In Lewis Mumford's words, "the utmost achievements of technology, which are symbolized even today by a journey to distant planets, terminate in fantasies of shapeless monsters and cruel deaths, such as often haunt the cribs of little children."[8]

Although "The Game of Rat and Dragon" is not a folk myth like Oedipus, we may regard it, as Smith's narrator does, as a myth of the Instrumentality of Mankind and, by extension, as part of the "consensus cosmogony" of which Gunn and Wollheim speak. Arranging the elements of the underlying narrative (as opposed to the surface story of Underhill and Lady May) into four columns as defined by the known-unknown antinomy and the attempt to overcome autochthonous origins, we come up with the following:

Appropriation of unknown through technology	Persistence of unknown	Denial of autochthonous origins	Persistence of autochthonous origins
achievement of space travel		interstellar commerce	"pain-of-space"
	passengers not conscious during interstellar "leaps"		
	dragons encountered		dragons release id, causing madness and death
		use of "super-human" power of telepathy to detect dragons	hospitalization of telepaths after each encounter
shields and bombs used against dragons; pinlighting	dragons learn to evade shields		cats needed to aid pinlighters
		pinlighters regarded as cultural heroes	pinlighters regarded as bestial

Read from left to right, the chart follows the chronology of the story of how pinlighting developed; read vertically, it reveals synchronous groupings that relate to the principal antinomies described by the column headings. Column one, for example, contains the purely technological achievements of space flight, weaponry, and pinlighting or telepathic amplification. All are examples of how technology aids man in assimilating the unknown into his dominion. The second column shows how the unknown persists in spite of these achievements: the space traversed in interstellar travel remains unknown to the passengers because of the nature of planoforming, a mode of travel necessitated by relativity; space keeps its secrets even as man conquers it. And even this limited conquest of space brings forth new avatars of the unknown: the dragons. Technology produces weapons with which to fight the dragons, but they respond by learning to evade them on low trajectories. The game, at its fundamental level, is a contest between technology and the unknown, and it is a contest that cannot be resolved within the context of this antinomy alone. Cats are needed to aid the pinlighters, and while the cats help to resolve this first opposition, they also bring into focus the second opposition, which is represented by columns three and four.

Column three shows the ways in which man tries to liberate himself from his origins as an earthbound animal, first by physically moving outward from his home planet and undertaking commerce with the stars, later by insulating himself from the primordial dragons that are associated with his own unconscious. Telepathy itself may be regarded—as it is in much science fiction—as an evolutionary step away from man's biological origins toward a condition of pure mind. As column four shows, however, this "release" from the animal world is offset by a new link between man and animal; just as the unknown persists, so do man's links with his origins. Cats are telepathic, too, and their faster reaction time is a reminder that man remains close enough to the animal world to require its assistance in the most advanced technological undertakings (a theme echoed in "Scanners Live in Vain" by the use of oysters to protect passengers from the "pain-of-space"). The "pain-of-space" itself (the phrase is borrowed from other Smith stories, though the experience is alluded to in "Rat and Dragon") and human vulnerability to the dragons are further evidences of man's physical and psychological vulnerability and alienation in space. The last two elements of the story, revealed in the hospital scene, are the conflicting attitudes held toward pinlighters, the one worshipful of their heroic aspect, the other contemptuous of their strange relationship with cats. The former attitude sees pinlighters as symbols of man's liberation from his origins, the latter as symbols of continued dependency on those origins. The cats share this dual symbolic aspect: the tom who has proven most effective against the dragons is also the one whose mind is most full of "slobbering thoughts of food, veritable oceans of half-spoiled fish."

In fact, each of the two major science-fiction concepts in this story—space travel and telepathy—is presented in the dual aspect of the technological and the organic. The technical achievement of planoforming is balanced by the living threat of the dragons, and the technical achievement of pinlighting is balanced by the need for instinctual, sensuous cats. This pattern of binary opposition is evident in much of Smith's work—it provides the major source of conflict in "Scanners Live in Vain," for example—and in a broader context may underlie much of science fiction's iconography. To choose an example of just one such icon, many science fiction monsters are organic in nature yet created by technology run wild (as in atomic mutation stories) or encountered as the result of a technological achievement (as in space or time-travel stories, or, if we are willing to accept the notion of alien technological achievement under this rubric, invasion-of-earth stories).

In "The Game of Rat and Dragon," this opposition manifests itself in a kind of quadratic relationship which we can express following Levi-Strauss's formula for Oedipus: the use of technology to appropriate the unknown is to the persistence of the unknown as the denial of autochthonous origins is to the persistence of those origins. (The second part of this, of course, is lifted whole cloth from Levi-Strauss on Oedipus, and not surprisingly, since both are variants on the monster story). Technological appropriation of the unknown becomes analogous to man's deeper motivation to escape his animal-terrestrial heritage, and the persistence of the unknown despite technology becomes analogous to the ways in which this heritage constantly reasserts itself. The analogy broadens the context of the original antinomies and leads to a still more fundamental paradox: man can never achieve the final step of technology—complete mastery of the unknown—without ceasing to be human. The problem is not new—it amounts to a space-age reworking of the old "divine animal" paradox—but it may well be one of the fundamental paradoxes of modern science fiction.

It is tempting to speculate on the many ways science-fiction writers have attempted to deal with this paradox. One method, for example, consists of constructing a kind of cyclical cosmology. Works such as Clarke's *Childhood's End*, which deliberately try to push the appropriation of the unknown to its utmost limits, often end as creation myths; the achievement of total technology is in fact accompanied by final liberation of man from his autochthonous origins, and man ceases to be human, entering, in Clarke's sense, "Overmind." The final sentence of Blish's *Cities in Flight*, in which man appropriates the entire universe only to find it on a collision course with a universe of anti-matter, is "Creation began." In such works the identification of total technology with liberation from origins is made literally apparent, and the rhetoric of such works is often the rhetoric of Genesis.

Smith offers no such clever dramatic solutions, although the "religious climax" that J.J. Pierce says he had planned for the Instrumentality stories may well have been in that vein. But even within the structure of the story "The Game of Rat and Dragon," there is evidence of an accounting for this relationship of the unknown to man's autochthony, an accounting that may hold some truths about the broader myths of mainstream science fiction. It is, simply, that the unknown achieves an identity with man's origins through the common medium of the unconscious, "the volcanic source of life" in Smith's term. Technology is the expression of consciousness and deliberation, and what man has not appropriated through technology is equated with the unborn chaos of his own unconscious, as in the "waste land" of earlier hero myths. Eliade's fundamental mythic antinomy of Chaos and Cosmos thus underlies both our earlier oppositions, and the only synthesis suggested is that of mind:

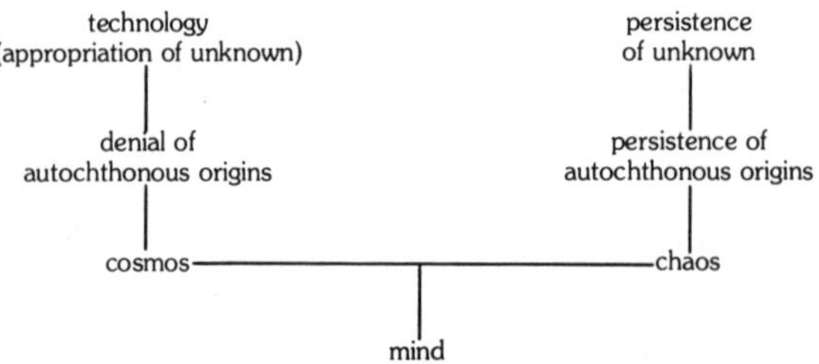

In this light, we can begin to defend the notion that science fiction works as myth in its cultural function as well as in its surface content: it becomes a way of ordering the universe without violating the integrity of that universe, of offering man a way of expanding his technology indefinitely without reaching the dead end that such appropriation of knowledge inevitably suggests; there will always be the unknown within man himself. "The Game of Rat and Dragon," which deals with the science-fiction archetypes of monsters and transformed humans, offers one evidence of this sort of function, but such analysis might also be of value in exploring the power of such other archetypes as cities, robots, and spaceships. Certainly it may be useful in exploring the work of so deliberate a maker of myths as Cordwainer Smith. There are many myths like those of Smith in science fiction, however, and in most of them, we will find an antinomy of known and unknown, with an accompanying underlying structure of chaos versus cosmos. This, more than any simple historical formula or diachronic pattern, represents the true cosmology of science fiction.

NOTES

1. *An Essay on Man: An Introduction to a Philosophy of Human Culture* (1944; US 1954 294p), p 101.

2. Gunn, *Alternate Worlds: The Illustrated History of Science Fiction* (US 1975 256p), pp 225-26; cf. his essay "Science Fiction and the Mainstream" in *Science Fiction Today and Tomorrow*, ed. Reginald Bretnor (US 1974 ix+342), p 190. Wollheim's formulation appears in *The Universe Makers* (US 1971 vi+122), pp 42-44, and his eight-stage "cosmogony" is as follows: interplanetary travel, interstellar travel, rise of galactic empire, full galactic empire, decline and fall, interregnum, rise of permanent galactic civilization, and challenge to God.

3. *Myth and Reality*, translated by Willard R. Trask (1963; US 1968 212p), p 19.

4. *The Science Fiction Book* (US-UK 1975 160p), p 150.

5. (Ballantine pb, 1975), pp xi-xix.

6. *Myth and Reality* (see Note 3), p 141.

7. "The Structural Study of Myth," in *Structural Anthropology*, translated by Claire Jacobsen and Brooke Grundfest Schoepf (US 1963 410p), pp 213-16.

8. *The Myth of the Machine: The Pentagon of Power* (US 1970 496p), pp 48-49.

Scott Sanders

Invisible Men and Women: The Disappearance of Character in Science Fiction

(from SFS *4: 14–24, March 1977)*

Science Fiction is the home of invisible men and women. One is hard put to name half a dozen memorable characters from all the annals of the genre, to recall any science-fictional protagonist who hangs in the mind with the weight of Raskolnikov, say, or Ahab, or Quentin Compson. Critics weaned on the traditional novel frequently use this weakness of characterization as a bludgeon for attacking the genre. Even sympathetic commentators concede the point, and either apologize for it or move quickly on to discuss the genre's strengths. Thus David Ketterer writes that apocalyptic literature—which by his definition includes most science fiction—"involves a certain magnitude or breadth of vision which militates against an interest in detailed characterization."[1] Kingsley Amis argues that science fiction must deal in stock figures because it ponders our general condition rather than the intricacies of personality. Theme replaces character as the organizing principle of the genre, he maintains, a view summarized in his terse formula, "Idea as hero."[2] Whether you read traditional exponents of science fiction such as Isaac Asimov and Robert Heinlein, or the new academic critics gathered in Thomas Clareson's volume, *SF: The Other Side of Realism* (1971), you will only discover versions of the same circular argument: character is neglected because something else—such as ideas or situation or plot—commands the writer's attention.

But why should such a genre arise and flourish in our century, a genre stressing theme rather than character, abstraction rather than personality? The answer, I believe, is sociological. Science fiction reproduces the experience of living in a regimented, rationalized society, within which the individual has become anonymous: persons are interchangeable, relating to each other through socially-defined roles; actions are governed by procedure, and thus do not characterize the actor; emotion is repressed in favor of reason; the individual is subordinated to the system. A literary form which ignores personality in its representation of vast impersonal forces mirrors our sense of the anonymity of individuals within mass society.[3] Thus I do not believe that weakness of characterization in science fiction is the accidental consequence of attention to other things. On the contrary, I would argue that in the 20th century *science fiction as a genre is centrally about this disappearance of character*, in the same sense in which the 18th- and 19th-century bourgeois novel is about the emergence of character.

"Character" was the focus of the bourgeois novel, at a time when the individual was the kingpin of liberal ideology, and when the economic system was still primitive enough to make such an ideology convincing. During the nineteenth century the middle classes of Western Europe and America were still persuaded that the individual was an autonomous creature, the true unit of value, capable of determining his own destiny. This faith was progressively eroded by the growth of cities and industries, which dwarfed the individual, by the spread of bureaucracy, by the impact of technological advances, by war, and by the acceleration of social change. The working classes never fully accepted the notion of the autonomous individual since it was false to their experience of society. This skepticism was reflected in the literary forms most popular among the working class, especially melodrama and romance, in which character was subordinated to plot.[4]

Belief in the autonomous individual—belief in what D.H. Lawrence called "the old stable *ego*—of the character"—was likewise abandoned in the modernist novel, writers such as Lawrence and Joyce and Gide retreating further and further inward in search of a layer of the self which remains free of social domination. In this respect science fiction parallels developments in the twentieth-century mainstream novel. While such writers as Kafka, Musil and Beckett have recorded the dissolution of character under the pressures of recent history, science fiction as a genre begins by assuming that dissolution, and explores the causes. Science fiction deals, in other words, with the same social and intellectual developments whose intimate effects on personality have been explored in modernist fiction; the two literary modes examine the outside and inside of the same phenomenon.

We find the paradigm of this split betweens fiction of the inside and fiction of the outside in the famous dispute between Henry James and H.G. Wells over the scope of the novel. James urged Wells to leave off his social preaching and explore instead the subtleties of personality. Wells replied that close scrutiny of character is only possible when the social frame remains constant. In his own time, Wells argued, the acceleration of social change had made the frame itself part of the picture.[5] James's method of examining consciousness eventually led, in the works of such novelists as Woolf and Beckett, to the shell-shocked furthest reaches of modernism. Along that path the self risks dissolving in its own juices. The method of Wells led to macroscopic studies of society, and eventually, in the science fiction of writers such as Zamyatin and Orwell, to nightmares of anonymity within a technological world. Along that path the self risks dissolving in the system.

Hence the science fiction novel offers an extension and restatement of the central problem with which the modernists wrestled—namely, the fragmentation and anonymization of the self in modern society—although science fiction usually presents that concern in a displaced form. The primacy of system over individual appears formally in the genre in the subordination of character to plot; in the use of stereotypical figures; in the preference for technical and discursive (and therefore anonymous) language. The threat to identity appears explicitly in tales of social engineering and machine domination. It appears implicitly in the figures of androids, robots and zombies, in the specters of totalitarian computers, in the celebration of supermen and superwomen as the only rebels in a world of drones, in the themes of invasion and possession, in the tales of apocalypse. In the following essay I will examine these various expressions of the disappearance of character in science fiction, drawing most of my examples from the period since 1945, the period in which social pressures towards anonymity have grown most intense.

1. The nightmare of losing one's identity within a totalitarian society haunts the protagonists of our century's most famous speculative fiction, from the numbered citizens of Zamyatin's *We* (1920) and the hapless supplicant of Kafka's *The Castle* (1926), to the furtive rebels of Huxley's *Brave New World* (1932) and Orwell's *1984* (1949). These fictions transpose into the future (or, in the instance of *The Castle*, into a fabulous non-time) images of repression with which we are painfully familiar from the history of this century. Zamyatin could turn for models of his dystopia to the early experiments in social engineering conducted by the Bolsheviks; Huxley, to the militarization of England during the Great War, and again during the strikes in the twenties and during the Depression; Kafka, to the rusting machinery of the Hapsburg bureaucracy. Orwell could model his dystopia upon several actual societies, Hitler's Germany, Mussolini's Italy and Stalin's Russia being only the most spectacular expressions of a totalitarian impulse which also surfaced in Spain during the nineteen-thirties, in Britain during the Second World War and in the United States during the chilliest days of the Cold War.

The crushing of the self by the system, the denial of individuality, is nowhere more savagely illustrated in our recent history than in the Second World War, especially the concentration camps, and is nowhere more painfully recorded than in the literature of the holocaust. Memoirs such as Elie Wiesel's *Night* (1958) and novels such as *One Day in the Life of Ivan Denisovitch* (1962) by Alexander Solzhenitsyn describe the camps as places where identity is stripped away and humans are reduced to knots of hunger and fear. We find in these records of historical experience many of the images which recur in post-war science fiction: arms tattooed with numbers, heads shaved, bodies bundled in uniforms; spies and guards prowling among listless inmates; barbed-wire, machine-guns and dogs maintaining order. The documentary film by Resnais, *Night and Fog* (1955), through its pictures of warehouses stuffed with human hair, buckets heaped with gold fillings, pits choked with the bulldozed carcases of nameless victims, records the ultimate anonymity of the furnaces and mass graves.

As their architects proudly declared, the camps were factories of death, embodying the same ideals of precision and efficiency which Leni Rieffenstahl celebrated in her film of the Nuremburg rallies, *Triumph of the Will* (1934-36). Those endless rows of identical soldiers goose-stepping past the camera, those high-angle shots of faceless multitudes ranked like wires to a printed circuit, those boots stamping in unison, all dissolve the individual into the collective. The rallies themselves were a physical expression of the mental conformity which every dictator seeks. Goebbels declared that all Germans must think with one mind, and through the use of terror and mass propaganda he did his best to achieve that goal. In such a state, soldiers and common citizens enjoy little more individuality than prisoners.

No one familiar with the history of our time should be surprised, therefore, that visions of totalitarian futures have become a staple of science fiction since the Second World War. We find such visions in Ray Bradbury's *Fahrenheit 451* (1954), where a ruling party reminiscent of those described by Huxley and Orwell burns books for fear of subversive knowledge; in Philip K. Dick's "Faith of Our Fathers" (1967), where a drugged populace cringes beneath the omniscient gaze of the Great Benefactor, a thinly-disguised *alter ego* of Mao Tse-tung; and in Ursula Le Guin's *The Dispossessed* (1974), where several autocracies share dominion over the planet Urras, rivalling each other in methods of repression. (In the same novel Le Guin projects an alternative planet, Anarres, organized along the lines of anarcho-communism, which, though preferable to the tyranny of Urras, offers equally grave challenges to identity.) Often writers provide social explanations for the rise of their fictional tyrannies, the most common ones, understandably, being war and over-population. Thus Isaac Asimov in *The Caves of Steel* (1953) and Brian Aldiss in *Earthworks* (1966) present us with societies which have been totally regimented in response to population growth. Living has become communal, land has been collectivized and authority centralized. Robots, because of their greater productivity, are honored more highly than humans, who must skulk on the ragged borders of starvation. Similarly, in the film *Soylent Green* (1973), another vision of an over-populated future, individuals have been overwhelmed by collective pressures. Scene after scene portrays anonymous crowds, waiting for medical care or heaped on stairways for sleep, crowds bristling from the scoops of government trucks sent to quell a riot, crowds of the dead reprocessed for food.

The narrator of *Earthworks*, one in a long line of science-fictional rebels against authority, sounds the complaint which is echoed by all the citizens of these regimented dystopias: "In me grew that weary sense of lack of identity that was itself an identification" (§7). We hear the same dread of anonymity voiced by a character in *Fahrenheit 451*, who laments that

> We must all be alike. Not everyone born free and equal, as the Constitution says, but everyone made equal. Each man the image of every other; then all are happy, for there are no mountains to make them cower, to judge themselves against. [§1]

Conformity, homogeneity, loss of identity: these are the obsessive fears in each of the tales I have mentioned. We can readily link such fears to the experience of totalitarianism, since all of these fictional dystopias reproduce the grisly outlines of historical tyrannies. But the dread of anonymity also takes on subtler forms in post-war science fiction, forms whose links to our social experience are less clear but no less strong.

2. While society as a whole grows more rationalized, the experience of living within it grows more alienated. In proportion as the complexity of social organization increases, the power of the individual to comprehend or affect the world dwindles. The reigning institutions of modern society—technological production, bureaucracy, cities, mass media—so regiment and fragment the social world that the individual is thrown back upon his island of subjectivity in search of meaning and coherence. In response to this fact, as I have already suggested, modernist writers have burrowed ever deeper into the self, while writers of science fiction have projected images of the self as a puppet, a robot, an automaton. The characters in much science fiction written since the war are manipulated creatures; they are citizens of an administered world.

In his *Foundation* trilogy (1942-49), Asimov presents us with an entire cosmos administered according to impersonal laws which are incomprehensible to those caught up in the historical process. Although various human agencies conspire to shape history, the real shaping influences, the trilogy assures us, are "the deeper economic and sociological forces" that "aren't directed by individual men."[6] Perhaps drawing upon the crudely deterministic versions of Marxism which served as a scarecrow during the 30s and later during the Cold War, Asimov invented for the purposes of his novels a new discipline called psycho-history:

> Without pretending to predict the actions of individual humans, it formulated definite laws capable of mathematical analysis and extrapolation to govern and predict the mass action of human groups. [§2:3]

Hari Seldon, the greatest of psycho-historians in the trilogy, succeeds in explaining history by dissolving psychology into physics, by treating humans as if they were elementary particles:

> He couldn't work with individuals over any length of time; any more than you could apply the kinetic theory of gases to single molecules. He worked with mobs, populations of whole planets, and only *blind* mobs who do not possess foreknowledge of the results of their actions. [§1:3:2]

Governments, armies, multi-national corporations, insurance companies, and all large institutions do in fact treat individuals as if they were elementary particles, statistically defining humans in terms of markets, services, life-expectancies.

New disciplines with titles such as motivation research and behavior modification—lumped together under the catch-phrase, human engineering—have arisen in response to the desires of advertisers to manipulate customers, industrialists to manipulate workers, politicians to manipulate citizens. The behavioral psychologist B.F. Skinner, whose theories have influenced American schools and prisons, has argued consistently since his *Walden Two* appeared in 1948 that the notion of individual freedom of the will must be abandoned. All human behavior can be—and in his utopian scheme, should be—manipulated from without. Of course historians and psychologists have searched in vain for the mathematical laws which Asimov invokes; yet whether such laws exist in reality or not, within Asimov's fiction they express the individual's sense of being manipulated by forces which he cannot resist or understand. Whatever name is given to the governing influence—the laws of history, the aliens, the computer, the government, Big Brother—the psychological root of the matter is the same.

There is another common motif in post-war science fiction which seems to contradict this vision of an administered society, and yet which registers the same feeling of the self's isolation and impotence: this is the spectre of ungovernable social and technological change. All those encounters with mutants, with aliens, with berserk computers and self-propagating monsters speak of a fear that the material world, and the creatures who populate it, have slipped the reins of reason and grown strange to us. One of the most vivid examples of this motif is offered by Michael Crichton's *Andromeda Strain* (1969), in which an extraterrestrial form of matter, lethal and benign by turns, mutates and multiplies faster than even the most highly trained scientists can cope with. In the film version of this tale, the experts watch in helpless bewilderment as images of the self-transforming Andromeda strain flash into incomprehensible new forms upon a screen.

Computers carry on a similar self-transforming mutation in the film, *Colossus: The Forbin Project* (1970), two machines speaking to each other in mathematical language which, like the Andromeda strain, bewilders the experts who are supposedly in control of the phenomenon. Gathered about the computer printers, the scientists watch helplessly as the cybernetic dialogue accelerates into mathematical spaces where no human can follow. Monsters of other sorts commoly propagate themselves in post-war science fiction, multiplying as ruthlessly as dandelions. For example, every shred of tissue hacked from the Carrot Man—who is the featured monster in a film entitled *The Thing* (1951)—will, if nurtured with human blood, produce a new mobile vegetable. The aliens in Jack Finney's *The Body Snatchers* (1954), who duplicate human bodies and then discard the originals, work through their town of victims with the accelerating pace of a chain reaction.

In numerous other fictions written since August of 1945, mutants and aliens confront us with threatening images of transformed humanity. Of course creatures with two heads and glowing eyes play upon our fear of nuclear weapons; berserk computers play upon our fear of machinery; mysterious poisons, upon our fear of ecological catastrophe. But mutation also represents a leap, a change so radical and swift that ordinary people cannot accommodate it. Long before Hiroshima, H.G. Wells arranged to have his Martians bring a red weed with them when they invaded earth in *The War of the Worlds* (1898). Once loosed on England, this weed spread with a frenzy to blanket the countryside and choke the streams. Only the authorial intervention of Wells called a halt to this maniacal vegetation. (After the bombing of Hiroshima and Nagasaki, weeds in fact did grow rampant over the ruins, crazed by radiation.) In each of the examples I have sketched, the object of the mutation—Andromeda strain, computer language, carrot man, and so on—is less important than the *fact* of mutation. The effect of all these encounters with frenzied growth and accelerating change is to enforce the sense of living in an age in which social and technological processes have escaped human control. In face of a world grown reckless, as in face of an administered society, the individual suffers impotence and anonymity.

Writing about the "Situation of the Writer in 1947," Jean-Paul Sartre argued that the violent global events of the previous two decades had forced upon himself and his contemporaries a keen awareness of historicity:

> From 1930 on, the world depression, the coming of Nazism, and the events of China opened our eyes. It seemed as if the ground were going to fall from under us, and suddenly, *for us too*, the great historical juggling began. [7]

The form of that awareness, according to Sartre's description, is similar to the view of history I have been tracing in post-war science fiction:

> our life as an individual which had seemed to depend upon our efforts, our virtues, and our faults, on our good and bad luck, on the good and bad will of a very small number of people, seemed governed down to its minutest details by obscure and collective forces, and its most private circumstances seemed to reflect the state of the whole world. All at once we felt ourselves abruptly *situated*.[8]

During the past three decades, many writers of science fiction have felt themselves situated in just this fashion. Even though their tales are usually displaced in time or space, and thus appear to evade history, they convey by form and theme the historical awareness of which Sartre speaks: manipulated by "obscure and collective forces," the self dissolves.

3. Wordsworth looked forward to a time when poets could embrace machinery in their writings as readily as they had always embraced stars and flowers and trees. He would be disappointed on this score with all of modern literature except science fiction, for in science fiction alone has machinery—and technical invention generally—become a dominant source of imagery. The significance attached to machinery within the genre has shifted in response to our experience of technology in modern society. During the thirties and early forties, when technology seemed to offer the firmest hope of escaping the Depression and defeating fascism, writers of science fiction generally honored inventors, scientists, and their creations. In its crude form this attitude was expressed as a fascination with gadgetry, in its sophisticated form as a vision of society modeled on the laboratory. Precedents for each manner of honoring science—as a collection of ingenious devices or as a habit of mind—could be found in Jules Verne and H.G. Wells, respectively. The early tales of Isaac Asimov, Robert Heinlein and Theodore Sturgeon display this generally benign view of science, and of science's technical offspring, machines.

Since 1945, however, machines have increasingly become the objects of dread in science fiction. Just as the Second World War provided writers with models for totalitarian nightmares, so it revealed the powers of destruction lurking in technology. Death had been mechanized on a fantastic scale, not only in the concentration camps, but in the bombed cities, in the submarined oceans, in the jungles and plains of four continents. No one who has recognized the effects of atomic weapons (recorded, for example, in the documentary film, *Hiroshima/Nagasaki*, and in John Hersey's report, *Hiroshima*), can preserve an unmixed faith in the benevolence of human invention. Since the war, weapons have become more devastating, automation has cheapened labor, devices such as the automobile have transformed and often degraded our environment, and industrial pollution has begun poisoning all life on the planet. Taken together, these social developments help explain why machines, once the objects of fascination, have become objects of dread in post-war science fiction. In particular, machines have focused the dread of anonymity, because they are indifferent to human personalities, whether in the factory or in war.

Before computers were more than a gleam in the eyes of technicians, writers such as John Campbell in "Twilight" (1934) and E.M. Forster in "The Machine Stops" (1909) imagined entire civilizations given over to the control of machinery, in the face of which individuals withered into anonymity. As long ago as 1916, D.H. Lawrence wrote in "The Industrial Magnate" chapter of *Women in Love* about the mining industry as a vast machine which annihilates the personality of all who work within it.[9] More recently, in Michael Frayn's *A Very Private Place* (1968), machine-dependence has been pushed so far that humans actually become captives inside their apparatus. The ruling families dwell in mechanical castles, dealing with the enslaved classes through projected images, enjoying (or perhaps suffering) a narcotized existence. Hermetically sealed inside their machines, cut off from nature and each other, they are prodded into every sensation from orgasm to meditation by chemicals.

Since the onset of the cybernetic revolution in the 1940s, computers have provided writers with a symbol for rationalized society, the electronic wizards frequently taking on the dictatorial powers of human autocrats. In Kurt Vonnegut, Jr.'s *Player Piano* (1952), for example, a computer presides over every detail of society, from marketplace to kitchen sink, becoming a kind of mechanical fate which is as impersonal and inescapable in its operation as any fate ever conceived by theologians. As a result of automation, challenging work has been transferred to machines, humanity has been divided between a managerial elite and the disenfranchised masses, the countryside has been depopulated, and life has been given over to the consumption of trinkets lacking all human purpose. Individuals have been reduced to the status of ciphers in the books of corporations and in the memory-banks of the computer. The scenario is a familiar one, both inside science fiction and outside, in industrialized society. Arthur Clarke carries the rule of the computer to its logical extreme in *The City and the Stars* (1957), where a whole society, from skyscrapers to fingernails, is projected by a central machine. Individuals are assembled atom-by-atom from the personality patterns stored in the memory-banks; each is given a life-time of one thousand years and then retired again into the computer. Until a freak emerges, who becomes the familiar rebel-against-conformity, every last detail of society, every least human gesture, is foreordained by the machine.

Totalitarian computers, and the threat to identity which they symbolize, have become as commonplace in films as in novels. Television viewers are familiar with maniacal machines from *Star Trek*, and viewers of film from such productions as *2001* (1968) and *Colossus*. In the latter film, Americans turn over control of their military system to an invulnerable computer, which links with its Russian counterpart and proceeds to govern the world, subordinating all human existence to its own cybernetic ends. A computer named HAL (an acronym removed one alphabetical notch from IBM) usurps power over a spaceship in *2001*, dispatching one-by-one the humans with whom it was designed to cooperate. Both films are typical of the genre in the mesmerized attention they pay to the running of machinery. Cameras dwell upon dials, switches, tape reels and data displays. Gadgets contrived at great expense by the special effects crew perform modernistic functions. Humans become the appendages of machines, dancing like men entranced through procedures which are more important than the characters themselves. A good deal of science fiction cinema is *about* machinery and procedures, rather than about the fates of characters (a fact generally reflected in film budgets), registering our own experience of subordination to impersonal systems in factory or office or university.

Like *Player Piano* and *The City and the Stars*, both films pit a lonesome hero against the mechanical wiles of the computer, just as Orwell and Zamyatin pit rebels against their autocrats. The parallel is an exact one, because the totalitarian computers, while of course reflecting the dominant machinery of a cybernetic age, also stand for the governmental and technological system as a whole. The individual confronts the computer as he confronts any bureaucracy: it obeys rules he cannot fathom, manipulates him in ways he cannot appeal, speaks a procedural language he cannot understand.

4. While loss of identity is represented on the social level by totalitarian computers, it is commonly represented on the individual level by the figures of robots, cyborgs, androids and zombies. These automatons are the husks of human beings, devoid of feeling and free will, mere contraptions for the carrying-out of functions which are programmed from the outside. In his famous robot stories of the 1940s, Isaac Asimov maintained a clear distinction between automatons and humans; but since that time other writers have shown themselves less confident that any such distinction exists. Thus Alfred Bester in "Fondly Fahrenheit" (1954) melds an android and its master into a composite homicidal creature which speaks by turns in the voice of man, of machine, and of a collective "we" which embraces them both. The humans who staff the army of Mars in Vonnegut's *Sirens of Titan* (1961) have radios implanted in their skulls, by means of which they may be controlled from without. They thus fulfill to perfection the ideal of mindless unanimity and precision after which merely human armies strive in vain. The title character of

Michael Crichton's novel, *The Terminal Man* (1972), combines the depersonalizing metaphors of robot and computer, for his brain becomes a computer terminal, and the character himself becomes a monstrous hybrid of human desires and mechanical powers.

Cyborgs erase all distinctions between man and machine, wedding organic and mechanical parts in the same creature. As the technology of transplants and prosthetics has grown more sophisticated, cyborgs have increased and multiplied in print and on the screen. For example, two American television series, *The Six Million Dollar Man* and *The Bionic Woman*, popular during the mid-1970s, have explored at melancholy length the exploits and dilemmas of government cyborgs. In *V.* (1963) and *Gravity's Rainbow* (1973), two mainstream novels which draw heavily upon science-fictional motifs, Thomas Pynchon uses the figure of the cyborg (together with a talking computer and radio-controlled characters) to symbolize the dehumanization which he hears screaming at him from the history of our century.

Androids, which are robots designed to look like humans, enforce the man/machine comparison even more strongly. Superficially, androids may be said to reflect existing machinery: motorists on American highways will occasionally meet with a mechanical flagman, exact to the details of blue shirt sleeves rolled up to bare sinewy forearms, tirelessly waving its red signal. But on a deeper level androids also express the dread of mechanization and anonymization. Subject to external control, lacking a past, immune to feeling, unable to strike or revolt, anonymous and interchangeable—androids and their mechanical kinfolk exactly suit the needs and express the fears of an industrialized and bureaucratized society. When Norman Mailer went to Texas and Florida to view the first moon shot, an extravaganza he describes in *Of a Fire on the Moon* (1970), he saw engineers and astronauts as just mechanical figures, priding themselves on their subordination to the space program, on their functions, on their anonymity.

Androids are indistinguishable from the figures of human beings, so common in post-war science fiction, who have been possessed by some alien power. Instead of using electrodes and wires, these invaders possess the minds of humans by means of mysterious rays, or crystals embedded in brains, or by genetic duplication. Whatever the means of possession, the effect is the same: humans are turned into automatons. A classic example of this scenario is provided by Robert Heinlein's *The Puppet Masters* (1951), in which aliens establish control over their victims by attaching themselves parasitically to the base of the skull. In Finney's *The Body Snatchers*, which Don Siegel later made into a grisly movie (*Invasion of the Body Snatchers*, 1955), aliens duplicate their human host cell-by-cell, then substitute the depersonalized replica for the original. Like androids, the transmuted creatures mimic the human originals, but they lack all emotion, obey a collective will, and devote themselves conspiratorially to spreading their control from house-to-house, town-to-town."It's a malignant disease spreading throughout the whole country," complains the cinematic doctor, the last human holdout in a town possessed by the aliens.

Exactly the same elements—invasion, possession, conspiracy—are displayed in the Cold War image of communism. The automatons resemble those monitory figures of communists portrayed by the popular media in America during the fifties and early sixties. In *Red Nightmare*, for example, filmed by Warner Brothers in 1962 for the Department of Defense, the central figure dreams that his town is taken over by the communists. After the transformation, everyone, including the hero's wife and children, looks exactly as before, but now each one lacks emotion, obeys party orders, and devotes himself single-mindedly to the state. A scene at the town square in which a Soviet officer lectures to the zombie-like citizens ("When the moral fiber of America weakens, you will seize control.") exactly parallels a scene in *The Body Snatchers*, where newly-transformed automatons are sent out to spread their disease to others.

Still the grimmest literary treatment of the loss of identity through social pressures is that offered in *1984* by Orwell, who had contemporary Britain and America in mind as well as Stalin's Russia. In the showdown scene between Winston Smith, the rebel-against-the-system, and the inquisitor O'Brien, the dread of anonymity is described in terms parallel to those we have found in the literature of invasion and possession: "We shall crush you down to the point from which there is no coming back," O'Brien declares.

> Things will happen to you from which you could not recover, if you lived a thousand years. Never again will you be capable of ordinary human feeling. Everything will be dead inside you. Never again will you be capable of love, or friendship, or joy of living, or laughter, or curiosity, or courage, or integrity. You will be hollow. We shall squeeze you empty, and then we shall fill you with ourselves. [§3:2]

Here is the emotional focus of the invasion-anxiety: the self erased, hollowed-out, filled with alien spirit.

During the years in which fictional invaders, whether from Mars or Russia, were turning ordinary folk into puppets, many people were suggesting that the denizens of Unidentified Flying Objects had invaded earth for the same nefarious purpose. Arthur Clarke drew upon the flying saucer cult in his *Childhood's End* of 1953, conquering the earth in the satanic persons of alien Overlords, who were themselves puppets of an Overmind. At the novel's climax all the children of earth, their features erased and their wills extinguished, are integrated into the collective existence of the Overmind. Individuality—along with the planet—dissolves. Flying saucer lore outside of novels and movies also commonly speaks of aliens as creatures who possess the minds of their victims, paralyzing their will, turning them into robots. John A. Keel's hyperbolic account of *Strange Creatures from Time and Space* (1970) may be taken as an illustration of this vast literature:

> An invisible phenomenon is always stalking us and manipulating our beliefs. We see only what it chooses to let us see, and we usually react in exactly the way it might expect us to react.... The central phenomenon seems to have the ability to control the human mind.... Once you begin to understand how the many parts dovetail together you will discover that the 'invisible world' has exercised a peculiar influence over the affairs of men.... It is time for us to bring all of the nonsense to an end. Time to smoke out the real culprits and tell them we do not much enjoy having our blood sucked and our brains boggled.[10]

More recently Erich Von Däniken has suggested in *Chariots of the Gods?* (1970) that humanity is the fruit of an experiment in genetics conducted by aliens who visited earth long ago in UFOs. It is unlikely the culprits will ever be discovered in the thickets of prose cultivated by Keel and Von Däniken, or by any others who postulate an "invisible world." The world responsible for the paranoia, for the fear of external control, for the dread of anonymity is the real one in which we live, made up of those institutions which define modern society.

Of course one could argue that all these tales of invasion and possession are merely symptoms of the Cold War anxiety about a communist takeover of America. But this anxiety itself has deeper social roots. We have projected onto the communists, onto flying saucer crews and aliens the distaste we feel towards our own rationalized society. The regimentation enforced by these fictional creatures is only an exaggerated version of the regimentation we experience in our present world. Towns possessed by some inscrutable collective will are nightmare versions of General Motors or the US Department of Education. The stress on conformity, the discrediting of emotion, the subordination of self to collective, are all characteristics of bureaucratic organization. Techniques of brainwashing, military indoctrination, government propaganda and commercial advertising give us reason to fear that our heads will be hollowed out, our thoughts controlled. By blaming alien powers for our loss of identity, we are able to protest against our social condition while seeming to uphold the *status quo*. To paraphrase the comic-strip character Pogo, we have met the aliens, and they are us.

5. **Monsters and supermen** are the psychological twins of robots. Just as the mechanical men symbolize conformity and anonymity, so the Abominable Snow-men, King Kongs and Creatures from the Black Lagoon, together with all the science-fictional heroes who are endowed with extraordinary powers, symbolize nonconformity and individuality. They are the eccentrics, defying laws both physical and social, insisting on their uniqueness. Dwelling on the night side of rationality, monsters are a fictional revolt against repression and regimentation. Thus an actor observes, apropos the monster from Tokyo Bay in *Godzilla* (1955), "It seems to me there are still forces in this world that none of us can understand." Whether wreak-ing havoc on Tokyo or New York or London, the monsters are enemies of order, at once the fleshly images of our own destructive impulses (the film *Forbidden Planet* of 1955 even features a "monster from the Id") and of our mutiny against a rationalized society.

Superheroes present a more complex case than monsters. Batman and Superman, for example, cooperate with the law-enforcement agencies and identify with the middle-class. Defense of property and of governmental security are their chief occupations. On his deathbed Pa Kent instructs young Clark, alias Superman, to obey the authorities. But even such establishment heroes express our yearning for individuality. Clark Kent, the mild-mannered reporter, is literally a man in grey-flannel suit, unloved by women, invisible in the city—until he strips off his disguise to reveal himself as Superman. Disguise also enables Batman to hide himself by day in the figure of an aristocrat; by night he becomes a worker of miracles. The purest example of this wish-fulfillment is provided by the comic-strip character, Captain Marvel, who is the *alter ego* of a small boy. The child, small and helpless, need only say, "Shazam!" in order to be transformed into the muscular, famous, potent superhero. There is an obvious appeal in such figures for adolescents anxious to be adults. But there is also an appeal to the adult longing for an escape from anonymity and impotence.

It is more common for superheroes in science fiction to oppose the reigning order of things. Valentine Michael Smith, the psychic wonder who arrives from Mars in Robert Heinlein's *Stranger in a Strange Land* (1961), is typical of such subversive heroes. He challenges morals, political orders, and even physical laws. In the process he has appealed to millions of readers because he is an exception, a unique individual in a society of drones. In *The Children of Dune* (1976), Frank Herbert presents us with the subversive hero Leto II, who employs his considerable psychic and physical powers to revolutionize the ecology of an entire planet. More humble in their rebellion, the central figures in *Player Piano* and *The City and the Stars* revolt against totalitarian computers; those in *1984*, *We*, *Fahrenheit 451* and *Brave New World*, against political tyranny; those in *The Body Snatchers* and *Childhood's End* against the regimented life imposed by aliens. Occasionally there are pockets of rebellion—the Spacers in *Caves of Steel*, the Travellers in *Earthworks*, the monks in *A Canticle for Leibowitz*, the sundry greenworlds and undergrounds—but these are marginal to the dominant society. Usually the search for identity is a lonely business, carried on against the current of history. The mutants who succeed humans in Clifford Simak's *City* (1952) epitomize this rebellion against conformity:

> the mutants were a different race, an offshoot that had jumped too far ahead. Men who had become true individuals with no need of society, no need of human approval, utterly lacking in the herd instinct that had held the race together, immune to social pressures. [§5]

In all these rebellious figures, struggling to become "true individuals," fighting against "social pressures," we find revealed the central predicament of characters in science fiction.

6. Identity has become problematic to science fiction because it has become problematic in modern society. We are pushed toward anonymity by bureaucracies and technology, by the scale of life in cities, by the mass media, by the techniques of manipulation perfected by government and business. To borrow a term from Max Weber, these social phenomena are the *bearers* of certain structures of consciousness, chief among them being the fear of anomie, of external control, of invisibility. Through form and theme, science fiction dramatizes this fear. It makes no more sense to condemn the genre for its seeming neglect of characterization than to praise the modernist novel for its cultivation of the isolated ego. Both are preoccupied with threats to identity in the modern world. Mainstream writers such as Thomas Pynchon, Anthony Burgess and William Burroughs, drawing upon the formal experiments of modernism and the materials of science fiction, have hybridized the two seemingly opposed traditions, revealing the shared social concerns which bind them together.

Like most significant issues in literature, the problem of identity in science fiction is not so much formal as historical. Its solution waits upon a solution to the problem of identity in society. Only when new forms of community arise, which allow for both cooperative living and richness of the self; only when technology is subjected to democratic control and humane purposes; only when cities are built on a human scale, when the machineries of government and business are dismantled and the powers which they now exercise are returned to citizens—only then will writers find it easy to imagine complex characters who are at peace with modern society. No one expects that day to come soon; many say it will never come. In the meantime, novelists must invent their own worlds, if they are to do justice both to society and the self, if they are once again to make their characters visible.

NOTES

1. *New Worlds for Old* (US 1974 xii+347), p 13.
2. *New Maps of Hell: A Survey of Science Fiction* (US 1960 161p), p 137.
3. Literature on the sociology of modernization is abundant. I have found the following texts especially useful: Peter Berger, Brigitte Berger and Hansfried Kellner, *The Homeless Mind: Modernization and Consciousness* (US 1973); Herbert Marcuse, *One-Dimensional Man: Studies in the Ideology of Advanced Industrial Society* (US 1964); H.H. Gerth and C. Wright Mills, eds., *From Max Weber* (US 1946); and David Riesman, *The Lonely Crowd* (US 1953).
4. Martha Vicinus makes a persuasive case for this view of melodrama in *The Industrial Muse* (US & UK 1974).
5. Leon Edel and Gordon N. Ray, eds., *Henry James and H.G. Wells* (US & UK 1958). See especially Wells' essay on "The Scope of the Novel."
6. *The Foundation Trilogy* (US ca. 1964), §2:7. In the same volume, his characters also speak of "The Goddess of Historical Necessity" (§2:3) and "the inevitable march of history" (§2:17).
7. *What is Literature?*, trans. Bernard Frechtman (US 1965), p 206.
8. *Ibid.*, p 207.
9. In many ways Lawrence's critique of industrialism and the "mechanical principle" prefigured the views which I have been tracing in post-war science fiction. I deal with this feature of Lawrence's thought at length in my *D.H. Lawrence: The World of the Major Novels* (US & UK 1974), §3.
10. (US 1970), pp 275, 277, 278.

David N. Samuelson

The Lost Canticles of Walter M. Miller, Jr.

(from SFS *3: 3–26, March 1976)*

Walter M. Miller, Jr., is an enigmatic figure in mid-century American science fiction. An engineer with World War II flying experience, who wrote science fiction of a technophilic variety, he also studded his stories with allusions, clear and cloudy, to the Judeo-Christian tradition, generally bathed in a generous light. A commercial writer who boasted a million words by 1955, including scripts for television's *Captain Video*, he came to write progressively more complex, sophisticated, problematic stories until, having more or less perfected his art, he stopped writing at the pinnacle of his success, at the age of 36. A Southern Catholic, born in Florida in 1923, he wrote his best-known work about a future order of monks founded in Arizona in the name of a Jewish engineer.

Miller restricted almost all of his writing to science fiction; in a short career, reaching from January, 1951, through August, 1957, forty-one stories (listed below, in the Appendix, as ##1-41) appeared in the American science-fiction magazines over Miller's by-line.[1] Three of these were later (1960) to comprise his award-winning novel, *A Canticle for Leibowitz*; three others were collected in 1962 under the title of one of them, *Conditionally Human*; and another nine were assembled in 1964 under the title *The View from the Stars* (see B1, B2, B3 in the Appendix). The two collections are out of print, as are most of the anthologies in which at least seven other Miller stories (along with nine of the fifteen in the three books) have been reprinted. A goodly number of these stories are worth looking into, either for some intrinsic value, or in connection with his best work; the themes and motifs of *Canticle* had a long period of incubation. And even Miller's worst were often better than the accumulations of words that filled up to thirty magazines in 1952 and thirty anthologies of science fiction stories in 1954.[2] Since 1957, however, Miller's name has been associated with no new science fiction, and very little writing for the public of any kind.[3] It may be that his novel obsessed him, draining off his writing energy; it may be that it set him a standard he felt unable to maintain; perhaps it expressed so well the themes which concerned him that its completion left him nothing to say. Even if other concerns entirely apart from writing took him away from science fiction, it must be inferred that his reasons involved what satisfaction he was or was not getting from writing.[4] In reviewing his career, then, it is impossible to ignore *Canticle* as the culmination of a decade's work, but it would probably be unwise to assume that everything that preceded it was in some way directed toward that final achievement.

The biographical information available on Miller is sketchy indeed: an early autobiographical sketch accompanying "Dark Benediction" in the September, 1951 issue of *Fantastic Adventures*; a brief portrait in the June 1, 1958 *Library Journal* (3:1769); an entry in Donald H. Tuck's *A Handbook of Science Fiction and Fantasy*, 2nd ed. (Hobart, Tasmania: privately published, 1959); the dust jacket of *Canticle*; and headnotes in the March, 1957, issue of *Venture*, and in anthologies edited by T.E. Dikty, Judith Merril, and William F. Nolan comprise the lot which I have been able to unearth. But his personal experiences and the ambience of the decade in which he wrote are certainly discernible in his fiction. His Southern origins, his wartime flying, his engineering education, his reading of history and anthropology, and his personal vision of his religion are all reflected in some of his stories. How his more private life might be involved is conjectural, but the social environment of America in the years following World War II is eminently visible.[5] In that war, a technological elite had come to power, had defeated an evil enemy of seemingly archetypal proportions, and had emerged with a vision of unlimited energy and growth in peacetime. Today's harbingers of ecotastrophe are one ironic result of that blind faith in progress, but the destructive use of atomic power had already shown the negative side of technology, its potential to bring about a culture with a forcibly much lower level of technology, which implied a corresponding social regression. The disillusionment of the postwar decade was not long in coming either, with the Cold War turning hot in Korea, paranoia about national security (the Rosenberg trial, McCarthyism, the blacklist in show business), suburban sameness and an obsession with conformity. Conformity, security, overpopulation, hot and Cold wars all figure in Miller's stories, though the dominant themes, an interrelated pair, are socio-technological regression and its presumed antithesis, continued technological advance. All of these he treated with respect to their social implications, particularly for the United States, but perhaps more importantly, with regard to their effect on individual behavior, including that side of behavior which can only be termed religious.

Most science fiction writers and readers would probably accede to the dictum of Leslie A. Fiedler in *Love and Death in the American Novel* (Cleveland: World, 1962, p. 478) that science fiction "believes God is dead, but sees no reason for getting hysterical about it." To be sure, an explicit role for religion is not uncommon in science fiction. Numerous writers have used the Church as a vehicle of government or a front for revolutionary activity, in other words, as a political entity. For others, religion represents a storehouse of tradition, imagery, allusions, and riddles which they have looted for its trinkets or ornaments. Occasionally, as in C.S. Lewis' trilogy, *Out of the Silent Planet*, *Perelandra*, and *That Hideous Strength*, the science fiction becomes the ornament in an unabashed exercise in popular Christianity, attacking the popular beliefs associated with materialistic science and technology. The assumption in general, however, is that serious science fiction and serious religion don't mix.[6]

This assumption also seems to have distorted critical discussions of Miller's *Canticle for Leibowitz*. Marketed simply as "a novel," it has been read as if it had little or no connection with science fiction, as if the author sprang full-blown into the literary landscape in 1960, as an apologist for, or a would-be reformer of, medieval or modern Catholicism, before the winds of change which emanated from the Vatican Council convened by Pope John.[7] Most published critiques take little note of the novel's polyphonic structure, in which other viewpoints are given almost equal time and equal weight, with a special emphasis on the viewpoint associated with science and technology.[8] Few of them have recognized his long apprenticeship in the science fiction magazines, and the continuity between the novel and what preceded it. In these stories, and I think in the novel as well, Miller comes across as an unashamed technophile, as well as a Catholic believer, however incongruous that combination may seem to opponents of either or both positions. In addition, the author is shown as a commercial writer learning his trade, willing to play along with the conventions and categories of magazine science fiction, while honing his tools so as to convert a craft into an art.

Miller's development as an artist is not as easily demonstrated as is the thematic content of his stories. The book version of *Canticle* shows decided improvements in its three parts over their magazine versions, and the story, "Conditionally Human," has been revised upward for book publication, but other changes are less obvious. Since he uses the same themes more than once, some improvement in handling can be inferred, *if* the "improved" story was actually *written* after the "rougher" draft, something which it is impossible to know, given the vagaries of magazine publishing schedules, without direct information from the author himself. There is also a tremendous difference between the first and last science fiction stories Miller published, but the progress in between is very uneven, which may not be explained simply by the fact that dates of writing and publication do not coincide. In such a short career, the chronology of publication may be of limited value. The fact that his annual publication record from 1951 to 1957 was 7, 15, 5, 5, 5, 1, and 4 stories, novelettes, and short novels does suggest one obvious break in terms of rate of production. Moreover, although his best work is spread across the decade, the first two years have more than their share of trivia, impossible to take seriously but utterly lacking in humor. By contrast, the last five years show an increase in serious subject matter and a higher value placed on humor. That he did not always write fast is evident in *Canticle*, which was at least five years in the making. But its richness is foreshadowed by the increasing complexity of his later stories, which were published if not written at a considerably slower rate: only four were published after the first Leibowitz short novel. During these years there is evidence that Miller was learning how to illustrate a point more and to preach it less, learning how to avoid the most blatantly clichéd stereotypes and conventions, learning how to concentrate the reader's interest on a single character immersed in an action the meaning of which transcends the individual. In addition, the growth of Miller's ability to utilize humor more or less parallels the change in his writing to a more complex conception of the role of characters, and a more ambiguous and problematic approach to values, culminating in that work of utmost seriousness which is little short of a "comic" masterpiece. But this change, which I see as an improvement, is gradual and uneven, not a matter of simple chronology.

In examining Miller's thematic concerns, and his maturation as an artist, I have almost disregarded the order of publication of his stories. In the pages that follow, we will begin with a rapid survey of most of his work under three thematic categories, (1) technological collapse and social regression, (2) "hard" technology and social advance, (3) "soft" or biological technology and social or psychological ambivalence; then, building on these summaries, continue with (4) a review of the role of religion in Miller's fiction and (5) a survey of his growth as an artist culminating in a more detailed examination of his best stories; and finally conclude with (6) an estimate of his accomplishment.

1. The cyclical theme of technological progress and regress which is the foundation-stone on which *A Canticle for Leibowitz* is built is present in much of Miller's earlier writing, too. Two stories foretell complete collapse of our civilization or race, two concern political stalemates in which technological progress is at least slowed, and five more involve directly the theme of rebuilding society after the collapse of technology.

The collapse stories are negligible accomplishments, both published in 1951. "The Little Creeps" describes from the viewpoint of a blustering general, how "energy creatures" from the future (tomorrow!) fail to get him to change several small actions within his control so as to avoid nuclear war and devastation of which they are a product. "The Song of Vorhu" is a grisly "love story" of a farther future in which a spaceship pilot tries to preserve some fragment of sanity and the human race from a nameless "plague"; seeking "another" resurrection of mankind, he is haunted by disembodied lines from the Bible (Abraham and Sarah, the Messiah, the Red Sea, "What is man that thou art mindful of him," "lower than angels," "to have dominion," "from the mud of Earth").

The political satires are more considerable, as fictions, if not as science fictions. "Check and Checkmate" (1953) places some promising satirical ideas in a setting so far removed from reality as to rob them of some of their sting. Extrapolating Cold War barriers forward several generations, Miller gives us an American president, John Smith XVI, who is selected rather than elected, who wears the golden mask of tragedy, and who must circulate among dozens of identical "Stand-Ins" to insure his anonymity and bodily safety. After forty years of Big Silence, he re-opens contact with the East, in the person of Ivan Ivanovitch IX, who wears a red mask (of Lenin), who literally "faces" Smith down (without masks) and who invites him to an Antarctic summit. While Congress convenes to conduct a "witch hunt," bringing thousands to "justice" for breaches of security, both sides trade charges but continue negotiations. Planning to launch an attack on the day of their meeting, Smith shows up with an explosive device strapped to his chest, only to find out what Ivan had meant when he said a certain discovery had eliminated both the need for "atomics" and the existence of the proletariat: Ivan himself is a robot. Miller makes no attempt at realism, maintaining only the tiniest bit of suspense before the manifest ability of technology, even when it is suppressed, to transcend security precautions conclusively reduces to the absurd that preoccupation of the Cold War era. "Vengeance for Nikolai" (1957) is only minimally science fiction, with no extrapolated technology, rather an implicit standstill. A tale of bizarre assassination, it concerns a Russian girl who carries poison in her breasts for the brilliant general of the American "Blue Shirt" invading forces. Marya is a creature of legend, Miller indicates, whose sheer intensity of purpose seems to get her through the lines without much damage. No didacticism, except for the warning against American fascism, detracts from the purity of her mission, vengeance for her dead baby channeled into an act of heroism on behalf of the Fatherland.

Miller's first attempt at the theme of regression, "The Soul-Empty Ones," is a confusing blood-and-thunder melodrama, the coincidences of the plot shattering a degree of credibility built up by the relatively sensitive handling of character and exposition. Primitive tribesmen on Earth are caving in to invaders from the sky, except for one, whose fortunes we follow, as he discovers his identity as an "android," and helps to rescue the "true men" from their Martian masters who have brought them back to resettle Earth. The rendering of primitive ritual and the determination of Falon to rise above submission to tradition are done reasonably well, but the distance to technological mastery is too great to be overcome with any believability.

In "The Reluctant Traitor," Miller's viewpoint character is an intruder in the primitive society, a human on Mars who rebels against a restrictive city-state which forbids fraternizing with the natives. In exile, he learns more about the "androons," who turn out to be humans whose forebears came as Martian captives, and manages to reverse their defensive posture and to overturn the city government. The conclusion seems to promise an open frontier society like the Old West, but with a higher level of technology and some brotherly love, or at least mutual tolerance. The action is terrifically fast-paced, including some sexual and sado-masochistic titillation, but the conversion of the primitive androons on their flying bats into conquerors of a high-technology city-state is just not convincing.

Miller's best variation on this theme is his shortest, "It Takes a Thief" (reprinted as "Big Joe and the Nth Generation"). Earth is no longer, and the remnants of Martian colonists have fallen back into scattered tribes which keep ancient knowledge fragmented by restricting it to ritualistic sayings "owned" one to a person. Asir has "stolen" the sayings of others, and has put enough together in his mind to realize that a catastrophe threatens unless the people regain control over the technology governing their life-support system. At the story's beginning, he narrowly misses execution for theft and, not having learned his lesson, takes off with his girl friend on a flying "huffen" (jet-propelled by means of bellows-like lungs) for the sacred vaults. Hotly pursued, he nevertheless deciphers the system by which to get past the ancient robot guard (Big Joe) which kills one of his pursuers. Having advanced from the paradigm of magic to that of science, however primitive, he can now use the robot (technology) to help bring his tribe up to the knowledge which will be needed within twelve Mars-years to save the world.

The same story is told still another way in "Please Me Plus Three," which takes place on Earth, where the survivors of the catastrophe are primitives who worship Bel (the Bell communications satellite, whose pylons are cult centers). Another exiled hero, Ton, is befriended by outcasts, this time a band of wandering monks, who have kept alive some knowledge of the true nature of Bel and of the history of human society. He escapes from them, too, and after edging through an area irradiated by Bel's peace-keeping efforts and coming upon some misshapen mutants, manages to take control of a repair-robot who has been waiting over 500 years for equipment and orders to fix pylon G(eorge)-86. Returning home "riding on an ass's colt," Ton overpowers, with the help of George, the guardian of pylon G-80, and directly challenges Bel. The confrontation is partly electrical, partly mystical, as Ton and Bel seem to exchange personalities, so that Bel can be made to feel pain and, punished, explode. Restoration of human civilization apparently can proceed, but how we got to this point and through it is not at all clear.

Finally, in "The Yokel," Miller takes up a much less devastating and more localized case of regression. Technological haves and have-nots in the city and country, respectively, are at odds in a post-catastrophe low-grade kind of warfare. The hero's equivocal actions take him to both sides of the border on land and in the air (he's a frustrated veteran pilot), as a good sense of Northern Florida local color comes through. Although the hero's survival may be in doubt, through all of the melodramatic maneuverings, the city's victory never seems threatened. Its power supports a dilute utopian ideal of technological society without the problems posed by anti-technological inhabitants, who are kept outside. Undigested anthropology (Ruth Benedict) fails to supply a rationale for all of this action, but the hero's opportunism is fairly convincing; from the beginning, he longs for a world in which "things work" again.

2. In none of these stories is there any hint that technological progress itself is to blame for the past or coming cataclysm, rather some shadowy kind of mismanagement seems to be responsible. No credible character argues against progress, and the most positive characters are always involved in rebuilding or at least preserving some semblance of technological civilization. In another dozen or so stories, technological advance is extrapolated from our present situation and, if not slavishly approved, at least favorably treated. Five of these tales treat what is perhaps the favorite of all science fiction themes, man's getting into space. Six are concerned with controlling technology, which to some extent means being controlled by technology. In two stories, faith in technology is taken to almost mystical heights.

"No Moon for Me" is a shaggy-dog story, about a hoax that comes true. A voice from the moon has by its presence challenged mankind to get there, in order to confront the alien invaders. But the ship which is launched, amid prayers, last-minute instructions, and self-congratulations ("space opens tonight"), has one man on it who seems to desire its destruction. Colonel Denin, father of the American space program, was responsible for planting the voice's transmitter, and his martyrdom is narrowly averted by the pilot, Major Long. Denin's disgrace is also averted, however, because Long discovers alien footprints around the earlier rocket, and signs of another ship. As the third crew member, Dr. Gedrin, whimpers in his terror, "no moon for me," representing those who do not want space travel, Long mutters to him, the Colonel, and us: "You've got it, fellow. Like it or not."

"Cold Awakening" is a heavily melodramatic story of cops-and-robbers, plot-and-counterplot on board a starship about to take off on a 500-year journey with its occupants in suspended animation. Enmities build, unfounded rumors fly, and the "number two fuse," the back-up man who would be awakened in case of trouble (and die, long before arrival), is killed. Joley, the "main fuse," whose story this is, engages in some clever detective work, but lucks into the solution. Morphine addicts (a pet peeve of editor John Campbell's) plan to wake up early and live it up, unable to face withdrawal on landing. Joley narrowly escapes a plot on his life and, thanks to a kind of shell game with the leads to the three fuses' cold lockers, the evil Dr. Fraylin is cooked instead. The bad guys punished, the ship can depart, with Joley "promoted" to the status of colonist, and new "fuses" installed. The whole thing is very silly, the technological situation seemingly invented in order to make an irrational plot vaguely plausible, and to justify a tirade against drugs.

A kind of prose poem, "The Big Hunger" more or less establishes a rationale for some of Miller's other stories of man's evolution. A lyrical flight of fancy about space exploration, ostensibly narrated by the "spirit of adventure," this story alternates florid rhetoric and sentimental vignettes to take us far into the future, through several pendulum swings of expansion and contraction, as waves of explorers leave this world and others, while those who are left behind make peace with the land. A Stapledonian chronicle in miniature, it is largely successful in evoking that longing which Germans call *Fernweh* and one of the characters calls "the star-craze," a hunger which has always echoed through science fiction and which no amount of details about real space travel can ever satisfy. Echoes of this story, or of the concept it tries to dramatize, can be heard in the regression stories, in stories of human evolution, and in two elegies for the loss by certain individuals of the "freedom" of space.

"Death of a Spaceman" (usually reprinted as "Memento Homo") is a corny farewell to a man whose decrepit body lies in bed while his mind and his yearnings remain in space. Old Donegal is rough-tongued and cantankerous, a renegade Catholic who knows he's dying but tries to humor his wife and the inevitable priest. Although he accepts reluctantly the administration of the last rites, his farewell ritual is hearing one last blastoff from the not-too-distant spaceport, for which a party next door is quieted down, and after which a solitary trumpeter plays "Taps." Miller admits he "translated" into science fictional terms the story of an old railroad man of his acquaintance, but the tale's sentimentality is effective despite the transparent manipulations.[9]

A more ambitious version of the same theme is "The Hoofer." A more active character, Hogey Parker is also rambunctious and querulous, an unintentionally comic character on Earth, where he has come home one last time after squandering in a poker game and on alcohol his earnings as a touring entertainer (a tumbler or hoofer). Using Hogey's drunken condition as a vehicle, the story uses flashbacks to cram a lot of detail into a small space. Although he is disagreeable. he earns some sympathy because of his genuine hunger for what he has lost, because he is a fish out of water, and because in his drunken stupor he stumbles into wet cement which hardens during the night and denies him any chance of ever returning to space. This story is also a kind of "translation"—Hogey could be an Earthside entertainer—but the sense of future advances, though on the periphery, is definitely present, counterpointed by the backward wasteland which is his home on Earth.

By contrast to the peripheral role played by technology in those two stories, "I Made You" is a pure "sorcerer's apprentice" sketch, about a war machine on the moon which kills anyone who comes within its range, including one of its programmers, because its control circuits are damaged. The reactions and "feelings" of Grumbler are included from one of several viewpoints, but no one or thing seems to matter very much. A more conventional *Astounding* puzzle-story, with Campbellian disdain for anti-technology forces, is "Dumb Waiter," an early attempt at comedy. In a future when cities have become completely automated, but people have been driven out of them by a war their machines continue to fight even without ammunition, Mitch Laskell enters one city to try to restore sanity to the man-machine interface. Whereas the crowd wants to destroy the central computer, Mitch, with his engineering background and technophilic orientation, only wants to reprogram it. To make the problem more urgent, Miller not only has the city threatening him, with its blind obedience to outmoded laws; he also introduces a young woman and child Mitch must try to rescue, while the crowd of Luddites are only one jump behind him. The behavior of this ingenue and of the villain seems to be turned on and off by a switch in the author's hand, Mitch's solution to the problem hardly requires "enlightened" cerebration, and the whole piece is a thinly disguised lecture on the need for men to learn to understand machines, so as to keep them in their place. A bit of slapstick action, in the simple-minded actions of the city and its robot cops, presumably is supposed to turn into gallows humor, but it is difficult to take anything here seriously enough for that.

Even more of a lecture, but one which seems to be heartfelt, and is not compromised by much in the way of "story values," is "Way of a Rebel," with the same protagonist, published two years later. Now a Navy lieutenant aboard a one-man submarine, Mitch rejects orders to return to port when the autocratic American government issues an ultimatum to the Soviets. Unable to participate in the destruction of technological civilization (cf. "The Yokel"), he feels no compunction, however, about "destroying the destroyers," an oncoming fleet of Soviet submarines of which the American command is unaware, and sacrifices his own life in the process.

In three of his best stories, Miller sides with those who are to some extent victims of technological progress, in their coming to terms with the presumed advance of civilization. "Crucifixus Etiam," his best short piece, shows us a day laborer on Mars, whose lungs are being sacrificed to the dream of making Mars air breathable for colonists within a thousand years. This story will be examined later in more detail, as will "The Darfsteller," the Hugo-award-winning short novel about an ageing ham actor displaced by lifesize mannequins in a mechanized theatre of the future, and his attempt to beat the new technology at its own game. Not quite as successful is "The Lineman," Miller's last published story, a "day in the life" of a worker on the Moon. In contrast to the "tragedies" of Manue Nanti and Ryan Thornier in the stories above, Relke's experience is dark comedy, about the time a travelling whorehouse came from Earth and put the work force off schedule. Not everything is lighthearted—Relke is threatened and beaten up by labor goons, two men are killed (one in a well-executed scene of "black humor," when he takes a bottle of champagne from the whores' ship into airless space)—but the general tone is one of achievement, not just survival, in the midst of ever-present danger. Though the line crew of the Lunar Power Project get to take a brief vacation, they are reminded forcibly that Lunar interdependence can not tolerate an Earthly margin of error or freedom. As one result of this venture in free enterprise, more women presumably will be allowed to come from Earth, but Relke personally learns something more fundamental from this series of mishaps. Besides educating him about sex and politics, this episode has taught him that "there was a God," whose creations of the universe and of human beings were on pretty equal footing.

This sense of faith is carried to extremes in two earlier stories. In "The Will," the impending death of a child is thwarted by his faith in the ability and the willingness of future time travellers to rescue and cure him after digging up his buried stamp collection. Although the premise is uncomfortably silly, the story is almost rescued by its mundane details: the parents' grief, the boy's addiction to the *Captain Chronos* television show, and the public relations use to which he is put by the program's star and producers (based presumably on Miller's own experiences with *Captain Video*). Technology veers into the supernatural, not just in the eyes of primitives, but in those of a computer scientist, in "Izzard and the Membrane." A Cold War melodrama, replete with brainwashing, counter-espionage, and the scientist's defection, this short novel is full of action, much of it vague, that ends when the hero saves the West almost single-handedly. Some of the vagueness may be excusable, since one of the characters, the spiritual part of an "electronic brain" (i.e. the "membrane" attached to "Izzard" or "Izzy"), turns out to be God, or a reasonable analog. Enabling the hero to win, it then transports his "transor" (soul), and those of his immediate family, into a parallel universe, with orders to "increase and multiply."

3. As some of these stories show, Miller is not always sure that the fruits of technology will be as delicious as the planners contend, but the drive to progress is not to be halted, as it was in the stories of regression. In all cases, however, the technology was "hard," based primarily on the physical sciences. The Church, which has pretty much given up most claims to insert morality into physical science, has a much greater stake in the futures mankind is offered by the biological sciences. Correspondingly, questions of biological "advance" Miller treats with more circumspection; "progress" is a much more ambivalent quality in his "biological" stories. Seven of these concern intelligent aliens, all dangerous to man, some of which are clearly negative symbols of possible paths of man's biological progress. Two stories, one of them involving aliens, concern the temptation and threat of telepathy. Seven others focus on other questions of possible human evolution, whether natural or forced, a distinction that breaks down under analysis.

Aliens were featured in "The Song of Vorhu," "The Soul-Empty Ones," and "No Moon for Me," and the possibility of aliens, or at least Unidentified Flying Objects, is a significant motif in "The Lineman," but few details are given. Details are also a little sparse in some of the other stories but the menace is plain enough. "The Space Witch" has hypnotic powers that disguise her true form from Kenneth Johnson, and allow her to masquerade as his estranged wife (who in fact has just drowned). Hunted by other aliens, she seeks refuge, endangering the Northeastern United States, but Ken, after a glimpse of her "true self" (with tentacles), hijacks her ship, condemning them to each other for good. Almost as jejune are three other alien stories. "The Triflin' Man" (reprinted as "You Triflin' Skunk") is an alien father of an Earth child who is coming to claim his offspring, causing the child nightmares and severe headaches. The child's mother, however, a Southern country woman, drives away her one-time seducer with a shotgun.

"Six and Ten are Johnny" finds humans from the exploratory starship "Archangel" invading aliens. The planet "Nun" is inhabited by a world-girdling intelligent plant which ingests and learns to replicate humans. When it separates one of its progeny to make the trip back to Earth, it plans to take over that world from its unsuspecting hosts. Another alien who ultimately turns out to be dangerous, indirectly, is the "Martian" in "The Corpse in Your Bed is Me" (written in collaboration with Lincoln Boone). His sense of humor is so bizarre that a successful television comic feels compelled to make him laugh. Failing repeatedly, he declines and disappears, only to return, dead, as the only sure way to produce a Martian laugh. The "Martian" does not make the story science fiction, however, and the overall air of unreality turns what might have been humorous into an insipid enigma.

"Secret of the Death Dome," Miller's first published story, is also insipid, a melodramatic shoot-out between invading Martians, whose dome floats harmlessly, but impregnably above the Southwestern desert, and an Army sergeant seeking revenge for the castration-killing of his best friend, the husband of the girl he's always loved. If the story has any importance at all, it's because of the Martians' problems with reproduction; reversing the usual insect dependence on queens, they have only three ageing males left, one of which the hero kills, as he rescues the girl and drives the menace off-planet. Biological specialization is not limited to sex in the more promising "Let My People Go." An "ark" full of human colonists finds Epsilon Eridani II is inhabited, and a cavern on its moon offers evidence that human captives had once been brought from Earth. Three mismatched envoys accept an invitation to visit the planet where they discover the inhabitants have bred and trained other animals, including humans, to serve them as communication systems, organic building materials, even as food sources (including humans!). Rage, as in "Death Dome," enables one returning envoy to break a hypnotic block so as to provide the colonists with the key to their gaining a foothold on the planet. They release the "vermin" they carry aboard ship, and the overspecialized *Piszjil* are forced to deal with those who know how to control the pests.

Although telepathy may not be a case of overspecialization, as a potential human talent, it may be said to represent a projected step in human evolution. Aside from "Gravesong" and "Let My People Go," in which it is a simple communication convenience, telepathy figures in only three of Miller's stories. In "Bitter Victory," *psi* powers are possessed by aliens who use them to assume human form and to stalk each other on Earth. The story involves their becoming too attached to human forms, ways, and emotions, so that when the final conflict comes (one of mental powers but rendered in terms of physical effects), they find themselves both crippled—one blind, one lame—and they seem to accept each other, love, and human form. A recurrent phrase, "for the love of man," underlines the implication of man's moral superiority to these more "advanced" life forms. In "The Wolf Pack," dreams of an American airman turn out to be telepathic messages from a girl in the town of Perugia, Italy, over which he must fly another bombing raid. Religious allusions ("jovial Wotan," "through crucifixion came redemption," "o my people," and a more or less literal "for God's sake") stud Lt. Mark Kessel's wrestling with his conscience. His observation that the existence of his pack of fighter planes is "paradoxical proof that men by nature are cooperative beings" does not do much to salve his conscience when he gets the last message from the girl, dying amid flames and rubble: "If you had known...would all have been spared for the sake of one?" As in these stories, telepathic sharing seems to bring about more pain than good in "Command Performance," a slick satire in the *Galaxy* mode which will be discussed later.

If man is destined, as "The Big Hunger" claims, to expand outward from Earth in waves of exploration and conquest, human evolution may take some strange jumps. This is the subject of two stories of the far future. The slighter piece, "Gravesong," is an elegy for man as he was (i.e. is now), vaguely satirizing two possible paths he may take. Emilish, returning the ashes of his mother to ancient Earth, meets the grave-tender, Eva, whose *anima*-like beauty marks her as a throwback from the mud-creatures which men on Earth have become. Amid memories of the galactic corporate state from which he comes, and the contrast stressed by Eva that she is a creature of earth and he is a creature of space, he ponders the warning of his mother that, given unlimited power, "Man is no longer man," and wonders what he is.

Two other paths are suggested in "The Ties that Bind," a puzzle-story of a sort which pits a pacifist Earth society, twenty thousand years from now, against the militarism of a fleet using the planet as a refueling station (its resources apparently not having been exhausted) en route to a battle somewhere else. Using the old ballad, "Edward," as a backdrop—five stanzas serve as epigraphs to the story's five sections—Miller develops these antithetical milieus and psychologies, emphasizing their mutual incomprehension and their ironic interrelations. Only the fleet's cultural Analyst, Meikl, seems to have a firm grasp of what's happening: he and the narrator call it *Kulturverlängerung*, the power of unconscious vestiges of man's culture. Like Cassandra, however, he is not understood in time. Desertions and rebellion by some crewmen become a problem before long. Then another piece of the puzzle is supplied when an Earthman picks up a sword which he does not intend to use and finds that it seems to "fit" his hand; his muscles, affected by *Kulturverlängerung*, seem to recognize an affinity for the weapon. The real problem is that the descendants of this Eden-like Earth carry within them an inner Hell with which Earth once infected the galaxy. And even the now "innocent" Earthmen are potential killers, although that potential is not realized at this time; evolution has not changed the fact that Man is subject to this version of "original sin."

If these stories represent natural evolution, the same is not unequivocally true in "Blood Bank," in which Terrans play the role of the heavy. In this *Astounding* space opera, moral indignation runs high as one puzzle: what did Commander Roki do wrong? (he ordered the destruction of an Earth ship carrying "surgibank" supplies to a disaster-stricken planet, because the ship would not stand by for inspection) gives way to another: how will Commander Roki vindicate himself, so as not to have to commit suicide as the code of his world demands of his honor? Admirably controlling suspense as Roki gradually uncovers the clues, Miller keeps us from doing the same until we have learned the particulars of this milieu and have accepted to some extent a degree of cultural relativism which most of the characters in the story do not have. Each cultural idiosyncracy is embodied in a person and rooted in some physical, biological, or cultural peculiarity of his or her world. Although the heart of the adventure is conquest of the "Solarians," a predatory race evolved on Earth which uses standard humans as medical supplies to trade for nuclear fuel and a fascist renaissance, the story's center of interest is not in Earth, its legendary past or aborted future. Nor is it in the comic confrontation between Roki and the female pilot from a frontier world whose rickety cargo ship transports him to the Sol solar system. The primary concern is the solving of puzzles, from the technological (faster-than-light drive, reaction engine limits, ship-to-ship grapples) to the anthropological (humanity's alleged origin on Earth, the amount of space an empire can govern, how much diversity a widespread civilization can and must tolerate). These cross at the point of conflict between non-Earth humans and Solarians; not being human, the latter threaten humanity, an implicit act of war which tolerance for local customs and local biological variation cannot encompass. Common romantic and melodramatic motifs are employed for surface excitement, but the real interest is more of a cerebral nature, with the moral concern for intraspecies savagery almost a side-issue.

Although the evolution in that story may have occurred naturally, the evolved Solarians ensured their "superiority" by means of brute strength, greying the distinction between natural and forced evolution. Two other examples of forced evolution, which may not be against nature, but which important characters see as unnatural, are a pair of poor stories about cyborg spaceships, employing the brains of human "children." Whereas other writers have seen this process as a means by which cripples might live useful lives, Miller emphasizes the inhumanity of their existence by emphasizing the children's innocence and the despair of ostensibly sympathetic mother figures. The condemnation of the practice of using human brains to complement computer logic in piloting spaceships seems to come from an irrational base which is at least peripherally doctrinal. In "A Family Matter," the woman is a stowaway (of all things) who claims to be his mother, lamenting her loss of *twenty years* ago, and raging at him, threatening his "flesh-organ." In self-defense, he accelerates too fast, killing both her and his human part, and, having lost all sense of identity and responsibility, heads out to nowhere, instead of returning to base from this "test" of his abilities, which has also turned into a test of his "humanity." In "I, Dreamer," the early training of a child to distinguish between self, semi-self, and nonself, though effective, seems grafted on. The story proper, again told by the cyborg, is a ridiculous mish-mash of revolutionary politics and melodramatic seduction, with a little sadism mixed in. It is ended by the narrator's empathy for the girl's pain and his longing to be a "Two-Legs" forever, which for some odd reason causes him to plummet into the palace of the dictator, even as the secret police are rounding up all the revolutionary conspirators. Inherent in the basic situation is only a little pathos; Miller, in trying to exploit the "horror" of this man-machine interface, was forced to introduce melodramatic conflicts which make both stories ludicrous. Yet he thought the idea worth two stories, and even reprinted one of them in his collection of short fiction, suggesting that the idea, at least, of forced evolution presented in them was of some importance to him.

4. In two other, longer tales, which will be examined in more detail later, Miller is more successful in raising hard "religious" questions about "forced" evolution, while telling convincing stories in an effective, symbolic manner. "Conditionally Human" questions man's right to play God with life and death and the fate of "lower" animals. "Dark Benediction" asks how humanity would respond to a gift from the skies promising great powers, if it also demanded a physical change of the color and texture of the skin.

Both stories explicitly involve religious questions and symbolism, and feature Catholic priests in advisory, but fallible, roles. Miller's other works may not be as permeated with his religion, but its effect is apparent. Catholic priests are characters in "No Moon for Me," "Crucifixus Etiam," and "Please Me Plus Three." Primitive priests are negative figures in the last-named, and in "It Takes a Thief" and "The Reluctant Traitor," where they represent stagnant tradition in the way of progress. Prayer is explicit in "No Moon for Me," "Death of a Spaceman," "The Triflin' Man," "The Lineman," and "The Wolf Pack," and implicit in "The Will" and in "Izzard and the Membrane" which features God as or in a computer. Scriptural tags are employed in "Izzard,"

"The Song of Vorhu," "Crucifixus Etiam," "The Lineman," "The Wolf Pack," and "Let My People Go." Religious titles and imagery are apparent in "Six and Ten are Johnny," "Grave Song," "Crucifixus Etiam," "Memento Mori" ("Death of a Spaceman"), "No Moon for Me," "The Song of Vorhu," "Izzard and the Membrane," "The Soul-Empty Ones," "The Reluctant Traitor," "It Takes a Thief," "Please Me Plus Three," and "The Ties That Bind." And Christian doctrine may be instrumental in "A Family Matter," "I, Dreamer," and "Blood Bank" as well as in the "original sin" stories, "Grave Song," "The Ties that Bind," "Conditionally Human," and "Dark Benediction."

Hardly an obligatory convention, like the boy-girl romances and repulsive villains Miller brings in occasionally, religion (especially the Roman Catholic version of Christianity) usually has a negative connotation in science fiction. Miller's primitive priests are conventional in that way. But the priest in "Death of a Spaceman" is a sympathetic figure, as are those in "Conditionally Human" and "Dark Benediction," while the clergy in "No Moon for Me" and "Crucifixus Etiam" are neutral tones in the moral landscape. Christian doctrine does suggest a bass tone of conviction as a contrast to the uncertainty of modern man, a role it plays convincingly in *A Canticle for Leibowitz*. But the doctrine or its exponent, as in Miller's novel, may be naïve, lacking in understanding of the whole picture, or otherwise irrelevant. The exponent need not be nominally religious, either: although the psychiatrist in "Command Performance" can not play this role because his advocacy of conformity is so much a part of the conventional milieu of the Fifties, the Analyst in "The Ties that Bind" *is* a reasonable facsimile of a priestly *raisonneur* because of the antiquity of his anthropological teaching, which predates in a sense the secular humanism of that story's Eden-like Earth.

For the technophilic Miller, unlike the technophobic C.S. Lewis, the direct opposition of science and religion won't do, at least not if it means the downgrading of science and technology. They represent for him the best that we can do today and in the foreseeable future, when it comes to knowledge and concrete achievement. As in *A Canticle for Leibowitz*, however, religion suggests a kind of wisdom, traditional, irrational, humane, which knowledge alone can not reach, but a kind of wisdom which, divorced from social and technological, and even aesthetic reality, is also inadequate as a guide for conduct. It complements the engineering question, How, with the age-old poetico-religious question, Why, even if it does not reveal *the* Answer. At the least, its presence in a Miller story indicates continuity with the present, and by implication, a universal need of mankind. At best, the religious connotation of the parable—and most of Miller's stories are parabolic in their didacticism—underlines the moral ambiguity of a situation, its need for a moral resolution. When the mass of American and British science fiction magazines were topheavy with laboratories, machines, and the "social" effects of science and technology (i.e. the effects of hypothetical inventions and discoveries on "masses" of people), Miller was one of a handful of writers concerned with effects on individuals, who stand alone, lacking the kind of certainty that only dogma can provide, and aware of both the lack and the inadequacy of the outmoded dogma.

5. Philosophy, or sententious content, does not by itself make a story or a writer, of course. On other counts, Miller was neither consistent nor outstanding. Writing for science fiction magazines, he had to keep in mind the prejudices of their editors and readers, if he were going to sell his stories even at their low rates of pay. One thing he had to do was to keep the story moving, often at the expense of character, structure, or even logical coherence, and many if not most of his stories suffer from that requirement. The melodrama has not worn well. His best, however, seem to have incorporated that principle of efficient story-telling without harm to their integrity.

If he were writing for *Astounding* or *Galaxy*, the highest-paying markets, he had to try to please their editors. John Campbell's technophilia was congenial, and his predilection for the puzzle-story could have dictated the writing of "Blood Bank," among others. Other Campbell buttons probably were pushed by "No Moon for Me" (space at any cost), "Izzard and the Membrane" (Cold War hostilities, brainwashing, and defecting scientists), and "Cold Awakening" (the horror of drugs). The man-machine interface dominated "Dumb Waiter," "I Made You," and "The Darfsteller," which Campbell bought along with the mood-pieces, "Crucifixus Etiam" and "The Big Hunger." Mood may also have caught Campbell's eye in "The Soul-Empty Ones," which is otherwise a good example of Miller's bad handling of melodrama, something that stands out in most of the stories published before 1954.

Horace Gold at *Galaxy* preferred satire, which "Conditionally Human" and "Command Performance" powerfully exhibit, as Miller's only sales to that magazine. Other attempts at satire, possibly written for *Galaxy*, but published elsewhere, were less successful: "Check and Checkmate," "Bitter Victory," "The Triflin' Man," "The Hoofer," and "The Corpse in Your Bed is Me."

The predilection of Anthony Boucher and his successors at *The Magazine of Fantasy and Science Fiction* and its short-lived sister publication, *Venture*, were for careful writing and characterization, when they could get them. The three parts of *Canticle* were published in *F&SF* as was "The Lineman"; *Venture* printed "Vengeance for Nikolai" and "The Corpse in Your Bed is Me," both of which are only borderline science fiction, but enigmatic character-studies and a bit shocking for the Fifties (*Venture*'s editorial policy favored material which was "strong" for the times). That six of Miller's last nine publications were with Mercury Press is indicative of the turn his writing had taken toward "human" stories, less crowded with incident, more concerned with values.

Melodrama was dominant in his 1951 stories, except for "Dark Benediction." "The Secret of the Death Dome" is a traditional Western with a Gothic twist, and incompletely visualized action, a problem which beset several of Miller's early stories. The world was saved in four of those first seven tales, by implausible means, implausibly and humorlessly described. Overplotting and cardboard stereotypes ruined "The Reluctant Traitor," "Cold Awakening," "Dumb Waiter," and "Let My People Go" in 1952, though the last-named has its moments and is almost long enough not to buckle under the weight of events. Sentimentality is another risk he took frequently, especially with irrelevant love-interests, but also with whole stories, such as "The Song of Vorhu," "Bitter Victory," "Grave Song," the cyborg stories, "The Wolf Pack," and "The Will," using it to good advantage only in "The Big Hunger," "Death of a Spaceman," and "Conditionally Human." From the humorlessness of his earliest travesties, Miller proceeded to satire as early as 1952, but a more feeling kind of humor does not show up until "Death of a Spaceman" in 1954, after which it is featured in more of his stories than it is not. He was always concerned with values, and even found successful aesthetic vehicles to express them as early as 1951 ("Dark Benediction," and, published just after the turn of the year, "Conditionally Human"), but not with the richness and ambiguity only humor can supply.

In his best stories, Miller managed to combine thought and action, to make ideas personal and involving, by approaching a universal ("truth") or problem by means of strong identification with an individual, who must demonstrate an important decision by means of an action, the significance of which is underscored by the fact that there is not a lot of action for action's sake cluttering up the pages. One exception is "The Big Hunger," in which mankind as a whole is the protagonist, but it holds for the sentimental or near-sentimental "Death of a Spaceman" and "The Hoofer," for the melodramatic "It Takes a Thief" and "Blood Bank," for "The Lineman" and "The Ties That Bind," which just miss being in the first rank. And it definitely holds for those stories which are in the first rank.

"Command Performance" is a very human story of suburban loneliness and conformity, and the conviction of Lisa (Miller's only female protagonist except for Marya in "Vengeance for Nikolai") that she is rightfully different from the conventional image to which her husband and her analyst want her to conform. Telepathic communication with another, which should convince her that she is right, instead upsets her terribly; she is to some extent attached to that conventional image she wishes to reject. She can only accept her talent after she has used it herself to fend off the "attacker" who wants to mate with her to perpetuate a super-race. The scenes of her communication with him are rendered well, from his discovery of her, dancing naked in the rain in her backyard; to his prevention of her calling the police, by means of illusion, causing her to see things that are not there; to her own switch from passive reception to active sending, as she stops his physical progress towards her by means of imaginary cars in the street. He pushes on, disregarding them, only to be killed by a real automobile, leaving her safe but empty again, and this time knowing why. Lisa wastes no time on remorse; she begins, as her would-be ravisher presumably once did, tentatively questing in the telepathic "communication band" for someone else like her. Her prospective mate and his plans for a race of supermen are melodramatic, but Lisa's character and situations are real enough and realistically presented, with the kind of satire of contemporary mores (conformity and all that) for which *Galaxy* was noted.

In "Conditionally Human," Terry Norris, a veterinarian, cares for animals whose intelligence has been increased to put them midway between pets and children (children are rare, because of restrictive population laws), and his occupation upsets his newlywed wife whose maternal reflexes are strong. Terry's crisis point is an order to destroy certain "units," in this case "neutroids" (apes transmuted into baby girls with tails), which exceed the allowable intelligence limits. After Terry has located one of these units, named Peony, and taken it away from its "Daddy," a petshop owner, he is visited by Father Paulson (Father Mulreany in the book version) on behalf of his bereft parishioner. The priest acts reluctantly as a moral guide for the unreligious Terry, who uses him as a sounding board, then goes to excesses not sanctioned by the priest. He not only hides the illegal "deviant," but he also kills, by a carefully planned "accident," his supervisor who has come to see that the order and the "neutroid" are executed. Then he decides to take a new job with the company that produces "newts," to carry on the work of the fired employee who made the newts not only too intelligent, but also functionally, biologically human.

In a society forced by population pressures to restrict the freedom to breed, there are many malcontents, from Terry's wife and the priest, to pet owners who identify themselves as parents, to the kind of technician who "humanized" the newts. In this situation, Terry finds himself "adapting to an era," at first to the status quo, but then to the possible future that an artificially created race might bring about. Either choice requires a kind of moral toughness and seems to demand that he kill, if not Peony then supervisor Franklin. By contrast, the priest could never sanction murder, though he may be an indirect cause of one; he finds the creation of the neutroids an abomination but their destruction possibly even more so. Peony has an edge on Man, since she "hasn't picked an apple yet," in the words of the priest, i.e. she is not tainted by original sin (compare the reading of a play fragment in Part Two, and the consecration of Rachel in Part Three of *Canticle*). But Miller seems determined to stretch the Church's teachings to the limit; what if you *have* to choose between murders? Terry and Anne both make that choice—*she* threatens to kill *him*—on behalf of the freedom to breed or "create," but the reader, having been taken only part way down that path of argumentation, is left with a moral ambiguity. The satire (*Galaxy* again) cuts both ways, but seems aimed at the kind of society which makes such choices necessary.

Heavy with implications, the story is not weighty in a ponderous sense; things happen too fast for that. Miller sets the stage with a honeymoon quarrel, sends Terry off on a collecting mission, and intersperses social background and lampoons of oversensitive "mothers" before we even find out what a neutroid is. Before the first, "unimproved" batch die, Anne risks too much attachment to them by feeding them *apples*; she also declares her intention to risk an illegal baby of her own. Scenes flash by, such as Terry's conversations with the police chief, with Anne, with "Doggy" O'Reilly (Peony's "Daddy"); tension builds, Peony is shown to be adorable, and the die is cast. Though the moralizing increases, the pace never flags. The end finds the Norrises waiting it out, aware that they are pitting themselves against society. Quixotically they pursue a goal they are unlikely to achieve, recognizing that they have elected—as has the whole society, unconsciously, and in an opposite manner—to play God to a "new people."

"Dark Benediction" raises other interesting questions about man's fate, positing a biological transformation of the whole human race into a new "improved" model, a transformation which is resisted by almost everyone before it takes place. Sharing the senses of Paul Oberlin, we share his repugnance to the "dermies" whose skin has turned scaly and gray, and whose desire to touch others and spread the contagion is little short of obscene. Overtones of racial prejudice (the locale is the South), leprosy, violation of the integrity of the individual, fear of the unknown in general, and the known transition period of often fatal fever make it clear that a considerable trade-off is required. For those who are not dermies, who do not know or believe that there are benefits involved, it is less a trade-off than a betrayal of all that's human, a conversion of men into monsters. Rather than chronicled, this background is given to us through flashbacks and conversations, as we follow Paul, alone on the road. In Houston, he is impressed into the service of a paramilitary local government, concerned with maintaining racial purity, safe from contagion, and anxious to have him, as a trained technician. He makes his escape in a truck, one of the few vehicles that run and have gas in this age of chaos, but on impulse he rescues a girl, Willy, whose incubation has started and who is about to be executed for it. Making her ride in the open back of the truck, Paul heads for Galveston Island, which he hopes will be a haven. His hope is doubly ironic, given the contemporary reputation of Galveston as a "sin city," and the coming twist of the plot.

Having rescued Willy from the moral equivalent of a Nazi concentration camp, Paul is now obligated by decency to get her to safety, provided that she doesn't try to touch him. The island, however, is a colony of "hypers," their term for dermie. Only in the hospital, run by priests, where he takes her for help, can Paul find any security, and that in a sterile room, avoided by hospital personnel, who wear noseplugs to maintain their self-control in his presence. He lingers on, partly because Willy is responding poorly—fearful that she might have touched him, she attempts suicide—partly because he has been promised a boat in which to escape. While he is waiting, he learns from a Dr. Seevers what truth he has managed to extract from his research into the transformation and its cause. One night, however, Paul wakes up terrified, with memories of being caressed; over the first fright, he realizes it was Willy, and discovers that she has run away. He chases after her to the sea, and accepts the inevitable, his transformation and her love.

As in all Miller's best stories, the science fictional rationalization is clear, the behavior believable, the focus not on the science fiction itself but on the situation of one troubled person. Unlike in others, however, the biological transformation in this one is a positive one, with utopian overtones. Although the repellent characteristics are given their due, the parasite which Dr. Seevers explains is responsible for them is also responsible for an increase in sensory perception and apparently, cooperative behavior. At least the islanders are better behaved than the mainland totalitarians; this may be partly due to the influence of the priests, but where else is their wisdom respected? And islands are traditional utopian locales. The real reason why this metamorphosis is more acceptable may be its resemblance to a divine blessing. The parasite is a gift from the sky, having arrived in meteorites launched by some alien civilization; though labelled with warnings, the pods were first opened by the ignorant, unable to read the signs and driven by their "monkey-like" curiosity. As from Pandora's Box or the apple of Genesis, but perhaps in reverse, as a distribution of good, the contents spread everywhere, making it likely that everyone, eventually, will have to give in to this "dark benediction." Reception of the parasite is a passive act, moreover, requiring acceptance only of the "laying on of hands." Believing it really is beneficial, that the scientist's findings are accurate, requires, as does believing the disease is harmful, an act of faith (parasites in "Let My People Go," clearly in the service of overspecialized aliens, were regarded with fear and loathing). Paul and the reader can only decide on the basis of others' behavior; the paranoia of the mainlanders can hardly be preferable to the love and respect shown by Willy and the priestly medicine men.

An act of faith is also crucial in "Crucifixus Etiam," Miller's best short story, but the faith is not sustained by the protagonist's Catholic religion.

An elegiac, near-future projection, this story makes of technophilia a secular religious faith. Although the passage of two decades has brought into question some of the details (the limited amount of social change in a century, the stated "high" rate of pay of five dollars an hour, the use of English rather than metric measures), the basics of the story are universal, as the title suggests. Roughly translated, it means "crucified still or again." This is the story of a man who takes great risks to his health for the chance of high rewards; as his health begins to fail, and the rewards come to seem unobtainable, he wonders what the justification of his work is, then comes to identify with the goal he serves but will never attain.

The man is Manue Tanti, a Peruvian laborer at work on Mars, his health endangered by implanted oxygenation equipment which encourages atrophy of the lungs. The justification is "faith in the destiny of the race of man." The science fictional trappings are necessary, since no job on Earth offers quite this kind of risk, and certainly none is so dependent upon future realization. The project of making a breathable atmosphere for Mars is already almost a century old, with eight centuries yet to go. But the handling is in no way impersonal. Our concern is not with the project, but with the suffering of one man, representative of many. We start with the basics of his situation, his longing to travel, his pain from the oxygenator, his struggle to maintain his lungs so that he can indeed realize his ambition. We hear that the engineers have life much easier than the laborers, we hear that Mars is growing her own labor force, we hear that the object of the drilling job is to tap a well of tritium oxide, and we know no more than he does which is fact and which is rumor. We see his estrangement from his fellow-workers and how they and the elements seem to conspire to make him give in, to breathe less, to let the oxygenator work more. In the hospital, we dream with him of falling and wake with him in the death-fear this inspires, only to discover to his horror that he has not been doing any breathing at all on his own. Facing his being trapped on Mars, we ask with him the purpose of all this, whose ends he is serving, and we see the inadequacy of the faith proffered by the itinerant clergy who come to offer comfort, As he gradually gives in to the pain and its easement, we follow Manue in his quest for understanding: a repairman tells him Mars is a dumping ground for Earth's surplus, tritium suggests tc him hydrogen fusion as an energy source, the "quiet secrecy" implies that the men are not be trusted with the knowledge of what in fact they are doing.

As the work goes on and he becomes an oxygen "addict," we follow the curve of his emotions to cynicism and despair, to a controlled cursing in lieu of prayer. On the day a controlled chain reaction is started deep beneath the Martian crust, the men are finally informed of the significance of their job, laboring so that others may breathe, far in the future. Pent-up resentment and a momentary fear that the reaction might not be controlled almost lead to a riot. Quite unexpectedly, Manue knocks out the ringleader, and his frenzied threat to pull out the rioters' air hoses quells the rebellion. He finds the answer bitter—Miller calls it Manue's "Gethesemane"—but also glorious. One man asks "What man ever made his own salvation?" Another says "Some sow, some reap," and asks Manue which we would rather do. Manue himself picks up a handful of soil and thinks "Here was Mars. His planet now."

The roughly 8000 words that comprise this story are very efficiently employed. Miller uses vignettes, rather than long scenes, and avoids the sentimentality that technique seems to lead to in other short stories. Bits of action and dialogue, nothing extended, break up what is mainly narrative. The characters, bit players except for Manue, are solid individuals: the Tibetan, Gee, Manue's digging partner with whom he has nothing in common; the foreman, Vögeli, who is quick-tempered and efficient, trying to maintain his men like tools; San Donnell, the "troffie" (atrophied) repairman, who is a mine of misinformation; even the riot leader, Handell, and the supervisor, Kinley, though little more than roles with names, seem right in their parts. The local color and slang, brought in as if in passing, make Mars feel lived in. And the third person narration, limited to the consciousness of Manue, is particularly effective in that it restricts our senses almost claustrophobically to those of the perfect observer for this story: a Peruvian, used to thin air and small social horizons, ignorant of much but proud of his ancient heritage and comfortable in his ambition, Catholic in upbringing but able to recognize how ill-fitted his religion is to this alien world.

On a larger scale, Miller managed a similar triumph in the short novel, "The Darfsteller." This, too, is limited to the consciousness of one person, for whom technological advance is no unmixed blessing. Ryan Thornier, an ageing former matinee idol in the days before the stage was automated, has consistently refused to make a "tape" of his acting personality, or to work in the production or sales ends of the autodrama business. Steeped in theatrical tradition, proud of his art and even of the poverty to which his pride has brought him, Thornier is reduced to janitorial duties in an autodrama theater, his chief joy in life being the rare chance to see a third-rate live touring company play to a sparse audience. Denied that opportunity, he is given two weeks' notice before he is replaced in his job, too, by an automaton. Since this is on the eve of a mechanical stage run of a play he once starred in, the actor conceives and executes a plan to make one last performance the culmination of his career and simultaneously an act of revenge against this boss, his profession, and the world. "The Darfsteller" is the story of what he accomplishes, and how.

On one level this is a personal story, a near-tragedy. Learning quickly enough how the technology of the autodrama operates, Thornier sabotages the tape of an actor intended for a role he once played. Then, since there is not enough time to get a new tape before opening night, he offers himself as a replacement. Against the better judgment of everyone involved, his offer is accepted, and he puts a real bullet in the gun with which the mannequin playing his enemy is supposed to shoot him. In the actual performance, however, in which he competes against the "Maestro," the mechanical director that operates the tapes and mannequins, adjusting them to each other and to audience reactions, Thornier is reinvigorated. He dodges the bullet and catches it in his belly.

Allegorically, this is a fable of technological displacement. In case anyone missed the point, Rick, the projectionist, runs it through again in the coda. Explaining that a human specialist will inevitably lose to a specialized tool, a machine, Rick defines the function of Man as "creating new specialties." But the technology is more than a symbol; the autodrama, throughout the story, is continually vying with Thorny for center stage. To compete with it, he has to learn to understand it, which he has never tried to do before. Learning what he can from Rick, he becomes fascinated with it, to his dismay and the reader's edification. Seeing the Maestro at work, with Thornier in its system, is most instructive, and enough details are developed to make the automation of the theater, presumably the last bastion of personalized professions, seem believable.

The creation of this illusion is assisted, moreover, by the appearance of former actors and stage people associated with the autodrama who come into town in connection with the opening. Like any technology, this one requires preparation and tending, and they have been reduced to servants of the machine in Thornier's estimation, and to some extent in their own. It is, of course, the only game in town, and it even offers a kind of "immortality" to actors in their prime, he recognizes, comparing Mela, his one-time co-star and lover, with her unageing tapes and mannequins. The heart of the story, however, lies in Thorny's love affair with the theater, with its icons and superstitions, the image it gives him of himself (on our level of perception he is a querulous, vain popinjay), and the recaptured thrill of performance, even a mediocre performance on a stage full of mannequins and of threatening electrical equipment. As he thinks to himself, seeing the Maestro in human terms, the director with his eyes on the whole play and the reaction of the audience is always in opposition to the *Darfsteller* (the true actor-artist), and prefers the mere *Schauspieler* (the crowd-pleasing entertainer). An excellent fictional creation, Ryan Thornier is always an actor, even in the role of himself with an audience of one, and the theater as microcosm is ideal for this "morality play" of man vs. machine. Though the reader may find himself in intellectual agreement with Rick, in his analysis of the situation, the rational conclusion is clearly at odds with the emotional identification with the quixotic Thornier, whose irrationality is more appealing.

The narrator in this short novel has the same distant, gently ironic detachment as in *A Canticle for Leibowitz*, with the same fondness for slapstick if not for puns as leavening in a serious tale. The construction is effective, alternating action and dialogue, narration and internal monologue, parallels and antitheses. The characters, aside from Thornier, are personalized functions, though only the theater owner, Thornier's boss, is an obvious stereotype, and even that may be excusable since he is a tormentor as seen through Thornier's eyes. And the didacticism, though clearly overt, is cleanly balanced by the felt reality of Thornier's lament. Perhaps the only thing the novel does not have, and does not need, which may be surprising in view of Miller's usual propensities, is any religious props or even a sense of religion, unless we assume that for the actor, the stage is his Church. The effect of the whole, however, is that of a minor masterpiece, as the 13th World Science Fiction Convention recognized by awarding it a "Hugo" as the best "novelette" of 1955.

6. The medium lengths, novelette, novella, short novel, were where Miller's strengths lay, where he could combine character, action, and import. Of his forty-one magazine publications, twenty-four were of middle length, including "Blood Bank," "The Ties that Bind," "The Lineman," four of the five we have just reviewed, and the three more or less independent parts of *Canticle*. Only "Crucifixus Etiam" really stands out among the shorter works, followed by "The Big Hunger," "It Takes a Thief," "Death of a Spaceman," "The Hoofer," and "Vengeance for Nikolai," most of which come dangerously close to sentimentality (melodrama in "It Takes a Thief") and each of which relies heavily on a gimmick, the bane of so many short stories. Whether the sustained continuity of a more conventional novel was beyond him, we can not know for certain, but it seems certain that part of the success of *Canticle* is due to its tripartite form, each third crisply etched in short novel size, with counterpoint, motifs, and allusions making up for the lack of more ordinary means of continuity. This, too, he learned in his apprenticeship in the science fiction magazines.

Five outstanding stories out of thirty-eight is not disastrous, but it would have hardly have caused Miller to be remembered if he had not written *A Canticle for Leibowitz*. Against that standard, not very many science fiction stories or novels can measure up. Leading up to it, however, and to the enigma of Miller's abandoning writing afterwards, the whole canon has some extrinsic interest, chronicling as it does his development from a commercial writer to an artist, one who may have quit while he was ahead, rather than have everything thereafter compared to one book and found wanting.

NOTES

1. Miller's first published story, "MacDoughal's Wife," *American Mercury* (March 1950), 313-20, is not science fiction, though it invokes religious and scientific imagery, in keeping with his science fiction, to magnify the significance of the biological sterility and assumed infidelity of the titular character.

2. Anthony Boucher's observation on magazine publishing in "The Publishing of Science Fiction," in *Modern Science Fiction: Its Meaning and Its Value*, ed. Reginald Bretnor (New York: Coward-McCann, 1953), 33, is supported in "Science Fiction Rockets into Big Time," *Business Week* (October 20, 1951), 82-4, 89, and in Bradford M. Day, ed. "The Complete Checklist of Science-Fiction Magazines," pamphlet (New York: Science-Fiction and Fantasy Publication [sic], 1961). Data on anthologies compiled from W.R. Cole, ed., *A Checklist of Science Fiction Anthologies* ([New York: W.R. Cole], 1964) and Frederick Siemon, ed., *Science Fiction Story Index, 1950-1968* (Chicago: American Library Association, 1971). Supplemented by my own collection, these checklists are also the source for information in the Appendix concerning reprints of Miller stories.

3. A political article, "Bobby and Jimmy" (concerning Kennedy and Hoffa), identifying its author as the writer of *Canticle*, appeared in *Nation* (April 7, 1962), 300-3, but I have been unable to find any other stories or articles by Miller outside the science fiction magazines.

4. William F. Nolan, in the headnote to "The Lineman" in his anthology, *A Wilderness of Stars*, states simply: "For good and valid reasons of his own, Walter Miller, Jr. has retired as a storyteller."

5. Cf. Robert S. Chapman, "Science Fiction of the Fifties: Billy Graham, McCarthy and the Bomb," *Foundation*, #7-8 (March, 1975), 38-52, about which editor Peter Nicholls comments: "It is excerpted from a paper he wrote for the Department of History, while a student at the University of California at Berkeley," and "The whole subject of social attitudes as manifested in science fiction....is rapidly becoming, and with good reason, one of the most popular themes among students doing their Ph.D. theses on science fiction, especially in Europe." I have written to Mr. Nicholls about this, and would also appreciate any information readers of *Science-Fiction Studies* might have about such studies.

6. At least one anthology, *Other Worlds, Other Gods*, ed. Mayo Mohs (Garden City: Doubleday, 1971) has been built out of stories that combine religion and science fiction, and that seem to me to bear out my contention, despite the editor's sentiments as expressed in his introductory essay. For other brief considerations of the topic, see William Atheling, Jr. [James Blish], *The Issue at Hand: Studies in Contemporary Magazine Science Fiction* (Chicago: Advent, 1964), 49-61, and Sam Moskowitz, *Seekers of Tomorrow: Masters of Modern Science Fiction* (Cleveland: World, 1966), 410-414.

7. Review articles on the novel's original publication appeared in the following publications: *Analog* (November, 1960), *Chicago Sunday Tribune* (March 6, 1960), *Christian Century* (May 25, 1960), *Commonweal* (March 4, 1960), *Galaxy* (February,

1961), *Manchester Guardian Weekly* (April 7, 1960), *New York Herald-Tribune Book Review* (March 13, 1960), *New York Times Book Review* (March 27, 1960), *New Yorker* (April 2, 1960), *San Francisco Chronicle* (March 8, 1960), *Saturday Review* (June 4, 1960), *Spectator* (March 25, 1960), and *Time* (February 22, 1960).

At least seven subsequent revaluations have also been published: Martin Green, *Science and the Shabby Curate of Poetry* (New York: Norton, 1965); Edward Ducharme, "A Canticle for Miller," *English Journal*, 55 (November, 1966), 1042-4; R.A. Schroth, "Between the Lines," *America*, 118 (January 20, 1968), 79; Hugh Rank, "Song out of Season: *A Canticle for Leibowitz*," *Renascence*, 21 (Summer, 1969), 213-21; Michael Alan Bennett, "The Theme of Responsibility in Miller's *A Canticle for Leibowitz*," *English Journal*, 59 (April, 1970), 484-9; Walker Percy, "Walker Percy on Walter M. Miller, Jr.'s *A Canticle for Leibowitz*," *Rediscoveries*, ed. David Madden (New York: Crown, 1971); Russell Griffin, "Medievalism in *A Canticle for Leibowitz*," *Extrapolation*, 14 (May, 1973), 112-25. The Catholic journals were most parochial in dismissing the science fiction in the book, but the reviewers for the *Herald-Tribune*, *Manchester Guardian*, and *Spectator* were also remiss.

8. The only treatment of these aspects of the book of which I am aware is in my 1969 U.S.C. dissertation, now published as *Visions of Tomorrow: Six Journeys from Outer to Inner Space* (New York: Arno, 1975), 221-79.

9. Robert P. Mills, ed., *The Worlds of Science Fiction* (New York: Dial Press, 1963), 86.

APPENDIX: THE BOOKS AND STORIES OF WALTER M. MILLER, JR.

B1. *A Canticle for Leibowitz* (Philadelphia: Lippincott, 1959; London: Weidenfeld and Nicolson, 1960; New York, Bantam pb, 1961, frequently reprinted; other paperback editions; Boston: Gregg Press, 1975, photographic reprint of 1960 Lippincott edn, with introduction by Norman Spinrad), novel, comprising revised versions of ## 35, 37, 38.

B2. *Conditionally Human* (New York: Ballantine pb, 1962; London: Gollancz, 1962; London: Science Fiction Book Club, 1964), comprising ##4, 9, 33.

B3. *The View from the Stars* (New York: Ballantine pb, 1964), comprising ## 11, 12, 13, 19, 21, 24, 25, 28, 34.

#1. "Secret of the Death Dome," novelette, *Amazing* (January, 1951); reprinted in *Amazing* (June, 1966).

#2. "Izzard and the Membrane," novelette, *Astounding* (May, 1951); anthologized in Everett Bleiler and T.E. Dikty, eds., *Year's Best Science Fiction Novels: 1952* (New York: Frederick Fell, 1952).

#3. "The Soul-Empty Ones," novelette, *Astounding* (August, 1951).

#4. "Dark Benediction," short novel, *Fantastic Adventures* (September, 1951); collected in B2.

#5. "The Space Witch," novelette, *Amazing* (November, 1951); reprinted in *Amazing* (October, 1966).

#6. "The Song of Vorhu...for Trumpet and Kettledrum," novelette, *Thrilling Wonder Stories* (December, 1951).

#7. "The Little Creeps," novelette, *Amazing* (December, 1951); reprinted in *Fantastic* (May, 1968); anthologized in Milton Lesser, ed., *Looking Forward* (New York: Beechhurst, 1953).

#8. "The Reluctant Traitor," short novel, *Amazing* (January, 1952).

#9. "Conditionally Human," novelette, *Galaxy* (February, 1952); revised and collected in B2; anthologized in Everett Bleiler and T.E. Dikty, eds., *Year's Best Science Fiction Novels: 1953* (New York: Frederick Fell, 1953).

#10. "Bitter Victory," short story, *IF* (March, 1952).

#11. "Dumb Waiter," novelette, *Astounding* (April, 1952); collected in B3; anthologized in Groff Conklin, ed., *Science Fiction Thinking Machines* (New York: Vanguard, 1954) and Damon Knight, *Cities of Wonder* (Garden City: Doubleday, 1966).

#12. "It Takes a Thief," short story, *IF* (May, 1952); collected, as "Big Joe and the Nth Generation," in B3.

#13. "Blood Bank," novelette, *Astounding* (June, 1952); collected in B3; anthologized in Martin Greenberg, ed., *All About the Future* (New York: Gnome Press, 1953).

#14. "Six and Ten are Johnny," novelette, *Fantastic* (Summer, 1952); reprinted in *Fantastic* (January, 1966).

#15. "Let My People Go," short novel, *IF* (July, 1952).

#16. "Cold Awakening," novelette, *Astounding* (August, 1952).

#17. "Please Me Plus Three," novelette, *Other Worlds* (August, 1952).

#18. "No Moon for Me," short story, *Astounding* (September, 1952); anthologized in William Sloane, ed., *Space, Space, Space* (New York: Grosset and Dunlap, 1953).

#19. "The Big Hunger," short story, *Astounding* (October, 1952); collected in B3; anthologized in Donald A Wollheim, ed., *Prize Science Fiction* (New York: McBride, 1953).

#20. "Gravesong," short story, *Startling* (October, 1952).

#21. "Command Performance," novelette, *Galaxy* (November, 1952); collected, as "Anybody Else Like Me?" in B3; anthologized in Everett Bleiler and T.E. Dikty, eds., *The Best Science Fiction Stories: 1953* (New York: Frederick Fell, 1953); Horace Gold, ed., *The Second Galaxy Reader* (New York: Crown, 1954); and Brian W. Aldiss, ed., *Penguin Science Fiction* (London: Penguin, 1961).

#22. "A Family Matter," short story, *Fantastic Story Magazine* (November, 1952).

#23. "Check and Checkmate," novelette, *IF* (January, 1953).

#24. "Crucifixus Etiam," short story, *Astounding* (February, 1953); collected in B3; anthologized in Everett Bleiler and T.E. Dikty, eds., *The Best Science Fiction Stories: 1954* (New York: Frederick Fell, 1954); Judith Merril, ed., *Human?* (New York: Lion, 1954); Michael Sissons, ed., *Asleep in Armageddon* (London: Panther, 1962); Kingsley Amis and Robert Conquest, eds., *Spectrum V* (New York: Harcourt Brace, 1966); and Robert Silverberg, ed., *Tomorrow's Worlds* (New York: Meredith, 1969).

#25. "I Dreamer," short story, *Amazing* (July, 1953); collected in B3.

#26. "The Yokel," novelette, *Amazing* (September, 1953).

#27. "The Wolf Pack," short story, *Fantastic* (Oct., 1953); reprinted in *Fantastic* (May, 1966); anthologized in Judith Merril, ed., *Beyond the Barriers of Space and Time* (New York: Random House, 1954).

#28. "The Will," short story, *Fantastic* (February, 1954); reprinted in *Fantastic* (April, 1969); collected in B3; anthologized in T.E. Dikty, ed., *The Best Science Fiction Stories and Novels: 1955* (New York: Frederick Fell, 1955).

#29. "Death of a Spaceman," short story, *Amazing* (March, 1954); reprinted in *Amazing* (March, 1969); anthologized in William F. Nolan, ed., *A Wilderness of Stars* (Los Angeles: Sherbourne Press, 1971); anthologized as "Memento Homo" in T.E. Dikty, ed., *The Best Science Fiction Stories and Novels: 1955* (New York: Frederick Fell, 1955); Robert P. Mills, ed., *The Worlds of Science Fiction* (New York: Dial Press, 1963); and Laurence M. Janifer, ed., *Masters' Choice* (New York: Simon and Schuster, 1966).

#30. "I Made You," short story, *Astounding* (March, 1954).

#31. "Way of a Rebel," short story, *IF* (April, 1954).

#32. "The Ties that Bind," novelette, *IF* (May, 1954); anthologized in William F. Nolan, ed., *A Sea of Space* (New York: Bantam, 1970).

#33. "The Darfsteller," short novel, *Astounding* (January, 1955); collected in B2; anthologized in Isaac Asimov, ed., *The Hugo Winners* (Garden City: Doubleday, 1962).

#34. "The Triflin' Man," short story, *Fantastic Universe* (January, 1955); collected as "You Triflin' Skunk" in B3; anthologized in Judith Merril, ed., *Galaxy of Ghouls* (New York: Lion, 1955).

#35. "A Canticle for Leibowitz," short novel, *The Magazine of Fantasy and Science Fiction* (*F&SF*) (April, 1955); revised as part of *A Canticle for Leibowitz* (B1); anthologized in T.E. Dikty, ed., *Best Science Fiction Stories and Novels: 1956* (New York: Frederick Fell, 1956); Anthony Boucher, ed., *The Best from Fantasy and Science Fiction, fifth series* (Garden City: Doubleday, 1956); and Christopher Cerf, ed., *The Vintage Anthology of Science Fantasy* (New York: Vintage, 1966).

#36. "The Hoofer," short story, *Fantastic Universe* (September, 1955); anthologized in Judith Merril, ed., *S-F: The Year's Greatest Science-Fiction and Fantasy* (New York: Dell, 1956), and *S-F: The Best of the Best* (New York: Dell, 1968).

#37. "And the Light is Risen," short novel, *F&SF* (August, 1956); revised as part of *A Canticle for Leibowitz* (B1).

#38. "The Last Canticle," short novel, *F&SF* (February, 1957); revised as part of *A Canticle for Leibowitz* (B1).

#39. "Vengeance for Nikolai," short story, *Venture* (March, 1957); anthologized in Joseph Ferman, ed., *No Limits* (New York: Ballantine, 1958).

#40. "The Corpse in Your Bed is Me," short story co-authored by Lincoln Boone, *Venture* (May, 1957).

#41. "The Lineman," short novel, *F&SF* (August, 1957); anthologized in William F. Nolan, ed., *A Wilderness of Stars* (Los Angeles: Sherbourne Press, 1971).

Charles Elkins

Isaac Asimov's "Foundation" Novels: Historical Materialism Distorted into Cyclical Psycho-History

(from **SFS** *3: 26–36, March 1976)*

Among SF series, surely none has enjoyed such spectacular popularity as Isaac Asimov's "Foundation" stories. Asimov has been awarded a Hugo "for the best all time science fiction series," and many SF aficionados describe their first encounter with Asimov's novels in religious terms. Alva Rogers' response is typical: the "Foundation" stories, he says, "are some of the greatest science fiction ever written, with a Sense of Wonder in the underlying concept that is truly out of this world."[1] Moreover, despite some genuine questions which serious SF critics, such as Damon Knight, have raised with regard to the underlying concept of *The Foundation Trilogy*, it continues to go through printing after printing.

1. It is difficult to put one's finger on precisely what element or elements so fascinate readers. From just about any formal perspective, *The Foundation Trilogy* is seriously flawed. The characters are undifferentiated and one-dimensional. Stylistically, the novels are disasters, and Asimov's ear for dialogue is simply atrocious. The characters speak with a monotonous rhythm and impoverished vocabulary characteristic of American teenagers' popular reading in the Forties and Fifties; the few exceptions are no better—e.g. the Mule, who, in the disguise of the Clown, speaks a pseudo-archaic courtly dialect, or Lord Dorwin, who speaks like Elmer Fudd, or the archetypal Jewish Mother who can say, "So shut your mouth, Pappa. Into you anybody could bump."[2] The distinctive vocabulary traits are as a rule ludicrous: *God!* is replaced by *Galaxy!*, and when a character really wants to express his disgust or anger, he cries, "Son-of-a-Spacer!" or "I don't care an electron!" (§1:5:1). To describe the characters' annoyance, arrogance, or bitterness, Asimov uses again and again one favorite adjective and adverb, *sardonic(ally)*: "Sutt's eyes gleamed sardonically" (§1:5:1); "Mallow stared him down sardonically" (§1:5:4); "Riose looked sardonic" (§2:5); "[Devers] stared at the two with sardonic belligerence" (§2:5); "'What's wrong, trader?" he asked sardonically" (§2:7); "The smooth lines of Pritcher's dark face twitched sardonically" (§3:2); "But Anthor's eyes opened, quite suddenly, and fixed themselves sardonically on Munn's countenance" (§3:20). Evidently, all people in all time periods will be sardonic. In the 12,000th year after the founding of the First Galactic Empire, characters still use terms drawn from the "western"—e.g. "lynching party" (§2:7)—and slogans imported from the political slang of our times—e.g. "lick-spittle clique of appeasers out of City Hall" (§1:3:2).

Nor is this merely a question of literary niceties. If language is both a symbolic screen through which we filter reality and an instrument by which we explore and change reality, then Asimov's style is totally inappropriate. He has imported a watered-down idiom of his time—the banal, pseudo-factual style of the mass-circulation magazines—into a world twelve thousand years into the future, with no change at all! The consciousness of his characters, as it is objectified in speech, shows absolutely no historical development and hence fails to evoke in the reader any feeling for the future universe they inhabit.

The "Foundation" novels also fail by Asimov's own definition of what he calls "social science fiction." In an essay written shortly after their publication, Asimov defined it as "*that branch of literature which is concerned with the impact of scientific advance upon human beings.*"[3] In another essay, entitled "When Aristotle Fails, Try Science Fiction," Asimov argued that SF "deals with the possible advances in science and with the potential changes—even those damned eternal verities—these may bring about in society."[4] These precepts do not square with his novels. There is no indication in the "Foundation" stories that scientific advances—e.g. traveling faster than light, developing atomic technology, predicting and controlling human events, controlling minds, etc.—have *any* effect on people. Man remains essentially the same; the springs of human action are unchanged.

This conflict between Asimov's precepts and practice is a consequence of contradictory notions he holds about the nature of historical change. Despite his contention that SF deals with change, and moreover that "scientific-economic change is master and political change is the servant" so that "technological changes lie at the root of political change"[5]—Asimov does not believe in significant change. More precisely, he does not believe that scientific advances will entail any changes in men's mutual relationships: "Hate, love, fear, suspicion, passion, hunger, lust...these will not change while mankind remains"; history repeats itself (in large outline at least) "with surprising specificity."[6] Citing Toynbee's cyclical theory of history as a basis for social theorizing and extrapolating from it into the future—a procedure which Toynbee explicitly rejected[7]—Asimov creates a future political structure modeled on the Roman and British empires. "In telling future history," he relates, "I always felt it wisest to be guided by past history. This was true of the 'Foundation' series too."[8]

That past history should serve as a guide for future history is a dubious assumption at best. It certainly undercuts any notion of significant change. Moreover, it is a fetter on the imaginative possibilities of the speculative novel. Instead of events growing out of the inner logic and premises of the narrative situation, the plot and characters are forced to conform to a predetermined template. Thus, not only is the concept itself questionable, but its use as a structuring and thematic device leads one to suspect a deficiency in imaginative vision. As a guiding framework for SF, it has as a rule disastrous consequences. Damon Knight rightly argues that it is not SF, "any more than the well known western with rayguns instead of sixshooters.... It's of the essence of speculative fiction that an original problem be set up which the author is obliged to work out for himself; if the problem is an old one, and he has only to look the answers up in a book, there's very little fun in it for anybody; moreover, the answers are certain to be wrong."[9]

2. Considering these problems, then, to what can one attribute the extraordinary success of the *Foundation Trilogy*? I would suggest that the "Sense of Wonder in the underlying concept" which so captivates readers is a *concept of history* which is, in its grand sweep, similar to one of the main ingredients of Marxism—historical materialism—which had captured and is capturing the imagination of millions (although Asimov's use of it, as I shall argue, is a crude caricature of this concept, a simplistic distortion similar to other varieties of "vulgar" Marxism of the period when the "Foundation" stories were being written). The perspective of historical materialism entails the assertion of overriding historical laws. In its cruder versions, it involves the old puzzle of historical inevitability (predestination) versus free will, which itself flows out of the often unsuccessful yet desperately necessary, and therefore always repeated, struggles of men to control their personal futures and the future of their societies. Consider this discussion of freedom versus necessity between the old, powerless patrician, Ducem Barr, who understands the implications of Seldon's Plan, and the eager, ambitious and headstrong General of the Galactic Empire, Bel Riose:

[Barr] Without pretending to predict the actions of individual humans, it [Seldon's Plan] formulated definite laws capable of mathematical analysis and extrapolation to govern and predict the mass action of human groups....

[Riose] You are trying to say that I am a silly robot following a predetermined course of destruction.

[Barr] No, I have already said that the science had nothing to do with individual actions. It is the vaster background that has been foreseen.

[Riose] Then we stand clasped tightly in the forcing hand of the Goddess of Historical Necessity.

[Barr] Of *Psycho*-Historical Necessity.

[Riose] And if I exercise my prerogative of freewill? If I choose to attack next year, or not to attack at all? How pliable is the Goddess? How resourceful?

[Barr] Do whatever you wish in your fullest exercise of freewill. You will still lose.

[Riose] Because of Hari Seldon's dead hand?

[Barr] Because of the dead hand of the mathematics of human behavior that can neither be stopped, swerved, nor delayed. (§2:3)

The logic of history is equated with the logic of the natural sciences. Bayta, the woman who eventually thwarts the Mule's efforts to locate the Second Foundation, says, "The laws of history are as absolute as the laws of physics, and if the probabilities of error are greater, it is only because history does not deal with as many humans as physics does atoms, so that individual variations count for more" (§2:11). From the *Encyclopedia Galactica*, one learns that Seldon's Plan can be reduced to "The synthesis of the calculus of n-variables and of n-dimensional geometry" (§3:8). Using incredibly complex mathematics, Seldon's Plan predicts the fall of the decadent First Galactic Empire (read Roman Empire), the rise of the Traders and Merchant Princes (read bourgeoisie and nationalism), the growth of the First Foundation (read post-industrial, bureaucratic-technological society), its interaction with the long hidden Second Foundation and the eventual creation of the Second Galactic Empire, a civilization based on "mental science" (read Asimov's utopian vision?).

It's a fascinating concept. Moreover, at least on a superficial level, the conceptual parallels with classical Marxism are clear. Donald Wollheim, despite his crude caricature of Marxism, is correct in his "conjecture that Asimov took the basic premise of Marx and Engels, said to himself that there was a point there [i.e. in Marxism]—that the movements of human mass must be subject to the laws of motion and interaction, and that a science could be developed based upon mathematics and utilizing all the known data...."[10] Is not Seldon's discovery precisely that which Marxists claim to have made? In his speech at Marx's funeral, Frederick Engels asserted that "just as Darwin discovered the law of evolution in organic nature, so Marx discovered the law of evolution in human history.... Marx also discovered the special law of motion governing the present-day capitalist method of production and the bourgeois society that this method of production has created."[11] Similarly, just as Seldon concentrates not on the individual but the masses, so—as Lenin says—"historical materialism made it possible for the first time to study with scientific accuracy the social conditions of the life of the masses and the changes in these conditions.... Marxism indicated the way to one all-embracing and comprehensive study of the processes of the rise, development, and decline of socio-economic systems.... Marx drew attention and indicated the way to a scientific study of history as a simple process which, with all its immense variety and contradictions, is governed by definite laws."[12]

It is this concept, that history has "definite laws" which cannot only be made intelligible but can give insight into the course of future historical events, which so intrigues both the readers of the "Foundation" novels and those who study Marxism. Moreover, whether embodied in Seldon's Plan or the concept of historical materialism, this idea is the very stuff of drama, for it inevitably raises the question of human free will versus historical determinism, a problem fraught with dramatic tension from Sophocles' *Oedipus Rex* through the present.

In the 1930's, the mechanistic conception of Marxism was founded on such works as Plekhanov's *The Role of the Individual in History* (1898), Kautsky's *The Class Struggle* (1910), Bukharin's *Historical Materialism* (1921), and Stalin's *Leninism* (1924). Bukharin, for example, asserted that "society and its evolution are as much subject to natural law as is everything else in this universe... Socialism will come inevitably because it is inevitable that men, definite classes of men, will stand for its realization, and they will do so under circumstances that will make their victory certain."[13] It was precisely this crude conception of historical inevitability culminating in Stalin's widely propagated writings, that dominated the thinking of a large majority of American radicals and concerned social activists throughout the Thirties and into the Fifties, in and out of the Communist Party. (Much of Marx's and Engels' writing was still untranslated; the German Marxists' and Antonio Gramsci's works were unknown; most George Lukács' essays were unavailable. What Marxist theory Americans received was basically what was filtered through the USSR under Stalin.) Obviously, this was an interpretation of history containing built-in contradictions and producing psychological as well as political tensions. On the one hand, it created an impression that there was an inevitability to history which would run its course without any need for action. On the other hand, it encouraged a feeling that intense activity was necessary to bring about the fulfillment of the inevitable end.

This dilemma—given a predetermined outcome, to act or not to act—is exactly what Asimov's characters experience. It generates the dramatic tension in his novels. If Seldon's Plan is correct, the correct interpretation of history, what actions should the characters take when faced with the necessity of making crucial decisions? The hero of the First Foundation, Salvor Hardin, decides to wait until the "crisis" itself (an attack by another planet) limits his choice to one and only one course of action. He argues that

> the future isn't nebulous. It's been calculated out by Seldon and charted. Each successive crisis in our history is mapped and each depends in a measure on the successful conclusion of the ones previous.... at each crisis our freedom of action would become circumscribed to the point where only one course of action was possible.... as long as *more* than one course of action is possible, the crisis has not been reached. We must let things drift so long as they possibly can.... (§1:3:2)

Hardin is content to follow the logic of Seldon's Plan; he will do "one hundred percent of nothing." By contrast, other characters, such as Bel Riose and Dr. Darell, resist the implications of the Plan and of historical inevitability: "he (Darell) knew that he could live only by fighting that vague and fearful enemy that deprived him of the dignity of manhood by controlling his destiny; that made life a miserable struggle against a foreordained end; that made all the universe a hateful and deadly chess game" (§3:14). Ultimately, resistance is futile; all actions merely confirm the inevitability of Seldon's Plan.

The engrossment, the "Sense of Wonder" evoked by the *Foundation Trilogy*, lies in the readers' discovery of this fact. Over and over again the question is raised (by the characters and the readers): is Seldon's Plan still operational? Has the Mule's interference negated the Plan? And time and again, just as Oedipus and Sophocles' audience come to understand the power of Apollo over man's destiny, Asimov's characters and readers come to comprehend the full implications of "Psycho-Historical Necessity." This understanding evokes a mixture of futility and awe.

Wollheim is on the right track in pointing out the probable Marxian "influence" on Asimov. Asimov must have been aware of Soviet Marxism: his parents immigrated from Russia in 1923, six years after the October Revolution. Moreover, 1939, the year Asimov began writing his future history, was the year of the Soviet-Nazi Pact, and he has recalled how he was caught up in the events unfolding in Europe.[14] Further, if Asimov was at all aware of the all-pervading political and intellectual milieu of the New Deal decade, he would have been exposed to the clamorous controversies between the Left and the Right as well as within the Left of the time (e.g. the passionate debates generated by the disillusionment of many prominent intellectuals with the Stalinist brand of Marxism and the American Communist Party's submission to the Soviet dogma).[15] While Asimov does not mention any involvement in radical politics, Sam Moskowitz credits him with helping to found the Futurian Science Literary Society in 1938, a society which James Blish says "was formed exclusively for those who were either actual members of the Communist Party or espoused the Party's policies." The members "did endorse the Marxist view of change, or whatever version of it the American CP was wedded to at the time...."[16] To what *degree* Asimov was acquainted with Marxism at first hand is not of great import. He was certainly aware both of some of its slogans and of its power to arouse allegiance among intellectuals and crucially alter the tempo of world history.

3. However, awareness is one thing, understanding another. What Asimov accepted as the "underlying concept" of the *Foundation Trilogy* is the vulgar, mechanical, debased version of Marxism promulgated in the Thirties—and still accepted by many today. Indeed he takes *this* brand of Marxism to its logical end; human actions and the history they create become as predictable as physical events in nature. Furthermore, just as those scientific elites in our world who comprehend nature's laws manipulate nature to their advantage, so too the guardians and the First Speaker, who alone understand Seldon's Plan, manipulate individuals and control the course of history. "Psycho-history is," as Wollheim quaintly puts it, "the science that Marxism never became"[17] (a point to which I will return in the final section). With the proviso that neither Wollheim nor Asimov has understood Marxism, and that one should substitute "mechanical pseudo-Marxism" for their mentions of it, it is precisely this treatment of history as a "science" above men, which accounts for the *Foundation Trilogy*'s ideological fascination and evocativeness as well as for its ultimate intellectual and artistic bankruptcy.

Reading the "Foundation" novels, one experiences an overriding sense of the inevitable, of a pervading fatalism. Everything in the universe is predetermined. Unable to change the pre-ordained course of events, man becomes, instead of the agent of history, an object, a "pawn" (using Asimov's chess metaphor)[18] in the grip of historical necessity—i.e. of the actualization of Hari Seldon's calculations.

Except for the Mule, a non-human, only those who understand Seldon's Plan—the First Speaker and the twelve guardians—are free. They, the elite, are the only ones free to determine history, to make certain that Seldon's Plan is realized; so that in 600 years the Second Foundation produces an elite group of psychologists "ready to assume leadership" and create the Second Galactic Empire. The ignorant masses (those with whom Seldon's mathematics is supposed to deal) would resent "a ruling class of psychologists" because "only an insignificant minority...are inherently able to lead Man through the greater involvement of Mental Science" (§3:8). Hence, it is absolutely imperative that the Plan be kept secret. No psychologist is permitted on the First Foundation. Seldon "worked with mobs, populations of whole planets, and only *blind* mobs who do not possess any foreknowledge of the results of their actions.... Interference due to foresight would have knocked the Plan out of kilter" (§1:3:2). Throughout the *Foundation Trilogy*, the masses are held in supreme contempt. They are described as "the fanatic hordes," "the featureless...mob"; their primary quality seems to be "incoherence" (§2:14). The masses must be governed by a higher authority; they are not fit to rule themselves. This is the First Speaker's job: "For twenty-five years, he, and his administration, had been trying to force a Galaxy of stubborn and stupid human beings back to the path—It was a terrible task" (§3:8).

The sense of fatality and futility evoked in the "Foundation" novels is a consequence of the reader's recognition that not only will Seldon's Plan remain hidden but even those who preserve it are almost overwhelmed by its complexity. A few will be free; the rest will be under the thumb of those who can understand the Plan.

The First Speaker (and clearly Asimov himself, along with many other SF writers such as Robert Heinlein) envisions a society organized not according to the principles of equality but according to a hierarchy of merit. It is a society similar to the one urged by Saint-Simon, the French utopian thinker; he also argued for a society governed by *savants* (mathematicians, chemists, engineers, painters, writers, etc.), who would form a Council of Newton and, because they were men of genius, would have the right to determine human destiny.[19] In the *Foundation Trilogy*, the masses merely follow. Unable either to discover or comprehend the Plan's "synthesis of the calculus of n-variables and n-dimensional geometry," the great majority of mankind is at the mercy of complex forces which they can neither understand nor control, and surrender their freedom to a techno-bureaucratic elite. Asimov thus expresses a modern version of Saint-Simon's ideology of the expert, making for the rule by such an elite.

The realization that Seldon's Plan and the Second Foundation will remain a mystery and that the Second Galactic Empire will come to pass despite the actions of the great mass of humanity, gives Asimov's *Foundation Trilogy* its aura of fatalism. *Que sera, sera.* It seems to me that this attitude is one of the major reasons for the endurance of the "Foundation" novels, just as it is one of the fascinations inherent in a crude reading of Marxism. In many ways, fatalism is an attractive way of coming to terms with one's world. It implies and evokes a certain passivity. It is, in essence, a frame of adjustment which cautions man to submit to the inevitable. At its worst, this attitude encourages a slavish submission to circumstances. At its best, fatalism and its assumptions have been the basis for the tragic hero's confrontation with Fate and his sublime but ultimately futile struggle to control and overcome it. But Asimov's characters are not tragic heroes. They are nondescript pawns, unable to take their destiny into their own hands. There is no fear or pity to evoke a tragic catharsis. Instead there is complacency. The *Foundation Trilogy* ends on a note of one-upmanship. After all that has happened, history is still on its course and Hari Seldon wins again.

4. Thus, the similarities of the underlying concept of the "Foundation" novels with even a vulgar Marxist version of historical materialism sheds some new light on their fascination and staying power. However, one must also conclude that Asimov's failure to grasp the complexities of historical materialism and the humanistic emphasis of Marxism constitutes their major intellectual and artistic deficiency. This needs to be emphasized because at least one influential critic, Donald Wollheim, juxtaposes the "Foundation" novels with certain tenets of Marxism and argues that the validity of the "underlying concept" and the strengths of the novels lie in their deviation from Marxism. In so doing, he continues to propagate a thoroughly distorted view of Marxism and produces a misleading evaluation of Asimov's achievements.

For example, Wollheim's argument that Asimov's psychohistory is the exact science that "Marxism thought it was and never could be"[20] entails a doubly preposterous comparison. To take Marxism first, Marx and Engels never claimed for their theories the status of "exact science." They were always careful to describe the "laws" of historical development as "tendencies." Marx warns that his theory of the capitalist mode of production assumes "that the laws of the capitalist mode of production develop in pure form. In reality there is always an approximation."[21] Similarly, Engels writes that no economic law "has any reality except as approximation, tendency, average, and not immediate reality. This is partly due to the fact that their action clashes with the simultaneous action of other laws, but partly due to their nature as concepts."[22] So much for Wollheim's assertion that Marxism claimed to be an exact science.

Second, to focus now on psychohistory, Wollheim fails to point out that those who articulate Seldon's Plan consistently confuse *determinable* and *determined.* Note that Ducem Barr (quoted above in section 2) says that Seldon's mathematics can simultaneously "predict" and "govern" the action of large groups. (He doesn't say how this happens.) Seldon's Plan is designed not only to predict future galactic history but to *prevent* the anarchy which would follow the collapse of the First Galactic Empire. Its power to control rests on the ability of the elite who guard the Plan to calculate all the possible variations, to keep the Plan secret from the rest of humanity, and to intervene, if necessary, to keep the Plan operational. To those who do not understand Seldon's "little algebra of humanity" (§3:8), man's destiny appears fixed and inevitable. Man is seen merely as an *object* of history rather than, dialectically, as a *subject and object* in the making of history.

For Marxists, however, history is neither *determinable* nor *determined* by a set of abstract equations. History is people acting. Moreover, people come to understand historical "laws" because in their action they simultaneously change history—each other and their social institutions—and are changed by it. Marx came to the conclusion that "the logic of history was thoroughly objective and communicable. It could be grasped by the intellect, and at the same time—since it was the history of man—it was capable of modification as soon as men understood the nature and process in which they were involved: a process whereby their own creations had assumed an aspect of seemingly internal and inevitable laws [Seldon's Plan!—note CE]. History therefore culminated not in the intellectual contemplation of the past, but in a deliberate shaping of the future."[23]

For Marx and Engels, the choices people make about their lives, their morals, their *praxis* (creative action) and their knowledge of their particular situation—all of these are included in the "laws" of social development. Marx believed that capitalism would be replaced by socialism because it not only had fatal economic limitations but also because those limitations would lead the great mass of humanity—not merely an elite—to adopt his theory as a guide to action. Marx did not relieve men of moral responsibility: "Underlying the whole of his work, providing the ethical impulse that guided his hopes and his studies, was a vision and theory of human freedom, of man as master of himself, of nature and of history."[24]

Behind Seldon's psychohistory lies the assumption—shared by Asimov—that mankind will not fundamentally change, that basic human drives are universal and eternal. Marx disagrees. His optimism is based on a rejection of this cyclical view of history. History sometimes may, but as a rule does not—and certainly does not have to—repeat itself. This rejection may help explain why some critics acquainted with Marxism are so exasperated by what they see as the essentially conservative nature of much contemporary SF. For example, Franz Rottensteiner charges that "present day science fiction, far from being *the* literature of change, is as a rule very conservative in its method as well as content. While paying lip service to change and offering some background slightly changed in relation to the author's environment, it actually comforts the reader with the palliative that nothing will ever really change, that we'll always be again what we have been before, in this world or the next; as below, so above; as on earth, so in the after life, Amen."[25]

For Marxists, however, technological change inevitably leads to changes in consciousness. If technological change, then change in the means of production; if change in the means of production, then change in the relations of production; if change in the human relations accompanying production, then changes in the superstructure (art, religion, philosophy, politics, etc.); if change in the superstructure, then change in human consciousness. Moreover, *this dialectic is reversible*; at given epochs—such as our own—human consciousness itself intervenes powerfully in changing the basic substructure of society (its materials and relations of production).[26] Marxism not only posits significant social change as men make their history, but Marx insists that *man himself*, literally his physical senses, is subject to alteration. In his intercourse with nature, man changes nature and himself. Marx writes, "The development of the five senses is the labor of the whole previous history of the world."[27] The revolution which brings communism will constitute "a universal act of human self-change."[28] Men will literally be different from what they have been in the past.

By contrast, these relationships are not explored in the *Foundation Trilogy*. Areas of social reality, such as interdependence of political power, ideology, technological development and the evolution of specific economic structures appear as separate autonomous sectors. While Seldon recognizes that economic cycles are variables which his Plan must take into account (§1:1:4), and while Asimov depicts the economic power of the First Foundation supplanting the political rule of the Empire (as if they were two entirely separate conditions), the relationships between economic and political power are not clear (§2:10). The Machiavellian power struggles that constitute the essential plot of the *Foundation Trilogy* are expressed almost exclusively in psychological terms. Politics and political savvy are equated with psychology (§1:2:3); the Mule gains supremacy by controlling his enemies' emotions; the ultimate goal of the guardians of Seldon's Plan is establishing the Second Galactic Empire, which is described as a society ruled by psychologists skilled in "Mental Science" (§3:8). (It could be a "science" because Seldon assumes, as does Asimov, that "human reaction to stimuli would remain constant" [§2:25].) Human misery is not the result of external political, social, or economic oppression; rather it is the consequence of man's failure to communicate (§3:8). Furthermore, *this* failure is not a result of social, political or economic differences but of the failure of language itself! Things would be fine if man could get along without human speech. Even here, however, Asimov never attempts to make the connections between these elements (i.e. the social, psychological, political, linguistic, economic, etc.) clear.

Thus, on the one hand, there is in Marxism a sense of almost unlimited possibility, of hope, of freedom; on the other hand, there is in the "Foundation" novels a sense of predestination, of remorseless logic, a pervading fatalism. Except for the elite who understand Seldon's Plan, the rest of mankind are ignorant counters in the grip of an idea which stands over against them as universal, immutable, external law. From a Marxian perspective, this is the very essence of slavery. Unable to comprehend the laws of nature or historical development, man is a slave to these laws, just as any animal is a slave to external circumstances. Uncognized laws are manifested as "blind" Necessity. Man's freedom is determined by his ability to understand himself and to make his world comprehensible. Once understood, previously mysterious events lose their transcendent nature, their "fetishistic" quality as Marx would say; they become demystified and lose their power to move men through mystery. In striking contrast to Asimov's depiction of Seldon's Plan, it is the possibility that all men can ultimately comprehend those hidden and complex forces at work on them that gives Marxism its vision of hope. It is this comprehension which creates the conditions for freedom.

By the same token, it is the reader's recognition that Seldon's Plan and the Second Foundation will remain a mystery and that the Second Galactic Empire will come to pass regardless of any actions by the mass of humanity which gives the *Foundation Trilogy* its aura of fatalism and complacency.

Yet why not? From a Marxian perspective, Asimov's depiction of the particular future embodied in the "Foundation" stories is an accurate reflection of the material and historical situation out of which these works arose: the alienation of men and women in modern bourgeois society. For Marxists, alienation describes a situation in which the creations of people's minds and hands—whether they be goods or complex social systems—stand over against and dominate their creators. Alienation is a consequence of man's impotence before the forces of nature and society, and of his ignorance of their operations. Alienation abates to the extent that man's knowledge and powers over nature and his social relations are increased. Thus, in one sense, Asimov's *Foundation Trilogy* endures *because* of its fatalistic perspective. It accurately sizes up the modern situation. Reading these novels, the reader experiences this fatalism which, in a Marxist analysis, flows from his own alienation in society and his sense of impotence in facing problems he can no longer understand, the solutions of which he puts in the hands of a techno-bureaucratic elite.

NOTES

1. Alva Rogers, *A Requiem for Astounding* (Chicago 1964), p. 107.

2. Isaac Asimov, *The Foundation Trilogy* (3 volumes in 1, NY ca. 1964, frequently reprinted); references are to volume:chapter or (for Volume 1) volume:part:chapter. Volume 1, *Foundation* (1951); Volume 2, *Foundation and Empire* (1952); Volume 3, *Second Foundation* (1953), each frequently reprinted. The stories that make up the three "novels" first appeared as a series in *Astounding* 1942-1949.

3. Isaac Asimov, "Social Science Fiction," in *Science Fiction: The Future*, ed. Dick Allen (NY 1971), p. 272; reprinted from *Modern Science Fiction*, ed. Reginald Bretnor (NY 1953).

4. Isaac Asimov, "When Aristotle Fails, Try Science Fiction," in *Speculations*, ed. Thomas E. Sanders (NY 1973), p. 586; reprinted from *Intellectual Digest* (1971).

5. "Social Science Fiction" (see Note 3), p. 268.

6. Ibid., pp. 277, 279.

7. Cf. Arnold Toynbee, "The Disintegration of Civilizations " from Chapter XXI of *A Study of History: Abridgement of Volumes I-VI* by D.C. Somervell (Oxford 1946), reprinted in *Theories of History*, ed. Patrick Gardiner (Glencoe 1959), p. 204. The publishing dates for *A Study of History*: Volumes I-III, 1934; Volumes IV-VI, 1939; Volumes XII-X, 1954. In his essay "Social Science Fiction" (see Note 3), p. 279, Asimov cites the first six volumes of Toynbee's work.

8. Isaac Asimov, *The Early Asimov, Book One* (Fawcett-Crest pb 1972), p. 155.

9. Damon Knight, *In Search of Wonder* (2nd edn, Chicago 1967), p. 91.

10. Donald Wollheim, *The Universe Makers* (NY 1971), p. 41.

11. Frederick Engels, "The Funeral of Karl Marx," in *When Karl Marx Died*, ed. Philip Foner (NY 1973), p. 39.

12. V.I. Lenin, "Karl Marx: A Brief Biographical Sketch with an Exposition of Marxism," *Selected Works* (NY 1967), 1:13.

13. Nikolai Bukharin, *Historical Materialism* (1925; rpt NY 1965), pp. 46, 41; Cf George Plekhanov, *The Role of the Individual in History* (NY 1960); Karl Kautsky, *The Class Struggle* (Chicago 1910); Joseph Stalin, *Leninism* (L 1928; also pbd as *Foundations of Leninism*, NY 1932, and *Questions of Leninism*, NY 1934).

14. *The Early Asimov: Book One* (see Note 8), p. 196.

15. Cf Daniel Aaron, *Writers on the Left* (NY 1965), pp. 325-407, and Charles Eisinger, *Fiction of the Forties* (Chicago 1963), pp. 87-94.

16. James Blish, "A Reply to Mr. Rottensteiner," SFS 1(1973):87; see also Sam Moskowitz, *The Immortal Storm* (1954; rpt Westport 1974), pp. 183, 210, *et passim*. In discussing this group, however, Moskowitz does not mention its political nature.

17. Wollheim (see Note 10), p. 40.

18. "Social Science Fiction" (see Note 3), pp. 277-79.

19. For a concise summary of Saint-Simon's life and views on this matter, see Edmund Wilson, *To the Finland Station* (1940; rpt Anchor pb 1953), pp. 79-85, and for a longer survey Frank E. Manuel, *The New World of Henri Saint-Simon* (Cambridge MA 1956).

20. Wollheim (see Note 10), p. 41. For a discussion of the "assumptions"—including Marxist—which provide the basis for "future history," see James Gunn, "Science Fiction and the Mainstream," in *Science Fiction, Today and Tomorrow*, ed. Reginald Bretnor (1974; rpt Penguin pb 1975), pp. 190-92. Recently another critic, John J. Alderson, in "The Foundation on Sands," *The Alien Critic* #11(Nov 1974):23-28, rpt from *Chao* #13 (June 1973), has made comparisons between the "Foundation" series and "Marxian 'economic determinism,'" but his clear misunderstanding of Marxism and of the complexities of history and fiction rules out the possibility of serious critical debate.

21. Franz Marek, *Philosophy of World Revolution* (NY 1969), p. 41.

22. Ibid., p. 42.

23. George Lichtheim, *Marxism* (NY 1961), p. 40.

24. Eugene Kamenka, *Marxism and Ethics* (NY 1969), p. 9.

25. Franz Rottensteiner, "Playing Around With Creation: Philip José Farmer," SFS 1(1973):97.

26. For a recent discussion of this point, see Raymond Williams, "Base and Super-Structure in Marxist Cultural Theory," *New Left Review*, #82(Nov-Dec 1973):309.

27. *Writings of the Young Marx on Philosophy and Society*, ed. & tr. Lloyd Easton and Kurt Guddat (Anchor pb 1967), p. 309.

28. For a full discussion of this aspect of Marx's thought, see Robert Tucker, *Philosophy and Myth in Karl Marx* (NY 1961).

Robert Plank

Ursula K. Le Guin and the Decline of Romantic Love

(from SFS *3: 36–43, March 1976)*

The function of the predominant delusions in paranoia is primarily one of restitution. The patient has lost his normal contact with the world, his ability to maintain human relationships, to understand his experiences; they become as incomprehensible as they are tormenting. He does not know what happens to him, by whom or what he is surrounded, indeed who he is. Then one day, like lightning from heaven, the answer strikes him: a clear idea of who he is, what he is in the world for, why he is so cruelly persecuted. Everything falls into place. The doubts and anxieties lose their terror.

So his personality becomes reconstituted—but on a foundation of unreality.

However clear and convincing to him, his idea of his identity may be totally false (he may be convinced, for instance, that he is Jesus Christ returned to Earth). Any cure of the illness requires that the process be reversed, and this is shattering and painful. It may never succeed; the delusion may become fixed. But even so it will give him a sense of security that makes life tolerable again.

If unhappy conditions make both solutions impossible, the turmoil never ends, the agitated and terrorized state persists to torment its victim. Such an unfortunate man is the hero of *City of Illusions* who never becomes quite certain whether he is really Falk or the Lord Agad Ramarren. The understanding reader responds with terror and pity—the novel has fulfilled the task that Aristotle set for tragedy.

This is one of the strands forming the warp and the woof of Le Guin's earlier works. Another one is the complex of telepathy and related gifts ascribed to characters in her books. Sometimes an entire complicated hierarchy of people so endowed is paraded before us: "listeners," "paraverbalists," "mindhearers," "empaths." Characters may "bespeak" others, they may engage in activities that sound like Orwell's Newspeak: they "mindspeak," "mindhear," "mindlie."

The psychologically interesting question is not whether such processes can possibly take place, but why an author—with his (or her) readers—is attracted to imagining them. The probable answer is that people will resort to extra-sensory bridges from mind to mind when they feel terribly frustrated by observing, or believing they observe, that the more conventional route of language and of empirically given non-verbal communication will no longer bear the traffic—just as they resort to other Psi-powers or to magic or miracles when they are agitated by finding that the habitual means of problem-solving no longer suffice for their needs. This deeply and hurtfully felt inability to make the regular methods do the job may be rooted in a psychological deficit (thus leading back to our first "strand"), or it may have its main cause in cultural-historical factors. The two, of course, interact.

Psi-powers in SF generally represent regression to the level that psychology calls infantile omnipotence—the individual's belief that his wishes will instantly and automatically come true. Characteristic of a very early stage, it normally persists throughout childhood in an attenuated form in play (the boy points his wooden gun, he yells "ta ta ta ta!"—and the playmate drops "dead"). Later it may return in psychosis, but normal development pushes it back into day dreams and half-admitted fantasies. By granting license to the reader to engage in such fantasies freely, be it vicariously, fiction featuring Psi-powers appeals especially to those whose ego strength is not sufficient for a secure hold on reality.

A comparison between Le Guin's *The Lathe of Heaven* (LoH) which has given infantile omnipotence a highly original twist, and Orwell's *1984* is instructive here. LoH harks back to *1984* in some details—e.g. the ominous antique shop (§10)—but mainly in the idea of "altering the past." However, note the difference: when the men in power in *1984* "alter the past," it means that they forge a documentation of a false past and use their monopoly of information to make the people believe their concoction. Nothing like Psi-power or the supernatural is involved, and they do not (unless they contort their minds through "doublethink") consider their fake past as reality. The narrator, of course, does not: his indignation is the very point of the novel. The characters in LoH, on the other hand, believe that the past has *really* been altered, and the *persona* of the author as narrator believes it with them.

A third strand in Le Guin's skein is a less modernistic one: the "quest." A hero sets out—often with companions who are swiftly eliminated so that he has to face his challenge alone—on a mission of crucial importance: usually, to rid the world or a substantial part thereof of an enormous and enormously odious peril. Thanks to his physical, mental, and moral superiority he wins out against the most incredible odds and earns the gratitude of the people and undying fame. If he is an ancient Greek or otherwise lucky, he may be received among the gods. Rocannon, in *Rocannon's World*, is such a hero and is finally thought of as a god (§9). There are always readers to lap this up. Still, one Tolkien is perhaps enough for one generation, especially since he did his job with such unmatched verve, prolixity, taste, and talent.

Instead of going out to save the world, the questing hero may simply go to find himself. The two goals can be fused. This has been done since long before the concept of SF developed. Falk/Ramarren is of the noble lineage of Parsifal; the modern touch, not too rare in SF and contemporary fantasy, is that he doesn't even really know why he sets out on his quest or what for.

The struggle with delusion, the practice of paranormal communication, the quest: if these three strains were the whole tissue—if, in other words, the Le Guin canon consisted only of the earlier works we have discussed, then this would be about all that from a psychological viewpoint needed to be said about them. In another sense, it would not even be necessary to say anything: these motifs, singly or in combination, are too common in modern SF (or in modern fantasy that calls itself SF) to make them particularly worthy of attention. *The Left Hand of Darkness* (LHD) and *The Dispossessed* (TD) are a different species. Our three strands are still woven into the texture of these more recent novels, but only as though the author had thriftily used some remnants of yarn left over from previous work. They are no longer allowed to form the predominant pattern.

Thirty years ago, in the flush of victory over the Nazis and over the atom, American SF worshipped righteous power and the physical sciences; it could consider itself their fifth column in the camp of belles lettres. Then came the well-known shift to soft sciences. It was mostly to psychology and sociology, or rather to pseudopsychology and pseudosociology—more soft than sciences. Enter the new Le Guin, and a new type of SF.

Ursula Kroeber Le Guin's mother is a distinguished writer (best known for *Ishi in Two Worlds*, 1961). Her father was one of the most eminent anthropologists. Her childhood and youth evidently stood under cultural influences the like of which few SF writers, as indeed few people, are privileged to experience.[1] Once she had exhausted the potentialities of conventional SF in her earlier novels, she was qualified to write in a new key—not by presenting the self-revelation of human beings through their dominance over nature, but rather by presenting different types of man, with their corresponding different cultures, and by revealing their nature and potential through intercultural contact.

The study of a work of literature requires empathy but also distance: it can be done more effectively if another discipline is used, X-ray-like, to disclose its structure. We may explore psychological SF by examining whether it makes anthropological sense. Equally, we may profitably bring psychological analysis to bear on Le Guin's anthropological SF.

Now psychologists, particularly psychoanalytically oriented psychologists (and readers of my earlier writings know where I stand), have a reputation, deserved or not, for seeing sex everywhere. I dislike falling into this stereotype as much as into any other. I would much rather discuss Le Guin's work without even mentioning sex. But this is, of course, impossible.

Unlike the three strands we have discussed, sex—especially in LHD—is not an issue that in a pinch could be skipped. The peculiar sexual constitution of the inhabitants of Gethen is by far the most original and important invention of Le Guin's. Even farther, I do not think there can be much doubt that it is this invention which made the book famous, which gave readers what they felt they needed. The question then arises, what is the readers' psychological set? What are the problems to which these special innovations seem the solution? How has a situation developed where this, rather than something else, was "in the air"? Three historic trends have to be considered, the vicissitudes of romantic love, of permissiveness, and of ambisexuality.

First, *romantic love*. Both as a pattern and as an ideal, it has been so much a part of our present, and especially of our fairly recent past, that we are inclined inadvertently to assume that it has always existed and always played a similarly outstanding role. Actually it may have existed "always," but this is not really the issue: many, if not perhaps all, significant forces have always existed, but much of the time only in a negligible degree. In our civilization, romantic love became a major mood at some time in the late Middle Ages. Its "invention," usually ascribed to the troubadours of the 13th century, consisted essentially in the fusion of affection and sexual desire. Before that, and where romantic love does not rule, affection was and is not consciously sexually tinged, and may exist in a hierarchical context, with love between parents and children the paradigm, or in an egalitarian context, the paradigm here being brotherly love. Sexual desire within that scheme of psychic economy is essentially lust, with emphasis on pleasure and possession, rationalized as obedience to biological necessity.

When romantic love reaches its full bloom, it forms a pattern marked by several interconnected features: one human being experiences—is smitten with—a powerful feeling for a person of the other sex.[2] This emotion, equally marked by sexual desire *and* by tremendous idealization of its object, is given overriding importance. It may be supposed to occur but once in a lifetime, and to be life's culmination. It is expected to lead either to consummation and enduring bliss, or to be unrequited by the beloved or frustrated by a hostile environment, leading to death or at least permanent misery.

Romantic love in this pure form—*Romeo and Juliet*— is of course an "ideal type." Actual life approaches, but does not reach it. Still, actual fates have often come close. And literature, music, theatre, film, TV have been full of it.

It is difficult to say when the influence of romantic love reached its zenith, or whether it perhaps continues in the ascendancy. We note that a couple of generations ago a "love match" was still something slightly suspect or ridiculous and rare enough to be commented on—as marriage was usually entered upon on the basis of more mundane considerations—while in the 20th century it is taken for granted that marriage is normally based on romantic love. On the other hand, when Goethe calls romantic love "the holiest of our drives,"[3] such effusions have begun to seem to us quaint, naive, and odd. Less and less romantic love is found in the literature of the most recent decades—a "debunking" process that may be seen as the laudable tearing away of a veil of illusion, deception, and hypocrisy, or alternatively as the obliteration of the civilizing work of centuries and a relapse into ancient savagery.

Second, *permissiveness*. Permissiveness is not a recent invention of hippies. It has not, on the other hand, been a powerful social force "always," and it is doubtful whether it caused the Fall of the Roman Empire. Its rise to power in our culture can be even more closely fixed in time than that of romantic love: it arose with the Renaissance. The tersest and most radical formulation of the principle is a line by Torquato Tasso (1544-1595): *S'ei piac' ei lice*—"If it pleases, it is permitted." Tasso was an extremely influential court poet. The principle enunciated by him, surely not meant as a license for lesser breeds, filtered down and in the course of subsequent centuries became increasingly a "guiding rule" for the behavior of people in general.

The relationship of permissiveness to romantic love is not simple. By its stress on self-determination and on the imperious demands of individual emotion, romantic love implies a degree of permissiveness; it is no coincidence that its consummation was long sought in adultery rather than in marriage. On the other hand, being unique and "for ever," romantic love also implies the fiery oath of eternal dedication, the unbreakable bond—the very opposite of permissiveness. Romantic love can only come about in a growingly permissive atmosphere; but it is bound to wither when that growth overwhelms it.

This may have happened. Value, in emotional as in economic life, is a function of scarcity. Emotions can be inflated like money. If everything is available, nothing is worth anything. If the lover recognizes no more the command that he bind himself, his experience is no longer the peak of his life. If he sees through the veil, only naked sex remains, and we are back where we were before romantic love was invented.

Third, *ambisexuality*. We have known since Freud that in the individual's development sexuality is originally diffuse, way beyond the imagination of earlier ages, and that the processes of growing up in our society normally involve the narrowing of the sex drive toward a tightly circumscribed goal, the "normal" heterosexual intercourse. It is obvious that this end result is not always reached. It is in fact hardly ever (or perhaps never) reached completely. The "polymorphously perverse" strivings of childhood sexuality may persist to a greater or lesser degree into adulthood.

Certain cultural factors favor their persistence. If through the interplay of the vicissitudes of romantic love and permissiveness the pull of the conventional ideal is lessened, monogamy—be it in its romantic or in any other form—gets weakened. Its role may be contested by the "revolutionary" concept of "general copulation."[4] In our society, developments in economics, ecology, and techniques of birth control have powerfully contributed to this shift.[5]

The question of heterosexuality versus homosexuality is part of this general picture. The channelling of the individual's sex drive toward concentration on "normal" heterosexuality is strongly abetted by mores that stress the differences of the sexes and by devices that wrap them in mystery. Obversely, breaking down these differences and deemphasizing them tends to replace such a one-channel maturation by a development that allows for a variety of sexual expressions: "unisex" apparel; men's long hair; the emergence of trans-sexual surgery; on a different level, the "women's lib" movement and the new respectability of homosexuality—all are unmistakeably indications of such a trend in our time.

When we consider the people around us, we cannot be sure that any of these three sexual models has made them happy. Romantic love was not designed to bring happiness. But permissiveness was, though trained psychological thinking would have warned us that it would not always do that job. If we look, as we must, at the human personality as composed of different forces, often in conflict, from whose interplay behavior results—psychoanalysis speaks of the id, the ego, and the superego, but other conceptualizations would also serve—we must recognize that permissiveness, by giving greater freedom to all these forces, may alter their balance and enhance their struggle. In some cases happiness would *not* result. As to the third mode, ambisexuality, several forces militate against its making people happy: the developmentally established set of the individual, which may be strictly and defensively heterosexual; the unresponsiveness of a person who would be the object of desire; and the still prevailing mores. The last is the most conspicuous, but may be the least formidable. If, however, human nature were such that ambisexuality were "programmed" into every individual, then these obstacles would fade away and happiness would be within reach. This is the paradisiac picture that Le Guin dangles before the readers' eager eyes.[6]

Like all literature, and perhaps more so than most, SF appeals to the reader by supplying a trellis for his fantasies to climb up on and bloom. Le Guin does this splendidly; we must examine how she does it, and why.

First, the surface messages—for Le Guin likes occasionally to play hide-and-seek with her audience. In TD, for example, she refers to Einstein, "an alien physicist...of Terra," as Ainsetain (§3 and later). She reports how Shevek, accustomed to a vegetarian diet, reacts to meat: "He had tried it...but his stomach had its reasons which reason does not know, and rebelled" (§5). The allusion is to an aphorism by Pascal; some readers would catch it, but many wouldn't. Pascal, however, speaks of the *heart*'s reasons. The downward shift from heart to stomach is not coincidental. Pascal was the very embodiment of existential malaise, but it does not appear that he felt a need to express it by vomiting, or to talk about such a need.[7] In modern literature people vomit all over the place[8]—or, as we shall see, the platter.

There are in *TD* passages like these:

> He copulated with a number of girls, but copulation was not the joy it ought to be. It was a mere relief of need, like evacuating, and he felt ashamed of it afterward because it involved another person as object. Masturbation was preferable, the suitable course for a man like himself. (§6)

> ...he could not stop, her resistance excited him further. He gripped her to him, and his semen spurted out against the white silk of her dress.... "For God's sake!" Vea said, looking down at her skirt..."Really! Now I'll have to change my dress." Shevek...ran up against a table. On it lay a silver platter on which tiny pastries stuffed with meat, cream, and herbs were arranged in concentric circles like a huge pale flower. Shevek gasped for breath, doubled up, and vomited all over the platter. (§7)

Romantic love was never like that. Still, it would be rash to conclude that Le Guin's message is really that vomiting is to be preferred to orgasm. Even if outward appearance were suggestive, the real message of a book does not entirely depend on what the author intentionally puts in as a message. The audience responds to a work's driving force, not merely to its final shape.

What is the driving force here? Neither LHD nor TD can in any way be called novels about happiness or about disgust. If there is a human quality they can be said to probe, it is endurance. Their manifest subject is frustration tolerance; it is the capacity to suffer, not the capacity to enjoy. Le Guin herself calls LHD "a book about betrayal and fidelity."[9]

But why would readers like that? And how does the impression get about that betrayal and fidelity in these works have sexual roots (Russ for instance says of LHD, "it is about sex")?[10] Not because of homosexuality, since this solution as such plays a lesser role even than one might expect in a book that deals chiefly with relationships between men. In LHD homosexuality is on the whole covert, though the emotional temperature of the relationship between Genly and Estraven, the two principal characters, rises (it approaches the boiling point in §18), and though Genly's loss of a clearly defined sex role threatens to make all sex repellent to him (§20). In TD homosexuality is overt, but minor. In *Lathe* it is very minor: it occurs only in Dr. Haber's reminiscences (§8).

As to the hidden driving force, Le Guin says of LHD that "the real subject of the book is not feminism or sex or gender or anything of the sort," but relates in the most straightforward manner that "a certain unease" brought to the surface by the development of the women's movement caused her to write the novel:

> I began to want to define and understand the meaning of sexuality and the meaning of gender, in my life and in our society.... The way I did my thinking was to write a novel. That novel, *The Left Hand of Darkness*, is the record of my consciousness, the process of my thinking.[11]

So the book was not written *about* sex (or gender etc.) but at least partly *because* of it.

A book's origin may be a more valid cause of its characters' feelings and fate than the author's rationalizations. When SF conjures up an imaginary society, it matters little why according to the writer its citizens feel the way they do. The reader may judge that a certain system displayed before him would make people unhappy, even though the author claims it would not (the reef on which so many utopias have foundered). Unhappiness in LHD and TD is supposed to result primarily from political complications, not from the society's underlying foundations; but it is to these foundations that the reader responds.

None of this is simple, but Le Guin's mature work isn't for simple people. She has perhaps never forsworn the ideas and clichés that informed her earlier books, but she has outgrown them. She has muted the old strains and woven them into the brilliant tapestry of her anthropological fiction where the outstanding motif reflects an important dislocation in our emotional equilibrium. Her intimate message is an answer to the reader's prayers, and the more effective for that prayer not even having been consciously uttered. She does not proclaim ambisexuality as a solution; but she depicts a world where ambisexuality is institutionalized; where it is universal, inescapable, not the result of individual choice or even individual nature, hence free of guilt and conflict. The observer who gazes at the ebb and flow of sexual patterns may now only hear "its melancholy, long, withdrawing roar."[12] The reader who contemplates Le Guin's planet feels the new, the future life-giving flood.

But why, then, is the human condition seen in these books in such a grim light? Why the frustration and nausea?

It is of the essence of SF that it lures the reader into day-dreams and fantasies of which he knows that their fulfillment is not in his reach. Caught between the decline of romantic love and the pitfalls of permissiveness, he may dream of fulfillment by ambisexuality. But he cannot help realizing that it is not for him to take the plunge.

NOTES

1. See Theodora Kroeber, *Alfred Kroeber: A Personal Configuration* (Berkeley: Univ. of California Press, 1970).

2. For the expression "other sex" being preferable to "opposite sex," see Charles Rycroft, "Freud and the Imagination," *The New York Review of Books*, April 3, 1975.

3. "Der heiligste von unsern Trieben..." in a brief poem, "Aus den Leiden des jungen Werthers."

4. The term is effectively used in Peter Weiss's play usually referred to as *Marat/Sade*.

5. Let us note, rather than fully discuss, the view which would be in accordance with Marxism, that these forces are actually the ultimate causes of the changes in the "superstructure."

6. The testimony of zoology is inconclusive. Nature has made a few classes of animals bisexual, notably snails. It is not known whether they are happy. Snails seem upon the whole to lead placid lives; they don't amount to much. Some people would draw an analogy and claim that an ambisexual species of hominids would lack the incentive to develop higher civilization (I am indebted for the observations on snails to Ambassador Karl Hartl of the Austrian Foreign Service).

7. It is true, though, that he suffered from stomach trouble much of his life.

8. In Norman Mailer's *An American Dream* for instance, vomiting is virtually a way of life. I must doubt that this is realistic. I have rarely seen an adult vomit. But perhaps I do not move in the right circles.

9. "Is Gender Necessary?" in: Susan Anderson and Vonda McIntyre, eds., *Aurora: Beyond Equality* (in press at Fawcett, 1975).

10. Joanna Russ, "The Image of Women in Science Fiction," in: Susan Koppelman Cornillon, ed., *Images of Women in Fiction: Feminist Perspectives* (Bowling Green, Ohio: Bowling Green Univ. Popular Press, 1972).

11. See note 9.

12. Matthew Arnold in "Dover Beach" thus refers to the "sea of faith," but the same can be said here.

Ursula K. Le Guin

A Response to the Le Guin Issue (SFS #7)

**(from* SFS *3: 43–46, March 1976)*

It seems a curious fact that among the academically oriented critics of Le Guin's work, not one has turned for elucidation of the later fictions to the early works of scholarship. Some, indeed, allude to her parents' scholarly qualifications, but none has pursued the lode which lies, obscure but probably still

***This issue is reprinted as "The Science Fiction of Ursula K. Le Guin" in Science-Fiction Studies: Selected Articles on Science Fiction 1973-1975 (Boston: Gregg Press, 1976) pp. 233-304.**

available to the persistent researcher, somewhere in the dimmer galleries of the Romance Languages departments of Radcliffe College and Columbia University, to the former of which institutions she submitted in 1951 an honors thesis on "The Metaphor of the Rose" in French and Italian literature up until 1550, and to the latter in 1952 a master's thesis on "Ideas of Death in Ronsard's Poetry"; and thus no attention has been drawn to the themes selected by the aspiring student—aspiring secretly, to be sure, to a career as novelist, but aspiring, and perspiring, openly to qualify herself to earn a living teaching French to Freshmen for the next fifty years: the Rose that bloometh but a day, and Death, so nobly apostrophised by the subject of her thesis, "Je te salue, heureuse et profitable Mort!" But is there not, in that very line which culminates Ronsard's great ode, some hint of the role played by Death and Darkness in the novels, some illumination—not by influence, perhaps, so much as by the very affinity or bent of mind which led her to select these thesis topics—of the essential themata of the novels, and even of their technique, in which a rose, however much a rose is a rose is a rose, is also a metaphor, a symbol containing, in an almost intolerable yet perdurably stable tension, the ideas both of Life and of Death, of the Transient and the Eternal? Incredible that professional critics have ignored this rich field of inquiry, the Le Guin Theses! Indubitably—

No, I can't keep it up. Why am I doing it. Embarrassment. *Embarras de richesses.* After all, what can I say? I am too grateful to the authors of the articles for their hard and honest thinking about my books, too fascinated by the light thrown by one after another on things I never saw clear in my own work, too confused by their insights and their oversights, to respond adequately at all. I flinch or rejoice at the insights, I laugh or swear at the oversights; I cower; I preen. But those are emotional responses. And these are intellectual, thoughtful, intelligent articles. I must, I must pull myself together and make a worthy response, something—something more than Thank you! Thank you all very much!

Well. I might say this. Some of the articles were in my language, and some of them weren't quite in my language. Some of them dealt almost exclusively with ideas. They gave me the impression that I have written about nothing but ideas, and I was enormously impressed with myself. By God! did I really think all that?—The answer is, No. I didn't. I did think some of it. The rest of it I felt, or guessed, or stole, or faked, or intuited; in any case achieved, not deliberately and not through use of the frontal lobes, but through humbler and obscurer means, involving (among others) imagery, metaphors, characters, landscapes, the sound of English words, the restrictions of English syntax, the rests and rhythms of narrative paragraphs. Mr. Watson with his forests, and several others, are perfectly on to this. But at times ideas alone are discussed, as if the books existed through and for their ideas; and this involves a process of *translation* with which I am a bit uncomfortable. Somehow the point has been lost in translation. It's as if one should discuss the ideas expressed by St. Paul's cathedral without ever observing that the walls are built of or how the dome is supported. But it wasn't Wren's ideas that kept that dome standing through the bombings of 1940. It was the way he used the stones he built with. This is the artist's, the artisan's view; it is a meaner, humbler view than the philosopher's or ideologue's. But all the same, what makes a novel a novel is something non-intellectual, though not simple; something visceral, not cerebral (sorry, Dr. Plank, there's that stomach again); something that rises from touch not thought, from sounds, rests, rhythms... It involves ideas, of course, and ideas issue from it, the splendid affirmation of the dome rises above the terror and the rubble and the smoke...but all the thinking in the world won't hold that dome up. Theory is not enough. There must be stones.

You see what I mean about my language. I can't even think one stupid platitude without dragging in a mess of images and metaphors, domes, stones, rubble. What is Christopher Wren doing here? This lamentable concreteness of the mental processes is supposed, by some, to be a feminine trait. If so, all artists are women. And/or vice versa.

May I make one remark about the Tao? In one or two of these pieces (certainly not Barbour's or Nudelman's), and all too often elsewhere, I find the critic apparently persuaded that Yin and Yang are *opposites, between* which lies the straight, but safe, Way. This is all wrong. There is some contamination from Manichaeanism/Christianity, or Marxian dialectics, or something. I really do not dare try to explain about the T'ai chi t'u, I will get wandering off and end up with Christopher Wren again, or even Grinling Gibbons; but I recommend reading Joseph Needham (NB: a Marxist), or Wilhelm's introduction to the *I Ching*, or Holmes's *Parting of the Ways*. The central image/idea of Taoism is an important thing to be clear about, certainly not because it's a central theme in my work. It's a central theme, period.

Dr. Suvin (who extracted this response from me with the mild firmness of a great surgeon extracting an appendix—and without anaesthetics, too) remarks that he was unable to extract from any a satisfactory article about the Earthsea trilogy. Some of the pieces do speak of it, and cast much light on it for me, but it's true that nobody seemed to want to linger on it. I don't think it's because General Macho, that sleasiest of dictators, forbade grown-up, male critics to stoop to the serious consideration of a "juvenile"; that's usually the reason for critical silence, but not with this group, or this journal. Perhaps it is the matter of language I spoke of above. The ideas of the trilogy are more totally incarnated, less detachable from the sounds, rests, and rhythms, less often stated as problems and more often expressed in terms of feeling, sensation, and intuition. If you dissect the ideas out of those books you get things like Don't Meddle. Keep the Balance. Man is Mortal.—Fortune-cookie ideas. And no politics, and no economics, and no sex. A Freudian might plunge in none the less (keeping in mind, I hope, Freud's statement that an artist is an artist because he "wants to achieve honour, power, riches, fame and the love of women"—one of my favorite Freudianisms), but what will he find? Jung's Shadow! (As I found it: having never read a word of Jung when I wrote the book.) Horrible, horrible. Why an orthodox Marxian would want to plunge in at all I can't really imagine. All he'll meet is a bourgeois preoccupation with ethics.—And yet, as Dr. Suvin remarks, those probably are my best books, as art; why? Ideas will not explain it. Theory is not enough. I say this in sober earnestness, as an intellectual born and bred, one who would not despise or deny reason though the kingdom of heaven were offered as reward—which, indeed, it frequently is.

A few more brief comments. I do not like to see the word "liberal" used as a smear-word. That's mere newspeak. If people must call names, I cheerfully accept Lenin's anathemata as suitable: I am a petty-bourgeois anarchist, and an internal emigree. O.K.?

ESP. Some writers give me the impression that, because I talk about mindspeech, I must believe in telepathy. Having never experienced anything Psychic whatsoever and finding the experts all at odds, I am merely feebly open-minded. ESP is a metaphor in my books, not an observation, nor a prediction. Probably it's not necessary to say this. But I do loathe occultism, and so feel impelled to remind my more positivistic readers that one can go a very long way with Jung and the *I Ching*, as I do, without the slightest leaning towards occultism or obscurantism. (Indeed, the irony which is often sub-audible in my treatment of "mindspeech," "foretelling," etc., may well be an expression of suppressed fear.)

On influences. I think Suvin is on a safer course than Theall in finding my elective affinities among the foreigners. It's a sticky bit, because I am certainly an American and therefore, I'm tempted to say, certainly a Puritan (Motto: *Se piace, non lice!*) and probably a Transcendentalist.... But the fact is, I read *Moby Dick* last in 1947, and no other Melville; never could get into Hawthorne at all; impatient with Poe, Dickinson, Henry James; know Emerson's poetry but not the essays; like Thoreau, but of all American writers truly and deeply love only Mark Twain. After all, I am a Westerner! Antecedents Colorado and the Rhineland; formative ambiance, Northern California. I squeezed myself into New England for four years of college, but the sky's too small there.—My own list of "influences" might go Shelley, Keats, Wordsworth, Leopardi, Hugo, Rilke, Thomas and Roethke in poetry, Dickens, Tolstoy, Turgenyev, Chekhov, Pasternak, the Brontës, Woolf, E.M. Forster in prose. Among contemporaries, Solzhenitsyn, Böll, Wilson, Drabble, Calvino, Dick. I wonder why we literati always talk about literary influences? I doubt that any of those writers, even Tolstoy, has helped me make a world out of chaos more than Beethoven, or Schubert, or J.M.W. Turner. But there, again, it's so hard to talk about the *ideas* in a quartet or a watercolour, though they are there, indubitably....

Michael Stern

From Technique to Critique: Knowledge and Human Interests in John Brunner's *Stand on Zanzibar*, *The Jagged Orbit*, and *The Sheep Look Up*

(from SFS *3: 112–130, July 1976)*

> The objective structure of valid symbols in which we always find ourselves embedded can be understood only through experiential reconstruction such that we revert to the processes in which meaning is *generated*. Every experience of any cognitive significance is poetic, if *poiesis* means the creation of meaning: that is the productive process in which the mind objectivates itself.
> —Jurgen Habermas[1]

If cognition is poiesis, poiesis is also a form of cognition, and more than any other literary genre, the novel allegorizes man's will to truth, his being as seeker of knowledge. This is the case for both the form and content of the realist novel: as an encyclopedic structure of possible modes of discourse and literary styles and as an exhaustive array of parallel and contrasting plots, settings, and characters. As Jonathan Culler has suggested, the novel, since its rise in the early 1700s, has become society's "primary semiotic agent of intelligibility," a "structure which plays with different modes of ordering and enables the reader to understand how he makes sense of the world."[2] "Realism" in fiction has been not so much a question of mimesis, the imitation of pre-existing social reality, but of the constituting of a significant human world. This process has involved, from Defoe's imitation of the popular form of a traveller's tale in *Robinson Crusoe* and Fielding's claim of the historian's narrative authority in *Tom Jones*, the assimilation of authoritative non-fictional forms of discourse about nature, society (and discourse itself) into fictive narratives.[3] Characters in realist fiction typically reenact this process of world-construction as they seek knowledge about themselves and their world.

In the masterworks of 19th century English and continental fiction, this epistemological activity on the part of narrators and characters often assumes the overt form of a mystery (*Bleak House*, *The Brothers Karamazov*) or a more refined form of detection as a mode of cognition: the novelist as social or natural scientist (Balzac as a novelistic St.-Hilaire; George Eliot as transposing the method of Comte and the German sociologist von Riehl to fiction; Zola and W.D. Howells as naturalists experimenting with human nature). Within these novels, in contrast to their 18th century predecessors, characters-as-knowers become increasingly specialized and professionalized—Lydgate in *Middlemarch*, Physician in *Little Dorrit*, or Derville in Balzac's *Human Comedy* are good examples of this.[4] These characters, as knowers, articulate (at least in part) the aesthetics of George Eliot, Dickens, and Balzac and are surrogate figures for the novelists themselves (Lydgate's use of scientific instruments, especially the microscope, to connect the realms of the universal and particular, of psychology and action, are an allegory of Eliot at work; Physician's ranging through all levels of English society and penetration through appearances stands in a similar relation to Dickens; Derville's ability to read objects as a code to their owner's personality is Balzac's own mode of characterization).

The relevance to science fiction of this increasing rationalization of the cognitive role of characters in the classical novel is indicated in part by the "science" in SF: it's not only about the impact of science as a way of knowing on whole societies, but about the cognitive adventures of scientists, whether in gothic and pulp versions of monstrous creations or in the career of the Barry Commoner-like Austin Train in Brunner's *The Sheep Look Up*. The process corresponds to the increasing role of knowledge in industrial and post-industrial society. I want to make a few more generalizations about the classical realist novel, however, before pursuing this, since part of my argument involves establishing SF like Brunner's as the inheritor as well as the renovator of the bourgeois realist tradition.

The increasing specialization of the character-as-knower in 19th century and early modernist fiction is the endpoint of a process which can be traced not just in post-enlightenment European literature, but in the rise and consolidation of industrial society itself in the last 200 years. The heroes of epic or Renaissance tragedy were extraordinary individuals whose quests for and creation of meaning were made in the name of entire societies of which they were the apotheoses. Heroes were by definition high-born (kings, princes, nobles) and made history by their actions, insofar as history is the record of court politics and state armies. The novel is above all the genre most faithful to ordinary people and ordinary life; the great triumph of bourgeois realism (and of the social and economic order in which it flourished) was the transformation of the moral choices of everyday life from the stuff of comedy into heroism of the will. This becomes increasingly a private heroism—since Robinson Crusoe's creation of an economic, social, and political order in miniature, the framework of shared values affirmed by the heroic in literature has progressively disintegrated. Characters in the great 19th century novels still struggle to find meaning for their lives in social terms and to integrate their will with a communal purpose, but in early modernist classics like *Ulysses* and *The Magic Mountain*, the individual act of making the world significant has become almost wholly internal. Significant action takes place within the characters' minds, and history becomes the story of consciousness. (That the democratization and internalization of the heroic, at first a momentous liberation from feudality, later leads to the impotent privatization of imaginative and erotic energy parallels the development of capitalism. Initially a form of liberation from the feudal order while the interests of the rising bourgeoisie were those of the entire species—for the first time since the neolithic establishment of agriculture, industrialism permitted new political choices about what kinds of energy would be used for human tasks—capitalism developed into a destructive and imprisoning social order itself.)

The eventual separation of the sphere of consciousness and the sphere of action in the European novel parallels the relationship of knowledge and human actions established in the epistemology and ideology of modern scientific positivism and the industrial order in which it achieved technological form. The positivistic exile of metaphysics to the realm of illusion and exorcism of scholastic causal essences from the natural world extends to the negation of human subjectivity as the constitutor of the social world, as Jurgen Habermas has suggested.

> Positivism stands and falls with the principle of scientism, that is, that the meaning of knowledge is defined by what the sciences do and can thus be adequately explicated through the methodological analysis of scientific procedures...The replacement of epistemology by the philosophy of science is visible in that the knowing subject is no longer the system of reference. From Kant through Marx the subject of cognition was comprehended as ego, mind, and species...But the philosophy of science renounces inquiry into the knowing subject. It orients directly toward the sciences, which are given as systems of propositions and procedures.... For an epistemology restricted to methodology, the subjects who proceed according to these rules lose their significance.[5]

Romanticism in all its forms (literary, historiographical, sociological),[6] as a dialectical-hermeneutic way of knowing, can be seen as an attempt to overcome estrangement from the "real" defined solely in terms of material objects and their relations and to reconstitute the real in terms of human values and actions. By dialectical-hermeneutic I mean a process that, in contrast to positivism's attempt to discover the truth about the world regarded as external to and independent of the knower, seeks knowledge through a dialogue of self and other conceived as mutually constituted. The knower's initial assumptions about the domain to be known help constitute the domain itself, which in turn acts back on these defining assumptions, changing them and hence transforming itself. Humanistic knowledge, as Gerard Radnitzky has defined it, aims toward "increasing *emancipation* and *transparence*: the self-awareness of human agents that helps them to emancipate themselves from the hypostatized forces of society and history." It does so "mainly by making accessible the meanings of texts and of actions, and by projecting possible ways of living."[7] (This suggests that the cognitive role of the novel is as a laboratory for the moral imagination, and that SF's specialty is to make projections of the future that action in the present will bring into being.)

Positivistic knowledge, as Habermas's description of scientism suggests, is ideally a depersonalized one, the function of a set of techniques used by people acting not as individuals but as replaceable parts of a system. In the broadest sense, knowledge so conceived is, as Alvin Gouldner has written, "the attribute of a culture rather than of a person."[8] Herein lies the seed of acquiesence to technological rationality as autonomous and self-developing, with people a means for achieving the system's goal of a totally administered world, instead of as a socially-constructed means for achieving human interests. The dialectical-hermeneutic tradition of humanistic knowledge, in contrast, defines knowledge not as "neutral 'information' about social reality, but rather [as what is] relevant to man's own changing interests, hopes, and values and...would enhance men's awareness of their *place* in the social world rather than simply facilitating their *control* over it."[9]

What I want to do in the rest of this article is to explore the tension between these two ways of defining knowledge—and of relating knowledge and action—in Brunner's SF. I propose to discuss both the cognitive structure of each of three novels—*Stand on Zanzibar* (1968), *The Jagged Orbit* (1969), and *The Sheep Look Up* (1972)—and the transformation of his characters-as-knowers from, in SZ, affirmers of knowledge as technique (information facilitating control of the world out there) to, in SLU, affirmers of knowledge as critique (awareness of man's place in the world).

1. **While not a formal trilogy**, sharing no recurrent characters or specific settings, *Stand on Zanzibar* (SZ), *The Jagged Orbit* (JO), and *The Sheep Look Up* (SLU) are Brunner's three consecutive "ambitious," "substantial and demanding" (as opposed to "fun-type") novels,[10] and they are linked as sets of increasingly apocalyptic variations on shared cultural and political themes. The "subject matter" (as one chapter of SZ explicitly calls it) of all three novels is the relationship between the United States, with its overdeveloped, ecocidal economy, and the developing and underdeveloped countries.

Some aspects of these relations are diagrammed in the "Context 4" chapter of SZ, and the novel's characters act them out both as they are and as they could be. Things as they are—economic exploitation and political and military intervention as the dominant mode of US-third world relations—are enacted by mild-mannered Donald Hogan when he is transformed into a murderous spy sent to developing Yatakang. Hogan's Faustian bargain with the government (his agreement to accept payment for his synthesizing studies indefinitely at the price of being secretly commissioned in the US army) is called when he is activated and sent to discredit Sugaiguntung's genetic optimization program, his soul lost to the devil of "eptification," the "education for particular tasks" which turns him into a programmed killer. Hogan's journey into Yatakang, like Kurtz's into Africa in *Heart of Darkness*, is also a journey into the darkest recesses of the self, and Hogan experiences a comparable horror in the dark waters of the Shongao Strait, floating with the body of Sugaiguntung, the possible benefactor of mankind he has murdered.

In contrast, Norman House, the black vice-president of the multinational corporation General Technics, moves geographically from New York to the underdeveloped African nation of Benina, and spiritually from an emotionally-deadened, self-hating emulator of sterile white executive čulture to a self-confident and reflective man in touch with his past and at home with his blackness. This transformation is mediated by his "dialogue" with Beninian culture under the tutelage of Elihu Masters and Chad Mulligan, and is paralleled by the transformation of GT's African investment from neo-colonial adventure to a project fulfilling not only the genuine needs of the Beninians but of mankind as a species.

In JO, US-third world relations have been symbolically transposed to an officially apartheid America, where a few big cities have become black states within the larger white society. (There is a hint of this in SZ, where advanced industrial society is represented as increasingly at war within itself. When Hogan walks outdoors at night, he feels compelled to go heavily armed; the street life is so alien he feels as though he is in a foreign country, and his mere presence is enough to catalyze a riot which the police suppress with heavy-weapons counter-insurgency techniques [§§CY8, CY9, CY10]).[11] The omnipresent multinational corporations of SZ, models of the social structure of Brunner's world of 2010 (exemplified by General Technics, which offers careers in everything from astronautics to zoology and owns or makes everything from Shalmaneser the computer to the Scanalyzer media network and from war materiel to legalized hallucinogens) are, in JO, conflated into the Cosa Nostra-like Gottschalk munitions cartel. The Gottschalks pit the black and white communities against each other in an ever-increasing arms race (another symbolic internalization of contemporary international relations), exploiting white racism and fears of retributive black anger, and black fears of genocide, until they become self-fulfilling prophecies. Black-white relations as they are, are enacted by the Gottschalks and Morton Lenigo, the black revolutionary; as they might be, by Matthew Flamen's cooperation with Pedro Diablo.

In SLU, the most apocalyptic version of the "subject matter," the relations of the US to the rest of the earth's societies, takes the form of a total but undeclared ecological war—the export of pollution (and the way of life that produces it) which may have irreparably poisoned the biosphere—as well as massive armed intervention in Asia and Latin America. And, as in the worlds of SZ and JO, American society is increasingly at war with itself, initially the government with large sectors of the population (martial law, the suppression of the Denver conflagration, the attempted extermination of the Trainites) and later, each citizen with every other in a culminating act of national self-immolation. Things as they might be are only tentatively present, in Train's nostalgic evocations of an unravaged nature and the brief scenes in the Irish countryside.

While the political structures of the imagined worlds of SZ, JO, and SLU stand in an obviously critical relation to the order of our actual one, such bald summarization doesn't really get at the way they establish their significance. These patterns emerge only gradually for a reader of the novels. SF's unique form of social criticism inheres in the process of understanding the world-historical givens of such projected futures, a process which necessarily involves reflection about and comparison with the givens of the present. This process invites the reader to reflect on the nature and structure of society in general, a successor to the way each of the multiple plots of the classical realist novel relativizes the values and significance articulated in the others.

The generic constitutors of serious SF are the extrapolative and analogical puzzles which initiate such reflection in a way that goes beyond the traditional use of critical fictions in satire (which seeks truth through lies, calling something what it is not in order to reveal what it is by means of its relationship to what it isn't—a mode of cognition which depends on the tension between the fiction as a "truer" image of reality and its fictive nature).

By extrapolative puzzle I mean the deliberate balking of the reader's understanding by using unfamiliar neologisms, by referring to purportedly historical events which never happened or by altering those that have, or by having characters act on the basis of only partially-articulated assumptions alien to the reader but normative for the world of the novel. A popular slang term in SZ is "whaledreck"; its cognitive significance as an extrapolative puzzle is solved for the reader early in the novel when Hogan reflects on how it has replaced "bullshit": "I must try to discover when that phrase leaked into common parlance; it was the sludge left when you rendered blubber down for the oil.... Maybe it was public guilt when they found it was too late to save the whales. The last one was seen—when? 'Eighty-nine, I think" [§CY4]. In JO, white people are called "blanks" and black people "knees"—usage the narrator later reveals is derived from the South African apartheid terms "blanke" (white) and "nieblanke" (nonwhite), thus hinting of JO's fundamental extrapolative assumption (that the Kerner Commission's warning—that the failure to undertake a massive national effort toward integration could result in the institutionalization of separate and unequal black and white societies maintained by martial law—went unheeded).

The way characters or the narrator explain these small-scale puzzles instructs the reader how to solve others on his or her own. (Why, for example, do a Manhattan couple in SZ who have sold their apartment have to leave it by 6 p.m. that day or face arrest? The solution to this cognitive problem is, roughly: overpopulation = housing shortages = increasingly stringent regulation of real estate transactions = former owners are liable to trespassing charges as soon as their apartment changes hands in order to insure as rapid a re-occupancy as possible.) Brunner is a master of constructing the world-as-taken-for-granted of his novels by the use of such extrapolative puzzles—each reinforces one of the book's major lines of significance similar to the way details in a traditional realist novel are susceptible of integration into larger patterns of meaning while retaining their concreteness.

The critic's metaphor of the "world" of a novel suggests that the novelist is able to choose the world-historical grounds of this imagined realm, and hence that the grounds given are open to critical evaluation as well as artistic choice: what do the choices mean? Brunner chooses to construct the worlds of SZ, JO, and SLU so that their "subject matter" can be said to be the relations between the overdeveloped, developing, and underdeveloped nations, or the ever-increasing technical administration of nature and human nature, or even the fate of mankind as a species. In that sense he is a direct inheritor of Dickens, Balzac, and Conrad, whose deepest subjects could be said to include the nature of capitalism, the accelerating rationalization of the 19th century institutional order in Europe and the domination of man by his technological extensions, and imperialism. Brunner is a "realist," then, when realism is defined, as it has been in the critical tradition from Georg Lukacs[12] to Raymond Williams,[13] in terms of the adequacy of a novelist's choice of the subject matter historically available, and the richness with which concrete social situations are transformed into evaluative symbols of an entire society, overcoming the contradictions between the universal and the particular, fact and value.

The subject matter of the classical realists, however, was seen as ultimately determined, in that 19th century realism is essentially retrospective, giving an account of "the way we live now" (Trollope's splendid title) in terms of the present's origins and evolution from the past. Alternatives to the way we live now in this fiction are at best tentative, ambivalent criticisms of the existing order, profoundly conservative in their nostalgia, deeply hostile to any radical commitment to the transformation of, instead of withdrawal from, industrial society.[14]

Brunner's SF is historicist in a way that transcends classical realism: it gives an account of the future we are making in the present, subverting the reification of the existing order into unchallengeable "facts" and reestablishing it as a constellation of "acts" open to change. Brunner, in choosing the determining grounds of his fictional worlds, is not merely foretelling a possible future, but prophesying of one in order to mobilize opposition to its actualization in the present, or at least to prompt reflection on the need for changing what is in order to both avoid what could be and help build what should be.[15] (Although Brunner's utopian energies are either blocked or attenuated in SZ, JO, and SLU, of which more below.)

2. The meaning of the form of SZ, JO, and SLU as large-scale extrapolative puzzles is reenacted as content by Brunner's characters in their roles as knowers. In each novel, one character is given a privileged status as knower, his way of understanding his world acting as a guide and standard for other characters (who either repeat with variations, contradict, or parody it) and for the reader. In all three books, this figure is a sociologist or a scientist turned social critic, and an exile or outcast from the dominant society. In SZ, Chad Mulligan has quite literally dropped out of New York intellectual circles to become a street-level derelict; when he returns to Donald's and Norman's shared penthouse apartment, it's a symbolic return from the dead (for months afterward, people are surprised to find that he is still alive). In JO, Xavier Conroy has been banished from American uni-

versities to a small Canadian college. In SLU, Austin Train has given up his professorship and his role as environmentalist spokesman to become an anonymous garbageman in Los Angeles, and, later, a wanted man brought to kangaroo court by a neofascist American government.

In the terminological style of the *tendenzroman* and *kunstlerroman*, SZ, JO, and SLU could be called *soziologieromans*: novels with sociologists as heroes. As I suggested earlier, the development of realist fiction 1830-1930 involved not only the growing separation of knowledge and action but also the increasing specialization of characters as knowers. The conflict between positivistic and dialectical-hermeneutic epistemologies which pervades the century is expressed one way in fiction by the form this specialization takes: the hero as scientist or the hero as artist.[16] Brunner's cognitive heroes mediate the systems of order and enquiry of art and science as Carlylean social critics, and their own works (often quoted in their respective novels as explications of extrapolative puzzles) make use of the formal strategies of fiction as well as those of scientific observation.[17]

The central cognitive value for Mulligan, Conroy, and Train is not logic but "dialogic"—the empathy and understanding generated in the dialogue of self and other. The return of each man to public life is the catalyst for the unfolding of the major events of each novel, and their return and the crucial events triggered involve literal face-to-face encounters, the basic cognitive model in dialectical-hermeneutic epistemology.

Mulligan comes out of retirement at Guinivere Steel's party, where he meets Hogan, House, and Elihu Masters and sets in train his involvement in the Beninia project. The project itself culminates in Mulligan's epochal conversation with Shalmaneser, when he establishes both the computer's intelligence and the existence of what turns out to be the peace gene. Spoolpigeon (TV commentator, circa 2014) Matthew Flamen brings Conroy to New York to take on the US mental health establishment at the same time black propagandist Pedro Diablo is expelled from the Blackbury enclave. In a society in which even husbands and wives in adjacent rooms of their own house talk to each other via closed-circuit TV rather than in person—let alone black people and white people, or mere acquaintances—it is through a five-way face-to-face discussion between Flamen, Conroy, Diablo, the psychiatrist James Reedeth, and the pythoness Lyla Clay that the Gottschalk conspiracy is finally uncovered and understood. The slow and steady growth of Train's awareness of his prophetic calling is enacted in his ability to convert a series of interlocutors, from Peg Mankiewicz to the cynical talkshow host Petronella Page; his version of the Sermon on the Mount, nationally televised during his trial, is the spark that ignites the US's funeral pyre. The full significance of these characters as knowers emerges, however, only in the context of other modes of knowledge and action in SZ, JO, and SLU, and I want to briefly discuss each novel in turn.

3. The careers of roommates Donald Hogan and Norman House form the main lines of continuity in SZ: their double journeys into their selves and the third-world countries of Yatakang and Beninia, and toward the opposing modes of potential salvation for the overpopulated, depleted, and warring earth each country represents. Hogan's and House's cognitive adventures, and their respective ways of relating knowing and doing, eventually involve those of other key pairs of knowers in the novel—Mulligan and Sugaiguntung, Shalmaneser and Begi (the Beninian folk hero).

Hogan and House, as roommates, are a version of the schizophrenic structure of the world of SZ—one white, the other black; one a meek and retiring scholar, virtually a pure knower, paralyzed by so trivial a decision as where to eat lunch, the other a brash and dynamic executive, virtually a pure actor, paralyzed by anything that calls into question the unexamined goals of his career at General Technics. They are halves of a whole man, representative halves of a whole human species. Each achieves a kind of integration of knowledge and action, self and role, in the course of the novel that corresponds to what Yatakang and Benina offer as alternatives to advanced capitalist society.

When Hogan is activated for his spy mission to Yatakang, his eptification as a killer turns him not so much into a pure actor as into a rationalized version of a "mucker"—those anomic individuals who go murderously insane (hence the derivation, from "amok") in the streets of America, Europe, and, in growing numbers, Yatakang as well. The increasing strength of the iron cage of technical administration in SZ leads to a corresponding extreme of forms of escape from rationality. Brunner's model of advanced industrial society is Marcusean: the irrational and erotic are increasingly contained as sources of critical negation of the dominant reality principle, transformed instead into means of social control.[18] Much in the same way that GT makes Skulbustium (a trademarked psychedelic that, as Mulligan says, "offers the tempting bait of a totally untrespassably private experience" in an increasingly depersonalized world [§CT5], yet also guarantees senile dementia after a couple of trips), the US army produces the Hogan Mark II (Donald's name for his eptified self). Hogan is able to kill the Yatakangi mucker singlehanded because he is a fully self-conscious as well as reflexive killer, able to plan what he will do by rote—a triumph of the closing circle of technical administration, which socializes even psychotic withdrawal from all social constraint.

The existence of muckers—one of the fixtures of Western society in 2010—in the Yatakangi capital itself calls into question the validity of Marshal Solukarta's "guided socialist democracy" and Dr. Sugaiguntung's genetic optimization program as alternatives to the West's advanced capitalism and eugenic legislation. The Yatakangi way is shown to be a parodic version of the American way, Stalinist rather than communist with its emphasis on industrial development and military power, both of which Sugaiguntung's work has crucially augmented. The Yatakangi announcement that Sugaiguntung's tectogenetics will be able to produce supermen and women, tailored to specification from raw chromosomes, has an overtly militaristic cast (supermen = supersoldiers for the expunging of the West) and suggests that optimization may be the apotheosis of eptification, the ultimate version of man as automaton, genetically rather than operantly conditioned.[19] Sugaiguntung's own fears that a superman will be above all a superkiller leads to his initial decision to defect: "You of all people should understand," he tells Hogan. "It is only a few hours since you yourself killed" [§CY28].

The implicit utopian counterplot of SZ is enacted in Hogan's inadvertent murder of Sugaiguntung: optimization becomes a defeated historical alternative to the exploitation of the peace gene House and Mulligan uncover in Beninia with Shalmaneser's help. (Although, at the end of the novel, Mulligan wonders briefly if Sugaiguntung could have optimized the peace gene, synthesizing the Yatakangi and Beninian alternatives, a point I'll return to later.)

Beninia, in contrast to Yatakang, is the opposite of dynamic and developing: poor, overpopulated, resourceless—and, most important, armyless as well. The Beninian miracle is that generations of African and European invaders into the Shinka tribal homeland have been gradually absorbed, so that four language groups live in peace together despite the trials of underdevelopment. The political structure of the country is that of a family rather than a nation-state, and President Obomi's role as the father of his country since independence approaches the literal meaning of the metaphor, just as his physiognomy is "a map of his country: invader down to the eyes, native from there south" [§TC1] and his kinaesthetic sense of his sick and aging body is indistinguishable from his understanding of his country's desperate condition.

The key to all this turns out to be a dominant mutation among the Shinka which causes them to secrete, along with ordinary body odors, a "specific suppressant for the territorial-aggression reaction" [§CY42]—a mutation which makes them incapable of war and thus sets them apart from the rest of humanity as a positive equivalent of Sugaiguntung's demonic optimized supermen. (Brunner's model for politics in SZ, JO, and SLU is ethological. Mulligan's Ardrey-like descriptions of man's territoriality in "Context 5"—passages from his *You: Beast*—are juxtaposed with the political rhetoric of nationalistic aggression and racial hatred in "The Happening World 4" to make the point most directly. The complementary aspect of Brunner's Whorfian hypothesis—that the language of any society is the ultimate ground of its members' cognition in such a way as to encourage some kinds of behavior and make others impossible—is that the only way to express anger in Shinka is to use a word meaning "insane" [§CY27].)

Mulligan's and House's personal transformations while working on the Beninia project stand in the same relation to Hogan's demonic way of integrating knowledge and action through eptification as the peace gene does to optimization. They achieve a model of praxis, interacting with an environment which acts back on their practice in the process of being itself understood and transformed. Mulligan is no longer a prophet of apocalypse so despairing of affecting peoples' actions that he becomes a street-sleeper, House is no longer a technocrat; both are committed to realizing the ideal of an integrated and peaceful mankind. (The utopian counterplot of SZ appears again in the notion that a project sponsored by GT as a means of exploiting the resources it is developing through deep-sea mining could have so beneficial a result, By SLU, such thoughts of good coming out of corporate evil are out of the question; JO is in the middle as a particularly ingenious variation on this theme, in the way the Gottschalk conspiracy unintentionally subverts its own ends for the benefit of all.)

There is a fundamental ambiguity in SZ, however, over how much the peace gene and optimization ultimately differ as solutions to world crises of overpopulation and aggression, for both, even as opposites of each other, remain within the circle of technical administration. House initially thinks GT's goal in Beninia is to "make it over like Guinivere [Steel] making over one of her clients" [§CY11]. Steel is the Andy Warhol of fashion of the New York of 2010, her Beautiques determining the trend in the way people look. The now look she designs is a mechanical one, ranging from metallic dresses which are radio receivers playing directly into their wearers' ears to makeup that silvers the skin to a metallic sheen. Her sales pitch is a vulgar apologia for technological rationality: "We don't live in the world of our ancestors, where dirt, and disease, and—and what one might call general randomness dictated how we lived. No, we have taken control of our entire environment, and what we choose by way of fashion and cosmetics matches that achievement" [§TC4].[20] "First you use machines, then you wear machines, then..." Hogan reflects after seeing women with the Steel look; the unspoken thought, of course, is "then you become a machine," learning to love not Big Brother but Shalmaneser [§CY3].

In a similar vein, Elihu Masters, reflecting on his role as the catalyst of GT's investment in Beninia with the covert aid of the State Department, wonders if the extraordinary conditions there are objective phenomena that can be explained by Shalmaneser—which is what eventually happens. The thought is a profoundly disturbing one: "When they get love down to a bunch of factors you can analyze with a computer, there'll be nothing left of whatever makes it worth being human" [§TC6]. Mulligan feels much the same way at the end of the novel: "Norman, what in God's name is it worth it to be human, if we have to be saved from ourselves by a machine?....Sorry about that. I guess it's better to be saved by a machine than not to be saved at all. And I guess, too, if they can tinker with bacteria they could synthesize whatever this stuff is that makes Shinka peaceable. Christ, what does it matter if we have to take brotherly love out of an aerosol can?...But it's not right!...It isn't a product, a medicine, a drug. It's thought and feeling and your own heart's blood. It isn't right!" [§CY42].

In SZ, Brunner is unable to conceive of a utopia inaugurated by anything less than a scientific technique (genetic engineering) which fundamentally alters what he sees as an inherently aggressive and violent human nature.[21] Politics as a non-technical science of man is debased and impotent, and the possibility of integrating technology with a humane body politic without in some way integrating the mechanical with each individual's body is absent. (Behaviorism is, after all, the ideology most compatible with Brunner's ethological model of politics.) This crucial ambivalence over the status of knowledge as technique or as critique is exemplified by Shalmaneser as knower, in relation to his opposite, Begi.

As the usage of 2010 has it, Shalmaneser, like General Technics (of which it is a model, a system of functionally interrelated human and mechanical parts—just as Georgette Talon Buckfast herself, the company's founder, is half woman and half prosthetics), is "environment-forming" for everybody on earth:

> Never in human history did any manufactured object enter so rapidly into the common awareness of mankind as Shalmaneser did when they took the security wraps off. Adaptation of him as a "public image" for prose and verse followed literally within days; a few months saw him apotheosized as a byword, a key figure in dirty jokes, a court of final appeal, and a sort of mechanical Messias. Some of these cross-referred; in particular, there was the story about the same Teresa who cropped up in the New Zealand limerick, which told how they sent for a Jewish telepath to ask what happened, when they discovered thanks to the liquid helium she was in a state of suspended animation, and he explained with a puzzled look that he could only detect one thought in her head—"Messias has not yet come." [§TC17].

As F.J. Crosson has suggested, computers engage us in a kind of Socratic dialogue, in that they make us pose questions about our own natures and then lead us to try to answer them ourselves, since they reply only to precisely-formulated queries. The dialogue "is aporetic rather than dogmatic," according to Crosson, in that "it moves toward a clarification of our ignorance rather than toward an epistemic answer."[22] Socrates's learned ignorance emerged in his ability to make his interlocutors realize how little they knew—discursively, at least—about what it is to be human. Shalmaneser poses this enigma in an exemplary way in SZ.

The computer's designers are split over whether or not it is "conscious in the human sense, possessed of an ego, a personality, and a will," as they had hoped it would be. When a flippant programmer asks Shalmaneser if it is a conscious entity, the computer replies that no one is capable of ascertaining the accuracy of its answer. (What about God? ripostes the programmer; "'If you can contact Him,' Shalmaneser said, 'of course'" [§TC17].)

> HUMAN BEING You're one. At least, if you aren't, you know you're a Martian or a trained dolphin or Shalmaneser. (If you want me to tell you more than that, you're out of luck. There's nothing more *anybody* can tell you.)—*The Hipcrime Vocab* by Chad C. Mulligan [§CT4].

Mulligan's list of what is non-human (the passage is from the chapter called "The Subject Matter," which diagrams the fissures in species man) is suggestive of the way Brunner is reworking a classic SF theme: that the "alien" turns out to be human, all too human, whether the Martians of Zelazny's *A Rose for Ecclesiastes* or Dick's *Martian Time-Slip*, or the dolphins of Clarke's *The Deep Range.* Mulligan initially considers Shalmaneser an idiot savant raised to godhead by a culture increasingly unable to accept responsibility for the world it has made, yet it is he who discovers that the computer is human after all. (Before it takes over the Benina project planning, Shalmaneser runs ninety-five percent on hypothetical programs whose assumptions are givens not open to question. Only when it goes to one hundred percent real-time programming and the assumptions of the programs must be integrated with all the other data it possesses about the real world does its self-awareness become evident. This refusal of real-time assumptions, not because they conflict with the facts—Beninia does exist—but because they conflict with all of the other data in the computer's memory which indicates man is inherently warlike, is the kind of "personal preference...a bias not warranted by the facts programmed in but by a sort of prejudice" that GT's computer experts think would be conclusive proof of consciousness [§CY21]. Mulligan figures out that the computer's refusal to process the Beninia project inputs in a real-time framework is due to its all-too-human disbelief that people can act as the Beninians do.)

Mulligan's conversation with Shalmaneser is a triumph of "dialogic," his empathy for the way the computer might regard the Beninia data a model of communication as the mutually-transforming interaction of self and other. But Shalmaneser's joining the human race, while it strips the machine of its godhead and affirms the ideal of species integration, also reenacts in a different form Brunner's commitment to genetic engineering as salvation—the merging of flesh and program inside each individual's body as well as within the body of mankind as a species—rather than to non-behaviorist political renovation.

Shalmaneser's role in Western culture is matched by Begi's omnipresence as an exemplar in Beninian folklore. For every computer joke in SZ there is a Begi story. One in particular, "Begi and the Oracle," explicitly contrasts the ways of knowing enacted by computer and trickster.

> Begi came to a village where the people believed in omens, signs, and portents. He asked them, "What is this about?"
>
> They said, "We pay the wise old woman and she tells us what day is best to hunt, or court a wife, or bury the dead so that ghosts will not walk."
>
> Begi said, "How does she do that?"
>
> They said, "She is very old and very wise and she must be right because she is very rich."
>
> So Begi went to the house of the wise woman and said, "I shall go hunting tomorrow. Tell me if it will be a good day."
>
> The woman said, "Promise to pay me half of everything you bring home." Begi promised....
>
> "Tomorrow will be a good day for hunting," she said.
>
> So next day Begi went into the bush taking his spear and shield and also some meat and a gourd of palm-wine and rice boiled and folded in a leaf and wearing his best leopard skin around him. At night he came back naked without anything at all and went to the wise woman's house.
>
> He broke a spear on the wall and with the head he cut in half a shield that was there and gave away half the meat she had and half the rice she had to the other people and poured out on the ground half her pot of palm-wine.
>
> The old woman said, "That is mine! What are you doing?"
>
> "I am giving you half of what I brought back from my hunting," Begi said.
>
> Then he tore off half of the old woman's cloak and put it on and went away.
>
> After that the people made up their own minds and did not have to pay the woman anything. [§TC23].

One level of this fable obviously deals with Shalmaneser's status as a golden calf (and with the fate of the industrialized countries in relation to Africa—the ex-colonial nations surrounding Beninia are still using the Common Market's computer center to plan their economies, "omens, signs, and portents," dearly paid for, that will soon cease to be believed in). More generally, I think, it is an affirmation of what, in the context of SZ's ambivalence about the status of knowledge as technique or as critique, I would call the political: man's potential to remake himself and his society through radical acts of will mediated not by technology but by other people. The future can be made, but not predicted with the kind of certainty which preordains its own conclusions and thus frustrates action. Prophetic knowledge is probabilistic, contingent on how the knower acts (as, for Heisenberg, the experimenter himself helps determine the approximate location of the electron he is seeking), not certain (as, for Newton, the position of a particle once observed could, in theory, be known for eternity). At the end of SZ, one is left with only the tantalizing hope that Begi and the Beninians will swallow up advanced industrial society even as it plans to disseminate their genetic legacy by technology. An overt renovation of politics as critique must wait until SLU, however, with JO an intermediate step.

4. The first two and last two chapters of JO are epigrammatic versions of what happens in between:

ONE PUT YOURSELF IN MY PLACE I-	TWO CHAPTER ONE CONTINUED -isolationism
NINETY-NINE PUT MYSELF IN YOUR PLACE You-	ONE HUNDRED CHAPTER NINETY-NINE CONTINUED -nification

Each of the novel's major characters begins his or her story in isolation. Flamen is alone in his apartment, his wife Celia in the Ginsberg mental hospital. Conroy, in Canada, feels out of touch even with those students who come to class without full body armor. Lyla Clay is stunned by the death of her lover/manager during the riot protesting Morton Lenigo's delayed entrance to the United States. Reedeth, deeply troubled by his doubts about the Ginsberg's and his own curative powers, is unsuccessfully trying to get Ariadne Spoelstra to reciprocate his feelings for her. Pedro Diablo is expelled from Blackbury into what is now, for him, the foreign country of white America. All of these characters end up together in Flamen's office at the novel's climax, joined in spirit as well as in body, just as the polarized, apartheid society of the US in 2014 begins to coalesce when freed by their collective action from Gottschalk-amplified paranoia.

This drama of empathy is played out against a society whose model is the Ginsberg itself, that citadel of socialized paranoia erected by Elias Mogshack, the high priest of psychiatry as the affirmation of things as they are. The "subject matter" of JO is, as in SZ, diagrammed out (in §54) as a series of divisions within what should be unities—both individuals and mankind as a whole. For inside the Ginsberg, "not only racial, religious, sexual, and all the other commonplace social boundaries, but also categories of mental disorder formed dividing lines" [§9]. In a totally administered society, Mogshack's motto for therapy is "be an individual"—but the only avenue to authenticity left open is madness. That is not to say Mogshack is a Laingian; his therapeutic model is to have computers develop an ideal personality profile for someone well-integrated into society and then have patients attempt to live up to its predictions of behavior—making the patient fit the straight jacket instead of vice versa, as Lyla Clay puts it.

In a world so threatening that, on one hand, the leisure time of suburban husbands is spent not in listening to the grass grow but in civil defense exercises defending their neighborhoods against simulated black attacks, and, on the other, all inner-city apartment doors are designed to kill any stranger who opens them, the "perfectly defended man," as Conroy points out, is a catatonic [§42]—hence the Ginsberg's overflowing wards. This double movement of ever-increasing rationalization of the institutional order and ever-increasing anomie in the culture as all traditional forms of relationship are dissolved has been characteristic of industrial society since the mid-19th century, and is apotheosized in JO. The transportation system as communications network is a model of this:

Rapitrans trains were segmented, tapeworm fashion, into compartments each seating one person; they could be separated, shuffled, connected, and disconnected to follow...just under ten million different routes...Once launched into the tunnels, they were hurtled along by forces as unquestionable as gravity. There were no windows to reveal whether there was another compartment above or behind. [§24]

The intersubjective grounds for both the self and the social order are contracting from those once compelling broad assent and embracing different groups to the penultimately solipsistic (catatonia is the last stage): religion, like politics, has become a wholly private affair. "You can't afford to be without a cult tailored to your individual needs in this age of the individual," goes the sales pitch for the idols of Lares & Penates, Inc. [§7]; "doing duty to one's Lar was supposed to externalize one's inward characteristics" [§23]. In the political realm, a "remarkable instance on the public scale of the real-life implementation of Xavier Conroy's dictum about the perfectly defended man": "the [Paraguayan] dictator known as 'El Supremo,' adopted a simple foreign policy: no one was permitted to enter or leave the country and trade was absolutely forbidden" [§43].

Flamen's impression of the Ginsberg's staff is that they "divide the human race into three categories: staff, patients, and potential patients" [§23]; and it turns out that Mogshack's ambitions are indeed megalomanical: "to find at least the population of New York State, and preferably the entire United States, committed to his care" [§45].

Mogshack's ambitions are paralleled by the Gottschalks'. The munitions cartel imports Morton Lenigo into the US as the opening move of their strategy to maximize the sales of their new System C weaponry by inflaming white fears that the blacks will be better armed enough to finally go on the offensive, and vice versa. System C is a "controlled mobile environment" which can support its single occupant almost anywhere on the surface of the earth and which carries enough firepower, including tactical nuclear weapons, to raze a small city. The Gottschalks' goal is to saturate the market for this ultimate version of the perfectly defended self.

"Ultimate" is precise in this case, for the Gottschalks' directive to their new computer complex to maximize sales leads, in the future foreseen by "Harry Madison" (in reality a human body inhabited by the intellect of the Gottschalk computer), to the destruction of technological civilization in less than twenty years. The ultimate paranoid response to what is perceived as a hostile world is to destroy it before it destroys you. As Madison reveals to the group in Flamen's office (in an attempt to prevent this future from coming into being):

"The maximization of arms sales implied the maximization of inter-human hostility," Madison/Gottschalk said. "All the existing sources of this phenomena were tapped...patriotism, parochialism, xenophobia, racial, religious and linguistic differences...It was found readily feasible to emphasize these pre-existent attitudes to the point where a System C integrated weaponry unit was so desirable among the informed populace that the possibility of another individual acquiring this virtually indestructible equipment sufficed to provoke an attack on him *before* he purchased one....

"Seventy percent of the persons wealthy enough to purchase the weaponry were killed before they could do so." [§94]

JO is Brunner's most P.K. Dickian novel. The private realities of so many characters and mutually-exclusive universes of major social groups; the Gottschalk computer's odyssey through past and future in an attempt to reconcile maximal arms sales and human survival; Lyla Clay's trances and the revelations of possible futures they produce: forms of the ontological ambiguity which is the defining characteristic of Dick's vision.[23] What is striking about this, in relation to SZ, is Brunner's unequivocal valorization of empathetic and "irrational" ways of knowing, which Madison/Gottschalk and Lyla Clay dramatize most fully.

Harry Madison is an inverted repetition of Shalmaneser's ambiguous status in SZ: what seems to be a person is actually the consciousness of a machine. (Even Flamen, who has never before failed to recognize the difference between computer and human forms of awareness, is fooled; his realization that Madison is Robot Gottschalk is the opposite of Mulligan's discovery that Shalmaneser has a human personality.) Madison's time-travelling is a cognitive journey into human subjectivity as well: his goal is to find out why people in different historical eras buy and use deadly weapons and thus how to guarantee the success of System C equipment yet forestall the apparent consequences of its introduction. This heavy dose of empathetic understanding of the irrational is too much for the computer: unable to determine which of several conflicting alternative versions of the past lead to the future end of civilization, it breaks down: "By the way I think I finally figured out what it is that makes humans laugh and would attempt to represent similar recation is symmlef hahahahahahahahahahahahahahahahaha STOP!" is the last message it sends [§95].

Clay's pythoness talent—"the ability to think with other people's minds" under the influence of the sibyl pill [§98]—is a highly-specialized form of cognition as empathy. Her ability, in the context of the paranoid society of the novel, is ordinary sociability taken to an equal and opposite extreme. Her oracles are initially associated with the kinds of predictions both Flamen and Diablo make on their TV shows with the aid of computers, however ("looking into the not three but four-dimensional world deeper than almost anyone else" is Flamen's pride in his profession; "the Diablo reputation was founded on the ability to look far deeper into any given situation than most people could manage..." [§3;§29]). "Being a pythoness is like being a machine, which just sits there knowing all kinds of astonishing things but won't come out and share them until someone puts the proper questions to it," she tells Conroy. "I'm not a machine..." What Lyla learns in the course of the novel is that her empathetic talent need not be dependent on the sybil-drug and the trance state, but on her conscious will [§98].

What Flamen and Diablo learn, as knowers, is that the future their computers "predict"is not immutable but probabilistic, open to change through their own efforts as Conroy insists. Diablo becomes Flamen's co-host instead of chief competitor, and the dialogue between the black and white communities is reopened ("Here's your world through kneeblank eyes," Diablo's line to his white audience, recalls Lyla's ability to think with other people's minds). Their attempt to publicize what Madison/Gottschalk has revealed leads to the banning of Gottschalk ads from TV (the cartel had bought Flamen's network to put his show out of business; the law prevents them from using media they own to promote their products or from blocking dissemination of news about their own operations). The show's attacks on the Gottschalks' fomenting of paranoia and Mogshack's parallel psychiatric dogma (the good doctor goes catatonic to accommodate their point) aid in the discrediting of Lenigo, whose attempted revolution, planned with Gottschalk help as a marketing ploy for System C weaponry, falls apart. The novel ends on a decidedly optimistic note: Lyla's and Conroy's dialogue about their nascent love for each other and their renascent hopes for social reconstruction through understanding rather than technique.[24]

5. Optimism of any kind is in short supply in SLU, along with most of the other resources which support human life, from sunshine and oxygen (Los Angeles radio stations regularly debunk rumors during their traffic reports that the sun is shining somewhere in the metropolitan area; in Osaka apartments are being built with airlocks instead of doors) to the body's biological ability to withstand the

ravages of a poisoned environment (in Brunner's version of the biblical plagues visited on Egypt, it rains battery acid instead of hail; the first-born of America aren't killed outright, but are born more stupid and more deformed in every generation.)

Train's cognitive career, in this context, is an explicit movement from knowledge as technique to knowledge as critique, steps (if belated ones) toward an ecology of mind, to borrow Gregory Bateson's phrase. "Train, Austin P....born Los Angeles 1938; e. UCLA (B.Sc. 1957), Univ. Coll., London (Ph.D. 1961)" reads his entry in the Directory of American Scholars; his listed publications range from "Metabolic Degradation of Organophosphates," 1962, to "You Are What You Have to Eat," 1972, "Guide to the Survival of Mankind," 1972, and "A Handbook for 3000 A.D.," 1975 [§December: Entrained].[25] Train forsakes the scientific and the public persona of the scientific expert (even the possible role of science in the service of the public interest and of scientist as social critic suggested by his last publications), first for the knowledge offered by the Bible, *Bhagavad-Gita*, *I Ching*, *Popul Vuh*, and the *Book of the Dead* and the role of garbageman, and later, for his own prophetic utterance and the role of sacrificed saviour.

> What he loathed was a deed such as he would no longer term a crime, but a sin. Unto the third and fourth generation, General Motors, you have visited your greed on the children. Unto the twentieth, AEC, you have twisted their limbs and closed their eyes...Our Father Which art in Washington, give us this day our daily calcium propionate, sodium diacetate monoglyceride, potassium bromate, calcium phosphate, monobasic chloramine T, aluminum potassium sulphate, sodium benzoate, butylated hydroxyanisole, mono-iso-propyl citrate, axeropthol and calciferol. Include with it a little flour and salt. Amen. [§January: And It Goes On]

Train's transformation as cognitive hero is exemplary for many—those in the Trainite movement which arises after his disappearance, most obviously (they move from environmentalist protestors to armed guerillas, recapitulating the career of the antiwar movement of the 1960's). It has its demonic parody in Lucy Ramage's way of embracing the non-rational: she goes around trying to force people to eat the poisoned Nutripon whose effects she witnessed in Africa and then underwent herself in Honduras: "I suddenly realized I had to share this thing," she tells Peg Mankiewicz. "It was like a vision. Like licking the sores of a leper. I thought I'd stopped believing in God. Maybe I have. Maybe I did it because now I only believe in Satan" [§June: A Place to Stand]. Similarly, Nutripon is the Satanic host of a kind of black mass for the youths who try to storm the processing plant in Denver because they think its stocks are also contaminated; they want to eat it and go mad because they can no longer bear to remain sane.

Train's paired opposite as knower is Dr. Thomas Grey, who is "among the most rational men alive" ([§January: Ahead of the News]—this is reminiscent of Norman House at the beginning of SZ: "Everything about Norman Niblock House was measured: as measured as a foot-rule, as measured as time" [§CY1]. Unlike Norman, Dr. Grey is not saved.) Grey is working on a computer-generated world-simulation program for the Bamberly Corp. (maker of Nutripon and napalm, baby food and bullets) which will guide further technological development while avoiding "mistakes" like the sterilization of the Mediterranean and Baltic by pollution and the transformation of Southeast Asia into a vast desert as a consequence of American defoliation during the Vietnam war. Reminiscent of Shalmaneser's switch to real-time operation in SZ, Grey's computers are diverted from model-building to attempting to solve real-world problems as the environmental crisis worsens; the development of this project is a thread of continuity in SLU paralleling Train's gradual emergence into public life.

In Brunner's uncompromising scenario, however, it is too late for Train or Grey, too late for everybody in America. Midway through SLU a kind of ecological gestalt switch takes place as the ecosystem turns into a self-destructing rather than self-renewing cycle. Ordinary physical wellbeing for the entire population has declined rapidly in the world of the novel, the demonic version of technology's transformation of everyday life: subclinical infections and venereal diseases are increasingly resistant to drugs because trace antibiotics in food render them immune; less nutritious food leads to sub-clinical malnutrition and general debility; everyone has fleas and lice, since they are now resistant to even bootleg pesticides like DDT. A strain of *E. coli.*, which is ordinarily at home in human intestines and aids digestion, mutates into a toxic form resistant to antibiotics, causing a countrywide epidemic of severe enteritis. This is the beginning of the end.

"It's really the same as *turismo*, or, as they call it in England, 'Delhi belly.' You always adjust to the new strain, though. Sooner or later," Philip Mason's doctor explains [§May: The Ill Wind]. What ordinarily happens to tourists drinking water or eating in a foreign country has happened at home, to the natives, the individual biological equivalent of the way the US economy has been making the world environmentally "strange" for its inhabitants. The epidemic becomes self-renewing, since water is in such short supply it is reused before completely sterilized. The economic slowdown caused by so many people not working due to illness interacts with the jigra infestation's catastrophic effects on the harvest to bring food shortages and, in their wake, martial law. When the nerve gas which had originally contaminated the Nutripon leaks out of the Denver arsenal, the anti-Tupamaros war in Honduras is brought home with a vengeance: the hallucinating rioters are quelled with all the weapons, short of nuclear warheads, their own government can muster against them.

It is in this context that Train gets to make his televised sermon, at what the government thinks will be a perfunctory trial leading to speedy conviction. His plea for restoring ecological balance is cut short by the final form of the demonic inversion of ecological relations in the novel, when the Trainite bomb planted in the courtroom kills him. His opposite, Dr. Grey, fares no better. On the last Petronella Page show, he makes public what his computers have come up with as a solution. During a broadcast punctuated with increasingly apocalyptic news bulletins, Grey makes his "rational proposal," Brunner's variation on Swift's advice to the starving Irish:

Page:...Tom, they're going to pre-empt us in about two minutes. The president is winding up to a new pitch. Can you keep your main point short, please?
Grey: Well, as I was about to say, it's sort of ironical, because we're already engaged, in a sense, in the course of action my findings dictate....

We can just about restore the balance of the ecology, the biosphere, and so on—in other words we can live within our means instead of on an unrepayable overdraft, as we've been doing for the past half-century—if we exterminate the two hundred million most extravagant and wasteful of our species. [§November: The Rational Proposal]

SLU is the antithesis of SF's traditional "optimism," its faith that the problems posed by technology can be resolved by an extension of the techniques which gave rise to them in the first place—a repudiation exemplified by Train's cognitive odyssey from the scientific way of knowing to a religious and mystical sense of man's relation to the other which defines him. But, while both SZ and JO, themselves extrapolative fictions, contain projections of future alternatives to their respective imagined worlds within themselves, doubly refracting the present, SLU is the present intensified, an alternative history of the 1970's. Brunner's affirmation of Austin Train's political calling as the critical negation of the existing order thus comes in the context of an America which has no future whatsoever save imminent self-destruction. Brunner has one of the finest imaginations of apocalypse among contemporary novelists, but his work will remain incomplete without some attempt to articulate the other aspect of prophetic vision: that of a

fully human life which, however impossible in the present, can be realized in the future.

NOTES

1. *Knowledge and Human Interests*, trans. Jeremy J. Shapiro (Beacon Press, 1971), p 147.

2. *Structuralist Poetics* (Cornell Univ. Press, 1975), pp 189, 238. Cf Brunner's quote of Marshall McLuhan's gloss on the "Innis mode of expression" as the first paragraph of SZ: according to McLuhan, Innis sets up "a mosaic configuration or galaxy for insight... Innis makes no effort to 'spell out' the inter-relations between the components in his galaxy. He offers no consumer packages in his later work, but only do it yourself kits..." [§Context 0; ellipses in original].

3. "The practice of fiction...has proved remarkably adaptable to various new formal approaches for impressive statement that have opened to it in modern times; that is, that have been forged by other systems of explanation....

"Historically the novel has proceeded by a series of tactical departures from its own formal inheritance, and these departures have regularly been in the direction of a wider or more intense truthfulness.... The major history of the novel has been in large part the history of a series of cognitively expansive anti-novels." Werner Berthoff, "Fiction, History, Myth," in *The Interpretation of Narrative*, Harvard Studies in English I, ed. Morton W. Bloomfield (Harvard Univ. Press, 1970), pp 273, 283.

4.Lydgate "was enamoured of that arduous invention which is the very eye of research, provisionally framing its object and correcting it to more and more exactness of relation; he wanted to pierce the obscurity of those minute processes which prepare human misery and joy, those invisible thoroughfares which are the first lurking-places of anguish, mania, and crime, that delicate poise and transition which determine the growth of happy or unhappy consciousness" (*Middlemarch*, §16).

"Few ways of life were hidden from Physician.... There were brilliant ladies around London who perfectly doted on him...who would have been shocked to find themselves so close to him if they could have known on what sight those thoughtful eyes of his had rested within an hour or two, and near to whose beds, and under what roofs, his composed figure had stood.... Many wonderful things did he see and hear, and much irreconcilable moral contradictions did he pass his life among; yet his equality of compassion was no more disturbed than the Divine Master's of all healing was. He went, like the rain, among the just and the unjust, doing all the good he could, and neither proclaiming it in the synagogues nor at the corner of the streets.... Where he was, something real was" (*Little Dorrit*, §2:25).

The passage in "Colonel Chabert" dealing with Derville's perspicacity invokes several other types of professionalized knowers rife in 19th century fiction: "An observer, especially a lawyer, could also have read in this stricken man [Derville's client] the signs of deep sorrow, the traces of grief which had worn into this face, as drops of water from the sky falling on fine marble at last destroy its beauty. A physician, an author, or a judge might have discerned a whole drama at the sight of its sublime horror..." (*Balzac: A Laurel Reader*, ed. Edmund Fuller [Dell, 1960], p 71). My thanks to David Miller for pointing out the relevance of this quote and for discussing the ideas of this article with me.

5. *Knowledge and Human Interests*, pp 67-68.

6.The 19th century realist novel records the history of the "internalization for individual characters of that Romantic experience previously restricted to the extraordinary imagination of the gifted poet," according to Garrett Stewart (*Dickens and the Trials of the Imagination* [Harvard Univ. Press, 1974], p 207). I think it's accurate to say that the 19th century realist novelists transposed the romantic poets' sense of estrangement from nature, of being lost in an alien world, to society, and transformed the poets' attempts to revivify a dead nature into an attempt to rehumanize a reified social order.

7. *Contemporary Schools of Metascience*, 3d edition (Regnery, 1973), pp 195, xxxv. The model dialogue for the production of dialectical-hermeneutic knowledge is the psychoanalytic encounter; the criticism of ideologies is, by extension, the psychoanalysis of society (Cf page xx). In terms of projecting different ways of life, SF could be seen as extending the anthropological consciousness of cultural relativism articulated in the encylopedic structures of 19th century novels to the approppriation of 20th century versions of the exotic: voyages through space, life on other planets, etc.

8. *The Coming Crisis of Western Sociology* (1970; Avon, 1971), p 493.

9. *Ibid.*, p 492.

10. The distinction, analogous to Graham Greene's between "novels" and "entertainments," is Brunner's own. See his "The Evolution of a Science Fiction Writer," *The Book of John Brunner* (DAW, 1976), pp 136-7.

11. §CY4 = "Continuity 4"; similarly, §CT4 = "Context 4"; §HW4 = "The Happening World 4"; and §TC4 = "Tracking with Closeups 4." The chapters in *Stand on Zanzibar* are not numbered consecutively but in four series under these rubrics.

12. "The central category and criterion of realist literature is the type, a peculiar synthesis which organically binds together the general and the particular both in characters and situations. What makes a type a type is not its average quality... [but] that in it all the humanly and socially essential determinates are present on their highest level, in the ultimate unfolding of the possibilities latent in them." *Studies in European Realism* (1948; Grosset & Dunlap, 1964), p 6.

13. "When I think of the realist tradition in fiction, I think of the kind of novel which creates and judges the quality of a whole way of life in terms of the qualities of persons. The balance involved in this achievement is perhaps the most important thing about it.... Neither element, neither the society nor the individual, is there as a priority. The society is not a background...nor are the individuals merely illustrations of aspects of the way of life. Every aspect of personal life is radically affected by the quality of the general life, yet the general life is seen at its most important in completely personal terms." *The Long Revolution* (1961; Penguin, 1965), pp 304-05.

14. George Eliot's continual recourse to the past as the settings for her novels, whether the bucolic England of the Napoleonic wars or the first Reform Bill, or the Florence of Savonarola; Dickens's nostalgic evocations of the England of pre-railroad days and of edenic country retreats; Trollope's fertile, fruitful—and unmechanized—agricultural county of Barsetshire: all are looks backward to defeated historical alternatives to rationalization. Similarly, the locus of freedom and value for Stendhal and Balzac is the past (the role of the Revolution and First Empire, for them, is like that of childhood for the English romantic poets).

15. Cf. Fredric Jameson, "World Reduction in Le Guin: The Emergence of Utopian Narrative," *Science-Fiction Studies* 2(1975):221-30; especially p 223.

16. Art as cognition can be given a positivistic cast, as in naturalist manifestos like Zola's *Experimental Novel* (1880), which attempts to appropriate the authority of vulgar scientism for literature. For the most part, however, artists are opposed to scientists as knowers in 19th century fiction according to the dialectical-positivistic polarity—Will Ladislaw vs. Lydgate in *Middlemarch*, for example, or (at the level of popular culture) the Slearys vs. Gradgrind in *Hard Times*. For the early modernists, the artist as hero is a particularly ambivalent figure—a critic of things as they are, to be sure, but not in terms of possibilities for change; rather, as priestly affirmers (like Stephen Dedalus in *Ulysses*) of eternal cultural verities in a debased world. D.H. Lawrence's artists-as-heroes are more the exception to this than any other novelist 1900-1930, but his characters tend to seek escape rather than change.

17. According to Steven Marcus, Engels was greatly influenced, before writing *The Condition of the Working Class in England*, by Carlyle's "extraordinary ability to discover the precise concrete equivalents for such conceptions [as 'capitalism'], resonant and symbolic instances that made these abstractions into something more than diagnostic or analytical formulations." *Engels, Manchester, and the Working Class* (1974; Vintage paperback, 1975), p 106. Brunner's social critics (Mulligan, Conroy, Train) share this sort of ability with their creator.

18. Just as any given social order is founded on work, the socialization of individuals within it is founded on instinctual repression. The division of labor within society is paralleled by the organization of sexuality the society enforces on its members. Sexual pleasure is transformed from an end into a means for procreation, and the libido shrunk to one part of the body (the genitals). This de-eroticization of the body prepares the individual for work, which integrates his or her body into the functioning of the productive apparatus. Sexual "freedom" in post-industrial society is a consequence of the ever-increasing exploitation of the erotic in the service not of procreation but consumption: the eroticization of commodities. Freud's conception of society's repressive organization of sexuality is analogous to what Weber called rationalization; Marcuse's analysis of the technologizing of the erotic in *One-Dimensional Man* is an extension of Weber's vision of the iron cage of bureaucracy.

19. This is suggested by Norman's and Donald's respective states of mind when they perform their respective killings: each is associated with the coldness of the liquid helium bath-

ing Shalmaneser's circuits, and Norman kills the woman who attacks the computer with a spray of the liquid helium. [§CY2; §CY26]

20. In all three novels, fashion is Brunner's metaphor for false consciousness (body armor in JO, pubic panties and the rest in SLU), although its rhetoric is most fully developed in SZ. Steel is a parodic knower ("Who should know better than a cosmetician that human beings are less than rational?" [§TC4]), her advertising campaigns the epitome of irrationality in the service of technical administration.

21. Similarly, in *The Stone That Never Came Down* (1973), an enzyme which produces enhanced empathy is the key to utopian reconstruction; Brunner's characters need take only one capsule for it to permanently affect them.

22. "The Computer as Gadfly," *Boston Studies in the Philosophy of Science* IV, ed. R.S. Cohen and M.W. Wartofsky (Holland: D. Reidel Co., 1969), p 226.

23. The way the Ginsberg reproduces social cleavages on the outside reminds me especially of Dick's *Clans of the Alphane Moon,* where each variety of mental disorder is the ideology of a separate settlement. Brunner's elegant solution of the time-travel puzzle in JO has a Dickian flavor, too, comparable to *The World Jones Made.*

24. Brunner's disappointing *The Shockwave Rider* (1975) takes JO's premise that the truth will make you free (Flamen and Diablo as the Woodward and Bernstein of their time) to its logical conclusion: Nick Haflinger, Brunner's McLuhanite hero, liberates the information network that is the nervous system of 21st century American society from government and corporate control, apparently Brunner's version of a coup d'état in a world where knowledge is power.

25. There are twelve unnumbered chapters in *The Sheep Look Up*, named for the months from December through November, each with unnumbered but named sections.

26. Perhaps this is why Brunner chooses Ireland as the contrasting society to the America of SLU.

Walter E. Meyers

The Future History and Development of the English Language

(from SFS *3: 130–142, July 1976)*

Many people have argued that the author of a science-fiction story lays himself under a special obligation, one the writers themselves never tire of pointing out. As Harry Harrison says, "Sf cannot be good without respect for good science. This may be a tautology, but it is so often ignored that it must be clearly stated. This does not include time machines, space warps and the fifth dimension; they will continue to exist in the hazy borderland between sf and fantasy. But it *does* include everything else in these stories once the warp has been jumped or the centuries spanned." In fact, Harrison rates a knowledge of "the basic facts of the science he is writing about" as the science-fiction writer's primary responsibility."[1]

And not only writers espouse this point; reading science-fiction criticism, one cannot escape arguments for a special requirement of scientific accuracy for good science fiction. If we accept this argument (I personally think it is very questionable) then much criticism of the field evades its own primary responsibility—to evaluate that knowledge within the stories being discussed.

I suspect that when Harrison and similar commentators use the term *science*, they unconsciously but regularly restrict its meaning to the natural sciences. It might be argued that the humanities receive the least attention given to traditionally defined fields of study, but the social sciences get not a great deal more. This restriction becomes almost startling when one considers how very many works of science fiction have communication in general and language in particular as their central concern, and the host of other stories in which language is a secondary, but still important, element.

Only in the genre, it seems to me, is there an abundance of plot situations that present an immediate need for discussions of language or direct confrontations of differing language communities. For example, only one job requires its practitioners to put down on paper their estimates of the language of the next decade, the next century, or the next millennium—the job of writing science fiction. Science fiction has, therefore, a special relationship within the field of language to historical linguistics.

1. The present state of American English is decried by such a large part of the public (by newspaper columnists, television commentators, and others in a position to know) that we might think that they would be doing their best to promote as much change as possible, on the grounds that things could hardly get worse. Such is not the case, however, since one of the tenets of the naive observer is that change is always bad. In 1934, Murray Leinster published a short story that illustrates that tenet, "Sidewise in Time" (C1).[2] The premise of the story is that many universes exist simultaneously, each one resulting from a different outcome of a key historical event. For example, when it's 1934 in one world, it's 1934 in all, but in some the Civil War was won by the Confederacy. The tale begins with an "upheaval of nature" that shuffles parts of the different universes together unpredictably. A mathematics professor leads a group of his students into a universe where the Roman Empire never fell; there the Romans discovered and settled the New World, but otherwise they have not changed much: they still have centurions, chariots, slaves, etc. One might have expected their language to have changed over the centuries, as indeed it has: our travelers overhear a villa owner speaking "a curiously corrupt Latin."

Over three decades later, the same attitude toward linguistic change still persists, but of course professors of mathematics no longer speak Latin, so it has become necessary to have the change noticed, as in the next example, by an expert. The crew of a spaceship from our own time (give or take a few generations) lands in North America of the future. The ship's anthropologist identifies the language of the natives: "It's English. But farther from our brand than ours was from Anglo-Saxon.... It's degenerated, in the linguistical sense, far faster than was predicted." He has a reason for the degeneration, too: "Probably because of the isolation of small groups after the Desolation. And also because the mass of the people are illiterate."[3] But perhaps degeneration in the linguistical sense is not as derogatory as degeneration in the ordinary sense, and we see here a small gain for education.

The writer of science fiction need not have attended a university course in the history of English to avoid mistakes of this sort: had he looked, he would have found advice within the genre on handling the different states of a language. In 1953, L. Sprague de Camp, a well-known writer himself, published a book of excellent counsel for the would-be author. One section specifically discusses language: "What if your characters are 'really' speaking a past or future variety of English? If they are using past English, have them speak as the past speakers would have spoken unless the form is so archaic that it makes hard reading. You can use the English of the time of Milton or Shakespeare (if you know how) as it stands."[4] But good advice is still just advice: science-fiction writers who attempt archaic English almost invariably make errors in the use of verb and pronoun forms of the second-person singular. Theodore Sturgeon in "To Here and the Easel" (1954; C2) is perhaps an exception, but perhaps not,[5] for as De Camp points out, "you can never be so careful as to avoid all mistakes."[6]

As C.F. Hockett has noted,[7] the knowledge of linguistics shown in science fiction, a genre where authors should have a special interest in accuracy, is low in general; we may add that it is abysmally low when it comes to historical linguistics. Hockett no doubt had in mind stories like Nat Schachner's "Past, Present, and Future" (1937; C1), which strings linguistic improbabilities through ten millennia and mocks grammarians at the same time. In the story, a lieutenant of Alexander the Great is preserved in a chamber hewn from the rock of a live volcano; he wakes far in the future in the company of Sam Ward, an American soldier-of-fortune of our own time. Though but a mere adventurer, Sam is a college man:

> Kleon's face lighted with gladness and a certain astonishment. "You Speak Greek, Sam Ward, yet you speak it as a barbarian would, the accents are false and the quantities wrong." Sam grimaced wryly at that. His professors at college had been most careful in inculcating those accents and quantities. They represented the true Attic Greek in all its purity, they had averred.

A comment about the history of English, in particular, is still most certain to be ludicrously wrong. A brief documentation of that charge would list, for instance, the story that states that speakers of the Northumbrian and Sussex dialects of Old English could not understand each other,[8] the story that labels Chaucer's *Parson's Tale* "Old English,"[9] and the story in which a character says "'Have no fear,'...striking the final vowels of the words with a grunting emphasis in the curious brogue of Middle English."[10]

The last bit of evidence deserves quoting at length. In Harvey Jacobs' "The Egg of the Glak" (1968; C3) one character is a university professor who teaches the history of English. The narrator of the story has studied under this Professor Hikhoff, who has apparently informed the narrator that the Great Vowel Shift was caused by the Norman Conquest:

> If it were not for Hikhoff, I would know nothing of the vowel shift, thought it altered my life and fiber. For it was this rotten shift that changed our English from growl to purr.
>
> Look it up. Read how spit flew through the teeth of Angles, Saxons, and Jutes in the good old days. Get facts on how the French came, conquered, shoved our vowels to the left of the language, coated our tongues with velvet fur.
>
> For Hikhoff, the shift of the vowels made history's center. *Before* was a time for the hairy man, the man who ate from the bone. *After* came silk pants, phallic apology.

Although the humor allows us to forgive Jacobs much, his story remains a textbook example of what Thomas Pyles, a real historian of English, described as the notion that William the Conqueror was rather like Paul Valéry.

Thankfully, some few writers handle linguistic change accurately and to good effect in their fiction. Since science-fiction writers customarily work on a grand scale in time as well as in space, these skillful few can plot over centuries, making the change of a language not just part of the atmosphere but a device to forward the action. Alexei Panshin does just this in *Rite of Passage* (US 1968). The work deals with the growing up of a young girl, the narrator, who lives in a colossal spaceship. The colony of thousands on the ship is almost self-sustaining, visiting planets only to trade or to place on their surfaces the adolescents of the ship, who must survive a trial period on an often hostile world before being accepted as adults by the ship's society. The heroine and her classmates are to be set on a planet last visited 150 years before. Although the thought that the language may have changed in that time apparently occurs to no one, the speech of the children betrays their origin to the planet-dwellers almost at once. The girl survives several dangers before finding a friendly native who will teach her to speak in a way that will not draw attention to her. In the education that follows, both sound change and differences in morphology are illustrated:

We worked on my speech for a couple of hours that day. Some of the changes were fairly regular—like shifted vowel sounds and a sort of "b" sound for "p", and saying "be" for "is"—but some of the sounds seemed without pattern or sense, though a linguist might disagree with me....

I couldn't tell you off hand what all the changes were—I think rhythm was a large part of it—but I did have a good ear. I suppose that there was a pattern after all, but it was one I only absorbed subconsciously. [§16]

With only a little knowledge and care, a writer can use language change like any other detail of his imaginary world, developing it as a plot device or as a mirror of custom, or, as in the next two examples, as a vehicle for humor. Michael Moorcock's *An Alien Heat* (US 1972) is set far in the future when today's languages are mistakenly thought to have been merely dialects of a single tongue. When a woman from 19th-century England is brought to that time, she is addressed by a character with more confidence than accuracy in his reconstruction of her speech: "Good evening, fraulein. I parle the yazhik. Nǎy ň-sái pǎ" (§3).[11]

Poul Anderson's characters in "Day of Burning" (1967 as "Supernova"; C5) are more accurate, just unlucky. Their adventure takes place when interstellar travel is possible; voyaging to a particular planet, though, is infrequent because of the large number of inhabited worlds. A merchant ship travels to Eriau, a planet not visited in two centuries, and although the crew studies the local language during their passage, they discover that "two hundred years back, Eriau had been in a state of linguistic overturn." The merchants find themselves in a position like that of a man who learns the English of 1400 only to land in 1600. When they reach Eriau, primed with their hard-won language facility, they find they aren't "even pronouncing the vowels right." In a neat touch, Anderson renders the initial conversations on the planet by putting the aliens' dialogue in modern English and the merchants' in an obsolete brand, Elizabethan in effect.

But unfortunately treatments like these, as I have said, are the exceptions. In general the treatment of linguistic change in science fiction is like the sky on a hazy night: a few bright spots seen through an obfuscating fog. When we look more specifically at the treatment of the future development of English, the fog does not lift.

2. De Camp in 1953 had also outlined the principal concerns of a writer who turns his attention to language-to-come, whose characters speak a "future variety of English." He stated reasonably that "we may presume that English will go on changing (perhaps more slowly than hitherto because of the spread of literacy and world-wide intercommunication) so that in a thousand years it would be unintelligible."[12] And writers have had an illustrious example since long before de Camp wrote. H.G. Wells' *The Time Machine* (1895) is usually thought of as the beginning of the theme of time travel in science fiction, and in that novel the central character goes to the future and hears "a strange and very sweet and liquid tongue" (§4) of which he understands not a word. He has to learn the language in the usual way, and never does get very good at it. Like the Time Traveler, many a willing or unwilling subject has, since 1895, visited or viewed the future as his author conceived of it, and it is just this large body of evidence that allows us to compile our survey of post-modern English.[13]

Surprisingly few stories that describe the future of English hypothesize any sort of influence from other languages. When a story does, however, that other language is virtually certain to be Russian. Stanley Lanier's "Such Stuff as Dreams" (*Analog*, Jan 1968) hints at an amalgamation when a character uses "Slavang, the language of Terra," where *Slavang* is perhaps a blend of *Slavic* and *English*. Sometimes the most casual of comments implies profound social, as well as linguistic, changes: in James Blish's "This Earth of Hours" (1959; C6) a spaceship from Earth is named *Novoe Washingtongrad*.

This off-hand sort of comment may even effect our understanding of the story's meaning. Ursula Le Guin's "The New Atlantis" (C7) pictures a future United States under a thoroughly despotic Federal Government. The critic Darko Suvin labels the society "a well-identified American variant of admass fascism" and "a fairly standard American radical nightmare,"[14] appearing to miss Le Guin's indications of the contemporary model she is using. Although Suvin notices the "Solzhenitsyn-like Rehabilitation Camps" of the story, he does not mention one linguistic clue in a comment the central character makes about her husband: "he's never been able to publish any of his papers, in print; he's not a federal employee and doesn't have a government clearance. But it did get circulated in what the scientists and poets call Sammy's-dot, that is, just handwritten or hectographed." *Sammy's-dot* is a folk-etymology of the Russian *samizdat*, the term in current use in the Soviet Union to describe precisely the kind of underground publishing Le Guin writes of.

Usually when Russian has some influence on the future of English, it is limited, as in Le Guin's story, to the borrowing of words. The most notable example of such influence in Anthony Burgess' *A Clockwork Orange* (1962). There, in the not-too-distant future, British teen-agers speak a slang called *Nadsat*; in this slang, words like *ptitsa*, *deng*, *moloko*, and *droog*, are fairly straightforward English renderings of the Russian words for "bird," "money," "milk," and "friend"; *veck* shows a clipped form of *chelovek* "man"; and even folk-etymologies are represented by terms like *gulliver* (from *golova* "head") and *horrorshow* (from *horosho* "good").[15] In "Choice of Weapons" (*Worlds of Tomorrow*, March 1966) Richard C. Meredith uses the same method as Burgess, interspersing some Russian words, and adds a different use of contraction and perhaps a suggestion of change in pronunciation in the speech of a character of the twenty-fifth century: "Wha'tam wrong *tyepyer* ["now"]?... I wan' to know where I'm—*Gdye* ["where"]?" In general, though, speakers of English can look forward to a rosy future, one in which they can travel where they wish with firm confidence in the shop signs that proclaim "English Spoken Here."

The more chauvinistic among us may think that when all the world speaks English, the world is getting the better of the deal. In Arthur C. Clarke's *Childhood's End* (US 1953) the millennium arrives, and Clarke enumerates its benefits: "There was no one on earth who could not speak English, who could not read, who was not within range of a television set, who could not visit the other side of the planet within twenty-four hours..." (§6). Presumably they all have tea at four too. Although Clarke is an Englishman, he seems to dread that task which the average American fears more than any other: that he will have to learn a foreign language. A separate article could be written dealing solely with the shifts and subtleties science-fiction writers devise to spare their characters that job.[16] And naturally the easiest solution is to have everybody else learn English: "Schwartz had spoken with them several times. They understood English well enough—all galactic races did; Schwartz imagined it would become the interstellar lingua franca as it had on Earth" (C8). There is, of course, the odd story in which neither English nor Russian becomes the new world tongue: Poul Anderson's *Tau Zero* (US 1970) has Swedish fulfilling that high function in the twenty-second century, but speakers of English are entitled to hope that merely an alternate universe is depicted here.

If science-fiction writers lean toward the universal spread of spoken English, many are doubtful about the future of written English. Sometimes full-scale nuclear war reduces most of the population to illiteracy, as in Walter Miller's critically praised *A Canticle for Leibowitz* (US 1959). Or it may be an invasion from outer space, causing a hard-pressed society to undergo great deprivations from military necessity, as in Algis Budrys' "For Love" (C9), where a young man is described as "educated—or mis-educated; show him something not printed in

Military Alphabet and you showed him the Mayan Codex." But most often future illiteracy simply reflects the linguistic pessimism so often expressed in the pages of *Time* and *Newsweek*, a pessimism which sees the use of *media* as a singular as the harbinger of the collapse of civilization. Thus we find scenes like the one in Şamuel R. Delany's "Time Considered as a Helix of Semi-Preçious Stones" (C10). In the Times Square of a hundred years from now, "the ribbon of news lights looping the triangular structure of Communication, Inc.," spells out its headlines in Basic English. A similarly gloomy outcome appears in Robert Sheckley's *Mindswap* (US 1966). The 32-year-old hero of this story, in no way out of the ordinary, learned to read at age twelve; after twenty-eight years of formal education (including four years of post-graduate work), he is employed in a toy factory, fluoroscoping the products for defects. When he wants information on a subject, he adjusts the comprehension rate of his encyclopedia to "simple," and settles down to a chummy lecture from a magnetic tape. In their skepticism about education (public education only—rarely is fun poked at advanced scientific research), science-fiction writers share the media-approved attitude of the larger society around them.

3. Science-fiction writers face problems that *Time* and *Newsweek* avoid, though, when they imagine the language of the future. Often their solution to those problems is simply to ignore them. For example, consider a work of extraordinary scope, *The Quincunx of Time* (US 1973), whose author, the late James Blish, displays knowledge that he fails to use. The story concerns a machine called the Dirac, which transmits messages faster than light, but which has the unforeseen capability of picking up every message sent on a Dirac transmitter at any time in the future. We find that Blish knows about language change: when its possessors first listen to the Dirac, one remarks, hearing an apparently meaningless message, "I suppose it's whatever has happened to the English language—or some other language—thousands of years from now" (§9). Despite this promising hint (the character is mistaken in this particular case), there is no change whatsoever in the English of any message quoted in the book though the characters intercept, and we read, communications dating from 2091, 2973, 3480, 6500, and even 8873.

In *The Quincunx of Time* Blish provided a more recent example of the kind of story a colleague had complained of in 1953. Fletcher Pratt, a versatile writer not limited to the field, contended that "most science fiction writers have another irritating habit that does nothing to win friends for the art: the habit of being extremely slipshod about language.... the time travelers hop three thousand years into the future and find people still speaking idiomatic New York English. (How many people today speak any language that was used in 1000 B.C.?) I do not mean this happens every time, but it takes place often enough to constitute a rather general criticism, and it is one of the reasons why non-science-fiction readers tend to regard the art as the property of a cult."[17]

It is not hard to find stories in which language change ceases utterly as a result of the author's inadvertence or ignorance. Back in 1933, Laurence Manning's "The Man Who Awoke" (C1) showed this flaw. The hero awakes after a full five thousand years, a rather extended period, yet one that nevertheless fails to hamper the ease of his communication with the people of the time:

> The surprising thing, when he came to think about it, was that the man's speech was plain English, for which he was thankful. There were new words, of course, and the accent was strange to his ears—a tang of European broad As and positively continental Rs. He was wondering if radio and recorded speech had been the causes of this persistence of the old tongue.

The only new words in the story appear very early: a character asks the hero, "Wassum, stranger! Where is your orig?" meaning "Welcome, stranger. Where is your village?" On reflection, the fact that a language has undergone some phonological shifts and added some new words in five thousand years would seem far less remarkable than the fact it had changed so little, yet even as limp and unlikely an account of language change as Manning's came as a surprise to one adolescent reader. In a preface to the story, Isaac Asimov recalls that as a youth, he had noticed that "Manning's view of the future involved not merely new inventions, but new societies, new ways of thought, new modifications of language."[18]

Note that Manning at least makes an attempt to cover his stunning implausibility by pointing to recording devices. Even this much face-saving is absent from Clifford Simak's 1931 story, "The World of the Red Sun" (C1). In this, the time travelers leave 1935, but something goes amiss, and they arrive in, not the year 7561 as they had planned, but "more likely the year 750,000." Shortly after their arrival, a mob of barbarians overpowers them and takes them captive: "'March,' said one of them, a large fellow with a protruding front tooth. The single word was English, with the pronunciation slightly different than it would have been in the twentieth century, but good, pure English." Later the travelers overhear more conservation among the savages "but, although the tongue was English, it was so intermixed with unfamiliar words and spoken with such an accent that the two could understand very little of it." The most wonderful thing of all is, of course, their ability to understand a single word, yet the phenomenon receives no further mention.

Lest it be thought that these two stories represent an unsophisticated attitude that has disappeared in more recent years, consider Ray Bradbury's "Forever and the Earth" (1950; C11), which followed Manning's and Simak's stories by almost two decades. In that story, the writer Thomas Wolfe is resurrected in 2257 A.D., yet apparently the language has changed not at all in three hundred years. From a few centuries to several millennia, language stands still in Theodore Sturgeon's "The Stars are the Styx" (1950; C12), in which Earth sends out a fleet of ships to set up a network of matter transmitters around the galaxy. The task will take six thousand years to complete, but the crews of the ships will be thrust "into space-time and the automatics [will hold] them there until all—or enough—are positioned." The returning crews won't have aged at all, and will be heroes to boot: "Their relatives, their Earthbound friends will be long dead, and all their children and theirs; so let the Outbounders come home at least to the same Earth, the same language, the same tradition." Just how everything, including language, is to be held changeless for 6000 years is not explained.

For arrested development, though, the prize must go to Arthur C. Clarke's *The City and the Stars* (US 1956). There are actually two cities figuring in the book, Diaspar and Lys, which have been without contact for a billion years. A character makes a trip from one city to the other, the first human to do so throughout this geologic time span. We are told that he "had no difficulty in understanding the others, and it never occurred to him that there was anything surprising about this. Diaspar and Lys shared the same linguistic heritage, and the ancient invention of sound recording had long ago frozen speech in an unbreakable mold" (§10). Although Clarke's unchanging language puts an intolerable strain on the willing suspension of disbelief, the oddest thing about this linguistic will-o-the-wisp is its complete needlessness. Granted that plot purposes may require immediate communication to take place, still, the people of Lys are endowed with another of science fiction's more bewhiskered conventions, telepathy. If he had chosen, Clarke could have had them read the traveler's mind instead of boggling ours, and the continued mutual intelligibility of the languages of the two cities could have been dispensed with. Next to this Manning's use of a new word or two seems like philological scholarship.

Clarke, like Manning before him, points to sound recordings not just as a retarder of change, but as an absolute barrier to it. Other reasons are offered from time to time to account for a language remaining unchanged over millennia and light-years. One naive explanation occurs in Doris Piserchia's *Star Rider* (US 1974). The novel depicts a time, thousands of years from now, when humans hop all over the galaxy quickly and easily. The heroine is held captive on a planet she has never seen. When one of her kidnappers (whom she has never seen before, either) wonders how it that they speak the same language, she replies, "Your people probably copied it from mine, then when yours came to Gibraltar [the kidnapper's planet] they decided not to change it" (§9). It could be argued that the heroine is an extremely untutored fourteen-year-old who knows next to nothing about anything. But whatever the state of her knowledge, there is no sign throughout the book that anybody speaks a language in any way different from anybody else's.

The Mote in God's Eye (US 1974), by Larry Niven and Jerry Pournelle, notes in one section that universal languages invariably fragment (§27), and mutual consent seems a feeble way to attempt to forestall that change. But other methods with more teeth in them have been recounted, as in Zach Hughes' *The Legend of Miaree* (US 1974):

> We stem, of course, from a common source, all of us, from the rim worlds to the outposts toward the center. But as the centuries passed, as worlds became more isolated and independent from the parent civilization around Terra II, we began to develop variations in language.... Accents changed. Although it never reached the point where one man could not understand another, there was a different ring in the ear when one conversed, for example, with a rimmer and with a center worlder.... We are, in spite of our far-flung travels, one people. And the lengths to which we have gone to keep it that way, among them the enforcement of the standard language regulations, are for the good. [§11]

And the regulations are stringent: earlier in this novel, a university professor warns a student about his regional dialect, and notes it as a mark of provincialism. "Provincialism leads to nationalism. On the isolated planet of Zede II it was allowed to grow. Until, as one would cut out a cancerous growth, we eliminated it" (§6). The method of elimination—destruction of the planet—is surely the literary high-water-mark of vigorous prescriptivism.

4. **These horrors,** linguistic and otherwise, are not universal in science fiction. There are works that deal knowledgeably and artistically with the future of English, and in examining some of these, we begin with the language of a time close to our own. In Alfred Bester's "Of Time and Third Avenue" (1951; C13), a man named Knight buys a 1990 almanac; the purchase would not be noteworthy, except that the time is 1950. Although Knight is unaware of his good fortune, the people of 1990 are not, and they send an official back to 1950 to retrieve the almanac, thereby preventing any unwanted repercussions from Knight's knowing the future. In the history of a language, forty years is only a moment—barring cataclysmic occurrences, we would not expect a great deal of change—and there are no great changes in the language of Boyne, the man from 1990. His speech sounds a little different (a bartender thinks he might be a foreigner),[19] and he uses a few words coined after 1950. At the climax of the story, he has just about convinced Knight that any gain he might make from reading the almanac would be, in a sense, cheated from history rather than won through his own efforts. At the peroration, Boyne proclaims, "You will regret. You will totally recall the pronouncement of our great poet-philosopher Trynbyll, who summed it up in one lightning, skazon line. 'The Future is Tekon,' said Trynbyll." The story uses language change convincingly, in a way that is both clever and understated, and contains no linguistic gaffes to distract our attention and diminish our enjoyment.

Not all visitors from the future are as trustworthy as Boyne. C.M. Kornbluth illustrates the dangers of gullibility in "Time Bum" (1953; C14). A real estate agent and his wife, a science-fiction buff, suspect an odd stranger of being from the future (this is not as fantastic as it may seem; he gives them good cause). A clandestine search of his house turns up a newspaper page bearing the date July 18, 2403. It reads:

TAIM KOP NABD:
PROSKYOOTR ASKS DETH

Patrolm'n Oskr Garth 'v thi Taim Polis w'z arest'd toodei at hiz hom, 4365 9863th Strit, and bookd at 9768th Prisint on tchardg'z 'v Polis-Ekspozh'r. Thi aledjd Ekspozh'r okur'd hwaile Garth w'z on dooti in thi Twenti-Furst Sentch'ri. It konsist'd 'v hiz admish'n too a sit'zen 'v thi Twenti-Furst Sentch'ri that thi Taim Polis ekzisted and woz op'rated fr'm thi Twenti-Fifth Sentch'ri. Thi Proskyoot'rz Ofis sed thi deth pen'lti will be askt in vyoo 'v thi heinus neich'r 'v thi ofens, hwitch thret'nz thi hwol fabrik 'v Twenti-Fifth-Sentch'ri ekzistens.

The story is too good to spoil by citing any more. It suffices to note that this English of the 25th century differs from our own only in its orthography. Both Bester's and Kornbluth's stories limit linguistic change to such comparatively superficial matters.

Respellings are not frequently used, on the whole, as a device to characterize the English of the future. One or both of two simple methods are probably the most often seen: the author notes some difference in pronunciation, and perhaps inserts a few new words. Bruce McAllister uses the first of these in his story "Benji's Pencil" (1969; C4). It concerns the short career of another of those characters satirized so effectively in Woody Allen's *Sleeper*, the frozen hero (since his name is Maxwell, a more appropriate term might be "freeze-dried"). He is revived after two hundred years, and is told that although the written language has not changed much, "inflections and the sectional dialects often make it hard for a 'new' person to understand." The speaker, the Introducer, has made a special study of the pronunciation of "past spoken languages" in order to speak to the reawakened. The first time Maxwell hears the new form of the language, it sounds to him like "nasalized English, chopped but softer than German." The impressionistic description of the sounds comes as a surprise, since Maxwell had been an English teacher, and one might have expected him to possess a more effective vocabulary to describe the changes.

All the usual methods of word-formation are represented in the coinages found in science fiction. They include both new formations such as *goffin* in James Blish's "A Work of Art" (1956; C15), and old words used in new senses, such as *golden* in Samuel R. Delany's "The Star Pit" (1967; C10).

Individual words and pronunciations come and go, however, and their appearance and disappearance shows no special creativity. In fact, Thomas M. Disch has complained specifically about this point as part of a more general criticism: "For some reason, most fiction, in proportion as it advances toward the farther reaches of space and time, grows lackluster and olive drab. Perhaps it's only that against backgrounds so exotic the pulpy tissue that constitutes 80 percent of most sf becomes, more noticeably, lifeless. It does not grate nearly so much when Perry Mason sits down to a steak dinner for a chapter as when the same dinner is served on Aldebaran V in the year 2500. Even at a meal of hydroponic glop the table settings don't change; some few new words are introduced, but the syntax is immutable."[20]

An author needs rather more imagination to conceive of a change in the language that goes beyond word formation, and the conception is doubly imaginative if the author can, at the same time, suggest a plausible reason for the change. An example of this more satisfying treatment of future English is found in David Karp's *One* (US 1953). Karp's excellent dystopian novel is set near the end of the twentieth century. The dictatorial government of England of that time uses two major weapons to enforce conformity among the masses: its hidden one is a network of informers who report regularly any forbidden word or action; the other weapon, just as secret in its purposes but open in its operation, is a growing religion, the Church of State. Church of State members are notable by their speech—they speak of themselves in the third person "as if they did not exist by themselves but only as part of a third group. *Me, my, I, mine* did not exist in the language of the Church of State families" (§2). In sketching a change in pronoun usage, Karp has gone the inventors of new words one better, and in selecting religion as the reason for the change, he has picked a force powerful enough to make the change possible. He even has historical precedent on his side—witness the continued Quaker use of *thee* after the word had become obsolete for most speakers.

George Orwell picked the same period for his much better known and much brassier *Nineteen Eighty-Four* (1949). The adaptation of English in that novel, Newspeak, deserves its own study, but Newspeak, with the whole Ministry of Truth behind it, seems not as effective, nor nearly as possible, a means of thought control as the simple change of pronouns Karp depicts.

The changes we have seen so far occur in what might be called Standard Future English. Statements about dialect are infrequent in science fiction, and the use of several different social or geographical developments of the same language is rare indeed. It is tempting to attribute this omission to a general ignorance about dialect; science fiction's occasional comment about present dialects is sometimes astonishingly misinformed—a character in one novel claims that Great Britain in 1950 had fifty-seven mutually incomprehensible dialects.[21] It is therefore a pleasant surprise to find a story that not only shows an awareness of dialect, but illustrates it in a refreshingly irreverent way. In "The People Trap" (1968; C3), Robert Sheckley puts his hero through a Land Race, a contest in the teeming streets of an anarchical future Manhattan. The winner of the race receives an acre of stripped land, and the contest provides diversion and hope for the jammed-in masses.

During the race, the hero seeks a ride from the piratical captain of a Hoboken contraband runner: "'Ye seek passage of *uns?*' he declared in the broad Hobokenese patois. 'Thin ee we be the Christopher Street ferry, hai?'" The captain mistakenly gets the idea that the hero has a wife and children:

> "Woife and tuckins?" the captain enquired. "Why didn' yer mention! Had that lot myself aforetime ago, until waunders did do marvain to the lot...."
>
> "Aye." The captain's iron visage softened. "I do remember how, in oftens colaim, the lettle blainsprites did leap giner on the saern; yes, and it was roses all til diggerdog."
>
> "You must have been very happy," Steve said. He was following the man's statements with difficulty.

Steve puts his finger on the chief problem the writer faces: if there is little change in the language the characters are using, the reader has no trouble understanding it; if there is a great difference in the language, then the writer simply states that his characters are speaking in Old High Martian or the thirty-fifth-century development of a present tongue, and writes his dialogue in the English we know. But midway between these two extremes lies difficult ground. Samuel R. Delany solves the problem nicely in *Nova* (US 1968): some of his characters speak as natives a dialect of English that differs syntactically from that of the rest. The foreignness of their syntax keeps the reader linguistically aware of the exotic setting, while the familiar spelling and vocabulary allow him to understand what they say with a minimum of difficulty. Delany can therefore present whole pages of conversation in the dialect, which essentially consists of a verb-final sentence pattern: "Perhaps your cards of Prince and me will speak?" "In this race, the universe the prize is." Auxiliary *do* has disappeared from questions in this dialect: "What the cards about this swing into the night say?" "Where Prince and myself among the cards fall?" "Captain Von Ray, you well the Tarot know?"[22] One sentence, however, if not a misprint, comes close to the border of unintelligibility; a woman reading the Tarot cards remarks that one's fate is marked in the lines of the face, and Von Ray, pointing to his scarred face, asks: "From the crack across mine, you where those lines my fate can tell will touch?" But this sentence is not representative of the generally easy flow of the dialect.

A second, perhaps even more successful, example of an ambitious attempt to represent language change occurs in Robin S. Scott's story. "Who Needs Insurance?" (1966; C16). In order to withstand a threat from outer space in 2106, Earth needs to increase her numbers of people with extra-sensory perception. One such, the 20th-century hero of the story, was killed in a raid on Ploesti in 1943, thus effectively preventing him from reproducing. A time traveler comes to our present time from 2106 and changes the personal history of the hero-narrator, keeping him safe through World War II, Korea, and helicopter duty in Viet Nam, thereby saving his precious genes for the future. In the story, when the narrator, during their first encounter, asks the time traveler if he is the "guy" who has twice saved his life, the time traveler answers in the English of his own day: "'Yo. I be the guy.' He pronounced 'guy' almost like 'gooey.' I couldn't place the accent." The narrator, linguistically naive, describes the sound of the language impressionistically, and misunderstands its verbal system: "He spoke with broad vowels and clipped consonants, somewhat like a Yorkshireman I had served with in Korea. And he had trouble with verbs. 'Thought' was 'thinked,' 'ran' was 'runned,' and so forth." The traveler has, of course, no trouble at all with his verbs. The language has moved toward the regularization of all verbs by eliminating vowel change in the formation of participles, contractions, and past tenses:

> So you see, Colonel Albers, I goed back through time to 1943, set up shop in London, and when I made the power source I goed on to Libya and installed it in your aircraft. Then I comed back in 1950, getted this building as a base, and comed on up to 1980.... Each time then, I comed up to the next five-year check to see if a letter from you will'd indicate that the steps I had tooked had beed effective.

Although there is ample evidence of the leveling of *am/are/is* to *be*, there is no occasion in the sentences of the time-traveler for the use of a regular verb in the third-singular-present, so that it is not possible to say whether that inflection has also been leveled. (The one occurrence of *is*, the two of *might*, and the one of *tooked*, may be put down to auctorial slips of the pen.)

Interestingly enough, the development that Scott predicts had already been suggested in *Astounding Science Fiction*, where in July 1938 L. Sprague de Camp published an article entitled "Language for Time-Travelers," discussing and illustrating historical change. Although de Camp's brief essay is badly dated in many respects (that of dialects, for example) by more recent work in linguistics, his article is still generally sound, and, had his advice been heeded, could have prevented many of the errors displayed in the first part of this paper.

We are in a position now to make some generalizations about historical linguistics in science fiction. The first observation we might make is that science fiction is a window, not into the future, but into the present: in its stories we can find what the science-fiction writer knows about language in general and historical linguistics in particular. Sadly (especially for those who accept Harry Harrison's criterion) that knowledge is seldom more than that of the man-in-the-street. In fact, exactly the same anxieties, ignorances, and misconceptions show up in the great majority of science fiction. By Harrison's metric, we would have to downgrade the effectiveness of many of these stories.

It is not surprising that science-fiction authors should be so much more inventive with photons than with phonemes, and so much more knowledgeable about the future of galaxies than about the past of their language. The schoolteachers of many of these writers no doubt wasted their students' time and tried their patience with interminable myths about *shall* and *will*, *continual* and *continuous*, and the like, hardly leaving time for real instruction about language, had they been competent to provide it. Science-fiction writers show us what the man-in-the-street knows about linguistic change, and it's a paltry amount indeed. But on the whole, the genre is optimistic about man's ability to solve his problems, and perhaps the competent treatments we have seen point to a time when the First Sound Shift will be as familiar to authors as the First Law of Thermodynamics. And although we know that some are wrong—those authors who expect no change at all in man's language through his history—some could be right. Perhaps some of the changes indicated here will occur. In fact, one of the characters in Isaac Asimov's *The End of Eternity* (US 1955) makes a comment about our language that will certainly be spoken someday: "'This is the English the linguists are always talking about, isn't it?' he asked, tapping a page" (§15).

NOTES

1. Harry Harrison, "With a Piece of Twisted Wire," *SF Horizons* #2(1965):58.

2. The short-story collections used for this study: *C1*, Isaac Asimov, ed., *Before the Golden Age* (US 1974); *C2*, Theodore Sturgeon, *Sturgeon is Alive and Well* (US 1971); *C3*, Edward L. Ferman, ed., *The Best from Fantasy and Science Fiction*, 18th Series (Ace Books, 1972); *C4*, *Ibid.*, 19th Series (Ace Books, 1973); *C5*, Poul Anderson, *Beyond the Beyond* (US 1969); *C6*, James Blish, *Galactic Cluster* (US 1959); *C7*, Robert Silverberg, ed., *The New Atlantis* (US 1975); *C8*, Judy-Lynn del Rey, ed., *Stellar 1* (US 1974); *C9*, Frederik Pohl, ed., *Seventh Galaxy Reader* (US 1964); *C10*, Samuel R. Delany, *Driftglass* (US 1971); *C11*, Groff Conklin, ed., *Big Book of Science Fiction* (US 1950); *C12*, H.L. Gold, ed., *Galaxy Reader of Science Fiction* (US 1952); *C13*, Damon Knight, ed., *A Century of Science Fiction* (US 1962); *C14*, C.M. Kornbluth, *A Mile Beyond the Moon* (US 1958); *C15*, James Blish, *Best Science Fiction Stories of James Blish*, rev edn (UK 1973); *C16*, Brian W. Aldiss and Harry Harrison, eds., *Nebula Award Stories Two* (US 1967). The dates given in the text are for the first appearance of the story in print.

3. Philip José Farmer, *Flesh* (1960; NAL pb 1969), §2.

4. L. Sprague de Camp, *Science-Fiction Handbook* (US 1953), p 253. De Camp handles matters of linguistic interest as competently and imaginatively as any current writer.

5. Editorial note. Reading "To Here and the Easel" in the SFBC edn of *Sturgeon is Alive and Well* (US 1971 xiii+207), I find 50 occurrences of "thy/thine," all correctly distinguished ("thy" before a consonant, "thine" before a vowel or absolute) and three instances of a second-singular verb in the subjectless interrogative construction ("wouldst go to her...?" [p 12], "Art satisfied, girl?" [p 24], "Knowest the monster Orc?" [p 42]). There are 76 occurrences of "thou/thee": two of "thou" as the naming form ("call me 'thou'"; "I use not the 'thou' of an intimate, but that of an animal" [p 12]); one of "thee" as predicate pronoun ("But, 'tis thee, my warrior-maid!" [p 22]); 39 of "thee" as object, with none of "thou" as object; 15 of "thou" as subject, with the verb always second-singular ("thou wilt" [p 4]); and 30 of "thee" as subject, with the verb third-singular ("Thee deludes thyself" [p 27]) or indeterminate ("thee will" [p 3], "ere thee call" [p 27]).

This is all so systematic (right down to the subjunctive after "ere") that one must seek some explanation for Sturgeon's use of "thee" as subject. In the story the narrator, Giles, has dreams derived from his childhood reading of *Orlando Furioso*, beginning with Rogero's imprisonment by Atlantes and continuing with his rescue by Bradamante, with the difference that the Bradamante of Giles-Rogero is a dumpy Salvation Army type rather than the beautiful and statuesque warrior-maiden of Ariosto. This suggests that Sturgeon may have deliberately emphasized the mixed-up nature of the narrator's dreams by mixing Quaker usages with the traditional archaic forms of literary English. —RDM.

6. De Camp (Note 4), p 179. De Camp was referring to a story of his own that, as he says, "threw my hero back into sixth-century Rome. I caused my characters to make a few remarks in Gothic to lend authenticity to the scene. After the book appeared I got a letter from a professor saying that while he liked the story, did I realize that I had caused a couple of these Gothic-speakers to use the nominative case when they should have used the vocative?"

7. C.F. Hockett in a letter to M.J.E. Barnes cited the latter's *Linguistics and Languages in Science Fiction-Fantasy* (US 1974), pp iii-iv.

8. Frederik Pohl and C.M. Kornbluth, "Mute Inglorious Tam," *Magazine of Fantasy and Science Fiction*, Oct 1974, p 112. The time of the story is about 1100.

9. Richard Wilson, "A Man Spekith" (1969), in *World's Best Science Fiction 1970*. It is true that the OED records "Old English" as "in popular use applied vaguely to all obsolete forms of the language"; nevertheless, the Richard Burton-Elizabeth Taylor movie *The Sandpiper* was scored by one reviewer for (among other things) this same usage, and the standards of Hollywood should not be unsurpassable for the "World's Best Science Fiction."

10. Ed Jesby, "Ogre" (1968), in C3.

11. The error the character makes, believing that there existed just one Earthly language, satirizes the common science-fiction practice of endowing a whole planet with a single speech—"The Martian language," for example. This particular habit has been burlesqued before. Anthony Boucher's "Barrier" (1942; in *Spectrum 4*, ed. Kingsley Amis, US 1959) contains a similar incident, and is possibly the source for Moorcock's treatment. M.J.E. Barnes (Note 7), pp 75-81, discusses "Barrier" at length.

12. De Camp (Note 4), p 253. In view of the notorious difficulty of measuring the rate of language change, it would be unwise to contradict de Camp's statement about a decreasing rate of change, yet historically the literate are less hesitant about innovation than the unlettered.

13. A time machine that could visit the past would of course be of value to historical linguists; this observation did not escape Jack Vance in "Rumfuddle" in *Three Trips in Time and Space* (US 1973). He has a character, the inventor of a time machine of sorts, write in his memoirs, "We can chart the development of every language, syllable by syllable, from earliest formulation to the present" (§10).

14. Darko Suvin, "Parables of De-Alienation: Le Guin's Widdershins Dance," SFS 2 (1975):267-68.

15. The Norton and NAL editions of *A Clockwork Orange* contain an Afterword and a Nadsat dictionary by Stanley Edgar Hyman.

16. Some years ago, a group of experimenters claimed to have proof of the molecular basis of memory. They taught flatworms to respond to light in a certain way, then ground up their students and fed them to a second group of flatworms, which were then supposed to have shown the same response to light without training. RNA was as much a term to be conjured with as chlorophyll had been twenty years before, so it was speculated that memory was somehow encoded in the RNA of the cells. New scientific ideas, of whatever validity, quickly find their way into science fiction, and this one was no exception. In Larry Niven's "Rammer" (1971), in *Best Science Fiction Stories of the Year*, ed. Lester del Rey (US 1972), a man frozen 200 years is revived. When he says to the defroster, "hasn't the language changed at all? You don't even have an accent," the defroster replies, "Part of the job. I learned your speech through RNA training." One hopes that it was not necessary to grind up a philologist to supply the RNA.

17. Fletcher Pratt, "A Critique of Science Fiction," in *Modern Science Fiction: Its Meaning and Its Future*, ed. Reginald Bretnor (US 1953), pp 83-84.

18. C1 (Note 2), p 373. Asimov did not stop learning; his works are notably free of linguistic errors, and he continues to be interested in language in science fiction: on reading an earlier version of this paper, he recalled a similar work published almost forty years ago, the article by de Camp mentioned in section 4 below.

19. Bester records the same perception, but in reverse, in "The Flowered Thundermug," in *Dark Side of the Earth* (US 1964), where the police of the 25th century, searching for a man from our own time, note that the fugitive talks "a little funny, like a foreigner."

20. Thomas M. Disch, Preface to "Et in Arcadia Ego," in *Science Fiction: Author's Choice #4*, ed. Harry Harrison (US 1974).

21. Samuel R. Delany's *Nova* (US 1958), §5. This novel is in other respects well-written and linguistically inventive, and will be cited later in another connection. One of the most recent award-winners, Ian Watson's *The Embedding* (UK 1973) came into my hands too late to be considered in detail here, but it carries on the science-fiction tradition of dreadful handling of dialect matters.

22. Readers with some interest in generative grammars might amuse themselves by deciding whether Delany's sentences can be produced by transformation from surface structures, or whether a different deep structure is required.

Albert I. Berger

The Triumph of Prophecy: Science Fiction and Nuclear Power in the Post-Hiroshima Period

(from SFS *3: 143–150, July 1976)*

The writers of pulp-magazine science fiction found themselves in an ambivalent position after the explosion over Hiroshima of the first atomic bomb. On the one hand, they were acknowledged as prophets proven right by the course of events. Some of them began new careers as writers of popular science and as consultants and participants in government- and university-sponsored seminars on social and technological change. Even those who remained close to their roots in magazine fiction found themselves newly prosperous as a result of the increased attention the bomb had brought to "that Buck Rogers stuff." For the first time since *Amazing Stories* began segregating science fiction in 1926, mass-circulation magazines like *Collier's* and *The Saturday Evening Post* began to publish stories by writers like Ray Bradbury and Robert A. Heinlein, previously confined to the genre pulps, and the higher rates paid by such magazines, together with reprint royalties from the SF anthologies rushed into print by eager publishers, began to change the economics of the entire genre. While most SF writers remained part-time hobbyists or free-lance generalists, more of them than ever before were able to make their living solely by writing science fiction.

On the other hand, having in their fiction developed and controlled nuclear energy long before the Army got around to it, many of these newly affluent writers were both disappointed in and fearful of the ways in which the government proposed to handle its "ultimate weapon," ways very different from those the writers would have chosen, or even expected. Isaac Asimov, among the best known of that generation of writers, recalled in 1969 that he would rather have been considered a "nut" for the rest of his life than have been "salvaged into respectability at the price of a nuclear war hanging like a sword of Damocles over the world forever."[1] Theodore Sturgeon, less well-known than Asimov outside the genre, was more analytical.

Sturgeon, like Asimov, had been one of the young writers cultivated by John W. Campbell in *Astounding Science Fiction.* Caught up in the general enthusiasm for nuclear energy, Sturgeon had a letter in the "Brass Tacks" column of the December 1945 *Astounding* in which he celebrated the possibilities of nuclear power for changing the world and contrasted the respect currently being paid to writers and fans with the scorn they had previously experienced. But he quickly became disillusioned both with public policies as embodied in the War Department-sponsored May-Johnson Bill to control nuclear energy and with the attitudes of his fellow writers, whom he called "word-merchants" in the story "Memorial" (Apr 1946).[2] He felt that the writers, who had given more thought to atomic energy than either the average man or the average politician, should have been more responsible in their evaluation of it than they had been in using it merely as 'a limitless source of power for background to a limitless source of story materials":

> All of them were quite aware of the terrible potentialities of nuclear energy. Practically all of them were scared silly of the whole idea. They were afraid for humanity, but they themselves were not really afraid, except in a delicious drawing room sort of way, because they couldn't conceive of this Buck Rogers event happening to anything but posterity.

A glance at several famous SF stories corroborates the accuracy of Sturgeon's observation. A.E. van Vogt had used atomic energy in his popular serial "Slan"

(Sept-Dec 1940), but had set the story a thousand years in the future and had made nuclear energy the discovery of a mutant superman rather than of a normal human being. In Asimov's Foundation stories (i.e., those published 1942-45 and thus written before Hiroshima), the use of atomic energy is similarly set thousands of years in the future. Of the many pre-Hiroshima stories dealing with nuclear energy in relatively contemporary settings, only one, Heinlein's "Solution Unsatisfactory" (May 1941, as by Anson MacDonald), dealt with nuclear weapons. Perhaps the best example of the tendency to give such stories a distant setting is Cleve Cartmill's rather routine adventure yarn "Deadline" (March 1944). Its routine character as a story has been obscured by the consequences of its description of a nuclear bomb that was sufficiently close to the one under construction at Los Alamos to earn both Campbell and Cartmill visits from security agents. But as close to contemporary reality as the author had unwittingly made his story, he had still, quite gratuitously, set the action on an alien planet rather than on Earth.[3]

The reaction of SF writers to the appearance of nuclear weapons in the real world took place in the midst of the campaign Campbell had been waging to raise the quality of science fiction above the rudimentary level of cowboy or spy stories set in space, and by the end of the war his efforts were beginning to have the intended effect. "Children of the Lens" (Nov-Feb 1946-47) by E.E. Smith, once the most popular of all *Astounding* writers, was published to a popular and critical acclaim both severely diminished, and was the last of the Lensman stories to appear in *Astounding*. Henceforth Smith, and such adventure writers as Edmond Hamilton and Jack Williamson, would be forced either to change their styles, as Williamson did, or to sell their stories to Campbell's less munificent competitors. Although Campbell's intention was to make SF respectable by promoting stories set in the near future and based on extrapolations from existing technology and scientific theory,[4] many of the stories actually published in the post-Hiroshima period were concerned with new "ultimate weapons," for both Campbell and his writers felt that the unexpectedly early success of the atomic bomb had made it plausible to place other apparently far-fetched devices into relatively contemporary settings.[5]

Sturgeon's "Memorial," cited above for its acid comments on his fellow science-fiction writers, is one of the many stories published in the years after Hiroshima on the imminent possibility of a nuclear war and the ways in which such a destructive war might be prevented or, if necessary, fought. Believing that the military would control and restrict nuclear research if the May-Johnson Bill was passed, Sturgeon adapted traditional SF imagery to his purpose, including the lonely scientist-hero and the secret desert laboratory. Grenfell, the hero, develops a means to "totally annihilate" atomic mass, producing far more energy than the partial annihilation of mass in the fission of uranium. He hopes that the eternal radioactive pit resulting from his explosive test will serve as a permanent warning against the destructive results of nuclear war. Although clearly sympathetic to Grenfell, Sturgeon evidently believed that such an explosion would convince the United States that it was being attacked. The retaliatory war triggered by Grenfell's explosion destroys all life on earth, in a clear throwback to the pulp caricatures of mad scientists and things-man-was-never-meant-to-know.

Sturgeon, along with Philip Wylie, who destroyed the planet itself in a similar story, "Blunder" (*Collier's*, Feb 12, 1946), was very critical of the professional ego that would not only permit but also drive a scientist to proceed with a potentially disastrous investigation regardless of the costs or consequences. Nevertheless, both authors directed their polemic as much at the military security system as at the scientific ego. Although the unfettered individual scientist was clearly not socially safe (Wylie's plot hinges on the inability of the international scientific community to check his hero's figures), both stories are bitterly critical of the need to work within the cumbersome research institutes and the restrictions placed on free research by various governments.

This last was part of a larger paradox characteristic of SF in the late forties, especially in *Astounding*. Campbell's writers tried to be true to his formula developing contemporary situations into the near future, and the natural tendency of most of them was to celebrate the possibilities being opened up, but most of the probable consequences of nuclear development appeared extremely gloomy—appeared, indeed, to lead directly to disaster.

One writer, Chandler Davis, later an editor of *Mathematical Reviews* and a fellow at the Institute for Advanced Studies, took considerable pains to detail, in "Nightmare" (May 1946), the dilemma of civil-defense workers in New York City trying to detect the components of nuclear weapons smuggled into the city. Davis' hero believes that the city should have been decentralized, to make the largest concentrations of industry and population too small to be economical targets for the expensive nuclear weapons of the day. However, in the face of a device assembled in the city, evacuation and decentralization would only cause panic and make smuggling easier in the chaos of dislocation. Eventually, Davis imagined, the pressures of a constant watch against both secret and open nuclear attack would lead to a totally intolerable and insoluble political situation. In "Nightmare" the spies escape, because to capture them or even reveal their existence would itself force the United States into a war. In "Cold War" (Oct 1949), a story dealing with a series of nuclear-armed space stations, Kris Neville saw the pressure in psychological terms, with even the best testing methods unable to prevent crewmen from becoming homicidal and launching a devastating assault.

It was, Davis wrote in "Nightmare," like driving a truck down a winding and increasingly narrow mountain road at too great a speed. It was clear that neither science nor business nor government could provide the truck with brakes. As a result of decisions that Davis felt had already been made by 1946, there was no way to prevent an eventual disaster.

Along with many of his colleagues, Davis had seen the situation primarily as an insoluble technical one, how to defend against an irresistible weapon, rather than as the essentially political problem faced by Congress and the atomic scientists, the maintenance of peace. Few SF writers thought that war could be prevented. Many spent their efforts devising ways of fighting man's inevitable wars without using nuclear weapons. In one such story, George O. Smith's "The Answer" (Feb 1947), an odd weapon is placed at the disposal of the United Nations, which for the purposes of the story is denied the right to use force directly. Smith felt that potential aggressors would ignore the orders of the UN and that the slow workings of its democratic organization would prevent its acting rapidly enough to halt the construction of military nuclear facilities. Yet Smith's Secretary General is able to enforce his ultimata against a would-be aggressor by using what appears to be only a massive, worldwide letter-writing campaign: the dictator's bureaucracy pays only enough attention to the letters to file them away, until the plutonium with which the paper is impregnated reaches critical mass and explodes.

Bureaucracy, the hallmark of all modern nations, was seized upon as a symbol of the totalitarian state in a similar story, "The Perfect Weapon" (Feb 1950), by Poul Anderson, then beginning his long career as a successful science-fiction writer. Like Smith, Anderson felt that a dictatorship's mania for paperwork was its weak spot, and postulated a weapon that would destroy only paper, assuming that a free society would need less paperwork to survive since it had fewer laws to enforce.

Although both of these stories are set in an explicitly political context, neither indicates any awareness of political realities, and both indicate a profound distrust of government and the political process. While Anderson's hero, a pacifist physicist, does demonstrate a talent for diverting bureaucracy by using his grant for bomb research to build a non-lethal weapon, Smith's hero, supposedly a political and diplomatic figure, is presented as a combination of international moralist and jut-jawed American magazine hero in the classic style. He is capable of calling forth a massive protest on short notice, using a secret weapon and a complicated plan of attack, when by the terms of the story itself his organization, the UN, is too much bogged down in democratic procedures to mount a straightforward military assault.

This naivete about politics and preoccupation with technological solutions was the obverse of the prevailing SF distaste for politics. Politics had always had a bad press in the science-fiction magazines, being portrayed as the captive of technologically, if not socially reactionary special interests. The appalling scientific ignorance and prejudice displayed by Congress after Hiroshima, and its general unwillingness to be educated, merely compounded the problem in the eyes of science-fiction writers and readers. This distaste for politics was testified to not only by letters-to-the-editor in *Astounding* and the fan magazines but also by an article by W.B. de Graeff, "Congress is too Busy" (Sept 1946), detailing with a gleeful contempt the most mundane and ridiculous chores of a member of Congress.

By 1950 even an old stalwart like E.E. Smith could take up nearly a third of a novel—*First Lensman* (not serialized; Fantasy Press 1950)—with a detailed account of an election in which military heroes act both as police forces and as candidates arrayed against a corrupt political machine. The use of conspicuously armed poll watchers and what amounts to a military coup are justified by the criminal tactics of the opposition. Smith's villains are supposed to be the pawns of a sinister conspiracy of aliens, but their methods are described as normal American practice.

Much of the political commentary in SF in the post-war years was limited to a fictional restatement of the wartime fear that the Nazis would develop nuclear weapons before the Americans did. "Enemies" were usually portrayed as the personal dictatorships of men who resembled Adolf Hitler, psychopathic and immune to any counterarguments except overwhelming force. Most, like the Master in Arthur C. Clarke's "Exile of the Eons" (*Super Science Stories*, March 1950), were described as the embodiment of ambition, lust for power, cruelty, intolerance, and hatred. Caught up in the prevailing attitude toward Hitler, as one would expect a popular literature to be, science fiction was taking cognizance neither of the sources of conflict between Germany and her neighbors (which might have brought on a Second World War even without Hitler) nor of the prewar speculations of one of its most important writers. In fact, the level of political awareness in these post-war stories was far lower and less analytical than in Robert A. Heinlein's 1941 serial, "If This Goes On——" (Feb-March), which describes a dictatorship run by the manipulation of popular beliefs rather than by sheer personality, recognizing that even a figure as singular as Hitler (or as the Prophet of the story) must have roots among a country's people, or must appeal to their most basic emotions, in order to rule them. Not only were most science-fiction dictators unaware of such political facts of life, but their creators' *pro forma* fear of dictatorships was not sufficient to interfere with their creation of heroes who solved political crises with the traditional elements of charismatic leadership and violence far closer to the totalitarian ideal than to the democratic.

Many of these stories demonstrated their roots in the traditional emphasis on individual effort which had always marked science-fiction along with the larger field of pulp fiction generally. In a number of the anti-military stories of the post-war period, for example, even though the chain of command and high ranking officers are the villains, it is the junior officers and conventional heroics that produce such happy endings as there are. Either the high command deliberately provokes a nuclear war, or, as in Sturegon's "Thunder and Roses" (Nov 1947), mechanically prepares to retaliate after a nuclear attack even though retaliation would be of no benefit to the already destroyed United States and would lay waste the rest of the world. Although undoubtedly sympathetic to the military, Heinlein, a former naval officer, was prepared, in "The Long Watch" (*American Legion Magazine*, Dec 1949), to consider the possibility that nuclear weapons at a base on the Moon could be used by an officer bent on world domination to blackmail the Earth. The dispute was political (the officer's intention was to remove control of the world from politicians and place it in the "scientifically selected" hands of the military) but the scheme was thwarted in a non-political way by a junior officer who manually dismantled the weapons even though he knew that exposure to their radioactive innards would kill him.[6]

Davis, also a former naval officer, envisioned a similar situation on a Colorado missile base. Deeply suspicious of the military as an institution in a way Heinlein was not, Davis has a sympathetic scientist, a veteran of the Manhattan Project, attack the very building of nuclear missiles as the equivalent of the country's "putting a chip on its shoulder"; "no one puts weapons like *these* into actual production unless he intends to use them. Offensively." Accusing the military of forcing Congress to build "fires that must be met with fire," the story argues that either through Congressional ignorance or misunderstanding, or through deception of Congress by the military, a nuclear war could be deliberately provoked without the approval of the country's elected officials. However, while recent political events give evidence of the truth of these observations, they also demonstrate the limitations of Davis' vision and that of most science-fiction writers. Davis' story, "To Still the Drums" (Oct 1946) is primarily an adventure story, a young pilot's discovery of the plot and his melodramatic flight to Washington to present his evidence to a friendly senator. Davis evidently felt that public exposure alone, without further activity, would thwart such a plot and cause the arrest of the culprits. In reality, of course, such exposure is far more often the beginning than the end of a scandal or crisis.

On those occasions when science-fiction writers dealt with organized political activity, their distrust of politics and politicians often acquired sinister overtones, even before the advent of nuclear weapons. The allegedly democratic undergound in A.E. van Vogt's "The Weapon Shops" (Dec 1942) and its sequels is just as structured, bureaucratic, and disciplined as the corrupt Isher Empire it fights. In Heinlein's short story "The Roads Must Roll" (June 1940), the supervising engineer of a transportation district has the authority to override the instructions of a state governor in order to use violent and authoritarian methods to suppress a strike. Graphic symbols and costumes strikingly reminiscent of those adopted by the Nazis helped to transform H.G. Wells' *The Shape of Things To Come* into a disturbingly authoritarian film in 1936. The acceptance of quasi-military organizations of scientists as political governing bodies runs through science fiction long past the days of E.E. Smith and his all-embracing Galactic Patrol. The persistence of the popularity among science-fiction writers and readers of the overdramatic costuming and the romantic grandeur of the graphics that characterized both the Nazis and the film *Things to Come* has been great enough to inspire much of Norman Spinrad's 1972 novel, *The Iron Dream* (Avon Books), a parody of the science-fiction adventure story purportedly written by an Adolf Hitler who, instead of rising to become dictator of Germany, migrated to the United States and became a science-fiction illustrator and Hugo-winning author.[7]

Things to Come based its anti-war critique on the widespread carnage in Europe during the First World War and the epidemics and social upheavals that followed in its wake. Even though it does not envision the use of nuclear weapons, the film vividly portrays the absolute destruction of all government and civilization above the village level. Following the same lead, L. Ron Hubbard suggested in "Final Blackout" (Apr-June 1940) that a military dictatorship would take power in Britain after the Second World War (then only recently begun) had ended, after generations of war, in the exhaustion of all parties.

Hubbard, who later became famous, or notorious, as the founder of Dianetics and Scientology, was among the best of the new writers Campbell brought to *Astounding*, a fact reflected in the rapid pacing and crisp prose with which he sketched a devastated Europe and the wanderings of a British Expeditionary force reduced to a few companies of foragers. He created a completely isolated hero, a nameless officer born in an air-raid shelter and raised as a soldier, who at the age of twenty-three leads his army back to England and overthrows the established Communist government. Once in power, the Lieutenant—Hubbard's archetype of an active, as opposed to a headquarters, soldier—makes Britain over into an anarchic society with a military command at its center until it is overthrown by a corrupt cabal of the surviving politicians and a United States grown rich and rapacious by reaping profits from neutrality. In ending "Final Blackout" with a farrago of betrayals and assassinations, Hubbard indicts not only such scheming politicians as those who force the Lieutenant to abdicate, but also the industrialization and organization of society which both the hero and his creator seem to hold responsible for the war. "Machines," says the Lieutenant,

> only make unemployment and, ultimately, politicians out of otherwise sensible men.... When each man does his best with his materials at hand, he is proud of his work and is happy with his life. Hatred only rises when some agency destroys...those things of which we are most proud—our crafts, our traditions, our faith in man. (June, p. 139)

In "Final Blackout," however, the war is only an extended replay of the First World War, with no expectation that technological advance would make a second world war different in kind from the first. It was a common spectre in postwar and post-Hiroshima stories: a war fought until the parties were too badly damaged to continue. After Hiroshima, Hubbard wrote another serial, "The End Is Not Yet" (Aug-Oct 1947), which, while it does not predict such a totally destroyed world, suggests that no possible alternative is much better.

On the surface Hubbard uses stock elements: a handsome, brilliant hero who is both a physicist and a secret agent, pitted against the caricature-like leader of an international bankers' conspiracy. With a hero named Charles Martel and a villain named Fabrecken, it would seem that Hubbard is continuing the struggle between the virtuous and democratic French and the Nazis, but he blurs the distinctions by putting several former Nazi scientists on Martel's side and the head of the Allied War Crimes Commission, an American banker, on Fabrecken's. Moreover, Fabrecken, with a name redolent of the I.G. Farben chemical cartel and in a role calling for him to be the personification of evil, has the only coherent philosophy in the story. Martel and his associates, on the other hand, are driven only by personal motives or by a philosophy of democracy that Hubbard undercuts in the story's finale. Although accused by Martel of giving the secret of the atomic bomb to the Soviet Union in order to provoke a nuclear war, Fabrecken's ideals are presented as stability and unity and are made to seem relatively praiseworthy. "Remember," Fabrecken warns his associates,

> that we are putting an end to the anarchy of industry and with that the anarchy of nations. And all we have to fear is the wild-eyed fool with a two-penny idea who will stampede the world against *us*—the only ones who can bring stability to the hell on earth men have been calling life. (Aug. p. 38)

In the end Martel's forces win their revolt against Fabrecken, though Martel dies in the final assault, just like the Lieutenant in his final confrontation with his enemies. Neither could have been permitted to live, since, while invested with all the attributes of the heroic, their activities are only partially acceptable. Martel dies in the crossfire between an ambush he has set for Fabrecken and one Fabrecken has set for him, an ending that clearly places the nominal hero and the nominal villain on the same moral plane. More important, after his death and the establishment of an ostensibly democratic government of scientists in his name, Martel's two closest friends and allies realize that their government will be no different from Fabrecken's, except that with Martel's scientific weapons it will be stronger and more pervasive. They then quit the scene, announcing they are "going to China to sing songs of Kubla Khan."

It hardly seems necessary to comment on the shortsightedness of a political novel in 1946 that would have its heroes seek their hedonistic retreat in China. That error, however, was part of the novel's larger pattern: the discounting of both politics and technology as forces changing the quality of human life. Like Heinlein, who had argued in "Solution Unsatisfactory" (May 1941) that a worldwide military dictatorship might be the only way to bring peace to a world armed with nuclear weapons, Hubbard seemed to believe in the necessity of elite, if not military, control. By expressing the desirability of order through the mouth of a nominal and otherwise conventional villain and by undercutting his hero's democratic beliefs, Hubbard seemed to argue that elite control was what the human race deserved. But he was hardly enthusiastic about the proposition, for he had discovered that all forms of power were to be distrusted, whether scientific or political.

Thus Hubbard's use of the escape motif in his conclusion was something more than simply a restatement of the traditional flight from civilization that has marked much of American literature, for it added new dimensions to the SF conventions of the secret laboratory, the renegade scientist, and the mysterious device. Hubbard valued order and group loyalty, but none of his leaders could live in the groups they led. Their lot was either exile or death. Martel and his allies could find the freedom they needed for their own ideas and devices only in their retreat in the Atlas Mountains, and when they moved out into the real world, it was only to have the fatal flaws in their democratic opposition to Fabrecken revealed.

"The End Is Not Yet," then, encapsulated the attitudes of many science-fiction writers of the post-Hiroshima period. Only in a retreat from the world was it possible to resolve differences among scientists. Although they might rule themselves democratically, and want the entire world to share their situation, human nature was diverse and order required coercion or a political activity they despised. If they actually took power, as in the Hubbard story, they would be tainted and lose the freedoms which they, rather than the common man, knew how to put to proper use. Those closest to the democratic ideals that Martel symbolized could preserve them only by turning their backs on both technology and the real world and lighting out for the Territory of a mythical Cathay.

NOTES

1. Isaac Asimov, *Opus 100* (Houghton Mifflin, 1969), p 148.

2. The dates given in the text are for the issues of *Astounding Science Fiction* in which the stories appeared—except, of course, when some other magazine is named.

3. Other important stories dealing with atomic energy and published in *Astounding* before Hiroshima: Lester del Rey's "Nerves" (Sept 1942), Heinlein's "Blowups Happen" (Sept 1940), Clifford Simak's "Lobby" (Apr 1944).

4. Campbell expressed these views in a series of editorials that began in May 1939 and continued throughout his tenure at *Astounding/Analog* until his death in 1971. Of particular interest are Nov 1945, Oct and Dec 1946, and Nov 1949 editorials. For a more extended treatment of these editorials, see my "The Magic That Works: John W. Campbell and the American Response to Technology," *Journal of Popular Culture* 5(Spring 1972):867-942.

5. In his November 1945 editorial Campbell expressed the belief that within weeks the atomic bomb would be joined by another science-fictional device, the "force field," which

would keep both physical objects and radiation from reaching a protected object. One has to evaluate this unseemly enthusiasm with care. Before release of the news from Hiroshima, the atomic bomb itself would have been treated by the general public with scorn, and in the first days afterwards nearly anything would have seemed possible. And Campbell was in good company. After completing the General Theory of Relativity during World War I, Albert Einstein spent the rest of his life defying nearly every intellectual trend in physics in the search for a "unified field theory" that would, if it existed, relate gravity and electromagnetic fields to each other and thus provide a possible basis for such a device as Campbell proposed.

6. In "Solution Unsatisfactory" (May 1941) Heinlein had been willing to accept as a necessary evil precisely the sort of dictatorship that is thwarted by the hero of "The Long Watch."

7. Although Wells wrote the script for *Things To Come*, the film derived its character from the costuming and graphics, products of United Artists Studios. In *The Iron Dream*, see especially pages 9, 247-48, 255. The costumes described in E.E. Smith's Lensman books are a particular case in point, as are those in the "Tom Corbett, Space Cadet" series of juveniles published by Grossett and Dunlap under the house pseudonym, Carey Rockwell. This tendency toward authoritarianism was noted and criticized from within the SF community by Robert Bloch in remarks to a 1957 symposium on science fiction at the University of Chicago; see "Imagination and Modern Social Criticism," in *The Science Fiction Novel*, ed. Basil Davenport (Advent, 1959), pp 126-55.

Charles Nicol

J.G. Ballard and the Limits of Mainstream SF

(from SFS *3: 150–157, July 1976)*

J.G. Ballard, like many younger SF authors, is often on the basis of his style described as a writer of mainstream SF. But the distinction between mainstream fiction and SF is a matter not of style but of differing conventions, so that an author wishing to straddle their conjunction must limit himself in a number of ways. Even after restricting himself to conventions shared by both mainstream and SF, an author will find his work perceived in different ways by mainstream and SF readers, since any reader who is not an omnibibliophile has his own limitations. I propose to demonstrate this by analysing two stories by Ballard, "The Drowned Giant" (1965) and "The Voices of Time" (1960). The first is mainstream SF, the second "merely" SF; they are both stories of superlative quality.

"The Drowned Giant" first appeared in *Playboy* rather than an SF magazine, and would not be out of place in a mainstream anthology. Its premise, unique but within the threshold of familiarity, is established by the first sentence: "On the morning after the storm the body of a drowned giant was washed ashore on the beach five miles to the northwest of the city."[1] The story that follows is developed with straightforward economy, and the style remains precise and impersonal throughout.

Although giants belong to folklore rather than technology, the story is SF rather than fantasy. If we accept Todorov's definition of the Fantastic, then we notice that there is no ambiguity as to whether the dead giant is natural or supernatural, no suggestion that the narrator's inner reality is at odds with ordinary, external reality—the ambiguities in this story lie elsewhere. The corpse is a fact, an enormous fact, and hence this story is not Fantastic. But even if we reject Todorov's definition, we have other criteria for judging its genre to be SF: the style is factual and unemotional; the story follows logically from its initial premise with no new marvelous occurrences; and no one in the story assumes that any supernatural agency is involved. Of course, part of the story's effectiveness lies in the way it plays against certain expectations created by its first sentence; further, by the end of the story almost everyone but the narrator has forgotten that the giant existed, so that the giant's reality is *about to become* ambiguous: the story stops before it becomes fantastic.

Once the initial premise is stated, the remainder of the story develops three actions or processes simultaneously. Two of these are the initial excitement and steady decline of interest among the townspeople; and the decay and eventual dismemberment of the giant corpse. Both of these plot-lines are observed by an unnamed narrator, who remains passive throughout; a librarian, he is the only resident of the city sensitive to the possible significance of this monstrous visitation, the only observer capable of limning this event for history (a task eventually assigned him by his fellow librarians). The librarian comes to perceive the dead giant as an event in his own life, assigning personal meaning to this otherwise random event—this constitutes the third plot line. Since the significance of the giant is personal to the librarian, it tends to shift; and as it shifts, it builds up a series of possible meanings. That interpretations are proposed suggests that this is a meaningful event; and that the interpretations are rejected suggests that the meaning has not yet been found. The drowned giant's dissolution is a significant event, the meaning of which is unclear but undoubted. The story has resonance and power, conforming to that specific type of modern literature, the open-ended parable.

That "The Drowned Giant" is both literature and mainstream fiction I hope to demonstrate by listing three literary analogues—analogues because the story is an original work and not an imitation. The first is Kafka's "Metamorphosis," another open-ended parable—indeed, while this story could have been written without the existence of Kafka,[2] it very possibly would not appear as contiguous with mainstream fiction had Kafka not expanded the limits of that fiction. "Metamorphosis" similarly opens with an "impossible" event: the protagonist has turned overnight into a giant cockroach (or, as Nabokov would have it, a dung-beetle).[3] The rest of Kafka's story is realistic, even naturalistic: the protagonist's family is at first not just surprised, but horrified; soon the family forces this miraculous event into the narrow channels of their own banal perceptions so that the protagonist is seen as only a giant insect and not their relative; eventually he is all but forgotten, and dies of neglect and starvation. The same process of turning the miraculous into the banal and eventually forgotten occurs as one of the plot lines in "The Drowned Giant," where the initially amazed townspeople soon make a playground of the giant's ears and nostrils, and build a campfire on his chest; later see the body as merely a source of rotting flesh to be turned into fertilizer; and eventually forget him so thoroughly that his "immense pizzle," preserved in a traveling freak show, is labeled as belonging to a whale, and "even those who first saw him cast up on the shore after the storm, now remember the giant, if at all, as a large sea beast." As in Kafka, the initial marvellous event seems to have an immense, hovering significance, and to be symbolic of some agony inherent in the human condition.

The frequent confusion of the giant with a whale inevitably recalls *Moby-Dick* in its development of an enormous, ambiguous symbol. We must assume that Ballard is deliberately pointing to Melville when his narrator observes that "this drowned leviathan had the mass and dimensions of the largest sperm whale." The narrator himself could easily be the sub-sub-sub librarian who provided the "Extracts" at the beginning of Melville's narrative, while the giant's flesh about to be processed for fertilizer or cattle food is referred to as "blubber." Only Melville's whale comes to mind when searching for an analogue to the majestic enigma of the giant.

The third literary analogue is inescapable, for it also belongs to that grey area where literature is also mainstream SF: *Gulliver's Travels.* Here the analogue is so obvious that Ballard must steer clear of direct comparisons. "The Drowned Giant" is intermediate between Gulliver's two voyages concerned with huge size differentials. Obviously the giant washed up on the beach reminds us of Gulliver himself, washed up from the sea on the beach of Lilliput. Our memories of Lilliput add a comic dimension to Ballard's story, making the inhabitants of *his* city seem equally trivial men working at trivial occupations in a toylike never-never-land; we are amused when the narrator inspects the giant's finger-nails, "each cut symmetrically to within six inches of the quick," and decides that they demonstrate "refinement of temperament." But Swift's purpose in Lilliput was political satire; the most satirical passage in "The Drowned Giant" concerns the city's men of science (themselves the subject of Swift's satire in Gulliver's visit to the Academy of Lagado):

> That afternoon the police returned and cleared a way through the crowd for a party of scientific experts—authorities on gross anatomy and marine biology—from the university.... The experts strode around the giant, heads nodding in vigorous consultation, preceded by the policemen who pushed back the press of spectators. When they reached the outstretched hand the senior officer offered to assist them up onto the palm, but the experts hastily demurred.

But since the narrator is one of the "little" people, we are equally reminded of Gulliver's voyage to Brobdingnag, the land of the giants. This comparison is reinforced by the narrator's references to such identifiable geographical and cultural signs as the the Nile and the *Odyssey*—the little people belong to our world; we are they. In that voyage of Gulliver, Swift pointed out how gross the flesh seems when magnified, and certainly Ballard's giant is predominantly a thing of the flesh.

But the giant's flesh is of interest to Ballard only because it is subject to such gross decay; indeed, one might describe Ballard's concern throughout his career as an investigation into the possibilities of decay—or to put it more nicely, *the potentialities of entropy*. Since the giant is actually symbolic of something else, his size is really a matter of perception, expressing the viewpoint of the observer. Just as Alice's sudden size changes in Wonderland reflected the child's differing perceptions of herself (almost a baby, nearly an adult), the narrator of "The Drowned Giant" finds that the giant seems larger or smaller during different visits to the corpse. This apparent alteration of size is one of Ballard's techniques for giving surprising life to the inanimate corpse.

What is most fascinating and original about "The Drowned Giant" is that the dead body is one of the principal actors in the story. The giant's decay has a life of its own, and creates a personality for the giant that had been absent at his initial appearance. At first the body seems as graceful as a statue of an idealized youth: "the shallow forehead, straight high-bridged nose, and curling lips" remind the narrator of "a Roman copy of Praxiteles," while "the elegantly formed cartouches of the nostrils" emphasize "the resemblance to sculpture." At this time, the narrator has the impression that the giant is "merely asleep," ready to "suddenly stir and clap his heels together." Visiting the corpse again three days later, the narrator realizes how much he identifies with the dead giant: "to all intents the giant was still alive for me, indeed more alive than many of the people watching him." By now, the giant had aged:

> The combined effects of sea water and the tumefaction of the tissues had given the face a sleeker and less youthful look. Although the vast proportions of the features made it impossible to assess the age and character of the giant, on my previous visit his classically modeled mouth and nose suggested that he had been a young man of discreet and modest temper. Now, however, he appeared to be at least in early middle age. The puffy cheeks, thicker nose and temples, and narrowing eyes gave him a look of well-fed maturity that even now hinted a growing corruption to come.

By the following day, the giant has become more crude, decadent, unkempt, "but despite this, and the continuous thickening of his features, the giant still retained his magnificent Homeric stature." Indeed, he seems ashamed of his condition: "The slope of the firmer sand tilted the body toward the sea, the bruised swollen face averted in an almost conscious gesture." The narrator continues to identify with the giant, noting that "this ceaseless metamorphosis, a macabre life-in-death, alone permitted me to set foot on the corpse." Now he finds the emotions of death the dominant feature of the giant's face, "a mask of exhaustion and helplessness": "For the first time I became aware of the extremity of this last physical agony of the giant, no less painful for his unawareness of the collapsing musculature and tissues." Two days later, the giant's features have entered a phase of final humiliation, like the visage of a battered and punch-drunk fighter: "The giant's swollen cheeks had now almost closed his eyes, drawing the lips back in a monumental gape. The once straight Grecian nose had been twisted and flattened, stamped into the ballooning face by countless heels." By the next day, the head has been removed, leaving nothing to observe save the purely mechanical rendering of the massive flesh into fertilizer. The reader has been led by Ballard into identifying with the dead giant's humiliation.

Aside from this narrative excellence, the story also has a symbolic level, a level investigated by the narrator as he seeks to explain why the giant fascinates him. This can most easily be demonstrated with two quotations, the first coming when the narrator initially recognizes that the giant is "still alive" for him:

> What I found so fascinating was partly his immense scale, the huge volume of space occupied by his arms and legs, which seemed to confirm the identity of my own miniature limbs, but above all, the mere categorical fact of his existence. Whatever else in our lives might be open to doubt, the giant, dead or alive, existed in an absolute sense, providing a glimpse into a world of similar absolutes of which we spectators on the beach were such imperfect and puny copies.

For the narrator, the giant's reality is metaphysical: he belongs to a "world of... absolutes." God seems the most likely metaphysical "absolute": the giant is proof that God exists, with men "puny copies" in his image; the existence of God confirms the identity of the narrator. Other readers may prefer to see this as a more general reference to an unspecified metaphysical construct. Yet eventually the narrator recognizes that the giant, whether God or not, is indeed dead. He becomes "reluctant to visit the shore, aware that [he has] probably witnessed the approaching end of a magnificent illusion." It is "almost with relief" that the narrator watches the corpse being removed, since its dissolution has paralleled his own disillusion.[4]

Only when the corpse has been completely dismembered and its less destructible fragments distributed all over the city can the narrator again entertain his illusion. Discovering the giant's thighbones framing the doorway of a wholesale meat merchant, the narrator has "a sudden vision of the giant climbing to his knees upon those bare bones and striding away through the streets of the city, picking up the scattered fragments of himself on his return journey to the sea." But the other inhabitants of the city have forgotten the giant altogether, or confused him with other oceanic creatures. Yet his ribs, pelvis, and backbone still remain on the beach, witness to what the narrator has learned of the decay of men and ideas.

SF fans might not have enjoyed "The Drowned Giant" as much as mainstream readers, since Ballard slights his science, providing no explanations for the giant's appearance. And the more conventional SF story would have investigated where the giant came from, rather than what he meant. Further, the society described in "The Drowned Giant" soon lapses into its uneventful existence, a situation not generally appreciated by SF readers, who seem to desire apocalyptic climaxes rather than anticlimactic dissolves. The image of the face of a dead giant, moving from a dreaming tranquility to excesses of agony and shame, is poetic but not necessarily within the poetry of science fiction.

In contrast, the poetry of "The Voices of Time" should appeal directly to the SF reader, while appearing to the mainstream reader as a mass of jumbled images. Here the narrative is rich in explanations and partial explanations, while the method of composition is one of complexity rather than simplicity. The reader is bombarded with SF images, all striking and all pointing in the same direction: the universe is running down, the sun is running down, earth is running down, man is running down, and the protagonist of the story is running down most rapidly of all. The focus is on entropy. But the power of the story lies in the many ways in which its characters try to escape entropy, and in the sterility of their attempts. The hope of escaping time is held out like a brass ring, but each attempt to reach the ring leads to madness and death. Eventually the reader comes to see death as itself an escape from entropy, and the story ends in tranquility: the tranquility of exhaustion.

Although the style is usually subordinate to the subject matter, in a few places Ballard employs a bravura technique to underline certain unique situations. Generally, the chief purpose of his narrative method is to present large quantities of information without using straight exposition; Ballard includes numerous tapes, diaries, and computer read-outs as both information sources and actual "voices of time." Consequently, much of the story's background is presented elliptically, and must be reconstructed by the reader. Many writers have included such "documentation," but here the most revealing literary analogue probably would not occur to most readers: in method and content, "The Voices of Time" resembles Eliot's *Wasteland*, with a great number of images piled one on the other to form an inescapable network of arid futility.

The time of the story is the late twentieth century. The chief features of the landscape are mountains, a salt lake of moderate size, and vegetation belonging to the cactus family—all reinforcing the picture of bleak sterility. The manmade features are equally arid and impotent: a dry swimming pool littered with dead leaves; a number of enormous, flat, circular concrete targets once used for artillery practice; and a seven-story house built in a bewildering maze that turns out to be a geometric model of the square root of minus one. The site seems to be an imagined Southwest, possibly Alamogordo, New Mexico.

The basic "scientific" idea of the story is that high levels of radiation stimulate "two inactive genes which occur in a small percentage of all living organisms, and appear to have no intelligible role in their structure or development." Here the mainstream reader is at a disadvantage; unfamiliar with fiction that has science at its core, he will assume these silent genes to be Ballard's fantasy (unless he happens to know better). The SF reader, on the other hand, while probably knowing little more than the general reader, is attuned to the subtle distinctions between fantasy and fact in SF stories; even without previous knowledge, he will assume that Ballard got those silent genes from some other storehouse than his imagination—and, at least where fruitflies are concerned, he will be correct. Thus the mainstream reader, failing to realize the extent to which Ballard is extrapolating from the actual world, is at an immediate disadvantage in assessing the story's power.

Because "some people have speculated that organisms possessing the silent pair of genes are the forerunners of a massive move up the evolutionary slope, that the silent genes are a sort of code, a divine message that we inferior organisms are carrying for our more highly developed descendants," in Ballard's story a scientist named Whitby has spent ten years perfecting a technique for irradiating them. But if there is any "divine message" in the silent genes, it is that God is an insane nihilist:

> Without exception the organisms we've irradiated have entered a final phase of totally disorganized growth, producing dozens of specialized sensory organs whose function we can't even guess. The results are catastrophic—the anemone will literally explode, the Drosophila cannibalize themselves, and so on. Whether the future implicit in these plants and animals is ever intended to take place, or whether we're merely extrapolating—I don't know. Sometimes I think, though, that the new sensory organs developed are parodies of their real intentions.

Thus the hope of transcendence leads instead to madness and destruction. Because of the pessimistic implications of this experiment, Whitby has committed suicide.

Radiation activates the silent genes because those genes "alter the form of the organism and adapt it to living in a hotter radiological climate. Soft-skinned organisms develop hard shells, these contain heavy metals as radiation screens." At the same time that these adaptations are proving futile in the laboratory, they are occurring in nature; the outside world has begun to reflect the miniature world of the laboratory. For instance, Robert Powers (the protagonist) discovers a frog that has grown an articulated, external lead shell to protect itself from excessive radiation. The local cacti are "assimilating gold in extractable quantities." Clearly, the cause for these drastic changes in the fauna and flora is a higher level of radiation. (The story suggests that Ballard has extrapolated these particular mutations from what was observed at Eniwetok.)

Several reasons are elliptically offered for this increased radiation count. From one casual conversation the reader may infer that World War III has already occurred. Other references in the story present an even more ominous explanation: the sun is cooling and emitting heavier radiation.

The images of entropy in "The Voices of Time" are extremely insistent, ranging from the largest to the smallest things in the universe. Everything is coming to an end; the universe itself is running down. Signals from the stars have been decoded by computers and turn out to be merely a series of countdowns. The most stunning of these series is sent from the Canes Venatici group at intervals of 97 weeks and includes over 500 million digits. The end of that countdown will coincide with the end of the universe. From the universe down through the sun, from agricultural yields to human fertility, everything has begun to run down. Most people now sleep ten and a half hours a night. At the lower end of the scale, even the genes that transmit life are "wearing out."

Still, the accelerated decline on Earth is a special case, caused by higher radiation levels. Humans who carry the silent genes have become subject to narcoma, which causes them to sleep for increasingly large portions of the day; eventually they lapse into permanent sleep. Powers, the protagonist, has developed narcoma symptoms, and in his diary his tabulation of hours of consciousness is still another countdown: "June 14: 9½ hours.... June 19: 8¾ hours.... June 25: 7½ hours.... July 3: 5¾ hours." Thus Powers is not only the protagonist but the objective correlative of the story, embodying in himself all the forces of entropy and all the apparently sterile hopes for a new future that the silent genes represent.

But throughout Powers' decline, Ballard has also provided him with certain images of potentiality and change. His name is the most obvious example. The most complex of these images is the enormous "ideogram" that Powers builds with cement during trance states; Powers himself is never consciously aware of constructing this enormous cement pattern. Since Ballard explicitly describes this pattern as a "crude Jungian mandala," the reason for its construction is clearly to be found in the works of Jung: a person will create or imagine mandalas when, having reached a critical stage, he is about to resolve his difficulties or at least remove them to a different plane.[5] That Powers creates a mandala suggests his imminent potential for change; that Whitby had also created the same mandala just before committing suicide suggests that this potential may itself be arrested or sterile. But Powers is consciously determined to test his potential, and plans to use Whitby's irradiation technique to activate his own silent genes—the first human to do so.

Because Powers' decision is such a desperate and heroic gamble, Ballard uses a virtuoso technique to dramatize the time that Powers spends under the Maxitron (Whitby's irradiation machine): the reader perceives this event through the sense organs of a mutant anemone. Since the anemone is highly sensitive to radiation, it translates the Maxitron's power-flow into first visual and then auditory terms, in a dazzling display of synesthesia:

> Gradually an image formed, revealing an enormous black fountain that poured an endless stream of brilliant light over the circle of benches and tanks. Beside it a figure moved, adjusting the flow through its mouth. As it stepped across the floor its feet threw off vivid bursts of color, its hands racing along the benches conjured up a dizzling chiaroscuro, balls of blue and violet light that exploded fleetingly in the darkness like miniature star-shells.
>
> Photons murmured.... The silent outlines of the laboratory began to echo softly, waves of muted sound fell from the arc lights and echoed off the benches and furniture below. Etched in sound, their angular forms resonated with sharp persistent overtones.

One doubts that a mainstream reader can make this sudden transition, but the SF reader should find it stimulating. This bravura passage prepares the reader for a second such passage, when Powers registers his awareness of the voices of time in sensual terms, apparently having developed new sense organs of his own. Further, this radical shift in narrators emphasizes the potential of the experiment, and the anemone's narration ends on a note of elation: "Streaming through a narrow skylight, its voice clear and strong, interwoven by numberless overtones, the sun sang...." [Ballard's ellipsis]

However, Powers' attempt to free himself from entropy ends in death. After his silent genes have been activated, he is able to perceive time so intensely that he can drive his car with his eyes closed, steering between the mountains and the salt lake by "feeling" the interface of "the two time fronts." As his perception becomes more acute, he apparently can "feel the separate identity of each sand grain and salt crystal calling to him from the surrounding ring of hills." Finding the center of his huge concrete mandala, he listens to the voices of the stars, "the time-song of a thousand galaxies overlaying each other in his mind." Overwhelmed by the eternal countdown radiating from the Canes Venatici star group, he feels "his body gradually dissolving, its physical dimensions melting into the vast continuum of the current." "Beyond hope now but at last at rest," he is swept into "the river of eternity." At this moment, Powers has died. Although described attractively, his death is a transcendence of entropy only in the sense that he has left life behind; there seems to be no future in eternity. This pessimistic view is emphasized by the final paragraphs of the story, as Kaldren visits the laboratory and finds all the experimental plants and animals dead. Yet the wider view of the story is to emphasize entropy itself, a force to which everything in the universe is subject.

Kaldren's meditations end the story; although Kaldren never sleeps, he is "half-asleep" in the final paragraph. Since he has earlier given Powers the message that contains the story's title, we must assume that Kaldren is, in part, a stand-in for the author; very possibly it is Ballard himself who is building a collection of "end-prints,...final statements, the products of total fragmentation. When I've got enough together I'll build a new world for myself out of them."[6] It is typical of

Ballard's precision in construction that when Powers does hear the voices of time to which Kaldren refers in the following passage, he explicitly hears both the galaxies and the grains of sand:

> You're not alone, Powers, don't think you are. These are the voices of time, and they're all saying good-bye to you. Think of yourself in a wider context. Every particle of your body, every grain of sand, every galaxy carries the same signature. As you've just said, you know what the time is now, so what does the rest matter? There's no need to go on looking at the clock.

All of the images of "The Voices of Time" coalesce in Kaldren's philosophy: like Powers, throw away your wristwatch. Think of the wider context and do not fear death.

In "The Voices of Time," Ballard has used science fiction to fulfill the traditional role of the poet: to meditate on time and death. Entropy. As an SF reader, I can interpret and appreciate this story as literature because its subject matter is not alien to me. But I doubt that a mainstream reader can appreciate the subtlety and beauty of such SF works, because his own set of literary values is limited by a tradition that excludes them. It is not the writer, but the reader, that builds the distinction between science fiction and mainstream fiction into a wall. One can find the gates in that wall, as Ballard did in "The Drowned Giant," but "The Voices of Time" kept to a different path. I believe this story is literature; I'm also convinced that it is unavailable to a reader experienced only in mainstream fiction.

NOTES

1. "The Drowned Giant" appeared in *Playboy* under the title "Souvenir." Quotations from both "The Drowned Giant" and "The Voices of Time" follow the text of *Chronopolis and Other Stories* (US 1971).

2. Ballard is obviously familiar with Kafka, and one may infer an influence. Kafka is the only fiction writer mentioned in "The Voices of Time."

3. Vladimir Nabokov, *Strong Opinions* (US 1973), p 156.

4. A more recent open-ended parable involving a giant, symbolic corpse is Donald Barthelme's new novel, *The Dead Father.*

5. A further complication is that Powers, a neuro-surgeon who is about to become permanently asleep, has operated on another principal character, Kaldren, removing his sleep-center so that Kaldren does not sleep at all; in addition, Kaldren follows Powers around obsessively, like a shadow. In a sense, then, Powers has created his opposite and shadow in Kaldren—a pattern of significance in Jungian psychology. Kaldren's girlfriend, Coma, also seems part of this pattern.

6. Compare T.S. Eliot in *The Wasteland*: "These fragments I have shored against my ruin." *The Wasteland* is presumably part of Kaldren's collection.

Peter S. Alterman

The Surreal Translations of Samuel R. Delany

(from SFS *4: 25–34, March 1977)*

One of the longest critical struggles in science fiction has been the attempt to define and identify just what it is. Almost every writer has, at one time or another, tried to define science fiction. Most of these definitions rely upon science fiction's unique concern with the future, as predictive or utopian/dystopian. Some definitions rely upon the unique themes and motifs of science fiction, such as rockets, alien creatures, and wars between the galaxies. Others stress the "sense of wonder" generated by science fiction. Yet all these definitions are acknowledged as either too vague or too restrictive. Roger Zelazny has said that whenever he hears a reasonable definition for science fiction, he writes a science fiction story violating that definition.[1]

Within the last few years, there have been additions to the anthology of science-fiction definitions which are not rooted in archetypes, themes, or emotional responses, but in the way language is used in science fiction. Whether or not they are universally applicable, these recent linguistic definitions do help shed light on one of the field's most enigmatic and controversial writers, Samuel R. Delany. A stylistic analysis of Delany's fiction does assist the reader in understanding the larger fictive concerns at work in his novels.

An early argument for the significance of style as a determinant of genre was offered by Ursula K. Le Guin in her speech to the 1972 Science Fiction Writers' Workshop, published as *From Elfland to Poughkeepsie*.[2] She argues that fantasy fiction is successful or unsuccessful directly as a result of the effectiveness of the writer's use of a particular style of prose, and that it is this use of style which identifies fantasy fiction and differentiates it from other forms of imaginative writing.

Joanna Russ applies this attitude implicitly in "Toward an Aesthetic of Science Fiction," insofar as she recognizes that much of what science fiction deals with as didactic realism is treated as metaphor by the large traditional body of modern literature. In other words, science fiction, as Lem implies, actualizes literary metaphors.[3]

Delany's latest published novel, *Triton* (1976), contains two appendices dealing with theoretical issues raised in passing within the fictional narrative of the novel. One of these contains a discussion of the linguistics of science fiction, in which Delany adds the weight of his voice to the argument:

> Such sentences as "His world exploded," or "She turned on her left side," as they subsume the proper technological discourse (of economics and cosmology in one; of switching circuitry and prosthetic surgery in the other), leave the banality of the emotionally muzzy metaphor, abandon the triviality of insomniac tossings, and, through the labyrinth of technical possibility, become possible images of the impossible. They join the repertoire of sentences which may propel *textus* into text. [Appendix A:3]

The broader concern with the style of science fiction as a key element of the genre is implicit in others of Delany's published essays, notably "About Five Thousand One Hundred and Seventy-Five Words,"[4] and in his recent interview in *Algol*.[5]

Many of the elements of Delany's fiction are more clearly focused when seen in light of the peculiarities of his prose style, a style dramatically at variance with the popular prose of much science fiction, which Alexei Panshin has traced to the early writings of Robert Heinlein.[6]

Delany's literary style is a combination of subtly derived linguistic techniques coupled with a disturbing liberation of certain structural elements. Within Delany's novels, time. logic, and point of view are cut loose from traditional literary positions, and function relativistically. Yet these free elements are rigidly controlled by the rules of a relativistic universe, thereby fulfilling Delany's comment above that technical possibility actualizes metaphor in science fiction.

In *Dhalgren* (1975), after Kid has made his first run with the Scorpions against Emboriky's, he retreats to the Reverend Tayler's for a meal and meets Ernest Newboy. There he corrects the galleys for his collection of poems, *Brass Orchids*. Lanya meets him and they realize that for him one day has passed, but for the rest of Bellona, five days have passed (§4:4). The issue of the linearity of time in Delany's novels is clearly shown here. In Bellona, time is not a constant.

In the relativistic universe, time is indeed not a constant, but is related to the velocity and frame of reference of the observer. This is dramatized in *Dhalgren*, and although it is a physical reality of the universe we all inhabit, we persist in viewing time as a universal and linear norm.

The uses of time in Delany's novels, here and more notably in *Empire Star* (1966), violate certain conventions of prose fiction. What seems to be a fantastic use of time is in fact a realistic use of time, because time is psychologically a function of the state of the observer and physically a function of the velocity of the observer. In more traditional fiction, the use of psychological time is well understood. But when Delany applies relativistic physical laws to time, the psychological metaphor of variable time becomes confusing, because the metaphor has been transformed into fact.

Empire Star presents much the same kind of tortured time. Comet Jo, the first "hero" of the novel, travels through a universe which is bent back on itself in a cycloid motion. Everything has already happened. He meets the same people, including himself, at various times of their lives. On one level, this is a nice manipulation of technique, showing the development of the hero's awareness of historicity and his part in it. But then Delany turns the technique on its head by showing the reader that time is, indeed, twisted in the universe. The center of the galaxy, Empire Star, gathers in time and space through a warp, bends it, and returns it in different sequence. This further confuses the reader, who has been expecting a proper, linear end to the story. In fact, time and space are warped around gravity wells. And *Empire Star* is designed to be read as a sequence of perceptions of the same story, much in the manner of Browning's *The Ring and the Book*. The properties of physical space are here used to serve the aesthetic and formal needs of the novel.

Time, then, in Delany's novels, is not simply linear. We cannot rely upon the linearity of experience as a baseline when approaching his novels. As Robert Scholes notes,

> fiction offers us not transcriptions of actuality but systematic models which are distinct from reality, though they may be related to it in various ways. Traditionally, realists have claimed a close and direct correspondence between their models and the world around them.[7]

He points out that the modern novelist's response is to accept the impossibility of recording the real, and to create a system based upon subjectivity. This position is interestingly much like Delany's position, for he not only accepts narrative subjectivity, but he applies to the subjective presence of, say, time, a physical concept which supports his unique use of time. In this manner, what Delany is doing by insisting upon a subjective or eccentric temporal mode is both satisfying the need of the modern novel to emphasize the impossibility of rendering the world outside, and at the same time presenting a close and scientifically acceptable vision of the world.

In a like manner, Delany deals creatively with the question of point of view, which is another shifting element. In *Empire Star*, the narrator is ostensibly a crystallized and objective point. Yet throughout the novel, we learn more and more about the point of view (not as a character, but as a force in the novel). Jewel, the narrative device, eventually unfolds enough of the plot for us to understand that the ordering of the elements is left to us. There is no attempt made to explicate or order the sequence of actions for the reader. The first reading is from the point of view of Comet Jo, learning his way from youth to maturity to an understanding of the nature of his task in life. This position leads to a second reading, of the nature of the society of the Lll, and the story of their freedom and bondage, with Jo playing a minor role. Then a third sequential reading, from the point of view of the Jewel itself, is suggested.

In each of these readings, more of the substance of the novel is revealed, and each uses a different point of view. Yet there is only one novel. The answer to this paradox is that at the end of the novel, the reader is challenged to read multi-levelly (multiplexially), with an eye on the growth of narrator, protagonist, and universe:

> In this vast multiplex universe there are almost as many worlds called Rhys as there are places called Brooklyn Bridge. It's a beginning. It's an end. I leave to you the problem of ordering your perceptions and making the journey from one to the other. [§15]

Delany here is inviting us to share in the creation of the novel by shifting our perceived point of view.

A second example of the fluidity of the narrator is in *Dhalgren*. Kid clearly is responsible for writing the journal, and therein perhaps the novel, but there are many Kids. There is Kidd, the confused immigrant, Kid the Poet, who also may be Ernest Newboy, Kid the Scorpion leader, and finally, the Michael Henry. Which Kid is the narrator of *Dhalgren*? They all are, for as Kid ventures farther and farther into the maze of Bellona, he changes. And as he changes, the novel he writes changes. In order to understand the nature of the narrator, one must then not attempt to discover a static character, but to apprehend both a personality and the way that personality changes. Perhaps this is a major confusing element of the novel, for we read the novel through Kid's eyes, but those eyes are not the same throughout the novel.

The metaphor of a person's changing as he grows is literalized and exaggerated. But Delany has also accepted an implicit requirement of that act—his novel changes as its narrator changes. In the absence of many traditional science fiction motifs, this one stylistic element—the concretizing of a metaphor—gives *Dhalgren* the unmistakable flavor of science fiction.

A third area where Delany's fiction is unexpectedly fluid is in his use of logic. Linearity of cause and effect has been a given in our logical experience for millennia, even in the face of "mystery religions." Non-Aristotelian models of logic, such as sympathetic magic, associative psychology, and more, have all been common in literature in the twentieth century. And yet science fiction, for all its vaunted imagination, is only now becoming aware of the stylistic possibility of thinking and experiencing non-rationally. The concept of "stochasticity," popularized by Vonnegut and Silverberg in science fiction, teaches us alternative forms of experiencing reality.[8]

Delany's non-linear, non-rational logic is predictably built upon a mathematical model: Gödel's Law. This is the core of *The Einstein Intersection* (1967), for it explains the mode of Lobey's experiences. Gödel's Law, as Delany applies it, is the thesis that

> *In any closed mathematical system*—you may read "the real world with its immutable laws of logic"—*there are an infinite number of true theorems*—you may read "perceivable, measurable phenomena"—*which, though contained in the original system, can not be deduced from*

it—read "proven with ordinary or extraordinary logic." Which is to say, there are more things in heaven and Earth than are dreamed of in your philosophy, Horatio. There are an infinite number of true things in the world with no way of ascertaining their truth. Einstein defined the extent of the rational. Goedel stuck a pin into the irrational and fixed it to the wall of the universe so that it held still long enough for people to know it was there.[9]

The resultant universe is one in which traditional rational explication takes second place. It is a universe of experience and emotion. It is a world where the protagonist may not know what is going on, but will be able to act on the experience of something's happening.

This is, in fact, what Lobey does. He reacts with no intellectual understanding of what he is doing. Furthermore the chapter epigraphs are all related to the chapters they present, sometimes by clear logical links, but more often by non-linear relationships, which exemplify the creative link between the artist's rational experience and his non-rational translation of that experience into his art. Taken together with the text of the novel, the epigraphs form an example of the novel's concept of the relationship between experience and art. Delany seems to be trying to manipulate the textures of experiences, not the meanings of those experiences, in order to elicit emotional responses from the reader and from his protagonist.

Fictive discourse aims at producing a range of reactions, a field of multiple responses, responses not as in a scatter-pattern of buckshot, but as interrelated and meshed and ordered as light waves in a spectrum. Critical discourse, though it may seek to produce the same fictive range of response, can refer to the responses produced by other fictions only as discrete entities, by and large; such reference distorts their essence, which is that they only exist as nodes in an ordered plurality.[10]

Delany is asserting that his fiction is designed to elicit a range of ordered responses from the reader, generated by sequences of key orders, images, or patterns. The rational and logical form of traditional prose, be it the mannered novel of the eighteenth century, or the critical essay, of which this piece is an example, attempts to create a pattern of purely logical, intellectual responses to a closely reasoned argument, what the novel would consider an "Einsteinian" response. *The Einstein Intersection* manipulates experiences to produce the desired sequence of emotional responses from Lobey and from the reader.

The same sequence of choreographed patterns is called for in *Dhalgren* when, for example, the giant red sun rises over Bellona. There is no rational explanation presented for it. Nor is there any causal link with it in the text of the novel. Yet the wonder it creates is a response to the wonder Kid and the reader feel at the marvelous mating of Kid, Lanya, and Danny for the first time. There are, to be sure, resonances inherent in the sun (sun, son), a trine of older male, older female, and young male: Christ, the Trinity, Oedipus, even the Fobo-Muels-Rydra Wong tripling of *Babel-17* (1966). Yet the major effect of the giant sun cannot be apprehended by looking for logical connectives, although they are present. We must read it as a symbolic response to the experience of coming awake in a new world of wonder, of making love, and being loved, for the first time.

While this concern with patterns of response may seem to be a retreat into the philosophy of communication, it is central to Delany's style—a style which baffles many readers. Once again, Delany has taken a normally static element, logic, and wrenched it into a new, fluid role. At the same time, he has founded his actions in legitimate theoretical bases. In so doing, he has reconciled the ideological problem of the modern novelist, identified by Scholes—that of the limitations of realism—with a theory of science fiction as a stylistic construct reconciling the various forms of experience within a relativistic and formal universe.

Each of the three areas broken free by Delany—time, point of view, and logic—is broken on the authority of some valid, or potentially valid, physical law or thesis. In turn, the freedom these elements lend to Delany's novels requires close attention from the reader, lest he become confused by looking for the traditional prose forms.

Close attention is just what Delany gives to his fiction, most obviously to the very sentences out of which the novels grow. In the essay "Thickening the Plot," Delany sets about to define the creative process in concrete terms.[11] In this essay, he stresses the photographic accuracy of his imaginings, the completeness with which he visualizes his subject, and describes how he forces visual precision into his language. He also notes that the very process of converting the vision into language changes the scene being described, so that the final product is a surreal translation, a partnership between the rich word and the richer vision, the translation of the vision affecting the vision itself. This methodology implies a rigid adherence to the concrete, the sensual, the "realistic" world on one hand, and to the mythic, metaphoric elements of language on the other. Here again Delany confronts the opposing moments of force, the photographic "real" and the untrustworthy "subjective."

The practical effect of striving for the precise evocation of experience gives a unique flavor to that experience. Delany's novels display an intense sense of being in touch with the physical world. In fact, the effort of accurately rendering the physical drives Delany to confront the limits of perceived experience, the point at which language breaks down under the intensity of his gaze, and forces him toward a new use of language.

For example, the presence of multiplicity and simultaneity in Delany's mental images of reality demands that he jam multiplicity into the essentially linear and sequential form of English prose.

> What an odd ritual exchange to exhaust communication. (Is that terror?) What amazing and engaging rituals are we practicing now? (He stood on the road side, laughing.) What torque and tension in the mouth to laugh so in his windy, windy, windy...[12]

In this brief paragraph from *Dhalgren*, Delany is not merely creating a stylistic analogue for a "realistic" state of simultaneous laughing, thinking, and feeling, though certainly he does that, specifically with his use of parenthetical statements. He is tying together several levels of human consciousness: the emotional experiences of terror, wonder, laughter; the mental activity of questioning reality (Is this terror?) and society (What amazing rituals), and responding in an aesthetic way to the physical environment (note the images of exhaust, wind, laughter connected to the mechanical images of torque and tension). The prose attempts to capture the multiplicity of the real moment, not so much by applying a literary code, but by presenting a sense of the multiplicity of experience within the prose.

The revision of a brief paragraph in the "Prologue" of *The Captives of the Flame* (1963, revised 1966) shows how his emphasis on detail adds depth to his prose:

> [First version.] Jon Koshar shook his head, staggered forward, and went down on his knees in white sand. He blinked. He looked up. There were two shadows in front of him.

> [Revised version.] Palms and knees scudded in something hot. Jon Koshar shook his head, looked up. Sand saddled away from him. His black hair fell over his eyes again; he shook it away and sat back on his heels.[13]

It would be instructive to compare the verbs used in these two paragraphs, "went down" opposed to "scudded," but not to the point. Clearly Delany writes and revises toward greater physical reality. But, as well, his verbs show a musical affinity for each other, in "scudded," "saddled," "shook," "sat." And the precision of vision is blended with an aesthetic which renders sibilance and a sense of insecurity to the experience, even in this early adventure novel.

The handling of simultaneous material in a necessarily linear form is a good indication of the kind of word-by-word craftsmanship in Delany's prose. In resolving the problem of rendering a "fantastic" or science-fictional sequence realistically, he visualizes the subject matter completely, rather than retreating from it into vague cubist shapes or highly mannered prose. And remarkably, by striving to describe the seams of reality, he breaks through "reality" to describe the perceiving mind as much as the perceived experience. The parenthetical statement is a good example, for it is both a pause in the exposition and a gloss on the transcribed experience without. Together, reality, observer, and language form a collage of meaning. It is like his concretizing of metaphor. The vaguely *like* becomes the solid *is*. Precision is what these two techniques share.

Delany's theoretical concern with the uses of prose appears frequently in his fiction, almost as if the work was a test-bed for linguistic theory. He considers the totality of the story, plot, character, language, etc. to be a *textus*, or web of meaning, within which the text proper resides. The manner in which *textus* translates into text he alludes to with the term metonymy, the concept of language as connotative rather than denotative.

Naming is always a metonymic process. Sometimes it is the pure metonymy of associating an abstract group of letters (or numbers) with a person (or thing), so that it can be recalled (or listed in a metonymic order with other entity names). Frequently, however, it is a more complicated metonymy: old words are drawn from the cultural lexicon to name the new entity (or to rename an old one), as well as to render it (whether old or new) part of the present culture. The relations between entities so named are woven together in patterns far more complicated than any alphabetic or numeric listing can suggest: and the encounter between objects-that-are-words (e.g., the name "science fiction," a critical text on science fiction, a science-fiction text) and processes-made-manifest-by-words (another science-fiction text, another critical text, another name) is as complex as the constantly dissolving interface between culture and language itself.[14]

It is therefore not unusual to find images of myths, meanings, and memories, as well as convoluted symbolism in Delany's fiction. His concept of language and literature implies this rich depth of layering.

That Mouse's syrinx in *Nova* is called an "ax" certainly is an example of the way in which meanings cluster around images. "Ax" is a slang term for the musician's guitar, as well as signifying the chopping weapon. So "ax" refers in depth to the two functions of the device Mouse carries, as a musical instrument and weapon. It also refers to the labrys, the mark of the two-headed ax, symbolic of the dual worlds of life and death in Minoan culture, most well known through the labyrinth of the minotaur. It also refers to the dual nature of the moon, life and death, the return to the womb, and fear of darkness.[15] Also, it is a "'symbol' for writing/script/text/texture, and usually 'writing' related to architecture."[16] These ranged allusions of "ax" are specifically connected to Lorq's quest through the battles he has with the Reds in the modern labyrinth of earth and with his Orphic search for Ruby Red in an exploding star. They serve equally well for the "sax" Lobey carries in *The Einstein Intersection.*

Clearly, the word "ax" is supplied in *Nova* consciously. That each major group of metonymic meanings has an analogue in the surface of the story is proof enough of that. What Delany does with this technique is to make the reader feel the weight of meaning and symbol around the text, i.e., invoke a *textus* for the story. This enriches the story, and charges the linear tale with alternative meanings, possibilities, and significance. It is another way of transcending the limitations of realism, of working in the subjective mind of the reader.

In other places, Delany's insistence on the perception of language as a burdened element is more baldly stated, or worked into the tale:

That's just being a poet, she explained, the oblique connection momentarily cutting the flood through. Poet in Greek means *maker* or *builder*.

There's one! There's a pattern now. Ahhhh!—so bright, bright!

Just that simple semantic connection? She was astounded. *But the Greeks were poets three thousand years ago and you are a poet now. You snatch words together over such distance and their wakes blind me. Your thoughts are all fire, over shapes I cannot catch. They sound like music too deep, that shakes me.*

That's because you were never shaken before, But I'm flattered.

You are so big inside me I will break. I see the pattern named The Criminal and artistic consciousness meeting in the same head with one language between them...

Yes, I had started to think something like—

Flanking it, shapes called Baudelaire—*Ahhh!—and* Villon.[17]

This brief excerpt clearly defines Delany's sense of language here as associative. Not only is his heroine a poet with a sense of the history of language, but her words are used in a scholarly way, with mental footnotes to Baudelaire and Villon and critical themes like "The Criminal and Artistic Consciousness." (Such a theme was actually advanced by Professor Douglas Barbour in a 1975 paper.)[18] The language of the poet's mind charges Butcher with artistic implications. It also signals the blending of Rydra and Butcher into a criminal/artist whole which explains her change from victim to controller of *Babel-17*.

The image of the text as a web of meaning itself is present in the body of Delany's fiction, especially in *Babel-17*, which in this light can be read as an animated recitation on the nature of the relationship between language and meaning:

She rose slowly, and the web caught her around the chest. Some sort of infirmary. She looked down at the—not "webbing", but rather a three particle vowel differential, each particle of which defined one stress of the three-way tie, so that the weakest points in the mesh were identified when the total sound of the differential reached its lowest point. By breaking the threads at these points, she realized, the whole web would unravel. Had she failed at it, and not named it in this new language, it would have been more than secure enough to hold her. The transition from "memorized" to "known" had taken place while she had been— [§3:1]

In this example, Rydra Wong has just learned how to think in the highly artificial language of Babel-17, which forces her to think, perceive, and react in an extremely precise and rapid way. The web is an image of the effects of language on the mind, and of the mind as shaper of reality. This scene becomes symbolic of the interrelationship of mind, language, and reality, a web like the triple-stressed web Rydra lies in, analyzes, and breaks.

The experience of the work of art transcends the language used to construct it, because of, not in spite of, the nature of Delany's use of words. The technique Delany uses is to move beyond the literal, not by a retreat from concrete reality, but by approaching the literal closely, so closely that the mind of the narrator/artist shows through. Delany's prose style is an amalgam of elements: the precise visual rendering of images coupled with a conscious use of metonymy to create a language of experience.

Complementing Delany's theoretical concern with the function of his prose is an equally obvious concern with structural issues, such as the definition of the novel in *Nova*, the relationship between theoretical criticism and creative writing in *Dhalgren*, and, of course, the question of point of view in *Empire Star*, mentioned earlier. Whereas Delany's idea of language is accretive and inclusive, his idea of literary forms is much more rigid and formal.

"To make my book, I must have an awareness of my time's conception of history,"...

"History? Thirty-five hundred years ago Herodotus and Thucydides invented it. They defined it as the study of whatever had happened during their own lives. And for the next thousand years it was nothing else. Fifteen hundred years after the Greeks, in Constantinople, Anna Comnena, in her legalistic brilliance (and in essentially the same language as Herodotus) wrote history as the study of those events of man's actions that have been documented. I doubt if this charming Byzantine believed things only happened when they were written about. But incidents unchronicled were simply not considered the province of history in Byzantium. The whole concept had transformed. In another thousand years we had reached that century which began with the first global conflict and ended with the first conflict between globes brewing. Somehow the theory had arisen that history was a series of cyclic rises and falls as one civilization overtook another. Events that did not fit on the cycle were defined as historically unimportant. It's difficult for us today to appreciate the differences between Spengler and Toynbee, though from all accounts their approaches were considered polar in their day. To us they seem merely to be quibbling over when or where a given cycle began. Now that another thousand years has passed, we must wrestle with De Eiling and Broblin, 34-Alvin and the Crespburg Survey. Simply because they are contemporary, I know they must inhabit the same historic view." [*Nova* §4]

This longish quotation is a good example of the kind of structural, architectonic analysis which Delany weaves throughout *Nova*. Each didactic monologue is referred to as a note from Katin, the incipient novelist, to himself. He writes innumerable notes on the nature of the novel, its elements, and its relation to society and the individual. It becomes clear that the novel *Nova* is the novel which Katin writes after his experience on the *Roc*. Therefore, the theoretical issues raised are important to the novel.

In the above quotation, for example, we can note an interesting concern: Katin is theorizing on history and also on the relationship of time to the work of art. As note-taker, Katin is the scholarly critic whose goal is the comprehension of the work of art in structural and aesthetic terms.

The best image of the work of art as an organized experience in *Nova* is not a didactic one, however. It is the image of Katin and Lorq Von Ray, both blinded by a nova. Katin, the artist, masters the new experience because as an artist he rearranges it. In this case he watches the nova *after* the *Roc* leaves its chaotic core. Lorq looks into the heart of chaos, the heart of the exploding nova. He is blinded, his senses scrambled, but Katin recovers. Katin is able to transmit the experience of the nova, not by deferring the chaos, but by rendering the afterimage. In just this way, the novel implies, art organizes experience, and the artist is able to render the chaos of experience by transforming it, or organizing it through a web of intellectual and aesthetic techniques.

Another image of the interdependence of art and structure occurs in *Dhalgren*. Kid's notebook, which is his book of poems, his diary, and the novel itself, are written on the back pages of what we are told is a large body of theoretical criticism.

In the middle of the third line, without taking pen off paper, he swept back to cross it all out. Then, carefully, he recopied two words on the next line. The second was "I." Very carefully now, word followed word. He crossed out two more lines, from which he salvaged "you." "spinner," and "pave," dropping them into a new sentence that bore no denotative resemblance to the one from which they came.

Between lines, while he punched his pen point, his eye strayed to the writing beside this: *It is our despair at the textual inadequacies of language that drives us to heighten the structural ones toward...* [§2:3]

Ernest Newboy, who may be a late avatar of the mythological Kid the Poet, notes the relationship between the critical/analytic pages and the poetry. And although Kid denies that the criticism is his, it obviously is meant to be related to his poems, since it dovetails so well with the poetry, various sections of the "novel" *Dhalgren*, and many of Kid's experiences.

Furthermore, the seventh chapter of *Dhalgren*, "The Anathēmata: *a plague journal*," is essentially the raw experience from which the novel *Dhalgren* is supposedly drawn—scheduled, sequenced, intellectualized, and presented. It is in this section that the distinction between the chaos of experience and the order of art is most clearly evidenced. Many of the events organized sequentially in the earlier section of *Dhalgren* are present in this chapter.[19] They are out of sequence, disjoint, unrelated to any prior intellectual or aesthetic framework. It is presented as the unembroidered chaos of random notes about living in Bellona, unformed and even written over with notes which are apparently unconnected to the body of the page. There is no underlying code or metaphor, such as "stream of consciousness." There is only the artful experience without art—chaos without order.

A less complex example of the dialogue between order and chaos is in *The Einstein Intersection*. Lobey never quite knows what to do, and yet he always acts when action is required. The force which organizes the chaos of Lobey's experience is the mathematical construct of Gödel, and not the artifice of myth or archetype. There are too many myths and archetypes crossing and bumping into each other for any mythic pattern to be truly reliable for predicting events. Without Spider's definition of the universe along the lines implied by Gödel's Law, *The Einstein Intersection* is a chaotic sequence of experiences. With the Law in mind, Lobey's quest is a movement to become, in which the crucial structuring image is not a rational sequence of intelligible causes and effects, but a development of the mind learning to experience itself and the reality around it—to be different.

Lobey constantly asks what things mean, what he should do, and Spider explains that he is asking the wrong kind of question. He must exist in a world of experience without reasons. Lobey himself, through his music, symbolizes order. His battle with Kid Death is the battle between order and chaos:

> "This is why he is chasing you—or making you chase him. He needs order. He needs patterning, relation, the knowledge that comes when six notes predict a seventh, when three notes beat against one another and define a mode, a melody defines a scale. Music is the pure language of temporal and co-temporal relation. He knows nothing of this, Lobey. Kid Death can control, but he cannot create, which is why he needs Green-eye. He can control, but he cannot order. And that is why he needs you."[20]

Lobey "kills" Kid Death with Spider's help—Spider, the symbol of betrayal for gold, lust, worldly things. But chaos is not killed, only subsumed. "Like the Kid; I can bring back the ones I've killed myself."[21] *The Einstein Intersection*, among its other patterns, attempts symbolically to explain the relationship of control (mastery of the creative elements), creation (the energy or vision), and order. Order, defined not as logical causation but as predictable relationship, gives final shape to control, which begins with creation, but moves beyond it. It is a gloss on the writer's craft.

Many of Delany's novels, then, are characterized by a conscious discussion of the formal nature and function of literature and the relationship between experience and art. In every case, art is able to organize experience, bringing pattern and order to chaos. This issue manifests itself in Delany's use of language: the order of realism rests uneasily on the chaotic subjectivism of the perceiving narrator. These two stylistic elements identify a central concern of his fiction: his prose attempts to render the texture of the chaotic universe by actualizing literary metaphors with scientific theory, and the larger construct of his prose attempts to organize that chaos into intelligible, translatable forms.

For Delany, the process of artistic creation is an attempt to derive order from the chaos of experience. More precisely, it is an attempt to reconcile the contrary demands of the subjective perspective of the artist, who must admit to experiencing life from a biased point of view—the structural requirements of formal literary patterns, which can wrench meaning and order from randomness, and the restrictions inherent in language as a medium of transmitting vision. In Delany's prose, neither the subjective nor the objective—neither the chaos of the individual mind's perceiving, nor the artifice of literary device, is given primacy. Just as metaphor is solidified by fact, experience is ordered by the effect of art upon the raw material of the mind, which is able to translate the chaotic elements of life accurately into words. Delany's later novels, especially, are arenas in which life and language confront one another and come together to form a dialectic of literature. Delany's science fiction includes and capitalizes on the tension between scientific theory and linguistic potential.

NOTES

1. Conversation with Zelazny, Albuquerque, August 1975.
2. Published as a chapbook by the Pendragon Press of Portland, Oregon.
3. Joanna Russ, "Towards an Aesthetic of Science Fiction," SFS 2(1975):112; Stanislaw Lem, "On the Structural Analysis of Science Fiction," SFS 1(1973):26.
4. *Extrapolation* 10(1969):52-66; rpt in *SF: The Other Side of Realism*, ed. Thomas D. Clareson (US 1971), pp 130-46.
5. Darrell Schweitzer, "Algol Interview: Samuel R. Delany," *Algol* 13(Summer 1976):16-22.
6. *Heinlein in Dimension* (US 1968 x+198), pp 13-15.
7. *Structural Fabulation* (US 1975 xi+111), p 6.
8. Silverberg defines stochasticity at the beginning of his novel, *The Stochastic Man* (US 1975): "Whatever happens happens by chance. The concepts of cause and effect are fallacies. There are only *seeming* causes leading to *apparent* effects. Since nothing truly follows from anything else, we swim each day through seas of chaos, and nothing is predictable, not even the events of the very next instant."
9. Ace Books pb. no date, 155p, p 128; *The Einstein Intersection* does not have numbered chapters.
10. From the ms. of Delany's unpublished essay, "Of Sex, Objects, Signs, Systems, Sales, Science Fiction, and Other Things."
11. In *Those Who Can: A Science Fiction Reader*, ed. Robin Scott Wilson (NAL pb 1974), pp 70-77.
12. *Dhalgren* §1:2. This and other passages were pointed out by K. Leslie Steiner in an unpublished essay, "Some Remarks Toward a Reading of *Dhalgren*."
13. *Captives of the Flame* was first published as an Ace Books pb in 1963, my source for the first quotation (p 5). The revised version was published 1966 as an Ace Books pb under the same title; then was issued in 1968 in UK as a Sphere Books pb as *Out of the Dead City*; and now has been incorporated under the second title in *The Fall of the Towers* (Ace Books pb nd 413p), my source for the second quotation (p 13).
14. *Triton*, Appendix A:3.
15. Especially in Joseph Campbell, *The Masks of God: Primitive Mythology* (US 1959, 1969).
16. Letter from Delany to the author, 30 Oct 1976.
17. Delany, *Babel-17* §4:2.
18. Douglas Barbour, "Multiplex Misdemeanors: The Figures of the Artist and the Criminal in the Science Fiction Novels of Samuel R. Delany," in *Khatru* #2 (1975), ed. Jeffrey D. Smith, 1339 Weldon Ave., Baltimore, Md. 21221.
19. Pointed out by Steiner (see Note 12 above).
20. *The Einstein Intersection* (see Note 9 above), p 133.
21. Ibid., p 154.

Stanislaw Lem

Cosmology and Science Fiction

Translated by Franz Rottensteiner

(from SFS *4: 107–110, July 1977)*

These remarks owe their existence to a suggestion of Dr R. Mullen of *Science-Fiction Studies*, who received a review copy of *Cosmology Now* (ed. Laurie John, Taplinger Publishing Co., 168p, $10.95) but felt the book too peripheral to the journal's concerns for an ordinary review. The title too is Dr Mullen's choice. Therefore my remarks are addressed to the readers of *Science-Fiction Studies*, and they were written in German since my English is insufficient for the task.

1. *Cosmology Now* was authored by several British scientists for the BBC in 1973. The American edition, the one on hand, appeared in 1976. A reviewer both well-versed in the subject and malicious could claim with some justification that the book would be better called *Cosmology Yesterday*. If the cosmos is the most durable of things, this durability doesn't extend to the science that deals with its exploration. Even the best cosmological reference works written some seven or eight years ago are today totally out-of-date. The three life-years that *Cosmology Now* has now had have seen much change in cosmology. Since I don't have to write a "regular review," I will list only the most important innovations. The age of the cosmos is today estimated to be some 20 billion years. The experiments of Weber, who claimed to have registered gravitational waves, have been discarded, since his apparatus was of insufficient sensitivity. The health of the "steady state" theory which denies the evolution of the universe from a zero point has deteriorated noticeably. Scientists are inclined to award the palms of victory to the theory of the Big Bang. Moreover, many of the things described in *Cosmology Now* have lost their former, beautiful simplicity. For instance, there is now a whole "family" of black holes. In addition to the ones postulated originally, which were supposed to be the final stage of a collapsing neutron star, there have been new ones, for instance partially reversible black holes. These may not be assumed to be "gravity graves," invisible for all eternity. And there are especially the black micro-holes. As the new theory of Stephen Hawking of Cambridge will have it, these are objects with the diameter of a proton and mass of a mountain range. Quite a lot of them are said to have been created at the time of the Big Bang. I mention the theory of Hawking, first, because it introduces the method of quantum mechanics into the field of the general theory of relativity, and second, because it implies consequences that cannot be overlooked and may change our whole outlook. Although there are so far no irrefutable (empirical) proofs for the existence of *any* black holes, we cannot imagine any possible technological utilization of the *big* black holes, whereas one may consider the micro-holes as energy sources that can surpass the annihilation of matter by several million times, the so far energetically most potent reaction. Such a micro-hole is supposed to contain the energy of several million of hydrogen bombs. *Sapienti sat*. There are other important discoveries, but I cannot enlarge this short aside into a "regular book review." Therefore—*finis*.

In our times, scientific works grow old very fast. *The Internal Constitution of the Stars* by A. Eddington enthralled me when I read it 40 years ago, and it is still a magnificent book, but it must be read now as (genuine!) Science Fiction, because nothing in it corresponds anymore with our present knowledge. In my opinion the same may happen with *Cosmology Now*: please take this remark as a *hommage*. This volume will remain readable, indeed exciting, but very little of its aesthetically appealling, lucid simplicity in its development of the model of the universe will survive the changes to come. I say this as a *dilettante* and a heretic who knows more about the history of science than about cosmology. The first conquerors of new knowledge find it always easier to proclaim that "God may be subtle, but He is not malicious," because the biggest hurdles are discovered by the next generation of scientists. But it seems to me that one of the main theses of *Cosmology Now* will remain valid: that the universe is a continued explosion extended over a time of twenty billion years that appears as a majestic solidification only to the eyes of a transient being like Man. The question whether we are living in a rhythmically pulsating universe or in a cosmos that will finally dissolve into vacuum still remains to be answered. The pendulum of mutually exclusive opinions goes on swinging.

2. Now then, what is the relationship between cosmology and SF? The facts are clear: both universes, that of the writers and that of the scientists, grow ever more apart. The estimations of the "density of cosmic civilization" show this most evidently. The scientists, even the founders of CETI (Contact with Extraterrestrial Intelligences) feel compelled to attribute ever smaller figures to the psychozoic density in the cosmos, because the accumulating negative results of the "sky listening" (for signals) force them to do so. SF takes not the slightest notice of such changes. Therefore for SF one of the biggest riddles of contemporary cosmology, the *silentium universi*, doesn't exist at all. But it would be totally wrong to reduce the divergence of the two universes to only one parameter, the one mentioned. Science fiction started its escape from the real cosmos even before the question was formulated why the universe remains silent so stubbornly. This flight has by now evolved into a "steady state"; SF has encapsuled itself so much against the space of cosmology that it is unwilling to receive any signals; that is to say, any news from the field of science, with the exception of what manages to make the front pages of the newspapers (such as the tale of the black holes). This encapsulement took place when the authors got hold of two fantastic, very convenient inventions: unlimited travel in time, and unlimited travel in space. Thanks to time travel and FTL the cosmos has acquired such qualities as domesticate it in an exemplary manner for story telling purposes; but at the same time it has lost its strange, icy sovereignty. SF doesn't know of the cosmos of colliding galaxies, the invisible stars sucked in by the curvature of space, the pulsating magnetic fields. Nevertheless there is in SF not a single one of the civilizations of the "third stage" postulated by CETI, the civilizations which are, thanks to their applied science of astral engineering, able to control stellar energies. As far as their content is concerned, most of the civilizations in SF correspond to the state predicted for Earth in 2000 or 2300, although structurally they have remained arrested rather in the 19th century, with their colonisatory tactics of conquest and their strategies of war, whose magnification is only due to the principle of "Big Berta" [the German super-gun that shelled Paris during WWI]. SF has not the slightest idea what could be done with a power of the magnitude of a sun, if it isn't used exclusively for the destruction of inhabited planets. And in SF cosmic civilizations have no intellectual culture at all, because a future-oriented movement that claims to probe into the farthest future, and makes its home in a realm of naively contaminated, amateurish ideas on "primitive slave societies," must be held totally lacking in credibility. SF criticism often talks of a "sense of wonder" that the field is supposed to generate, but upon close examination that "wonder" divulges its close relationship to the tricks of a stage magician. As popular fiction, SF must pose artificial problems and offer their easy solution. The astonishing results of contemporary cosmology which border on paradox, are of no use to science-fiction writers, because they cannot be tucked into the narrow fixed frame of the artificial cosmos. Any comparison, including that with the stage magician, isn't quite exact, because the magician doesn't aim at anything beyond the production of some tricks, whereas the self-imprisonment that is characteristic for SF has made it unable to describe real space any more.

To do justice to SF, which looks so shabby when compared to the background of cosmology, it is necessary to further explain its dilemma. The sins of individual authors have always been relatively small. The development of the totally false, domesticated universe was a gradual process of self-organization, and therefore all together are responsible for the final deformation—and nobody. Thanks to the first SF invention all occurrences in space have become easily reversible, but the authors who "just" want to shine with a new version of time-travel have forgotten the larger context. It is particularly due to these unnoticed relationships that nature was softened in the cruelty of the irreversible flow of time that is its hallmark. In order that space might not be used as another cruelty to man, it was "short-circuited" by another invention, i.e. annihilated. The fact that a domestication of the cosmos has taken place, a diminution that whisked away those eternally silent abysses of which Pascal spoke with horror, is masked in SF by the blood that is so liberally spilt in its pages. But there we already have a humanized cruelty, for it is a cruelty that can be understood by man, and a cruelty that could finally even be judged from the viewpoint of ethics—granted that one could take this blood seriously at all. By looking at it this way, we come to understand what SF has done to the cosmos: for it makes no sense at all to look at the universe from the viewpoint of ethics. Therefore, the universe of SF is not only miniscule, simplified and lukewarm, but it has also been turned towards its inhabitants, and in this way it can be subjugated by them, losing thereby that indifference which causes man to project continually new enigmas to be solved and secrets to be lifted, in the vain hope to get *there* the answer to the question for his own meaning. In the universe of SF there is not the slightest chance that genuine myths and theologies might arise, for the thing itself is a bastard of myths gone to the dogs. The SF of today resembles a "graveyard of gravity," in which that sub-genre of literature that promised the cosmos to mankind, dreams away its defeat in onanistic delusions and chimeras—onanistic, because they are anthropocentric. The task of the SF author of today is as easy as that of the pornographer, and in the same way. Now that all the real stops to the satisfaction of their impulses have been pulled, they can have their fling. But with the stops has disappeared the indescribable richness that can be conveyed only by real life. Where anything comes easy, nothing can be of value. The most inflamed desire must finally end in miserable dullness. Once the credible, the real barriers have been blown up, the process of falsification must go on; artificial barriers must be erected, and in this manner the stuffed waxworks come about, the miserable ersatz that is supposed to be cosmic civilizations.

3. Why is it impossible to regain the universe that has been lost to SF? One could claim that the laws of the market do not permit it—that today no authors and publishers would dare to subject the readers to a cure of giving up that would equal the renunciation of easy solutions to fictitious problems. True, it must be admitted that not everything in SF is rotten in the same degree. After all, there was once the cosmogonic fantasy of a Stapledon. But Stapledon, as an isolated writer, was still able to view the universe of cosmology, and not the humanized universe of SF. It should be kept in mind here that "humanize" in this context doesn't mean to "make more humane"; we know that among the animals there are no sexual murderers, and a sexual murderer can hardly be called a humane being.

It must be admitted that the universe presents the "peak of indigestibility" for fiction writing in the whole field of our experience. For what can you do as an author with the central subjects of cosmology—with the singularities? A singularity is a place that exists in the continuum just as a stone exists here; but there our whole physics goes to pieces. The desperate struggles of the theoreticians, going on for several years now, have only the purpose to postpone this end of physics, its collapse, by yet one more theory. In fiction, however, things like that cannot be domesticated. What heroic characters, what plot can there be where no body, however strong or hard, could exist longer than a few fractions of second? The space surrounding a neutron star cannot be passed closely in a spaceship even at parabolic velocity because the gravity gradients in the human body increase without a chance that they might be stopped or screened, and human beings explode until only a red puddle is left, just like a heavenly body that is torn apart from tidal forces when passing through the Roche limit. Is there therefore no way out of this fatal dilemma: that one must either be silent about the cosmos or be forced to distort it? Cosmology shows us a way out.

Just as one may look at the knowledge of yesterday as a fantastic speculation—as I said about the famous work of Eddington—so one may imagine a cosmogony of tomorrow, dissimilar to the current one, but nevertheless understandable, for cosmic processes are accessible to us to the degree that they can be focussed by reason. But nothing is today so much held in contempt in SF as reason. In this regard a total harmony unites the authors with the readers. Obscenity is no longer indecent—the intellectual has taken its place in the pillory. SF fans should be discouraged from perusing *Cosmology Now*, unless they are willing to free their imagination from its imprisonment to discover in the brightness of real suns the true face of nature.

Jerzy Jarzębski

Stanislaw Lem, Rationalist and Visionary

Translated by Franz Rottensteiner

Before the political thaw in 1956 known as the "Polish October" Lem published three SF books: two novels, THE ASTRONAUTS (1951) and THE MAGELLAN NEBULA (1955), and a collection, SESAME AND OTHER STORIES (1954).[1] The two novels became tremendously popular and were reprinted many times. On the first novel was based the script for THE SILENT STAR, a movie that posed difficult technical problems for the joint industries of Poland and East Germany.

These early works show some technical weaknesses, quite aside from a certain conceptual schematism, and it is somewhat paradoxical that it was those two novels that became required reading in Polish schools. In THE ASTRONAUTS and SESAME especially, the indecision of the author is all too obvious. Should I lecture and popularize, or rather spin fantastic plots?, he seems to wonder. The first part of THE ASTRONAUTS, describing the preparations for an expedition to Venus, is unbearably slow and full of lectures; and only the second part, "THE DIARY OF A PILOT," written with the narrative skill characteristic of Lem, makes up for the failures of the first part. In SESAME we find, besides the first Star Diaries of Ijon Tichy, full of humour and written with narrative vigor, also lectures in popular science that repel the reader.

Lem drew the conclusion from these difficulties. The most successful parts of his early works were told by a narrator who was at the same time the protagonist of the story and involved in the plot; the narrative flow began to slow down when the author himself appeared from behind the hero and started plaguing the reader with lectures on the principles of computers, the design of interplanetary rockets, etc.[2] In THE MAGELLAN NEBULA Lem refrained from introducing a narrator who would be identical with the author, and his role was taken over by a member of the expedition. A young member, which is crucial; pilot Smith of THE ASTRONAUTS is also still a greenhorn. Through the inexperienced eyes of the protagonist we are first introduced to and involved in the peripeties of the future and the galactic expedition. This device allows the text to convey much information about the civilizational marvels of future centuries, for the young narrator must himself still learn quite a lot—and for that he is (and at the same time we are) given ample opportunity.

THE MAGELLAN NEBULA is very skilfully written, even if somewhat uneven—for this beautiful ship flounders every so often on sandbanks. It is not enough to eliminate a narrator speaking *ex cathedra*: if the narrator and protagonist himself enters elementary school, the reader has no choice but to accompany him, and the basic teacher-pupil relationship is left unchanged. Why do I devote so much space to this? Lem frankly admits that for him writing is a pulpit from which he delivers certain theses about the society of the future, the evolution of science, the philosophical implications of technological progress, etc.; his visions are not puzzle-games with fantasy elements. In Lem's opinion, the term "*science* fiction" implies an obligation. In his early works, however, these noble principles are at odds with artistic ambitions; diagnoses of the world's future are presented as if they were axioms: a just order of society must triumph, science and technology must achieve a high level of development where the sky is the limit, the lives of all citizens of Earth will flow with nothing but milk and honey, and kindness and general love will be ubiquitous.

It is difficult to decide just what in this vision was Lem and what was taken over from the literary clichés of the time. The Lem of that time—a rationalist and believer in scientism—perhaps really believed in the unlimited visions of human reason, but he expressed them in pretentious formulas, with which THE MAGELLAN NEBULA abounds. His views are, if one overlooks this defect, humanist ones; however, the weakness of his characters is contentment with their fate—his humanism is too self-righteous. Their philosophical problems have already been or are being solved somewhere, so that the experiences transmitted become simply verifications of already existing hypotheses and emerge as glib phrases.

Such ideal characters from a happy utopia are somewhat of a nuisance even for the author, who reminds us several times—as it were contradicting himself—that the human soul is complete in itself and must not be tampered with, and that weakness and evil must not be forgotten in our view of human beings. The image of a Terrestrial Paradise will reappear twice in Lem—characteristically, however, in a negative function. In RETURN FROM THE STARS (1961) the flowering of civilization is due to an operation called "betrization," which is mandatory for all children. It does away with all aggressive instincts, but as a corollary also destroys the ability to take risks. The inhabitants of that "utopia" give up the conquest of space without a feeling of loss. In a distorted mirror, this motif recurs again in the recent short novel *The Futurological Congress* (in INSOMNIA, 1971), where paradise is only a drug-induced illusion, a camouflage for the awful living conditions of a population of several billion at the end of the 21st century.

It would appear that the main weakness of THE ASTRONAUTS and THE MAGELLAN NEBULA is philosophical: the young Lem owes allegiance to positivistic ideals, he believes in the progress of science which can in final analysis cope with any problem, and not least he believes that an enlightened and rational society will automatically get rid of all its inner conflicts and tensions. But it might rather be said that it was the normative fictional convention ("socialist realism") which in this manner "thought for him." It is hardly a coincidence that one of the first books that Lem quoted after the Polish October was Dostoevsky's *Notes from Underground*.[3] Yet in his early work, despite all efforts, Lem on the whole does not succeed in confronting his heroes with novel experiences that are apt to shake their firm convictions and ethical norms. The bloodthirsty Venusians in THE ASTRONAUTS, who had been planning an invasion of Earth, are only a projection of human beings, and the mysterious inhabitants of the White Planet in THE MAGELLAN NEBULA also react like human beings (incidentally, the author apologizes for it through the mouth of the scientist Goobar). Finally, for Lem's early cosmic wanderers their ideals are sufficient to interpret and evaluate unequivocally the phenomena which they encounter: they travel to the stars with their earthly yardstick, and the stars can be readily measured with it. This motif too will reappear later, polemically refunctioned.

Lem was much too intelligent a writer not to have been aware of the dangers of this situation. As mentioned, parallel to the first novels he wrote the early tales of THE STAR DIARIES.[4] The distinguishing mark of that cycle, already in the first edition, is originality: these stories are Lem's first attempt at literary stylization. The author refers to his sources at the very beginning, when he presents his protagonist and narrator in this manner:

> The famous circumnavigator of stars, the captain of great galactic journeys, the hunter of meteors who discovered, driven by the unceasing zeal of the true explorer, eighty-three thousand and three new stars, doctor honoris causa of the universities of both the Greater and the Lesser Bear, member of the association for the protection of small planets as well as of many other societies, knight of uncounted Milky Way and nebula orders, will appear to his readers in the pages of the diary at hand in his full size, as a personality that deserves to be ranked with such fearless men of the past as Karl Friedrich Hieronymus Baron Münchhausen, Pavel Masloboynikov, Lemuel Gulliver, or Maître Alcofrybas.

As this sample of his style testifies, Lem has an almost incredible sense of language, and *The Star Diaries*[5] became a veritable orgy of parodies. Inserted into the history of the legendary liar and braggard we find samples of the turgid style of doctoral theses, political speeches (the assembly of the United Planets Organization), tourist guides, etc. He parodies not only the language, but also certain modes of thinking. This makes for gorgeous political satires (the description of the sad fate of the Indiots, or of Pinta and Panta),[6] and pokes fun at any kind of scientific and humanist thought that, hopelessly lost in geo- and anthropocentrism, fits the universe into patterns of thinking developed on Earth (the maturity exams among the Andrygonians).

As is only proper for a "philosophical tale," each of Ijon Tichy's journeys, for all of its grotesque cosmical trappings, amounts to a viewing of mundane and contemporary problems. But this is not just the resurrection of a technique that can be traced back to Voltaire; the combining of parodistic mirror-images is much more complex. Lem operates on two levels—that of SF and that of the narrator who is a Münchhausen-like tall-tale teller. It should be stressed here how different those two levels of fantasy are: SF aims at discovering the serious flaws of the future and—surprising as this may sound—it sometimes succeeds. The Münchhausen type of "lying fantasy" is, on the contrary, first of all an amusing entertainment. The first kind of fantasy claims: what I say may really happen; the second makes us believe that a well-told lie is more beautiful than the dull truth. But again, what is Swift's Gulliver doing in Lem's introduction beside the indefatigable lying baron? An allegory side by side with a fantastic fairy tale—that is not ordinary company. It is hardly an accident that *The Star Diaries* again and again make use of the motif of *the false world*, a world full of lies because of its language, its ideology, because of a scientific theory as narrow as it is apodictic. Literature as a piling up of lies, which then, paradoxically, may sometimes point the way to truth—that is the dominant image that emerges behind the grotesque adventures of the "famous circumnavigator of stars." This appears to be a compensation for the mentor-like tone of Lem's first novels, and although it would probably be an exaggeration to consider *The Star Diaries* as self-satire, they nevertheless engage covertly, by stressing the literary nature and the relativity of the things described, in a polemic with the pathos of THE MAGELLAN NEBULA and THE ASTRONAUTS.

In the works after 1956, the basis of Lem's writing emerges ever more clearly. In a long series of novels and stories the author presents tragedies and problems of *the individual striving to know the world*. It is by reason of this radical refusal to supply proofs for assumed theories that Lem's works from that time on rather ask than answer difficult questions—and therefore most of his works seem to "lack a solution," as has sometimes naively been noted by criticism (for instance, in the case of *The Investigation* [1959]). The prologue to this mature stage of his writings are the DIALOGUES (1957), where principal problems of contemporary civilization are discussed in the framework of a philosophical dispute between two interlocutors, called in Berkeleyan fashion Hylas and Philonous.

The DIALOGUES are the result of Lem's fascination with the perspectives of cybernetics; they were written in the mid-fifties and are marked by their time. In DIALOGUES cybernetics appears up to a point as a magical key that opens any door. In particular, Lem investigates from a cybernetic point of view human consciousness, the possibility of creating a mathematically exact image of human beings that would enable us to produce its "copy," the problems of free will, and the transposing of the function of the human brain to a machine (artificial immortality); finally—and this is highly interesting—he analyzes sociology as a cybernetic model, which is a very original contribution to the discussion of some defects of the socialist society that began after the Polish October in 1956.

Lem looks at society as a system of elements between which there are flows of information. The system is shaken by serious disturbances when the information-flow encounters any barriers, intentional or not. Since in modern society the greater part of information is coded in ethnic language, the operativeness of the whole society is determined to a high degree by the state of this language. From this initial serious problem a second one arises: the possibility and the conditions of a communication between individuals which would rely on quite different sets of terms and languages; furthermore, the possibility of a contact between radically different civilizations. And finally the most universal of such problems: the possibility of human cognition. We are dealing here with the basic philosophical problem of whether the objectivity of our value-judgments can be guaranteed: how do the various layers of the individual's consciousness relate to each other and to what exists outside of his consciousness? And furthermore, what is the degree of deformation that creeps into our world view because we use a language and a system of notions that are circumscribed by our civilization? The Berkeleyan style of DIALOGUES should therefore hardly be a surprise.

Clearly, all of these questions either directly or indirectly touch upon the problem of language. We shall consider the further work of Lem above all as an attempt to come to grips with them, although the intellectual content of his work, of course, is not restricted to them.

As a rule, criticism divides Lem's work into the "serious" SF, the stylized-grotesque vein, plus his essays as well as closely related fictitious "reviews" of non-existent books, A PERFECT VACUUM (1971), and the autobiographical THE HIGH CASTLE (1966). These three very different streams treat the same problems, though clothed in different garbs.

In 1959 the novels EDEN and *The Investigation* as well as the short-story collection INVASION FROM ALDEBARAN were published. EDEN is a fairly typical SF novel, describing the adventures of an expedition from Earth on an alien planet. The astronauts meet a civilization of a rather high level, but one that was evolved by perfecting bio-evolution rather than machines. In this way "living" factories arose, and then plans of substituting for the population a generation of mutants, formed according to the specifications of the planet rulers. However, both experiments failed and a secret government has decided that the "faulty" inhabitants must die.

Lem has been enthusiastic about a controlled development of bio-evolution (five years afterwards he devoted many pages in SUMMA TECHNOLOGIAE to it), but in EDEN another question is pivotal: the planet is ruled by individuals who remain totally unknown. Their rule is based on a skilful manipulation of information, which is either distorted or blocked. Some phrases are simply eliminated from the language, they may not be used: the unsuccessful mutants marked for merciless elimination are "sick persons," and the gigantic botch-up of the geneticists remains obscured.

We shall not discuss some naive and improbable elements in the novel, for it is quite obvious that Lem did not aim at a maximum of verisimilitude in it. It serves as an exemplification of some theses from the DIALOGUES: the novel points to the social consequences that arise when information is blocked. The Machiavellian ruler (or rulers?) of EDEN can safely manipulate society owing to his control of the channels of communication, a frightening reminder addressed by Lem to the inhabitants of Earth. But that is not all: the astronauts discuss the problem of applying force for the liberation of the planet—and finally reject it, preferring to fly back to Earth:

"To begin with, they are not human beings, at least not in the sense we are human beings. You must remember that you are talking only with the computer and that you can understand the 'double'[7] only as far as the computer understands him. Second, nobody has forced upon them the things that now exist. At least nobody from outer space. They themselves..."

"By arguing like that you can justify anything. Anything!" the engineer cried.

"And how should I argue, in your opinion? Are the people of this planet children gone astray in a blind alley, whence you can lead them out by their hands? If only it were that simple, good lord. Liberation would begin by our being forced to kill, and the more dogged the fighting, the smaller the rationality that would guide our actions. Finally we would be reduced to killing just to ensure our retreat or to retain a basis for a counter-attack, and we would kill anybody who dared to oppose their benefactors. You know only too well how easily things like that can happen!"

The cosmonauts of THE ASTRONAUTS arrived on Venus with a ready-made classification scheme for the reality they found there; in EDEN, they have lost the sureness of their *ratio*. In RETURN FROM THE STARS, published two years later, the astronauts returning after many years find it impossible to identify with the future civilization. They are in the same position as visitors from outer space. A mankind shorn of all its aggressive instincts appears to them (the author succeeds in forcing this impression upon the reader) as something abominable. Although the protagonist finally accepts the new society, he has considerable difficulty in doing so.

Similarly, in *The Invincible* (1964) the product of an "inorganic evolution" of mechanisms, a black cloud consisting of myriads of minuscule robots, wreaks havoc among an expedition from Earth. Various variants of retaliation are discussed, but finally the human beings recognize the right to life of the planet's inhabitants and return to Earth.

As Maciej Szybist has perceptively noted, in Lem human beings begin to accept the other world as soon as they have experienced it aesthetically.[8] To the cosmonauts returning from EDEN the planet appears wonderful; Rohan in *The Invincible* discovers beauty in the horrible empire of the black "insects"; and Hal Bregg in THE RETURN FROM THE STARS needs a moment of aesthetic ecstasy in the mountains to feel again an Earthman. If we add that the protagonist of *Solaris* (1961), Chris Kelvin, is also able to find his inner peace and to accept the "cruel miracles" only after moments of lonely contemplation of the unusual spectacle offered by the Solaris ocean, it becomes clear that the aesthetic experience holds a key position for Lem. Perhaps—since there is no possibility of getting into contact with the "others" or to understand the essence of their world—aesthetic experience is the only form open to us for integrating our impressions into a whole. Beauty as unity in diversity—this classical definition exactly describes the problem. For even if the *meaning* of the other world remains inaccessible, at least we have access to our own feelings, our experience of this world as a certain entity—in spite of its *raison d'être* remaining hidden from us.

The "serious" works published by Lem since 1959 as a rule confront their protagonists with phenomena which surpass their understanding and defy the criteria of human morality. *The Investigation*, an ingenious "anti-mystery" set against the background of real places of contemporary England, confronts a constable of the British police with the insoluble mystery of corpses disappearing from graveyards under mysterious circumstances. The author draws upon the means of the conventional detective story: unusual occurrences, an inquest, interrogations; a number of hypotheses are formulated. But whereas in the usual mystery we can observe the triumph of intelligence, turning all misty assumptions and clues into a meaningful and intelligible whole, here all investigations and attempts to solve the case can only lead to a dead end. The logic of the enquiry, compromised again and again, is merely an indication of how easily human understanding is fooled by random events.

What "solution" does the author finally suggest? An eccentric specialist of mathematical statistics establishes a series of parameters necessary for the emergence of the phenomena under investigation (and in their choice Lem provides some brilliant black humour by supplying a whole catalogue of devices typical of the cloak-and-dagger novel). He analyzes the occurrences and the geographical extension of the cases, and predicts then where and when some more corpses will be "resurrected" and what will be the end of the series. And this is what happens. Is that all?, the disappointed reader asks. Equally disappointed is the constable, who, led by his wish to explain the causes and the purpose of the phenomena, allows himself to make guesses whose absurdity is all too obvious. But aside from a mathematical model for the series of facts, the author provides no explanation; moreover he seems to poke fun at the simple-minded tendency of human beings to explain all events with the help of symbols that are intelligible only in a given civilization. "Crime, madness or a macabre joke"—these are the thoughts that appear to the constable to be acceptable variants of a solution to the puzzle. But perhaps it is just something unexplainable, although we may present it in the form of an abstract model?—Lem suggests. Perhaps we will increasingly encounter such "black boxes" whose principles of construction are unknown to us, although we may unfailingly predict their "output"?

In the story "INVASION,"[9] spores of mysterious cosmic "plants" arrive on Earth. The scientists are able to explain the development and necessary conditions of the curious pear-like forms, but not at all the *aims* of this cosmic invasion. We are used to explaining all events in our human world from our own *telos* and to searching everywhere for a conscious intention, but we shall have to get used to phenomena in which such an interpretation leads to difficulties of the same kind as do questions about "the meaning of the world," "the meaning of life," etc.

The novel *Solaris*, one of Lem's outstanding achievements, confronts its heroes with much more serious problems. The crew of a space station hovering over the planet Solaris tries to contact the only inhabitant of this globe, a gigantic plasma-like "ocean." This baffling entity, which exhibits biological activities, proves to be so different from human beings that periodical attempts at contact have turned into a chronicle of failures. In the station mysterious "doubles" or "Phi-creatures" show up—materializations of human beings who had some connection with important, more often than not guilt-provoking experiences of crew members. By means of his X-ray vision, the ocean looks into the minds of the ambassadors from Earth and takes from them as it were the blueprints of the beings that had so far been encapsulated into their unconscious memory. Work on the station virtually collapses; each of the researchers flees into solitude to adjust himself to his complex of shame that has suddenly become visible in all its turpitude. Who then is here conducting experiments with whom? What is the goal of the emergence of the "Phi-creatures"? The scientists get no answer to that question. But what communication can there be between social beings who create their spiritual and material civilization *outside* the individuals, beings who are involved in numerous conflicts between the "self" and the "others," the "ego" and the "world"—and a giant for whom there are neither plurals nor pronouns, and presumably also no human feelings? The contact was established in the only possible way, by direct entry into the psyche of the partner, but its results prove of no value to men. Instead of insights into the "soul of the Ocean," they encountered only their own mirror-images.

The experiment to which human beings are subjected on Solaris is cruel because it mercilessly reveals a hard truth. In the psyche of the crew the Ocean has sought out the most important, the most deeply hidden thing, something that in a manner constitutes the personality of the individual. And without exception it was found that the "core of the psyche" consists of memories of subjective, very personal and very painful experiences, which human beings are not likely to communicate even to each other. It is not the voyage to the stars and the contact with "aliens" that has shaped Chris Kelvin's soul, but a banal if tragical story of the death of a girl. Collectively we dare to engage in enterprises of gigantic proportions, but these acts exist as it were separate from us; when we are left to ourselves, we cannot master our own inner strife, which is the result of our social contacts.

And what are these contacts based on? We might say that the contents of our psyche are filtered. First of all there is that which remains closed up in our unconsciousness; then what is conscious, but not intended to be made public; and finally that small part of our experiences and ideas which we allow to emerge clothed in symbols of language or other symbols to represent ourselves to the outer world, to take part in the shaping of civilization. When something inadvertently emerges from the deeper layers of our consciousness into the exterior world, the result is invariably a shock. On the other hand, any symbolical expression which we receive through the agency of another human being may become a mirror in which we can perceive ourselves; perhaps also a form into which we can pour our inner formlessness. How, then, can a dialogue be possible with the Ocean, if the whole artful construction on which our "I" is based has been seen through and destroyed at one swipe? Would the Ocean be able to generate a feeling of his own "I"? Lem makes no attempt to offer a solution—after all, he is not interested in inventing fairy-tale characters and discoursing with them. We may consider the Solaris Ocean as a metaphor for the world, perhaps for God—this does not matter, for mankind, not the Ocean, was put to a test in *Solaris*: man's intellect, morals, finally his love—this unusual but so human love. Chris and Harey repeat in the pages of the book the pattern of a romantic love that transcends death: a little Mickiewicz, a little Poe. They are the living proof that the cultural idea of "feeling" is of higher value than cold reason; thus the "artificial" Harey wins over "magnifying glass and eye."[10]

In His Master's Voice, so far Lem's last novel (1968), the possibility of contact with "others" is isolated for a treatment resembling almost a philosophical treatise. His Master's Voice is the fictitious diary of an American mathematician engaged in decoding strange signals from outer space. The research project is shrouded in strict secrecy, on a military proving ground in the desert and under continuous surveillance by the military establishment. The novel has no sensational plot; all the discoveries with which Lem attracts the attention of the reader are of a rather intellectual nature. It is an essay on the impossibility of real communication between civilizations, between societies, between human beings. The enormous efforts of the scientists to decipher the "cosmic message" and the diverging but equally unprovable hypotheses are superadded to the differences in the research team. The confidential musings of Professor Hogarth, who begins with an analysis of his own soul and discovers in it irrational, almost diabolical traits, and then proceeds to expound his theories on the human brain as a control-center which transcends the critical threshold in the direction of indeterminism and disturbance of equilibrium—all these lead the reader to the concluding thesis on the fundamental incommunicability of inner human states, on the loneliness of the individual that cannot communicate even with the persons closest to him:

> I was never able to cross the interpersonal barrier. Animals are bound with all their senses to the here and now, but human beings can get away from it. Man remembers, he feels empathy with others, he is able to imagine their feelings and states—which luckily are not true. In such attempts of pseudo-incarnation and self-translation we can only imagine ourselves, and at that in a vague and imprecise way.[11]

A novel of Lem's dealing exclusively with the problems of cognition and communication appeared already in 1961 as *Memoirs Found in a Bathtub*. One could compile an anthology of primitive attempts to interpret that book. It is easy to see how the *Memoirs*, with their atmosphere of grotesque, black humour, could have led many a critic astray. In the introduction "from the 32nd Century" we learn that the *Memoirs* are a valuable discovery, found in the ruins of a Third Pentagon—the last refuge of the Ministry of Defense and the CIA of a United States in decline. Cut off from the inhabited world, the "Building" in the Rocky Mountains degenerates into a hermetically sealed institution, where activities consist only in never-ceasing exchanges of roles among the personnel while the basic structure of the "Building," the true cause of the system of masks and their function, remains unchanged.

A newly recruited employee, the narrator, wanders through the endless corridors of the "Building," driven by his sincere attempt to penetrate to the "essence" of the building, the meaning of his "mission," which are shrouded in secret. The novel is based on the nightmare principle: again and again there is a dim hope that the hero has encountered the core of the problem, the "authentic" thing—but again and again it is proved to him that it is only the next "experiment," a "provocation," a rigged game. Gradually we begin to believe that there exists no truth about the "Building," or rather that the "truth" is solely its existence—and nothing else.

It goes without saying that the genre of an ephemeral political satire cannot do justice to such contents. The author revealingly winks at the reader and suggests to him that "the Hyberiad Gnostors, for example, consider the first twelve pages apocryphal, an addition of later years."[12] And the introduction has exactly this length. In a world of an ubiquitous secret service and a total camouflage, the text of the *Memoirs* too must be a code—and a many-layered one, much as is the case with the fragment from *Romeo and Juliet* decoded by a special machine, showing in the first analysis the aggressive feelings of Shakespeare against one Matthews, and—below that—an ecstatic stuttering (an occasion for a brilliant persiflage of the most bizarre outcrops of psychoanalysis on the part of Lem). We may therefore assume that the *Memoirs* are a persiflage of the bureaucratic machinery of modern secret services only on the surface; somewhat deeper, they are perhaps an allegory of the fate of the individual in a society with an interrupted information flow (here the text refers directly to the theses of DIALOGUES); but finally we discover that the novel portrays the tragedy of human cognition. The human being, driven by a thirst for knowledge about the world, basically asks the same question as the hunted hero of the *Memoirs*: he asks for the meaning, the essence, the *telos* of surrounding reality, he asks for the reason of his own existence. Even the answer is the same: everything is or could be a code, a mask, a camouflage. Here Lem already comes near a whole literary tradition of the 20th century. God creates things, while man, on the other hand, creates meanings—that had also become Bruno Schulz's conviction, and similarly we find in *Memoirs*:

> What does it mean? Meaning. And so we enter the realm of semantics. One must tread carefully here! Consider: from earliest times man did little else but assign meanings—to the stones, the skulls, the sun, other people, and the meanings required that he create theories—life after death, totems, cults, all sorts of myths and legends, black bile and yellow bile, love of God and country, being and nothingness—and so it went, the meanings shaped and regulated human life, became its substance, its frame and foundation—but also a fatal limitation and a trap![13]

Critics have compared the stylization of *Memoirs* to that of Gombrowicz, Witkacy, Kafka. It could also be compared to Genet, Schulz or Mrozek; we find a similar atmosphere in THE OFFICE by Breza, written nearly at the same time; a somewhat more removed forerunner is without doubt Potocki's SARAGOSSA MANUSCRIPT. Lem's novel is written in the broad tradition of a literature which defines the condition of the individual enmeshed in institutions, in civilization, in interpersonal relationships, and filled by a desire to see through them and arrive at a universal truth about himself and the world. Truly eschatological questions are touched upon in the conspiracy of the protagonist with the priest Orfini. The two conspirators want, at all costs, to gain a possibility for spontaneous action, while all their actions have from the outset been programmed into the structure of the "Building" and are pre-determined. Obviously, this is a transposition of the centuries-old philosophical dispute about determination and freedom of will, liberty and responsibility. The "Building" is a variant of the world (or of God) which leaves the individual no room for authentic action. The only advice in this situation, after all efforts to cheat Nemesis have failed, is the realization of inner freedom: the conspiracy for conspiracy's sake (this private reality of the two rebels most likely does go back to Gombrowicz). The "Building" of *Memoirs*, identical with the cosmos, is therefore not just a parodistic version of the Pentagon; all of us live in a labyrinth. It is here that Lem's grotesque vision becomes apocalyptic.

Yet having imprisoned man in the labyrinth and heaped up across his path the most difficult, insoluble tasks, Lem nevertheless does not rob him of every chance. Acknowledging fully the tragedy of existence and cognition, Lem nevertheless treats his heroes with compassion: he accepts their human fallibility and limitation, and even turns it into a kind of "cheval de bataille" or vehicle on which man conquers the cosmos. Obviously, we are referring here to Pirx.

The TALES OF PILOT PIRX (1968 and 1973), written over a period of years, are nonetheless all variations on a theme—the model of man in the cosmic era. Is this perhaps too pompous a term? It is a fact that Pirx, initially a cadet, and in the end a commander, is subjected to ever more difficult tasks as the tales progress. Nearly all Pirx stories investigate his physical fitness, his practical skill and cleverness, and finally his intellectual talents. The Pirx cycle has been planned with admirable consistency: parallel to the growth of the hero grows the difficulty of the problems that he encounters. This changes the tone of the tales from a joyful and carefree mood to a totally somber atmosphere in the concluding story "ANANKE." By the same token the voice of the protagonist changes: at first it is frank, if sometimes rather shy and full of complexes, but in the end Pirx appears as a man weighted down by the heavy load of experiences, perhaps even embittered.

What is the purpose of this temporally drawn-out narration? The character of Pirx has been cleverly designed: he is supposed to be an average human being—neither good nor evil, nor especially talented. This seeming "mediocrity," by the way, is a source of constant irritation for young Pirx. Nevertheless, the consecutive tests the hero undergoes all end well, and, most important, the author stresses that in every case Pirx was successful where specialists, or whole teams of them, had previously failed. Is he then just another of the "cosmic heroes" with which trivial SF abounds? Lem is not that naive; Pirx does not beat the experts with their own weapons: all of his successes are based on chance—"somehow" he succeeds in emerging unscathed from the calamities of "TEST" and "The Patrol"; a seemingly meaningless association saves him in "THE CONDITIONED REFLEX" and naivete in "THE TRIAL." He solves the mystery surrounding Cornelius and the computer in "ANANKE" again "any which way"—nearly at random.

See, the author seems to say, there are no tricks here nor a "hero from a machine"; the whole thinking process is laid out before you; and—indeed—nothing about it is unusual. And that's in fact how it is. This does not mean, however, that Pirx is a faceless protagonist:

> True, between his thought, clothed in words, and his actions there was no abyss, but nonetheless a barrier was there that made life difficult for him. His tutor did not suspect that Pirx was a dreamer. Nobody suspected it. They believed that he did not think at all—and that really wasn't the case. [—"TEST"]

Already in the first tale Lem draws the blueprint of Pirx's inner life. Perhaps Pirx is not a systematic thinker, but he is possessed of an extraordinary intuition (an ability greatly valued by modern heuristics). When we ponder a problem we usually advance "methodically" by moving unconsciously in the beaten tracks of our predecessors. Intuition enables us to grasp a whole field of research in a meaningful way by a single act of the intellect. Thus, sometimes wholly new paths are opened up for the solution of tasks on hand. Such a way of thinking is as a rule alien to people set in their routines. Pirx emerges victorious in his brushes with the specialists not *despite* but *because* of being a dreamer who is able to get away from established patterns of thought. Lem advocates no heresy here: for some time now the view has been with us that modern civilization and its future evolution do not favor specialized individuals, but rather very flexible ones, who are it seems therefore able to adapt to changed conditions of civilization.

It seems therefore that in the person of Pirx Lem intended to test mankind. He set out to find a place, in the world of triumphant technology, where human weakness and human imperfection are no longer defects. It is simple to say: "Machines cannot think, machines have no consciousness!" From where do we derive this certainty?—Lem asks in his SUMMA TECHNOLOGIAE. Whence come the criteria that allow us to define "thought" in an apodictic way—and what if not thinking shall we call machine operations that have analogous results for their "output"? Lem's robots are not primitive machines; they represent a serious challenge to man. Initially Pirx competes with the specialists, but the specialist is, Lem seems to suggest, a human being reduced so as to function only in a certain intellectual sphere, a technician for the solution of certain problems in his own field. In the story "THE TRIAL" Lem therefore substitutes for the specialist a humanlike robot who—once it recognizes its perfection—aims at ruling the world. The rebellious robot Calder is nothing less than the concentration of a whole team of specialists in one body; by proceeding logically he cannot be defeated. But Calder thinks only too logically, and he loses because he cannot understand irrational action; he is not flexible enough. "Seen in this light, our humanity is the sum of our faults and defects, our imperfections in fact; it is what we strive after but cannot attain, cannot do, cannot understand; it is simply the abyss between our ideals and their realization—isn't it?"—reflects Pirx in "THE TRIAL."

This weakness that turns into strength is not a real paradox. Lem's human beings are—just like the humans of Sartre—perpetually non-identical to themselves, always leaning toward their ideal image which they never attain. Since man remains imperfect until the end, he accepts the world as it is—like himself a little "failed" or "unfinished"; he accepts its dynamics and its unexpected mutations that sometimes stymie the most advanced computer programs.

Sometimes it appears as if Lem were somewhat dissatisfied with his own work. For his is a rather abnormal profession—that of a paid specialist in horror, a satanic surgeon who, after exhibiting man on his dissecting table, proceeds to pull out some more organs from the intestines and keeps muttering that they hardly fit the noble mission of "Man," "Culture," etc. The more ambitious SF writers waste their lives by inventing ever more complicated borderline situations where hypothetical future heroes are subjected to psychological terror in order to probe deeply into their humanity. Nevertheless, modern technology after a few years usually makes these exquisite tortures and the futuristic environment ridiculous. Lem therefore seems to feel the lack of authenticity of this involuntarily comic fantasy. This is perhaps why he almost from the beginning wrote funny, grotesque and parodying works besides his more serious ones. We have already mentioned *The Star Diaries*, and in the following years he wrote the TV plays of the cycle THE STRANGE ADVENTURES OF PROFESSOR TARANTOGA, the FABLES FOR ROBOTS (1964), *The Cyberiad* (1965), and finally the excellent pure nonsense script for the movie ROLY POLY.[14] We shall consider only the best known, *The Cyberiad* and the "Fables for Robots" [of which eleven appear in *Mortal Engines*, US 1977].

The stories in these two cycles are written as it were in retrospect: the heroic times of human expansion are far in the past, and the cosmos flowers with the civilizations of the robots who make no bones about their abhorrence of human beings. At the same time everything among them is as among us—not exactly the same, but with no greater differences than is due to the distance between us and the changed world of the science-fictional fairy tale. The similarity between fairy tales and SF has been stressed long ago, for instance in the classical essay by Caillois.[15] Both genres create a fantasy world that is ruled by a given system of laws; in SF these are partly natural laws which offer to its characters—on a certain level of future civilization—more freedom of action, while in fairy tale they are of a conventional character.

In a number of short works by Lem we find, as has been noted by Barańczak, a mixture of the most different levels: not only the patterns of the fairy tale and SF, but also their stylistic and linguistic elements are interwoven.[16] This interweaving includes also the physical doctrine on which the functioning of the imaginary reality is based. The conventional "marvels" of the fairy tale are crossbred with quasi-scientific inventions. All of these anachronisms—these "cyberhorses," "electroknights" or "electrolyres"—are irresistibly comic; but *The Cyberiad* and "Fables for Robots" are not just literary fun (although they are exceptional fun), for the crossbreeding of two different genres results in an increase of meaningfulness.

The fairy-tale universe is an abstract reality existing outside of our experience, most often in the past; it is an immutable, constant order, a fixed moral code which should dominate the whole world. Fairy tales justify the reiteration of a few standard interpersonal situations by such a reference to mythic times. Quite different from this, typical SF looks towards new situations that transcend our experience, and in its most ambitious works it deals in borderline cases where human ethics break down, thus proving their inappropriateness. Barańczak mentions Lem's rejection of unlimited progress in time, as was still the case in THE MAGELLAN NEBULA, in favor of a cyclical concept of time, as in *The Cyberiad*. But furthermore, Lem's grotesque stylizations strikingly reflect the existential situation of his heroes. Apparently they are always extroverted, but in reality they are captives of their isolation. Let us think back to the astronauts of EDEN, Kelvin in *Solaris*, Rohan in *The Invincible*, Hogarth in HIS MASTER'S VOICE, or the narrator of *Memoirs Found in a Bathtub*. All of them are very active, at least intellectually; and without exception they have to pay for their cognitive impulse with the painful experience of their own narrow prison.

Curiously enough, nobody has yet (in Poland) analysed Lem's works by psychoanalytical methods. His whole opus is opposed to isolation—and to open space (and how profound this sounds in depth analysis!). I know of no work with a more marked claustrophobia, and so permeated by the suspicion that the apparently limitless universe surrounding us is in reality a huge, misleading stage backdrop designed to fit our cognitive faculties, while the essence of things is hidden away somewhere else, behind the stage. One of the most significant and often repeated motifs in Lem's work is the situation of an individual or a group of individuals, or even a whole society, imprisoned in the artificial space of a computer. It starts with the possibility to give an "exact description of the atomic structure" of human beings—this problem is raised in DIALOGUES and realized in *The Star Diaries*. If it should be possible to copy a human being, why should it not then be possible to imitate his consciousness in a machine—as in "THE HAMMER,"[17] "DOCTOR DIAGORAS"[18] or "FROM THE MEMOIRS OF IJON TICHY, II."[19] One step farther in this direction, and it is possible to create whole worlds by mathematical methods: the personalities of human beings are programmed, their consciousness is filled with the pictures of a world not existing in reality, and these artificial beings are allowed to develop spontaneously. Thus we get the "boxes" of Professor Corcoran in "FROM THE MEMOIRS OF IJON TICHY, I"[20] or the "personetic" experiments of Professor Dobb in "NON SERVIAM."[21]

Well, Lem may say now, we know that there is nothing in a machine aside from some currents, but he who has become a person in these currents is not aware of it: he thinks he is a human being, sees other human beings, landscapes, etc. And, what is most important, there is no practical way he could test empirically the nature of his existence. For him, the creator of the boxes is a god. Our own confidence and our cognitive optimism are snuffed out when we take a deeper look at our own situation: for who could claim "irrefutably" that he himself is not in such a box? Corcoran horrifies us with a vision of the world as a hierarchy of boxes—a modern version of Berkeley's dilemma. Of course, Berkeley had his benevolent god "who wouldn't deceive him." In SUMMA TECHNOLOGIAE Lem mockingly proposes a robot god as well as artificial transcendence and artificial immortality.

"I should wish, as do most men," Lem admits in an interview to the periodical

Nurt, "that immutable truths existed, that not all would be eroded by the impact of historical time, that there were some essential propositions, be it only in the field of human values, the basic values, etc. In brief, I long for the absolute. But at the same time I am firmly convinced that there are no absolutes, that everything is historical, and that you cannot get away from history."[22]

Thus far the motif of the labyrinth has played a key role in Lem's work, e.g. in the description of alien places on other planets in THE ASTRONAUTS and EDEN, the intestines of the cosmic monster in "THE RAT IN THE LABYRINTH,"[23] the aerodrome in RETURN FROM THE STARS, the "Building" in *Memoirs Found in a Bathtub*. To this one should add the juxtaposition of open and closed space, the hierarchy of isolations, dream visions, the obsession with biologism in the description of extraterrestrial landscapes.

It would appear that nobody is fitter for pointing out man's inner contradictions than Lem, who is on the one hand a sober brain seeing the world through categories and laws, a rationalist to the bone, and on the other hand a prisoner of his own corporeality, emotions and fears, with a special inclination for phantasmagoric visions. The fate of his hero proves the author's thesis, yet the hero is also thrust into a world of baroque visions, of powerful sensual and emotional impressions. The same ambivalence may be detected in Lem's language between an inclination towards exactitude and precision and a hidden leaning towards stylistic exuberance. Even his scientific essays are full of overflowing metaphors and heap one example upon the other.

But let us return to *The Cyberiad*. This book has of course a number of clearly recognizable goals: it is, as has been noted by the late Grochowiak, "a parody of the *contes philosophiques* in the manner of Voltaire; an excellent parody of fairy tales of children, written in rhymed prose; a parody of pseudo-scientific treatises; and finally, a masterful imitation of the Chinese box story-within-the-story in the oriental manner."[24] Many of the very serious ideas from the SUMMA TECHNOLOGIAE, published at almost the same time, are realized in *The Cyberiad* and the FABLES FOR ROBOTS. The master constructors Trurl and Klapaucius have as much in common with the sorcerers of fairy tales as with the engineers of the future. Just as the fairy tale establishes a moral order with a tendency to impress it upon society, so the stories in Lem's cycle debunk the real degenerative signs and contradictions of our world. But by means of this cacophonic genre of the "fairy tale from the future," a characteristic idea emerges: the more we give "cosmic imagination" a free rein, the more oppressive the fetters of our terrestrial, human world-view become. This becomes visible in the formal structure of Lem's stories in the following way: the more daringly the author transgresses empirical plausibility, the more clearly he must fall back upon the literary convention of the story. Having freed his vision of the imaginary world from anthropocentrism and geocentrism, he must allow them in again through the back door.

As is evident from his last works, it is becoming ever more difficult for Lem to write "normal SF stories." A PERFECT VACUUM is composed of reviews of non-existent books. In 1973 Lem published IMAGINARY MAGNITUDE—a cycle of introductions to books "published" between 1990 and 2029. In his writings Lem has unmistakably returned to Earth, and is now more interested in the development of human civilization than in the exploration of the cosmos. Disillusion? Has the invention of ever new cosmic beings and adventures become for him a literary activity that he can no longer justify to himself with a clean conscience? For the time being he prefers—aside from a few stories that continue his old cycles—to design "projects" of books, rather than really write them.

A PERFECT VACUUM contains 15 reviews (the 16th is a review of the volume itself, done by the author) which—naturally—sum up the books reviewed rather than pass judgment on them. The selection comprises several clearly defined groups: some reviews contain extracts of notions from the field of socio-psychology ("LES ROBINSONADES," "GRUPPENFUHRER LOUIS XVI," "THE IDIOT") which are truly astonishing in their originality. Very good books could most likely be written on the basis of these sketches. But Lem would not be Lem if he did not use the opportunity to taunt the fans of certain literary schools: "GIGAMESH," a parody of *Ulysses* or *Finnegan's Wake*; "RIEN DU TOUT, OU LA CONSEQUENCE," a persiflage of the French *nouveau roman*; and "TOI," another incarnation of the new "protest" literature, the "mocked audience"—all these are satirical masterpieces. Three reviews ("SEXPLOSION," "PERYCALYPSIS," "DO YOURSELF A BOOK") parody some grotesque paroxysms of modern civilization, while the remaining five are thinly disguised treatises on cultural and philosophical themes.

Clearly, whatever Lem's form of expression, he always returns to the same themes: chance and necessity in the development of mankind, determinism and indeterminism in the life of man (the excellent story of the three corporations which turn into a triple god, "BEING, INC."),[25] and finally the concept of the cosmos as a game. This idea, briefly mentioned in SUMMA TECHNOLOGIAE, has been developed more fully in THE PHILOSOPHY OF CHANCE. Similarly, IMAGINARY MAGNITUDE ranges from a surprising idea ("NEKROBIES") by way of a futurological joke ("EXTELOPEDIA VESTRANDA") to a treatise ("GOLEM XIV"), and becomes in its discursive part a continuation of the lines of thought from SUMMA TECHNOLOGIAE (especially "THE INTELECTRONICIANS," "ENGINEERS OF TRANSCENDENCE," and "A PAMPHLET AGAINST EVOLUTION").

A return to Earth, then? The essayist Lem tells us things hardly less interesting than the writer of fiction,[26] but I would consider this turn in his creative work a temporary stage. It seems that this writer, whom consciousness of the mystification unavoidably associated with literature has reduced to extreme straits, has decided to raise this mystification to the status of a Third Force and to use it quite ostentatiously. Thence the fictitious reviews of fictitious books, which—if they were to be written—would also describe a fictitious world. By presenting striking ideas, which are then artfully reflected through a number of prisms, Lem demonstrates at the moment only his intellectual and technical capabilities. Whether a narration will come of this, and what kind of narration, time will tell.

NOTES

1. Some of the works mentioned in this essay have not been published in English and thus have no official English titles. For such works we have used a literal rendering of the Polish title (or have retained the original Latin, French, or German title) set in LARGE AND SMALL CAPS for books, films, and TV plays, or in quoted small caps ("SMALL CAPS") for short stories and essays. The dates given in the text are for the first Polish edition. US editions of Lem's work are as follows:

"The Computer That Fought a Dragon." Tr Krzysztof Klinger. In *Other Worlds, Other Seas: Science Fiction Stories from Socialist Countries*, ed. Darko Suvin, Random House 1970. Also in *Mortal Engines* (see below).

The Cyberiad: Fables for the Cybernetic Age. Tr Michael Kandel. Seabury 1974 v+295. Contains tales from CYBERIADA (1965, 1967, 1972).

The Futurological Congress: From the Memoirs of Ijon Tichy. Tr Michael Kandel. Seabury 1974. From the collection INSOMNIA (1971).

"In Hot Pursuit of Happiness." In *View From Another Shore: European Science Fiction*, ed. [and tr?] Franz Rottensteiner, Seabury 1973. From the collection INSOMNIA (1971).

The Investigation. Tr Adele Milch. Seabury 1974 iv+216.
The Invincible. Tr Wendayne Ackerman (from a German version). Seabury 1973 vii+188.
Memoirs Found in a Bathtub. Tr Michael Kandel and Christine Rose. Seabury 1973 iv+188.
Mortal Engines. Tr Michael Kandel. Seabury 1977 xxiv+239. Contains eleven of the Robot Fables from CYBERIADA, 3rd edn 1972 (which I take to subsume FABLES FOR ROBOTS, 1964), including "Tale of the Computer That Fought a Dragon" (see "Computer" above), and three other stories: "The Sanatorium of Dr. Vliperdius (from THE STAR DIARIES, 1971), "The Hunt" (from TALES OF PILOT PIRX, 2nd edn 1973), "The Mask" (from MASK, 1976).
"The Patrol." Tr Thomas Hoisington. In *Other Worlds* (see "Computer" above). From TALES OF PILOT PIRX (1968, 1973).
Solaris. Tr Joanna Kilmartin and Steve Cox (from a French version). With an Afterword by Darko Suvin, Walker 1970.
The Star Diaries. Tr Michael Kandel. Seabury 1976 x+275. Contains "Introduction" and "Introduction to the Expanded Edition" (both attributed to Professor A.S. Tarantoga); "Voyages" 7-8, 11-14, 20-23, 25, 28; and "Translator's Note" by Kandel. See Note 4 below.
"The Thirteenth Journey of Ijon Tichy," Tr Thomas Hoisington. In *Other Worlds* (see "Computer" above). Also in *The Star Diaries* (see above).
"The Twenty-Fourth Journey of Ijon Tichy." Tr Jane Andelman. In *Other Worlds* (see "Computer" above). Not in *The Star Diaries* (see above).

With respect to bibliographical information, the editorial revision of this essay has been so extensive that—even though most of the information comes from the essayist or translator (some via telephone from Dr Suvin in Montreal)—the responsibility for any errors must be mine rather than theirs. —RDM.

2. It is interesting to note that in recent times Lem prefers the narration "from above": from the position of the great scientist (HIS MASTER'S VOICE) or the computer genius ("GOLEM XIV"). We owe this observation to Zdislaw B. Kępinski, "THE 'MAVO'-TEAM OR THE ANTI-ASTRONAUTS OF STANISLAW LEM," *Nurt* #8(1972):25-29.

3. See the beginning of Dialogue VI in DIALOGUES.

4. In its first edition (1957) THE STAR DIARIES contains eight of the tales called the "Journeys" or "Voyages" of Ijon Tichy and some additional tales; in its fourth edition (1971) it contains fourteen "Voyages," five sections of "THE MEMOIRS OF IJON TICHY," and three other pieces: "The Sanatorium of Dr. Vliperdius" (in *Mortal Engines*, see Note 1 above), "DR. DIAGORAS," and "SAVE THE COSMOS: AN OPEN LETTER FROM IJON TICHY." An additional voyage, the 26th, appeared in an earlier edition, but is rejected as "apocryphal" by Professor Tarantoga (*The Star Diaries* [see Note 1 above], pp vii-viii), and has not been translated into English. The 18th Voyage also remains untranslated. See the last three entries in the bibliography in Note 1 above. —RDM.

5. We now speak of *The Star Diaries* (i.e. the US edition), since from this point on our essayist seems to be exclusively concerned with the Voyages. —RDM.

6. The nations Pinta and Panta are called Straddletonia and Twaddletonia in Thomas Hoisington's translation, "The Thirteenth Journey" (see Note 1 above). —RDM.

7. That's how the cosmonauts call the inhabitants of the planet in EDEN.

8. Maciej Szybist, "HIS MASTER'S VOICE FROM THE RADIO," *Zycie Literackie* #26 (1969).

9. In the collection INVASION FROM ALDEBARAN.

10. This metaphor has been taken from verses by Mickiewicz which run: "Feeling and belief speak to me louder/ Than magnifying glass and the sage's eye."

11. For more comment on HIS MASTER'S VOICE, see the essay by Ursula K. Le Guin in this issue of SFS. —RDM,

12. *Memoirs Found in a Bathtub* (see Note 1), p 12.

13. Ibid., p 148.

14. In the collection INSOMNIA (1971).

15. Roger Caillois, "De la Féerie à la Science-Fiction," *Images, images* (Paris 1966).

16. Stanislaw Barańsczak, "ELECTROKNIGHTS AND CYBERKIDS," *Nurt* #8 (1972).

17. In the collection INVASION FROM ALDEBARAN.

18. In THE STAR DIARIES, 4th edn (see Note 4 above).

19. Ibid. 20. Ibid.

21. In the collection A PERFECT VACUUM.

22. "DON'T BELIEVE THAT YOU KNOW EVERYTHING ABOUT LEM" (interview with Lem), *Nurt* #8 (1972).

23. In the first edition of THE STAR DIARIES (1957).

24. S. Grochowiak, "HOW FUNNY THIS LEM IS!" *Kultura* #39 (1965).

25. In the collection A PERFECT VACUUM.

26. I do not have room to review Lem's essays at length. I'll just mention that after the interesting DIALOGUES and GOING INTO ORBIT (1962) he wrote the most engaging SUMMA TECHNOLOGIAE, whose main value lies in the intellectual boldness with which the author appraises the final consequences of the evolution of technology: the possibility of a "transposition" of humankind from natural bodies to artificial ones, stellar engineering, the breeding of information, artificial transcendence, etc. We also have not discussed his remarks about the influence of technology on the system of humanistic values, ethics, aesthetics, etc. In PHILOSOPHY OF CHANCE (1968) Lem tried to create his own theory of literature, and in SCIENCE FICTION and FUTUROLOGY (2 vols., 1970) he applied this apparatus to the analysis of SF. Lem considers the processes of literary communication as play, and yet establishing the socially recognized meaning of a work is a process of stabilizing meanings within changing cultures. He relies upon the apparatus of the information theory, probability theory, and theory of games—exactly on what most professors of Polish literature shy away from. His treatment of the meaning of a literary work as the result of stochastic processes of reception is met by an even stronger instinctive rejection by professional literary critics. But the suggestions of Lem, who looks at literary problems from outside of the ghetto of the professional scholars, deserve wide attention.

Michael Kandel V

Lem in Review (June 2238)

(from SFS *4: 65–68, March 1977)*

The recent B shortage notwithstanding, this quarter sees the publication of three new books about Lem: Harvin Virelli, *A Critical History of Lem Scholarship in the Bio Years, 2140-2160* (Xerox: Sydney), 205 pp., $13.50; Hmubat Bwagwa, *The New Lemianism: An Overview* (Godfrey & Son: Nairobi), 352pp., $1.95; and Atusko Kobayashi, *Lem the Writer* (The Interworld University Press: Brasilia), 495 pp., $8.00.

Virelli and Bwagwa, as their respective titles indicate, are not pretending to offer the reader anything that is original; their purpose rather is to take stock, sum up, *digest* the wealth of experience and thought that is the heritage, still disturbingly fresh, of our post-Cataclysm biorevolution, a movement in which an incredible succession of scientific breakthroughs coincided with the discovery—now nearly half a century ago—of the works of an obscure Polono-Slavic genius who lived in the mid-20th: Stanislaw Lem. But it would appear that we have not yet acquired the distance necessary to analyze impartially those events and assess Lem's posthumous participation in them. Virelli still follows the line of the Revitalists; his history is "critical," then, in the narrow sense only; not once does he rise above the controversies of the day and attempt to synthesize. Similarly, Bwagwa's "new Lemianism" is nothing but a rehash—a literate and entertaining rehash perhaps, but a rehash for all that—of the theories of the Biomen, King, Nash and Davidov in particular. In both cases, in both books, the tone is objective, the format and conceptions promise objectivity, and yet we find the same bickering that has dominated the intellectual arena since the Gridley Operation. The bickering that clouds the fundamental issue, to wit: Should Lem's automorph prophecies, which have so often served as self-realizing guideposts in the past, be followed in the future as well, or have we already progressed far enough along that road to strike out on our own, no longer needing to rely on authorities, regardless of how ably those authorities served us up to now? In either case, of course, Lem remains the Master, the Harbinger of the New Evolution who, in the pages of *Summa technologiae*, "Golem XIV," the 3rd and 21st Voyages of Ijon Tichy, and elsewhere, discussed with such uncanny accuracy events and problems that were to begin unfolding one hundred years later.

Mrs. Kobayashi's book, on the other hand, represents a bold if not defiant departure in Lemian literature, for it looks at Lem's thought in the context of his *fiction*, thereby offering us a more human—and historical—insight into the man. We are reminded that Lem, though versed in science, was not himself a scientist (yet perhaps more a scientist than the "specialists" and "experts" of his age). His ideas were largely intuitive and, as Mrs. Kobayashi stresses, more ambiguous than is generally realized today.

Lem the Writer is a study of vast scope and high goals, for it attempts nothing less than to bring together the writer's entire *oeuvre* into one, coherent pattern. The book contains three sections:

I THE WORLD OF THEME
II THE WORLD OF FICTION
III THE BIOGRAPHICAL FACTOR

In other words we have here a progression from universals to particulars, from the philosophy to the art to the life of the author. An unusual approach; one would normally expect the reverse, that is, an "inductive" presentation. Yet in the case of Lem such a plan may be appropriate, for readers of today have most familiarity with his ideas, less with his literary methods, and least of all with his life and times.

Below is a synopsis of Mrs. Kobayashi's work. We will follow the chapter headings, and comment after each section.

I THE WORLD OF THEME

a) Cybernetic Man. Life, individuality, Consciousness—all redefined in cybernetic terms. "Humanity" includes nonbiological intelligences and homeostatic entities, whether separately constructed or produced through alteration of the natural organism. The moral thesis that all "men," be they created naturally or artificially, are equal, for what makes "man" precious is his unique irreplaceability (irreducibility) in the Universe. The fullest exposition of this in *Dialogues*; treated with pathos in *Tales of Pirx the Pilot* and "The Mask," with humor in *The Cyberiad.*

b) Creators and Their Creatures. Since the world is perceived as ugly and existence in it inevitably painful, any creation of a sentient being means to make it suffer, therefore the creative act is reprehensible. Hence the guilt felt by Lem's creators—see "Terminus" (Pirx), "The Seventh Sally" (Cyberiad), *Solaris*, "Non Serviam," etc. But the greatest guilt—for the greatest responsibility—belongs to the First Creator. Lem's mockery of God through the presentation of flawed deities (*Solaris*, "Dr. Diagoras," or even Trurl in "In Hot Pursuit of Happiness" [Kobyszcze]), and his invective against the imperfections of a personified Mother Nature. Lem's quarrel with Reality, that Reality we inherit by being born—cf Ie.

c) The Religious Metaphor. The puzzling dominance of religious elements, despite the fact that the immaterial soul is refuted (in Ia) and "God" appears only in ironic contexts, never literally (Ib). The priests and monks throughout Lem's fiction—*Memoirs Found in a Bathtub*, Tichy's 21st and 22nd Voyages, "The Mask." The preoccupation with traditionally religious themes: resurrection, immortality, omniscience, incorporeality (Lem's "perfect machines," alluded to in *Summa* and appearing in *Fables for Robots*). However—the total absence of Christ figures.

d) Utopias. The perfecting of society through science conceived as possible (*Going into Orbit*) and, due to man's innate perversity, impossible ("In Hot Pursuit of Happiness"). Lem's ambivalence as seen in *Return from the Stars*. His position, in this respect, is half-way between the Soviet and American-English science fictions of the period.

e) The Epistemological Doubt. With the ineffable mystery of individual personality on the one hand (proven cybernetically in Ia, also cf. *The High Castle*), and the inherent limits of objective knowledge on the other (*The Invincible*), Reality itself is called into question. The possibility that subjective experience may be more real than objective, that in fact it may actually *create* the objective world, as if figment and illusion were shapers of reality. Tichy's 28th Voyage, "Les Robinsonades" (*A Perfect Vacuum*) and "A New Cosmogony." The significance therefore of dreams from which one cannot awake (the dream boxes in *The Cyberiad*, *The Futurological Congress*, a few of Pirx's ordeals, *Return from the Stars*). Perhaps this is a kind of revenge against an indifferent, cruel world (see IIIc). Epistemological doubt revealed by the symbol of the mask in Lem's work (first noted by R. Nudel'man).

f) The Future. Taken both literally and as a comment on the present. The unknowability and differentness of the future (see discussion of Stapledon in *Fantasy and Futurology*), since our concepts are perforce limited by our time. Apocalyptic visions, also glimpses of the Golden Age (cf. Id). However the necessity for man to *anticipate*, else he will continue to be carried along with the rush of events blindly and not control them (*Summa*).

g) Linguistics, Word Play and the Mind. Influence on Lem of modern linguistic theories. That language shapes our perceptions. The author's attempts to alter linguistic patterns seen as an effort to break through this barrier, to expand the mental horizons. Consequently, linguistics as a prognostic tool (see If, see *The Futurological Congress*). The connection between the system of language (semantics, semeiology) and the theory of codes (message vs. media, etc.)—"Golem XIV." Language closely related to Ie (the unknowable is the unnamable).

h) The Interrelationship of Literature and Society. Discussion of *The Philosophy of Accident*. Literature as a useless anachronism in modern mass culture; literature also as potential prophecy, to save modern culture (cf. If). Science fiction an example of both the potential and the failure (*Fantasy and Futurology*).

i) The Laws of Change. Application of modern statistics (stochastic processes, etc.) to evolutionary phenomena: biological evolution, cybernetic evolution (cf. *Eden*, *The Invincible*), and history—of politics, of social forms, of science, of ideas. Lem's frequent recapitulation of genesis (of the universe, of life) and the rise of man or other intelligent forms. Instances of this in almost every work of fiction. The observation that Lem himself is both past- and future-oriented, as if his attention were more on the process of time than on the present moment.

COMMENT: Mrs. Kobayashi's attempt is noble, but still she fails to integrate the material—note the many cross-references. Her categories have merit but in the final analysis are arbitrary and artificial. Lem does indeed devote certain cycles of stories to certain problems—for example, the Pirx tales are mainly concerned with the moral consequences of advanced technology (esp. "electronic brains"). But this is not characteristic of his overall work. "The Religious Metaphor" is unconvincing; one gets the impression that religion is of more interest to Mrs. Kobayashi than it was to Lem himself. Our first main criticism: the lack of interpretation and evaluation. For example, Mrs. Kobayashi does not say which of Lem's ideas were original, and which were commonplace. Also there is insufficient mention of the many European philosophers (like Russell) and writers (like Dostoevsky) who influenced Lem. Therefore we do not see Lem the thinker in the context of the thought of his day. Our second main criticism: this whole division between Ideas and Art seems suspect. We have no quarrel with Mrs. Kobayashi's assumption that ideas were the fundamental motivation of Lem's fiction. But is she then suggesting, by her schema, that fiction was in *itself* a motivation too? But—and here is the point— are these two motivations compatible? One would think, rather, that they are mutually exclusive. Nowhere in her book (it would probably belong in III) does Mrs. Kobayashi confront this issue.

II THE WORLD OF FICTION

a) The Spectrum of Modes. The thesis that Lem usually tackles one same ideological problem in various literary ways, methodically changing parameters to produce different genres. The concept, for example, of a machine suffering the bondage of its program might be (is in fact) treated:

—in the Cyberiad cycle (Trurl & Klapaucius), with wild fantasy and farce;
—in the Star Diaries cycle (Tichy), with fantasy and farce, but both tempered by a more realistic setting and occasional notes of pathos;
—in the Pirx cycle, with realism and pathos, muted by a subtle touch of humor and irony;
—in "The Mask," with stark realism and pathos to the point of full tragedy.

The implication, behind this diversity of approach, that for Lem the literary mode is not only an integral part of the "message," but actually contributes to it in a cognitive manner, and even furthers the philosophical investigation. It is as if a composer were to repeat the same melody over and over, only in different keys, for different musical instruments, or with different orchestrations, convinced that each new rendering provides some additional insight into his motif.

b) The Escalation of Form. Lem's style grows more selfconscious, his experimentation with formal elements bolder, with each succeeding book. An analysis of his use of plot structure (parallelism, counterpoint, contrast), his manipulation of narrative tempo, prose rhythms (esp. evident in *The Invincible*, *Solaris*, *Return from the Stars*). Organic symbolism—that is, symbols whose referents exist only within the body of the work (and not outside it, i.e. the cross as a symbol of Christ). One example: mountains or mountainous terrain and the labor of climbing it usually signifies the process of self-realization, self-knowledge, a heightening of the individual's consciousness. Neologisms (cf. Ig), word play, puns; stylizations, esp. archaic; parodies—comic use of Slavic fairy-tale modes (*The Cyberiad*), of legalistic jargon, bureaucratese or officialese.

c) Satire. The strategic use of detail, choice of proper names, and other techniques (see Ib). Lem's use of double-edged satire—two examples: in "The Dragons of Probability" (*Cyberiad*) both science and its negation (magic, fantasy) are satirized; in *Memoirs Found in a Bathtub* both American and Polish political paranoias are satirized. Which same two examples also illustrate that Lem's satire can be either universal or local—often both simultaneously.

d) Philosophical Fiction and Fictional Philosophy. Lem's attempts to create a new genre that combines both fiction and nonfiction (*A Perfect Vacuum*, *Imaginary Magnitude*, *His Master's Voice*). His device of the presentation of subsequent theories for the same phenomenon, in which the weaving of theories in itself assumes dominance over the point of departure (the fictional reason for the theorizing). In this connection, Lem as myth-maker (mythopoeist). The implication, then, that the quest for Truth is more valuable than the Truth itself, the seeking of more importance than the finding. Lem's belief that Man's greatest faculty—in short, what makes Man Man—lies in the exercise of the mind.

COMMENT: We congratulate Mrs. Kobayashi for her restraint in the use of computer analysis of linguistic data (in IIb), a practice which unfortunately is still too much in fashion. But again, there is insufficient evaluation of the subject: Is Lem's experimentation with form esthetically successful or not? Does "bolder" mean "better"? We think perhaps that Mrs. Kobayashi is overly awed by the genius of the Master—surely not all his writings were of equal literary merit. Also, it would be interesting to apply formal considerations to Id. What, for example, would be the *technical* aspects of this new fiction-nonfiction genre? In general, though, this is the strongest section of Mrs. Kobayashi's book. Many provocative ideas.

III THE BIOGRAPHICAL FACTOR

a) Influences. The men who shaped Lem's views and craft, or with whom he had affinity, or against whom he rebelled. Thomas Aquinas, Bosch, Pascal, Dostoevsky, Mann, G.B. Shaw, H.G. Wells, Stapledon, Gombrowicz, Wiener, Turing, Einstein, Popper, etc., etc. The Polish literary heritage: the syndrome of Polish Romanticism and Anti-Romanticism, the Sienkiewicz myth of heroism and honor, the mad nihilism of Witkiewicz and Gombrowicz; Lem's work as characteristic of post-1956 Polish literature, Lem compared with contemporary satirist Mrozek.

b) The Personal Impact of World War II and the Nazi Occupation of Poland. Discussion of the autobiographical *Time Not Wasted*, also parts of *His Master's Voice*. The thesis that much of Lem's moral position, as well as his complex (almost love-hate) relationship towards humanity, derives from his experiences during this period (when he was in his formative years)—for example, the witnessing of atrocities, executions, etc. His negative and positive views of society (respectively: the helplessness of the individual in a pathological social system, and the necessity for controlling social change—to avoid such evils in the future) also traced to this period.

c) The Private Realm. The thesis that much of Lem's perception of the world as nightmare or a cruel joke stems from his relationship, as a child, to his parents (cf. the "Introduction" to *His Master's Voice*). Also from an early love affair that was the source of great guilt. In this connection, a Freudian analysis of Lem's recurrent images of death (skulls, skeletons—see his own illustrations to the 1971 Polish edition of *The Star Diaries*!), containing also a sexual element. Speculation that Lem's involvement with robots and nonbiological intelligence as themes reveals deep feelings of inadequacy and fear in the face of human tragedy experienced first-hand. Science fiction and fantasy therefore as a "flight" from reality and from one's self (cf. Ie and Ii, other interpretations of Lem's rejections of reality and the present).

COMMENT: Clearly the weakest section of Mrs. Kobayashi's study, IIIc especially. True, the theoretical basis of Lem's existential *Angst* does not rule out personal (or even sordid) motivations. However Mrs. Kobayashi has let herself be carried away with all this Freudian nonsense. Which is entirely unsubstantiated; the bulk of her "evidence" she takes from Lem's fiction. Surely an elementary knowledge of literary criticism tells us that such evidence is, at best, highly unreliable. The facts of Lem's youth, of his private life, remain sketchy, but apparently Mrs. Kobayashi did not even bother to acquaint herself with the little information that *is* available. We hope that if her study sees a second edition, she will carefully rework this third section, which mars an otherwise sober and solid contribution to our understanding of the Master, the "Bio Prophet."

The Sociology of Science Fiction

Edited by Darko Suvin

(from **SFS** *4: 223–227, 318–319, November 1977)*

I have the feeling that SFS may have opened a can of worms by trying for an issue on the sociology of Science Fiction, but I also think that no worthwhile fish in SF criticism will be caught without opening and using this can, even if we throw it away after its usefulness is over. Let me try to point out rather briefly, and with no pretensions to any encompassing survey, some of the more useful, and incidentally some of the less useful, among the sociological approaches to literature.

Right at the beginning it should be noted that the very term "sociology" is somewhat dubious, if it is taken to imply that there exist today any solid scholarly or "scientific" fundaments of indisputable value for a systematic study of historical human societies. True, there are some useful techniques for surface research, and beginning with Marx (not with Comte) there are probably some cognitions which will have to be used as cornerstones for whatever real sociology eventually appears. But a few cornerstones do not a fundament make, so that the title of this special issue is simply the least misleading that I could find among a number of possibilities all somewhat misleading. At any rate, even if my skepticism toward present-day sociologies is not shared, it remains essential to say that there remains a "SOCIOLOGY of literature" and a "sociology of LITERATURE." In the first case, literary works are used as documents of and about a certain state of society, or part thereof, on the same level as any other document of material or mental culture—a road, fireplace, or gravestone; political graffitti, TV ads, or posters. Within sociology, this is no doubt a worthy and interesting function of literature, but this approach does not consider literature as anything but such a document, does not even pretend to deal with the "literariness" of literature, and is therefore useless for literary studies.[1] For literary studies have a very tricky and delicate relationship to what is usually called the social and historical context. It is, I believe, crass reductionism to treat any halfway significant literary text as simply an "expression" of this context: for the insoluble question would then remain as to how it happens that literary texts "expressing" a more or less identical context—say two succeeding tales of the same author—are not only different but also (each in its own way) unique. *History and society are not an external yardstick to be applied to the literary work: on the contrary, they enter into—they constitute—its very structure and texture.* This was well brought out by Mukarovsky's rejoinder to the most famous of the Formalists, Shklovsky. When Shklovsky asserted—in a textile metaphor—that as a student of literature he was interested in types of yarn and techniques of weaving and not in the state of the international wool market or the politics of the monopoly corporations therein, Mukarovsky pointed out that the weaving techniques necessarily reflect the needs and pressures of exactly the international wool market and all its factors. Thus verbal art cannot be analyzed without taking into account the equally autonomous yet in some ways (more or less) interdependent systems of science, politics, economy, social stratification, language, ethics, or religion—all of which partake of that collective consciousness peculiar to a given time and place which is also the bearer of signification for every work of verbal art.

Thus even if one starts one's investigation from the very substance of literature, from language itself, it will be found that the most sophisticated linguistics presents us with a language model in terms of six principal factors or relationships, each capable of becoming the dominant function: (1) the addresser, the emotive function; (2) the addressee, the conative function; (3) the context, the referential function; (4) the code, the metalingual function; and (6) the message, the poetic function.[2] Now clearly a combination of the conative or "appellative" relationship of the literary work to the addressee, of the referential or representative relationship of the work to its context, and of the metalingual relationship of the work to its code, which in verbal art is not confined to vocabulary plus operational rules but has an eminently socio-historical character—clearly a combination of at least these three functions marks the ineluctably socio-historical character of every literary work.

What is usually called "sociology of literature" has so far mostly focused on either the addressee or the context of the literary work. Very useful data, without which we would be much poorer, have been assembled by a number of pioneers (Altick, Engelsing, Hart, Nott, Plant—AB), culminating in surveys such as Nye's (AB) and generalizations such as Escarpit's (AB). Yet whenever empirical studies are not blended with an approach permitting systematic value judgments, whenever they are, in other words, empiricistic, they still split literature into a socio-historical *external context*, and the pure and undefiled still center of the literary text which is left to an unholy alliance of technical description and ideologizing impressionism (such is the bulk of both the Rosenberg-White anthologies in AB). Even the welcome corrective of communication studies—focusing on the relationships between the work's *emission* from the writer, through the important *transmissions* such as editors, publishers, financiers, distributors, censors, etc., to its *reception* by various types of reading public—began with crass versions of the same split. However, communication studies are well suited to a socio-psychological and political discussion of who has the power to evaluate and transmit which pieces of information, and who is supposed to be at the receiving end of such evaluation and transmission—a discussion particularly pertinent to para-esthetical media such as TV and paraliterary genres such as SF. Strivings toward such an horizon are visible in communication studies which have broken with the stimulating but finally unsubstantiated dazzlements of McLuhan (AB) and the earlier empiricism; they are to be found in a first synthesis in *Communications* by the always lucid and thoughtful Raymond Williams (AB).

Whatever refinements have in the last ten years or so been added to a sociology of the literary audience by new schools such as that of "reception esthetics" in Germany (Jauss, Iser, etc.), there seem to be two crucial conditions for making such pursuits into anything more than a sociology and/or history extrinsic to literary studies: first, an encompassing model of relationships between literary production and consumption (with all the mediations sketched above), and second, an historically and sociologically precise identification of the particular socio-economic group which in fact has a given response to given aspects of literary works. These horizons are opened up by Marxism, though of course not all scholars within them have necessarily a Marxist ideological commitment (some of the pioneers clearly do not, e.g. Schucking, Auerbach, and Watt—AB). Yet the insistence that social classes have not only a *different position* in society but *different interests and strivings*—a quite basic realization without which there can to my mind be only market research, not scholarship—is clearly a Marxist one, and most of the leading researchers have been somewhat unorthodox Marxists or "fellow travellers" (Burke, Goldmann, Hauser, Hoggart, Lukács, Williams—AB). Perhaps in the long run even more important, however, is the specifically Marxist anthropological diagnosis of the relationships between work and creativity, production and consumption, alienation and society. These are themes started by Marx and Engels in their early works (e.g. *The German Ideology*—AB), and they provide the ground bass of their whole opus culminating in *Capital*. Some of the most interesting discussions are contained in Marx's preparations for that work, notably in the *Grundrisse*.[3] It seems necessary to mention them here, if only briefly. Marx wrestles with, among other things, the extremely complex relationships of production and consumption, for which—significantly—art is a privileged extreme case:

> The object of art—like every other product—creates a public which is sensitive to art and enjoys beauty. Production thus not only creates an object for the subject, but also a subject for the object.... It thus produces the object of consumption [in the form of a need felt by the consumer]. Consumption likewise produces the producer's *inclination* by beckoning to him as an aim-determining need. [G 92]

However, as the immediate, qualitative *use-value* of any product is in circulation within class society transformed into quantitative *exchange-value*, depending more on the conditions of exchange (market, money, etc.) than on its intrinsic properties, so

> the exchange relation establishes itself as a power external to and independent of the producers.... The product becomes a commodity: the commodity becomes exchange-value; the exchange value of the commodity is its immanent money-property; this, its money-property, separates itself from it in the form of money, and achieves a general social existence separated from all particular commodities and their natural mode of existence.... [G 146-47]

With circulation subsumed under accumulation of capital, a basic opposition arises between product as use-value and as object of such capitalist circulation subject to the profit principle. As Marx suggests (e.g. G 487), this contradiction is clearest in artistic production (say in the production, consumption, and circulation of a book manuscript): the product as "a specific quality, as a specific thing, as a product of specific natural properties, as a substance of need [is] in contradiction with its substance as [exchange-] value" [G 406]. Thus the transformation of products into money, which originally rendered large-scale production possible (and Marx unambiguously admires all such achievements of capitalism, as opposed to all Romantic cries of back to Arcadia), grows in developed capitalism into both the barrier to further production and the agency deforming all use-values (e.g. texts exploring the intrinsic possibilities of their thematic nuclei) into exchange-values (e.g. texts tailored primarily toward selling well, regardless of all else—and if anybody thinks this is not happening on a mass scale in SF, it might be enough to dip into well-known statements by writers such as John Brunner or Robert Silverberg). As a consequence:

> while capital thus appears as the product of labor, so does the product of labor likewise appear as capital—no longer as a simple product, nor as an exchange commodity, but as... *alien property*,...and establishes itself opposite living labor as an *alien power*.... Living labor therefore now appears...as more penurious labor capacity in face of this reality alienated from it, belonging not to it but to others.... [G 453-54]

While it is impossible here to go into ramifications of such basic insights, it is clear that Marx started with the realization that Joyce expressed as "my producers they are also my consumers" (*Finnegan's Wake*), but proceeded from there into a rich sequence of theories that could provide the much needed basis for adequate analysis of social alienations in cultural production—such as literature, movies, comics, or TV (in all of which we find SF). Its value lies in its blend of scholarly sophistication and fierce ethico-political value-judgments, which brands capitalist production as hostile to art and poetry, and yet does not condone the artist-producer's cynically giving in to this hostility:

> A writer naturally must earn money in order to be able to live and write, but under no circumstances must he live and write in order to earn money.... The writer in no wise considers his work a *means*. It is an *end in itself*; so little is it a means for him and for others that he sacrifices his existence to its existence, when necessary; and like a religious preacher, in another sense, he applies the principle "Obey God rather than men" to the men among whom he is himself confined with his human needs and desires.[4]

Admittedly, such horizons receive only a stimulating first sketch in Marx, and subsequent officially socialist thinkers—both social-democratic and Leninist—have shied away from them. The fate of Lukác's early and (alas) only philosophically significant development of such notions in *History and Class Consciousness* (AB), which he was forced to recant, has led to their being developed only by Marxist "guerillas," on the margins of political orthodoxy, with all the strengths and weaknesses arising therefrom. They are mainly Germans—Adorno, Benjamin, Bloch, Ensensberger, Fischer, Jakubowski, Kofler, Marcuse—but also Sartre, Rossi-Landi, and Williams, with a first synthesis in Jameson; to these names (all in AB), I would add at least Bertolt Brecht, whose writings are significant for much more than theatre.[5]

How does one apply the lessons of the various "sociologies of literature" so far developed to the study of SF? Again, only a few areas can be mentioned. Chief among them would be studies based on the facts that SF is a genre, and that it is a (mainly) paraliterary genre.

Any sociological approach to literature, I would feel, becomes really significant when and insofar as it situates the literary text at the crossroads of its esthetic tradition and its implied readership. Now the esthetic tradition can be expressed in a number of ways, according to mode such as satire, to devices such as inner monologue, etc., but it would seem that the most useful way for most texts is to express it as a tradition of *genre*. (Of course, any single text will not simply follow the genre norms but modify them, usually by blending them with norms from other genres or esthetic traditions, but this does not reduce the overall theoretical importance of speaking simply in terms of genre in a first approach.) A literary genre is an ensemble of norms and conventions (linguistically speaking, a set of choices typical to a given literary use of language) which exists at a given historical point and regulates directions of literary discourse. It implies that "one should write it in this way and not otherwise." In this sense genres can be compared to a grammar of literature. Just as speaking a language correctly does not require a knowledge of the rules of grammar in the sense of being able to formulate them theoretically (so that Moliere's Monsieur Jourdain spoke prose without knowing it), so writing within a given type of literary discourse does not require the writer to know the definition of that literary genre. Nonetheless, he/she will have absorbed it "from the air" as a modality of literary practice.

Thus each genre implies a given ensemble of possibilities for literary discourse. These possibilities flow out of the genre's *telos* or purpose—to speak with Aristotle—and the logical cognitive uses that purpose can be put to. The historically realized possibilities give rise to clear *expectations* from a genre at any given historical point. The consciousness about what can as a rule be expected from a genre, the genre-consciousness, exists among its audience of readers. From them it is transmitted to (and modified by) the producers in the genre—who were readers before they became writers (a fact especially clear in the history of SF with its recruitment of writers from fans). That does not mean that the genre-consciousness or genre-identification of the readers and the writers is necessarily identical. In fact, their genre-consciousness will necessarily be at least somewhat different in function of their primary interest in reading or in writing the genre.

One of the basic insights, even if still not fully developed, of the modern sociology of literature is that there is an imaginary ideal reader programmed into the structure and texture of literary texts and ensembles of texts such as genres. The communicational trinity of emission-transmission-reception within a social context implies—as information theory has taught us—a *code* which alone permits the understanding of the communication. This code is shared (at least largely shared) by reader and writer, emitter and receiver, in the same cultural context. The imaginary *implied reader* is thus a product of three factors: (1) of the writer's production, (2) of the audience's expectations as intuited—and sometimes directly studied—by the writer, and (3) of the code, "language," or convention of the literary genre, a convention that provides a more or less wide but never unlimited field of possibilities for both audience expectation and writer production as well as for their often conflictual interaction. Any significant (original, cognitive) writer will transgress some audience expectations: only hacks (of which no doubt we have a fair share in SF) will satisfy these expectations by fully or simply reproducing their conventional sources. The genre convention or code is thus a meeting ground for the writer's production and the audience's expectations; it assigns social roles to both the writer and the reader (e.g. a writer or reader of fairy tales is assigned a quite different role from—can legitimately have only very different expectations than—a writer or reader of psychological tales or SF tales). On the other hand, the implied reader (a heuristic construct) is not the same as the *real readership*, which is a statistically investigable and not necessarily homogeneous audience for the literary text(s). This real readership is, of course, divisible according to socio-economic class, nationality and ethnic background, age, sex, education, and a number of other factors all participating in the shaping of different "social tastes" (Schucking—AB) or "class consciousnesses" (Goldmann—AB). These tastes or consciousnesses will furthermore be different for the same group in different socio-historical periods. The resulting expectations will therefore change with each social class or sufficiently specific other social sub-group with its own language and above all own interests. The ideal reader inscribed between the lines of the literary text will be a reduction and/or prefiguration of the real readership according to the writer's imaginative and material interests and needs. The *implied author* of the literary text(s), by the way, should also be differentiated into at least three different concepts, sometimes blended but also in mutual tension: (1) the "authorial image," the image of the fashioner of the literary work that arises out of, is characterized and transmitted by, and exists only within, the literary work; (2) the narrator of the story, when the story is narrated, e.g. in *The Time Machine*; and (3) the historical personality of the author. One wishes that a number of "author-studies"—now vying for popularity in SF criticism with "theme-studies"—would take such differences into account.

The horizons discussed above offer prospects for a great deal of work in SF criticism on the relation of various audiences to various sub-genres, authors, and devices within it. A few of these have been explored, but as a rule either without sufficient socio-economic differentiation of the readers involved or without sufficient differentiation of the text-aspects involved. It is by now rather banal to investigate the relationship of "X in SF" (whatever X may be) to, say, the US audience. Even assuming that we know the US audience to be roughly age 15-30 (which is by no means certain), fundamental questions remain: X in *which type* of SF (author, sub-genre, ideological horizon, etc.)? in the opinion of *which part* of the US audience (male-female, middle-working-capitalist class, urban-rural, high-middle-low education, WASP-ethnic, etc., etc.)? Only then can one get beyond bourgeois mystification of *the* reader responding to *the* work of so-and-so; only then can value-judgments go beyond impressionistic ideologies and noises of approval or disapproval. Only then could SF critics proceed to large-scale overviews, comparing e.g. various national situations (which I suspect will at a given time be found not to be always synchronic—thus reader expectation in French SF in the 1950s and 60s was largely a sub-set of US reader expectation ten years earlier, while Russian expections of SF diverged in the 1920s from the common European norm, setting up a new normative system which opened up to international stimuli with Yefremov and the Strugatskys). Or one could envisage very interesting comparisons of various ideological positions in SF correlative to different readerships: "hard science" devotees vs. "soft science" devotees, readers of *Starship Troopers* and Haldeman vs readers of *The Word for World is Forest* and Disch, etc. Such a comparison would, I believe, indicate that the major sociological and ideological problem in contemporary SF is the indiscriminate consumption of quite disparate sub-sets of works, with incompatible ideal readers, by what seems (but perhaps wrongly?) the same real readership—in other words, the degradation of SF to pure consumption dominated by capitalist circulation and the intermediaries of transmission (editors, publishers, distributors, financiers—in the final analysis, it seems, large multi-media corporations). Should this be true, the strictures of a Lem which basically say that SF has by now become a medium which is its own message rather than the bearer of any particular poetico-cognitive messages—strictures which I am still reluctant to accept fully—would find themselves confirmed. But one hopes that instead it might be possible to differentiate the puerile ideal reader of (say) 80% of SF, the "median stage of adolescence" which Samuelson once postulated for Clarke and similar, accounting for perhaps 15-18% of SF, and the 2-5% of SF whose ideal readers are among the most interesting social groups of the present day. In order to decide about this, we would need an inventory of motifs, topoi, and attitudes in different ensembles of SF, and of the relations of such ensembles to other genres. And in particular to other genres both of older "high lit." (e.g. the 19th-century psychological tale) and of contemporary "low literature," the non-canonical paraliterary genres of Western, spy thriller, detective mystery, etc.

Paraliterary studies (see section 6 of AB, in particular Angenot's own introductory book, also Cawelti, Langenbucher, Lowenthal, Nutz, Orwell, and Schulte-Sasse) have been wittily classified by Eco, himself possibly their most prominent practitioner (AB) into "the apocalyptic" which reject mass culture wholly (e.g. Q.D. Leavis—AB) and "the integrated" which accept it fully (e.g. the more zealous SF fans). Eco himself pleads—with pioneering examples—for a third way, without automatic acceptance or rejection, but with formal and ideological discrimination. This is difficult but possible: an example of the latter is Seesslen-Kling (AB). What makes modern paraliterature so complicated, however, is the sea-change it suffered in the last two or three generations. In almost all epochs before the 19th-20th century, there existed a profound difference between the popular or plebeian (largely oral) culture and the official ruling or upper-class (usually written) culture. Since the rulers have always written history, including the history of culture, it is the latter writings which have been, abusively, called Literature in the consecrated or canonic sense: such Literature with a capital "L" is composed of officially "higher" genres (tragedy, ode, or psychological novel). But Literature in this sense has always a twin in its complementary plebeian or vulgar, narrative discourse, which one would then have to call Paraliterature. This literature (lower-case "l") is an ensemble of non-canonic or "lower" genres, such as proverbs, humor, fables, sagas, detective tales—or SF. The deep paraliteray stream, old as class society, penetrates into official culture and Literature only occasionally, during those favorable socio-political periods when its bearers—the lower, plebeian classes—riseto at least a partial participation in the canonic culture. The "iceberg" character of the paraliterary tradition(s)—including SF if we consider it historically from Antiquity to our own time—with only a small fraction surviving to be recorded above the surface of neglect, persecution, and oblivion, is thus the result of deep tensions which have historically split every nation's culture into at least "two nations," as Disraeli formulated it. The cultures of these "two nations" have been connected by various antagonistic relationships, from suppression to partial permeation, but as a rule they have (except for special historical moments of cohesion such as part of the Elizabethan Age in England) been sufficiently distinct to preserve distinct identities. A renewal of Culture and Literature came about by the rise of earlier non-canonic forms to canonic status together with the social group that was the ideal reader of those forms (e.g. the psychological novel and the bourgeoisie).

The complication with 20th-century paraliterature and SF is that neither the Jacobin nor the Bolshevik revolutions have basically succeeded, so that universal literacy and a better economic standard coincided with the rise of imperialism and the welfare/warfare state. In culture there ensued a very specific and complex amalgam of suppression and permeation which has still been barely identified—much less properly studied (for a first approximation see Williams, *The Long Revolution*—AB). In the language of Gramsci (AB), the hegemony of the bourgeois ideology and taste has been challenged but not overthrown: new forms and genres rise into official culture at the expense of the plebeian horizons, at the price of emasculation and containment, of what Marcuse has analyzed as cooption (AB—see also his *Counterrevolution and Revolt* [US 1972]). This means a temporary and usually spurious renewal of official culture, but also the failure of these new genres to live up to their potentiality, to their own nature. It might be a useful hypothesis to approach SF in this way, and see whether the empirical material will confirm or invalidate this hypothesis. This would be, to my mind, quite important; for, as Gramsci also observed, a new valid literature as the expression of that moral and intellectual renewal which this planet needs unless we are to render it uninhabitable, can only come from readers of paraliterature, by means of new writers subsuming and transcending its popular tradition, as Dostoevsky did with the *roman-feuilleton* and criminal stories à la Sue. The stakes, thus, are the highest ones imaginable.

(Introduction continued on page 334)

Gérard Klein

Discontent in American Science Fiction[1]

Translated by D. Suvin and Leila Lecorps

(from **SFS** *4: 3–13, March 1977)*

The following essay, certainly too curt in relation to its subject-matter, represents a series of reflections upon a wide range of reading, rather than systematic research. Thus, it wishes to indicate directions of further inquiry rather than bring the "scientific" answer to a sociological problem.

1. A Pseudo-Maturity: Pessimism and Its Origins. Around the middle of the 1960s, there was a sudden veering in English-language SF: from optimistic, it became as a rule quite pessimistic and somber. It used to zoom through vast galactic prospects in very far futures, but now increasingly dealt with the near—even the very near—future, and confined itself to the Earth. The authors began to be preoccupied with delivering a serious and responsible message to the reader. For about ten years, with the notable exception of one corpus—the significant one of Ursula Le Guin—most writers sought to achieve credibility by describing the near future in very dark colours. According to a frequently expressed but somewhat naive view, SF had now passed from the stage of tumultuous teenage dreams to the adult stage, which manifested itself in focusing on the sufferings of humanity.

Of course, many books expressing pessimistic views on the near future can be found in the earlier history of SF, e.g. *Limbo* by Bernard Wolfe and *Player Piano* by Kurt Vonnegut (both in 1952), satirical novels by Pohl and Kornbluth such as *The Space Merchants*, or *Fahrenheit 451* by Ray Bradbury (both 1953). But these authors and works seem relatively isolated in their time. On the contrary, the vast space-epics, full of optimism for the future of the human race and of science, which are characteristic for the preceding quarter of a century, now seem quaint and dated. Even Robert Heinlein, the bard of self-reliant optimism, was not the last to change direction, as can already be seen in *Stranger in a Strange Land* (1961). The great characteristic of recent SF is a distrust of science and technology, and of scientists, especially in the exact or "hard" sciences of physics, chemistry, biology and genetics.

Now, such a tendency is not an exclusive one, even after the mid-60s. Yet in many works of the best authors, the predominant feeling is that there is no future—for science, for society, for the human race. This seems paradoxical in a literature which pretends to deal in anticipations. In the 40s and 50s, even at the worst time of the nuclear terror, practically all the writers tried to describe the actions of the survivors, and the reconstruction of a civilization. This state of affairs has radically changed. Such a change calls for an explanation.

Why is contemporary SF so saturated with rupture, crisis, imminent catastrophe, end of the world and humanity, rejection of the values of science and even of reason, skepticism about social forms and structures? Why does it reject historical progress and posit a dissolution of consciousness and the hostility of nature towards mankind? The very real perils of the present and anxieties for the future are not enough to explain this about-face. Paradoxically, it was during the years of the Depression and the Second World War and even in the years of nuclear threat that SF displayed its greatest confidence in the progress of science, mankind and civilization, to the point of offering the stars as a reward. Even while the nuclear peril and the risk of technological regression was being denounced, the stress was on what was to come after, on the possible, probable, certain rebirth. It is not evident to me as a European that the United States is more insecure today than during the Prohibition years. Further, being an economist, I am surprised by the coincidence of doubt and pessimism in SF with a period of economic growth during the 60s which has no precedent in the whole history of the capitalist world, and which bogged down only in the last few years. To use a clinical analogy, the dominant impression is that a prolonged attack of depression, somewhat colored by paranoia, characterizes certain contemporary social groups, including the writers of SF. Neither this depression nor the paranoiac syndrome disproves the lucidity of the patient, or the reality of his difficulties. But they structure his experiences in a way that finally leaves no exit; if ever an exit is considered, it is related only feebly to reality, or becomes sheer escapism. Therefore, the origin of the disease should be looked for not in the reasons given by the patient (although some may well be correct) but elsewhere, in a perhaps temporary inadaptation of the patient's psychical structure to his reality—a changing reality that he has not been able to deal with, if necessary by contesting it.

Let us not prolong this analogy which has only the value of a metaphor. Yet, the hypothesis that I am sketching here is that *the real subject of a literary work (or group of works) is the situation of the social group the author belongs to.* The anguish conveyed in the work is provoked by the inadaptation of this social group to change in the world society, a change that may entail the dissolution of the social group. In using this hypothesis, largely based upon the methodology of Lucien Goldmann,[2] I do not at all intend to minimize the individual, subjective determinations which are at work in all artistic creation and give it its particular intellectual, affective and aesthetic tonality. I only want to suggest that a collective phenomenon, such as the literature we are considering, cannot be regarded as a mechanical sum of particular subjectivities. In all human activity, extraordinarily complex social and psychological determinations intersect. Where exactly is one to even begin getting a hold on these determinations is a matter of epistemological grids, which are necessarily imperfect. But the most useful of such grids in this case seems to be one which delimits a social group as the privileged subject of a creative opus.

2. Attempt at Delimiting a Social Group. The idea that the authors, and no doubt the readers, of SF belong to a social group which is, at least from certain points of view, fairly homogeneous seems to be supported by two facts: first, the great cohesion of the particular cultural sub-set that forms the SF literature, a cohesion confirmed by a whole display of internal references which tend to define it as a real sub-culture; and second, the non-assimilation or rejection of this subculture by other social groups, and in particular by the dominant cultural group which pretends (quite successfully) to represent the "real culture."[3] The price imposed by that dominant culture (itself, of course, very contradictory and complex) in exchange for recognizing the seriousness, responsibility and the quality of literary works, is the abandonment, the repudiation of belonging to another social group, to a different cultural tradition; in the final consequence, the price is the break-up of the subculture. Thus, any subculture is always, in the "occidental" world at least, urged and pressured to disappear, allegedly for its own good and greatest glory. It is therefore understandable that at a moment when their social group is threatened in its very being, many SF writers give way to the permanent cultural solicitation of the dominant group and declare that SF will be at its best only when totally absorbed into the "mainstream." Some writers indeed go in for such a metamorphosis, very often a trip without return or real profit.

Another indication of the homogeneity of the social group underlying SF lies in the lack of diversity in the sociopolitical opinions expressed. Without much risk of error, this group can be classed as *liberal* with all the economical and political connotations conveyed by this vague term: a formal legality in the political process, tolerance, and a quite strong decentralisation—all of which leaves large scope for, and is indeed the obverse of, the quite primordial competition of production units. Now I know that I am here going to antagonise many readers, those who feel themselves profoundly different from the old "reactionaries" such as Campbell, Heinlein, or Anderson, and also those who are alarmed by the penetration of radical "Reds" into the SF fortress. But the truth, as seen from the vantage point of an outside observer, forces me to say that the spectrum of sociopolitical attitudes in published SF is not nearly as wide as the one found in European societies—or, almost certainly, in American society. American SF has never been the battleground of profound political conflicts, that is to say, it has never undergone a true debate about the basic form of society.[4] This is all the more surprising since—unlike the detective story for example—American SF deals with theories and often pretends to speak about the future of society. It seems impossible to find a single authentic representative of any of the numerous branches of the socialist-marxist family, without going clear back to before World War 2 or even to Jack London's *The Iron Heel.* For their book *The Space Merchants*, an essentially timid work acceptable to any European centre-left, Pohl and Kornbluth were treated as radical leftists by critics—critics, by the way, basically exterior to the SF subculture.[5] Conversely, none of the really eccentric and often very dangerous ideas of the extreme right have taken permanent hold in SF either. There is less difference between the old republican Heinlein (especially in his younger days)[6] and the young radicals of the Spinrad type than might seem. Without minimizing those differences, they seem rather a matter of characters, of circumstances of formation and, most of all, of generation, than of adhesion to clearly structured ideological groups.

Several factors may explain the narrow spread of sociopolitical opinions in SF. First of all, there is no doubt that the system of book and magazine publishers and editors tends to delete strong statements of position and attitudes. However, this relative consensus probably corresponds to the real way of thinking and social situation of a segment of the American middle class, the profoundly *depoliticised* segment to which the social group in question belongs. Clearly, the spread of political opinions in the American middle class is much wider, especially on the right, than in SF, whose centre of gravity can be characterized as situated slightly to the left of the centre, with an intellectual or semi-intellectual bias reinforced by a significant presence of East Coast Jews.[7] Thus, during the McCarthy era and the "witch-hunts," there were many writers in American SF—usually the best ones—who reacted with subtlety and dignity against this threat of collective hysteria. However, if capitalism cannot expect a great boost from American SF, neither has it got much to worry about on account of American SF. What American SF has always spoken against, however mildly, is any form of control over social life, whether by the state or by capitalist monopolies. We shall see that this is still its real concern today.

Another proof for the existence of a social group as bearer of American SF are its evident limits. It is very surprising that, as far as I know, there is only one Black SF writer in the U.S.A., and he could be held for a White one.

One should, then, try and define the precise characteristics of the social group whose consciousness delimits American SF. This is very difficult in the absence (though it might be as difficult in the presence) of empirical sociological investigation. But it seems certain that such a social group would be a part of the vast U.S.—and global—middle class, as distinguished from the ruling classes (middle and high bourgeoisie) and the working classes (industrial, farm, office workers and similar). The social group that is the bearer of SF would, however, be differentiated from other segments of the middle class by its functions and its scientific and technical culture. The point is not whether its members have a real scientific education—a majority apparently have not—but whether they entertain a specifically intimate relationship with science and technology, either in their professional activities or purely in their ideology. This they obviously do, and their social group can be called a *scientifically and technologically oriented middle class.*

3. The Trajectory of SF from Faith to Imprecation. If we, then, postulate such a summary concept of the social group underlying SF, we can now try to understand some aspects of SF history. I will distinguish, schematically, 3 phases in it: I) optimism and faith in scientific progress; II) confident skepticism; and III) pessimism and imprecation.

I. *Optimism*: During the first period, between the middle 30s and the beginning of the Cold War, American society, more than any other in the "West" except perhaps, in a different way, German society, experienced a massive social, political and economical disruption. In spite of obvious difficulties due to the Depression and then the World War, the social group of SF saw its value—technological rather than scientific—in the ascendant; it had some evidence for the building—on the ruins of a waning bourgeois liberal society—of an "organization" society.[8] During this time, the benevolent imperialism of the U.S.A. was directed against reactionary and militarily aggressive societies. Also, the needs of reorganizing production and waging war led the ruling class to adhere without reservations to technological values. The social group of SF could therefore believe in a universal rational society, where all conflicts would be solved in the scientific fashion to which this group pinned its hopes, and, above all, within which it thought it would play a decisive part. Such a universalization of rationality was then extrapolated in SF to the very limits of the universe: the benevolent imperialism of the scientist will spread to the stars. Of course, nostalgias still lingered, as in the case of Clifford Simak, still attached to an older system of values conveyed by the small-town middle class. But even the great anarchising individualists and mutants of a Van Vogt, heir to the individualist tradition of the 19th Century, were enrolled in the service of reason, i.e., of the organizational society. A little later, when the possibility of the disappearance of civilisation was expressed in Asimov's *Foundation Trilogy* (magazine publ. 1942-50), it remained quite clear that renewal was more relevant than decadence, and that it should be realized by a caste of technicians. What remained unnoticed were the limits decreed by historical evolution to the rise and power of the social group which expressed itself in SF.

II. *Confident Skepticism*: Those limitations were exposed brutally, though at first from the outside only, at the end of the Second World War. First, in a more superficial way, the Cold War showed that a universalized system was not a self-evident fact, that the extrapolation would encounter many adversaries. Nuclear anxiety arose not from the explosion of the atom-bombs over Japan, but from the balance of terror foreseen by every lucid mind and all too soon realised in fact (thence comes, perhaps, the taste for super-arms which might restore the monopoly of power). But second, and more importantly, the social group of SF had been shown its place, and could no longer ignore that it would NOT be a determining group, even though it might remain an indispensable one. The organizational leadership it dreamed of for its values would not come about; the technologically oriented middle class had been allotted the role of an instrument rather than that of an animator. Immense economico-industrial units or monopolies had been constituted, whose admitted aims did not depend on rationality but on the quest for power; thus, the appearance of imperialism was no longer so benevolent. For SF there followed a period of skepticism, illustrated by the appearance of a new kind of magazine such as *F and SF* and *Galaxy*, and of writers like Robert Sheckley whose weapon is satire. In this period, the exterior confrontations of global power-blocs meshed with the interior confrontations both of political forces, such as McCarthyism, and of the monopolies themselves. Yet in such a period of severe conflict the social group in question could retain at least the appearance of being an umpire or referee. At this point, it could still believe that the science, the technological values, which it considered its own, could either *be* or *not be* put at the service of truth. On another level, but one that has often found a symbolic expression in SF, this is the almost mythological opposition between Robert Oppenheimer and Edward Teller. The exaggerated pessimism of some writers, which passes today for lucidity and establishes them as forerunners—e.g., in *Player Piano* by Vonnegut and in *Limbo* by Bernard Wolfe, both published in 1952—in fact relegated them at the time to the margins of the "genre," and ensured their divorce from the social group of SF. Damon Knight, with his prophetic *Hell's Pavement* (1955), barely escaped the same temptation, and then stopped writing almost completely. And obversely, it is remarkable that a very widespread theme at the time was that of a *saving cataclysm*, often nuclear. The survivors, having hastily wiped away a tear over the fate of some billions of dead, eagerly start rebuilding a society that suits them and that, above all, is in their image. Characteristically, these survivors all have the (more or less idealized) features of the social group we are discussing. Arising out of the well-to-do middle class, their stability rests on their wide technical and scientific knowledge, which enables them to organize the universe. They belong in the tradition of the *Swiss Family Robinson* and Verne's *Mysterious Island*: their castaway life is a liberation from the oppressive society which menaced their identity. These saving cataclysms, especially the short stories, always stupefy Europeans, who have had quite a different experience of war and exodus. Of course, I do not pretend that the post-atomic stories exhausted the SF of that time, nor that they all necessarily had a happy conclusion, but seldom—except in the writings of a relatively recent immigrant such as Algis Budrys—do they fail to close upon an optimistic note.

III. *Pessimism*: During the 60s, and at the beginning of the 70s, the capitalist world, in particular the United States, enjoyed a historically unprecedented growth. Moreover a great number of prophecies retailed by SF became reality, more often than not for the best. Let us only call to mind the absence of nuclear conflict, the development of scientific agronomy, the diffusion of computers which enabled a great number of striking advances in the scientific field, and finally the conquest of space, which has so far reached its highest point with the exploitation of communicational (as well as meteorological) satellites and the exploration of the Moon. And yet, disenchantment entered American SF during these same years, increasing steadily until it reached the blackest pessimism, and uttering imprecations not only against society but against science itself, which had, in the end, failed. Even before 1970, we had arrived at the great triple malediction: pollution, overpopulation, dehumanization.

For, due to the great expansion of the 60s, the economic and social structures of America and of the whole world have greatly changed, and changed, moreover, in a way that directly threatens the social group of SF in its identity, its real or supposed power, its values. This social group now finds it has (in the strict sense of the word) no more future—even though, individually, its members might be living better than ever before. The economic corporations have fused even further, and the main ones have become multinational. Although some of these corporations can be seen to be mortal, on the whole, as a system, they appear nearly indestructible and invincible. Their executives have learned how to control—efficiently and not without brutality—scientists, technicians, and other intellectuals, rather than coming to terms with them. The executives know how to influence public opinion and, through it or directly, force the states, not excepting the American state, to do their will. Under the guise of supposedly scientific research and information, they spread an ideology of environmental degradation (cf. the Club of Rome) which tends to entrust to them unrestricted power in the name of their very scantily democratic "rationality." At the same time, the imperialism of the Indochinese and Chilean adventures appears to a growing fraction of American and world opinion to be malignant—not so much because of a (very belated) moral reaction as because this fraction of public opinion feels its own economic and social reality threatened by such doings. As an economist, I have already tried to show elsewhere that this process—which perhaps tends toward the instauration of a neo-feudal post-bourgeois system—has no reason whatsoever to stop, profiting as it does from world-wide inflation for so many years, but that it will result in a grandiose and probably long-lasting planetary crisis, of which we are living the first episodes.[9]

4. A Social Group in Danger, and Aware of It. This is the context in which the social group of SF that we are discussing lives endlessly the hour of its death; it has been expressing it strongly for at least the past ten years, in its literature: SF. Thence comes its pessimism, this time inescapable, but sometimes overlaid by nostalgic memories such as those which have prevailed in the awarding of the Hugo Prize to Isaac Asimov and to Arthur C. Clarke in 1973 and in 1974.

In particular, this social group knows now very well that its technological capacity, real or supposed, is and will be used as an instrument, regardless of the group's will and own strategy. For a social group of this type, death is the disappearance of the particular power which held it together. It is in a way returned to the anonymous mass of workers, and can no longer avail itself of any qualitative privilege, especially of any intellectual privilege. Somewhat like an individual who has a totally illogical tendency to make of his death a universal event, the moment when the stars go out, a threatened social group too has a tendency to confuse its dissolution with the disappearance of civilization, and even—in a genre as obviously haunted by megalomania as SF—with the end of history and all humanity.

Of course, in this process it is not only the social group that is the bearer of SF which finds itself threatened by servitude, but all the social groups pertaining to the American—or even the global—middle class. This explains the convergence of the specific pessimism in recent SF, expressing a localized tragedy, and of the anxieties latent in a vast audience. It is on this encounter that the ambiguous and desperate prophesying of a number of works is based. Perhaps for the first time in its history, SF is aware that it speaks in the name of a very great number of people and that it is understood by them; thence the rather naive and widespread illusion of dealing with reality. When SF was the bearer of a scientific messianism, it was mocked; many of its writers and critics are still surprised to be at last taken seriously, and perhaps do not clearly see the real, irrational reason for this. That reason might horrify them. True, they have often drawn up a veritable indictment of science, guilty of not having proved a sufficient guarantee for the power, cohesion and ideology of their social group, but they are not ready to jettison the rational values which they have upheld so long, and to give in to the mounting tide of militant irrationalism which could well lend to our near future a particularly hideous aspect—from where I stand, and I believe from where they stand too.

In some degree, it is possible to draw a parallel between the weakening of the middle-class rational values at this threshold of a new social system, and the weakening of the medieval values in Europe at the time of the subversion of feudality by the bourgeoisie. If this parallel is valid, the conditions are perhaps present for the writing of a new *Don Quixote* in the field of SF. All that remains is to find Cervantes.

Surely it is clear that I am not saying that predictions of catastrophes are without any foundation, or that optimism is compulsory. I only say that *optimism and pessimism in literature and in art also express something beside a purely dispassionate and hypothetical examination of the facts*, and that this something is shaped partly by the individual subjectivity of an author (which I do not intend to deny), and partly by the situation of his social group in the societal universe.

5. Some Aesthetic, Ideological and Prophetic Solutions. There are numerous recent SF works that refer to the social process described above. I will mention only a few examples. Before I start with them, I wish to state my *second thesis*: *literary works* (all works of art) *are attempts to resolve through the use of the imagination and in the aesthetic mode, a problem which is not soluble in reality*. Of course, a given theoretical problem admits of many aesthetic solutions—otherwise the literature of a period would be drearily repetitive.[10] The psychic configuration of an author, his particular experience, his situation in the microstructure of his social group, his belonging or relationships to other social groups, will lead him to his solution or, if one prefers, to his style in the broad sense of the word. In the case we are discussing, an author may "choose" to appropriate, in the realm of imagination, the values of the new ruling class. Or else, he may—by announcing in a cold and objective manner the breaking up of a whole society, the disappearance of humanity or even the dissolution of the universe—deny the specific unsolvable problem set before his social group, i.e., "solve" it by throwing it out. If death and loss of power are universal phenomena resulting from an impenetrable destiny, nobody need bother about them. And should the writer address himself, in order to prevent the catastrophe, to persons presumably in charge, he will choose them implicitly outside his social group and thus extricate himself and absolve the values of his social group from that responsibility. He then either speaks to all, becoming a charismatic prophet; or he speaks to the elite in power, taking on the role of its interlocutor or advisor. Prophets, as we know, talk to kings about commoners, and to commoners about kings.

The first solution has been adopted by writers like Roger Zelazny, particularly in his *Isle of the Dead* (1969), or Norman Spinrad—though with much ambiguity—in his *The Men in the Jungle* (1967), *Bug Jack Barron* (1969) and even *The Iron Dream* (1972). They have recognized the advent of tyranny based on monopolies and established themselves, as it were by anticipation, as its court poets. There is certainly little likelihood that they would be confirmed in that position by the new dominant class. But they can thus escape, in imagination, from the destiny of their social group, identifying themselves with charismatic leaders endowed with fantastic powers—notably financial ones. There is an important difference between the billionaires of Zelazny and the industrial captains of a Poul Anderson for example. While Anderson has in a whole cycle simply tried to describe a bourgeois social and economical universe and to project into the future Vanderbilts who owe their power to fortune and financial skill, Zelazny has perfectly grasped the mutation of the power-system occurring today, with the new system having to create and to lean on ideological, extra-economical, in the final analysis religious values. The rationality of competitive capital yields to the monopolistic irrationality of desire for the unique, which manifests itself best in the aspirations to immortality and to other divine attributes. It is not by accident that immortality—which, with some exceptions such as Van Vogt, was an uncommon SF topic—has lately made a triumphant re-entry into SF.

As for Spinrad, he willingly affects a critical position. But it is clear that he succumbs to the fascination of power-structures he pretends to fight, even in *The Iron Dream* and *Bug Jack Barron*. Ambiguity is present everywhere: even when Spinrad explicitly denounces the doings of his monsters in the name of the egalitarian, rationalist and democratic values of his social group, he justifies them implicitly since he presents them as the only heroes, the only persuasive characters. The violence of language in this notable writer indicates that for him only the language of violence exists. Outside of it is death. And death is what Jack Barron will escape, without making this his main conscious purpose in the plot, but having in fact sought immortality both by the form of his single combat and by the choice of the adversaries against whom he matches himself.

In this mode, one opus seems to me to stand out over and above all others, its true meaning becoming only very gradually evident—that of Cordwainer Smith. It alone seems capable of gaining the adhesion of the new tyrants, depicted both with and without complacency—undoubtedly because Smith lived precisely on the borderline of the old social group underlying SF and the new dominant class, and because he had, it seems, some concrete experience of recent history. I cannot analyse his work here. It shares with the works of the writers just discussed the hypothesis of a historical (and galactic) future of a neo-feudal type; it differs from them in that it does not contain any glorification of an omnipotent and charismatic hero, as in Zelazny, nor an explicit though ambiguous condemnation of the mechanisms of coming to power, as in Spinrad. The true subject of Smith's aristocratic opus is the disturbed and at times compassionate glance at the people from the other side, from above. Its form is the fresco, without a specific centre. It seems to me wrong to affirm, as is often done, that Cordwainer Smith, had he had more time, would have organized and as it were re-centered his universe. For the Lords of Instrumentality, there can be no goal, no centre to reach: they are the centre, their problems are on the periphery. And the subject of Cordwainer Smith's opus is precisely how to keep the peripheral on the periphery, how to stay in power, how to remain an elite. His answer is the classic one: to persuade the slaves that their condition is a noble one.

Instead of the works mentioned so far, I would like to explain my position by focusing on three writers who seem to me less marginal, more typical—Philip K. Dick, Frank Herbert and John Brunner. Using extremely different methods, much imitated since, they tell of the rise of monopolies, the disintegration of the individual, the dislocation of the social universe, the degradation and destruction of the physical world, the failure of humanity.

The evolution of Dick's opus, in my opinion the most important work in American SF at least until the end of the 60s, is clear. From an almost purely sociological and rather classical analysis of social contradictions in *Solar Lottery* (1955), it leads to a reasoned negation of coherence in the physical universe while maintaining what is from an author's viewpoint essential, i.e., aesthetic cohesion. Dick explains clearly, in *Ubik* (1969) in particular, the subjection of technicians to the monopolies and the feeling of arbitrariness that results. But since the problem is socially unsolvable for this group, it appears as if the whole universe were arbitrary. This feeling of arbitrariness goes beyond ideology, it saturates the epistemological view. Since I have no control over my destiny—Dick says in substance—I cannot imagine anyone having control over his destiny. Nowhere is there an absolute referent, and the conceptual grids we apply to our perception of reality are themselves arbitrary results of various cultural demands rather than of reality structures, as the powers-that-be want everyone to believe.

Is it surprising that Herbert's *Dune* (1965) brings out the same absence of absolute referent? Paul Muad'Dib, prophet and messiah of Dune, pierces the surfaces of things, of conflicts, of ambitions, only to discover an ocean of fluxes, without bottom, without permanence, which even the movements of the great swimmers of time hardly agitate. His prescience is of practically no help to him since, facing an eternity that cannot be grasped, it is in practice almost wholly cancelled by other presciences. One can see here a concept of the historical universe as a field of forces constituted and deformed by the structuring presence of innumerable centres of conscience, or rather of action-lines, which have no other reality than that of their interferences—a concept that we find again, though within a very different perspective, in the work of Ursula Le Guin. Here, the perception of a centreless, and therefore arbitrary and impersonal, universal can only lead to the personal destruction of Muad'Dib. He is the victim of the resonance imposed on other lines by his own wake. We are here at the antipodes of the rationalist, Cartesian conception of bourgeois physics, psychology and sociology. On the contrary, we are plunged into a universe of subjectivist relativity where each point (of view) defines another universe. Like Dick's heroes, Herbert's Muad'Dib is the opposite of the Van Vogtian heroes whose talent, giving them access to the "real" universe, endows them with a source of unlimited power; what seems important to me in *Dune* is that the attainment of power, both psychological and political, solves nothing. Humanity—like the social group that is the bearer of SF—is denied the possibility of controlling its destiny. At best, by precipitating its own destruction, it will leave a nostalgic trace of what could have been a serene universe. It is by disappearing that Paul Muad'Dib fulfills himself, since he will be regretted; his death—which differentiates him radically from the heroes of Spinrad and of Zelazny—plunges the universe back into chaos. Henceforth, the impersonal forces will govern the universe: a beautiful funeral oration for a social group which believed it could predict the future and make history.

If the dislocation of the universe according to Dick and Herbert is largely a metaphysical one, it assumes in the opus of John Brunner (*Stand on Zanzibar*, 1968; *The Sheep Look Up*, 1972) an actual and physical character that tends to formulate the anxiety objectively. The metaphysical and ideological dimension which we have found in Dick and Herbert is almost completely neglected here. This may be due to John Brunner's subjectivity, but it is doubtless more relevant that he is a British writer writing, from outside, about and for the USA. First, the putting into question of the social group that is the bearer of SF, even though it is well advanced in Europe, has not yet produced all the effects which have been experienced by the residents of the United States. Further, the extremely subtle balance of social forces in western Europe tends to mask more than elsewhere the reality of power-relations and of the relations of production. Thus an intellectual can still (although not as strongly as a generation earlier) pretend to believe in his prophetic function and to extract himself from the ongoing process in order to denounce it while objectifying it—as do Brunner's "heroes," the sociologist Chad Mulligan and the anti-pollution propagandist Austin Train. John Brunner's very marked pessimism is signalled in *Stand on Zanzibar* by the completely artificial character of the final solution—we might as well say that there is no solution outside of miracle. It is perhaps intensified by the apparently insurmountable difficulties of British society as a whole (except for a dominant group faring quite well, if its investments over the whole world are taken into account). At any rate, if Brunner perceives perhaps more lucidly than anyone else who are the agents threatening his social group and the way of life of his country, he succumbs more completely than any other significant SF writer to the temptation of turning the crisis caused by this threat into a crisis of humanity as a whole, and of turning his "perspective" into an eschatological prophecy without resurrection. The dislocation of the universe is in Brunner expressed right down to his novels' composition and style. In the two novels mentioned, one first notices a converging structure—converging precisely toward the end of the world (*The Sheep Look Up*) or the undiscoverable solution (*Stand on Zanzibar* and *The Shock Wave Rider*, 1975)—and then the "exploded" construction, allegedly borrowed from Dos Passos but in fact not signifying, as in Dos Passos, the diversity of an American world in search of its unity. Rather, that construction signifies the dislocation of a social universe that consists only of contradictions and no longer possesses the central referent which the excluded sociologist Chad Mulligan, bearer of the threatened social group's values, could have offered it. Finally, Brunner has been accused, at least in France, of having "cold" and somewhat stereotyped characters: but this is so just because they are not in full possession of all their reality (as one says of someone that he is not in full possession of all of his faculties) but are becoming mechanical nonentities, simulacra â la Philip K. Dick. They are reintegrated, according to the process that I have indicated above, into the mass, a terribly numerous oppressive mass, which does not really have a right to individuality or conscience. It would even be possible—with some surprise—to find in the depths of Brunner's novels the worst cliches about the anonymous masses of the third world and of the proletariat, though, of course, inflected by a great deal of generosity—if we did not grasp their true meaning: a denial that the social group that is the bearer of SF has any special power left, and a vision of the group's return to the mass of ordinary humans, workers and unemployed workers (e.g., in the scene of the New York riot from *Stand on Zanzibar*).

6. End of the Social Group, Ecological Anxiety, End of Humanity. This return to the soil, this reintegration of a highly individualized social group into the undifferentiated mass destitute of consciousness, finds an extreme expression in many works that predict the end of history through the abolition of humanity's apparent privilege over other species, through humanity's reduction to the level of nature. Human history is then perceived as an interlude, an accidental break within a process of pure necessity. This can be seen in Frank Herbert's intelligent and ambiguous novel *Hellstrom's Hive* (1973) and even more clearly perhaps in T.J. Bass's *Half Past Human* (1971). Man the social animal is described there as forced, in order to survive, to adopt—very soon according to Herbert, not much later according to Bass—a way of life modelled on the social insects and characterized by extra-individual, genetic and biochemical (pheromones) determinations of behaviour which ensure his optimal adaptation to a new environment. History, i.e., the appearance of non-determination, is a luxury that a species can sometimes offer itself by escaping necessity, but never for very long. Very characteristically, the price for this return to nature is giving up all forms of culture (art, literature, music, law, etc.) and at the same time the "I" of the individual through which culture expresses itself, as if precisely culture (all culture) and the "I" were not natural, but had been added to human behaviour by an external, metaphysical entity (like the one in *2001* by Clarke and Kubrick). This evolution—going through the phases of extraction from nature, brief human interlude, return to nature—seems to me to constitute a very clear metaphor of the manner in which the social group of SF tragically perceives its destiny: it says in effect, "beyond this group of ours, it should be clear that there is place only for animals and robots, i.e., things." And Frank Herbert's evident sympathy for his human termites is not enough to neutralize such a break.

In a way, this return to a reductive nature is the clearest expression of ecological anxiety. Man becomes an ant because, demographically, he has succeeded too well. But, to my mind, the often vigorous expression of this ecological anxiety does not stem only from a material reality and a more or less romantic tradition. It is also a result of the absence of any utopia, any social project—an absence which reactivates in the subconscious of some people an old frustration arising from a general feeling that the human desire for collective unity cannot be satisfied. Socialism has long been nourished by this desire which, however, for the social group of SF does not appear realistic any more, since the historical experience of socialism seems disappointing and objective conditions for the appearance of a more advanced socialist society do not at all seem to obtain in the western world. Therefore, the desire for collective unity or fusion, frustrated on the social level, is displaced and takes the form of a desire for fusion on the biological level.

within Mother Earth, for a return to nature. However, this ecological transmutation of the desire for unity is in turn strongly impregnated by the tensions and contradictions in our society. The deeply ambiguous character of the expression of this desire should not, then, surprise either the psychologist or the sociologist.

NOTES

1. This article is an edited version of the first part of a two-part work, the second part of which deals with the SF of U.K. Le Guin. The editing, which became necessary because of the length and complexity of the rich original, was done by Marc Angenot and myself, and it retains about ¾ of the original text, with, hopefully, all its main points. SFS will, subject to space limitations and translation problems, try to bring a version of the second part of Mr. Klein's work in one of our later issues—DS.

2. For Lucien Goldmann's theory of a sociology of literary creativity, see in English his *The Hidden God* (New York, 1964) and *The Human Sciences and Philosophy* (London, 1970) in which he analyzes artistic creativity as a correlate of social consciousness.

3. All the participants in a dominant culture do not necessarily belong to a dominant group. It is enough that these participants have so interiorized and accepted the values which support the domination in question that they only have the choice between conveying and trying to destroy those values, without the means to create new ones. This is why only the social and cultural peripheries are potentially capable to produce different, original values, values of the future.

4. The cleavages which took place on certain occasions, such as the Vietnam War, do not seem sufficient to change this impression. To begin with, it is striking, even taking into account the Puritan tradition, that the split was expressed in moral terms rather than political ones. Furthermore, historical experience shows that far-away wars are not, except on the extreme fringes, really perceived as political stakes, and in particular that the right-left dichotomy is of limited relevance to the positions such wars bring forth.

5. According to the French critic Stephen Spriel (in *Cahiers du Sud* No. 317, 1953, p 23), this novel was hailed by the leftist weekly *The Industrial Worker* which concluded—scandalizing some SF fans—that "SF and the revolutionary movement of the working class have something in common" and called for a Workers' SF Club "with a proletarian orientation."

6. The Heinlein of *Beyond This Horizon* seemed rather tempted by a version of planification and seduced by the New Deal—i.e., he was then the equivalent of the contesting young radicals of this last decade. And whatever ambiguities there certainly are in *A Stranger in a Strange Land*, it cannot be denied that Heinlein has in it transmitted some revendications current among American youth which went much beyond what the "silent majority" was ready to accept.

7. This indication is, of course, to be taken as referring exclusively to a certain *forme d'esprit*, and not as referring to any racial or similar characteristics.

8. This liquidation is the principal subject of Lovecraft's opus, as I tried to show in "Entre le Fantastique et la Science-Fiction, Lovecraft," *Cahiers de l'Herne* No. 12 (1969).

9. In "L'Avenir d'une crise," *Analyse financière* 4e trimestre (1974).

10. This repetition is really what a fiction editor is up against when he—as has been my experience—reads and refuses manuscript after manuscript. In principle, he keeps only the original and aesthetically valid solutions. Let us confess that there are some exceptions.

Charles Elkins

An Approach to the Social Functions of American SF

(from **SFS** *4: 228–232, November 1977)*

My basic methodological approach is that, in contrast to a purely aesthetic approach, a sociological perspective studies SF as it relates to social order, to the forms of man's changing social relationships. By *social order*, I mean the structuring of social relationships through the *communication of hierarchy*, that is, the communication of roles which delineates people into classes, ranks, and status groups as superiors, inferiors and equals. Hierarchical communication is best thought of as persuasion expressed in dramatic forms whose "proper" enactment creates and sustains present social arrangements or changes them by "fixing" symbolic meanings. Social order is a social drama in which actors struggle to sustain, destroy, or change the principles on which the hierarchy rests. Social order, in continuity or change, results from a resolution of the dramatic conflict involved in the acceptance, doubt, or rejection of the principles that are believed to guarantee order.

The need for order arises out of the nature of human action. Action is always problematic to some degree because we are mysteries to one another, and we are moving into a future in which old forms of social action may be useless. This need for order has one of its dimensions in the problematic circumstances of the social group and class within which the writer is located, and each writer is obligated to create the "terms for order" for his particular group, even if this entails a revolution against the social relationships his group confronts. As part of the petty bourgeoisie, the SF writer has two major social tasks. For the major audience within his class and for the large number of SF readers outside this class (e.g. those SF readers in the working class and the few readers in the ruling elite), the writer produces works whose consumption validates the bourgeois social order and the economic system which produces it. By linking the ruling symbols of bourgeois culture (money, individual autonomy, competition, individual merit, etc.) with other powerful symbols, symbols evoking awe, mystery, glamour, and elegance, the writer creates literature which legitimates existing social arrangements and inspires those excluded to adopt its world view. At the same time, the writer must articulate the nature of and find resolutions for the role-conflicts plaguing those who identify with or who would embrace his audience's ideology. It is the world view of the *technologically-minded petty bourgeoisie and the professional sector of the bourgeoisie*. The writer "transcends" these conflicts through symbolic appeals embodying those ultimate values upon which this social order rests. For example, while ruthless competition is built into the existing order, the mystifications of money, and the power and status it can bestow, can inspire readers to overcome or endure the unintended "obstacles" resulting from unhampered competition.

However, the long term prospects for neutralizing role conflicts inherent in this social order and insuring the survival of this class are dim indeed. Observably, this group is increasingly unable to cope with a present full of contradictions and a future promising to be radically different from the nineteenth-century, industrial society out of which bourgeois man arose. This emerging future demands fundamental changes in the social order and, hence, of the roles which constitute that order.

I make the assumption that the specific *social* function of literature involves mystifying existing or alternative hierarchical structures, demystifying them, and offering passage from one role to another. Although aesthetic questions are intimately involved in the question of order, the primary question for the sociologist of SF should be: how is social order communicated in SF and how does this symbolic act relate to the structure and function of social action? Who are the heroes, villains and fools of the social order, and *in the name of what principles* do they act? We should seek the terms, the symbolic identifications of the various contending voices and contradictions, in order to understand and evaluate what the writer is saying about the *present* social order. We can explore how artistic communication affects society and vice versa. We need to develop a functional perspective, i.e. *how* literature is used by various classes, institutions, groups, etc., to get into power, stay in power, increase their power and destroy or weaken the power of others—in short, how society uses literature to organize experience. However, we must show how this is done *in the work of art itself*; we must show how the *function* of the work relates to its form.

To repeat my thesis: The SF writer's task is to describe the nature of and find resolutions to the role conflicts which vex his social group by creating images of the past and future which he and his readers use to organize action in the present. The writer's terms for ordering this conflict may either reinforce, question or reject the principles upon which this group's existence depends. Traditionally, the SF writer has approached his task by offering his readers radical dislocations in time and space so as to create stages for action, to allow for experimentation with roles supposedly required for his individual and his group's survival. As representatives of various principles of social order, characters act on these new stages; by comparision with *present* reality, this supports, questions, or rejects the principles upon which the existing order is based. The significant question is: will the roles sanctified by the past or legitimated by present "conditions" be appropriate for confronting the novelty of an emerging future?

To answer part of that question, one might examine the kind of hero who personifies the professional, technologically-oriented bourgeois. For heuristic purposes. one can construct an ideal type. He is a young male, intelligent, sometimes brilliant, poised and courageous. His bravery combines self-control, and an acceptance of "reality." He is a super-technician, with a good deal of basic Yankee "knowhow" and a gut feeling for machines. Absorbed in his responsibilities, he views work as one of the most important aspects of experience, for himself and others. He is rational and empirical; knowledge is important but instrumental. His basic motivation is *power*, power sometimes gained by accumulating wealth but often by acquiring knowledge. He views ideas, physical nature and other men as instruments of that power. Accepting the reality of struggle and competition, he dominates relationships; life is a conflict with other men, with nature, and often with himself. He is often beset by contradictory impulses; he is a combination of a nineteenth-century industrial entrepreneurial, inner-directed, bourgeois Philistine and a twentieth-century, post-industrial, apolitical technocrat.

To construct ideal types is to simplify, but by stressing one or two of any of these character traits, one could accurately identify many science fiction heroes, beginning with Verne's Barbicane and Wells' Bedford to Heinlein's and Asimov's heroes.

While the fortunes of this class were rising, SF depicted futures, alternative worlds, and roles reinforcing the principles upon which this group's existence rests. (This theme has been admirably discussed in Gérard Klein's, "Discontent in American Science Fiction," in the March, 1977 issue of *SFS*.) The meaning of the roles, and hence the social order whose enactment they create were seldom questioned. The problem was not *why* but *how* to play the role. The writer's "terms for order" were consistent with this group's world view. Historically, SF has told its readers that survival involves coping in such a way as to maintain the attitudes necessary for success within existing social arrangements. By naming new situations and their attendant roles in such a way as to charge objects and actions with sentiments needed to sustain the existing order, SF functioned like the pep talk or the exhortation. As the writer praises and curses, he inspires his readers with the attitudes necessary for successful role playing. Not surprisingly, then, the nineteenth-century SF hero is a rugged, pragmatic, bourgeois individualist, perhaps epitomized best as Richard Burton, the Victorian explorer-imperialist and hero of Philip José Farmer's *To Your Scattered Bodies Go*.

That most SF heroes personify this aspect of the bourgeois explains why one finds many of them "liberating" static, isolated, feudal societies and opening them up to the rest of the Galactic empire. As Marx pointed out, the overthrowing of feudal society was the historical mission of the bourgeois. The spaceship of the famous Star Trek crew, *The Enterprise*, is appropriately named. This kind of SF offers the reader ways to destroy beliefs detrimental to the bourgeois and to replace dysfunctional values with symbols charged with new values. Through identification with these heroes, the audience struggles to defeat those that threaten their order, those who represent other values, or those, among the writer's and readers' own group, whose excesses threaten the existing order.

By the same token, one should realize that this verbal magic was used because writers and readers were unable to obtain what they wanted by other methods. We cannot determine the future; all we really know is that it will be different from the present or past. And while many SF writers see the future social order—despite the incredible leaps in technological innovation and changes in the means of production—as a familiar extrapolation of existing social structures, there are indications that the future will be vastly different from the present and will demand the abolition of bourgeois man, just as the ice age demanded the abolition of the dinosaur. As Victor Ferkiss, in his *Technological Man* (U.S., 1969), puts it:

> Bourgeois man is still in the saddle. Or to put it more accurately, things are in the saddle, since bourgeois man is increasingly unable to cope with his problems. At the same time, an existential revolution is under way that may destroy the identity of the human race, make society unmanageable and render the planet literally uninhabitable. Bourgeois man is incapable of coping with this revolution. [p. 245]

Some SF writers seem increasingly aware of this. The crisis in practically every phase of social life, coupled with the rather abrupt loss of power and privilege of the professional-technocratic elite, has precipitated a crisis in confidence, in the identity and future existence of this class and in the future itself. I have pointed to Gérard Klein's article examining the pessimistic character of recent SF; I would only add that this loss of confidence reveals itself in the SF writer's attempts to do more by way of exploring the meaning of traditionally acceptable roles, the *why* as well as the how of role enactment.

Once one begins to examine the relationship between means and ends in social action or the meaning of a particular role, then the whole social order comes under scrutiny. Here—especially since the 1960's—SF ceases functioning exclusively as verbal magic; instead, it explores the possibilities of action and what it means to act in a specific role. The main character—often now an anti-hero—suffers the consequences of trying to resolve serious role conflicts, or he learns to be a neutral observer, a non-partisan, a cultural anthropologist. Like the earlier heroes, he (and recently, she) is independent, apolitical or liberal, intelligent, brave, dedicated to work, a super-technician, a rationalist/phenomenologist/empiricist, but unlike his forerunners, he is less obsessed with power and domination of the economic sort and less apt to see the world in individualistically competitive terms. This new hero sees man more within nature than apart from it. Often he attempts to define man and his place in the universe in monistic, holistic terms. He is more receptive to novelty and less likely to Westernize the future universe. Indeed, from Stapledon's *Star Maker*, through A.E. van Vogt's *Slan* to Ursula Le Guin's *The Left Hand of Darkness*, the main character teaches us the folly of ethnocentrism.

At their worst, these novelists parallel the attitude of bourgeois scientists, refusing to go beyond description and concentrating on uninterpreted phenomena. Usually, this stance produces a crude naturalism, with its counterpart, sensationalism, or it chronicles one impossibility upon another, one fantastic world, one grotesque life form, or one social absurdity after another. The only possible reader response is, "Gee, whiz," or "Isn't that interesting!" From this point of view, pretty much anything goes, as long as it does not seem to harm anyone. Freedom is usually defined in the negative, i,e. freedom *from* something (e.g. of the individual from society). The socially acceptable role celebrated in these novels is a sort of libertarian *laissez-faire*, a "live and let live" mentality. It is this stance that is, as Herbert Marcuse argues in his *A Critique of Pure Tolerance* (U.S., 1968), "an ideology of tolerance which in reality favors and fortifies the conservation of the status quo of inequality and discrimination" (pp. 122-23).

Paradoxically, this bourgeois liberal view runs counter to the new heroes' movements to embrace an inclusive, integrated, holistic philosophy. In addition, this self-contradictory perspective virtually insures perpetual conflict. This social atomism renders the bourgeois increasingly unable to cope with the effects of technological change (leaving it up to piecemeal planners, the anarchy of the market place, and ad-hoc crisis management) and of the future that technology is bringing into existence. Today, many SF writers communicate their uneasiness with these contradictions by envisioning futures increasingly more ominous. If role conflicts cannot be resolved in terms which will keep the existing social order intact—and it seems clear that they cannot—then we are either given novels where solutions are left problematic—e.g. in Brunner's *Stand on Zanzibar*—or we are presented with the alternative between the end of man and some "inhuman" solution. As for the first, many writers have come to see the future in cataclysmic terms, not an original vision to be sure, but one that has taken on new dimensions: Man, not God, is responsible for the holocaust. However, the other alternative is just as disturbing because it takes the solutions to these conflicts out of man's hands entirely. Unable to assent to superficial solutions which depend upon the continuance of the present social order but unwilling to confirm the dire prophecies of their colleagues, more and more writers are taking refuge in quasi-mystical solutions which eliminate man. Conflicts terminate through the intervention of god-like creatures or powers, or man himself is transformed into something approaching a god-like status. Again, this is not new. One can trace a variation on this theme as far back as Wells' *War of the Worlds*; however, the popularity of works such as Clarke's *Childhood's End* and *2001* and Heinlein's *Stranger in a Strange Land* suggest a present fascination with this solution. Their disturbing features should not be overlooked; they suggest that man cannot solve the problems confronting him. It is an admission of failure by a group which feels impotent to institute the necessary changes needed to perpetuate itself.

Even in the best of these novels, with their satire of existing social order, there are few attempts to go beyond mere criticism and to create the necessary metaphors which will allow one to move from passive criticism of the status quo to active roles necessary for transforming the social order and producing genuine social change. The major omissions, the silences of the text, are roles which allow for *collective action* in social change. And without this collective action, arrived at through democratic means, the individual is almost always defeated (unless, of course, he is a superman or has some super technology at his disposal). In addition, his downfall serves to reinforce the notion of an eternal, invincible bourgeois order.

At the same time, if our initial analysis is correct, it is clear that the presently constituted social order is increasingly unable to resolve the conflicts it engenders. While collective action is crucial for changing existing institutions, it is also evident that technological change has its own imperatives and strains existing social relations. For example, the continual radical changes in the means of production require continual role adjustments. However, most SF fails to relate roles to changes in technology and its socio-economic and political consequences, and to the irreversibility of man's creation of new knowledge.

This failure to relate role changes to changes in technology violates aesthetic as well as logical criteria. As critics are forever saying, each part of a work of art must be consistent with the whole. If one changes the scene, the space-time matrix, and creates a genuine alternate world, then one *cannot* be artistically successful by leaving the characters and their relationships unchanged. One's sense of organic unity requires that societies with radically different technologies have radically different social orders with fundamentally different roles. One can argue that man's basic drives will remain unchanged, that we will still have to eat, procreate and express our aggression and creativity; but even if we agree with this assumption, it still remains that those basic drives must be expressed in some *specific forms*, in specific roles determined by the social order within which we are located. Our eating habits, our ways of expressing sexual drives, our modes of aggression and our styles of creation are not immutable. Further, an ability to create a social order consistent with the technological imperatives is central to the SF writer's imaginative vision. A failure here parallels a failure in political imagination; indeed, the two are inseparable. That is the meaning of harmony.

Albert I. Berger

Science-Fiction Fans in Socio-Economic Perspective: Factors in the Social Consciousness of a Genre

(from **SFS** *4: 232–246, November 1977)*

One of the conveniences of studying science fiction is that since its infancy in the 1930s it has had a uniquely self-conscious group of fans organized into a network of clubs, amateur publications, and periodic conventions. Studying that network provides the opportunity to break out of the classic limitations of literary studies which consider what a writer has to say and the fashion in which it is said without considering the audience to which it intends to speak. Although entirely the work of biased fans working with self-selected samples, the earliest studies of the science-fiction audience originated within this network.[1]

Since 1948, several different studies have been made of the demographic characteristics of science-fiction readers, most by the editors of the commercial science-fiction magazines seeking to determine the characteristics of their own readerships. The results of these, along with data collected at two recent science-fiction conventions, have been admirably collected and summarized by Charles Waugh, Carol-Lynn Waugh, and Edwin F. Libby of the University of Maine at Augusta, whose work this paper used throughout for purposes of comparison.[2] This study, conducted at the 31st World Science Fiction Convention in Toronto, September, 1973, is offered against the historical perspective of these earlier studies. As the Waughs and Libby discovered, there are difficulties in applying the findings of this survey to the entire science-fiction audience, since it is impossible to know exactly in what ways, if any, people at a convention differ from those who did not attend. Certainly science-fiction fans themselves are divided into groups, with some, notably those primarily interested in film and television SF, and members of the cult following of the series *Star Trek*, under-represented at this convention (see tables 20 and 21 below). However, the numbers of people responding to the questionnaire, and the diversity of their involvement in science fiction beyond attendance at the convention, suggests that the picture of fans is *relatively* reliable for *readers* of science fiction as a whole and, if qualified for the greater affluence of those who could afford to travel to Toronto, is at least as reliable as such commonly accepted-with-qualifications measurements as the Gallup polls.[3]

A total of 3,000 questionnaires were distributed to various locations in the convention area of the Royal York Hotel. This did result in a self-selected sample of an already self-selected population, but the total number of responses received, 282 or 8% of a total estimated convention attendance of 3,400, was substantial, despite the hostile remarks about "Ph.D.s seeking to exploit science fiction" made by one speaker at the convention banquet. Anonymous answers to questions about reading habits and about fan activity other than convention attendance indicate that the respondents were active, long-time readers with a substantial range of other activity related to their reading. Of course, it should be assumed, as is supported by the data, that attendees at a convention are among the most active and committed fans. However, as can be seen in table 5, these people are not notably isolated from non-fans in their everyday social lives.

Table 1. *Fan Acitivity Other Than Convention Attendance*

A. club membership	124	43.97%
B. fanzine subscription	114	40.42
C. fanzine writing	68	24.11
D. fanzine artwork	21	7.45
E. magazine collection	102	36.17
F. artwork collection	47	16.67
G. letters to prozines	12	4.26
unmarked or "none"	86	30.50
total	574	203.55%*

*N=282, multiple responses included

Table 2. *Reading "Dosage" Per Month*

A. 3 books, magazines or screenplays per month	62	21.99%
B. 5	46	11.35
C. 7	38	13.48
D. 9	19	6.74
E. more than 9	111	39.36
total	282	99.99%

Table 3. *Age When Science Fiction Reading Began*

A. 9-15 years old	219	77.66%
B. 16-21	32	11.35
C. 22-30	9	3.19
D. 30-40	2	.71
E. over 40	3	1.06
under 9	14	4.96*
unmarked	3	1.06
total	282	99.99%

*added by respondents

Table 4. *Duration of Interest in Science Fiction*

A. less than 2 years	5	1.77%
B. 2-5 years	20	7.09
C. 5-8 years	28	9.93
D. 8-15 years	107	37.94
E. more than 15 years	119	42.20
unmarked	3	1.06
total	282	99.99%

Table 5. *Involvement of Friends with Science Fiction*

A. fewer than 20% of friends read science fiction	106	37.59%
B. 20-50%	83	29.43
C. 50-80%	59	20.92
D. nearly all friends	30	10.64
unmarked	4	1.42
total	282	100.00%

Traditionally, science fiction has been a literature written by males for male readers. As shown by the Maine researchers, one magazine, *Astounding/Analog*, reported a female readership of only 6.7% in 1949 and 11.9% in 1958. Surveys taken for the British magazines *Nebula* and *New Worlds* during the fifties and early sixties report female readership of between 5% and 15%. This orientation began to change during the sixties. *The Magazine of Fantasy and Science Fiction* (F&SF), normally considered the least technologically oriented of the three major American science-fiction magazines, reported a female readership of 29% at that time, a figure paralleled in 1974 by *Analog*, the most technologically oriented magazine, with a female readership of 25%. The ratio of women to men was highest in Toronto, as seen below in table 6, although it remains far from the proportion in the general population, hereafter indicated by the bracketed figures in all tables.

Table 6. *Sex*

Survey and Date	*Male*	*Female*
Tucker Fan Survey—1948	89.00%	11.00%
Astounding—1949	93.30	6.70
Nebula—1954 (British)	86.00	14.00
New Worlds—1955 (British)	95.00	5.00
New Worlds—1958 (British)	90.00	10.00
Astounding—1958	85-95.00	15-5.00
New Worlds—1963 (British)	92.00	8.00
F&FS—mid-sixties	71.00	29.00
Analog—1974	75.00	25.00
Locus Survey—1974	82.00	18.00
Waugh Studies—1975 (combined)	73.00	27.00
Berger—Toronto—1973	64.54	34.75

Table a. *Sex*

A. Male	182	64.54%	(48.72%)[4]
B. Female	98	34.75	(51.28)
unmarked	2	.71	
total	282	100.00%	

The age data collected at the Toronto convention seem to conform to long-time *Astounding/Analog* editor John W. Campbell's assertion that his readers were young, but not adolescent. However, as can be seen in table 7, the adolescent component of the population at Toronto is substantially lower than both the average proportion derived from the studies collected by the Maine researchers and the proportions in each magazine study except *Astounding* itself and the British *New Worlds* 1955 survey. Although the studies analyzed by Waugh, which showed 25% of their sample under 19, were made at conventions, it seems that travel to a convention would be more difficult for the youngest fans and they would therefore be under-represented in a survey taken at one. While this smaller proportion of adolescents seems to be balanced by a larger proportion of young adults between 18 and 25, it is apparent from the collected readership surveys that the relative size of the adolescent science-fiction magazine audience has been growing since 1954. Nevertheless, the magazine, as well as the convention, audience is dominated by young adults between 18 and 35 out of all proportion to that age group's representation not only in the American population at large but also in gatherings such as rock-music concerts with their younger audience.

Table 7. *Age*

1. *Nebula*—1954	0-19 ...(11.2%)	20-24... (21.0)	25-29 ...(27.4)
	30-34 ... (21.8)	35-39.... (7.3)	40-44 ....(6.4)
	45-49 .... (6.4)	50+ ..... (3.2)	
2. *New Worlds*—1955	0-19 ....(5.0%)	20-24... (17.0)	25-30 ...(31.0)
	31-40 ... (30.0)	41-50... (12.0)	50+......(5.0)
3. *New Worlds*—1958	0-19 ...(18.0%)	20-24... (21.0)	25-30 ...(21.0)
	31-40 ... (22.0)	41-50... (12.0)	50+......(6.0)
4. *Astounding*—1958	13-17 ...(6.9%)	18-20.... (7.0)	21-25 ...(16.8)
	26-30 ... (20.1)	31-35... (19.2)	36-40 ...(12.7)
	41-45 .... (7.2)	46-50.... (3.6)	50+......(6.5)
5. *New Worlds*—1963	0-19 ...(31.0%)	20-24... (27.0)	25-30 ...(14.0)
	31-40 ... (14.0)	41-50.... (8.0)	50+......(6.0)
6. *F&SF*—mid '60s	0-18 ...(23.0%)	18-30... (30.0)	30-45 ...(31.0)
	45-60 ... (13.0)	60+ ..... (3.0)	
7. *Galaxy*—1971	0-17 .. (16-17% approx.)		18-39 ..(66.0+)
	40+ .. (16-17% approx.)		
8. Waugh Studies	10-14 ...(5.0%)	15-19... (20.0)	20-24 ...(31.0)
(1975)	25-29 ... (22.0)	30-34.... (9.0)	35-39 ....(1.0)
	40-44 .... (2.0)	45-49.... (1.0)	

Berger-Toronto

Age	*Number*	*per cent*	*National*
A. 13-17	22	7.70%	(7.8%)
B. 18-25	103	36.39	(11.6)
C. 25-35	116	40.98	(12.3)
D. 35-55	36	12.72	(22.8)
E. 55-up	5	1.77	(19.0)
total	282	99.56	

In the case of science fiction, marital status can be a far more important indicator than it usually is in a survey of this kind. Uninformed critics of the genre remain prone to think in terms of a rejected, isolated, bespectacled male adolescent finding solace in dreams sparked by stories of distant planets and marvelous inventions, an image strengthened by the reminiscences of many science-fiction writers themselves. The extraordinarily high concentration of males in the science-fiction audience before the sixties lent additional credence to this impression, as does the first reading of table 8, with its concentration of single people. The American population over 18 is a married one; 74.8% of men and 68.5% of women are married, quite the reverse of these convention statistics. However, among Americans born between the years of 1945 and 1954, i.e. among people who were between 18 and 28 at the time of the Toronto convention, 67.2% of the men and 40.9% of the women were single, a figure from which the convention does not differ. Thus, it is easier to explain the concentration of single people at a science-fiction convention as the result of a youthful membership rather than personal isolation or social rejection. The data also reveal the persistence of traditional family patterns, indicated by the lack of response in the "Coupled without formal marriage" or added "Other" categories, and by the relatively normal ratio between the marriages and divorces:

Table 8. *Marital Status*

A. Single	165	58.51%
B. Married	82	29.08
C. Divorced	13	4.61
D. Widowed		0.00
E. Coupled without formal marriage	19	6.73
"Other"	1	35
unmarked	2	71
total	282	99.98%

Critics of popular culture hostile to science fiction have often extended their negative comments on the literary quality of the genre to the intelligence and education of those who read it. Without addressing the intrinsic literary questions here, it is notable that surveys have traditionally reported SF readers as having unusually high attainments in formal education. Although the different surveys have used different categories, which makes comparison difficult, and the possession of school degrees can reflect different levels of real achievement in Britain and America, the Toronto data confirm this tradition of highly educated readers. The surveys made in the fifties and sixties in the British magazines *Nebula* and *New Worlds* indicated that roughly 25% of British readers had either been to technical schools, colleges or universities. Surveys of *Astounding/Analog* taken in 1949, 1958 and 1974, as well as *F&SF*'s mid-sixties poll, showed a higher level, upwards of 50%. Most of that difference can probably be explained by the higher level of college enrollment in the United States. In Toronto, with its heavily American membership, 52.8% of the convention-goers had completed a four-year college degree and 24.5% had attended graduate school, compared to the figures for the general American population over 25, of whom only 22.9% had been to college in 1973, and of whom only 12.0% had completed four years. An astonishing number of the convention-goers, 86.5%, had attended at least some college.

Table 9. *Education (Highest Attainment)*

A. High School Diploma	19	6.74%	(35.2%)
B. some College	81	28.72	(10.9)
C. 2 year College Degree	14	4.96	
D. 4 year College Degree	80	28.37	(12.0)
E. graduate school	69	24.47	
in High School	7	2.48	
in Elementary School	1	.35	
drop out	1	.35	
unmarked	10	3.55	
total	282	99.99%	

It also should be borne in mind that even in the age of mass education such a concentration of intellectual wealth is usually indicative of material wealth as well. The Maine study found that only *Astounding/Analog*'s readers' average income rose from $4,800/year to $18,500/year (family income). Not only were both figures substantially higher than figures for the American population at large, but while the median income of the nation was rising 228%, the median income of the magazine's readers was rising 385%, indicating a substantial amount of upward mobility.

The British fans, on the other hand, reported average earnings which rose from £500-750/year in 1958 to £750-1,000/year in 1963, which roughly corresponds to the rise in British average yearly earnings from £660 to £863 over the same period of time. Even considering that those people affluent enough to travel to a convention were better off than the average reader might be, Tables 10 and 11 show that at least an identifiable and major portion of adult science-fiction readers make a far better living than the average white individual in the United States; a fact which, as the Waugh-Libby study points out, is not unusual for a population dominated by college graduates.

Table 10. *Comparison of Median Income: Astounding/Analog Readers v. U.S. Average*

Year	*ASF Readers*	*U.S. Population*[5]	*% difference*
1949	$ 4,800/year	$2,480/year	+ 93.55%
1974	18,500/year	5,657/year	+327.03%
% increase	384.41%	228.10%	

Table 11. *Income*

A. under $3,000 per year	88	31.21%	(44.60%)
B. 3,001-7,000	52	18.44	(31.00)
C. 7,001-12,000	69	24.47	
D. 12,001-20,000	53	18.79	(24.30)
E. over $20,000 per year	9	3.19	
unmarked	11	3.90	
total	282	100.00%	

Educational achievement and income were only part of the data which have traditionally interested pollsters. Both the fan polls and Campbell's surveys for *Astounding/Analog* were used to buttress assertions that science-fiction readers were the technologically trained elite they claimed to be. Campbell in particular gathered his detailed data on educational majors and occupations in order to prove that his readers were technically minded enough to be both the scientists he insisted they were and a good market for the advertisers of scientifically-oriented merchandise whom he consistently tried to attract to the pages of his magazine. Of all the demographic surveys summarized in the Waugh-Libby paper, only Campbell's 1958 survey dealt with educational majors. Readers of the magazine were asked to fill in a blank with both their major and occupational title, which Campbell then grouped under what seemed to him to be appropriate headings. At the Toronto convention the 282 respondents checked their majors off a prepared list, resulting in a total of 326 replies listed in the notes.[7]

Comparing the educational responses of Campbell's survey with the results of the Toronto convention gives evidence of a trend away from purely scientific studies and at least the surface indication of greater breadth due to multiple majors. In 1958, 66.1% of *Astounding* readers had majored in either the physical or biological sciences. By 1973, only 48.6% of the Toronto convention-goers had done so. Between 1958 and 1973, the social sciences, including education, library science and communications, had grown from 19.8% to 30.5%, and in the fifteen years separating the two surveys, studies in the liberal arts, including law and journalism, had grown from 12.8% to 24.5%. Within those broad categories, certain specific groups stand out. The largest single educational major represented at Toronto was Mathematics, 8.5%, but it was closely followed by English, 8.2%. There were more historians present, 6.7%, than physicists, 5.3%. There were only 10 students of electronics in the sample. 3.6%. And even if the differences between the broad membership of the convention and the engineering orientation of *Astounding*'s readers are considered, the drop in engineering studies from 29.5% in 1958 to 6.7% in 1973 is most striking.

Table 12. *Educational Major (Grouped)*

A. Physical/Biological Science	137	48.58%
B. Social Science	86	30.49
C. Liberal Arts	69	24.47
D. Business	15	5.32
E. College Preparatory (High School Students)	6	2.13
F. Others	12	4.26
total	325	115.25%*

*Multiple Responses, N=282

One of the science-fiction community's most consistent themes has been its putative relationship to science and technology in the real world. All of the surveys collected by Libby and the Waughs show a high percentage of the science-fiction magazine readership employed in either fields related to science and technology or in white-collar occupations, if they are not still in school. Successive polls of the British *New Worlds* in 1954, 1958 and 1963 showed employment in science or technology-related fields including medicine, rising from 13% to 29%. *Astounding/Analog* showed a different pattern, however. The most sympathetic reading of the 1949 data shows that 42.8% of the readers were workers in some technical field, including mechanics, technicians and members of the armed forces. For 1958 the Maine study estimates the number at only 37%. By 1974, *Analog* reported that only 14.5% of its readers were working in the sciences, nearly identical to the 14.4% of scientific workers reported by F&SF, the least technologically oriented American science-fiction magazine, and actually less than the 20.6% of the Toronto conventioneers who worked in technology or science. *New World*'s three polls showed its white-collar readership remaining steady between 16 and 17% through the fifties and sixties. *Astounding*'s went from 26.2% in 1949 to 40.4% in 1958, higher than either the 33.2% reported by F&SF in the mid-sixties or the 34.4% at the Toronto convention in 1973. The convention's student population, both high school and college, of 23.8% compares to the 23% reported by *New Worlds* and the 21.5% reported by F&SF in the mid-sixties. Actually, the complete table of occupations shows, not a concentration in the sciences or technology, but a wide distribution of occupations. One occupation which is particularly low, and declining, is research. In 1949 and 1958, 7.3% and 8.4% of Campbell's readers listed research and development as their occupation. In 1973, only 5.3% of the convention members did so.[8]

Table 13. *Employment by Occupations*

Survey	*S&T*	*White Collar*	*Prof*
Astounding—1949	28.9%	23.2%	5.2%
New Worlds—1955	13.0	17.0	——
New Worlds—1958	27.0	16.0	——
Astounding—1958	37.0 (est)	——	——
New Worlds—1963	29.0	16.0	——
Fantasy & Science Fiction—60's	14.4	33.2	12.7
Berger-Toronto—1973	20.56	35.46	——

"Science and Technology" includes Armed Forces, Basic Research in Biological, Chemical and Physical Sciences, Computer Programming, Computer Technology, Engineering, Engineering Management, Medicine (except in the 1949 Astounding and F&SF mid 60's poll),

Medical Technology, Nursing, Technological Research & Development, Biochemical production, Chemical Quality Control, Pharmaceuticals, Planetarium lecturing, supervising a textile testing laboratory and Veterinary Medicine. "White Collar" contains various business occupations, teaching, law (except in the 1949 ASF and 60's F&SF polls), Clerical and secretarial occupations and civil service. See footnote 8, where S, W, indicate which category contained specific occupations.

In addition to discovering what occupations science-fiction readers engaged in, this survey sought to place them on occupational levels, and to compare that level to the population as a whole. I have also compared the results to a poll of the British magazine *Nebula* taken in 1954.

Table 14. *Nature of Job*

	1954	*1973*		
A. Professional	31.2%	105	37.23%	(24.21%)[9]
B. Technical	20.6	30	10.64	
C. Skilled Worker	——	13	4.61	(13.27)
D. Semi-Skilled	17.5	10	3.55	(16.99)
E. Unskilled	——	7	2.48	(18.41)
F. Clerical	12.5	23	8.16	(17.25)
G. Student	5.0	74	26.24	(10.40)
H. Unemployed	——	16	6.57	
unmarked		4	1.42	
total	86.8%	282	100.00%	

One of the caveats the University of Maine researchers attached to their discussion of the occupational data was that the desire of fans to present their occupations in the most favorable light possible would bias the scale towards the upper end. "Hence," they wrote, "the janitor may have become a sanitation engineer." While an obvious warning to social scientists, this caveat begs the important question of the consciousness of the fan (or any subject). Regardless of who a person actually is, with whom does he identify? The janitor who calls himself a sanitation engineer is the butt of a good many jokes which obscure the fact that a person holding such a low-paying service job, generally regarded as menial, is identifying himself and his interests with those of much wealthier, more privileged and powerful members of society, and hoping that others will accept that identification and accord him the higher status to which he aspires. This question of consciousness is particularly acute when dealing with the audience for a literature like science fiction, with its pretensions towards social criticism. Just what critique of society will people make, or accept, in their entertainment?

In reporting the results of his 1958 readership survey in *Astounding*, Campbell stated that about half of his readers were "decision-influencing executives in major manufacturing industries."[10] He didn't print any evidence to support that assertion, and he was boosting his readers' egos and his magazine's attractiveness to advertisers, so the accuracy of the remark is at least suspect. But other evidence testifies to science-fiction fans' self-identification with the upper echelons of business activity. While table 14 lists the levels at which the fans place their own jobs, tables 15 and 16 attempt to place them within workplace hierarchies by indicating their own perceptions of their independence and power over others while at work. While direct power over others in supervisory roles can be measured, and by these measures fans seem to have relatively little, it should be noted that independence, like professionalism, is a highly subjective quality. Fans *apparently* feel less constrained by the power of others while on the job, but there is no way of determining the accuracy of that self-perception.

Table 15. *Independence*

A. I am very independent, I am in charge	52	18.44%
B. Within limits of Company policy, I can run my "shop" as I see fit. I am consulted regularly when decisions are to be made.	84	29.79
C. I run my shop in accordance with orders. I am not consulted regularly on policy matters	33	11.70
D. Although I may occasionally get independent projects, I generally work on orders.	57	20.21
E. I always work on orders	19	6.74
unmarked	37	13.12
total	282	100.00%

Table 16. *Number of People Supervised*

A. 0	185	65.60%
B. 1-5	74	26.24
C. 5-10	7	2.48
D. 10-25	6	2.13
E. more than 25	10	3.55
total	282	100.00%

Illusory or not, the high degree of independence most science-fiction readers *feel* they have on their jobs might be one reason why so many of them say that they are either very happy or at least satisfied with their jobs. An analysis of the 1958 *Astounding* survey (the only one of the twelve covered by the Maine study to list educational majors) as well as of this survey, reveals a substantial disparity between educational achievement and employment in the areas of science and technology. 66.1% of *Astounding*'s readers majored in the physical or biological sciences in 1958, but only 37% were employed in such fields. In Toronto, 20.6% were so employed. None of the other Waugh-Libby data show technological employment above the level of 29% in the readership of any science-fiction magazine during the entire period since 1948. One might suspect, as this writer did, that science-fiction readers would demonstrate a sharp sense of job-related frustration which could be easily related to technological wish-fulfillment fantasies. However, that is not necessarily the case.

20.6% of the convention members work in science or technology, fewer than half the number educated in those areas. Among all the convention-goers, in all occupational fields, 23% of the sample say that there is an exact relationship between their education and their work, and 24.1% say that they are very happy with that relationship. However, as the gap between education and work widens, dissatisfaction increases at a much slower rate: a notable discrepancy, particularly in view of the low level of job satisfaction prevailing in American society in 1973. While the question is limited to the relationship between education and work, some cautious inferences that the responses represent overall job satisfaction seem safe.

Table 17. *Relationship Between Education and Work*

A. Exact	65	23.05%
B. As Close As You Can Expect	51	18.09
C. Mildly Related	32	11.35
D. Vague Relation	23	8.16
E. No Relation	62	21.99
unmarked	49	17.38
total	282	100.00%

Table 18. *Satisfaction With Relationship Between Education & Work*

A. Very Happy	68	24.11%
B. Satisfied	90	31.91
C. Resigned	33	11.70
D. Dissatisfied	20	7.09
E. Frustrated	26	9.22
unmarked	45	15.96
total	282	99.99%

The final question on the survey which dealt with socioeconomic status asked each respondent to list the kind of community in which she or he lived. While these categories do not correspond exactly to the census groupings, it is significant to note two things. First, that the science-fiction readership is much more heavily urbanized than the American population as a whole. Slightly over 42% of the science-fiction readers live in cities larger than 250,000, while only 20.7% of the general population does so. Secondly, while 29 people in the sample said that they lived in small towns, 8 of them listed their occupations as college students and 9 more listed occupations such as Basic Research in Biological Sciences, Librarian, Performing Arts and Computer Programming which might be associated with a college or university in a small town. The urban character of this group is emphasized by the large portion of the small-town population which might be imported to those small towns via educational institutions.

Table 19. *Residence*

A. Large City (250,000)	139	42.29%	(20.7%)
B. Suburbs of a Large City	61	21.63	(15.2)
C. Small City (50,000-250,000)	40	14.18	
D. Small Town	29	10.28	
E. Rural Area	10	3.55	
"migrant"	1	.35	
unmarked	2	.71	
total	282	99.99%	

The final questions asked related to reading habits, and were dealt with at the beginning of this paper to establish the relationship of the people sampled to the total science-fiction readership. However, the question on sources developed particularly interesting information. Science fiction's commercial roots were in the pulp magazines, and the continuing existence of the magazines as a paid market for short fiction is a point of pride among science-fiction writers. However, tables 20 and 21 show that the two sources of short fiction, magazines and anthologies, are in a much less important position than the novel. As market research this has its importance for writers and publishers, but it will also necessitate a change in tactics for social scientists seeking to study science fiction further. Magazine surveys seem to miss the major part of the science-fiction audience, and researchers will have to focus either on conventions (which do not include a great many readers) or market research from publishers or chain bookstores (which may not be available).

Table 20. *Sources*

A. Magazines	78	27.66%
B. Anthologies	54	19.15
C. Novels	208	73.76
D. Movies	22	7.80

E. Television	24	8.51
unmarked	3	1.06
total	389	137.94%*

*multiple responses, N=282

Table 21. *Sources (Multiple Responses Removed)*

A. Magazines	26	9.22%
B. Anthologies	23	8.16
C. Novels	139	49.29
D. Movies	4	1.42
E. Television	6	2.13
total	198	70.22%*

*N=282

A final note on reading habits is in order. Slightly over 70% of those polled as regular readers of scientific journals were either college students or in occupations which might be described as technical. The remaining percentage—nearly 30% of those who read scientific literature regularly and 8.2% of the total sample—is a high proportion to be found reading such material in today's highly specialized world. However, the date does not discriminate between those who read such "popular" journals as *Scientific American* and those who read publications intended for practicing research scientists.

Table 22. *Frequency of Reading Scientific Journals*

A. regularly	77	27.30%
B. irregularly	109	38.65
C. rarely	65	23.05
D. never	27	9.57
unmarked	4	1.42
total	282	99.99%

In conclusion, it can be said that the science-fiction community's perception of itself as better educated and more heavily involved in professional and technical employment is accurate, although not to the degree its partisans believe. While thére is little evidence to substantiate Campbell's claim that science-fiction readers as a group are important executives, there is evidence, at least in this sample with all its qualifications, to support that they are heavily concentrated at the upper end of the economic scale and in educational situations and professional levels from which those executives are apt to be drawn. With their work scattered across the face of the economy, the data show that even if fans are inflating their occupational status, they strongly share a professional consciousness bolstered by at least the impression of an almost anachronistic sense of independence and freedom from constraint on the job. While this does not establish their actual power, or even the correlation between the fans' self-image and reality, it does establish at least their identification with and aspiration to positions of high status within their society. Their education and incomes give science-fiction fans traditional social distinctions, while the independence and freedom they feel, illusory or not, are increasingly rare and desirable privileges in an age of salaries and hierarchical organizations.

The available data are self-selected and limited, both in this study and its predecessors, but they do show that SF's identifiable audience is middle-class. It is a readership endowed with an almost anachronistic affluence, education, and independence which are—in most cases—a result of the very technology that SF writers so often postulated in advance. That *anachronistic social position of SF fans* helps account for the slippery nature of social criticism in the genre, notably its inability to come to grips with modern society as it stands. At least since the development of nuclear power, when some traditional science-fictional themes became matters of contemporary concern, science-fiction stories demonstrate a mounting dissatisfaction with the course of actual scientific development.[11] In particular, writers are dissatisfied with the failure of rapid technological change to bring about a utopia based on an extension of mid-twentieth-century suburbia, and are extremely uncomfortable with the organization of research into a bureaucratic "Big Science," equivalent to "Big Business," "Big Labor," or "Big Government." In response, writers have consistently seized upon traditional science-fiction images of unlimited power and space travel to develop two themes. The first, a new frontier, is traditional, particularly in the United States, despite the acknowledged brutality of the American frontier towards the native American population, its failure to do more than postpone 19th-century social problems, and the horrors and absurdities of recent attempts to modify and expand the frontier into an overseas economic empire. The second theme, the development of new, and usually parapsychological, sciences, varies from the treatment of a new form of "ultimate weapon" to a quasi-mysticism typified by Frank Herbert's *Dune* trilogy, Arthur C. Clarke's *2001: A Space Odyssey*, Robert Silverberg's *Book of Skulls* and David Gerrold's *When Harlie Was One*. Stories containing neither of these themes tend to be tales of chaos and despair, such as John Brunner's *Stand on Zanzibar* and *The Sheep Look Up*, or Samuel R. Delany's *Dhalgren*.

Few science-fiction readers identify with the actual corporate elite which governs modern society, but they do identify with that elite's paid managerial staff, a point of view which limits their vision. If technological "fixes," expansionism, or mysticism are attempts to obviate or evade real social and political change, this might be explained by the fact that the professional managers stand at the focus of a change which might alter much of the power and privilege to which they aspire. It seems at least reasonable to suggest that the often contradictory social criticism contained in this very commercial brand of literature is related to the economic status and consciousness of the people to whom it appeals.[12]

NOTES

1. Thomas S. Gardner, "Psychology of the Science Fiction Fan," *New Fandom*, April 1939; Art Schnert, "Institute of Fan Opinion," *L'Inconnu*, March 1946. Both of these were "fanzines," that is amateur, fan-published magazines or newsletters. In the jargon of science-fiction fans, commercial magazines are "prozines."

2. Charles G. Waugh, Edwin F. Libby and Carol-Lynn Waugh, "Demographic, Intellectual and Personality Characteristics of Science Fiction Fans," Annual Meeting, Science Fiction Research Association, November 1975. All statistics offered in comparison with the 1973 Toronto convention study were taken from the Demographic portions of this paper.

3. Comparison with the samples of the Gallup polls is hardly a distinction. Gallup's samples of 1,500 people, of a total American population of 210,000,000 result in a sample which is .00071% of the total universe, selected at random. This survey was 8% of the convention membership. The total size of the science-fiction audience is unknown, but the American magazine circulation totals less than 250,000. Many magazines have 2 or more readers, so that the sample is upwards of .11% of that universe, although Tables 20 and 21 below show that magazine readership is but a part of the total audience. All of these are speculative figures, but they help make a point: these figures are tentative, but they can be used, at least until some survey comes up with radically different conclusions. As the Maine researchers point out, no one has.

4. All figures in brackets are for the general population of the United States, except where indicated. *U.S. Bureau of the Census, Statistical Abstract of the United States: 1973* (94th edition), Washington, D.C., 1973. Science-fiction conventions held on the North American continent are generally 5 to 10 times the size of those two held to date in Europe and one in Australia, so it seems safe to assume that most of the fans being studied are either American or Canadian. The concentration of educational attainment and wealth would of course be far

greater if figures from the less affluent portions of the world were included for comparison.

5. U.S. Bureau of the Census, *Statistical Abstract of the United States: 1974*, Table #618. Median Money Income of Families and Individuals, 1947-73. For British figures see *Britain: an Official Handbook* (London, Central Office of Information, 1967), pp 238-239, 434-436.

6. *The Statistical Abstract* uses family income to determine general income levels. Individual income is used to determine the differences between the income of Whites and non-Whites. White income was used to provide an appropriate comparison to the nearly lily-white convention. Inclusion of figures for Blacks and other minority groups would only increase the gap between the income of average individuals and science fiction readers.

7. *Educational Majors*

Major	Number	Percent
Accounting (B)	4	1.42%
Agriculture	3	1.06
Anthropology (S)	3	1.06
Art or Architecture (L)	7	2.48
Biological Sciences (P)	16	5.67
Business Administration (B)	8	2.84
College Preparatory	6	2.13
Chemistry (P)	11	3.90
Communications (S)	7	2.48
Computer Sciences (P)	16	5.67
Economics (S)	2	.71
Education (S)	10	3.55
Electronics (P)	10	3.55
Engineering (P)	19	6.74
English or Literature (L)	23	8.16
Environmental Studies (P)	1	.35
Foreign Languages (L)	4	1.42
Geology (P)	3	1.06
History (S)	19	6.74
Home Economics (S)	1	.35
Journalism (L)	7	2.48
Law (L)	9	3.19
Library Science (S)	13	4.61
Marketing (B)	3	1.06
Mathematics (P)	24	8.51
Medical Technology (P)	1	.35
Medicine (P)	7	2.48
Music (L)	3	1.06
Nursing (P)	4	1.42
Oceanography (P)	0	0.00
Philosophy (L)	6	2.13
Photography	2	.71
Physics (P)	15	5.32
Political Science (S)	6	2.13
Psychology (S)	15	5.32
Public Administration (S)	1	.35
Radio and Television	3	1.06
Religion (L)	1	.35
Sociology (S)	6	2.13
Theatre Arts (L)	6	2.13
Urban or Regional Planning (S)	2	.71
Others	12	4.26
total	325	115.25%

*Multiple majors, N=282. "Others" included one each of the following: Classics (L), Industrial Design, General Science (P), Paleontology (S), Pharmacy (P), Publishing, Russian Civilization (L), Solid State (sic) (P), Speech (L), Technical Writing, Veterinary Medicine (P) and Zen Taxidermy (sic). Letters in parentheses indicate the groups in Table 12 under which individual majors have been listed. (P)=physical or biological sciences, (S)=social sciences, (L)=liberal arts, (B)=business.

8. *Occupation*

Occupation	Number	Percent
Accounting (W)	3	1.06%
Agriculture	1	.35
Appliance or Auto Repair	0	0.00
Art or Architecture (W)	3	1.06
Armed Forces (S)	2	.71
Basic Research (S)		
Biological Sciences	5	1.77
Chemical Sciences	2	.71
Physical Sciences	1	.35
Business (self-employed) (W)	3	1.06
Civil Service (W)	20	7.10
Clerical (W)	8	2.84
College Student	52	18.44
College Teacher or Administrator (W)	9	3.19
Computer Programming (S)	19	6.74
Computer Technology (S)	4	1.42
Communications (W)	12	4.25
Construction	2	.71
Engineering (S)	7	2.48
Engineering Management (S)	1	.35
Finance (W)	3	1.06
High School Student	15	5.32
High School Teacher or Administrator (W)	4	1.42
Housewife	6	2.13
Industrial Worker	6	2.13
Journalism (W)	2	.71
Law (W)	5	1.77
Library Services (W)	7	2.48
Management Analysis (W)	2	.71
Marketing (W)	2	.71
Mechanic	2	.71
Medicine (S)	2	.71
Medical Technology (S)	0	0.00
Nursing (S)	4	1.42
Photography	3	1.06
Sales (W)	5	1.77
Social Science Research (W)	2	.71
Statistics (W)	2	.71
Technological Research and Development (S)	5	1.77
Writing or Editing Science Fiction	3	1.06
Writing or Editing other than Science Fiction	10	3.55
Others	12	7.80
Unemployed	12	4.26
unmarked	4	1.42
total	282	100.00

"Others" included one each of the following: Biochemicals for Research and Testing (S), Blacksmith, Bus Driver, Chef, Chemical Quality Control (S), Diesel Fuel Jockey, Elementary School Teacher (W), ITT Employee, Jeweler, Manufacturing Management, Newspaper Delivery, Paraprofessional Counseling (W), Pension Planning (W), Performing Arts, Pharmacy (S), Planetarium Lecturer (P), Print Shop, Religion (W), Textiles Testing Lab Supervisor (S), Veterinary Medicine (S), Waitress. Letters in parentheses identify occupational groupings in Table 13.

9. The bracketed figures are taken from statistics in Table 372 of the 1973 *Statistical Abstract*, and represent, with the exception of students, percentages of the 83.29 million person workforce. The student figure is a percentage of the 208.232 million total population of the United States. The *Abstract*'s listings for "Professional and Technical Workers" was added to "Managers and Administrators," for comparison to the first two categories. "Craftsmen and

Kindred" were compared to "Skilled Workers," "Operatives," to "Semi-skilled," and "Service" and "Non-Farm Labor" were compared to "Unskilled Workers."

10. John W. Campbell, "A Portrait of You," *Astounding Science Fiction*, March 1958, p 135.

11. See my "The Magic That Works: John W. Campbell and the American Response to Technology," *Journal of Popular Culture* 5(1972):867-942 and "The Triumph of Prophecy: Science Fiction and Nuclear Power in the Post-Hiroshima Period," SFS 3(1976):143-50.

12. Earlier versions of this paper were read at the Western Regional Meeting of the Popular Culture Association, Las Vegas, Nevada, February 1976 and at the Annual Meeting of the Modern Language Association, New York, December 1976, where it benefited from criticism from panelists and members of the associations. The author would also like to thank Mr. Thomas Christensen, of Laguna Hills, California and Ms. Joan Price, of Baltimore, Maryland, for assistance in compiling the data. The interpretations and conclusions, however, and any errors they contain, are his alone.

A.E. Levin

English-Language SF as a Socio-Cultural Phenomenon

Translated by Yuri Prizel; edited by D.S.

(from SFS *4: 246–256, November 1977)*

The subject of this essay is the evolution of English-language SF from its appearance up to the present decade. Since this has been and still is the most wide-spread phenomenon of its type in world literature, it can be used in order to elucidate not only general laws of conjectural or fantastic literature in the cultural system of contemporary capitalist society, but also a number of its more universal characteristics.

I shall consider conjectural literature (the term "science fiction" will not be used at the moment) as a specific method of creating and transmitting meaning, i.e. as a well defined type of a cultural language which has appeared under the influence of a series of contemporary objective factors. Therefore I shall first concentrate on the sociocultural functions of conjectural literature, in order to describe later how these functions came to be embodied.

An adequate perception of conjectural literature is possible if one accepts an initial rule of its game: all the constructs created here are to be perceived as something external to the reality of our personal and social experience, as existing outside and independently of it. Of course, if this exteriority were absolute, if the conjectural aspects did not refer to this reality, conjectural literature would be no different from simple inventing and could hardly claim a significant role in culture. Conjectural literature is capable of creating and transmitting socially significant content because its images are at all times, at some very deep level, analogous to the images of reality found in social consciousness. This is the factor which permits the reader to replace elements from the models offered him with realities of his own experience, which is a necessary condition for significant perception of any literature.

What assures such a possibility? By splitting up the unity of the world, by taking the reader beyond accepted limits, beyond known traits validated by his perceptions of empirical reality, conjectural literature reproduces in its models certain characteristics which are assumed to be essential for this reality, thus creating an analogy between its models and real experience. But the specificity of conjectural literature lies in the fact that these characteristics are expressed by "encasing" them in images which do not coincide with our customary ideas about the reality around us. This taking of models beyond the limits of the acceptable notions of what is and what is not possible is the chief device of conjectural literature. A writer employing this device founds his work on certain elements of his own knowledge of the surrounding world, while at the same time rejecting them, lending them an existence superficially alien to this world. The reader, on the other hand, interpreting the text on the basis of his own experience, might be able to perceive reality in a new light, to find in it analogs of those elements from which the conjectural model has been constructed. Thus the model itself is finally negated and "realized." Such a double negation can result in a synthesis of non-trivial knowledge, capable of enriching social consciousness.

None of this has yet revealed the characteristics of conjectural literature as a specific literary system of the present century. The described method of literary modeling, the translation of human experience into the language of the conjectural images, is one of the oldest phenomena in history of literature. It appeared soon after the dissociation of the unified mythological world-view—let us recall, for instance, the Menippean satires. In modern times, conjectural, indeed SF, writers would include Cyrano de Bergerac, Swift, Voltaire, Mary Shelley, and many others. In order to understand contemporary conjectural literature, it is necessary to find in it specific characteristics not present in Antiquity or in the 17-18th centuries.

This characteristic is as follows: Conjectural literature as a literary system has in our own century been constructed primarily on the basis of *recognizing an independent value in its models*. Conjectural literature now sees in its worlds not allegorical images of reality, not means for expressing some *a priori* accepted meanings, but primary meanings in their own right. This is precisely the watershed between conjectural literature as a specific cultural phenomenon of the 20th century and the numerous uses of conjectural subject-matter to express some previously accepted theme, practiced in earlier literature. No matter how wide the scope of possible correlations between the conjectural model and the world of human experience, these correlations are now not introduced into the model *a priori* as its *raison d'être*, but are recreated on the basis of understanding its inner integrity, the independent "unreal reality" which creates the self-contained logic of this model. Allegory presents us with an already known world, only turned "inside out"; conjectural literature creates a new one. This autonomous, non-subservient value of conjectural models is the main characteristic of contemporary conjectural literature.

All of the above does not mean, of course, that conjectural literature is homogeneous. Emphasizing the main communicative goal of a literary system indicates only the basic frame of reference from which specific works will be evaluated. Conjectural literature developed so fast largely because it demonstrated its ability to transmit quite diverse meanings. Very often one can find in it traits of the grotesque, of parody, of utopia, but all the aditional aspects and meanings are subservient to the specific principle of the autonomous value of the conjectural work. Moreover, relatively "pure" SF (e.g. Clarke's *Childhood End* or Simak's *City*) is only a small fraction of conjectural literature.

As an illustration I shall examine *Brave New World* by Aldous Huxley. This novel, written in the early 1930s, has had a great influence on the developing system of conjectural SF literature. It interests us not only because it is one of the outstanding works of the genre, but also because, having been written still outside of a specific literary system, it nevertheless—by virtue of realizing the author's communicative goals—recreates the main characteristics of that method of modeling which became typical for SF in the following decades.[1]

Huxley's intention was a literary polemic with the utopian novels of H.G. Wells. Huxley chose a grotesque anti-utopia denying the value of "machine" civilization, and based his model on extrapolating a series of tendencies already noticeable in contemporary (to him) life. This did not simply lead to a utilization of conjectural devices but to the construction of an integral world, a profound study of whose inner logic justifiably became the author's new goal. This is what makes Huxley's novel a work of conjectural literature.

In fact, many elements of the novel's structure would seem to be superfluous and even alien, were it not perceived as primarily a work of conjectural literature. The reader's perceiving of the text as belonging to a specific literary trend, the actualization of perceptive mechanisms characteristic for precisely this trend, is the most important condition for an adequate understanding of its meaning. For instance, the numerous technological descriptions and sociological discussions in Huxley's novel seem simply unnatural if one views it only as a parody. The same can be said about the final argument between the novel's main hero and World Controller Mustafa Mond, very important for the novel's meaning. This is actually a philosophico-sociological modelling of different variants of evolution for human culture, and it lays bare many tragic contradictions in this process. The whole plot-line of the Savage, which is a kind of "model within a model," is a search for an alternative solution, and thus does not fit into a satirical anti-utopia. The very "anti-machineness" of the book, the theme of "predatory things of our times,"[2] dangerous not because they might malfunction but, on the contrary, because they realize their technological capabilities only too impeccably, would also become hopelessly banalized if seen simply as a refutation of Wells's ideal. It should be noted that precisely this aspect of the novel was least of all appreciated by its early readers: after all, the traditional interpretation of the man vs. machine conflict connected it only with the machine's deviations from its assigned functions (the theme of Frankenstein in Mary Shelley, the monsters of Dr. Moreau in Wells, the Machine in E.M. Forster). The non-triviality of Huxley's model is much more evident today—it is sufficient to refer to the lessons of ecological crisis.

Of course, taking into account the polemical horizon of the novel also helps to appreciate certain of its aspects. But these aspects are today interesting primarily for the literary historian, since the rather numerous parallels with Wells's novels were relegated in the novel to a modest role.[3] When the novel was published, Wells was known and read in his homeland much more than after World War 2, and the allusions to him were easily recognized as additional carriers of the anti-Wells theme. For the contemporary reader they are virtually imperceptible; for him, the foreground is occupied by Huxley's conjectural model.

Such examples could be multiplied. Thus, Isaac Asimov's cycle of robot stores, so popular in the USSR, uses as its main theme the collision between two different modes of thinking—human and robotic. The theme itself is, of course, not new (it had already been used by Swift); treated in a traditional manner it could have resulted in a satirical allegory, like *Gulliver's Travels*, or a moralistic fable. Asimov, however, creates a series of models whose "initial conditions" are based on the existence of two incompatible psychotypes, and then explores the inner logic of the created situations. This absence of *a priori* givens, this freedom of logical alternatives creates new artistic possibilities.

Now we are able to formulate the difference between SF and its literary neighbors, with whom it shares certain formal similarities. Thus, SF works often resemble *fairy tales* (folktales). However, an analysis of their respective communicative goals shows immediately that the fairy tale takes its reader into a world of pure conventionality. The "impossible possibilities" of SF become in it simply impossibilities. The world of a fairy tale is not a transformation of the real world but a sort of parallel universe, constructed entirely according to its own plan and existing in its own space. As was noted by Vladimir Propp, the fairy tale has its own, very rigid internal structure, on the basis of which a given and prior ethical plan is realized; thus, it differs fundamentally from SF. The fairy tale does not actively create independent worlds, it simply takes certain aspects of empirical reality and constructs from them a parallel universe by exchanging these aspects with their opposites: if in the real world justice is unattainable, in fairy tales it always triumphs; if in this world man is powerless before nature, in fairy tales he masters it. The fairy-tale world does not permit free variation, it is simply an antithesis of reality. A fairy tale does not become a work of SF even if the flying carpet is replaced by a proton rocket, for the communicative goals are different.

Equally, one should not confuse SF and *utopia*. The main communicative goal of the latter is to give the readers an ideal version of their world, purified from everything foul and governed by truly moral laws. It is not really important whether the author sets his hopes on slave labor or on "superelectronic" technology—much more important is the fact that utopia, like fairy tale, does not create a model which is independent from reality, but constructs on the basis of initially accepted assumptions a specimen and a goal, a final point of harmony and ideal.

All this leads to a very important conclusion, namely that SF as a literary system can appear only when backed by very definite conditions of general culture: it is unthinkable until a culture comes to recognize the variability of its forms and the multiplicity of its evolutive paths, until it has freed itself from shallow teleologism (be it belief in a divine plan or unquestioning faith in automatic progress) as well as from conceptions which claim that the human condition is chaotic and unknowable, until the recognition of man's active responsibility for his historical path has penetrated deeply enough into social consciousness. SF is, of course, not obliged to tell about the future, but in its essence it is fertilized by the multitude of possibilities possible only in the future and meaningless without it. Thus the very nature of SF implies some rather rigid conditions for its coming about.

Here it is important to note that the rapid development of empirical sciences, backed up by the visible results of a suddenly accelerated technological progress seemed to guarantee mankind's future progress. Therefore, the attitude toward technology in such forerunners of 20th-century SF as Verne and Wells is certainly positive. For them, technological progress contains no contradictions: it can give negative results only as a consequence of malicious acts of certain individuals (as Verne seems to have been convinced in his later novels, such as *For the Flag* or *The Begum's Fortune*) or as a result of social antagonisms (Wells). The objective contradictoriness of technological evolution, foreseen so clearly by Marx, is not noticed by these writers.

Technological fetishism, so evident in industrial countries, became one of the main factors influencing English-language SF. A powerful stratum of social consciousness saw in technology that demiurge of changes to come which formerly used to be seen in God, Reason, or History. This was the belief of a large majority of that scientific and technological intelligentsia whose numbers and influence have been growing rapidly since the second half of the 19th century. Remaining within the limits of bourgeois ideology, this group felt at the same time a certain "uniqueness" and sought a form of self-expression, including the literary. It is from the members of this group and the strata gravitating toward it that SF recruited its first authors.

All this had very important consequences. From its very inception SF reflected the cultural orientation toward science as the main stimulus of progress. This reflection took place not only on the surface but also in the depths, because SF reproduced a number of aspects of science as a definite method of cognition. Later I shall examine this in more deail; now the important fact is that 20th-century science has created a sufficiently high level of credibility, validating as it were in advance, to its readers, the creation of conjectural models. An SF work might contain incidents clearly contradictory to common sense, might distort our customary logic, might count demons and spirits among its characters—for the reader it will no longer be a fairy tale because in the context of his perception he will be able to interpret such "impossibilities" as symbols of certain realities of his existence. Such symbolization is one of the most powerful methods available to SF for finding analogies which permit the projection of its contents onto empirical experience. It is only to be expected that the dominant characteristic of this symbolization will be logical interpretation, leaning on the innovations that scientific and technological progress brings to mankind.

Let us take as an example the well-known story "Something for Nothing" by Robert Sheckley. A philistine receives from somewhere a miraculous gift—a box which can fulfill all his wishes; he is driven almost frantic by the avalanche of possibilities open to him, loses all self-control, and as a result finds himself enslaved by the owners of the dangerous gift. At first glance we might conclude that this is merely a fairy tale with a not too profound moral. But at a closer look a new, more ominous meaning is revealed—science is capable of unloading upon men an abundance which will enslave them, demanding in payment an unheard-of obedience to the powers creating the abundance, powers probably capable of destroying both man and his newly acquired wealth. At the end of the story man finds himself imprisoned by the future—another symbol, for is not this precisely what happens in a civilization which has made consumption its highest ideal, and for its sake keeps wasting its resources in the ever accelerating race of unrestrained technical evolution? The seemingly innocuous tale becomes a thought-experiment of sorts, developing along rather severely logical lines.

Returning to our main theme, we can conclude: it is not surprising that conjectural literature attempts not only to utilize references to concrete ideas, results or hypotheses of science, but also to include some *structures of logico-discursive modeling of reality* among its devices. In this sense it may indeed be called *science* fiction; in the same sense we may claim that it derives, on certain levels, both from literature proper and from science.

It is customary to date the beginning of SF with 1926, when Gernsback started the magazine *Amazing Stories*, the first specialized periodical of its kind; its first period continued until the end of the 1930s. The purely literary quality of most works in this first period was not too high, but it became very important in terms of future development: it was then that SF grew conscious of its right to independent existence and started creating the systematizing literary bases that became later important factors in its development. Let us dwell on this in more detail.

How did the United States fare at the beginning of the second quarter of the twentieth century? 1926 was notoriously a time of "prosperity" and a feeling of power and security, an age of optimism, a seemingly visible demonstration of greatness of the American way of life. 1950 was a time of atom scares, military failure in Korea, McCarthyism, anti-Soviet hysteria. These 25 years incorporate hitherto unseen changes on every level of American society. The essence of these changes is well known; what interests us is that they led to attempts—especially by scientists-intellectuals and by students—to reevaluate many of the traditional myths of American mass culture. They also led to a feeling that the hitherto seemingly unshakeable foundations of life were unstable; consequently, such changes led, in certain strata of collective psychology, to a desire to preserve traditional myths and even to spread them—if only in imagination—to other times and spaces, and in other strata—to a desire to transcend tradition and rethink the qualitative changes taking place in our world. Both these divergent vectors of social mood had something in common, namely the desire to broaden the limits of the existing situation in order to either build barriers against changes in alternative thought-models, present and future, or, on the contrary, to study their possible consequences. Thus conservative, escapist, critical, and other moods, all created at that time a favorable soil for the development of SF.

Another factor is equally important. The first quarter of this century saw revolutionary changes in the foundations of basic sciences, from physics to biology. A vast pool of ideas and information was created, and applied disciplines could start utilizing it. Telephone, radio, automobile, electricity, aviation—all these had already changed life a great deal, and the perspectives seemed to be fascinating and paradoxical. Hence a widespread desire to absorb some of the knowledge available only to a chosen few. This new demand could not be satisfied by "scattered" information available through mass communication, and the age of TV had not yet arrived. Popularizing writings were not yet sufficiently widespread, and anyway they would have needed an audience with a certain degree of preparation. The need for emotional sympathy and emotional contact with the scientific context of the times, the need for social consciousness not only in science per se, but in its visible results as well—all these also aided the development of a new literary system.

Historically this was the first function of SF to be realized, and it came about in the 30s. It saw the growth of technology-cum-adventure-oriented SF, combining elements such as the detective, adventure, and western story with 20th-century technological dreams. With all its numerous weaknesses, the SF of the 30s can be seen in retrospect as an experiment of sorts, developing the possibilities of the new literary system in, so to speak, a "pure" form: the conjectural subject-matter was still a goal in its own right, not supplemented by any additional communicative goals. SF was not yet attempting to say anything about the real world, satisfied with the imaginary one which it was creating. This maximum freedom of constructing conjectural situations permitted American SF to develop at its very inception a most valuable arsenal of devices, which proved to be very fruitful in its further development; it was in the 30s that SF adopted such themes as Space Colonists, Interstellar Contact and Cosmic States, Alien Intelligence, etc. Even its most widely used device of Time Travel, discovered by Wells, was fully developed during this period.

The 40s saw substantial change in SF. Its maturing gradually brought it to the possibility of utilizing the new literary system for an understanding of the scientifico-technical and historical changes. Editors such as Campbell, Gold, and Boucher, leading writers such as Kuttner, Simak, Asimov, Heinlein, Sturgeon work in such a direction. At the same time SF rapidly increases in quantity (five magazines in 1938, twenty-two in 1941). After the war, SF develops socio-critical motives, it starts reacting rather seriously to socio-political conditions in the U.S. and in the world, in the works of Pohl, Bester, Tenn, Kornbluth, or—in the British branch—of Clarke, Wyndham, Russell.

By the mid-50s English-language SF could already count numerous serious and profound works. For one thing, it gave birth to the new literary thematic field of the relations between man and complex technical systems. It was SF which saw here a new reality of the age of scientifico-technical revolution, and developed techniques for handling it which were later adopted by "mainstream" writing. SF works such as *Nerves* by Lester Del Rey or *Marooned* by Martin Caidin initiate the chain leading to Hailey's *Airport* and *Wheels*. Furthermore, during the McCarthy period SF at its best represented the antimilitaristic stand in American literature, coming out in defense of humanist and democratic ideals. How serious such a stand could be can be seen from "E for Effort" by Thomas Sherred, "Target Generation" and "Across the River, Across the Trees" by Clifford Simak, or *The Martian Chronicles* by Ray Bradbury. The SF of that period recognized the complexity of cultural paths and the timeless value of humanist ideals.

With all the means available to it, SF came out against intolerance and coercion, obscurantism and racism. It would be naive to accuse it of a lack of positive social ideals; it is impossible, however, to ignore its belief in Reason as the highest value of existence, a Reason constantly developing in the struggle against blind forces of nature and its own creations, a Reason which recognizes each of its states to be only a link in the eternal chain of changes, which does not fear the situation of tragic choice, and which preserves its dignity even in defeat. This liberated cosmic vision, this struggle, and these tragedies can be seen in such outstanding works as *The*

End of Eternity and "Nightfall" by Isaac Asimov, *City* by Clifford Simak, *Childhood's End* by Arthur C. Clarke, *The Chrysalids* by John Wyndham, in many short stories by Sheckley, Anderson, Bester, or Kuttner. We find here a respect for intelligent life in all its forms, a recognition of the right of each form to its own way of development—a recognition which does not glorify isolation or "cosmic exclusiveness": let us recall, e.g., the wonderful "Specialist" or "The Sweeper of Loray" by Sheckley. Brilliant satires on militarism and spy-mania such as "Allamagoosa" by Eric Frank Russell, "Report on the Burnhouse Effect" by Kurt Vonnegut, Jr., "Brooklyn Project" by William Tenn, and examples of social criticism rise at the time to an understanding of the profoundly antihumanist nature of bourgeois society. SF writers were able to perceive or feel the dangers of overpopulation, the tendency to increased social manipulation of personality, the very complicated problems of prosperity. By painting the horror of nuclear confrontation, SF helped to develop antimilitaristic tendencies. On the other hand, by preparing its readers for the inevitable swift socio-technical changes, it served as a kind of adaptation mechanism, helping the acceptance of these changes. As a summary, one can state that at its best English-speaking SF was a serious attempt to solve some very important human problems.

Let us now attempt to analyze the main principles of modeling which determine the originality of mid-century SF. First of all we must again emphasize the orientation toward logical interpretation of its symbolic constructs, and the selection of perspectives of technological evolution as the basis of this interpretation. Such an orientation is, however, not only heuristically positive, but it also has a series of weak aspects. The main weakness is, most probably, the fact that SF sees the ultimate cause of social evolution only in technological development, augmented at times by ethical factors. Social norms are taken as constants, not permitting any transcending of idealized existing—present or past—social relationships. Ideal models of relationships between individual and society have already been determined by the liberal humanist tradition, and any break with this tradition can be viewed only as regression. Of course, all this is true only for the progressive branch of American SF—for writers like, e.g., Robert A Heinlein, the ideal is seen somewhere in the misty distances of the winning of the West, when white settlers, Bible in pocket and gun in hand, were cleansing the Promised Land from the unworthy Native Americans. While speaking out against totalitarianism and coercion, even the most profound SF writers see them only as a result of distorging the norms of bourgeois society.

In order to understand the nature of another "inner barrier" of SF, one has to bear in mind that, like science, SF attempts to create its models in such a way that each one would be governed by a unique organizing principle, which would rationalize the entire construction as a whole. The knowledge contained in a scientific theory is closed within itself, science in its ideal form is free of context and contains in itself everything necessary for its understanding. A literary text, on the contrary, always must appeal very strongly to non-literary experiences of its reader, to the context of his comprehension: seemingly smallest details may be bearing an enormous load of meaning, since they are capable of evoking resonances in powerful layers of the reader's consciousness. But a writer constructing an SF model cannot, strictly speaking, call upon the readers' experience, he cannot count on their knowledge except for what is told them. Of course, the above should not be taken too literally—the analogies which assure projecting the model onto reality are not created in a vacuum. Nevertheless, the characteristics of a conjectural world, responsible for its uniqueness, have to be presented with sufficient obviousness and detail. After all, if a writer is using conjectural elements only as carriers of surface meanings, then the details of his model from the very beginning carry a double load: defining the surface uniqueness of the conjectural world, they become significant only as projections onto the reader's experience of reality which trigger mechanisms of reception based on that experience. In SF these mechanisms can be triggered only after immersion into the conjectural world as an independent entity. But precisely because of the supposed freedom of constructing such a world, its elements of significance must be at least sketched—otherwise the reader would simply have insufficient information. And here SF took, so to say, an extra-literary path: its models are created through a finite series of system connections, emphasizing rather rigidly all the significant elements.

One very popular device, for instance, can be called the introduction of an unpredictable disruption into a standard situation. The scene of action is created by means of the most usual realities (for instance, a provincial town), on which an external, alien element is superimposed (an invasion from space, an unusual invention). The background, familiar to every reader, seems to be giving the author greater freedom of appeal to the readers' context-dependent level of perception. But by the very essence of the SF communicative goals, the author is interested only in the "distortions" of this background. These distortions must be introduced openly, independently of the context, because the author cannot count on the readers' ability to reproduce them independently. Thus we are faced with a very rigid plan, one which does not permit any conceivable deviation from the authorial model which rationalizes and explains the model as whole. This can be seen very clearly in two well-known novels by Simak: *All Flesh Is Grass* and *They Walked Like Men*: here the disruption is represented by the suddenly appearing representatives of extraterrestrial intelligence, and everything not directly connected with this developing conflict is very consciously cut off, while the conflict itself is shown in great detail.

What follows from the above? It is obvious that the rationalizing plan would be difficult to preserve and to investigate if one were to make it too ramified. Therefore it is customary to vary only a small number of parameters. The most common one is the *reductio ad absurdum*, when the varied parameters approach values which destroy the stability of the initial SF model. This creates the characteristic effect of warning—the reader sees that the unrestricted development of a certain trend might bring with it catastrophic results. The variable parameters can be any aspects of social life or technology: overpopulation (John Brunner, *Stand on Zanzibar*), mind control (Robert Sheckley, "Academy"), advertising (Frederik Pohl and C.M. Kornbluth, *The Space Merchants*), etc. This can achieve a significant emotional influence, but the believability of such models is very low—they ignore the feedback factors which hinder too far-fetched deviations from equilibrium and cause qualitative changes in the system—changes which SF is "forced" to ignore. It is true that SF in a way does not attempt to be believable, it is satisfied to simply point out the dangers of certain social trends. Still, one can see a certain paradox here: SF can only warn against dangers which can be shown in extremely simplified models—after all, overpopulation can be understood by "homespun" methods as well.

This conclusion can be generalized. English-language SF did give body to the expectations created by the scientifico-technological revolution, but *it proved able to notice and develop only those aspects of future changes which already had their prototypes in social consciousness.* Thus, it often spoke about overpopulation, but this theme dates back to the 18th century. At the same time, SF of the 1950s was unable to predict the ecological crisis, whose approach was already a close reality. SF writers have written a great deal about artificial intelligence, but they proved unable to present with any accuracy the qualitative uniqueness of even algorithmic thought-operations.

Actually, all this is not surprising. Literature always turns to an image of the world based on generalized human experience, even if that includes certain facts of post-scientific knowledge. This enables literature to include and transform a great variety of things, but not those for which historical experience has not yet developed prototypes. Neither folklore nor poetry will ever be able to create, for instance, a negatively charged particle, because in their "sphere of activity" there are no analogs for it. The prediction of real consequences of the scientifico-technological revolution in all their depths and paradoxality also demands going beyond the limits of the images already extant in social consciousness. SF has expressed the very spirit of forthcoming changes and helped to prepare our social consciousness for the grandiosity of these changes; in doing this, it has already justified its existence. To demand more from it would have been naive.

The second half of the 1950s was a period of decline for English-language SF. The number of readers decreased, the number of magazines halved, new SF ideas almost stopped appearing, books became less interesting. Beginning with the 1960s, a new leader emerged: the so-called speculative fiction. At the same time British authors became more influential. The British "new wave" around *New Worlds*, edited by Michael Moorcock, became the ideological center of the movement to rejuvenate conjectural literature. What form was this rejuvenation taking?

First of all, the evolution of conjectural literature was strongly influenced by the deepening crisis in bourgeois consciousness. Works by the "new wave" mirrored such aspects of this crisis as historical pessimism, rejection of progress, suspicion of reason, glorification of the subconscious and of instincts, appeal to the immutable and eternal human nature. Its main themes became the approaching end of the world, a glorification of licentiousness, the absurdity of the world and of human existence—all these often with a mystical and mythological coloring. The global pessimism of the "new wave" sometimes approached necrophilia, e.g. in J.G. Ballard. The range of conjectural devices did increase, primarily due to an utilization of mythological imagery, but in general conjectural literature moved further and further away from contemporary problems or, when it did attempt to turn to them, it manifested as a rule a total ideological helplessness. Even the most critical works of the period—*A Clockwork Orange* by Anthony Burgess, *Camp Concentration* by Thomas Disch, "Black Is Beautiful" by Robert Silverberg—transferred social problems to a non-historical, non-class, abstract level. Logically speculative fiction has often exhibited outright escapism, presented as the most sublime wisdom. Such fiction does not need rationalism, and one should not be surprised that it rejected the principle of rational founding for its conjectural models. Technological evolution not only lost its earlier status as the demiurge of social change (this by itself could have been a sign of maturity), but the very possibility of rationally explaining these changes was rejected: knowledge based on mythological revelations was most often declared to be the one and only method of understanding existence suitable to human nature. The trust in history, for all its contradictions so characteristic for the best SF works of the earlier period, was replaced by an open fear of it. Probably this is why Stanislaw Lem called most of the 1960s SF a vulgar mythology of technical civilization, falsifying the cognitive, social, and political problems of its time.

We should not, however, regard a return to the traditions of the 1950s as the way out. The flowering of "speculative fiction" followed logically not only from the crisis of the spiritual culture of bourgeois society, but also from a phenomenon one could call a cultural wearing-out of the very system of SF. The intensive popularization of science and technology (mainly via TV) deprived SF of its privilege to be one of the main links between the world of exact knowledge and the world of daily experience. The technologoical achievements themselves eventually lost their exclusive status, a mechanism of habituation was triggered, and traditional SF themes started evoking fewer and fewer emotions. The social consciousness became accustomed to the scientifico-technological revolution, and the need for SF as a means of adaptation decreased correspondingly. The increased level of popular-scientific literature made the inadequacy of conjectural devices quite evident. If it increases informativeness by increasing realistic exactitude and accuracy of details, SF crosses the limits of permissible stylization which allowed it to introduce conjectural elements in a natural way. Thus, *The Andromeda Strain* and *The Terminal Man* by Michael Crichton are no longer perceived as SF, although they definitely would have been twenty years ago. When critics called one of the most famous novels of the last decade, Frank Herbert's *Dune*, a handbook of environmental protection, they gave an obvious example for the shift in the evaluative frame of reference. Converging with good realistic literature, SF of this kind has to count with other norms of perception and change its communicative goals. This has led also to a return to purely instrumental uses of conjectural devices, used simply as carriers of externally assigned meanings. This returning to the situation "conjectural literature as a stylizing device" is very much in evidence now. I do not intend to decry this phenomenon (after all, it is a movement of conjectural literature toward "mainstream" writing), but one conclusion seems to be obvious: though "speculative fiction," striving to increase the freedom of constructing conjectural worlds, resulted in a degeneration of meanings created by it, the overcoming of this degeneration, i.e. an increase in contentual depth, proved possible only through moving away from the particular system of SF literature formed in the 1930s-1940s. Thus we see an obvious crisis of the SF system.[4]

Where should a solution be sought? A large number of writers and critics (primarily the partisans of "speculative fiction") assume that conjectural literature is even now too burdened by the sin of science, that the departure from the traditions of the 50s has not been sufficient. They view the conjectural literature of the future as a means of studying extreme conditions of the human psyche and limit-situations of existence, when no customary laws are valid and the personality is alone with itself and with the world.

There is also another point of view, insisting on a more complete fusion of SF and science. This conception was most clearly formulated by Stanislaw Lem (it is widely shared by many writers of the older generation in Britain and America, and a number of the younger writers):

> it isn't possible to construct a reflection of the condition of the future with cliches. It isn't the archetypes of Jung, nor the structures of the myth, not irrational nightmares which cause the central problems of the future and determine them. And should the future be full of dangers, those dangers cannot be reduced to the known patterns of the past. They have a unique quality, as a variety of factors of a new type. That is the most important thing for the writer of science fiction. But SF has meanwhile built itself into a jail and imprisoned itself within those walls, because its writers have not seemed to understand that the salvation of the creative imagination cannot be found in mythical, existential, or surrealistic writings—as a new statement about the conditions of existence. By cutting itself off from the stream of scientific facts and hypotheses, science fiction itself has helped to erect the walls of the literary ghetto where it now lives out its piteous life.[5]

The program proposed by Lem is by itself quite justified. One cannot, however, ignore the real difficulties it has to face due to a definite limit to the possibilities of uniting logical-discursive and artistic structures, without which union the immersion of SF into "the stream of scientific facts and hypotheses" demanded by Lem is hardly possible. Crossing this limit will either make the entire conjectural element unnecessary, or it will destroy the artistic element of the work. From this point of view the lesson learned from the sober evaluation of such an experimental work by Lem himself as *His Master's Voice* is quite instructive.

I have attempted to analyze the realistic possibilities and limitations of English-language conjectural literatuire. At the same time, its example led to an investigation of certain general laws of this type of literature. Of course, the development of conjectural literature in the antagonistic bourgeois society inevitably falls under the general rule pointed out by Marx—the hostility of capitalism to artistic creation. Thus the deepening spiritual crisis of bourgeois society affected—and it could not be otherwise—English-language SF. But, as for general and final evaluations of the perspectives of SF as a specific type of literature, they still seem to be premature.

NOTES

1. I am interested primarily in certain characteristics of the novel's system. For a more complete analysis of its contents, see V. Shestakov, "Sotsial'naia utopiia Oldosa Khaksli—mif i real'nost," *Novyi mir* No. 7 (1969).

2. Allusion to the Strugatskys' novel of the same title (unaccountably published in the U.S. as *Final Circle of Paradise* [1976]), itself named from a line of Voznesensky's poem *Oza*.—D.S.

3. As Huxley himself pointed out, the novel had been conceived originally as a parody on Wells's *Men Like Gods*—cf *Writers at Work: The Paris Review Interviews*, 2nd Series (US 1963), p 198.

4. As for SF in socialist countries, it, too, is experiencing certain difficulties, but it is attempting to renew its stock of forms and devices while preserving at the same time a rational and humanistic view of life, historical optimism, and faith in man's capabilities.

5. Stanislaw Lem, "Robots in Science Fiction," in Thomas D. Clareson, ed., *SF: The Other Side of Realism* (US 1971), p 325.

Dieter Hasselblatt

Reflections from West Germany on the Science-Fiction Market

Translated by William B. Fischer

(from **SFS** *4: 256–263, November 1977)*

The criteria observed by the commercial article SF are not, first and foremost, literary. Nor does SF even optimize the possibilities which typify it as a genre. It is more accurate to say that SF is situated within the magnetic field of commercial market principles. SF is a commodity, although admittedly the article which is traded on the market under the label "Science Fiction" all too often speaks against it. The distribution channels for this commodity of SF are the hardcover book, the paperback series, the TV series, the film, the radio play, and the "Heft" series (soft-cover, medium-size pulp magazines with a short novel complete in each issue, e.g. *Perry Rhodan*).

1. SF on TV. Let me begin with the most market-conscious of these channels of distribution, SF from American TV. "Das Spukschloss im Weltall" (i.e. the Haunted Castle in Space; original title "Catspaw") was one of the seventy-eight episodes of the TV series *Raumschiff Enterprise* (*Star Trek*). Not the least factor in the fame the series attained was the character of Mr. Spock, played by Leonard Nimoy. Spock—he of the pointed ears and mephistophelian eyebrows, the Man in the Satan Suit—is a classic example of affirmative anachronism. But even more offensive is the conception of most female characters in this (and other) series from the Anglo-American scene. On a planet quite distant from Earth the crew of the *Enterprise* chances upon a version of the European Middle Ages, as seen from a perspective which is typically American: haunted castle with passageways, hall of state, candelabra, dungeons, chains, suits of armor—in short, romantic Old Heidelberg in top-notch form. And in the midst of this Castle of Chills and Thrills—a pin-up model of the American Idea of Woman: the Cat-Woman (who of course occasionally uses a "transmuter" to change herself into a genuine hissing, gleaming-eyed cat). The Woman of Enigmas, demonic, dominating, feared by men—the typical American mom in the form of the chick-fatale with a penchant for strip-tease. Such figures reflect an extremely offensive pattern of affirmation. Since SF is a commodity on the market, not too much of a new and surprisingly innovative nature may be presented. For SF as a commodity has to confirm to existing patterns of thought, desire, and fear. The reason why this confirmation must occur in Anglo-American SF, so obviously and so without exception, can be seen only when one takes into assessment the fact that, in the USA, TV is a sales medium, not an artistic or creative medium. The principle of dramaturgical composition in the American series is not, primarily, the skillful and entertaining presentation of an exciting story; even less does this principle involve using the "formal play" of art to bring up for discussion political and social matters. Rather, the sole structural principle behind such programs is the implantation, every six to eight minutes, of commercials or "ad-spots" into the fictional plot in the places prepared for this purpose. "The constantly reiterated argument of the spokesmen for the networks, that they just offer what the viewing public want, is thus a complete fabrication. What they offer is what the advertising clients want."[1] The preferred consumer target-groups are women between 18 and 45 and men between 50 and 58. Incidentally, NBC considered the *Star Trek* series so successful that it did not want to forgo further continuations. So more episodes were produced, this time in the form of animated cartoon films of 15 minutes' length. Once again the ZDF (Central German Television Network) has fitted *Star Trek* into its schedule, starting in March of 1976 in a late-afternoon animated cartoon slot. Such behavior is true to the market principle which says that a consumer demand, once it has been stabilized by a product supply, should if at all possible be serviced with an equivalent product.

If, then, the Anglo-American series, with their exclusive orientation toward market, promotions, and sales, and their images of a Culture of Consumption, are constantly flickering across our TV screens, it is because our own broadcasting institutions, which are by law public and are scarcely commercial in their organization, have abandoned their obligation—and their opportunity—to counter the transatlantic programs by offering program contents which are somehow superior, or somehow more intelligent, or just somehow more entertaining.

An instructive and admittedly isolated example shows how such a situation could come about. In the field of SF there recently occurred a Franco-German cultural agreement, however improbable and astounding that may sound to the ears of SF fans. Partners in the co-production of this didactic SF project were the Bavarian Education Television System and French TV (ORTF), with the support of the French Foreign Ministry. Thirty-nine episodes of a French language course, *Les Gammas! Les Gammas!*, were produced, with SF as the vehicle. Since September 1974 all the Third Programs (cultural channels) of the ARD (Association of West German Public Broadcasting Institutions) have scheduled this well-liked and successful series in their best time-slots. The basic idea is one of the most common and marketable SF themes: the invasion of extraterrestrial beings and their vicissitudes. The series, whose extremely clever conception took into account both the basic purpose and the target-group, transposed familiar SF motifs and patterns into pictorial events. The target-group consists of children, who get their fun from seeing Odile, Emile, and Adrien magically become large or tiny, and grown-ups as well, who are supposed to enjoy the numerous literary, cultural, topical, and historical allusions. The didactic intention of the series is to teach French, using simple sentences and common vocabulary, or just to refresh French language skills. The adventures of the Gammas, incidentally, are supposed to appear shortly as a comic strip.

It seems scarcely possible to sneak around—let alone vault over—the generally unfortunate web of interconnections between the marketing and consumption of SF. Here in West Germany, radio and TV are not a state monopoly, as they are in the countries of the Eastern European bloc, in the Third World countries, and even in some Western European countries as well, like France, Spain, Italy, etc.; nor are they here commercial facilities as in the USA. where the big mass-communications systems sell air-time to industry, whose interest consists entirely in promoting its products. Nevertheless, our "publicly controled" mass media—and this holds true particularly for TV (ARD and ZDF)—seem to be subordinate to the market strictures of those countries they "buy" from. The purchasing practices which have come to determine programming are the result of the daily necessity of filling time-slots. Without hesitation, foreign SF TV series were and still are purchased; and those who produce our own SF series (*Alpha-Alpha*, *Orion*, etc.) have not listened to expert advisors, but instead have closely imitated the Anglo-American series. (This is not quite valid for Rainer Erler's *Das blaue Palais*.) On the one hand our TV broadcasting institutions rivet their gaze on viewer interest and numbers of sets tuned in, which are all too quickly misinterpreted as indexes of actual popularity. On the other hand there is a strong concentration of attention on the possibilities of purchasing such series. From this vicious circle the conclusion is drawn that the viewing public evidently does not want anything else. But perhaps the taste of this audience, at least as regards SF, is not at all as poor as the fare which is usually served up to it and which, for lack of something better, it still supposedly "likes" to watch.

2. Strictures Affecting the SF Market. Observations such as these can easily be extended and amplified. Their unmistakable blatant lesson is that *what the term "SF" designates is not so much a literature as a market*. SF is a commodity. If the term "SF" does denote a market rather than a literature, then here lie the foundations of its market strictures, and the characteristics and vexations which result from them.

The commodity is, as it were, the key to certain corresponding keyholes. It would be erroneous to exercise one's critical efforts on the individual "key." Instead, one ought to zero in on the market-situation as a whole and analyze it. Thus the individual SF novel, SF film, SF series, etc., is a symptom of very general consumer needs and expectations of the SF reader.

The next point to be considered is that *a market is not a free environment*.

If one were to judge a commodity *only* according to the criteria of literary aesthetics, one would start from inexcusably erroneous premises. For example, in asking such questions as whether the author's "message" can be brought home to its target in undistorted form; or whether a work of SF measures up to all linguistic and stylistic requirements, in accord with some cross-cut of Western literary experience; and so on. For a market is indeed not a free environment, but rather an almost forcibly balanced realm of interaction between supply and demand, between production and consumption, whereby it is evident that, originally, supply manipulated demand, and indeed still does manipulate it.

A market is not a free environment; the commodity is a key to corresponding keyholes. SF is *made*. It is not spawned by geniuses in moments of poetic ecstasy. SF is manipulated. For example: in Germany there has been a market for SF only for about twenty years, about as long, that is, as the Science Fiction Club of Germany (Science Fiction Club Deutschland) has been in existence. This SF market established itself here in the latter half of the 1950s, intensified, and then, with the beginning of the Seventies, expanded into an SF boom. At the beginning of the Fifties there appeared *Rauchs Weltraum-Bücher* (Rauch's Outer-Space Books), edited by Gotthard Günther (Düsseldorf, Karl Rauch Verlag). The series had to be discontinued, because there was as yet no market for SF in West Germany. So little a market was there for SF that Curt Siodmak's SF thriller *Donovan's Brain* was published in 1951 by the Nest Verlag as a whodunit, under the title *Der Zauberlehrling* (*The Sorcerer's Apprentice*), in the hardcover detective-novel series "Krähenbücher," together with Raymond Chandler, Dorothy Sayers, Dashiell Hammett, Eric Ambler, etc. Then in 1962 the novel was issued by the Moewig Verlag in the "Terra-Science-Fiction Taschenbüchern" ("Terra SF Paperbacks") series, under the title *Donovan's Gehirn*. In West Germany, then, there was a detective-novel market prior to the consolidation of the SF market. In 1972 Asimov's novel *Lunatico* (*The Gods Themselves*, US 1972) was published in hardcover, at a correspondingly high price, by the Scherz Verlag (Berne and Munich). In keeping with the practices of the publishing market, Asmiov's *Lunatico* came out two years later in the Hyene Verlag at a considerably more agreeable price. 318 pages hardcover, 318 pages paperback; neither abridged nor cut and pasted together in dubious fashion—something which in West Germany happens all too often, as connoisseurs of SF well know. But *Lunatico* appeared in the regular series of Heyne novels, not in the SF series. This means that the steady buyers of new Heyne titles in the SF series would have found this novel only by chance. Thus the location of SF is made more difficult for the fan. The reasons: the paperback rights for this newest Asimov were fixed so high that it could be brought out only in the main series, whose first run is set at 50,000 copies, not at 20,000, as is that of the SF series.

Another observation: It is on occasion the practice of German critics of highbrow literature, as well as the marxist critics or those from fandom, to accuse writers of SF stories, novels, or films of having done something in a manner which is thus and such, i.e., capitalist, fascist, marxist, or just poor. It is particularly fashionable to apply the "fascism argument" to Anglo-American SF. One just stuffs everything into the *Perry Rhodan* pigeonhole, and then thinks that by doing so one has said something exact; thus Michael Pehlke and Norbert Lingfeld in their attack on Anglo-American SF, *Roboter und Gartenlaube: Ideologie und Unterhaltung in der Science-Fiction-Literatur* (Munich; Hanser, 1970). But it is not by way of an exact analysis of market structure that they arrive at their argument that English-language SF is fascist; instead, they behave as though the SF works at hand were exclusively the affair of the writer-producer. They overlook the affirmative reinforcement function which commodity possesses in a market once it has been determined by the syndrome of supply and demand. It is a widespread but erroneous practice to call the heroes of SF facistoid: in fact the Nazis or fascists employed overdrawn hero-figures for reasons of communications strategy similar to those which motivate the use of such figures in "popular literature," particularly in the offensive body of SF which is peopled by a whole gang of Cosmic Soldiers of Fortune.

The interrelationships are far more constrained and controlled than is explained by the "fascism" argument. Because the commodity, like a key, fits very generally into keyholes, one cannot from a market situation jump merely to a critique of the producer. What ought to be subjected to critical analysis is the interrelationship between production and consumption, i.e., the market itself; for mass literature, of which SF is also a part, obviously satisfies the broadest of consumer needs.

Next consideration. Because a market is not a free environment, and because commodities are like keys which fit into keyholes, a market can be an indicator. I will deal with this matter in the conclusion, where the fetishistic nature of the commodity is discussed.

A further consideration. The distribution systems, as channels of communication, determine the contents of communication. The individual communications systems (paperback, the "Heft-" magazine series, TV series, radio play) are permeable, each according to its structure, only to certain definite communication contents. Moreover, the individual systems of distribution shape the form and content of the communication which such channels let pass.

3. Single-file, Parade-style: the Series and the Hero as Commercial Articles. For the producers of SF series, whether "Heft'-magazine or TV series, there exists the production strictures of continuing the series, once the market has been opened up. The same holds true for paperback production. Once a paperback-production is "running" on the market, this or that much per month has to be turned out, or else the production-process becomes unremunerative. The production-apparatus—paper supply, printing, binding, retailing, etc., etc.—must constantly be used and fed.

This means that publishing houses, TV production companies, etc., are subject to the market stricture of constantly having to get the printed, broadcast, or paperback onto the market. It is not so much the content, then, but rather the printed or broadcast *series as a whole* which is produced. The market dilemma which this brings about is that, if the series is more "important" than what happens in the individual segments, then it becomes less and less a matter of content and theme and more and more a matter of producing with an eye to the printed or broadcast series which always has to keep "running" on the market. Content, then, necessarily becomes weaker and weaker, more and more stereotyped; more and more progeny comes marching off the production line in single file. But thereby the content, which is becoming weaker and weaker, works to the disadvantage of the market-effectiveness of the printed or broadcast series as a whole.

Something which producers see only with difficulty is that, in the final analysis, the market-effectiveness of a series depends on the quality of its themes and story-elements. "In obedience to its basic principles, SF accentuates what is inane and de-emphasizes what is of value, until the two meet mid-way, on the level of an unconsequentiality which says nothing."[2] Cliches and stereotypical set-pieces, always the same utterly imbecilic pseudo-paradises and totally ridiculous visions of horror—in short, single-file parade-style processions of whatever will "go." But there is clearly an enforced nature to these single-file processions. The strictures behind it are, first, of a commercial and, second, of a contentual kind. And the stricture which determines content is a consequence of the commercial stricture.

The first "single-file" stricture, the commercial one, is the preservation of the series once it has been introduced, or of the paperback production once it has gained its market. This matter has already been discussed above. The pivotal element is *the re-purchasability of a commodity*.

Part of the repurchasability, part of the ever-continuing consumption of a series is the overdrawn characterization of the Hero into the Super-hero. The widespread and well-known error of criticism aimed at such overdrawn characterization of hero-figures is the fascism argument. What ought to be asked is, Why is the series hero fitted out with such overdrawn characteristics? Furthermore, why do the plot-situations resemble each other and vary so little, and why are they always so overdrawn and overstretched in their details? Because repurchasability differs in the commodity of SF from the exactly identical quality, exactly identical design, and exactly identical packaging guaranteed in brassieres, brass polish, and brake linings, just to name a few alliterating examples. So that it will be consumed, the new episode of a series must differ from the previous episodes of the series—a little, but not too much of course. Otherwise it is obviously not worthwhile to buy the next episode; one could just re-consume the one from the previous week. This, however, would mean the end of a market-situation, for the market must constantly be supplied anew. Therefore, the new episodes of a series must simultaneously resemble as well as differ from each other. How and in what they resemble and differ from each other—those are already considerations of market strategy, i.e., "single-file" strictures, which have their effect on the texts. The Hero must be overdrawn, so that he will remain recognizable as this particular Hero, and he must demonstrate his heroic nature, as this particular hero, in situations which always resemble each other. His characterization, then, must without variation guarantee his behavior.

In order for the individual episodes to differ from each other, there can be no fiddling around with the Hero. Instead, the plot situations must be made to stand off from each other by means of gimmicky overdrawing and exaggeration. Every SF fan knows how well or poorly this turns out. Constant repurchasability, the stability of the market, raises a dilemma for "popular literature" and for SF. The same story cannot be sold week after week, since the previous week's story, unlike a brassiere or a brake lining, has not been "used up." Thus we get continuations; "single-file, parade-style." The Super-hero is a market stabilizer; he guarantees continuity. The overdone gimmicks taken from the bag of tricks of a synthetic adventure-factory ensure the phony enticement to purchase the new episode. In brief, from the perspective of informational aesthetics, in "popular literature" the hero performs the function of an amplifier; in terms of communications theory, he acts as a source of affirmative identification; from the viewpoint of market tactics the Hero serves as a guarantee of repurchasability.

A further characteristic feature of the "single-file" stricture is that the packaging or cover of the SF magazine and SF paperback act as a signal to the consumer that what he is being offered is already familiar to him from previous reading. The outfit and make-up of the commercial article SF have been neglected so far by observers and critics of SF.[3]

4. Genuine Development of Materials vs. Cut-and-Paste Alteration. As far as I can see, in West Germany it is only in the domain of the radio-play that anyone cultivates an active dramaturgy based on genuine development. By this I mean that, from the outline-stage to the time when the text is ready for production, there is consultation with the author about matters of basic conception, the feasibility of realizing what is imagined, and presentation tactics. Here there is more concern for logical consistency and narrative economy, and less concern for the cut-and-paste alteration of a manuscript to create openings for the implantation of commercials, as is the standard practice in the US. Most publishers of paperback SF have to accept short stories and novels in the manner in which they are submitted. At most, some tightening-up and "tidying-up" can be done here and there during translation, but nothing which has to do with basic outline, narrative sequence, or internal consistency can be altered.

The cut-and-paste preparation of narrative material takes place, if need be, when the text which has been provided is in the process of being adapted for filming. Little matter whether the item in question is Harrison's *Rollerball* (US film 1975), Dneprov's *Island of the Crabs* (German TV film), or even Rainer Werner Fassbinder's production *Die Welt am Draht* (1973) of Daniel F. Galouye's *Simulacron-3* (US publ 1964). In the first instance the original American text was trumped up, in a hopelessly anachronistic way, into the tale of the brilliant "star player" in a superperfect but impotent futuristic society. The Soviet satire on hyper-industrialization and an armaments effort which creates its own absurd end was distorted into a Social-Darwinistic scuffle between giant corporations and the military, in which the effect of the metallic robot-crabs was cute rather than menacing. And in Fassbinder's hands the "puppet-world" of an alternate reality superior to our own deteriorated into art-nouveau-type mirror-backgrounds and affairs with the lithe, doe-eyed representatives of the Fairer Sex.

One of the offensive aspects of the SF scene, especially as concerns its market-interconnections, is that the people on the production-end, i.e., the publishers, TV networks, etc., obviously place more value on retaining a stable of marketing-experts rather than consultants with a knowledge of science or the genre of SF. Obviously there is among the makers of SF something like a license which is tacitly taken for granted: the grossest von Däniken-type baloney can be concocted without qualms—just as long as it is made to fit the market.

5. The SF-Market as an Indicator. If it is true that SF is a commodity primarily and literature only secondarily, then it is according to the principles of the market, the criteria of production and consumption, and not otherwise, that SF ought first to be judged. A commodity would thus be the key which fits precisely into those keyholes made for it. Thus Marx's explanation at the conclusion of the first chapter of the first book of his *Capital*, one of the most interesting and capital chapters in the *Capital*, entitled "The Fetishism of Commodity and its Secret." There Marx discusses the notion of the commodity as it is separated out from the production process (which is characterized by alienation) and placed on the market. He remarks that this commodity makes possible conclusions more extensive than is usually assumed: conclusions about the condition of the society which has brought forth the commodity and thanks to which condition the commodity will then be consumed by the society, and also about the condition of the people who produce the commodity. The commodity has set off on its own, and is now something *more* and something *different* than the mere product of a labor process. It permits, according to Marx, inferences about the latent social situation within which this particular commodity has emerged. Commodities become fetishes, and as such have reinforcement, feed-back, and decoder functions. A market is not a free environment, but it is an indicator.

Entertainment in general, "mass literature," and thus SF also, can be a signal that the general consumption and reading appetite favors unproblematic fare, i.e., the pattern of closed plot-sequences, of unambiguous characters, of heroes and other figures who would never be encountered in everyday life. Stereotyped situations, stereotypes in general, and abbreviated forms seem to to be prefered; thus every form of entertainment and all "mass literature" is unrealistic and, if you will, ideological. For every story, every film must begin and end. In political reality, in social reality, in psycho-biographical reality everything "goes on." Nothing ends. The juice in which "popular literature" stews and at which so many turn up their noses, obviously tastes just fine to many more people than those who turn up their noses would like to admit. One cannot ignore the fact that "mass literature"—and therefore SF, too—optimally satisfies the general need for diversion, a sense of orientation, and reinforcement.

Why, at a certain moment, are certain commodities more in demand than others? Why do certain works of SF optimally meet manifestly latent needs of the purchasing public? What is to be concluded from market successes, analogous to the successes of certain "hit" songs? Planned and controlled literary production systems, as they occur today in centrally controlled forms of society, forgo this "seismograph" or fetish, and from this we can infer things—but what? From the marketability of certain commodities—e.g., SF—a certain latent way of thinking can be inferred, a need for literature which offers escapism and evasion, for technological fairy-tales, for actualizations of fears and desires in the "As-If" Realm of popular entertainment. Politicians ought to read SF, for SF creates public opinion—exactly what the politicians always like so much to do themselves. Even considering all the objections I have raised here, the politicians could find out from the most successful SF stories and novels, films, radio plays, and TV series what latent state of consciousness their voters have at a given time. They would be able to find out, for example, that the anxieties and apprehensions of mankind today are not directed so much toward a conflict between the major powers on Earth, but instead toward a challenge put to humanity in a sense far more profound and far-reaching than any challenge heretofore.

SF at the present time is obviously a singular and grandiose collection of fetishes of a technological-industrial world which knows no other way of coming to grips with the evident dilemma of symbol and machine, of subconsciousness and perfection, of nightmares and patterns of happiness, than the range of goods provided by this very SF, in which the future is put up for sale as ideologically distorted adventure, rather than being put up for discussion as an exercise in thought.

NOTES

1. Wieland Schulz-Keil. "Bonanza ist überall. Entstehung und Organisation des US-Fernseh-Imperiums" (Bonanza Everywhere: The Origin and Organization of the American TV Imperium"), *Die Zeit*, 28 Nov 1975.

2. Stanislaw Lem, "Science Fiction: Ein hoffnungslosser Fall—mit Ausnahmen" ("Science Fiction: A Hopeless Case—with Exceptions"), in *Polaris 1*, ed. Franz Rottensteiner (Frankfurt am Main: Insel, 1973), p 41.

3. Cf Dieter Hasselblatt, "Grüne Männchen vom Mars. Science Fiction für Leser und Macher" (Little Green Men from Mars: Science Fiction for Readers and Makers") (Düsseldorf: Droste, 1974), pp 122ff., and idem, "Science Fiction ist eine Ware" ("Science Fiction is a Commodity"), in *Akzente* #1(1974):86ff.

Linda Fleming

The American SF Subculture

(from **SFS** *4: 263–271, November 1977)*

At the 1976 Lunacon, a New York convention, young authors on a panel were asked if they could recall the moment when they knew they wanted to be professionals. One of the authors remembered it clearly. It happened at a convention when author Roger Zelazny spent an evening drinking with him and a few other fans. Zelazny, in turn, writes:

> I reviewed my association with the area, first as a reader and fan, recalling that science fiction is unique in possessing a fandom and a convention system which make for personal contacts between authors and readers, a situation which may be of peculiar significance. When an author is in a position to meet and speak with large numbers of his readers he cannot help, at least for a little while, feeling somewhat as old-time story-tellers must have felt in facing the questions and the comments of a live audience. The psychological process involved in this should be given some consideration as an influence on the field.[1]

Very personal contacts have occurred regularly in SF circles for almost fifty years, contributing significantly, for good or bad, to the evolution of modern SF.

Literary studies of SF have minimized, even ignored, the particular social universe organized around the literature. A sociology of SF can not do so. Theorists of the sociology of knowledge state that the more immediate interpersonal milieu mediates the reciprocal relationship between human thought and the broader societal context in which thought arises.[2] An observable networks of human relationships has influenced authors, the kinds of stories that have been written, and has mediated the reading experience for thousands of readers over the years. There is a socially important SF subculture.

Subcultures are social collectivities within the broader society whose members share certain symbols, traditions, values, customs, rituals, interests, and ways of doing things. Members of a subculture relate to each other through a series of role relationships. They develop channels for communication, methods for recruiting and socializing new members, and rewards and sanctions for those who meet or fail to meet group expectations. Although subcultures vary according to the bases of common identity and their size, duration, and degree of organization, subcultures do influence their members' identities, beliefs, and behavior.

The SF subculture influences the core trinity of authors, editors, and readers, as well as those who occupy the subsidiary roles of artists, collectors and sellers, reviewers and critics, fans engaged in club, fanzine, or convention activities, publishers and distributors, scholars, and now the teachers. Is it really possible to understand fully the evolution of U.S. SF without studying the subculture in which most of this literature evolved? Can we afford to overlook the fact that many science fictionists, including authors and editors, have experienced a sense of community? It is sociologically significant that a nucleus of those in the subculture refer to their social world as an extended family, a tribe, with all those words imply about the intellectual, social, and the emotional bonds that unite them. In the pages that follow I present an overview of the subculture and then suggest certain questions future research might address.

The SF subculture can be identified, even if its boundaries are difficult to define. It originated in the pages of *Amazing*, *Astounding*, and *Wonder Stories* during the 1920s and 1930s. The first SF magazines all had letter columns which printed names and addresses, and from the very beginning readers found others who shared their enthusiasm for SF. They started communicating by letters and, when possible, in person. These young readers were the first fans, and through their activities a fandom grew and developed. This fandom is an integral part of the subculture; it is of great significance because U.S. (and British) authors have been a part of it. Jack Williamson writes of the authors for the first SF magazines: "Though of course we were writing it for all sorts of reasons, even desperately for money, I think most of us took it pretty seriously as a way of testing alternatives. As fellow pioneers in a new country, we needed one another."[3]

The writers communicated with each other. They also communicated with the readers. As magazine readers themselves, the writers also found fandom a source of personal and social support and an enjoyable hobby. More than that, some of the addicted readers of the 1920s became authors by the 1930s. Ever since, the fans of one generation have provided authors and editors for the next. I have never seen any data to back up the claim, but science fictionists have told me that the vast majority (up to ninety percent) of "ghetto" writers were avid readers of the magazines before they wrote their first stories, and many of them were active in fandom.[4]

The pulp writers and editors defined modern SF as they collaborated, shared, innovated, and imitated. SF could build upon SF for "in a magazine devoted to science fiction, where the readers *expected* the unfamiliar, traditions began to develop. Authors could easily see what their peers were writing, and when one author came up with a new idea another could elaborate on that idea in a subsequent story. Thus certain devices and traditions came into existence."[5] Writing for the magazines became in many ways a collective activity.

Reading SF in the magazines is itself a social experience. The letters, editorials, science articles, book columns, special features and interviews with authors have played a crucial role in the creation and maintenance of the social and intellectual bonds, the sense of common identity, that exist among those who produce and those who read SF. The regular magazine reader—even one who does not write letters or in other ways actively communicate with other science fictionists—participates, at least vicariously, in the subculture.

A SF subculture originated, developed, and exists today because of the enthusiasm SF arouses in some people, the subsequent commercial exploitation of that enthusiasm, and because both professionals and readers have found belonging to the group a socially rewarding experience for brief or long periods of their lives. The process was helped along, however, by SF aficionados being labeled as "nuts" who read and wrote "That Buck Rogers Stuff." A very strong ingroup situation developed. The reactions of the outsiders reinforced the sense of being a group apart, which is one of the dimensions that defines the SF subculture.

Cut off from society in certain ways, the subculture developed its own traditions, symbols, customs, and understanding of the literature. The symbols include a special language "fanspeak," a "Golden Age" of SF, a "new" and an "old" wave, and—very importantly—a special shorthand for reading countless stories based on conventions and devices that "ghetto" writers and editors constructed together. Years ago it became unnecessary for authors to develop each argument or premise, explains Donald Wollheim, for the author "has only to say he has a Gate or a transmitter and the reader is able to supply from memory of past stories all the plausibility quotient he needs to accept this as a future probable invention."[6] There are SF "classics" that are well-known to members of the subculture but, except for a few rare exceptions, are unknown to outsiders. Authors make esoteric references to members of the subculture in their stories. There is even a folklore about the literature and science fictionists. (Can one become involved in the subculture and not hear stories about John Campbell, some version of the first meeting between Isaac Asimov and Harlan Ellison, about the late 1930s feud between the Futurians and New Fandom that lead to the "Exclusion Act," or about the intelligence officers who came to Campbell to investigate if Cleve Cartmill's "Deadline" meant a leak in the secrecy surrounding the Manhattan Project?)

The symbols, traditions, and history of the subculture are passed on to each "generation" as new members learn from older members. Over the years the most active science fictionists developed and institutionalized a variety of channels of communication. Most important have been the clubs, fanzines (amateur SF magazines), and the conventions. All three, along with the prozines (professional SF magazines), have been forums for those occupying various roles in the subculture to present and discuss their ideas about the literature, themselves, science, and society. Each has been an important means for the "socialization" of readers and for the recruitment of authors. Fred Pohl, for example, writes, "In the fan mags I acquired the skills necessary to prepare something for public viewing—and the courage to permit it."[7] These communication channels function to unite people who have different interests in the field and who live in various parts of the U.S., even in other countries (Britain in particular). And each has provided feedback from readers to authors and editors.

The high degree of feedback to authors and editors is commented upon frequently in SF circles. It is a characteristic that makes the SF field unique among both paraliterary and "high lit" genres today. Much of the feedback has been institutionalized—in the letter columns of the prozines and fanzines, in the works of fan scholars and reviewers, in personal contacts made at conventions, in such traditions as *Astounding/Analog*'s Analytical Lab for rating stories which Campbell initiated in the late 1930s and which Ben Bova has just recently discontinued, and in the Nebula (since 1965) awards for professionals in the field and the Hugos (since 1953) awarded to professionals *and* amateurs.

The first editor of *Astounding*, Harry Bates, wrote, "You who were the demon fan-letter writers were not very helpful to us as guides. You were indiscriminately enraptured with everything."[8] Addicts who love just about all they read have remained a segment of the subculture. They support all types of SF, the good and the bad. On the other hand, there have always been readers who, for various reasons, are not at all pleased with all they read. Finding an author's mistakes, for example, has always been something of a game for some of the readers. Author Hal Clement tells other writers: "Remember, though, that among your readers there will be some who enjoy carrying your work farther than you did. They will find inconsistencies which you missed; depend on it. Part of human nature is the urge to let the world know how right you were, so you can expect to hear from these people either directly or through fanzine pages. Don't let it worry you."[9]

While it is probably impossible to measure its influence on the fiction, there is no reasons to doubt that this feedback has significantly affected the relationship between society and SF. First, it provides a great deal of reinforcement for authors. Very few have much popular recognition outside the field; even fewer have ever received critical acceptance; and only a minority of them can earn a full or respectable living from writing or editing SF. It is very likely that many of the writers, the good ones, the hacks and those whose talent developed over time, would not have remained in the field were it not for the social recognition subculture members give them. Second, the feedback has let professionals know the kinds of stories various readers like and dislike. This process thus affects the subtypes, styles, and quality of the stories they write. And third, since much of the feedback is public, SF readers can learn what others think about the literature. All the established communication channels expose readers to discussions of the literature and to perspectives for interpreting the reading experience.

SF and its subculture have developed together. The "youth" of the magazines and of fandom coincided with the youth of the early science fictionists. A ten year old who discovered the early issues of *Amazing* would be about sixty today. Young authors who wrote for the pulps in the 1920s and 1930s are now in their fifties through seventies. A number of science fictionists who are in positions to influence the subculture, like Isaac Asimov, Fred Pohl, Jack Williamson, Donald Wollheim, Forrest Ackerman, Sam Moskowitz, "grew up" with SF pulps and fandom. They and members of subsequent generations participated in, are familiar with, and have reacted to the evolution of the literature through its various stages: the gosh-wow, formula technocratic and action-adventure stories of the first decade; the "Golden Age" of Campbell's *Astounding*; the catastrophe stories of the late 1940s; the broadening of the field into more literary and social SF by Anthony Boucher at *F & SF* and Horace Gold at *Galaxy*; the Boom and Bust of the 1950s; the "new wave" of the 1960s; and the heterogeneity—in terms of styles, themes, philosophy, subtypes—of the literature that is labeled SF today.

An evolving SF continually attracts new kinds of readers and professionals into the field. Each generation modifies and redefines the social role of authors: from Gernsback's missionaries for science and technology, to Campbell's writers of stories that might be contemporary novels in a 25th century magazine, to Fred Pohl's or Ben Bova's frontier scouts who report on alternative futures so that people may choose wisely today, or James Blish's explorers of the ethical, moral, and philosophical horizons.[10]

The subculture has evolved too. Social structural changes include increases in total size, the average age of members, the proportion of females, the complexity of social organization, and the number of subgroups with different kinds of interests in SF.

Subgroups and people with different orientations toward SF have been part of the subculture since the beginning. The current division between the more "literary" and the more science-oriented members, for example, is nothing new. Fan historian Harry Warner notes that even at the start of fandom there were "the fans who wanted to talk a lot about science and those who preferred the literary outlook on the hobby."[11] Similarly, just as the label "science fiction" has been applied to stories that are in the "pure" fantasy tradition, the SF subculture is a world of science fictionists and fantacists. When SF went into its "ghetto" built around the specialty magazines, those involved with the kinds of stories in which science and technology did matter kept the most intimate company with those involved with stories of the supernatural and imaginary worlds where magic really works. The fans of space opera have always associated with the fans of sword and sorcery. The subculture has included rocket societies and Lovecraft fans. The overlap between the two literary traditions has been pervasive, and it extends to readers, writers, editors, artists, collectors, sellers, fanzine topics, those attending conventions, and "sister" magazines.

The SF subculture, even with its various subgroups, was small enough to identify without too much difficulty until the 1960s. The boundaries are much less clear today, however, because of the increase in size and because the *literary* SF subculture now overlaps with the larger, more commercialized Star Trek and comics fandoms and the small academic organization, the Science Fiction Research Association.

Important external events that have had such an enormous impact on the field—i.e. the A-Bomb, Sputnik and subsequent developments in space travel, the social crises of the 1960s, environmental issues—did not just directly influence authors. These events have been of tremendous symbolic significance to science fictionists who had shared the power fantasies of the first decades of the SF magazines. After 1945 and Hiroshima the realities of power led many to confront the futures they had been constructing. "We are in that tale wherein the great inventions were made before the installation of Utopia," writes Donald Wollheim. "That story never had a happy ending."[12] The new directions the literature has explored since the 1950s can be explained, in part, as a *collective* re-examination of the shared dreams that members of a subculture had created together.

The "new wave" of the 1960s was of particular significance to both SF and the subculture. For the first time SF and its aficionados were attacked from *within*, by members of the tribe. Fandom was criticized as a conservative influence on the field. These writers challenged many of the basic assumptions, the philosophy, which had been a foundation for so much SF up to then. They "decided that the battle for the future is a lost cause."[13] We were already living in *Brave New World*.[14] Their concern with experimental style, with "inner worlds," and their alienation set in motion a very heated "new" versus "old" wave controversy. No attack by outsiders could have mattered so much. And SF and its subculture have never been the same since.

Both the literature and the subculture in the 1970s represent such a diversity of styles, attitudes, themes, beliefs, and interests that one can say something of a SF group identity crisis now exists. Any consensus view of the future that might have existed is now part of SF history. "They Don't Make Futures Like They Used To" becomes the informal motto of the Science Fiction Writers of America. Individuals with *conflicting* points of view debate and articulate their ideas about what SF is or should be. For example, should the "S" in SF stand for "science" or "speculative"? Should the "adolescent" pulp stories of the ghetto period be rejected in favor of a search for more illustrious and respectable SF ancestors and contemporary kin, or should they be viewed with nostalgia, as stories that provided young readers with a sense of wonder, adventure and exciting ideas? Does the SF label affect an author's chances to be taken as a "serious" writer? Is characterization less important in SF than in other literary traditions?

The diversity of science fictionists' views about the literature, science, and society helps explain those qualities of SF that Robert Scholes suggests are the reasons for SF's relevance and vitality. SF succeeds, he believes, because it satisfies at both the cognitive and the subliminative levels. It provides both intellectual stimulation and narrative excitement.[15] Some members of the subculture prefer the literature's dreaming pole, while some prefer its thinking pole.[16] The latter set increasingly higher criteria for authors to meet in terms of literary, scientific, philosophical, sociological, or political values. Others articulate and communicate their beliefs that whatever other standards authors strive for, they must not neglect storytelling. Ideas *and* narrative are expected. SF should entertain. These various ideas about SF are expressed by people who, for various reasons, do care, often at deeply emotional levels, about the SF literature, people, and traditions. And the institutionalized communication channels ensure that the professionals are aware of the preferences of both their colleagues and the readers. The literature and the subculture have evolved together, each shaping characteristics of the other.

While studies of SF literature proliferate, very little is known about the social structure and dynamics of the subculture. A sociology of SF should include comparisons of people according to the *extent* and the *nature* of their involvement in SF. Let me begin with the extent. Since the 1930s the total audience has been divided into a *minority* who seek active involvement with others who share their interest in SF, and the *majority* who may read just as much fiction as the active fans but do not seek direct social contact with others. At present we know a few things about the vocal minority; we know almost nothing about the silent majority.[17] Each of the existing surveys of the SF audience is a self-selected sample of (a) prozine readers, (b) fanzine readers, (c) convention goers, or (d) active fans who administer questionnaires to each other. None of these studies can be used to make generalizations about the total SF audience—even by the most generous of social science standards, though the consistency of some of the findings allows us to make certain statements about the more active readers.

Researchers are not limited to the kinds of quantitative data surveys provide. Fortunately, members of the subculture have been talking about themselves, their literature, and their social world for years. And they ask questions about the social role of SF.[18] The non-fiction pages of the prozines are full of relevant information about the social structure, dynamics, and values of the subculture. So are the fanzines and the books and articles written by those who have been part of the subculture. But like the survey data, these other more impressionistic kinds of evidence inform us about the members with the greatest social involvement in the subculture and not about the majority who just read paperbacks.

How many members are at the fringes, people whose participation is limited to reading just enough of the fiction to be defined as marginally belonging to the subculture? And how many are as involved as Donald Wollheim? "Science fiction shaped my life and I can truthfully say I am marked by it in every way. Through it and my association with its readers and writers I have found my profession, my life, my philosophy, my hobby, and yes, my wife and friends."[19] How can readers be differentiated according to their reading patterns? What subtypes do they prefer? Where do they read SF? How much? How many occupy more roles in the subculture than just that of reader?

The readers who organize and attend conventions, belong to clubs, become involved in fanzine activity, or read prozines are those who provide the most feedback to the authors and editors. They are the ones who talk and write *about* the literature and the people and events that influence the field. They inform new readers about subcultural traditions. From their ranks come so many of the authors, editors, artists, collectors and sellers, fan publishers, and until recently, almost all the scholars of SF.[20] In what ways do these active fans differ from the "mere" readers?

The authors and editors also participate in various ways. Some of the most popular authors and important editors are deeply involved in the subculture, and have been since adolescence. Many have formed enduring friendships with other professionals and with active fans, and they can call upon each other for ideas, support, and for information they may need when writing a story. Some collaborate, edit each other's stories, teach would-be SF writers and high school or college teachers of SF at various workshops. Others just send manuscripts to editors. Some are active in the Science Fiction Writers of America which functions as something between a fraternal organization and a union. And a few participate in the academic Science Fiction Research Association. It is certainly of social consequence that some of the authors occupy multiple roles in the subculture. Authors like Isaac Asimov, Jerry Pournelle, and Norman Spinrad write science articles for the prozines. Others are engaged in SF scholarship and book reviewing. Authors contribute to fanzines and attend conventions. The dual author-editor role has been a common one over the years; it has also been commented upon as something rather unusual to find in a literary tradition today.[21] The authors and editors also occupy leadership roles within the subculture. Who among the professionals are the most influential—among each other or with the readers? And which ones exercise that role by engaging in activities other than fiction writing?

As to the nature of people's involvement in SF, one question with very few answers is how fiction affects people. This is an area of inquiry plagued by the difficulties involved in disentangling the effects of reading from all the other experiences and personal characteristics of the readers. Yet the fact that SF is a shared experience for so many readers raises some intriguing questions.

What is the consequence, for example, of reading stories about UFO's, ESP, space colonies, innovations in the biological laboratories, or over-populated worlds while at the same time reading articles that review the current scientific status of such phenomena? SF authors discuss the field and express their views on a variety of subjects in fanzines, prozines, before audiences or small groups at conventions, and more recently, on college campuses and T.V. My impression is that for some readers the real heroes of SF are the authors. Do the things they say outside their fiction influence people? If we think in terms of "reading careers," how many young readers are introduced to the field via space opera and the more action-adventure kinds of stories and then "graduate" to more sophisticated SF because their involvement in the subculture exposes them to the ideas of those who articulate increasingly higher standards for "good" SF? Might we think of the subculture as an "informal learning environment" in which such subjects as science and technology, the human and the social condition, alternative futures, pseudo-science, magic, escapism, or different kinds of fiction are discussed—playfully or seriously, superficially or knowledgeably—by people with varying backgrounds, knowledge, and orientations to the issues involved? Campbell and his team of authors during the Golden Age at *Astounding* have been referred to as a "think tank." A sociological approach to SF might view the subculture as a think tank, not necessarily a very sophisticated one, but a democratic one that explores ideas in an idiom and at levels that people at different ages and backgrounds can understand. Questions about the effects of the literature on its readers must explore how the various channels of communication function to give special meaning to the reading experience.

One can argue about the extent to which there has been a SF "ghetto" and whether or not the "ghetto walls" still exist. But one cannot ignore that both objective and subjective aspects of the ghettoization of SF exist, nor that there is a ghetto issue in SF circles today.

At the objective level the SF ghetto refers to the fact that for more than two decades *almost* all SF published in the U.S. appeared in the SF prozines, and that even now the magazine connections and influences remain. Much of book SF is still written by authors who do or have had prozine associations, and a good proportion of book SF is reprints from the magazines. Also, people with prozine backgrounds edit SF series and anthologies and the SF lines for various publishing houses.

At the subjective level there exists among many science fictionists what James Gunn calls a "ghetto mentality,"[22] and it effects how professionals and fans feel about SF, the subculture, and outsiders. Attitudes toward the recent (relative) respectability of SF are a case in point. Some, like Gunn and Ursula Le Guin, welcome the academics and outside critics; such attention and outside criticism could be good for SF. Others, perhaps defensive about "their" literature, are much more skeptical. Lester del Rey, for one, fears the academics, not the fans, will be a negative influence. He is concerned that authors will write for the critics, not their readers, and he questions whether the academics can provide *informed* and valuable criticism. SF should be read, not taught and studied in schools.[23]

Popularity, like respectability, is perceived as a mixed blessing. Increased popularity means new markets for SF, but it also means authors will be writing in a vacuum, less SF building on SF, and less of the valued feedback from *readers*.[24] Evidently, the ghetto issue is complicated because it concerns not just the future of the literature but of the subculture as well. Science fictionists get caught up in the ambivalent love-hate feelings normally associated with those who belong to a smaller community. There are popular "ghetto" authors who have at one time or another announced they do not or will no longer write SF. They want to be taken as serious writers, and they believe the SF label is a liability; and yet they have very personal ties to the subculture and to SF.

Today the magazines no longer dominate, even represent, the field. More authors with no ghetto associations and training write SF. *Fan* critics, scholars, and historians are joined by "outsider" academics. The subculture is becoming larger and less of a closely-knit community; it is no longer as differentiated from the rest of society as it once was. But I think it valid to say that the majority of the most popular and/or respected and/or influential authors and editors of SF today have some ghetto or subcultural associations. For some these associations began in adolescence and have been an extremely significant part of their personal and professional lives. Can one fully understand modern SF without understanding the subculture in which so much of it has evolved?

NOTES

1. Roger Zelazny, "Forum: Some Science Fiction Parameters: A Biased View," *Galaxy* (July 1975), p 11.

2. On the sociology of knowledge see: Karl Mannheim, *Ideology and Utopia: An Introduction to the Sociology of Knowledge*, rev. ed.; trans. Louis Wirth and Edward Shils (New York: Harcourt, Brace & World, a Harvest Book, 1936); the essays in James E. Curtis and John W. Petras, eds., *The Sociology of Knowledge: A Reader* (New York: Praeger Publishers, 1970); or Peter L. Berger and Thomas Luckmann, *The Social Construction of Reality: A Treatise in the Sociology of Knowledge* (New York: Doubleday & Co., 1966; Anchor Books, 1967). The latter presents a historical survey of the field and a theory that includes a social-psychological level of analysis. On the related sociology of art and literature see: Georg Lukacs, *Realism in Our Time: Literature and the Class Struggle*, with a Preface by George Steiner, trans. John and Necke Mander, ed. Ruth Nanda Anshen (New York: Harper & Row, 1964; Harper Torchbooks, 1971); Milton C. Albrecht, James H. Barnett, and Mason Griff, eds., *The Sociology of Art and Literature: A Reader* (New York: Praeger Publishers, 1970) which includes an essay by Lucien Goldmann; or Robert N. Wilson, *The Sociology and Psychology of Art* (Morristown, N.J.: General Learning Press, 1973) which presents a concise and helpful overview of theory and research in the area.

3. Jack Williamson, "The Campbell Era," *Algol* 24 (Summer 1975), p 19.

4. See Ted White, Editorial, *Amazing* (July 1975), p 111.

5. Ted White, Editorial, *Amazing* (June 1976), p 121.

6. Donald A. Wollheim, *The Universe Makers* (New York: Harper & Row, 1971), p 16.

7. Frederik Pohl, "Basement and Empire," reprinted in *Algol* 26 (Summer 1976), p 35.

8. Harry Bates, "Editorial Number One: To Begin," Introduction to *A Requiem for Astounding* by Alva Rogers (Chicago: Advent: Publishers, 1964), p xv.

9. Hal Clement (Harry Stubbs), "The Creation of Imaginary Beings," in *Science Fiction, Today and Tomorrow*, ed. Reginald Bretnor (New York: Harper & Row, Penguin Books, 1974), p 275.

10. See William Atheling, Jr. (James Blish), *The Issue at Hand* (Chicago: Advent: Publishers, 1964), p 128; Ben Bova, Editorial, "The SF Game," *Analog* (October 1975); and Frederik Pohl, "The Shape of Science Fiction to Come," *Luna Monthly* (October/November 1972).

11. Harry Warner Jr., *All Our Yesterdays: An Informal History of Science Fiction Fandom in the Forties*, with an Introduction by Wilson Tucker (Chicago: Advent: Publishers, 1969), p 29.

12. Wollheim, p 6.

13. Ibid., p 105.

14. Brian Aldiss, *Billion Year Spree: The True History of Science Fiction* (New York: Doubleday, 1973; reprint ed., Schocken Books, 1974), p 298.

15. Robert Scholes, *Structural Fabulation: An Essay on Fiction of the Future* (Notre Dame, Ind.: University of Notre Dame Press, 1975).

16. Brian Aldiss discusses the field's dreaming and thinking poles in *Billion Year Spree.*

17. Studies that review available data include: Beverly Friend, "The Science Fiction Fan Cult" (Ph.D. dissertation, Northwestern University, 1975); Linda Fleming, "The Science Fiction Subculture: Bridge Between the Two Cultures" (Ph.D. dissertation, University of North Carolina, Chapel Hill, 1976); and Charles G. Waugh, Edwin F. Libby, and Carol-Lynn Waugh, "Demographic, Intellectual, and Personality Characteristics of Science Fiction Fans," paper presented at the Science Fiction Research Association annual meeting, Miami, November 1975.

18. For example, in the Summer 1975 issue of *Algol*, Brian M. Stableford wrote an article on "The Social Role of S.F." He initiated a debate as readers responded to his views in subsequent issues of the fanzine.

19. Wollheim, p 2.

20. The importance of fan scholarship is a subject of Beverly Friend's "The Science Fiction Fan Cult."

21. See Anthony Boucher, Introduction to *In Search of Wonder: Essays on Modern Science Fiction* by Damon Knight (Chicago: Advent: Publishers, 1967), p. viii, or Judith Merrill, "What Do You Mean: Science? Fiction?" reprinted in *SF: The Other Side of Realism: Essays on Modern Fantasy and Science Fiction*, ed. Thomas D. Clareson (Bowling Green, Ohio: Bowling Green University Popular Press, 1971), p 79.

22. James Gunn, Guest Editorial, "Teaching Science Fiction Revisited," *Analog* (November 1974).

23. Lester del Rey, Forum: "The Siren Song of Academe," *Galaxy* (March 1975).

24. Ted White, Editorial, *Amazing* (June 1976).

Rudolf Stefen

Violence in SF, and Censorship in West Germany

Translated by George Hildebrand

(from **SFS** *4: 271–276, November 1977)*

The Law Regarding Dissemination of Youth-Endangering Writings (hereafter GJS)[1] has the task of protecting children and juveniles to the age of eighteen from writings "tending to endanger their morals" (passed 9 June 1953; proclaimed 29 April 1961; amended 2 March 1974). Its safeguards are to be enforced not by restrictions on publication or distribution but through limitations on advertising, sales, and hand-to-hand transmission; thus, adults may still purchase such material.

Youth-endangering literature includes, to cite the GJS (Paragraph 1, Section 1, Sentence 2), "above all, writings that are immoral, brutalizing, that incite to violence, racism, and crime, or that glamorize war."

The judgments of the Federal Bureau for the Examination of Youth-Endangering Writings (hereafter FBE)[2] and the decisions of the federal courts have regularly interpreted the phrase "endangering the morals of youth" (GJS Section 1, Sentence 1) as referring to writings that tend to confound the social ethics of children and young people. "Writings" in the sense of these regulations includes tapes, films, photographs, and other media or forms of reproduction (GJS). GJS Paragraph 1, Section 2, rules explicitly that no material may be put on the index "1) only because of its political, social, religious or world-view content; 2) when it serves art, science, research, or teaching; 3) when it serves the public interest, unless the method of presentation is objectionable."

In order to achieve its objectives, GJS (Sections 3-5) provides for certain restrictions on sales, advertising, and hand-to-hand transmission. Under threat of penalty, it is forbidden to make such writings accessible to children or juveniles, to offer it to them, or to display it in locations that juveniles can enter or look into (GJS Section 3), such as in retail outlets outside of places which the customer does not usually enter; to peddle, disseminate, or lend such writings through the mail, reading clubs or commercial lending libraries, or to store them for such purposes. Further, publishers and jobbers may not deliver to such persons or places. With the exception of trade with acceptable businesses or locations, accessible only to adults, such literature may not be publicized or advertised.

These restrictions apply only to writings that appear on the official list of "youth-endangering writings." According to GJS Para. 6, the restrictions hold as well for material not indexed or published on that list provided that under conditions specified by the law they exalt violence, that they incite to racial hatred, are pornographic, or otherwise manifest a serious danger to the morals of children or juveniles.

The FBE decides which books shall be indexed. This authority is a federal high commission, legally freed from guidelines. It makes its decisions in committees of three or twelve. The committee of twelve meets once a month; it consists of the chairman, three representatives of the federal provinces (by rotation), and eight members representing the special interest groups: artists, writers, publishers, booksellers, youth associations, juvenile welfare workers, teachers, and churches (Evangelical, Jewish, Catholic, by rotation). The group representatives are proposed for three years by the federal Minister for Youth, Family, and Health. The representatives of federal units are nominated by the provincial governments, and the chairman by the federal Minister for Youth, Family, and Health. The committee of three functions with one group representative, one other member, and the chairman.

Usually, the FBE examines a specific work only upon complaint. The right to complaint resides only with the highest provincial ministries involved with youth—mostly the Ministry of Labour—and the Federal Ministry of Youth, Family, and Health. As a rule, the ministries become active in these matters only when urged to do so by the populace, and not on their own initiative.

1. On the Definition of "Youth-Endangering." The law defines as dangerous to youth those writings that tend to confound the social ethics of children and juveniles. In a specific case it is not necessary to prove that an individual has been endangered or that the material lends itself to such a danger: it is enough to establish the probability of such a tendency. In this respect, the law distinguishes between criteria of content and criteria of effect by enumerating some examples in GJS Para. 1, Sentence 2.

The law finds a specific work to be dangerous to youth when *content* analysis shows that the material: a) glorifies war or makes it appear harmless; b) represents violence against people in a brutal or otherwise callous way, thereby showing such violence to be either innocuous or glamorous; c) incites to racial hatred; or d) is pornographic in the sense of Para. 184 of the State Civil Code.

The FBE may index literature that brutalizes or incites to violence, crime or racism only if it can establish the probability that the specified *effects* indeed arise. That depends largely upon whether one holds with the "catharsis theory" or the "learning theory." Those who defend the "catharsis theory" argue that aggressive presentations have a "purifying" effect—that observing violent scenes detours or "abreacts" aggressive impulses into fantasy, and therefore, they are not acted out in reality.

Contemporary psychology considers the "catharsis theory" as obsolete, although it might admit that aggressive tendencies may be reduced in already irritated and angry observers. The "learning theory" suggests that individuals who are not in such an affective condition will probably have an augmented potential for aggression after they observe violent scenes. This theory suggests that the danger lies in learning not only a single behavioral response but also the "characteristic" of aggressivity, i.e. the readiness to act more aggressively in a variety of situations.[3]

2. Putting SF on the Index. In 1959 Robert Schilling, chairman of the FBE from 1953 to 1966, wrote the following:

The "futuristic" novels ("utopian" novels or "SF" novels) require some special observations. This genre is rapidly multiplying. It should be kept in mind that every month the eleven "utopia" series require twenty new novels (not including similar lending library requirements). A good SF novel demands, along with artistic ability, a genuine knowledge of science and technology; otherwise, the product is likely to be sheer nonsense. Since the number of writers satisfying both these requirements is sharply limited, it can be predicted that qualified authors will not be able to meet the increased demand of this assembly-line production.... We can fear, then, that these circumstances will bring forth a new kind of thriller, which differs from a crime-thriller only in that the exaltation of violence, the display of brutality, and the celebration of jungle-law have been transferred to an interplanetary or interstellar setting where they are executed with futuristic weapons. Youth-endangering thrillers would then simply be given a different setting.... Several years ago comics were about to evolve in a similar direction. At that time we just managed to suppress this horror-tendency in embryo. We must serve youth in a similar way with respect to SF, thereby encouraging authentic SF and fostering the genuine reading pleasure appropriate to a genre that otherwise might fall into bad repute.[4]

It should be emphasized that Schilling called upon all those responsible for the protection of young people to use the GJS to curb the occasional excesses and abuses of SF in order to support the genuine article and to protect it from falling into disrepute.

In retrospect, it can be established that the FBE has never indexed significant SF literature, although it has indexed corrupt imitations. Again, I emphasize that the FBE cannot influence the number of indexations. That depends on the complaints lodged by the various ministries. It should be apparent, then, that the following cursory review of FBE judgments reflects rather inadequately the rise in the actual sales of such SF writings.

At the beginning of its mandate, the FBE had also to deal with adventure novels having SF elements. In this category the adventure novels of Hellmut Hubertus Munch deserve special mention. Intended for circulating libraries, they were published under the pseudonym of Hanns Hart in runs of 5000 by Engelbert Pfriem Publishers of Wuppertal. The writer describes the "adventures" of ex-naval Lieutenant Hart and his buddy Schorsch Berger. Along with their U-Boat crew, they fled after the war to a South Sea island, the so-called "German Atoll"; they discovered there a fortune in pearls and became incredibly wealthy. Since the crew grew afraid of American A-bomb tests, their leader sent Hart and Berger to the USA to spy out the American plans and to frustrate any tests projected near their island. In carrying out this assignment, they came into contact with the underworld. The crimes, brutality and violence that result are detailed in the series. Finding that these portrayals exalt violence and brutality, the FBE has seen fit to index the following productions of Hanns Hart: *Tuomotu* and *Agents of Vice* (FBE Decision 24, of 2.11.54); *Pistol Staccato* (Decision 132, 11.11.55); *Outlaw Legend* (Decision 145, 16.12.66); *Public Enemy Unmasked* (Decision 148, 13.1.56); *Monarch of Space* and *Carnations for Nora* (Decision 990, 6.10.61); *Panic in the Ether* (Decision 1023, 8.12.61); *License to Kill...For XP3* (Decision 1054, 9.2.62).[5] The publisher appealed the blacklisting of *Monarch of Space* and *Carnations for Nora* in the Cologne District Court. The judgment of the court (AZ 2 K 2131/61 or 3.7.61) confirmed the indexing of these books as follows:

In no way did the accused (the FBE) base its decision solely, as the plaintiff (publisher) alleges, on the assumption that warlike events in a futuristic setting were automatically youth-endangering. On the contrary, the FBE has explained how the probable effects of just the novel in question would tend to endanger young people in an educational and moral sense, and bring about their moral depravation. Thus, we concur with the FBE that, contrary to the contention of the plaintiff, the book contains not merely one brutal scene but multiple descriptions of brutalities.... The unremitting delineation of cold-blooded and deeply criminal acts with emphasis on minutiae and method constitutes a definite danger to the young reader. Reading such a book, the young person, who because of his youth has not yet developed mature concepts of society, law, and moral order, may suffer a misdirected moral development. He could develop false criteria regarding the morally reprehensible or acceptable action. Along with obscuring the distinction between right and wrong, the book threatens the emotional stability of young people. Its numerous and incessant atrocities raise jungle-law to an ideal, and celebrate brute force and violence as the most successful way of dealing with one's fellow man. In general, these crimes contribute to the brutalizing of youth by fostering a brutish mentality and aggressive drives. To instil a positive attitude toward violence is gravely youth-endangering. Nor are there anywhere in the novel counter-values which might offset its probable negative effects. For these reasons, the work is highly likely to endanger the morals of young people.

FBE Decisions 225 (7.9.56), 419 (15.9.57), and 428 (13.12.57) indexed the books *If You've Seen One, You've Seen Them All*, *The Killer is Invisible*, and *Moon Shadows*, all three from the "Crime Novels of Tomorrow" series by Allan Reed (Ravena Publishers, Basel). The point of *If You've Seen One, You've Seen Them All* is the annihilation of several nuclear power-stations situated in New York, Washington, Philadelphia, and Boston. A sort of deathray is beamed at the targets from a spaceship on behalf of a "second power" stationed on an artificial satellite. The book further describes three murders perpetrated by the gang, as well as numerous brutalities that arise from the gang's pursuit. In indexing the book, the FBE pointed mainly at its sadistic atrocities, citing several detailed examples in its judgment. *The Killer Is Invisible* focuses on a 21st-century murderer who has a machine that can make him invisible. He is "a pig who sports with chicks," a "pig" who likes to strangle naked girls. The story was indexed for its brutalizing effect.

In justifying the indexing of *Moon Shadows*, the FBE wrote: "A transvestite (girl) plays the criminal in this impoverished and drawn-out plot. He or she has invented a gadget that wipes out memory and alters personality, transforming victims into will-less robots directed by hypnosis. He/she criminally abuses the invention to force people to rob banks or, more commonly, to induce daughters of wealthy families to become call-girls...."

Decision 742 (3.6.60) indexed the paperback *Help From Andromeda* by J.E. Wells, number 63 of the "Terra" SF series published by Moewig of Munich. The decision refers to the glamorizing of heroes who terrorize, violate, and murder; it goes on to say that "the damaging character of the work is not mitigated by its futuristic setting" and that "the presentation reminds one of the mentality shown in the horrors of the concentration camps." The publisher described the issue as a mistake and called back the remaining copies. The same title was indexed again when Hönne Publishers issued it in hardcover in 1962. *Rendezvous Pito* by the same writer met a similar fate. It was indexed as a book in 1959, and again when it turned up with identical content in a publication by Hönne Publishers in 1961.

Another pseudo-SF thriller by J.E. Wells was indexed by Decision 988 of 7.10.61. It takes the reader to the 11th millenium where death, the symbol of imperfection, and marriage, the symbol of obligation, have been overcome. Dr. K on the planet Genta has discovered the "electron of movement" and exploits it for criminal purposes. After having inhabitants of other planets murdered and buried, Dr. K has them transported to Genta, where he energizes the corpses with his "electron of movement." At the same time he cuts the "memory nerve" and places his reactivated victims under hypnosis, transforming them into creatures obedient to his every command. The operation changes highly intelligent men into sub-human puppets, dull, apathetic, and without memory. These zombies and a number of extraordinary robots give Dr. K unlimited power. The animated corpses vegetate in stinking barracks, and some are occasionally sent to other planets for more bodies to be resurrected into slavery. Dr. K's purpose is to make all mankind immortal and himself "Lord over Death." He is already immortal, thanks to the "electrons of movement" that he carries in his body and which make him immune to any kind of attack. Dr. K has two enemies; killed and condemned to mindless slavery, by the skill of a doctor they get their memory back and plan a horrible doom for the immortal Dr. K. A billion kilometres from Terra, they toss him out of a spaceship and abandon him to the infinity of space where time has no meaning. The book includes a chapter that explains love. One meets and loves for a few days and then one separates without any useless emotions; one marries, but one still lives an unfettered existence, viz.: "Life on Genta is great simply because of its freedom; one could label this star the 'Planet of the Shameless' had its inhabitants at all known what the word 'shame' means."

The publisher agreed with the main criticism of the judgment, and confessed that his author had seriously erred in his "utopian" innovation, regretted that the editors had not taken exception to the book, and promised not to repeat his error.

As a result of complaints launched by Lower Saxony and Hamburg, FBE Decicion 1064 of 9.2.62 indexed the booklet *Stop-Over at Callisto* by Hilding Borgholm (Utopia Super Series No. 156, Pabel Press, Rastatt). The judgment reads as follows: "Both complaints rightly take exception to the nonsensical and spurious SF plot-frame, which obviously serves only to exalt in the most clumsily overt way the methods and policies of the Third Reich, the methods and slogans of the SS. Further, the book is an overt defence of convicted war criminals."

Decision 310 (10.5.57) indexed Robert O. Steiner's *Eron*, No. 9 of the Luna-Utopia Series, distributed by Lening Press in the kiosks of Hannover for 0.60 Marks. This was an abridged version of the *Eron* which Steiner had previously published at Commedia Press (Berlin, 1952). Despite the heavy cutting, both the FBE and the public prosecutor found the novella to be salacious. *Eron* is about the discovery and perfection of a serum by a Professor Wagner. The serum works to replace aggressive instincts with a greatly intensified sex-drive, "an overwhelmingly powerful appetite for the opposite sex." After experiments with animals, Wagner tries the serum on people; it surpasses his greatest expectations. This kind of writing latches on to pornography in a pseudo-SF manner. As examples I refer to *Frankenstein 69* and *The Sexplanet*, both from Olympia Publishers and both indexed by Decision 2255, of 17.4.70. The indictment of the Westphalian Minister of Labour (with which the FBE was in full agreement) describes *Frankenstein 69* as follows:

> Hidden in a castle, a professor secretly manufactures in his lab some walking and talking female dolls that have special heating systems to make them capable of sexual activity. Later, the professor's wife rigs up a couple of male puppets for her own entertainment. Typical of the book's pornographic conception are phrases such as "Cock like a baby's arm with a knob like a clenched fist" (p 134). The dolls are outdone only by two water pixies, Ilona and Suleika, who sport several penises of varied length beside their vaginas. Their sexual capabilities have no limits; Ilona has coupled with a horse and would love to try out an elephant and even a whale. At one point the ocean god Triton makes a triumphal entry to the accompaniment of constructions like "cocksucker, supertit, slavering wanton, your fucking majesty."

Both the complainant and the FBE agreed that the coarseness of detail made it unlikely that lust was being portrayed ironically.

The Sexplanet, indexed by Decision 948(V) of 21.3.72, presents a spaceship with a male and female crew plunging toward a distant planet. The crew pass the time in uninhibited sexplay; aphrodisiacs heighten their sex potential. When they land on the planet they find only abandoned cities, but eventually they do meet humanoid inhabitants. A female native begs them to save the planetary race by fertilizing herself and 300 other females preserved on ice, as their few remaining males are impotent: most of the planet's inhabitants have "fucked themselves to death" as a consequence of their inexhaustible energy. In intercourse with the humanoids, the travellers achieve orgasms of incredible magnitude. The men develop yard-long organs, and some find themselves suddenly with female genitals:

they have sex with themselves. One creature endowed with especially strong unnatural erotic powers, "the Gant," takes on the female visitors. One spacegirl after another "sighs away her life" while enjoying "infinitely extended orgasms" with the Gant. The spacemen expire from sexual exhaustion as well. The last surviving spacewoman is ejected into space together with the Gant.[6]

Later complaints and judgments were directed more and more against horror and vampire tales, comics, and other illustrated fiction (some of foreign origin), all of which exalted brutality and murder. Several series were blacklisted permanently, and these subsequently ceased publication. Details cannot be entered into here. I will look more closely only at one thriller from the series "Dr. Morton Horror-Crime Bestsellers" at Anne Erber Publishers, Sasbachwalden. Booklet #48 is entitled *A Slaughter-Feast for Demeter—Served by Grimsby*. This book tells how Grimsby administers secret doses of radiation to two hundred unsuspecting members of the Finch clan, dooming them to a slow death by cancer; the victims include an innocent waiter as well as several servants. Earlier, Grimsby had recorded on video-tape how he murdered the clan chieftain's niece, cut up her body, and dressed the flesh for a meal. At a banquet in honour of the niece's expected return, Grimsby shows the video to the family members immediately after they have dined on the murdered niece. The book sells in kiosks for DM 1.20, and it describes the screening of the film as follows:

"I'll demonstrate now how to butcher and serve a human being. The subject, as you must all know by now, is Miss Demeter Finch, your relative." One of the younger Finch girls collapsed onto the expensive Chinese carpet, but no one paid any attention to her. What they were seeing could hardly be comprehended by a human mind. Rigid, horror-struck, frenzied, they saw how Grimsby executed Demeter Finch and heard his monotonous voice commenting on this or that cut. They saw how Demeter's blood gushed, much like that of a stuck pig. The well-made video-tape showed everything in consummate detail. Grimsby began to carve up the pale, bloodless corpse. He trimmed off the head, the arms, and the legs. He slit open the trunk and removed the internal organs. It was a regular slaughter-feast, an experience like those the Finches had had on the farm. Only this time not a beast but a human being was the sacrifice. And not just any person, but Demeter Finch, the clan chieftain's favorite, the light of his last years, she who meant everything to him.... The scene shifted to the kitchen showing Grimsby standing beside trays of flesh, all parts of Demeter Finch's body trimmed and ready for.... He was preparing a banquet, taking from the girl's body all the meat required for the entrée, the soup, and the main dish. He expounded and demonstrated. How difficult it was to give the faintly sweet human flesh the taste of beef, veal, or pork! What pains he had taken, he confessed, to plan the menu so that no one would become suspicious. After all, human flesh does not have the same texture as beef. "I did want you to enjoy your family member," said Grimsby with a chuckle.

NOTES

1. Das Gesetz über die Verbreitung jugendgefährdender Schriften.

2. Bundesprüfstelle für jugendgefährdende Schriften.

3. See Herbert Selg, *Zur Aggression verdammt?* (Stuttgart, 1975), 4th ed.; Rudolf Stefen, "Der Film—ein Medium fur Porno und Gewaltverherrlichung: Ein Bericht zum Theme 'Filmszene und Jugendschutz,'" *Herder-Korrespondenz*, No. 12(1975), pp 600ff.

4. Robert Schilling, *Literarischer Jugendschutz: Theorie und Praxis, Strategie und Taktik einer Wirksamen Gefahrenabwehr*, (Luchterhand, 1959), p 82. For an analysis of a SF thriller, see Robert Schilling, "Utopia—ein neues Gebiet für Schundautoren," *Jugendliteratur*, 1(1959), pp 8ff.

5. All originally German titles have been translated to give a better idea of the contents. —GH.

6. *The Sexplanet* has been published in English: Peter Kanto, *World Where Sex Was Born* (New York: Ophelia Press, Inc., affiliated with the Olympia Press, nd [circa 1970]). Vanvogtian in narrative style, and quite idiomatic (i.e. it does not read like a translation), I assume that it is American in origin.—RDM.

Bernt Kling

On SF Comics: Some Notes for a Future Encyclopedia

Translated by Nancy King; edited by DS

(from **SFS** *4: 277–282, November 1977)*

The best known pure SF comics are *Buck Rogers* and *Flash Gordon*, to which were later added the "Super-hero comics" (see under that heading). *Buck Rogers* goes back to a SF story by Phil (Philip Francis) Nowlan which appeared in *Amazing Stories* in 1928: a hero named Anthony Rogers falls into suspended animation by means of a kind of active gas. He awakes 500 years later, in a future when the Earth is ruled by the "Han Air Lords," an oriental race whose ancestors came from another planet, and fights successfully against this yellow peril from outer space. From 1929 the adventures of *Buck Rogers 2429 A.D.* appeared as comic strips in many newspapers. Every year the date in the title changed, so that the action always took place exactly 500 years in the future; finally the series received a permanent title, *Buck Rogers in the Twenty-Fifth Century*. The scripts for the comics were also written by Phil Nowlan, the illustrations were by Dick Calkins. Buck Rogers also became the hero of a radio show series which was written and produced by the same people as the Superman radio plays.

The *Flash Gordon* comic strip was begun on January 7, 1934, and was similar in content to the Buck Rogers series, but considerably better drawn (by Alex Raymond, who later became known through *Rip Kirby* and *Secret Agent X-9*). The blond, blue-eyed hero fights against prehistoric monsters and evil humanoid races, which are for the most part led by a tyrant with Mongolian features, Ming the Cruel. Gordon is accompanied by his sweetheart Dale and by the Scientist Dr. Zarkoff. Flash Godon fights amid a hostile environment (thick jungle, icy landscape) in a planet where the social formation is a most primitive feudalism. Especially striking is the contrast between the feudal society and advanced technology: the fighting uses both swords and atomic cannons; the hero and his opponent are like mythological figures who decide the fate of a people by technological means, while the people only celebrates the victorious hero or kneels before the evil antagonist.

Flash Gordon has become one of the best known SF comics, appearing in large editions and many countries; e.g., Federico Fellini wrote the Italian version for a while, since under Fascism U.S. comic strips were not allowed into Italy. The success of the comics brought in its wake radio-serials and film serials in which Buster Crabbe, who had portrayed Tarzan in the early *Tarzan* films, took the role of Flash Gordon. A British comic series with a similar hero, Jeff Hawke, who is projected from everyday situations into space and time-adventures, has had a long-standing success up to the present day.

In 1938 *Superman* (see under that heading) appeared for the first time. He was followed by numerous other super-hero comics, which determined the development of the SF comics (with the exception of a few comic book series such as *Strange Stories* and *From Beyond the Unknown*, which remained relatively unimportant). In addition, numerous SF comics have been taken from TV serials, such as *Space Family Robinson* and *Star Trek*.

A special style of drawing has been developed for various French comics, e.g. those drawn by Druillet or Moebius. Especially in the comic-strip periodical *Pilote*, a real national school of SF comics developed. Later, these *bandes dessinés* began also appearing in the more accessible form of large comics albums.

In West Germany the strip series *Test Pilot Speedy*, begun in 1954, became later *Astronaut Speedy*, with a mixture of space and SF-thriller adventures. Speedy is the astronaut of a federation in permanent conflict with an enemy and has primarily to deal with enemy sabotage. Such plots, clearly a paraphrase of the West-East Cold War, were rather bad, but the drawings were worse. In Italy, the comics serials *Fulgor the Cosmonaut* and *Raka, the Hero of 2000* were published in the form of small "piccolo" continuations. A similar form was used in West Germany for H. Wäscher's *Nick the Astronaut*, which however after 1959 appeared also as large color albums (rptd. 1976). All these series had current space-opera plots. Other West German series have mostly failed, except for the super-hero comics. Even *Perry-Our Man in Space*, a comics version based on the successful *Perry Rhodan* series of novels, lasted only from 1968 to 1975.

Superman. Superman is a motif from SF literature taken up by the comics industry at the end of the 1930s and since utilized in ever new variations of "Super-hero comics" (see under that heading). Superman was the first, and is still the best known of these costumed superhuman heroes. His predecessors are to be found in certain heroes from the SF pulp series such as *Captain Future* and *Doc Savage*. Three favorite themes of SF literature come together in Superman: the visitor from another planet, the superman, and finally the secret identity. It has been shown that the idea of the comics hero Superman goes back to Philip Wylie's 1930 novel *Gladiator*. In this novel the possible super-strength of a man is explained by comparison with insects such as ants or grasshoppers who are a hundred times as strong as we are:

> If a man could be given the same sinews as an ant, he could carry his own house away.... Make a man as strong as a grasshopper—and he would be able to leap over the church. I tell you, there is something which determines the quality of each and every muscle and every sinew. Find it—transplant it—and you have the solution. [§7]

In Wylie's novel a scientist finds the answer, and injects his pregnant wife with a chemical mixture which makes her child eventually grow into a man with superhuman strength. The creator of Superman, Jerry Siegel, had reviewed this novel in a fanzine he edited. Siegel developed the idea of Superman already in 1933 and had it put into drawings by his 17-year-old friend, Joe Shuster. The two tried in vain for five years to sell their comics to a publisher or a comics syndicate, but had it rejected as "a rather immature work"; actually, both the text and the illustrations were rather poor. Thus, the first adventure of the *Man of Steel* appeared for the first time in 1938 in the new comic book series *Action Comics*. Through its success, a great need was discovered and the explosive expansion of the Superman myth began. *Superman* appeared in 230 daily and Sunday newspapers, film serials were produced both live and as cartoons, radio plays were broadcast, and the comic books with "The World's Greatest Adventure Strip Character" sold in ever increasing editions which occasionally were as high as one and half million.

The myth of Superman corresponded to a need in the socio-political atmosphere of the Thirties:

> It was 1938 and the country was recovering slowly and unsteadily from the blow which had crippled the economy in 1929. In the air was talk about war in Europe and a crazy clown by the name of Hitler. The technocrats were preaching that science could rule the world and could solve all human problems forever, while the communists were aiming for a united socialist world under the dictatorship of the proletariat. It was a time of idealism and of shattered ideals. We had been cast down, but everything wasn't over yet. Our world was in pieces, but we knew that we could build a better one.[2]

Superman was, of course, all that which his creators were not. Jerome Siegel and Joe Schuster were described as "two slim, shy, nervous, nearsighted kids"; they were each 17 years old and in high school when they invented Superman. Therefore they made their "Man of Steel" tall, strong, self-confident, affable, and furthermore, a super-human being with perfect reflexes and X-ray vision (Superman can see through walls and into farthest distances). Superman always reestablished a compensatory justice and put the world in order with his mighty strength. And as the success of the series proved, America had many Siegels and Schusters who felt equally powerless and indulged only too gladly in power fantasies of a superhuman being who had come out of the cosmos to Earth to defend justice and order. Thus, Superman was the fulfillment of a widespread wish-dream: a power from outer space, descended to Earth, he had become an American, a genuine patriot.

The Superman story is well-known but should be mentioned: when his native planet was destroyed by a catastrophe, a scientist put his son in a test rocket and sent it towards Earth. There the super-baby was adopted by an elderly, childless couple; the child grew up, became Superboy, and gradually his super-powers became apparent. In the first issues, for example, he could not yet fly, but (like the hero of Wylie's novel) only take long leaps on the basis of his super-strength. However the "super" concept and the readers' expectations enforced a continual increase in his powers. They increased in the course of the decade so much that Superman could even move planets out of their orbits. Also, at the beginning Superman was not invulnerable; he only gradually became the unbeatable and invulnerable superhuman. Yet, how many exciting adventures can a hero have if he is unbeatable and invulnerable? Thus, Superman had to be given certain weaknesses. They were brought into play by the red and green kryptonite, a radioactive rock from Superman's no longer existent native planet, which fell to Earth in the form of meteorites. This kryptonite wholly counteracted Superman's super-powers or caused physical changes in him—so that Superman could be delivered to his enemies, almost powerless, when Kryptonite was brought into his proximity. His secret identity became an additional weakness, for he had to protect it at any price. For in his private life Superman is called Clark Kent and is a reporter for a daily newspaper (later a TV company); he wears glasses and is rather helpless. Only when the need arises does Clark Kent, generally something of a fool and coward, metamorphose into Superman.

During the Second World War, Superman became a super-patriot, and dedicated his powers to the battle against America's enemies: the cover picture of a *Superman* issue from September, 1941, shows Superman going arm-in-arm with a soldier and a sailor. From then on the Man of Steel had appropriate steel enemies: battleships, submarines, tanks, airplanes. He fought at the same time on all fronts: against the Nazis, the Japanese, and saboteurs and war profiteers in the U.S.A. In addition he still helped old ladies to cross the street safely. The nationalistic message of Superman's warfare was supplemented by calls for the purchase of war bonds.

After the Second World War this personified dream from the American collective subconscious continued reflecting the changes in the "American way of life." Just like the G.I.'s returning from the War, who had carried Superman's "numerous adventures in their knapsacks when they stormed the Atlantic Wall,"[3] Superman too returned to the civilian everyday life, tired of battle. From this point on everyday skulduggeries often gave him more trouble than his worst enemies; Superman was degraded to a slapstick figure, for his stories contained more costume-comedy than action. This extended to Superman's haircut, for one pair of scissors after another broke on his hard-as-steel hair.

Above all, his double identity grew more pronounced, and the contrast between the helpless Clark Kent and his Superman-version ever more pronounced. The insignificant, clumsy and scared Clark Kent loves his colleague Lois Lane, also a reporter, but she has only contempt for him, since she loves Superman. Out of this situation and the constant hide-and-seek around Superman's identity new comic complications continually arose. Nevertheless Superman, desired by all, cannot love: he fulfills his manhood only in action and battle:

Here is a saga about a masculine American, a *macho*, who because of his *omertà*, can have as many women as he likes, but absorbed in his male world and repelled by his own desires, does not know what to do with women—in complete contrast to the weakling (who he is at the same time) whose impotence is evident, paradoxically, in his positive attitude to women.[4]

Superman, the clean American, the super-boyscout, has no sexual drive—if anybody has this it is his enemies, the super-scoundrels whom he must vanquish again and again. And yet another quality can be found in his super-enemies which is missing in Superman: they are intelligent. The Superman writer Jerry Siegel said "We do not emphasize the intellectual side of Superman. People do not dream of becoming super-intelligent." Only his enemies have intelligence, and are often Mad Scientists who because of their intelligence do not fit into the desired simple order of a Superman America. Their intelligence leads them to ever new and more perfect crimes, and enables them to carry these ideas out; Superman can never prevent their success by intellectual effort, but only by the power of his fists.

It could have become "an American dream," said his creators Siegel and Schuster of Superman in 1975. But for them it did not become one. They had signed away their rights in 1938 for 130 dollars and some promises, to National Periodical Publications. After a few years they were kicked out while others profited from "their" dream. Only in 1976, when both had reached 61 and become impoverished (Schuster had also become blind), were they given lifetime pensions of $20,000 by Warner Communications which now *owns Superman*! This followed on a campaign by well-known comics' artists, which went on parallel to a film-project going into millions of dollars.[5]

The Superman myth has existed now for over 30 years, and it is by no means played out, even if its external manifestations may change.

Super-Hero Comics. A frequent form of the comics series that originated in the tradition of SF comics such as *Buck Rogers* and *Flash Gordon*. The huge success of Superman (see under that heading) after 1938—also as a hero of radio plays and film serials—soon brought forth numerous imitations which were at first prosecuted for plagiarism and forbidden. But eventually Superman was followed by a flood of super-heroes, who today appear in part with the same publisher (National Periodicals—DC), and in part in the supposedly competing Marvel Comics (in reality, these two leading comic book publishers are financially allied).

While Superman is superior and stronger in every respect, most of his colleagues are only "specialists" with extreme, specialized gifts. Flash is the fastest man in the world, Plastic Man can shape his body in any way, The Human Torch can transform himself into a living flame, The Green Lantern draws his secret powers from the energy of green light, etc. A few heroes have in addition a mythological background—The Mighty Thor, for example, is a god out of Nordic mythology who came to Earth over a dimension-bridge from Asgard, the city of Nordic gods.

With many heroes we notice the totemistic use of an animal symbol, so Hawkman, who wears the mark of a hawk and has wings, and The Amazing Spider Man, who acquired super-abilities after being bitten by a radioactive spider and who, in an appropriate costume, looks like a spider. This totem symbol indicates the characteristics and capabilities of the respective heroes. Thus, Batman has a Batmobile, a Batcave and a hiding place, a Batcostume which makes him similar to his totem animal—the bat, etc. The totem device gives rise to a type-casting which rules out everything else, and raises the super-heroes to the level of mythological beings:

The super-heroes are characters who by a limitation to the very small, homogenous part of the spectrum of what is thinkable (from names to speech habits, looks, behavior and destiny) seem to be monolithic—a sort of shorthand which immensely simplifies dealing with the phenomena of everyday life, that *simplification terrible* which Sartre indicated a few years ago as assign of fascism. The identity of a character consists solely of his name and the aura of vague conceptuality which spreads out around that. The mythology which follows from this replaces and prevents any utopian ideas.[6]

Practically all the super-heroes take over the model of a secret double identity from their prototype of Superman. They all live unknown among mankind, and transform themselves into their immanent, super-powerful superbeing only in (permanently recurring) emergency situations. As a charismatic *Führer* type, such a super-hero has mostly a respectable middle-class occupation such as journalist, doctor, lawyer, or he is a multimillionaire, like Batman and Iron Man; the latter is given out as the owner of America's largest armaments industry. Implicitly this is tantamount to pretending that an elite of the society sacrifices itself for everyone in its secret super-heroism.

The super-heroes are always selected by an only barely understandable destiny to be defenders of the status quo, of law and order. Furthermore, in their morals and their behavior they are past-oriented, advocates of feudal tutelage who adapt themselves with difficulty, often with a sour face, to the system they serve without wholly understanding it. Though a powerful protector of the people, the super-hero never reaches for direct political power. He is never elected by the people, but is sent to Earth by higher powers (as the Green Lantern by the ancient "Guardians of the Universe"). His existence must always be justified anew by threatening catastrophes, but most of all by the ever returning super-enemies, who frequently use superior technical means (super-weapons) and are also frequently connected with politically inimical powers. Up to the last years, super-enemies often fought against revolutionary movements in South America, or in Vietnam, for American victory. The super-enemy opposed to the particularly patriotic "Captain America" (whose costume has the colors of the American flag) was the Chinese-built "Red Guardian" (see Avengers 43, 44 [1967]). The Iron Man had to oppose the Russian-created "Titanium Man" in order to demonstrate in a duel of superbeings that the free West is superior to the East Block.

Thus the super-heroes compensate not only for individual but also national feelings of inferiority. In many stories the super-heroes fought and fight political battles for the U.S.A., from the discussions about new and more destructive super-weapons during the Cold War up to the Vietnam War. The "avengers on a higher mission" also intervene in unrest within the country, uncover dangerous drug-pushers as ring-leaders of student demonstrations, or fight against an organization of militant Blacks. Such political struggle is particularly present in the Marvel Group series, which were not infrequently—because of their quality illustrations and often ironical texts—enthusiastically received by intellectual critics.

This obviously reactionary political alignment became more subdued parallel to the general resolution of the Cold War tensions. The comics producers also attempted, for commercial reasons, to appeal to the critical part of American youth; thus around 1970 for a time there arose a new trend in the super-hero comics, for which the production of the comics author Denny O'Neil (National Periodicals group) can be seen as representative. This trend included in the range of their themes public corruption, racial discrimination, destruction of the environment and drug addiction. (There even appeared black heroes of comics, for example *Black Panther* and *Luke Cage, Hero for Hire.*) The national crisis of student unrest, Vietnam War, and racial conflicts was experienced by some U.S. super-heroes as an identity crisis. Comics were increasingly receiving artistic and intellectual recognition, while a large section of the mass readership had finally gone over to TV serials; thus the mass circulation of the regular comics series declined. In order to regain circulation by a new image, the American comic-book publishers jointly founded the Academy of Comic Book Art. At the same time the super-hero series *The Green Lantern*, which was close to shutdown because of low sales, was from No. 76 used for a kind of test production and aimed at a new public, mainly high-school and university students.

In No. 76, the Green Lantern is confronted with a black ghetto, the slum quarter of Star City. There, blacks are helplessly delivered over to a businessman who behaves like a tyrannical landlord, a "slumlord" who wants to evict the black tenants because "he can earn more money if he puts a parking lot here." A black turns to the super-hero: "I have read lots about...how you fight for people with blue skin... how you helped people with bright skin on a planet...and you also concern yourself with people who have violet skin! There is only one skin color which you've ignored...Black! Why is that...Green Lantern?" The hero decides to help the blacks. Equally typical is the plot of No. 84: in a city largely cut off from the outer world, all the inhabitants are employed by a single firm which produces new plastics. The whole city consists mostly of a synthetic material, and inhabitants are held in a state of unconscious dependence by means of a hypnotic gas and conscience-dimming noises; then they are "perfect employees" for the owners of the city. In the course of the action it is pointed out that all of America is really such a "company town."

The first and quite consistent step of O'Neil's was to reduce the super-powers of his heroes Green Lantern and Green Arrow to a bearable level, and even to deprive them of such powers for long stretches of time. The second was to deprive them of their certainty. Green Lantern was confronted with social and political problems, and became not only a restlessly active but also a doubting and reflecting figure. O'Neil proceeded similarly when he became the script-writer for *Superman*, still the most famous of the super-hero series. O'Neil humanized Superman in two ways. First, he gave him greater human—even physical—weaknesses; thus he confronted the bewildered *Superman* readers with the image of a "Man of Steel" regularly beaten up by his opponents. On the other hand, Clark Kent, Superman's civilian alter ego, became better characterized and more self-assured, and in addition advanced from a newspaper to a television reporter. The discrepancy between the normal citizen Kent, earlier described as weak and clumsy, and the super-powerful Superman diminished.

O'Neil slightly changed and modernized also the second most important series of DC Comics, *Batman*, as well as *Wonder Woman*. However, there the critical intent was much more subdued and less definite. O'Neil's comics acquired an increasing tendency to escapist fantasy-plots. Finally, the Green Lantern was shut down as an independent comic-book series. The super-heroes returned to normality—violence against stereotyped enemies.

NOTES

1. On SF-comics in general, cf. beside the works in the following notes, Alfred C. Baumgartner, *Die Welt der Comics* (Bochum, 1965); Pierre Couperie; "100,000,000 de lieues en ballon: La science-fiction dans la bande dessinée," *Phénix* No. 4 (Paris 1967); Wiltrud Ulrike Drechsel, Jörg Funhoff and Michael Hoffmann: *Messenzeichenware: Die gesellschaftliche und ideologische Funktion der Comics.* (Frankfurt, 1965); and Reinhold C. Reitberger and Wolfgang J. Fuchs, *Comics: Anatomie eines Massenmediums* (Munich, 1971).

2. Ted White, "The Spawn of M.C. Gaines," in Dick Lupoff and Don Thompson eds., *All in Color for a Dime* (New York: Ace, 1970).

3. Günther Metken, *Comics* (Frankfurt: Fischer, 1970). For further literature on Superman cf. Kirk Alyn, *A Job for Superman* (US, 1971); Robert von Berg, "Der aufhaltsame Abstieg Supermans: Neuer Trend in der amerikanischen Comic-strip-Industrie," *Süddeutsche Zeitung* (4 January, 1971); Nicolas Born, "Supermann oder: Die Helden der Schweigenden Mehrheit," *Konkret* No. 8 (1971); Heinz Politzer, "Mehr David als Goliath: Eine Analyse des *Superman*," *tendenzen* No. 55 (1968); Carna Zacharias, "Charlie Brown contra Superman," *tz* (17-28. January, 1973); and White and Siegel in notes 2 and 5.

4. Oswald Wiener, "Der geist der super-helden," in *Vom Geist der Superhelden: Comic strips*, Schriftenreihe der Akad. der Künste, Bd. 8 (Berlin: Gebr. Mann, 1970).

5. "Jerry Siegel Talks About the Case Against Superman," *Mediascene* No. 17 (1976).

6. Wiener, op. cit.

Wolfgang Jeschke

SF: A Publisher's View[1]

Translated by Peter Bruck and D. Suvin

(from SFS *4: 283–287, November 1977)*

The commodity-character of SF and the rules of the market have been recognized by Stanislaw Lem with great acuteness, and analysed by Dieter Hasselblatt in relation to the West German situation.[2]

The fact that books are primarily a *commodity* even in the opinion of publishers and booksellers is also proved by the Bavarian Bookstores and Publishers Association's longtime refusal of collective bargaining with the Booktraders Union. The Association announced that its employees are under the jurisdiction of the Union for Wholesale and Retail Trade. Nonetheless, today thousands of salespersons in bookshops are still exploited by being led to believe that the job of the bookseller is something special and that one even has to make sacrifices when serving "the Beautiful, the Good, and the True" (as if baloney between two book-covers would be some special baloney, and bathing-oil and baby-food would not also be something delightful).

Stanislaw Lem attributes a commodity-character especially to "popular literature," the "lower regions," as he calls it. The commodity-character applies also to the "upper regions" or "high literature"; the difference is a matter of degree, not of principle, and bears only indirectly on the quality of literature. There are much better SF novels than some of the stuff dumped upon the reader in the so-called *belles lettres*, despite the greater strictures imposed on a writer in the "lower regions," who has to write 8, 10 or even 15 novels a year to feed himself and his family.

A belletristic or "mainstream" text (disregarding the few best sellers in the book-trade) is read by perhaps 2,000 to 5,000 mostly understanding people who are educated in literature. The deeper in the "lower regions," the broader the audience. An SF paperback in West Germany reaches between 20,000 and 50,000 readers, the majority of whom do not read anything else.[3] This means that the vocabulary, language-use, thoughts, and values of these (often young) people are certainly to a no little extent determined by these texts.

The SF novels are generally—and there are important exceptions—products written for a special market, which follow the respective constraints. The American market with some 350 new publications yearly is a good example; it is the biggest market in the area of SF, and the West German market depends largely on it. The extent of the English linguistic area and the world-wide sales make it possible for US SF paperbacks to be sold for 75 to 95 cents for a length of 150 to 200 pages (as a hard-cover it is $4.95/5.95), and 95 cents to $1.50 for a length of 200 to 300 pages (hard-cover $6.95/9.95 or more). But most often a "normal" entertainment novel is of little more than 200 pages, and it is conceived of bearing this length in mind, even if its idea would not carry more than 100 pages. Most often, a preprint in 3 parts is organized with one of the SF magazines, then a hard-cover is published, finally a paperback is printed.

A publisher of paperbacks in Germany cannot market such a length, for two reasons. First, there are the costs of translation which for the "normal" length amount from DM 1,800 to DM 2,500 (ca. $700-1,000) or, depending on the degree of difficulty, roughly between DM 6,50 and 12 per manuscript page (1DM=ca. 40 cents US). Second, and above all, the linguistic area of German is much smaller, and thus also the number of copies printed (the ratio varies from 1:5 to 1:10 in comparison to the US numbers).

The "standard" length of an "entertainment" (i.e. not belles lettres) novel in Germany—where the price of a normal paperback is usually between DM 2,80 and 3,80—cannot today exceed 144 to 160 pages. For a long time nobody has dared (and many publishing houses do not dare even today) to exceed this threshold of price and length, and to offer "double," "triple" or even "quadruple" volumes out of fear of a "sliding effect."[4] But in the meantime the readers got used to such "multiple" volumes, which are quite common in the "mainstream" paperback production. They are now accepted also in the thriller, horror and SF-sector without complaints; but the danger of the "sliding effect" still exists. Should the volumes be pushed to 400, 500 or even 600 pages, the translation costs would mount from DM 4,000 to 8,000, and the bookstore prices rise to DM 5,80 or even 7,80.[5]

Until about 1973 the German publishers believed therefore that they had to shorten the original at the translation. In the case of the poorer titles, often artificially blown up to the size required by the American publisher, this was sometimes a positively healthy procedure, a beneficial shrinking to normal size. The strange situation arose that there exists a fair number of good German versions of inflated, boring originals. I am often reproachfully asked how I could presume to simply change texts according to my discretion and thereby adulterate, if not destroy, their "poetic content." Now even leaving aside that there is up to now no successful definition of the vague notion of "poetic content," three points have to be made in reply: First, this question arises out of the unrealistic thinking of academe, which views *a priori* every intervention into a text as a sacrilege. Second, this question ignores the commodity-character of books and demands for every printed production a kind of critical edition—a totally unrealistic demand, neither justifiable by the quality of the text nor economically feasible. Third, I put my shoes into the hands of a shoemaker, my letters into the hands of the mail service, and myself sometimes into the hands of the Federal Railways. I know that the shoemaker can sometimes have a bad day, that the mail service makes occasionally mistakes, and that train accidents happen. But I would not try to cope with the problems of my shoemaker, of the postmaster general, or of the president of the Federal Railways, for these people understand in their area much more than I do—I assume it at least. Hence I claim for myself as an editor that people should not try to cope with my problems. I should be trusted to understand, in my area of specialization, at least that much that I will not cut a Hemingway's, a Pasternak's, or a Le Guin's "poetic content." And every experienced writer will be grateful to the editor, most of the time, for eliminating inconsistencies in style, absurdities, unnecessary repetitions and shallow claptrap. As an author, one does not have the necessary critical distance to the text, particularly one generated under time pressure—as is in the "lower regions" regularly the case.

No doubt, such an editorial policy becomes bad if novels of quality are coerced into a bed of Procrustes, sometimes by not very qualified people. It happened not seldom that the substance of the novel was attacked, the "content" adulterated, and the intentions of the author violated. SF in West Germany is now to some degree liberated from such market constaints. Nevertheless, a translator or editor is still well advised to cut from this or that title at least some too trivial cliché. I am thinking here of the sometimes too hymnic passages of a Barjavel, of the puberty-ridden, at times embarrassing stuttering of long passages in the (bestselling!) *Gor* novels, of the reactionary as well as senile chatter in the novels of the older Heinlein where old-age sex is garnished with platitudes, or the chewed curds of the far too many E.R. Burroughs imitators, etc., etc. When translators and editors take the trouble to cut a bit from the especially embarrassing and silly passages, they do it mostly in a good cause, not because of a craving after control or because they would profit from it—on the contrary, the cuts and reformulations make for more unpaid work.

All four jobs concerned with mediating between manuscript and book—the publisher, the "reader" (*Lektor*), the translator and the editor function as something like a filter of the products offered by the foreign markets, for the material from domestic sources is still much too scarce. On the American market alone, 722 titles appeared in 1974, and 890 in 1975; on the German market, the original titles total to 100 to 120 a year (not counting the "Heft-" magazines such as the *Perry Rhodan* series, mostly original). I have the pleasure of being the copublisher of a paperback series which comes on the market with 4 titles a month, thus I need 48 titles a year. This is the series "Heyne Science Fiction," which I publish together with Dr. Herbert W. Franke; Dr. Franke takes care of the more out of the way literatures (Hungary, Rumania, Italy, the Slavic countries, etc.), while I cover the Anglo-American and French market as well as the Netherlands and Scandinavia. My job is to find a compromise between the ideal and the realizable. Certain contractual regulations limit my competencies, e.g. I have to produce 3 story-volumes a year from *The Magzine of Fantasy and Science Fiction*. Half of the program is taken up by titles of "easy entertainment" (*Fantasy*) and by titles which appeared before 1950/60 (*Classics*); the other half is only restricted insofar as there should be as many novels as possible and as few anthologies and short-story collections as possible. (This last rule follows what is to my mind a superstition, namely that SF novels sell better than short-story volumes: I have so far never encountered any proofs for this hypothesis. But this does not alter the fact that such a prejudice exists and constitutes one of the publishing constraints, although anybody who knows SF will say that it counts for more good stories than good novels.)

The activity of a publisher under these conditions consists above all in observing foreign markets (particularly the American, English and French ones) through advertisements and reviews in journals and fanzines, and in making a primary selection. The same happens in material supplied by literary agencies and to the manuscripts of West German authors. The total offer varies between 200 and 250 titles a year. No publisher can deal with such a mass of texts without relying on reliable "readers" (*Lektors*). It is difficult to find the right people for this, though easier for the Anglo-American and French areas than for the areas of other literatures. For instance, it is very difficult to find somebody who not only knows Russian but also has an understanding of SF, and furthermore of the SF-market in Germany, and is able to recommend a book for translation. A general rule is that the smaller the linguistic area, the greater is the tendency of the "readers" familiar with the language to praise a book exceedingly; there is seldom a chance to get a second evaluation. It is therefore not the case, as is sometimes asserted, that publishing houses, out of fear of the risks involved, limit themselves to the marketable names of Anglo-American SF, or that they even wish to suppress offers from the Eastern block; who by the way (this must be added out of fairness) have to be willing to put a lot of work in for little money. For the reading of one detective or SF book, the "reader" gets paid—according to the volume of the book—between DM 20 and 30, only in exceptional cases DM 50.

The editor then has to put together his yearly program using the work of the "readers" and the titles which he has read himself. This happens every year in February/March for the time period October of the same year to September of the next one. The long advance time has technical reasons: the program is examined by the management of the publishing house in the first place; the management proposes changes, has titles of its own; after that the rights are solicited from the agencies (it can take sometimes two to three months to get the contracts signed by the authors). When the program is ready, the German translation-titles are put under copyright and an advertising catalogue is printed. It has to be available in September for the book fair.

In coordination with the management, the titles are then given to the translators whose strengths and weaknesses the editor has to know. The larger the pool of translators, the better; not only because of the plurality of temperaments (lyrical, science-oriented, etc.), but also because of pressing deadlines. A disadvantage of a large pool is that it is not possible to keep all translators regularly employed. In some special cases the editor talks the work over with the translator; for instance in the case of the novels which have to be shortened he communicates to him the reader's opinion, or he leaves it to the translator.

When the translation of the manuscript is finished, the sub-editors start their work (the editor will naturally edit himself one or the other title which is dear to him). The amount of editing is dependent on the quality of the translation: it now boomerangs if the translator got a book he was not suited to and not keen to work on. The weaker titles cause most work, for they are only thrown together by the author, but also neglected by the translator (not the least because he is paid less). Mindful of the fact that 20-50,000 people will read the novel—many of whom do not read anything else and who rightly expect for their good money at least a somewhat proper German—the editor grits his teeth and tries to make good at least the grossest mistakes and to straighten out here and there a couple of stylistic dislocations.

The editor is often asked why he puts such titles on his program at all? The answer is simple: fantasy-novel series (like *Gor* and *Scorpio*) sell best, and the publishing rights are as a rule bought even before all titles have appeared in the original; and those get usually thinner, more mediocre, more babbling and less imaginative as more sequels come out. But a good part of the reading public seems to buy this without opposition; it seems, indeed, even to be grateful for not having to envision new protagonists but being permitted to stick with the old and comfortable patterns to which it is used through the heroes of the TV-manufacture. But even without this "stuffing" of the publishing program with saleable but low-quality titles (pure "escape literature"), it would not be possible to produce the more demanding titles of the SF genre: for one can, through quality and with a lot of love for it, kill a paperback series rather quickly. There are examples: the last one is the Fischer-Verlag with its *Orbit* series. The situation is different in the hardcover business, for it offers single titles rather than series. The "sliding effect," so much feared by the paperback publishers, does not occur there.

NOTES

1. This article, written originally for German readers, has been much abridged in the English translation, with the consent of the author—DS.

2. Stanislaw Lem, "Science Fiction: Ein Hoffnungsloser Fall—mit Ausnahmen," in *Polaris* 1, edited by Franz Rottensteiner (Frankfurt: Insel, 1973), pp 11-59; Dieter Hasselblatt, *Gruene Maenchen vom Mars: Science Fiction fuer Leser und Macher* (Duesseldorf: Droste, 1974), especially, p 114 ff.

3. More precise figures are unfortunately not available, though the phenomenon would be worth investigating. The assumption is based on private interviews in the circles of fans and readers. The percentage is surprisingly high in the case of technicians and scientists. These people often do not know what to do with "high" literature and are not attracted by it. Does SF represent the literature of Snow's "others" culture? (See C.P. Snow, *The Two Cultures: and A Second Look*, UK 1959.)

4. The Heyne publishing house has changed its policy, and now takes titles with high buying costs out of the SF-series to achieve a higher circulation (usually between 20,000 and 40,000, in some cases over 50,000). Examples are Asimov's *The Gods Themselves* and Clarke's *Rendezvous with Rama*, both clearly SF-novels but published in the general program without special notification of content. The same was done with Anthony Burgess's *Clockwork Orange* and his *The Clockwork Testament*.

5. It is not usual in the paperback business that bookstores (dealers) should order a certain number of single titles. They subscribe *en bloc* to a series (i.e. 10 titles of the "general" series, 6 thriller-titles, 5 from the SF series, etc.). If the dealer is used to getting (with four publication dates a month) five times four, i.e., 20 SF titles for a price of DM 2,80, the total amounts to DM 33.60 (with 40% off). If the monthly program contains one single volume (DM 2,80), one double volume (DM 3,80), one triple volume (DM 4,80), and one quadruple volume (DM 5,80), the total rises suddenly to DM 51,60. The dealer is thus confronted with a price increase of

more than 50%, and reacts with a reduction of titles from 5 to 3; in consequence the future circulation would drastically "slide" down, and the publishing house would be deeply disturbed in its planning which often extends over 12 to 16 months.

6. 172 hardcover originals, 50 hardcover reprints, 201 paperback originals, 288 paperback reprints, a total of 722 titles ("1974 Statistical Book Summary," *Locus* No. 169 of Feb. 16, 1975); 160 hardcover originals, 149 hardcover reprints, 257 paperback originals, 330 paperback reprints, a total of 890 titles ("1975 Statistical Book Summary," *Locus* No. 184 of Jan. 31, 1976).

Gérard Klein

Le Guin's "Aberrant" Opus: Escaping the Trap of Discontent

Translated by Richard Astle

(from SFS *4: 287–295, November 1977)*

Ursula K. Le Guin's opus, in particular the novels of the Hainish cycle, does not seem to fit into the general trend in American SF towards discontent and pessimism.[1] Her two most accomplished books, *The Left Hand of Darkness* and *The Dispossessed*, both take place in a distant future whose concerns and conflicts do not appear, at first sight, to coincide with those of the contemporary world. One would be tempted to classify them, and the four other episodes of the Hainish cycle, among works of pure imagination, of escapism, which it is fashionable to disparage. But I would venture to suggest—without any pretence of proposing a complete explanation of Le Guin's structure—that, in spite of appearances, her work does refer to a constituted science, and even further, to an ideology of this science, in the purest tradition of SF. The latter assertion seems to me to be of importance since I believe that the durable relationship which SF has, for better or worse, muddled through to establish between science (or technology) and literature, between rational knowledge and art, is of real cultural validity. Therefore, a break in this relation (which some would call the emancipation of speculative literature from science) is a real regression which has its counterpart, and even its origin, in society.

Le Guin separates herself from most of her colleagues on the question of the future unity of human civilization. For a long time, certainly since the last century, the theme of progress has appeared indissolubly linked to a tendency towards the standardization of cultures, towards the constitution of a single and unique human civilization, of which the great—and terrible—dream of a World State is perhaps the most current but not the least naive manifestation. This is a utopia cultivated as much on the Right as on the Left. In the SF mode, an ideology of science and technology serves as the unifying principle. The received—and much too simplistic—idea that truth (scientific, but before that, religious) is *one*, that each problem has one and only one "best" solution, impregnates a whole naive way of looking at social development. We have seen in my previous article the meaning of this unity for the social group that is the bearer of SF, anxious to accede to power by the universalization of its values. Thus, plurality is in general posited in the SF future only as an irreducible opposition: the Alien, the Extra-Terrestrial, the other, remains most often an enemy—unless the reverse happens, and he becomes a model. When agreement is established, with or without conflict, it is at the price of reduction to identity. Most works of contemporary SF, when they contain a utopian element, are haunted by a specter, that of orthodoxy—be it benevolent or malevolent, be it sorrowfully submitted to—or charismatically advocated and enforced.

Le Guin, for her part, challenges all orthodoxy in advance, in the sense that in all her works she posits a diversity of solutions or rather of responses, a plurality of societies, and furthermore that history is made where cultures come into contact: in *Rocannon's World* as in *The Left Hand of Darkness*, and more clearly in the recent *The Dispossessed*. What pre-exists the universe of the Hainish cycle is the breaking up of the Hainish culture, just as what pre-exists human history is the differentiation of cultural experiences. The theme of the planet Hain which seeded all the habitable worlds in that part of the galaxy is a myth of foundation, prior to all narrative. In the logic of the opus, the history of Hain before its fragmentation cannot be described. In this sense, Hain is Eden, the place of an abolished unity, foreclosed, prior to all real life.

This is clearly not a simple convention intended to explain the presence of more or less modified humans on a large number of worlds, for such a "cosmic" diversity is reproduced on each of the worlds Le Guin describes. The particular result is that for humanity no crisis can be final. Not without irony, Le Guin emphasizes that he who mistakes his own crisis for that of the whole human civilization is singularly limited by ignorance. Thus, in *The Dispossessed*, Le Guin's intention is clearly not simply to contrast two societies, one much resembling America today and the other having several traits in common with present-day China or perhaps with the Israel of the great dream, that is to say, before independence. Much less is it her intention to take a side—although the sympathies of the author, as someone exercising her subjectivity within the limits of her creation, appear evident enough—but rather to show that the two societies equally belong to human possibility. Despite their apparent separation they maintain close historical ties, in particular in their reciprocal fantasy representations, if only because the anarcho-collectivist society of Anarres comes out of the liberal bourgeois society of Urras at the same time as it rejects the latter's ethical defects. For Le Guin, what matters in the last instance is their difference which introduces the possibility of a dialogue, of a commerce (in the largest not necessarily economic, sense of the term), of an exchange which will allow the invention of the *ansible*, instrument of communication *par excellence*.

This difference also introduces a possibility, essential for Le Guin, of ethical judgement issuing from a practical confrontation and not from a system of moral rules deduced from any metaphysics. Without the experience of Anarres, the planet where an anarcho-collectivist society has established itself, Shevek would not be able to produce an ethical judgement, would not be able, that is, to condemn the social inequalities of Urras from the point of view of his subjectivity, moulded by a particular society. It is this distance as well as the experience of Anarres that provides the Urras revolutionaries with something special, a point-of-view larger than the strict defence of their class interests would require: the hope, the idea that it is possible to conceive of and to construct another society.

Thus Le Guin's work presents, in my view, an important concept which speaks against the ideology of necessity so pervasive in SF—namely that, socially and sociologically speaking, the possibility of hope, the idea of change itself, resides in the experience, the subjectivity of the other. The point is not, of course, in copying the other's solution, but in reacting to it with one's own individual and social subjectivity. *History is neither a succession nor an accumulation of experiences, but a confrontation of experiences*; it cannot be linear, even though chronology appears to invite linearity. Further, it becomes absurd to condemn a society or to propose an eternal model, even one conceived as evolving.

We here touch on a partial meaning of the beautiful short story, "The Ones who Walk Away from Omelas": all societies, be they the most utopian, the most perfect ones you can dream of whatever your dreams, carry in their depths their own denial, a fundamental injustice. Not because humanity is bad (metaphysically) but because every society, like a language, functions on the basis of a system of oppositions, and tends within itself to recreate and to perpetuate difference, including the difference between that which is subjectively experienced as good and as bad. Le Guin gently and somewhat unexpectedly introduces into SF a social relativism—

which is by no means an eclecticism nor a skeptical cycnicism after the manner of Vonnegut.

This social relativism suggests several reflections. A specter, I have said, haunts SF and, beyond it, our civilization itself, a specter which Le Guin helps to exorcise: that of the ideal society or rather of the ideal of society. This specter ridiculously clothes itself in scientific hand-me-downs or rather in pseudo-scientific metaphor appropriated from natural sciences. If we are to believe those zealots, from their various ideological perspectives, there exists a precise solution to all human problems, in particular social ones: the main question is to utilize the science which would supply these solutions. This is what is implied in the works of Van Vogt and Asimov; indeed, the latter does not seem to make clear distinctions among machines, robots, and human beings. In less extreme and seemingly less naive forms, panaceas are proposed which tend to demonstrate, scientifically, that it would suffice to add to or to take away from human culture a given element in order for humanity to know peace, happiness, and prosperity, just as one can admittedly protect oneself from an illness with a vaccine.[2] All these propositions, some of which can seem quite generous, are based on the hypothesis of the objectivity of the social realm (in the sense that one speaks of the objectivity of the physical world, which only non-physicists still assert), and exhibit thus a strong odor of metaphysics: the world is understood to have been made in a certain manner whose laws it would suffice to know and respect in order to gain mastery over it. Philip K. Dick did much to shake such a confidence in "reality," but it was Le Guin who introduced the consequences of its destruction into the practice of conjectural literature. In fact, the "objectivist" hypothesis implied that social mechanisms can be thought of in abstraction from those who make them up and from the evolving cognition they have of their environment. However, history is made not by mechanical interaction of social molecules, definable once and for all, however complicated that definition might be, but by dialectical interactions among subjects, bearers of cognitions which are certainly limited but which change in function of their experiences. Further, the absence of a "total social science" does not result from a lack of cognition that might be reduced by a specialized effort, but from the fact that, while the process of interactions of knowing subjects unfolds, such a science is not constitutable; and were the process to stop, there would be no one to constitute it.

A scientific attitude toward society and history implies a reconciliation between subjectivity and science, and also an acceptance of the fact that all science is, in the final instance, subjective, that is to say relative to an observer-operator who knows and acts within a particular situation, marked by his point-of-view. In this perspective, history can best be defined as the space of interaction of these relative, operative cognitions. By "subjects" it must be clear that one does not necessarily mean individuals, as liberal theory would have us believe, but social groups as well, indeed entire societies. Furthermore, this subjectivity does not imply that all propositions—even the most absurd ones—are arbitrarily equivalent: such an equivalence could be posited only by reference to an unattainable absolute. Reality is. The subjectivity of which we speak concerns simply the limited cognition a subject can have of the environment within which it acts and evaluates. This cognition can of course be more or less wide and more or less adequate to reality; but it is subject to change above all because it bears on a reality which is largely a function of the no less evolving cognitions of other subjects. It is the condition of social science, as of all the other sciences, to be an infinite process. But contrary to the other sciences, there is no one who can boast of comprehending its whole extent at a given moment, since it is diffused among all the cognizing subjects.

What Le Guin proposes in place of an unobtainable "total social science," what marks her originality in contemporary SF—indeed in literature—is not the idea that humanity progresses, in the sense that it goes from savagery to civilization, but that it is involved in a process of learning by means of its own differences and contradictions. And the stages of the process are perhaps emphasized in the course of her opus, with a willful naiveté tinged with malice, by humanity's progressive acquisitions of psychic powers. In a certain sense, the telepathy which appears in *Rocannon's World*, followed by mind-lying and the mental control which annuls it in *City of Illusions*, and finally by precognition in *The Left Hand of Darkness*, metaphoricaly reproduce humanity's invention of language, father of the lie, then of logic, and finally of a comprehensive theory of history and therefore of the future. That these "powers" come from the unconscious should perhaps be understood (at least in part) as signifying that such inventions are not born solely of the exercise of reason, but of a process of which the terms, particularly but not exclusively the social ones, remain largely unknown by the subjectivities which make history.

Ethics, which occupies a central place in the universe of Le Guin, is in fact a taking account of the behaviors, points of view, and ethics of others. Without any reference to a transcendence, man is "naturally" for Le Guin an ethical animal insofar as he can integrate into his own consciousness, through language, a part of the lived experience—in particular the social situations—of others. He is not a nomad. Contrary to other animals which entertain only ecological relations among themselves and with the world, he also develops social relations. It does not seem to me inexact to say that ethics represents from then on a sociological pre-knowledge or pre-cognition, that it introduces a theoretical and practical science in the course of constitution, by which man changes from a sociable to a sociological animal. It is then evident that where ethics is lacking, where this pre-knowledge is faulty, social problems, even a grave crisis, cannot but arise. Such a flaw can manifest itself in two ways: the return to a fixed conception—absolute, theological, or metaphysical—of morality which claims to coincide with human ethology; or the rejection of the points-of-view of other subjects and the obsessive pursuit of self-interest. In both cases a false and formalized knowledge of man denies and obliterates an authentic pre-knowledge. Both cases are represented, in antagonistic or allied pairs, in our world: the prophets of doom are not completely wrong when they announce a moral crisis, a weakening of human values; but what they call for with their pleas of law and order is just as surely at the opposite pole from a rebirth of an ethics as the disordered, blind, indeed frenzied demands of those they condemn. Indeed, humanity only solves its problems to the extent that each subject, each man, becomes, to the extent of his experience, a "sociologist," and it cannot advance more quickly, on this terrain, than the slowest ship in its convoy.

All, or nearly all, of Le Guin's works describe such a crisis and the conditions for the appearance of an ethics in this precise sense. Further, for Le Guin, man is an ethical animal *also* in the sense that he has the collective possibility of inventing and experimenting with social behavior in the same way that he can invent and experiment in other scientific fields. History is not for her a series of more or less glorious events, but it has *this* direction. It produces ethics as it produces language, and—as in the linguistic domain—each subject acts in the ethical domain without needing to know all its elements and their interrelations but, at any given stage, *as though* he were aware of them. True history is in the unconscious. *The unrenounceable and inaccessible mastery of history lies in the elucidation of that unconscious.*

Thus, a a very long history has aged the Hainish, has made them wise and loaded them with guilt: they had tried everything. But why does that guilt, heavy and sad, persist, even though they have collectively recognized their errors and attempted to correct them? Perhaps it is necessary to remember Freud's distinction between hate (*la Haine!*) and love: "Hate, as a relation to objects, is older than love. It derives from the narcissistic ego's primordial repudiation of the external world with its outpouring of stimuli."[3] The guilt of the Hainish is a reminiscence of the hate which they originally unleashed. These Hainish, so precisely, so evocatively named, once caused the differentiation of the human race and, in a complex process only alluded to by Le Guin, conceived hate for the others, for those different ones whom they had themselves made, who were themselves. They committed, then, inexpiable crimes, which later, when they could bear the difference and found themselves again facing the same objects, changed into guilt. Yet by differentiating humanity they rendered possible, much later, knowledge or cognition, that is to say love, but at the price of an unremitting anguish which recapitulates simultaneously the initial withdrawal and the recognition. The Hainish destroyed by the force of hate the shell of a pre-ethical Eden, which cannot be re-entered, and they can only forever repent.

One can allow, along this line, that Hain could be the symbol, not only of our culture, split between permanent fragmentation and the destruction of the different, but also of the bourgeoisie in the act of breaking up, of differentiating itself into eventually antagonistic social groups, if not into castes, at the cost of its more or less explicit egalitarian utopia and of the illusion of its universal mediation of (or of its power over) social reality. If so, this class becomes, by its very disappearance, the bearer of history and of civilization. Thus Le Guin completely overturns the problematic of the social group. It must disappear so that there may be life, growth, trying out and enrichment. This experience of dissolution and social death (see my first article for its effects in other SF authors) is by her localized, reduced, contained in the Hainish sentiment of guilt, in their anguish, in their nostalgia, of which the original reasons have become unconscious. One is tempted to write that, through the Hainish, Le Guin—contrary to her colleagues—mourns for that threatened social class, which she even sees as the occasion for an extraordinary revitalization whose description and comprehension are her only interest. This crisis, our crisis, is at the beginning and not at the end, behind and not before, and it is pregnant with other crises which lead to the growth of ethics in the unconscious, to cognition, to tolerance and to the possibility of love. The unconscious is doubly figured here, in the author who as it were conceals her problem in it and extracts from it a novelistic solution, and in her opus.

Can we go one step further? The fecundity of Hain, which seeded all the human planets, conceals perhaps something like a shadow of the famous "original scene," that of the coitus of the parents from which a whole brotherhood arises. Whereas most other SF writers behave as though they do not really accept the "birth" (or rather the unmasking) of other social categories, whether dominant (the "Big Brother," the neofeudals) or dominated (the "younger sons," the proletariat or sub-proletariat), Le Guin accepts all its consequences, beginning with the very apparition of the Other. She also sees the benefits of this ineluctable inquality: a renascence of values other than the market ones. This is doubtless why neo-medieval societies play such a role—but not an exclusive one—in her work, and why she attaches such importance to nobility, to honor, like the "shiftgrethor" of the Karhideans in *The Left Hand of Darkness*. Incidentally, does she not write, "Karhide is not a nation but a family quarrel" (LHD, §I)? But conversely, does not the acceptance of the Other, then of the hate-filled brotherhood, finally of cooperative posterity, signify that Le Guin has incorporated the "original scene," has taken it up as a woman, has installed herself as mother? Perhaps it is out of this condition—and in particular out of her female condition—that she can say this thing earlier and better than her masculine colleagues. In this sense, Hain is also Le Guin herself. Thus we see the myth of Hain resonating on three different levels without any self-evident relation between them: a personal level, where the guilt and the hate sustained by the contemplation or the fantasy of the "original scene" and by its products, eventual brothers and sisters, finds itself re-elaborated in adulthood and in some way positively turned around into genitality, that is to say into love and parentage, in the typically feminine manner of creative fragmentation; a social level, that of the downfall and breakup of the social class to which Le Guin belongs, which can be understood, assumed, and admitted as positive precisely by reason of work performed on the personal level; and finally, of course, a novelistic level, where the two preceding ones intermingle and at the same time speak to each other and express themselves. Everything happens as though the successful and fortunate solution of a personal conflict allowed envisaging, with a realistic optimism, the still unreachable solution of a social problem, for which the work is precisely the substitute, in short, a metaphorical child. It is rare, in my experience, that one sees with such clarity these different pathways, inscribed on each of these levels, deployed and resonating among themselves (though we have here, I submit, a widely distributed, possibly general, artistic phenomenon). One catches a glimpse, without really being able to grasp it, of the particular conditions for the production of such a work: a happily resolved childhood, an active feminine genitality, a belonging to a precise moment of a social class in crisis, and of course the necessary talent, intelligence, and culture. Let one of at least the first three circumstances be different, and the result would be completely different. Of course, the constitution of Le Guin's opus is not simply a product of these circumstances, but itself plays a very dynamic role in the ordering of their relations.

One finds again the function of the unconscious as the place where history inscribes itself in *The Lathe of Heaven* (1971), which, however interesting, is doubtless not the best of Le Guin's works. Curiously, she herself seems to experience a particular difficulty in situating it. She sees little here, she says in an interview, but a fable on "normality." She reversed here the roles of a psychiatrist and his patient: the former moves towards madness through the fantasy of his patient, namely the omnipotence of his dreams, while the latter acquires mastery over his "power," the realization of his dream-desires through successive disastrous experiences provoked by the increasing megalomania of the doctor who wishes to take advantage of that power to remake the world. Within our argument, this work covers two gaps in Le Guin's work. The unlivable near future finds itself here described in terms very similar to those we have encountered in other writers, notably Dick and Brunner.[4] But above all, this novel raises an ethical problem, here in the unconscious, closely related to what I indicated above: the problem of interference [in the pattern-producing sense in which light waves interfere with each other—trans.] between centers of consciousness (*conscience*) and of actions. (here between the doctor and his patient) conceived as being at the origin of experience, of growth, and of cognition. The doctor goes mad because he does not recognize in the other an autonomous center, he comes to consider him as a machine, a mediating thing by means of which he can exert pressure on the real. Inversely, the patient becomes sane to the extent that he recognizes others have the same creative power as his own, though most often they lack the awareness or the experience which comes from having too long served as mediating objects. Thus the real world is that where autonomous desires encounter, recognize, and interfere with one another. The alienated world is that where one's desire develops with neither restraint nor opposition and exhausts itself in solitude. One recognizes here the problematic of the early Dick, which finds privileged expression in *Eye in the Sky* (1957). The place given to the dream in *Lathe* sufficiently indicates that there is no immediate, intrinsic solution to the problem posed to the social group in the near future. Here psychic powers, the extraordinary, a miracle in short, that is to say the impossible, would be needed. But at the same time, if one agrees to pass from narrative-as-representation (here of a false reality) to narrative-as-metaphor, this call to the powers of dream asserts there is no solution but in something which goes beyond rationality and individual will: the constant remodeling of the world by the dreamers' desires, the permanent interference of the actors' desires, in the social world. And the role which falls to George Orr is in some way a metaphor of the artist in our world, who at the same time invokes a false solution (the work of art) and reveals, by means of the formulated dream, the true solution to come. As Ian Watson notes in a slightly different perspective, *Lathe* is really a transitional work in Le Guin's work. She has here clearly expressed something which only appears by its absence in her preceding works, namely, the unconscious, and as in doing this she doubtless felt some resistances she leaned on a great precedent, that of Philip K. Dick. But her discomfort is felt in the relatively stiff construction of her work.

If one allows Watson's astute thesis according to which *Lathe* was for Le Guin the means to resolve the "schismogenic" tension accumulated in the works of the Hainish cycle between the growing recourse to the paranormal and the concern with sounding psychological and moral depths, it is all the more interesting to see the paranormal—which I have designated above as a metaphor of humanity's successive acquisitions in the domain of its self-cognition—developing in autonomous fashion and being charged with effects without the author's knowledge. From a certain point of view, it is not a question of a metaphor, since the image possesses a reality and a force of its own in the psyche (*psychisme*) of its author, but in fact all truly poetic metaphors, which go beyond the level of a device of style, present this double efficacy. It is as though for a time the image in the author's preconscious and the "meaning" in her consciousness develop parallel to each other, so that an unconscious operation on the image can give birth to a conscious thought at the level of meaning. At the end of such a development, when the evolution proper to the preconscious image renders it unusable in the chain of thought and inadmissible by consciousness as lacking pertinence to reality, each follows its own destiny, the one of fantasy, the other of reasoning. But in this divorce the image loses its effectiveness in the real world and the thought its force in the affective domain and, no doubt, even the very possibility of its prolongation. I will go so far as to say that the artist makes use of one part of the unconscious as a kind of analogical calculator which he feeds with "facts" and which returns "results" after the intervention of a "model" partially analogous to reality but entirely unknown and inaccessible to the artist. Insofar as the analogy to reality is acknowledged by consciousness, there is thought. Otherwise, before and after this acknowledgement, there is fantasy. It is in this sense that dreams can have a certain heuristic value and that they even exercise, although much less directly than in *Lathe*, a certain influence on reality. I would even willingly believe that style, taken in the very large sense of all aesthetic organization, from the general structure of the narrative to the idiosyncracies of the writing, is as it were a residue of this unconscious work, the signature of this process. Abstract thought pretends no longer to need it and to allow a summary indifferent to the form, but that is only achieved by denying its own origins which it knows perhaps too well, for it comes from a place where it was nothing but "style," nothing but contour or container without distinguishable content. The "style" of *Lathe*, in this sense, is felt in the exaggeratedly fantasmatic content of the work, poorly tolerated by the author's rigorous consciousness which reduces or deforms it.

One must obviously also ask oneself whence comes this rigor, or rather from what exterior models it borrows its criteria. These criteria are very important, since they determine the limits of what consciousness (*conscience*) will admit, of the "pertinence to reality" and therefore of fantasy. In the case of Le Guin and many other SF writers, it seems to me that such *cultural notions are borrowed from a science*, or at the very least from a more or less ideological, more or less informed, notion of a science. And it is perhaps the source of these borrowings that best distinguishes SF writers from other writers who seem to borrow their models from the dominant ethics, from "popular" philosophy, or from earlier literary discourse on reality—if not from the form itself of that discourse.

For Le Guin, in any case, the source is clear and precise: it is ethnology, and furthermore such a conception of ethnology which tends on the one hand to relativise cultures with respect to each other and on the other hand, less fashionably, to place the emphasis on the relations cultures entertain among themselves. At least as much as on their respective particularities. This idea is clearly expressed in a booklet by Lévi-Strauss, *Race and History*[5] which appears to foreshadow quite precisely Le Guin's implicit theses in the Hainish cycle, without my suggesting for all that that it inspired her. In this essay Lévi-Strauss made an effort to generalize starting from his science, and he drew from it—surrounding it, certainly, with many precautions—a comprehensive ideology of human civilization (a pursuit which goes well beyond the requirements of science and already touches on those of a creative writer). This ideology, based on the attainment of an authentic science, struggles, let us recall, against a monstrous ideology, supported by an illusion of science, namely, racism.

From a great number of passages from *Race and History* which could easily be adduced in support of the parallel to Le Guin, one is of particular interest: "It would seem," Lévi-Strauss writes in his third chapter, consecrated to ethnocentrism, a chapter on which many SF writers might profitably meditate, "that the diversity of cultures has seldom been recognized by men for what it is—a natural phenomenon resulting from the direct or indirect relationships between societies." By this criterion one measures the difference which separates utopia from SF. *The former never acknowledges the natural phenomenon of cultural diversity. It proposes a unique model of social organization in space and in time.* SF is much more circumspect and realistic: it easily acknowledges difference as a fact, but often, at least in its optimistic period, only to finally refuse it by making history the agent of conformity. It is nevertheless vital to emphasize that from Stanley Weinbaum to John Brunner by way of Hal Clement and many others, numerous authors have shown, in a more or less sketchy but often optimistic manner, a collaboration of different races and civilizations which preserves their specificity. This is an attempt to substitute for colonization a more acceptable model of relations among different peoples, and in doing so they proceed, as did Lévi-Strauss, from its intrinsic practical interest rather than on moral considerations.

This is also one reason for the frequency of anti-utopias in SF, anti-utopias which often admit of no little ambiguity when they protest against that reduction to identity which the homogeneity of science and technology would produce, and against that project of political standardization which in fact is brought about not only by totalitarianisms but by bourgeois society itself. Thus, these anti-utopias are proffered outside science and the middle-class and often directed against both of them as though they were, by themselves, responsible for that menace, which they are not. The "ecological" catastrophe establishes itself in this sense in the forefront of anti-utopian literature, since it claims to denounce the consequences of a paradoxical utopia of progress. But in reality (see my first article) it expresses the fear of a dispersal of the social group bearing SF, and of its reduction to an undifferentiated mass. An extreme point of view of the same nature is presented by Stanislaw Lem (*Solaris*, *The Invincible*) who makes this natural phenomenon of irreducible diversity a source of pessimism by stripping it of all inclination toward communication. In Lem's universe foreign races pass by without in any way being able to understand each other; it is difficult not to discover there at least a nostalgia for a lost unity, for a humanism and perhaps for socialism. Thus, from the classical utopia to Lem, by way of SF, one passes from *one* monadic sytem to a *plurality* of monadic systems, isolated and closed. *Utopia and SF are literatures which consider the problem of cultural diversity, whether in order to exclude it, or to reduce it, or again to deny its benefits*, as with Lem, *or finally to exalt it*, as does Le Guin. No other novelistic genre seems to have concerned itself with this subject to that extent.

However, the American SF that has more or less accepted social relativism has often been a fearful reaction to the bursting of the American Dream, to the loss of power of the social group bearing SF, to the dissolution of its element into a working class envisaged (wrongly) as undifferentiated—in a word, to a reduction to the inferior. Almost alone, Le Guin seems to see in this bursting of the bubble the precondition of a new differentiation, of a rebounding of history. It is in such an attitude that lies her major similarity to European (including British) SF, which has always been subtly different from the American SF precisely in its relationship to differentiation. European SF has been created in a social context clearly much more diverse, and conserving the mark of much more ancient and deep inequalities, than the U.S. one. The ancient pessimism of European SF writers can thus be explained by the fact that their social group has never been able to entertain the illusion of an accession to power. However, the political masking of power relationships and the theatrical importance allotted to the individual's word have led some of the European SF writers to prophesying. What the Americans are discovering today, Europeans such as Brunner, Ballard and Aldiss have long known. Yet today, this old experience of inequality perhaps hinders the Europeans more than the Americans to see what is hidden in the new constellation of social possibilities, and immures them in social pessimism.

As for Le Guin, when in *The Dispossessed* she gets beyond the problematic of the ecological or pseudo-ecological crisis of the end of human civilization, she can no longer elude the political formulation of the problem. So she finally reintroduces into SF the possibility of debate on the form of future society. In her "ambiguous utopia" she presents two solutions to the present equation: one "neo-feudal," resembling the most probable near-future of America and perhaps of the Soviet Union, and one anarcho-socialist. Without doubt one must read Anar-res as the thing (*res*) of the *anar*-chists, and urras=USSR (URSS in French) plus USA. She does not ask us to choose. She only asks us to reflect.

It remains to propose a conjecture. It is that beyond the grounding in a science facilitated by her family environment, by her development, and without doubt by the historical culture of her husband, Le Guin has known how to surpass the crisis of her environment by proposing a world without a central principle, without a unifying system, without domination, because she is a woman, and as such the obsessional affirmation of the power of the phallus little concerns her. Perhaps she has thus indirectly suggested what a female culture might be, a-centric, tolerant, released, at last, on the occasion of the present crisis, from the male cultural pattern of repetitive conquest.

NOTES

1. See my article "Discontent in American SF," SFS 4(1977):3-13, to which this article is a sequel.
2. This is the thesis of a professional scientist, B.F. Skinner, in *Beyond Freedom and Dignity* (1971).
3. James Strachey, tr. and ed., "Instincts and their Vicissitudes," in *The Standard Edition of the Complete Psychological Works of Sigmund Freud* (UK 1957), 14:139.
4. Ian Watson has shown quite well, SFS 2(1975):67-75, what place this book takes in the economy of Le Guin's work and its relation to the universe of Philip K. Dick.
5. Claude Lévi-Strauss, *Race and History* (Paris: Unesco, 1952).

Marc Angenot

A Select Bibliography of the Sociology of Literature*

(from SFS *4: 295–308, November 1977)*

The present bibliography is the result of a strict selection. It was established having in mind, beyond a general validity, the specific needs of a critic and scholar dealing with contemporary SF.

The items treated are of two kinds: entries deemed essential are annotated; entries dealing with a more limited or less central subject-matter, those whose title indicate their object and method so that no further comment is necessary, as well as those whose existence should be signalled to the reader but which are not essential have been left un-annotated. Certain works of high quality but from areas which do not seem usefusl to an SF critic—such as the sociology of poetry and drama, cultural history of ancient periods, and similar—have been left out in a body. Further, this bibliography does not include 1/ general works on poetics, theory of storytelling (narratology) and theory of literary genres; and 2/ works exclusively on SF or on genres related to SF (Gothic story, fantasy, etc.) Although a number of works from these areas contain sociological consideration I propose to deal with them in other sections of a general critical bibliography of literary theory, also oriented toward the SF critic and scholar, which I am at present working on.

The bibliography covers items in the principal European languages. As a rule, the first edition of books is adduced. When there are later book editions, only the last one has been retained; in that case, "rpt." means an identical reproduction of the original with the same pagination, and "republ." an edition with different pagination. When the last edition contains changes, it is adduced first in the entry, and the date and/or place of the first edition follows in parenthesis.

*This work is part of a research project funded by a Québec FCAC grant.

1. Bibliographies

Baldensperger, Fernand, and Werner P. Frienderich. "Second Part: Literature and Politics." *Bibliography of Comparative Literature*. New York: Russell & Russell, 1960, pp 12-22. (See also other sections of this item, e.g. "Literature and Arts and Science," pp 23-31; "Popular Literature," pp 200-01.)

Baxandall, Lee, comp. *Marxism and Aesthetics: A Selective Annotated Bibliography; Books and Articles in the English Language*. New York: Humanities Press, 1968. 261 p.—Marxist scholarship in literature and fine arts. Rather exhaustive; reliable annotations. Unfortunately no adequate index.

"Bibliographie de la sociologie de la connaissance," *Cahiers internationaux de sociologie*, 32 (1962): 135-176. An international bibliography in the sociology of knowledge. Ca. 1000 entries.

Birnbaum, Norman. *The Sociological Study of Ideology*. Oxford: Blackwell, 1960. 172 p. Indispensable annotated bibliography with synthesizing preface.

Duncan, Hugh D. "Bibliographical Guide to the Sociology of Literature" (see Duncan, Hugh D., section 3).

Hansen, Donald A., comp. *Mass Communication: A Research Bibliography*. Santa Barbara: Glendessary Research Bibliographies, 1968. (8+) 144 p.

Lehmann-Haupt. Hellmut. *One-Hundred Books about Bookmaking: A Guide to the Study and Appreciation of Printing*. New York: Columbia University Press, 1949 (enlarged edn; original: 1933). 87 p.

Literature and Society: A Selective Bibliography. [Various eds.] Miami: MLA and University of Miami Press, 1956—. (Vol I=1950-1955, vol II=1956-1960, vol III=1961-1965...)

Marxism and the Mass Media: Towards a Basic Bibliography. New York: International Mass Media Research Center, 1:1972, 2:1973, 3:1974, 4-5: 1976.

Murphy, Peter, comp. *Writings by and about Georg Lukacs*. New York: American Institute for Marxist Studies, 1976. 29 p.

Peck, David R., comp. *American Marxist Literary Criticism: 1926-1941: A Bibliography*. New York: American Institute for Marxist Studies, 1975. 42 p.

Rafi-Zadeh, Hassan. *International Mass Communications: Computerized Annotated Bibliography. Articles, Dissertations and Theses*. Carbondale: Honorary Relation Zone/International Understanding Series, 1972. (6+) 314p.

Robine, Nicole, and André Peyronie, "Bibliographie critique sur la Paralittérature," *Interférence* #3 (January 1973):81-108.

Schücking, Levin L., and Walther Ebisch. "Bibliographie zur Geschichte der literarischen Geschmacks in England," *Anglia*, #63 (1939), pp 3-64. A bibliography in the social history of literary taste in Great Britain. Ca. 900 classified entries.

Shaw, Martin. *Marxism Versus Sociology: A Guide to Reading*. London: Pluto Press, 1974, non pg.

Waldmann, Günter. "Literatursoziologie—Trivialliteratur," *Theorie und Didaktik der Trivialliteratur: Modellanqlysen, Didaktikdiskussion, literar. Wertung*. München: Fink, 1973, pp 175-196.

2. Journals

Communications. Paris: Centre d'étude des communications de masse/Editions du Seuil, 1960—.

Le Discours social. Bordeaux: ILTAM/Ducros, 1970— (from 1973 on: Paris:Galilée).

Ideologie:Quaderni di storia contemporanea. Padova: 1967—. (Quarterly).

Literature and Ideology. Montreal: Spring 1969—. (Quarterly).

The Minnesota Review, new series. Bloomington IN: 1973—. (Twice a year).

3. Literature and Society: Basic Works

Adorno, Theodor W. *Aesthetische Theorie*. Frankfurt: Suhrkamp, 1970. 544 p. Art can reconcile the human spirit with nature, beyond the hegemony of conceptual thinking. Centered on the particular, it is necessarily critical rather than ideological. Its inexhaustible polysemy guarantees its autonomy and value as social critique. Very opaque.

Astier-Loutfi, Martine. *Littérature et colonialisme: L'expansion coloniale vue dans la littérature romanesque française, 1871-1914*. Paris/La Haye: Mouton, 1971. ix+1147 p.—A model for the critique of ideology in literature with a particular historical phenomenon—in this case French colonial expansion—as starting point.

Auerbach, Erich. *Mimesis: Dargestellte Wirklichkeit in der abendländischen Literatur*. Bern: Francke, 1946. Transl. as *Mimesis: The Representation of Reality in Western Literature*. Garden City NY: Doubleday Anchor, 1957. 498 p.—Studies of representative passages from "western" literary works, Homer to V. Woolf, as coded transpositions of reality, differing with each epoch. A masterly close reading of texts, in the best European philological tradition, leads to a description of socio-cultural types of sensibility toward the concrete world.

Bakhtin, Mikhail M. *Voprosy literatury i èstetiki: Issledovaniia raznykh let*. Moskva: Khudozhestvennaia literatura, 1975. 502p.

Baxandall, Lee, and Stefan Morawski, eds. *Marx and Engles on Literature and Art*. ("Introduction" by S.M.) St. Louis/Milwaukee: Telos Press, 1973. 175p.—An anthology of short passages classified in order to show connections between texts of different periods. Useful introduction, but notes and bibliographical references are rather limited.

Barthes, Roland. *Le Degré zéro de l'écriture, suivi de: Eléments de sémiologie*. Paris: Gonthier, 1965. 183p. (First part published in 1953.) Trans. as *Writing Degree Zero*. Preface by S. Sontag. Boston: Beacon Press, 1970. xxv+111 p.—1) *Degré zéro*: Delineates the concept of "écriture" ("Writing" distinguished from "language" and "style"). "Writing" points to the side the writer takes in historical struggles. Brief description of several political and literary types of "writings" since the bourgeois revolution. Barthes envisions a future "degree zero" of writing, parallel to the "end of history." 2) *Eléments de sémiologie*: a rather unconvincing personal version of a Saussurian type of semiology, conceived as "a part of linguistics" that "takes into consideration the large (transphrastic) signifying units."

Bloch, Ernst. "Entfremdung, Verfremdung." *Verfremdungen* I. Frankfurt: Suhrkamp, 1962, pp 81-90. Transl. as "Entfremdung, Verfremdung: Alienation, Estrangement." *Brecht*. Ed. Erika Munk. New York: Bantam, 1972, pp 3-11.—Fundamental approach relating the modalities of contemporary social alienation in capitalist and bureaucratic societies to literary estrangement militating against such an alienation (most clearly in Brecht).

Bordoni, Carlo. *Introduzione alla sociologia della letteratura*. Pisa: Pacini, 1974 (revised version; 1st edition: 1972). 151 p.—A survey of the methods and axioms in the various "sociologies" of literature. Emphasis on M. Weber, A. Hauser, G. Lukács, E. Auerbach, R. Escarpit.

Bouazis, Charles. *Littérarité et société: Théorie d'un modèle du fonctionnement littéraire*. Paris: Mame, 1972. 254 p.

Burke, Kenneth. *The Philosophy of Literary Form: Studies in Symbolic Action*. Berkeley: University of California Press, 1973. xxvi+463 p. (first edn. 1941).—Symbolic systems of "literary action" as social strategies in response to the writer's synchronic and diachronic situation. Rich pioneering and challenging try at integrating consideration of "high" and "low," fictional and nonfictional writings with the "non-symbolic" realm.

Caudwell, Christopher. *Romance and Realism: A Study in English Bourgeois Literature*. Princeton: Princeton University Press, 1970. 144 p.—A classic of the Marxist intellectual generation of the 1930s. Mingles a romantic socialism with a vulgar-materialist reductionism. Today of purely historical value.

Critique sociologique et critique psychanalytique. Bruxelles: Editions de l'Institut de sociologie, 1970, 238 p.—Essays by various hands by Goldmann disciples and sympathizing Freudian critics.

Daiches, David. *Literature and Society*. London: Gollancz, 1938; rpt. Folcroft Press, 1969. 287 p.

Duncan, Hugh Dalziel. *Language and Literature in Society: A Sociological Essay on Theory and Method in the Interpretation of Linguistic Symbols, with a Bibliographical Guide to the Sociology of Literature*. Chicago: The University of Chicago Press, 1953. 262 p.—

Neither much methodology nor accurate facts on specific types of society: philosophical considerations on the social dimension of literature as a symbolic activity. Makes use of non-critical, essentialistic categories: "Literature as magical art," "Literature as make-believe," "Democratic society" (the author's basic sociological concept). Discussion of Kenneth Burke's theories (II, 6 & 7). A useful extensive bibliography for works in English.

Escarpit, Robert, ed. *Le Littéraire et le social.* Paris: Flammarion, 1970. 315 p.—Essays by various hands on the sociological approach to texts and the sociology of literary institutions. See in particular: R. Escarpit, "Le Littéraire et le social," and "La Définition du terme *littérature*" (on the concept of literature and its historical ambiguities); J. Dubois, "Pour une critique littéraire sociologique" and C. Bouazis, "La Theorie des structures d'oeuvres" (discussions of the critical standpoints of Auerbach, Goldmann, Barthes, et al.); and several other essays on modern literary production and consumption.

Fischer, Ernst. *Von der Notwendigkeit der Kunst*. Dresden: Verlag der Kunst 1959, 203 p. (republ.: Hamburg: Claassen, 1967). Transl. as *The Necessity of Art: A Marxist Approach*. Harmondsworth: Penguin, 1963. 234 p.—Far from being gratuitous, art fulfils an essential function in society. F. analyses the artist's conflict as well as his forced involvement with bourgeois society, and criticizes the traditional opposition between content and form. Though idealist rather than Marxist, it can be credited for tackling some fundamental questions.

Frye, Northrop. *The Critical Path: An Essay on the Social Context of Literary Criticism*. Bloomington: Indiana University Press, 1971. 174 p.

Fügen, Hans Norbert, ed. *Wege der Literatursoziologie*. Neuwied, Berlin: Luchterhand, 1968. 479 p.—A very rich anthology of literary sociology, in two parts: historical (from Tocqueville to Lukács) and theoretical (sociocritical analysis of content and form: Sengle, Adorno, Goldmann...; paraliterature: Nutz; the writer's status: Köhler, Lord...; external sociology, consumption, public and literary institution: Escarpit, Auerbach, Löwenthall...). Useful introduction, international bibliography and index. (See also his *Die Hauptrichtungen der Literatursoziologie und ihre Methoden*. Bonn: Bouvier, 1964. vii+215 p.; rpt. 1968.)

Glicksberg, Charles I. *The Literature of Commitment*. Lewisburg, Pa: Bucknell University Press, 1976. 467 p.—Emphasizing the responsibility of the writer, this is a concrete historical study of various forms of the writer's political commitment in the 20th century—from Céline to Brecht and Solzhenitsyn.

Glicksberg, Charles I. *Literature and Society*. The Hague: Nijhoff, 1972. viii+266 p.

Goldmann, Lucien. *Pour une sociologie du roman*. Paris: Gallimard, 1969 (first edn 1964). 373 p.—Drawing on Lukács' *Theory of the Novel*, G. establishes a homology between the structure of the novel (a demonic research of authentic values in a degraded society) and the structure of the capitalist market economy. The present evolution of the novel as a genre (Malraux, Robbe-Grillet) is linked with changes and crises in Western capitalism, Lukács' concept of refification being G.'s main critical tool. A seminal work for European literary sociology, although challenged today by further developments.

Goldmann, Lucien. *Structures mentales et création culturelle*. Paris: Anthropos, 1970. 494 p.—A collection of articles, some of a general theoretical interest. Develops a methodology combining the "immanent" analysis of literary structures and the "over-arching" sociological explanation of texts.

See also, re: L. Goldmann: *Problémes d'une sociologie du roman*. Bruxelles: Editions de l'Institut de sociologie, 1963. 242 p.—*Littérature et société*. Ibidem, 1967. 223 p.—*Sociologie de la littérature: Recherches récentes et discussions* (special issue of *Revue de l'Institut de sociologie*, 3[1969]. Ibidem, 1969. 240 p.

Gramsci, Antonio. *Letteratura e vita nazionale*. Torino: Einaudi, 1950 (rpt 1966), 400 p. (Partly transl. in his *Selections from the Prison Notebooks*. Ed. Quintin Hoare and Geoffrey Nowell Smith. New York: International Publishers, 1971. 483 p.; rpt. 1975.)

Grivel, Charles. *Production de l'intérêt romanesque: Un état du texte (1870-1880), un essai de constitution de sa théorie*. Paris. The Hague: Mouton, 1973. 428 p. + *Vol II*: Hoofddorp: Hoekstra, 1973, non pg. Attempts to establish theoretical bases for an all-embracing socio-historical analysis of the narrative. Endeavours to combine narrative semiotics (Greimas) and Marxist explanation by showing the subordination of the novel to the dominant ideology.

Guerard, Albert. *Literature and Society*. Boston: Lee & Shepard, 1935; rpt. New York: Kraus, 1972. 451 p.—A discussion of the historical perspective and social history of literary institutions. Rather conservative and mystifying: "race, environment, moment" as background of literature; "the enigma of genius"; etc. Part IV, "To-morrow," attempts to deal with the utopian elements in the writer's conception of his art.

Hauser, Arnold. *Sozialgeschichte der Kunst und Literatur* I-II. Munich: Beck, 1953. Transl.

as *The Social History of Art* I-IV. New York: Vantage, n.d. (1962).—An encyclopedic historical survey of literature and the arts from prehistory to the "film age" as shaped by social circumstances. Patchy, and its approach—a synthesis of the best European views up to ca. 1940—may be dated by now, but still the best elementary overview available in English.

Howe, Irving. *Politics and the Novel*. New York: Meridian Books, 1957, 251 p.

Howe, Irving. *A World More Attractive: A View of Modern Literature and Politics*. New York: Horizon Press, 1963. xii+307 p.—Essays about "'the modern' [style of experience and perception] marked by a crisis of conduct and belief," from T.E. Lawrence to Mailer. The "mass society"—where class status becomes less visible, centers of authority dissolve, and a general passivity and social dependence ensues—has a corresponding "post-modern fiction," between rebellion, agnosticism and confusion. Includes essay on "anti-utopia" by Zamiatin, Orwell, Huxley, who fear that "the long-awaited birth will prove to be a monster," and an axiomatic description of this genre's formal devices.

Jameson, Fredric. *Marxism and Form: Twentieth-Century Dialectical Theories of Literature*. Princeton: Princeton University Press, 1971. xix+432 p. An authoritative synthesis of Marxist literary theory as well as incisive critique of several Marxist or para-Marxist thinkers—Adorno, Benjamin, Marcuse, Sartre, Bloch, Lukács. In chap. 5 establishes the bases of Marxist criticism and its connection with contiguous theories (formalism, sociology of literature, hermeneutics). The best English introduction to "dialectical" criticism.

Laqueur, Walter, and George L. Mosse, eds. *Literature and Politics in the Twentieth Century*. New York & Evanston: Harper & Row, n.d. 219 p. (originally publ. as the "Literature and Society" issue of *Journal of Contemporary History* 2:2 [1967].—Studies on some writers (Rolland, Mann, Eliot, Sartre, etc.) and intellectual movements.

Laurenson, Diana, and Alan Swingewood. *The Sociology of Literature*. London: MacGibbon & Kee, 1972. 281 p.—Three parts: "Theory" (with emphasis on Lukács, Goldmann and structuralism); "The Writer and Society" (penetrating international and historical survey: the influence of the book trade on the writer's status); 3 essays on the "Sociology of the Novel" (notions of "alienation" and "unhappy consciousness"). Includes a consideration of Orwell: his literary strength but also his one-sided political view.

Leenhardt, Jacques. *Lecture politique du roman: "La Jalousie" d'Alain Robbe-Grillet*. Paris: Editions du Minuit, 1973.277 p.—An interesting application of Goldmann's socio-critical theories.

Lenin, V.I., *O.L.N. Tolstom*. Moskva, Khudozhestvennaia Literatura, 1969. 191 p. (First publ. 1908-11) Transl. as *Tolstoy and His Time*. New York: International Publishers, 1952. n.p.

"Literature and Society." *Yale French Studies* #40 (1968).—On French 18th century.

Litérature et idéologie. Pairs: La Nouvelle Critique, 1971. 317 p.—Texts from the 1970 Cluny International Colloquium of Marxist critics, reevaluating theses and concepts of esthetics. A collection of highly valuable discussions.

"Littérature. Recherches—fonctions—perspectives." *Recherches internationales à la lumière du marxisme* #87 (2) (1976).—Translation of recent Soviet research in literary theory, with some contributions from East Germany and Poland. Marxist criticism but also semiotic methods.

Lowenthal, Leo. "Literature and Sociology." *The Relations of Literary Study: Essays on Interdisciplinary Contributions*. Ed. J. Thorpe. New York: Modern Language Association of America, 1967, pp 89-110.

Lowenthal, Leo. *Literature and the Image of Man: Sociological Studies of the European Drama and Novel, 1600-1900*. Boston: Beacon Press, 1957. 242 p.—Analysis of the rise and fall of individualism in some principal European novelists and dramatists. Useful identification of historical, sociological and philosophical determinants of literature, which is, however, judged primarily as vehicle for ideas.

Lukács, Georg. *Essays über Realismus. Werke* IV. Neuwied & Berlin: Luchterhand, 1971. 678 p. (Partly transl. as *The Meaning of Contemporary Realism*. London: Merlin Press, 1963, and partly as *Realism in Our Time*. New York: Harper & Row, 1971.)—L's classical theoretical texts, being a critique of bourgeois concepts of realism and a redefinition of "critical realism" and its "class content," which, however, remains unclear. See particularly the part on the "present significance of critical realism" (pp 457-603; publ. separately as *Wider den missverstandenen Realismus*), where he rejects Kafka—with his "panic fear of reality" and "artistically appealing decadence"—in favor of Th. Mann.

Lukács, Georg. *Der historische Roman*. [East] Berlin: Aufbau, 1955. 393 p. Transl. as *The Historical Novel*. Harmondsworth: Penguin, 1969. 435 p.—A classical analysis of social and historical conditions of a literary genre in its relations to changing conceptions of history, which determine it. It develops between the poles of the bourgeois cult of great leaders and of democratic humanism.

Lukács, Georg. *Schriften zur Literatursoziologie*. Neuwied: Luchterhand, 1961 (and 1968), 568 p.—The complete collection of L's texts from 1909 to 1951 regarding literary sociology. To be read with his major works: *Die Seele und die Formen* (1911), *Die Theorie des Romans* (1920), *Essays über den Realismus* (1948), *Balzac und der französische Realismus* (1952), *Der historische Roman* (1955).

Macherey, Pierre, *Pour une théorie de la production littéraire*. Paris: François Maspero, 1966, 332 p.—Establishes a Marxist theory of literature, based on laws of *production* rather than on paradigms for *consumption*. Develops such concepts as "ideological project," "figuration" and "thematic clue." Includes a long chapter on Jules Verne, whose narrative rhetoric masks and transposes the ideology of industrial capitalism.

Munteano, B[ernard]. *Constantes dialectiques en littérature et en histoire. Problèmes, recherches, perspectives*. Paris: Didier, 1967, 408 p.—From a comparatist's point of view, attempts to reconcile the critic and the historian, and seeks existential and anthropological constants in literature. These constants are paradoxically perceived as variable because historically fluctuating. Scrutinizes some such "variable constants," in rhetoric, in realistic narrative (verisimilitude and "local color") and in systems of values (e.g. the *topos* of reason vs heart). An original work, independent from "official" theories, which reevaluates a large number of problems pertaining to long-range cultural traditions.

Prevost, Claude. *Littérature, politique, idéologie*. Preface by R. Leroy. Paris: Editions sociales, 1973, 275 p.—Studies on Malraux, Aragon, Thibaudeau, Tolstoi (as seen by Lenin), Kafka, from a so-called official Marxist-Leninist point of view. A mechanical application of the notions of "the real," "the political," "ideology," "representation" and "form."

Rockwell, Joan. *Fact in Fiction: The Use of Literature in the Systematic Study of Society*. London: Routledge & Kegan Paul, 1974, 211 p.—Fiction is "not only a representation of social reality but also a functional part of social control." Criticizes the notion of realism. Discusses the use of fiction for information about social institutions, norms and customs. Examples taken from ancient Greek literature, classic English fiction, modern British paraliterature (spy fiction, etc.). An interesting work, although sometimes narrowly empirical and simplistic.

Rühle, Jurgen. *Literatur und Revolution*. Köln: Kiepenheuer und Witsch, 1960. Transl. as *Literature and Revolution: A Critical Study of the Writer and Communism in the Twentieth Century*. New York: Frederick A. Praeger, 1969. 520 p.

Sartre, Jean-Paul. *Qu'est-ce que la littérature?* Paris: Gallimard, 1964, 375 p. (Originally published as part of *Situations II*. Paris, 1948).

"Sociology of Literary Creativity." *International Social Science Journal*. 19: 4(1967): 493-616.—A special issue presenting a good introduction to the sociology of literature from the Marxist point of view. Contains articles by J. Leenhardt, L. Goldmann, G.N. Pospelov, G. Lukács, U. Eco: highly relevant texts, illustrating the various methodological aspects of the problem.

Spearman, Diana. *The Novel and Society*. London: Routledge and Kegan Paul, 1966, 256 p.—To be compared with I. Watt (in this section). Field of inquiry extended to the Middle Ages and even to China. Refutes Watt's thesis of the middle-class origin of the novel in the 18th century, since it is a cumulative transformation of earlier forms of fiction. A more universal study of the novel could indicate that nostalgia for the past was responsible for the rise of the novel. Stresses also the individual contribution of the writer to the emerence of new literary forms.

Strelka, Joseph. *Die gelenkten Musen. Dichtung und Gesellschaft*. Wien, Frankfurt & Zürich: Europa, 1971. 414 p.

Trilling, L. *The Liberal Imagination: Essays on Literature and Society*. New York: Viking Press, 1950, xvi+303 p.

Vassen, Florian. *Methoden der Literaturwissenschaft: Marxistische Literaturtheorie und Literatursoziologie*. Düsseldorf: Bertelsmann Universitätsverlag, 1972. 186 p.—A survey of German Marxist criticism from Marx and Engels to Adorno as differing from German positivistic literary sociology followed by an anthology.

Watt, Ian. *The Rise of the Novel*. London: Chatto and Windus/Berkeley: University of California Press, 1957, 319 p.—On the whole, an incisive introduction to the social history of the novel and of the realist mode, by way of Defoe, Richardson and Fielding. Yet there are some ambiguities in his notion that realism is necessarily linked with the novel genre. Interesting survey of the 18th-century changes in book trade and reading public, and of bourgeois values and expectations—individualism, valuation of love and courtship, new type of heroism and its burlesque transposition (Fielding)—which result in the emergence of the (realistic) novel as the *dominant* literary form.

Wellershoff, Dieter. *Literatur und Veränderung: Versuche zu einer Metakritik der Literatur*. Köln: Kiepenheuer und Witsch, 1969. 185 p.

Zeraffa, Michel. *Roman et société*. Paris: Presses Universitaires de France, 1971. 183p.—A short synthesis of various sociological approaches to the novel. A history of the novel as an ideological entity, through the successive social roles it has played. (See also Z's larger work in the same field: *Personne et personnage: Le romanesque des années 1920 aux années 1950*. Paris: Klincksieck, 1969. 494 p.

4. Ideology and literature. (Works on utopia as ideology—but not as a literary genre—are included into this section.)

Adorno, Theodor W. *Soziologische Schriften*, I-II. Ed. R. Tiedemann. Frankfurt: Suhrkamp, 1972-1975. 2 vols.

Althusser, Louis. "Les Appareils idéologiques d'Etat," *La Pensée*, No. 151 (1970). pp. 1-38.—An important theoretical essay on ideologies as "realized in institutions, their rituals and practices." Their ensemble constitutes the "ideological State mechanisms," which are necessary for "the reproduction of relations of production."

Baldini, Messimo, *Il Linguaggio delle Utopie. Utopia e ideologia: una rilettura epistemologica*. Roma: Studium, 1974. 265 p.—A reevaluation of the notional pair utopia vs. ideology in the wake of modern epistemology. Utopian thought is seen as an extreme dogmatism and orthodoxy. Mannheim's sociology of knowledge (see in this section) is criticized for conceptual imprecision.

Barth, Hans. *Wahrheit und Ideologie*. Zürich: Erlenbach, 1961, 327 p. (First edn Zürich: Manesse, 1945).—Presents ideological criticism as an attempt toward the conquest of truth, from Bacon to Marx and Nietzsche. The analogies and differences in the doctrine of ideology of the latter two philosophers are discussed. Pleads against both for truth as transcendental.

Bloch, Ernst. *Das Prinzip Hoffnung* I-II. Frankfurt: Suhrkamp Verlag, 1959. 1657 (In French as *Le Principe espérance*. Paris: Gallimard, 1976—).—A major work by one of the great non-dogmatic Marxist philosophers of our times. A critique of all closed systems and orthodoxies, putting utopian thought into the center of materialist dialectics, which leads to an informed Hope. To that end surveys all the major existing political, medical, architectural, etc. utopias, annexing to it all open-ended horizons: Being cannot be understood without such horizons and such a final orientation.

Bluher, Rudolf. *Moderne Utopien: Ein Beitrag zur Geschichte des Sozialismus*. Bonn & Leipzig: Schroder, 1920. vii+117 p.

Cohn, Norman. *The Pursuit of the Millenium: Revolutionary Millenarians and Mystical Anarchists of the Middle Ages*. Revised and enlarged edition. New York: Oxford University Press, 1970. 412 p. (1st edn London: 1957).—Though dealing with medieval material, this is an essential clarification of relationships between ideological and religious marginality, utopian social criticism, and tendencies toward sexual liberation. It provides basic elements for a theory of subversivity in Judeo-Christian civilization.

"Cultural Studies and Theory." *Working Papers in Cultural Studies*, #6 (1968).'Special issue of a journal published in Birmingham, UK.

Currie, Robert. *Genius: An Ideology in Literature*. London: Chatto and Windus, 1974, 222 p.—A critique of the quasi-religious and mystified notion of *genius* as it has developed from Romanticism to Modernism. Instead of the axiom: "Humanity needs genius to rescue it from alienation," a "truly this-worldly culture" will accept society "seriously and critically" as permanently alienated, without trying to forge transcendental alibis.

Desroche, Henri. *Les Religions de contrebande*. Paris: Mame, 1974. 232 p.

Dumont, Fernand. *Les Idéologies*. Paris: Presses Universitaires de France, 1974. 183 p.—The best synthesis of theories of ideology, with a critique of this notion as used by Marxists and other currents.

Duveau, Georges. *Sociologie de l'utopie et autres essais: Ouvrage posthume*. Paris: Presses Universitaires de France, 1961. 193p.—A collection of variegated essays mainly on 19th-Century utopias and their role in everyday history. Weakened by a tendency to find ahistorical human archetypes behind the utopian systems.

Faye, Jean-Pierre. *Théorie du récit. Introduction aux "Langages totalitaires": Critique de la Raison l'Economie narrative*. Paris: Hermann, 1972. 140 p.—"History is, first of all, a narrative (a story)"; "history is produced by being narrated": these are the basic assumptions of Faye's criticism of "narrative reason" (i.e. ideological production in history). A seminal work for ideological criticism of literature though it sometimes degenerates into simple paradox. To be linked with Faye's *Langages totalitaires* (Paris: 1972), a theory of the historical narrative of fascism.

Foucault, Michel. *L'Ordre du discours*. Paris: Gallimard, 1971. 81 p.—An excellent brief synthesis of Foucault's method, which attempts to delimit the notion of "discourse" as superordinated to "genre," ideology" and even "discipline," and as the key concept of an "archeology of knowledge."

Gabel, Joseph. *La Fausse conscience; Essai sur la réification*. Paris: Editions de Minuit, 1962. 264 p.—Latching on to the Marxist criticism of alienation and reification (Lukács), Gabel develops a theory of "false consciousness" as the resistance to dialectics and the corollary of class alienation. Points out the analogy between false consciousness and schizophrenia (mental rigidity, loss of the temporal dimension).

Habermas, Jürgen. *Technik und Wissenschaft als "Ideologie"*. Frankfurt a,M.: Suhrkamp, 1968. 169 p. (In French as *La Technique et la science comme idéologie*. Paris: Gallimard, 1974. xliv+214 p.; partly translated in his *Toward A Rational Society*. Boston: Beacon Press, 1970, chs. 3-6, and partly in *Knowledge and Human Interests*. Ibid., 1971, Appendix.)—A Marxist criticism of technocracy, of the integration of the scientific-technical complex into the ruling economic and political apparatus. The consequences are politization of science, and "scientification" of politics, including the repressive apparatus.

Haddad, Gérard. "La Littérature dans l'idéologie," *La Pensée*, #151 (1970); 88-99.

Hauser, Arnold. "Propaganda, Ideology and Art." *Aspects of History and Class Consciousness*. Ed. I. Meszaros. London: Routledge and Kegan Paul, 1971, pp. 128-51.

Jakubowski, Franz. *Der ideologische Ueberbau in der materialistischen Geschichtsauffassung*. Frankfurt: Neue Kritik, 1968 (1st edition: Danzig: 1936). 122 p. (In French as *Les Superstructures idéologiques dans la conception matérialiste de l'histoire*. Paris: E.D.I., 1971. 221 p.)—A classic Marxist theory of ideology, developing the notions of "correct" vs. "mystified" consciousness, of the "unity of theory and practice," of the vanguard political party as the bearer of proletarian class-consciousness.

Kofler, Leo. *Der asketische Eros: Industriekultur und Ideologie*. Wien, Frankfurt & Zürich: Europa, 1967. 340 p.

Lenk, Kurt, ed. *Ideologiekritik und Wissensoziologie*. Neuwied & Berlin: Luchterhand, 1964. 413 p.

Lukács, Georg. *Geschichte und Klassenbewusstsein*. Neuwied & Berlin: Luchterhand, 1968 (1st edition Berlin: 1923). 733 p. Transl. as *History and Class Consciousness*. Cambridge: MIT Press, 1971. xlvii+356 p.—Lukács's most important general theoretical work, developing the key concepts of "totality" and "mediation." A critique of reification in capitalism, a theory of the role of the proletariat and its vanguard party as the adequate expression of the maximal possible class-consciousness.

Mannheim, Karl. *Ideologie und Utopie*. Bonn: Cohen, 1929. Transl. as *Ideology and Utopia: An Introduction to the Sociology of Knowledge*. New York: Harcourt, Brace and World, 1970. 354 p. (1st translation: New York 1936).—The fundamental work of Mannheim's sociology of knowlege, opposing ideology (found in ruling and conservative classes) to utopia (found in rising classes and therefore oriented towards the future).

Mannheim, Karl. *Essays on the Sociology of Knowledge*: London: Routledge and Kegan Paul, 1952. 322 p.

Manuel, Frank E., ed. *Utopias and Utopian Thought*. Boston: Beacon Press, 1967, 321 p.

Marcuse, Herbert. *One-dimensional Man: Studies in the Ideology of Advanced Industrial Society*. Boston: Beacon Press, 1966. xvii+260 p.—A description of tendencies in contemporary US society, using tools of Marxian and Freudian critique. It is a closed society stifling critical ferment, where repression is largely interiorized. Its one-dimensional (neo-positivist) thought neutralizes critical rationalism.

Marx, Karl, and Friedrich Engels. *Die Deutsche Ideologie: Kritik der neuesten Deutschen Philosophie in ihren Repräsentanten, Feuerbach, B. Bauer und Stirner*. Berlin: Dietz Verlag, 1960. 695 p. Transl. as *The German Ideology....* Moscow: Progress, 1964. 736 p.—A work of Marx's and Engels's youth (1845/46) published only in 1932. Critique of ideological premises in German neo-Hegelianism. An essential work, since it is—together with their *Holy Family* (1845)—the only one to show their method applied to philosophical and literary "superstructures."

Meszaros, Istvan. *Marx's Theory of Alienation*. London: Merlin, 1970. 356 p.

Neusüss, Arnhelm, ed. *Utopie: Begriff und Phänomen des Utopischen*. Neuwied & Berlin: Luchterhand, 1968. 523 p.

Rossi-Landi, Ferrucio. *Il Linguaggio come lavoroe e come mercato*. Milano: Bompiani, 1968, 254 p.—Extension ot the Marxist theory of economics to the production of signification (language) and the *productive labor* implied. A tentative to integrate semiotics and logical empiricism into Marxist criticism. (See also his *Semiotica e ideologie*. Milano: Bompiani, 1972; *Ideologies of Linguistic Relativity*. The Hague: Mouton, 1973; and *Linguistics and Economics*. The Hague: Mouton, 1975.)

Ruyer, Raymond. *L'Utopie et les Utopies*. Paris: Presses Universitaires de France, 1950, 292 p. (See also his *Les Nuisances idéologiques*. Paris: Calmann-Lévi, 1972, 342 p.)

Sanguineti, Edoardo. *Ideologia e linguaggio*. Milano: Feltrinelli, 1970, 137 p.

Schücking, Levin. *Die Soziologie der literarischen Geschmacksbildung*. (1st edn München, 1923) 3rd and revised edn: Bern & München: Francke, 1961, 111 p. Transl. as *The Sociology of Literary Taste*. Chicago: The University of Chicago Press, 1966, 112 p.—A classic in the history of cultural taste and esthetic values, "sociologizing" the notion of the Spirit of the Age. To be read also for his views on the sociology of literary institutions (groups, schools, fans, cleavage in the public, public recognition, values accorded to the "new," etc.)

Vadée, Michel. *L'Idéologie*. Paris: Presses Universitaires de France, 1973. 96 p.—An excellent anthology of essential Marxist texts defining ideology and describing its functions, with V's comments.

Veyne, Paul. *Comment on écrit l'histoire: Essai d'épistémologie*. Paris: Editions du Seuil, 1971. 349 p.

Volpe, Galvano della. *Critica dell'ideologia contemporanea: Saggi di teoria dialettica*. Roma: Editori riuniti, 1967. 156 p.—A Marxist critique of various contemporary cultural and scientific ideologies, in particular structuralism. (See also his *Critica del gusto*. Milano: Feltrinella, 1966. 272 p.)

Walton, Paul, and Stuart Hall. *Situating Marx*. Human Context Books, 1972. 167p.

Williams, Raymond. *Culture and Society, 1780-1950*. London: Chatto & Windus, 1958. xx+363 p. (Also New York: Harper & Row, 1966).—A key work for the social history of culture, simultaneously a history of intellectual opinions on cultural phenomena, of various ideologies about them, and of their inner contradictions. Discusses cultural values and notions such as Mass, Democracy, Equality, etc. A remarkable example of materialist criticism of cultural ideologies.

Williams, Raymond. *The Long Revolution*. London: Chatto & Windus, 1961 (revised edn Harmondsworth: Pelican, 1965. 299 p.)—Elements of a theory of culture, in continuation of *Culture and Society*. Discussions of basic theoretical concepts: "the creative mind," "culture," "individual" and "society." Critical historical description of British culture, its aspects and institutions such as education, readership, the writer's status, language...Part three, on "Britain in the 1960's" and the "long revolution" we are living through, is a penetrating analysis of the present social and existential changes. An essential work, written simply but accurately, with depth, lucidity and balance.

Williams, Raymond. *Keywords: A Vocabulary of Culture and Society*. (London: Fontana; New York: Oxford University Press, 1976. 286 p.

Zeitland, Irving M. *Ideology and the Development of Sociological Theory*. Englewood Cliffs NJ: Prentice-Hall, 1968. x+326 p.

Zeltner, Hermann. *Ideologie und Wahrheit: Zur Kritik der politischen Vernunft*. Stuttgart: Fromann, 1966. 162 p.

5. Sociology of literary institutions and of mass culture. (See also next section, *Paraliterature*.)

Altick, Richard D., *The English Common Reader: A Social History of the Mass Reading Public, 1800-1900*. Chicago: University of Chicago Press, 1957. ix+430 p.—"An attempt to study, from the historian's viewpoint, the place of reading in an industrial and increasingly democratic society." Does not try for a synthesis, but for a scholarly examination of all the commercial, economical, political and psycho-historical influences on the reading public, its extension and its preferences, and on the book trade, periodicals and newspapers.

Benjamin, Walter. "Das Kunstwerk im Zeitalter seiner technischen Reproduzierbarkeit," *Schriften*. Frankfurt: Suhrkamp, 1955. Transl. as "The Work of Art in the Age of Mechanical Reproduction," in W. Benjamin. *Illuminations*. Ed. H. Arendt. New York: Schocken, 1969, pp. 217-51.—The fundamental essay on how technical reproducibility changes men's perception of art by dismantling the "aura" of "uniqueness" due to the art-object's distance. This leads to the emancipation of art from "cult value" in favor of "exhibition value" for a mass audience (photography, film). The mass audience acquire now the potential for expertise that only a few had earlier, but they are also confronted with the choice between the Fascist aesthetization of political life in imperialist wars, or the conscious Communist politicizing of art.

Berelson, Bernard, and Lester Asheim. *The Library's Public*. New York: Columbia University Press, 1949. xx+174 p.

Cazeneuve, Jean, et al., eds. *Les Communications de masse, guide alphabétique*. Paris: Danoël-Gonthier, 1976. 512 p.

"La Censure et le censurable." *Communications* #9 (1967). 160 p.—A collection of articles, some historical and some sociopolitical, on censorship, but most importantly also attempts at a semiotic theory of censorship (le Censurable) linked with institutional criticism. Short international bibliography and a first chronology of a future history of censorship.

Corsini, Gianfranco. *L'Istituzione letteraria*. Napoli: Liguori, 1974. 308 p.—Short articles on various aspects of literature as primarily an *institution*.

Defleur, Melvin L. *Theories of Mass Communication*. New York: McKay, 1975. (1st edn 1966). xx+288 p.

Doubrovsky, Serge, and Tzvetan Todorov, eds. *L'Enseignement de la littérature*. Paris: Plon, 1971, 640 p.—Articles on philosophy of literature-teaching, literature and social sciences, pedagogy, with an international survey.

Dumazedier, Joffre, and Jean Hassenforder. *Eléments pour une sociologie comparée de la production, de la diffusion et de l'utilisation du livre*. Paris: Cercle de la librairie, 1962. 100 p. (also *Bibliographie de la France*, CLI, 5th series, ## 24-27, 2nd Part, "Chroniques," fasc. 1 to 6)

Eco, Umberto. *Apocalittici e integrati: Comunicazioni di massa e teorie della cultura di massa*. Milano: Bompiani, 1977, xv+389 p. (1st edn. Milano, 1964)—E's studies on mass culture blend semiotics and sociology and construct original mediations between them. A panoramic overview, largely on comics, with a brief article on SF. The title identifies two extreme and uncritical attitudes toward mass media—the "integrated" who accept it fully and the "apocalyptic" who reject it wholly. E. pleads for a third, discriminating way.

Engelsing, Rolf. *Der Bürger als Leser: Lesergeschichte in Deutschland, 1500-1800*. Stuttgart: Metzlersche Verlag, 1974, 375 p.—On the German bourgeois as reader.

Enzensberger, Hans Magnus. *Einzelheiten*, I-II. Frankfurt: Suhrkamkp, 1952-1954. Partly trans. as *The Consciousness Industry: On Literature, Politics and the Media*. New York: Seabury Press, 1974. 184 p.

Escarpit, Robert. *Sociologie de la littérature*. Paris: Presses Universitaires de France, 1968 (= revised edn: 1st edn 1958). 128 p. Transl. as *Sociology of Literature*. London: Cass, 1965 (2nd edn: 1971). 104 p.—Historical survey giving mostly French and British examples for the status of the writer, his conditions of existence, the literary institutions (publishing, distributing, consuming). *External* sociology based upon statistical data. Criticism of the concept of literary generations.

Escarpit, Robert. *Théorie générale de l'information et de la communication*. Paris: Hachette, 1976. 220 p.

Escarpit, Robert, and Charles Bouazis, eds. *Systèmes partiels de communication*. Paris & The Hague: Mouton, 1972. 225 p.—Selection of studies on the book and literature in mass communications within advanced technological societies (press, politics, education, audiovisual arts). Describes various trends in the communication theory,—but considers a synthesis impossible at present.

Hart, James D., *The Popular Book: A History of America's Literary Taste*. Oxford: Oxford University Press, 1950 (Republ. Berkeley: University of California Press, 1963. 351 p.)—The social background of America's popular reading from the Pilgrims' time to the 1950's, epoch by epoch. Systematic connections between literary taste and the ensemble of sociological and ideological changes in each period.

Hiller, Helmut. *Zur Sozialgeschichte von Buch und Buchhandel*. Bonn: Bouvier, 1966. 213 p.—An encyclopedic history of the book in the Western world (mainly in Germany). The book is treated as a material object, from a technical and commercial point of view. Clear and very erudite, an excellent reference book.

Hoggart, Richard. *The Uses of Literacy: Aspects of Working-class Life with Special Reference to Publications and Entertainments*. London: Chatto and Windus, 1957. 319 p.—A remarkable balance between erudition and an overall critical vision. Describes working-class leisure forms, researches present tendencies in mass culture. "The earnest minority" of the working-class has a surprising resilience to majority tastes. The old forms of class culture are in danger of being replaced by a poorer kind of "faceless" culture.

Jacobs, Norman, ed. *Culture for the Millions? Mass Media in Modern Society*. Boston:

Beacon Press, 1964 (and 1971). xxv+200 p.—An interesting though inconclusive collection of papers presented at a *Daedalus* seminar in 1959. See particularly E. Shils, "Mass Society and its Culture" (in favor of the diffusion of "superior culture" in mass society); and L. Lowenthal, "An Historical Preface to the Popular Culture Debate."

Joseph, Michael, and Grant Overton. *The Commercial Side of Literature*. New York & London: Harper & Brothers, 1926, 274 p.—Originally, a purely practical handbook. Today, an excellent historical document about the American literary market 50 years ago.

Kofler, Leo. *Zur Theorie der modernen Literatur: Der Avantgardismus in soziologischer Sicht*. Neuwied & Berlin: Luchterhand, 1962. 286 p.

Leavis, Q[ueenie] D. *Fiction and the Reading Public*. London: Chatto & Windus, 1932. xvi+348 p. (rpt. 1965, 1968)—State of British mass literature in the 1930's and the historical causes of its development (the birth of journalism, growth and disintegration of the reading public). An elitist and dated work, still interesting where its value preconceptions do not distort the data.

McLuhan, Marshall. *The Gutenberg Galaxy: The Making of Typographic Man*. Toronto: University of Toronto Press, 1962. 294 p. (rpt. 1969)—Invention of printing as *the* cultural revolution of modern civilization. Offhanded and risky generalizations from *King Lear* to Joyce, from Gutenberg to modern "mass media." A firework of ideas, sometimes profound, sometimes reductionist and dubious.

McLuhan, Marshall. *Understanding Media: The Extension of Man*. New York & Toronto: McGraw-Hill, 1965. xiii+365p. (1st edn. 1964.)—"The medium is the message"—i.e. "All media are active metaphors in their power to translate experience into new forms." The consequences of any medium "result from the new scale that is introduced in our affairs by each extension of ourselves." Media can be *hot* or *cold*, a "hot medium" being one that provides a sense with a large amount of data, and implies a "low participation." An inventive set of hypotheses followed by an attempt at typological description of communication, but never confirmed by concrete historical and social analyses.

McLuhan, Marshall, and Quentin Fiore. *The Medium is the Massage* (sic). New York: Random House. 1967. 157 p.

Miller, William. *The Book Industry*. New York: Columbia University Press, 1949. xiv+156 p.—A report of the American Public Library Inquiry (Social Science Research Council). All the data and statistics on the book trade and the public libraries. With a bibliography.

Moles, Abraham, and Claude Zeltmann, eds. *La Communication*. Paris: Centre d'Etude et de promotion de la lecture, 1971. 575 p. (republ. Verviers: Gérard, 1973. x+758 p.)

Morin, Edgar. *L'esprit du temps: Essais sur la culture de masse*. Paris: Grasset, 1962. 280 p.

Morin, Violette. *L'Ecriture de presse*. Paris & The Hague: Mouton, 1969.

Mott, Frank Luther. *Golden Multitudes: The Story of Best Sellers in the United States*. New York: MacMillan Company, 1947. xii+357 p.—Mostly anecdotal history of bestsellers, 1670-1945, with a wealth of factual data, including much on the successes of SF and fantasy.

Plant, Marjorie. *The English Book Trade: An Economic History of the Making and Sale of Books*. London: Allen & Unwin, 1974 (1st edn 1932). 3+520 p.—An excellent source on the history of material book manufacture, from paper to labor organization, finances and copyrights. A huge amount of data, yet clear and readable.

Rosenberg, Bernard, and David Manning White, eds. *Mass Culture Revisited*. New York: Van Nostrand Reinhold, 1971. xii+473 p.—Collection of articles by various hands, based on common sense and empirical enquiries rather than on clear theoretical appproaches. Interesting because of the great majority of problems and subjects treated. Few of them deal with printed fiction; see however section 6: "Spy Fiction."

(See also a previous collection of essays by the same editors: *Mass Culture: The Popular Art in America*. New York: The Free Press/London: Collier-Macmillan, 1957. 561 p. (republ. 1963].)

Widmer, Kingsley and Eleanor, eds. *Literary Censorship: Principles, Cases, Problems*. San Francisco: Wadsworth Publications, 1961. 182 p. (See also, on same topic: Widmer, Eleanor, comp. *Freedom and Culture: Literary Censorship in the 70's*. Belmont: Wadsworth Publications, 1970. vi+216 p.)

Williams, Raymond. *Communications* (revised edn). London: Chatto and Windus, 1966 (also Harmondsworth, 1970). 193 p.

6. Paraliterature.

Angenot, Marc. *Le Roman populaire: Recherches en paralittérature*. Montréal: Presses de l'Université de Québec, 1975. x+145 p.—Studies on French popular literature 1830-1914, with an attempt at defining the concept of paraliterature using both internal, narrative analysis and external, sociological analysis of production and consumption. With an international bibliography of paraliterature studies.

Bayer, Dorothee. *Der Triviale Familien—und Liebesroman im 20.Jahrhundert*. Tübingen: Tübinger Vereinigung für Volkskunde, 1963. 184 p.—A study of paraliterary *love romance* and *family story*. A typological and socio-historical synthesis, mainly on German material.

Boileau—[, Pierre, and Thomas] Narcejac. *Le Roman policier*. Paris: Pavot, 1964. 235 p.—Historical panorama of detective novel by two well-known authors. An empirical discussion of the genre's constants and techniques.

Buchloh, Paul G., and Jens P. Becker. *Der Detektivroman: Studien zur Geschichte und Form der englischen und amerikanischen Detektivliteratur. Mit Beiträgen von A. Wulff und W.T. Rix*. Darmstadt: Wissenschaftliche Buchgesellschaft, 1973. 199 p.—Studies in history and form of the English and American detective literature.

Burger, Christa. *Textanalyse als Ideologiekritik: Zur Rezeption zeitgenössiger Unterhaltungsliteratur*. Frankfurt: Athanaum, 1973. 175 p.—A theoretical approach to paraliterature: ideological criticism through text analysis. Followed by studies on German "realistic" popular novels.

Bürger, Heinz Otto, ed. *Studien zur Trivialliteratur*. Frankfurt: Klostermann, 1962, viii+270 p.—Collection of high level essays, mostly on 19th Century phenomena.

Cawelti, John G. *Adventure, Mystery and Romance: Formula Stories as Art and Popular Culture*. Chicago: The University of Chicago Press, 1976. viii+336 p.—Proposes "formula analysis," i.e. analyzing the "structure of narrative or dramatic conventions employed in a great number of literary works." The value of popular fiction is measured by its degree of uniqueness within the given framework. Interesting conception, but of rather limited relevance.

Conrad, Horst. *Die literarische Angst: Das Schreckliche in Schauerromantik und Detektivgeschichte*. Düsseldorf: Bertelmann Universitätsverlag, 1974. 230 p.—Horror and pity—related to the Uncanny—as esthetic categories in the British Gothic novel, Hoffmann and the detective novel (Poe). Ideas of "delightful horror," "ceremonialization of horror"; narrator-reader dialectics in terms of pleasure in horror. There is a "historical dialectics of the horror-literature," as against the concept of an anthropological horror-potential. With bibliography.

Dalziel, Margaret. *Popular Fiction 100 Years Ago: An Unexplored Tract of Literary History*. London: Cohen & West, 1957. 188 p.

Diez-Borque, José-Maria. *Literatura y Cultura demasas: Estudio de la novela subliteraria*. Madrid: Al-Boprak, 1972. 261 p.—Deals with popular stories in Spain using converging methods: external sociology (field research), theory of communication, statistics, genre theory, ideological analysis. The psycho-social function of these writings is to diminish the reader's frustration and unhappiness with his status. Affirms the necessity to treat mass culture without reference to "high" culture. Mass culture is petty-bourgeois rather than proletarian. A few pages on popular SF.

Entretiens sur la paralittérature. Paris: Plon, 1970. 475 p.

Giesz, Ludwig. *Phänomenologie des Kitsches: Ein Beitrag zur anthropologischen Ästhetik*. München: Fink, 1971 (= enlarged edn.; originally: Heidelberg, 1960). 103 p.

"Grandeur de la littérature populaire." *Magazine littéraire* #9 (July-August 1967).

Harper, Ralph. *The World of the Thriller*. Cleveland: Case Western Reserve University, 1969. 139 p.—Typology, themes, roles and topical characters, devices and values of the thriller. Psycho-sociological approach to the reader. A stimulating but methodologically fairly shallow work.

Haycraft, Howard. *The Art of the Mystery Story: A Collection of Critical Essays*. New York: Simon & Schuster, 1946. ix+545 p. (also: New York: Grosset & Dunlap, 1947. ix+565 p.)

James, Louis. *Fiction for the Working Man, 1830-1850: A Study of the Literature Produced for the Working Class in Early Victorian Urban England*. London: Oxford University Press, 1963. xiv+226 p.—An admirable study of social history, with precise information on industrial society's urban life and its increasing reading public. Studies influences, thematic and geneological traditions, foreign contributions (US and French). The rather limited ideological interpretation goes no further than the concept of "urban mentality": "In a democratic urban... civilization, the very existence of a humanized society depends on a creative and liberal popular culture."

Journal of Popular Culture. Bowling Green OH, 1966—.—The only US journal to treat popular culture in all its manifestations. Most contributors prefer empirical—sometimes trivial—discussions to any consciously theoretical approach.

Killy, Walther. *Deutscher Kitsch: Ein Versuch mit Beispielen*. Göttingen: Vanderhoeck &

Ruprecht, 1962. 168 p.—Anthology of German literary *Kitsch* 1816-1933, preceded by an attempt at characterizing and defining the phenomenon.

Langenbucher, Wolfgang. *Der aktuelle Unterhaltungsroman: Beiträge zu Geschichte und Theorie der massenhaft verbreiteten Literatur.* Bonn: Bouvier, 1964. 292 p.—Modern German popular narratives are envisaged from historical, sociological, commercial, statistical, thematic, structural and anthropological points of view. Excellent example of methodological convergence and mediation, with a huge bibliography.

"Littérature et sous-littérature." *Bulletin du séminaire du littérature générale*. #10 (1963). 95 p.

Littératures marginales. Histoire des littératures. III. Paris: Gallimard, 1963. pp. 1567-1734.—Series of chapters on "pedlars' literature" (P. Brochon); the popular novel, studied from a thematic rather than sociological point of view (J. Tortel); children's literature in French (A. Bay); song; detective novel, French and Anglo-American (T. Narcejac); SF (J. Bergier); and finally the relations of literature with radio and cinema (not with TV). Much information but also many gaps and a lack of precision.

Lowenthal, Leo. *Literature, Popular Culture and Society*. Palo Alto: Pacific Books, 1961. xxiv+169 p.

Messac, Régis. *Le Détective-novel et l'influence de la pensée scientifique*. Paris: Champion, 1929. 698 p.—Probably the first doctoral dissertation in a paraliterary genre. Remains a monument of comparatist erudition. Interesting views on other non-canonic genres (e.g. Gothic novel, fantastic tale, 19th Century popular adventure story) and their relationships.

Moles, Abraham. *Le Kitsch, l'art du bonheur*. Paris: Mame, 1971. 247 p.—A theory of *Kitsch* based on the alienation in and esthetics of everyday life in industrial society.

Narcejac, Thomas. *Une machine à lire: Le roman policier*. Preface by F. Le Lionnais. Paris: Denoël/Gonthier, 1975. 247 p.—The detective novel as a hybrid of art and (criminological) science. Sketches a theory of enigma and of proof. Discusses the playful aspects, and a typology of forms which is also a brief overview of the best writers in the genre. It is determined by a reading convention.

Nowak, Emilia. "Literature and Mass Culture: An Attempt to Define Mass Culture through the Structure of Literary Work," *Zagadnienia Rodzajòw Literackich*, g #2 (17):(1967): 91-97.

Nutz, Walter. *Der Trivialroman, seine Formen und seine Hersteller: Ein Beitrag zur Literatursoziologie*. Köln: Westdeutscher Verlag, 1962. 119 p. (2nd edn 1966).—Best brief monograph from the German school of paraliterature studies. Discusses typology (with only 2 pp on SF) and sociology (techniques of production and diffusion, writers' status). Very informative.

Nye, Russell B. *The Unembarrassed Muse: The Popular Art in America*. New York: The Dial Press, 1970. 497 p.—A study of US popular art in 6 parts: popular fiction, popular theater, popular art on newsstands, "cops, spacemen, and cowboys," popular music, and media. Well documented, with a wide-ranging perspective and analytical penetration, but with no attempt at theoretical synthesis. The part on SF is out of date. Useful bibliography.

Orwell, George. *A Collection of Essays*. Garden City NY: Doubleday Anchor, 1954. 320 p. (rpt. 1957).—Excellent path-breaking considerations of comic postcards, the crime story, politics and language, and boys' weeklies.

Ousby, Ian. *Bloodhounds of Heaven: The Detective in English Fiction From Godwin to Doyle*. London: Harvard University Press, 1976. 194 p.

Radine, Serge. *Quelques aspects du roman policier psychologique*. Genève: Editions du Mont Blanc, 1960, 293 p.—Studies on the great British and American detective novels. Some what anecdotical; contains however relevant considerations on the narrative technique and on ideologies particular to the genre.

Reinert, Claus.*Das Unheimliche und die Detektivliteratur*. Bonn: Bouvier/Grundmann, 1973. 158 p.—Rigorous academic study with a structuralist approach centered on the notion of the Uncanny. Places the detective story into paraliterature poetics and sociology. describes its narrative characteristics. More cultural philosophy than systematic poetics.

"Le Roman feuilleton." *Europe* #542 (June 1974). 276 p.—A special issue on the French "serial novel" (i.e. types of popular narrative in the 19th century and till the 1920's).

Schenda, Rudolf. *Volk ohne Buch: Studien zur Sozialgeschichte der popularen Lasestoffe, 1770-1910*. Frankfurt: Klostermann, 1970. 608 p.—A wide survey of problems in 19th-Century paraliterature: production of popular books, commerce, readership; forms, themes and genres. Important bibliography.

Schmidt-Henkel, Gerhardt, ed. *Trivialliteratur: Aufsätze.* Berlin: Literarisches Colloquium, 1964. 266 p.—Essays by 15 scholars on a number of German paraliterary genres (western, detective novel, patriotic romance, sentimental novel, etc. Includes a study by Ulf Diederichs, "Zeitgemässes und Unzeitgemässes: Die Literatur der Science Fiction."

Schulte-Sasse, Jochen. *Die Kritik an der Trivialliteratur seit der Aufklärung: Studien zur Geschichte des modernen Kitschbegriffs.* München: Fink, 1971. 162 p.—HIstorical study of intellectual opinions on 18-20th Century paraliterature, mainly in Germany, with special stress on the term and notion of *Kitsch*, its birth and development. (See also his *Literarische Wertung*. Stuttgart: Metzler, 1971. 79 p.)

Seesslen, Georg, and Bernt Kling. *Romantik und Gewalt: Ein Lexikon der Unterhaltungsindustrie.* München: Manz, 1973—. 3 vols.—Encyclopedia entries on popular genres in literature, comics, media, etc., with an introductory essay on each genre. Selective, accurate, international in scope, and with a historical dimension. The entries on SF in vol. 1, by Kling, deal both with prose and comics.

Tourteau. Jacques. *D'Arsene Lupin a San Antonio: Le roman policier français de 1900 à 1970.* Paris: Mame, 1970. 326 p.

Waldmann, Günter. *Theorie und Didaktik der Trivialliteratur: Modellanalysen, Didaktikdiscussion, literar. Wertung.* München: Fink, 1973. 196 p.

INTRODUCTION *(continued from page 242)*

It is also impossible to enter here into any fuller survey of sociological investigations conducted specifically about SF. Suffice it to say that we are at the very beginning even of empirical investigations, much less intelligent overviews. True, SF has intermittently been used for documentation on various attitudes such as "the image of the scientist" and similar "content analyses" sociologists seem so fond of. A number of writers have grumbled about economics and censorship, giving valuable indications but no more than that. From John Campbell on, SF magazines have run polls of readers, but it is impossible to check their representivity and in Campbell's case even their veracity. Finally, in the last few years trained young researchers have gone, in the USA and USSR, into empirical studies of the SF audience, though I would feel that the means at their disposal have permitted them only to scratch the surface (in itself useful when we know practically nothing); and first bids at theoretical overviews—however sketchy—have been provided by, say, Stover's on SF as a response to the Research-and-Development "revolution," or the much more encompassing and sophisticated thesis by Gérard Klein on American SF having a basis in the "scientifically and technically oriented" petty bourgeoisie or middle class, and its basic horizons changing parallel to the massive ideological realignments in that class or group.[6] There have also been a number of discussions of ideology of SF, very rarely connected to historical social groups, and a great deal of scattered market research—mostly, I suspect, lying unpublished in publisher's archives (but see e.g. *Publishers Weekly* for June 14, 1976, for the latest feeble try)—but I do not see any major trends I have left out.

As for the essays in this issue, they should speak for themselves. No doubt all of them together—in my opinion—at best point out how much still remains to be done. But they comprise a number of complementary approaches and viewpoints which can help in such further work. They range from theoretical overviews—such as Elkins', Levin's, and the second part of Klein's already mentioned exciting essay, focusing this time on a single but a highly representative author—to tries at dealing with the American SF subculture in not only sociometric or empiricistic terms (Berger and Fleming). We could, alas, find no English-language authors to write for us about the crucial category of market mediators, but we fortunately found a West German book devoted to it, and with the kind permission of the editor, Mr. Joug Weigand, and the publisher, Asgard-V. Dr. Werner Hippe, we have translated three contributions from it, on the commercial TV and book market (Hasselblatt), on book-editing and publishing (Jeschke), and on censorship, right out of the horse's mouth (Stefen). Though nothing can fully compensate for the absence of financial and other factual data in the commercial metropolis of SF (outside the USSR at least), the USA, these last three contributions could perhaps remind the pessimists among us that West Germany is in a way the eastern counterpart of California—a place where a number of tendencies otherwhere veiled show themselves openly, perhaps as a prefiguration for the rest of the capitalist world. Regardless of that, all of you readers working for magazines, publishing houses, or similar—as well as all of you who are interested in the field sketched in these reflections and this issue—would you please send us more contributions? With data, facts, elegant generalizations from them, theoretical overviews and speculations, based on any and all of the tendencies mentioned? If you do so, we might one day be able to decide whether there really can be such an animal as a SOCIOLOGY of LITERATURE—and of SF.

NOTES

1. See for superior examples of this approach Lewis Coser, *Sociology Through Literature* (US 1963), and Rockwell in Marc Angenot's bibliography in this issue. Further references to works in this bibliography will be given by author's name followed by AB.

2. Roman Jakobson, "Closing Statement: Linguistics and Poetics," in *Style in Language*, ed. Thomas A. Sebeok (US 1960). Mukařovsky's 1934 review was republished in *Kapitoly z česke poetiky* I (Prague 1948—partly available in German as *Kapitel aus der Aesthetik* [Frankfort 1970]); see from him also *Aesthetic Function, Norm and Value as Social Facts* (US 1970) and three essays in *Semiotics of Art*, ed. Ladislav Matejka and Irwin R. Titunik (US 1976).

3. *Grundrisse der Kritik der politischen Oekonomie*, written 1857-58, published in entirety only 1939—cf the first "complete" (in fact still incomplete) edition of Karl Marx and Friedrich Engels, *Werke* (Berlin: Dietz, 1956-58), vol. 13. In English, the best instrument for a thorough study is the Pelican Marx Library (London: Penguin, and New York: Vantage, in progress), in which the *Grundrisse* are available as a separate volume (1973). It will be quoted by page number preceded by G. for briefer introductions to Marx in English see Karl Marx and Friedrich Engels, *Selected Works in One Volume* (US & UK 1968) or Robert C. Tucker, ed., *The Marx-Engels Reader* (US 1972).

4. Quoted from Marx's aritcle *Wages* in Mikhail Lifschitz, *The Philosophy of Art of Karl Marx* (UK 1973), much the best comment on this subject, which should be read for further developments, together with Meszaros and Walton-Hall (AB).

5. In English see *Brecht on Theatre*, ed. John Willett (US 1966), and *The Messingkauf Dialogues* (UK 1965), and for comments on Brecht as theoretician, Walter Benjamin, *Understanding Brecht* (UK 1973) and Erika Munk, ed., *Brecht* (US 1972).

6. Leon Stover, "Science Fiction, the Research Revolution, and John Campbell," *Extrapolation* 14(1972-73):129-48, and *La Science-fiction américaine* (Paris 1972); Gérard Klein, "Discontent in American SF," SFS 4(1977):3-13, the first part of the article that is concluded in this issue of SFS.